THE ESSENTIAL BRUNSWIK

THE ESSENTIAL BRUNSWIK

Beginnings, Explications, Applications

Edited by
KENNETH R. HAMMOND
THOMAS R. STEWART

OXFORD
UNIVERSITY PRESS

2001

OXFORD
UNIVERSITY PRESS

Oxford   New York
Athens   Auckland   Bangkok   Bogotá   Buenos Aires   Calcutta
Cape Town   Chennai   Dar es Salaam   Delhi   Florence   Hong Kong   Istanbul
Karachi   Kuala Lumpur   Madrid   Melbourne   Mexico City   Mumbai   Nairobi
Paris   São Paulo   Shanghai   Singapore   Taipei   Tokyo   Toronto   Warsaw
and associated companies in
Berlin   Ibadan

Copyright © 2001 by Oxford University Press

Published by Oxford University Press, Inc.
198 Madison Avenue, New York, New York 10016

Oxford is a registered trademark of Oxford University Press.

Library of Congress Cataloging-in-Publication Data
Brunswik, Egon, 1903–1955.
   [Papers. Selections]
   The essential Brunswik : beginnings, explications, applications
edited by Kenneth R. Hammond and Thomas R. Stewart.
      p.   cm.
   A selection of the author's English language papers, 1935–1957.
   Includes bibliographical references and index.
   ISBN 0-19-513013-8
   1. Psychology.   2. Brunswik, Egon, 1903–1955.
I. Hammond, Kenneth R.   II. Stewart, Thomas R., 1944–   III. Title.
BF121 .E8   2000
150′.92—dc21   00-022509

9 8 7 6 5 4 3 2 1
Printed in the United States of America
on acid-free paper

Dedicated to Egon Brunswik

PREFACE

Because Egon Brunswik's papers are scattered throughout the literature in various obscure publications, no more than a handful of psychologists have ever read any of his original papers or know where they are or what they consist of. Dissatisfied with this state of affairs, the editors approached Joan Bossert of Oxford University Press with the suggestion that the Press publish a collection of Brunswik's papers on behalf of the Brunswik Society. If that were done, we thought, the original papers would be brought to the surface, could be found in one place, and would thus be made more accessible. Oxford concurred, and we proceeded on the assumption that we would do no more than publish a collection of Brunswik's papers.

But we soon came to our senses. We realized that Brunswik's ideas had failed to be persuasive in his own time, and that merely to collect and reproduce them would not be likely to be much more effective now than in the past. In addition, we had often heard the complaint that Brunswik's papers were very difficult to understand. In short, we realized that we would have to take steps to make the content of the original papers more accessible intellectually as well as physically. And with the help of many others, that is what we have tried to do in this volume. Each (but not all) of his English-language papers from 1935 to 1957 is accompanied by comments indicating the context in which the paper was developed, what its objective was, and why it is of significance today.

It would be a mistake, however, to assume that Brunswik's failure to communicate effectively was due to a habit of careless writing. In fact, it was the opposite; it was the precision of his writing and the complexity of his ideas that defeated those who were not motivated to pursue them. This point is important and we illustrate it with an anecdote.

The faculty of the psychology department at Berkeley was stunned and saddened by Brunswik's death in 1955 and sought to find a suitable memorial for him. Edward Tolman, in particular, was anxious to preserve his memory and thought that publishing a translation of Brunswik's 1934 book from German to English would be appropriate. So Tolman set about making that translation himself, but he soon found that it was beyond him. He explained this in a conversation with me (KRH), and asked for suggestions. I offered to ask Karl Muenzinger, then chairman of the psychology department at the University of Colorado, whose first language was German, whether he would undertake the task. Muenzinger agreed but soon gave up. Professors of German were asked, but after a brief review, none would try. Then, help came from Lewis W. Brandt, who was both a professional translator and a psychologist. He succeeded in going further than the others, and his translation of a few pages of Brunswik's book were reproduced in *The Psychology of Egon Brunswik* (Hammond, 1966b; see pp. 514–534). What is most interesting, however, is Brandt's explanation (reproduced here from memory) for why he could not complete the translation: "The difficulty is not that Brunswik is a poor writer; on the contrary, what makes the task difficult is that he is such a *good* writer in German that it is almost impossible to translate him into English. That is, he is so very very careful to express his ideas exactly and precisely, to choose exactly the right expression and the right German neologism, that it becomes very time-consuming to find the correct English meaning, and sometimes I cannot do it." It is that style of work, devotion to precision of expression, that makes Brunswik's work difficult for readers not accustomed to reading carefully every word of a text; Brunswik cannot be skimmed. Examination of any paragraph, or any diagram, will soon show how much care Brunswik put into getting every detail right. (When KRH was a student at Berkeley he had occasion to present to Brunswik a seminar paper containing a diagram. When Brunswik returned the paper his first comment was to note a tiny error in the diagram; he then explained, somewhat apologetically, "To me, diagrams are sacred.") Words were sacred, too.

But there is more to it. Brunswik's ideas were not ignored by the prestigious psychologists of his day because his presentations were demanding, or because he failed to communicate effectively; rather, it was because he communicated all too well. What made his demand for change particularly galling to the establishment was that it was made on their own terms. That is, Brunswik accepted the scientific, empirical, behavior-oriented, "objective" approach of the American psychologists of the twentieth century and used it to show his contemporaries that they were on the wrong path. In current jargon, he worked "within the system" to show its leaders that drastic changes in their conception of their science were necessary, that their theories were misguided, and that their methodology was defeating them. In short, he put forward a full frontal attack on the psychology of the day and employed the guiding principles of his opponents as weapons.

It must be recognized these were not the ideas of someone who merely wished to tinker with conventional theory and method; they were the ideas of a true revolutionary. And they were the ideas of a practical man as well as of a theoretician. Therefore, in this volume, we present Brunswik's papers that contain his fundamental theory (Part I) and his explications of that theory (Part II) and show how it has been applied to a wide variety of current topics (Part III). For example, the main ideas of probabilistic functionalism have resulted in the conduct of over 250 studies of "multiple cue probability learning," a fact that surely would have astounded Brunswik (see Holzworth, this volume). We conclude with a collection of essays on Brunswik, the man and his ideas (Part IV).

We gratefully acknowledge the contributors to this volume, each of whom is a distinguished scholar and productive researcher. The quality of their work and the value of their contribution will be readily evident to the reader. Two contributors, Michael Doherty and Ray Cooksey, deserve special thanks for their valuable advice throughout the process of planning and preparing this book, and for their thoughtful reviews and comments on several of the chapters. We are indebted to Sue Wissel and Mary Luhring for assistance in preparing manuscripts and especially to Joanne Orologio, who spent many hours formatting manuscripts and preparing the reference list for the book.

Boulder, Colorado   K. R. H.
Albany, NY   T. R. S.
September 1999

CONTENTS

Part II Explications: Iconoclasm at Work

A. Demonstrations of a New Methodology: Representative Design

B. Demonstrations of a Comprehensive Theory

C. Final Thoughts

Part III Applications

A. *Theoretical and Methodological Contributions to Psychology*

B. *Overviews of Applications to Substantive Problems*

Part IV Brunswik the Man and His Ideas

CONTRIBUTORS

Kenneth R. Hammond / University of Colorado
Thomas R. Stewart / University at Albany, State University of New York
Leonard Adelman / George Mason University
Linda Albright / Westfield State College
Mitchell G. Ash / University of Vienna, Austria
Frank Bernieri / University of Toledo
Mats Bjorkman / Uppsala University, Sweden
Gregory L. Brake / Microsoft Corporation
Ruth Bussey / Boulder, Colorado
Gérard Chasseigne / Université François-Rabelais, France
Ray W. Cooksey / University of New England, Australia
Michael E. Doherty / Bowling Green State University
Ludovic Duponchelle / Ecole Pratique de Hautes Etudes, France
Bo Earle / University of Washington
David C. Funder / University of California, Riverside
Gerd Gigerenzer / Max Planck Institute for Human Development, Germany
John S. Gillis / Oregon State University
William M. Goldstein / University of Chicago
DeVere Henderson / George Mason University
Ralph Hertwig / Max Planck Institute for Human Development
James H. Hogge / Peabody College of Vanderbilt University
R. James Holzworth / University of Connecticut
C.R.B. Joyce / Royal College of Surgeons in Ireland
Patrik N. Juslin / Uppsala University, Sweden
Peter Juslin / Uppsala University, Sweden
Alex Kirlik / Georgia Institute of Technology
Gernot D. Kleiter / University of Salzburg, Austria
Elke M. Kurz / Max Planck Institute For Human Development, Germany
Thomas E. Malloy / Rhode Island College
Sheryl Miller / George Mason University
Etienne Mullet / Ecole Pratique des Hautes Etudes, France
Jeryl L. Mumpower / University at Albany, State University of New York
Barbara A. Reilly / Georgia State University
John Rohrbaugh / University at Albany, State University of New York
María Teresa Muñoz Sastre / University of Toulouse, France
Stephen G. Schilling / University of Michigan
Alexander J. Wearing / University of Melbourne, Australia
Robert S. Wigton / University of Nebraska College of Medicine
John H. Wright / University of Chicago

THE ESSENTIAL BRUNSWIK

Introduction

Kenneth R. Hammond

Thomas R. Stewart

Probabilistic functionalism is the best broad descriptive term we have for Egon Brunswik's work; it is the one he used, and it is far preferable to *Brunswikianism*, a label he would have found to be in bad taste. But the phrase *probabilistic functionalism* is somewhat forbidding, and its meaning is not immediately obvious; thus, newcomers are confronted at the outset with an uninviting title. Although the mystery will disappear for the reader of Brunswik's articles in this volume, we offer here a brief explanation to facilitate understanding his approach to psychology.

Recall the scene in psychology during the period 1930–1960, the time during which Brunswik carried out his work. American behaviorism ruled the discipline, and learning theorists (Clark Hull and Edward Tolman, together with the general theorist Kurt Lewin) were the rulers. Filled with great optimism that bordered on arrogance, learning theorists set the tone and the general principles that governed theory and research. The primary principles were derived from stimulus-response psychology and were directed toward the discovery of the laws of learning. Determinism was at the basis of these laws, and determinism is exactly what Brunswik took as his target. He did so by introducing the idea of an environment that included probability relations among the variables of interest. The "probabilistic" part of the phrase is now easy to understand and accept (thanks in large part to Brunswik's work), although it certainly was not in the period in which he was arguing for it. As the papers in this volume illustrate, Brunswik spent a good deal of time and energy fighting for the acceptability of probability—not only in the environment but also in the organism—a concept that many found shocking.

Brunswik also pushed aside the stimulus-response approach in favor of the idea of organisms possessed with intentionality, and it is the concept of intentionality that gives rise to the idea of functionalism. *Functionalism* has acquired many meanings during the twentieth century; at this point, we need to note only its implication that the organism's behavior is somehow organized with reference to some end, or objective. Functionalism implies a "utilitarian, adjustment-centered biological conception of psychology which may be traced to Charles Darwin's views on the struggle for existence" (1952, p. 55). That description of functionalism, together with his emphasis on probabilism, indicates Brunswik's orientation toward psychological theory. And although the probabilistic aspect of probabilistic functionalism has been largely absorbed into current psychology, the Darwinism of functionalism has not. (But see Chapter 42 in this volume on "How Probabilistic Functionalism Advances Evolutionary Psychology.") Thus, the term *probabilistic functionalism* covers his general work, and we are entitled to use it to refer to his overall network of concepts and methods.

A considerable amount of empirical research was carried out under this rubric because Brunswikian views persisted from the early 1930s to the present, a life span of seventy years, a rarity in psychology. At first, Brunswik's ideas and concepts were dealt with mainly by ignoring them (see Doherty, Chapter 10, and Gigerenzer, Chapter 44, this volume), but for the past twenty-five years they have been steadily creeping into the mainstream. They are being silently absorbed into conventional psychology, however. It is a *silent* absorption because they are being absorbed without either an acknowledgment of their source or an understanding of Brunswik's intended meaning; worse still, critical concepts now appear in modern psychology in a distorted fashion. In what follows, we describe the development of the absorption of Brunswikian concepts into modern psychology events for three reasons: First, for reasons of history and scholarship it is important that basic Brunswikian concepts be described accurately; second, the reader who has been exposed to current distortions should be offered the original meaning of these concepts early in the text in order to reduce further misunderstanding; and third, the description of the absorption (even though misguided) of Brunswikian concepts into modern psychology demonstrates the current need for them, much as Brunswik argued a half century ago.

The Absorption of Brunswikian Method and Theory into Modern Psychology

During the first part of the twentieth century, academic psychologists demonstrated beyond doubt that they could carry out laboratory experiments that met stringent scientific criteria and could make use of sophisticated statistical methods for analyzing their results. The result was an explosion of publications. At the beginning of the twenty-first century, however, psychologists met a new problem, explaining what significance their research holds for the society that supports it. Further demonstration that experiments *can* be done is no longer important. What is important is justifying the generalization of results from experiments, that is, demonstrating that psychological research carries meaning beyond the laboratory, or even beyond the specific conditions of one laboratory experiment to another.

Psychology has been slow to recognize this problem; indeed, many psychologists will argue that such demonstration is not merely unnecessary, but insulting. The scientific productivity of the work, they will claim, should be enough. Nevertheless, during the latter half of the twentieth century, the need for demonstration of the meaning of their work has grown and become apparent to many psychologists, and that is because continuation of research funding depends on it. Recognition of that fact can be seen in the creation of a special federation of psychological societies whose purpose is to explain to representatives of the federal government why it is important for them to provide funds for psychological research, a practice otherwise known as lobbying.

It is commonplace for special seminars to be held in which the scientists explain why their research is important to members of Congress and their staff members who can then ask, "Why should the government provide money for that?" Convincing answers to such questions rest on the ability to generalize results beyond the laboratory situation. It was during this period of a demand for results that carry meaning beyond the laboratory that psychologists began to borrow concepts from Brunswikian psychology.

Methodological Absorption

Absorption of Brunswikian methodology began implicitly; there was no explicit declaration by anyone that researchers should adopt Brunswik's notion of representative design as a means for generalizing their results. But some researchers did, and in some surprising ways.

Representative design

The term *representative design of experiments* refers to the arrangement of conditions of the experiment so that they represent the conditions to which the results are intended to apply. Brunswik thought of *represent* here in the same sense in which *represent* is used when one says that the sample of subjects in the experiment "represent" the subjects in some population that is not included in the experiment. Thus, he was arguing that the logic of induction should hold for conditions as well as subjects. This argument seems rather innocent and straightforward, but it is diametrically opposed to a formidable tradition.

During the 1940s experimental psychology had taken over Sir Ronald Fisher's theory of the factorial design of experiments, successfully applied in agriculture, in which the conditions of the experiment are arranged *orthogonally* in order to test the effect of a variable (e.g., a fertilizer). In these circumstances the agriculturist determines the *circumstances of the application* (see Hammond, 1996c) as well as the *circumstances of discovery*. Thus, if a fertilizer is discovered to have a significant effect in the experiment, it is applied; and because the agriculturist controls the conditions of application to fit the circumstances of discovery, no induction over uncontrollable conditions is necessary for the agriculturist. But psychologists do not control the circumstances of application; consequently, the *conditions* toward which generalization is intended must be represented, just as the *subjects* in the experiment must be represented, and for the same reason. When making the inference from subjects included in the experiment to those not included, we depend on the statistical logic of induction, which, of course, depends on the subjects' representation. Brunswik argued that the same logic must hold for the conditions. When we make the inference from conditions included in the experiment to those not included, the validity of our inference depends on how well we have represented the conditions not present in the laboratory.

In adopting the agriculturists' design of experiments, however, psychology had borrowed a methodology that had no need for the logic of induction over conditions because they would be the same as those in the experiment. Therefore, psychologists had borrowed a methodology that defeated its possibilities of inductive generalization beyond the specific conditions of the experiment. Thus, in making his demand for representative design, which called for the application of the logic of induction on both sides of the experiment, Brunswik was calling for what Sigmund Koch would later call an "indigenous" methodology for psychology.

Brunswik called his innovation "representative design" because he wanted to convey the idea that the conditions of the experiment should be designed to represent the conditions outside the experiment *toward which the generalization was intended*. It must be emphasized that he did not mean that all experiments must represent the conditions of the *natural* world by means of statistical sampling, although he undertook one such a study in order to drive his point home (Brunswik, 1944). He simply argued that the logic of induction should be applied in both directions, that the circumstances toward which the generalization was intended should be specified (as with subjects) and that these should be included in the experiment if the generalization is to be justified. And he often used the expression "double standard" to indicate that psychologists employed the logic of induction in one direction only (over subjects) but *claimed* generalization over conditions without justification. This argument is most easily seen in terms of "subject and object sampling."

Subject and object sampling

When Brunswik introduced the need for both "subject and object sampling," he did so in order to emphasize the equal status of the environment with the subject (see especially his 1957 article). In the case of social perception, in which persons judge other persons, the idea of "object" sampling was fairly easy to grasp; the "objects" to be judged were simply other persons just like the subjects, so the idea of sampling these "person-objects" was clear, and the method was the same (see Albright & Malloy, Chapter 22; Funder, Chapter 28; Gillis & Bernieri, Chapter 31; and Mumpower, Chapter 33, this volume, for examples). It may seem incredible, but articles regularly appear in American Psychological Association (APA) journals describing experiments in which many subjects (conforming to the logic of induction on the subject side) but only one or two or three "person-objects" are used, thus ignoring the need for sampling on the object, or environmental, side (for an early demonstration of this "double standard," see Hammond, 1954).

The idea of subject and object sampling may be clear in the field of social perception, but when we move away from that field, and the "objects" are not persons, the idea of sampling from the environment is not as easy to grasp. For example, many decades later, Robyn Dawes (1998) would imply that to demand such sampling impossible, if not silly; Then, there is the further problem of sampling questions. Hammond, Hamm, and Grassia (1986) have suggested that not just people but "items" and even tasks should be sampled in order to achieve "external validity." But Dawes wanted to know exactly what is this population of questions from which we can randomly sample? Where is a population of "decision-making" or of "probabilistic-judgment" tasks from which we can sample? The problem of justifying the sampling of tasks is even more daunting than sampling from a population of people.

Of course, Dawes's question is exactly the question that should *always* be asked: To what population of circumstances—test items, task conditions—do we wish to generalize our results? To what set of circumstances do we wish the results to apply? And that is a question that should be asked before the experiment begins, not after it is finished. Brunswik's contribution was to urge psychologists to provide a rigorous method for answering that question.

The issue of generalization came to James J. Gibson's attention as well as Brunswik's, when in the 1940s psychologists were testing air force pilots for the accuracy of their distance perception by asking them to adjust two rods in a visual tunnel. From the point of view of generalization to the pilot's visual task, this test was an absurdity. Yet, this double standard continues. For example, when researchers first studied the question of whether people (in general) were overconfident of their knowledge (in general), they used a "sample" of subjects. (We put the word *sample* in quotes because *canvass* would be a better word; they followed convention and used the available college students, as is customary.) But the researchers did not simply select students they thought to be appropriate—that is, cooperative, or intelligent, or not-so-intelligent—to be their subjects. They used a "sample" of subjects because they wished to generalize their results to people in general.

They took a different approach, however, when they chose *questions* to test their subjects' general knowledge. In this case, they did not use a random "sample" of questions; they *selected* questions they thought to be appropriate. And no one disputed that method; it is traditional. The standard method all undergraduate students are taught is this: Sample *subjects* in order to generalize to those not included in the experiment, but do not sample *conditions*; simply arrange experimental conditions to test the hypothesis, without any regard for justifying a generalization to conditions not included in the experiment.

That difference can prove to be fatal. For example, in the study of overconfidence someone did dispute that traditional method, and as the reader may well guess, it was someone who understood Brunswik's admonition about subject and object sampling and took it seriously. Peter Juslin noticed the arbitrary selection of knowledge questions and proceeded to replicate the previous experiments using knowledge questions *randomly sampled* from a specified source; now the logic of induction would be applied to both sides of the experiment, not just to the subject side. Did that make a difference? Yes; the results were opposite to those obtained with the personally chosen questions; the overconfidence phenomenon dis-

appeared (see Juslin, Chapter 36, this volume). In this case, then, Dawes's question was easily answered: The population of questions of interest was an independent knowledge source from which questions could be sampled. Thus, the question about generalization was answered; unfortunately, it was answered after the experiment was conducted rather than before. But Juslin took an important step; he showed exactly what was meant by representative design and how to achieve it.

But this question is not always so easily answered. As Dawes's question demonstrates, it is difficult to grasp the idea of representative design when it extends beyond social perception to impersonal cognitive tasks. There is one study, however, that made the attempt to present a Brunswikian theory of tasks and to show what it means to sample them.

Hammond, Hamm, Grassia, and Pearson (1987) studied the judgments of expert highway engineers. They studied each of 21 highway engineers separately over nine conditions, and they sampled tasks within each condition. For example, in one condition, the engineers made judgments of the safety of highways based on moving pictures (taken from a car) of forty different highways, the safety of which was known from their accident statistics. There was a large pool of such pictures and a sample of $N = 40$ was used. The engineers' judgments were based on this sample, and because the statistical properties of the sample of tasks was known, the appropriate statistical tests could be made. Similar procedures were carried out for the capacity and esthetic qualities of the highways. The population of tasks was specified, and the statistical properties of samples were made clear, just as Brunswik had made them clear in his study of perception in the natural world in 1944 (Chapter 4, this volume). It is easier to grasp the idea of sampling conditions if we introduce the distinction between formal and substantive sampling.

Formal versus substantive sampling

When Brunswik talked about sampling task conditions, he was referring to the formal, statistical properties of tasks as well as their substance. Mere sampling of persons to be "objects" to be judged in a study of social perception is now a step recognized by nearly all researchers to be as necessary as sampling the persons who will be judges. But examining the statistical properties of an impersonal judgment task remains a puzzle to most psychologists. Brunswik, however, put this matter very plainly, thus: "Generalizability of results concerning the . . . variables involved must remain limited unless at least the range, but better also the distribution . . . of each variable, has been made representative of a carefully defined set of conditions" (1956b, p. 53). Harlow (1959), the famous animal researcher, overlooked this simple suggestion when he reported, "Tall, unstable stimuli . . . elicit avoidant, hesitant behavior" on the part of monkeys. Had he attempted to specify the "range and distribution" of "tall, unstable stimuli" in his laboratory experiment and compared these to range and distribution of tall, unstable stimuli (trees) in the natural habitat of monkeys, he would have been spared this absurd generalization. Chasseigne and Mullet (Chapter 39, this volume), on the other hand, provide an excellent example of how the consideration of the formal properties of a judgment task can be productive. They found that elderly persons have difficulty in making use of cues that have an *inverse* relation to a criterion. Thus, interest in the formal properties of tasks (in their case, the form of the functional relation between cue and criterion) led them to discover facts about the cognitive activity of elderly persons.

Although the research on multiple cue probability learning made such considerations a necessity (see Holzworth, also Stewart, this volume) and thus a standard part of research design among Brunswikian researchers, the consideration of formal, statistical properties of judgment tasks is still infrequent among researchers not acquainted with Brunswikian theory. Too often, the question of the ecological validity of cues, the intercorrelation among cues, and the overall uncertainty in tasks is not considered in the description of the task, or in the function of the task in testing of hypotheses.

We have described in detail the concept of representative design because it is often misunderstood. Although psychologists were energetically seeking a means for generalizing their results, they did not explicitly urge that representative design replace the methodology borrowed from agriculture. They made the unfortunate mistake of pursuing the generalization of results by borrowing the wrong concept, namely, *eco-*

logical validity, a mistake discussed in detail in the comments on Brunswik's 1949 paper (this volume).

"Real life" versus the laboratory: A false choice

Psychology now finds itself locked on the horns of a false dilemma: Should it pursue the goal of generality by demanding that research be generalizable to "real life" (aka the "real world"), or should it pursue generalizability by holding onto its traditional laboratory research paradigm? Despite the emptiness of the term *real life*, there are supporters of both points of view. On the one hand, there is a group of researchers who have followed Neisser's astounding declaration in 1976 that the work on memory over the past 100 years has been "largely worthless" (Cohen 1996, p. 20). According to Gilliam Cohen, "[Neisser] claimed that the experimental findings are trivial, pointless, or obvious, and fail to generalize outside the laboratory" (p. 2). Ulric Neisser had made his views clear in his 1976 book titled *Cognition and Reality* and had invoked the concept of *ecological validity* to explain them (p. 48). He explained that the term had been introduced by Brunswik but added that Brunswik's use of the term "was slightly different from the one that is popular today." Unfortunately, Neisser offered neither Brunswik's definition of the term nor his own and thus left us without any idea of what he was talking about.

But there are those who still have faith in the conventional design of experiments. This view achieved considerable visibility when Banaji and Crowder (1989) sharply criticized the "real-life" advocates in 1989. One who took their critique seriously was Margaret Matlin (1997), who wrote in the textbook *Cognition*, "Probably the wisest conclusion about this controversy is that *both* the laboratory and the real world approaches can advance our understanding of human memory" (p. 168). She supported her view by citing the well-known researcher Endel Tulving as follows: "There is no law that says that good fact or ideas can come out of one type of approach only if some other approach is suppressed. As in other fields of science, there is room for many different kinds of fact and ideas about memory and for many approaches" (p. 169).

The real trouble with introducing the terms

real world or *real life* and the reason that they should be abandoned is that they are simply low-grade escape mechanisms; their use makes it unnecessary to define the conditions toward which the generalization is intended. One need only assume (without evidence) that everyone knows what these terms entail. But their emptiness merely allows escape from the necessity of developing a theory of the environment from which such definitions will have to be derived and thus avoids the necessity of being specific about environmental conditions. Sooner or later, psychologists will have to treat the matter of generalization seriously, and when they do, they will have to come to grips with Brunswik's theory of the environment and its methodological companion, representative design.

Theoretical Absorption: Quasi Rationality

This concept has its source in Brunswik's theory and research, which indicate that a perceptual judgment is a *compromise* between proximal and distal information (see Kurz & Hertwig, this volume). When he began (about 1940) to broaden his interests beyond perception to thinking, however, "compromise" began to be associated with "rationality." Curiously, he began this new course not by a long theoretical disquisition on rationality but with a striking experimental demonstration of the differences in the *distribution of errors* associated with perception (normal distribution) and thinking (truncated distribution with outliers). (See the excerpt from his 1956 book, this volume.)

This was a bold and imaginative innovation, still to be appreciated by cognitive scientists. But nothing was said about quasi rationality in earlier publications; no articles were devoted to the development of the concept of *quasi rationality*; it does not appear in his writings until 1952, when, in his monograph titled "The Conceptual Framework of Psychology," he wrote, "An attempt was made directly to compare perception and thinking in terms of the differences in the statistical distribution of error." He then concluded, "All evidence may best be summarized by designating perception as 'quasi-rational' rather than a rational system."

The use of the modifier *quasi* is critical. It indicates that perception does no more than *re-*semble rationality; it is not a true replica of rationality, and thus, perception is not a fully rational process. The use of the term *quasi rationality* thus opens the door to the *simulation* of a cognitive process, for it indicates that Brunswik did not intend quasi rationality to be a *duplication* of rationality. The distinction between duplication and simulation is often overlooked, but in the case of quasi rationality, it must not be, as becomes apparent in the next step taken by Brunswik.

If quasi rationality only resembles rationality, the question is: Where does the resemblance begin and where does it end? He answered this question by undertaking a "rational reconstruction" (his term) of quasi rationality, and he found a way that had a lasting impact: "In an attempt at the rational reconstruction of the ways of the quasi-rational, with its reliance on vicarious cues each of which is of limited validity, one may best refer to a remark of Robert Thorndike comparing the impressionistic or intuitive judge of men to a device capable of what is known to statisticians as multiple correlation" (Brunswik, 1952, p. 24). (Thorndike had in 1918 carried out such a study.) Thus, by 1952, Brunswik had found a rational model that resembled his concept of quasi rationality in the mathematical statistical technique of multiple regression, for it possessed properties similar to those he had specified for quasi rationality. That is, because the properties of the multiple correlation model begin with those properties he had *earlier* specified for quasi-rational cognition—namely, multiple variables, limited validity of each, intercorrelations (redundancy) among them, and a measure of achievement between distal variables (judgment and criterion)—the multiple correlation model did provide a rational reconstruction of quasi rationality. The one property of the multiple correlation model he did not discuss or critically examine was its organizational principle, summation. Nor did he mention its larger implication: The multiple correlation model is but one example of the *linear model*. (It is important to note that the theory came first, *then* the adoption of the statistical model. This is an exception to Gigerenzer's, 1991, description of how psychologists adopt theories from "tools.")

In addition to establishing the multiple correlation "device" as the *explication* of the meaning of quasi rationality, by 1956 Brunswik had taken a second step; he advocated its potential use as a *model for cognitive activity* itself. That is, it was a model that could be used to make the concept of quasi-rational cognition explicit, and that could therefore (it turned out) be used to *simulate* quasi-rational cognition. Did Brunswik claim that the multiple regression equation should serve as a simulation of cognitive activity? The answer to that question lies in some brief remarks (1956b, p. 110), in which he indicates that the multiple regression model should and does simulate cognitive activity:

> Further mathematical steps in the evaluation may perhaps be *patterned after* (italics ours) a model first introduced into the study of functional problems in perception by Else Frenkel-Brunswik in her analysis of clinical intuition (1942; 1951, p. 362), that is, multiple correlation. For facial cues an example of such an analysis of impressional values was undertaken from the materials underlying our figure 6, using Nose-height (N) and Forehead-height (F) in relation to the response quality, likability (l). The intercorrelation between N and F was ascertained as .27, and their respective impression validities relative to likability as .30 and .28. The multiple correlation between Nose-Forehead and apparent likability is then computed as $R_{NF} = .41$. Prediction of response even from low-utilization cues could be built up to a considerable extent by such a procedure. And the same procedure could be used symmetrically for ecological validity so that eventually an understanding of the mechanism of the super ordinate functional achievement arcs (correctness, fig. 5) could be obtained.
> (p. 110)

Brief as Brunswik's paragraph is, in fact, it says it all; predictions of a person's judgments even from "low-utilization cues" could become very high, a conjecture that has been borne out many times. His recognition of the fact that the same procedure could be used "symmetrically" on the ecological side has also been proved correct, as has been the case for his hope that "an understanding of . . . the functional achievement arc (correctness) . . . could be obtained," as the lens model equation demonstrated mathematically by 1964 (see Tucker, 1964) and as researchers have demonstrated many times since (see, for example, Stewart, Chapter 27, this volume).

This succinct paragraph offers clear evidence that Brunswik had decided that the multiple cor-

relation equation was an appropriate model for the simulation of cognitive activity, not only in connection with visual perception, but with regard to clinical judgment, and judgment in general, at least in those cases in which multiple fallible indicators are involved. Despite its brevity, the paragraph is clear and unequivocal in its commitment.

If the simulation of quasi rationality begins with the multiple regression (or linear) model, where does it end? It ends with the specification of the above properties; it does not extend to the behavior of the neurochemistry of the brain, or any action of the brain; it ends with a rejection of that sort of reductionism. It also ends with the idea of *duplication*; there is no suggestion that the use of the multiple regression equation entails the duplication of cognitive activity. It is necessary to describe these limits to which the multiple regression model resembles cognitive activity, for, absurd as it may seem, the use of this model to simulate cognitive activity has often been criticized as if it implied that persons rapidly make all the tortuous calculations required by the multiple regression model. Simulation does not imply duplication.

Richard Thaler is the only psychologist that has appropriated this term, and he did so without knowledge of Brunswik's prior use (personal communication). This term appears in the title of his book *Quasi Rational Economics* (1991). His usage cannot be compared with Brunswik's, however, because no definition of the term is given by Thaler.

The concept of *quasi rationality* appears during the writing of the 1952 monograph, and it is in his 1956 book that Brunswik expanded his interest to the topic of thinking as well as perception. This can best be seen by examining the pages 89–93 of the 1956 book, which we reproduce here because it signifies the widening scope of Brunswik's interests to include rational, analytical cognition as well as quasi-rational perception (Chapter 30, this volume).

It is natural to compare Brunswik's "quasi rationality" to Herbert Simon's term "bounded rationality." Both seem to indicate or imply a form of cognition that somehow approximates but does not duplicate rational cognition. As Hammond has explained in detail elsewhere (Hammond, 1996c), however, there is a large and important difference between these two concepts. Quasi rationality is intended to describe the process that controls the empirical accuracy of judgments based on multiple fallible indicators; in contrast, bounded rationality is intended to describe the problem-solving process that is limited to a bounded segment of the "problem space." Simon's emphasis is on rational analytical cognition within a bounded problem space, thus his aptly named concept "bounded rationality." There is no room for intuition in bounded rationality: All cognition is rational and analytical. In quasi rationality, however, there is a place for intuition; depending on task conditions, the process may closely resemble intuition or may closely resemble rational analytical cognition (see Hammond, 1996c, 1999). There is a place in cognitive science for both bounded rationality and quasi rationality, but they should not be confused.

Quasi rationality also allows room for the combined use of rational/analytical cognition and intuitive cognition, in what is also called common sense. An example of how analytical and intuitive cognition can be combined can be found in Whitecotton, Sanders, and Norris (1998), who examined "the intuitive combination of human judgment and mechanical prediction under varied information conditions" (p. 325; see also Blattberg & Hoch, 1990; Hoch & Schkade, 1996).

Brunswik's life ended before he got very far with this expansion of the scope of his theory. But the ideas that appear on pages 89–93 did move some of his students to consider analytical as well as intuitive cognition and inspired the development of cognitive continuum theory. These ideas were later expanded to employ the metatheories of *correspondence* and *coherence* (see Hammond, 1996c, 1999) to describe the work in the field of judgment and decision making.

Brunswik was clearly a correspondence theorist; his research focused entirely on the empirical accuracy—the *competence*—of physical and social perception, the correspondence between judgment and object. Neither he nor his followers ever seriously pursued the issues of coherence competence and, as a result, it must be acknowledged that current Brunswikian psychology does not address the entire cognitive problem. On the other hand, cognitive psychology, with few exceptions, seems to have forgotten that correspondence competence is a necessary part of any animal's existence, including the human animal's,

and its attention has been almost entirely concentrated on finding failures of coherence competence, no matter how trivial. Thus, we are faced with a field divided into two spheres of interest that lack conceptual contact, despite mutual functional demands.

Why Now?

Why is this absorption of Brunswikian concepts taking place now? The answer to this question lies in the current demand for *justified generalization of research results in the field of psychology*. Now, more than ever before, psychologists are seeking—and the sponsors of their research are demanding—legitimate methodological generalization for their work so that results will carry meaning beyond the restricted conditions of the laboratory. Yet, at least one clear answer to that demand was already present in Brunswik's work. Regrettably, that answer was ignored. Nevertheless, if no explicit acknowledgment of Brunswik's answer appeared, the current implicit absorption of Brunswikian concepts into the mainstream indicates that (almost) all want to be Brunswikians now—whether they know it or not—because they want and need what Brunswikian theory offers: a theoretically compatible methodology, indigenous to psychology, that provides a defensible means of generalization over conditions. Against this trend of implicit absorption, the editors and the authors of this volume trust that by making available Brunswik's original papers, together with elucidating commentaries, as well as demonstrations of the theory and research that have followed from his work, current confusion will be reduced and the purposes of the field of psychology will be advanced.

Thirty-five years ago Kenneth Hammond (1966a) wrote:

What does the future hold for Egon Brunswik's probabilistic functionalism? What part will it play in the unfolding of the science of behavior? All those who knew Egon Brunswik agreed that he was a brilliant man and an earnest scholar. The question is—was he a brilliant man who wasted his life on ideas that were so tangential and so unorthodox that they could be of no use to the graduate student, the young professor, those who are carving the new face of psychology? Or did he lay the groundwork for a new point of departure, slow to be recognized but sure to be overwhelming in its final impact? Only history, of course, can give the final answer. (p. 77)

Thirty-five years of history are too few to provide a definite or "final" answer, but all the signs are pointing to the more positive view. There have been many empirical studies in the academic area, many applications, and a growth in theory as well. Although Brunswikian ideas are being incorporated into mainstream psychology, their recognition occurs too often implicitly (and in a distorted fashion) rather than explicitly (and correctly). The editors of this volume hope that the greater availability of Brunswik's original articles and the related comments of our many contributors will lead to a greater understanding of the work of this brilliant and innovative psychologist, who may well have provided the answer to psychology's most pressing problem fifty years ago.

PART I

BEGINNINGS

The Grand Ideas Introduced

The Organism and the Causal Texture of the Environment [1935]

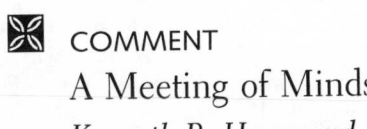 COMMENT

A Meeting of Minds

Kenneth R. Hammond

Edward C. Tolman, then perhaps the outstanding academic psychologist in the United States, and chairman of the psychology department at the University of California at Berkeley, spent part of his 1933–1934 sabbatical in Vienna. There he met Egon Brunswik, an assistant in Karl Buhler's laboratory, and discovered they were kindred souls. They found that "our previous separate investigations had led us quite independently of one another to a common point of view as to the general nature of psychology." That discovery led Tolman to invite Brunswik to spend the next year (1935–1936) in Berkeley.

That sounds very matter of fact, but what price would one pay to have overheard these conversations, which we can imagine to have gone something like this:

> [Tolman?] Why, that is strange! Your views of perception are a mirror image of my views of learning!
>
> [Brunswik?] And your views of learning are the mirror image of my views of perception!
>
> [Tolman?] And we even hold common views about the nature of psychology, what the science of psychology should be! What a coincidence that we should meet! We must write about this; you must come to Berkeley!

Note that these two had discovered not merely a common point of view regarding a theory of learning or perception but "a common point of view as to the *general nature of psychology*," and that sweeping conclusion led them to publish their views in an article titled "The Organism and the Causal Texture of the Environment" in the *Psychological Review* (1935). That publication date means that they must have written it in Vienna.

The phrase "a common point of view as to the general nature of psychology" was critical; it would turn out to have both strong positive and strong negative results; it would mean the widening of the horizons of psychology, as well as the erection of a barrier to the acceptance of their views. For by this statement, they brought themselves within the purview of Thomas Kuhn's "structure of scientific revolutions," as described in his book of that title. That is, on the positive side they were declaring themselves to be more than "normal scientists," as Kuhn put it; they had announced themselves to be revolutionaries. But revolutionaries are unwelcome in science unless they first provide empirical advances that lend credence to their views. Brunswik and Tolman's 1935 article certainly did not accomplish that, although they set about achieving that goal, each in his own way.

It is now more than a half century later. What draws us to this article now? Exactly what was their common view of the "general nature of psychology"? How was it different from the conception of psychology generally held by others in their time? or from the view(s) held by psychologists today? Did it make a difference in the behavior of psychologists then, or does it now? More important, should it?

The principal difference between the view advocated by Brunswik and Tolman and mainstream psychologists, then and now, lies in what they considered the point of departure for psychology, namely, a *theory of the environment*. They began with the idea that the natural environment—the natural environment that E. O. Wilson envisioned as the origin of *Homo sapiens* in his "Biophilia Hypothesis" (Wilson & Kellert, 1993)—would demand a certain form of cognition and behavior from the organisms that inhabited it, an environment that would exert its selective pressures accordingly. Their plan was to begin with a consideration of the nature of that environment and to seek out those characteristics that it would demand, and that would provide the basis for the selection of organisms, and *then* to theorize about the nature of those organisms that would successfully come to terms with that environment. That was a new idea because psychologists had traditionally done the opposite; they first speculated about the nature of the organism and confined their theorizing to it, independent of the nature of the environment; in fact, they hardly gave the environment a thought. That difference in approach remains largely true today. And that indifference toward the environment accounts for the failures of generalization of results, as Brunswik would later show, not only from the laboratory to the outside, but from one set of laboratory conditions to another.

Brunswik and Tolman were quite clear and specific in their premises about the characteristics of the natural environment; it mediated information from the unseen to the seen—distal variables to proximal variables or, better, depth variables to surface variables—in a probabilistic fashion. There was redundancy among signs, and there

were misleading as well as valid signs, and on one point they had no doubt: There were few unequivocal signs. Similarly, on the behavioral side, there are multiple paths to a goal, a premise that would lead to the symmetry later exhibited in the well-known lens model (about which much below). All this suggested to them that, if this were so, then psychologists' experiments should entail *more than* the variation of a *single* sign (isolated from all other variables), nor should signs be *unequivocally* related to significates; rather, they should entail probabilistic relations—Brunswik would later call them "uncertainty-geared relations"—whenever appropriate and thus expand the limits of generalization of results. In short, psychologists should *expand* their notion of what a laboratory environment should entail. They should not be slaves to a methodology that offered rigor but was theoretically empty; theory and method are *not* independent. In psychology, the wrong method was being applied to the wrong conception of psychological problems.

Later (1956b), Brunswik would be very specific about what generalization should entail, but here, we should turn to a second feature of their view that was entirely new, one that followed from their notion of a textured environment. Their new idea was that a collection of *fallible* inputs could result in an almost *infallible* perceptual achievement, and that a collection of fallible endeavors could result in an almost infallible success in learning to achieve a goal. The idea that infallibility could arise out of fallibility led to a probabilistic psychology, a descriptive psychology more like geography than physics, which was then—and still is—the model for most academic psychologists. All this—and more, explained in greater and greater detail as their lifework continued—was at the core of their common view of the "general nature of psychology."

REPRINT

The Organism and the Causal Texture of the Environment

Edward C. Tolman and Egon Brunswik

Having found that our previous separate investigations had led us quite independently of one another to a common point of view as to the general nature of psychology, we decided upon this joint article.

I

Each of us has come to envisage psychology as primarily concerned with the methods of response of the organism to two characteristic features of the environment. The first of these features lies in the fact that the environment is a *causal texture (Kausalgefüge)*[1] in which different events are regularly dependent upon each other. And because of the presence of such *causal couplings (Kausalkoppelungen)*, actually existing in their environments, organisms come to accept one event as a *local representative (Stellvertreter)* for another event. It is by the use of such acceptances or assertions of local representatives that organisms come to steer their ways through that complex network of events, stimuli and happenings, which surrounds them. By means of such *local representation (Stellvertretung)* the organism comes to operate in the presence of the local representative in a manner more or less appropriate to the fact of a more distant object or situation, i.e. the *entity represented (das Vertretene)*.[2]

The second feature of the environment to which the organism also adjusts is the fact that such causal connections are probably always to some degree *equivocal (mehrdeutig)*. Types of local representatives are, that is, not connected in simple one-one, *univocal (eindeutig)* fashion, with the types of entities represented. Any one type of local representative is found to be causally connected with differing frequencies with more than one kind of entity represented and vice-versa.

And it is indeed, we would assert, this very *equivocality (Mehrdeutigkeit)* in the causal "representation"-strands in the environment which lend to the psychological activities of organisms many of their most outstanding characteristics.

It appears also that, whereas the one of us, Tolman (**33**), was led to emphasize these two facts of *local representation* and of *equivocality (Mehrdeutigkeit)* by a study of the relations of *means-objects (Mittelgegenstände)* to *ends (Zeilgegenstände)* in the learning activities of rats, the other, Brunswik (**2**), was led to emphasize these same concepts as a result of an examination of the relations of *stimulus-cues* or *signs (Reize als Anzeichen)* to *Gegenstände*[3] as a result of a study of the relations involved in the "Konstanz"-phenomenon in human perception.[4]

We observe animals making and using tools, entering paths, ingesting food, avoiding dangerous objects, and the like. But in each such case the tools, the paths, the foods, the dangerous objects are behaved to only because of their role as means-objects. They are behaved to, that is, in their roles as the most probable "local representatives" whereby to reach or avoid such and such more ultimate, "represented" positive or negative, goals. For it is the reaching or avoiding of these more distant represented goals which are of final importance to the organism. And further, we also observe these same animals, responding selectively, (and perhaps in the ordinary case relatively correctly), to immediate entities (*e.g.*, the detailed structure of light-wave bundles, and the like) in their turn, as the most probable local representatives, *i.e.*, cues, for such tools, paths, foods, dangerous objects, etc. And here, also, it is the character of these more distant "represented" objects which have the greater determining significance for the organism. Light-wave bundles, and the like, are to be correctly selected as the most probable local representatives, *i.e.*, as cues, for such and such object-characters, just as the latter must themselves be correctly selected as the best

Reprinted from *Psychological Review* (1935), 42, 43–77.

local representatives (*i.e.*, as means-objects) for the finally to-be-reached or to-be-avoided goals. Without the ability to rely on these two successive types of local representation no higher forms of organism could have developed and successfully survived.

Finally, it is to be pointed out that because of the equivocality (*Mehrdeutigkeit*) that always to some degree obtains in both such steps, *i.e.*, in the relations between cues and means-Gegenstände and in those between the latter and goals, the organism is led in both instances to the assertion of "hypotheses." That is, whether in the process of selecting the correct means-object (Gegenstand-complex) to reach a given goal or in that of selecting the correct cue-Gegenstände for perceptually identifying a means-Gegenstand, the organism is forced to venture an hypothesis.[5] We would here introduce, that is, the term hypothesis as not only appropriate and inevitable for the case of discursive thought, for which it was originally coined, but also for such simpler lower-order situations as are here involved in immediate perception and in the simpler sorts of means-end activities. Thus, whether the case be that of a father, who, as a result of his reading and previous experimentation, ventures a discursive verbalized hypothesis to the effect that the conditioned reflex is the fundamental principle of all learning and proceeds thereupon to try to make his children love Latin as a substitute-stimulus for chocolates; or whether it be that of a rat, who, from having been run through a discrimination-box and having found the lighted alley always open, tends "hypothetically" to choose this alley continuously for some time afterwards (whether or not the latter then still leads to food); or whether, finally, it be that of a monkey or a human being who, upon having projected upon his retina the characteristically fuzzy grading-off edge of a dark area, sees this dark area as a shadow and not as a separate spot with a blacker surface-quality; the essentials are the same. In each such case the organism behaves "as though." That is, he ventures an hypothesis. He may be right; but he may also be wrong. A fuzzy edge in the given case may surround not a shadow, but a spot with separate surface-color.[6] The lighted door in the given instance may lead, not to food, but to electric shock. The giving of Latin before chocolate may result not in the child's coming to love Latin, but merely

in an unpleasant propensity to secrete saliva while studying Latin.

An hypothesis "asserts" that a given "*a*" is the local representative of a given "*b*." But the connections between types of local representative and types of entities represented are, as we have said, practically never "one-one." Any given type of "*a*" is probably always capable of being in varying degrees and representative of a number of different types of "*b*." And any given type of "*b*" is probably always capable of being represented with different degrees of frequency by each of a number of different types of "*a*." Any particular hypothesis therefore that a given "*a*" on a given occasion means a given type of "*b*" will have only a certain probability of being valid. The degree to which such an hypothesis will tend to be valid or merely superficial and hasty will vary with the degree to which, "normally," the given type of cue-Gegenstand does tend to be coupled in "relatively one-one" *i.e.*, univocal, (*eindeutig*) fashion with the given type of to-be-perceived (*intendiert*) means-Gegenstand or upon the degree to which the latter does tend to be normally coupled in "relatively" one-one fashion with the given type of goal-Gegenstand.

As we have indicated, it is to be one of the main tasks of this essay to indicate the further significance for the psychologies of perception and of means-end action of just such lacks of complete *univocality*.

But first we wish to present a single simplified scheme for combining perception and means-end action into one picture (on the oversimple assumption of univocality).

II

Figure 1.1 is a diagram to represent the combined perceptual and means-end activities of an organism. This diagram involves the simple but incorrect assumption (to be corrected by later diagrams) of solely univocal, one-one (*eindeutig*) correspondences between goals and means-objects and between the latter and cues. In this figure the area above the v-shaped continuous line (*i.e.*, a "v" with a curved bottom) represents the environment, whereas the area below this line represents the organism. Let us suppose that *b* indicates a *behavior-object* (*Hantierbarerkörper*) *i.e.*

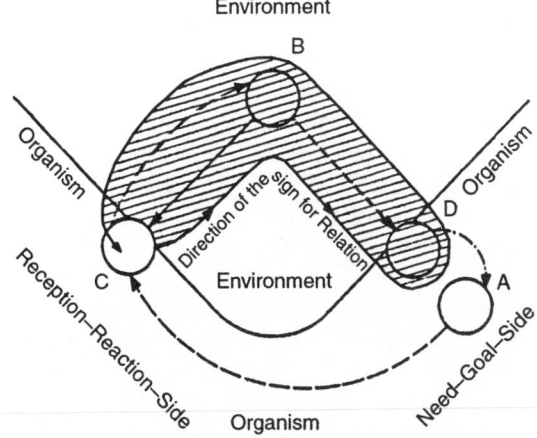

FIGURE 1.1 Organism and behavior object — with assumption of univocal, one-one, couplings between cues, means-objects and goals. The cognitive lasso principle.

a possible means-object in the visual field, *e.g.* food, which, as such, has the characteristic that it is an appropriate possible cause (with the cooperation of the organism) for resultant satiation, *d*. Independently of the organism this object *b* radiates causal trains, *e.g.* light-waves, in many directions. And part of these lead (continuous arrow *bc*) to the sensory surface of the organism. Let us assume, further, that other objects of the same variety as *b* have previously sent visual influences of this same sort to the organism. And let us also suppose that previous trial and error activities on the part of the organism have demonstrated the *behavior-manipulability (Hantierungstauglichkeit)* of these *b* sorts of object. And, finally, let us suppose that the outcome of such behavior-manipulations led in each past case to satiation *d*, *i.e.* let us suppose previous experience by the organism of the *utilitability (Erfolgstauglichkeit)* of things like *b*. The total organized experience resulting from all these previous causal currents means the present readiness of a system of "hypotheses" concerning the various different actual or possible causal chains connected with *b*, — that is, as to the probable suitability of any new *b* as a means for reaching, *i.e.*, as a cause for resulting *d* and also as to the fact that the given peripheral stimulus at *c* probably results from (has probably been caused by) a *b* sort of object.

If, now, as a result of some internal activity, say hunger *a*, there comes an influence from the *need-goal-side (Bedarf-Erfolgseite)* of the organism to the *reception-reaction-side* of the latter (broken arrow *ac*), resulting in an opening of sense-organs and in the activation of this hypothesis-system, this latter together with the peripheral stimulus-configuration coming from *b* will lead to a reactional event *c*. In this reactional event *c* the peripheral stimulus has assumed the function of a *sign, cue, (Anzeichen)* indicating an actual *b* and "transitively" through *b*, a possible final *d*. In this event *c* the total past and present causal complex — indicated in the diagram as surrounded by the dotted loop — is anticipatively lassoed (*Lassoprinzip*). *C* thus has the character of a *sign-gestalt (Zeichengestalt)*.[7] It appears, therefore, further, that if the situation be one of univocal relations or, that is, if it be a situation in which the anticipatory achievement of the lasso will be in all cases of this type correct, then it can be said that the means-object and also the goal have been by means of this lasso or sign-gestalt, *intentionally attained (intentional erreicht)* (Brunswik, 2).[8]

We note next that broken arrows indicate those causal chains in which the activity of the organism itself is necessary. Thus the broken arrow *cb* (issuing from the sign-gestalt *c*) is intended to depict the actual manipulation of *b*, grasping, eating, etc. And the outcome of this manipulation of *b* is indicated by the broken arrow *bd*. This latter action is to be conceived as resulting out of such manipulation, that is, as occurring without further independent activity on the part of the organism and it brings about the final goal situation *d*. Finally, after the attainment of *d* there will occur (after some interval of time) as a result of physiological processes (which need not concern us here) a new appearance in the organism of the need a (broken line da). And thereupon the whole circular process will once again be set into action.

III

Figure 1.1 presented the scheme of an organism in its environment for a very simple case—namely, that in which one step only is involved both on the left-hand and on the right-hand sides of the diagram. But organisms often meet situations involving a succession of cues or a succession of means-objects or both. Figure 1.2 is therefore now presented to show types of further extension of the diagram which are necessary for cases involving more than one step between cue and behavior-object or between the latter and the final goal.

The nature and meaning of Fig. 1.2 will be understood most easily if you apply it to a concrete example. Let us suppose that the organism in question is a child in his crib and that the object b is a piece of chocolate. We shall suppose further, however, that the latter is beyond the child's own reach.[9] He requires therefore some second object as a secondary means to the chocolate. And let us suppose further that there are in the room both good-willed and less-favorably willed individuals. The child can use the assistance to be provided by the good-will of one of these good-willed individuals. This good-will will serve, in short, as the second means-object b_1, suitable for achieving the first means-object (the chocolate,

b). But this good-will b_1, this secondary means-object, lies shut-up within the psycho-neural make-up of the other individual. It can send no direct cues to the sense-organs of the child. The perception of it has to be mediated causally through some external characteristics in the other person's face. The facial expression of the other individual must, in short, serve as an intermediate cue c_1 between the final cues c_1' on the child's retina and the ultimately to-be-perceived means-object b_1—the good-will (or the bad-will) of the other individual. Such an example thus presents a double step on both the reception-side and the means-side of the activity. The retinal effects on the child's eyes serve as local representatives, signs, for the facial expression of the individual. And this facial expression as a local representative serves in its turn as a sign (or sign-system) for the will (good or bad) of the other individual. Again, on the right-hand side of the diagram, the will of the other individual is a local representative of, and the means to, the presence of the chocolate and then this chocolate is, in its turn, the local representative of and the means to (through perhaps some still further steps) final satiation.

It is evident that the general scheme of Fig. 1.2 could be extended indefinitely to allow for long trains of intervening means-objects or long trains of intervening cues, or both. Or again, it could easily be modified to allow for various special types of case such, for example, as that in which two means-objects have to be behaved to simultaneously—or in which one and the same object will serve both as secondary cue and as secondary means.[10].

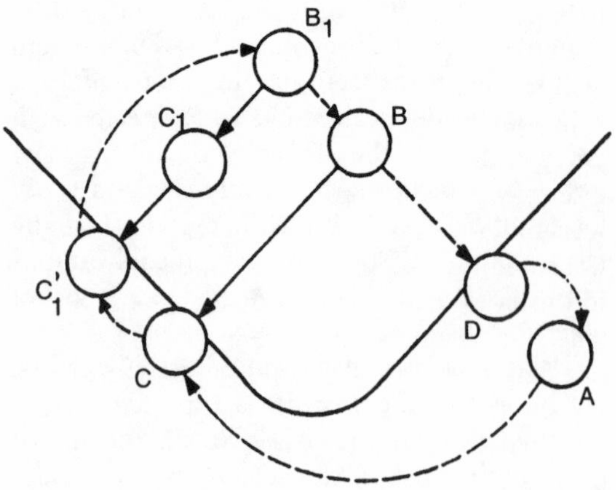

FIGURE 1.2 Example of lengthened means-goal and cue-means chains.

Consider now still another type of possible extension of the original diagram which may also sometimes be needed. It must be noted, namely, that any single behavior-object such as *b* must in reality be conceived as subdivisible into three distinguishable aspects. The first of these parts or aspects (groups of Gegenstände) (see Fig. 1.3) we shall designate as the *discriminanda* properties of such an object. These discriminanda would be such properties (Gegenstände) as the object's color, shape, size, etc., which are the relatively direct causes of the immediate sensory cues. They are the properties whereby the object is differentiated, discriminated from other objects. As the second part or aspect of a single behavior object we would designate its *manipulanda*-properties. The manipulanda of an object are, so-to-speak, its essential, behavioral core. They are the properties which make possible and support such and such actual behavioral manipulations. They are the object's grasp-ableness, pick-up-ableness, chew-ableness, sit-on-ableness, run-through-ableness, and the like. Finally, as the third aspect or part of a behavior-object we have what we shall designate as its *utilitanda* properties. The utilitanda of a behavior-object lie, so-to-speak, on that side of it which points towards further means-objects or towards an ultimate goal. They are the ways in which the object, given the manipulanda, or its manipulanda and discriminanda combined, can be useful as a means for getting to further objects and goals. Thus, for example, a behavior-object such as a maze alley which has the manipulanda of run-through-ableness will, as such, also have the utilitanda of leading to objects which are distant in space. Or a behavior-object such as a piece of chocolate will have, by virtue of its manipulanda character as something chewable, the utilitanda character of something which will lead towards a full stomach. Or, still again, the behavior-object, the good-will of another individual, will have, by virtue of its manipulanda character of possessing a substitute pair of hands and feet, the utilitanda character of bringing about the reaching of objects which from the position of the original organism are, as such, unattainable. Or, again, a picture which has both the discriminanda properties of a certain pattern of color and the manipulanda properties of thinness and hang-up-ableness will have the utilitanda-properties of aiding in the establishment of a par-ticular set-up for a certain type of æsthetic satiation.[11]

It is to be noted, however, that in this discussion and in Figure 1.3 we have again been assuming for simplicity's sake only univocal relations. But such univocal relations do not really obtain. Quite different discriminanda may be coupled on different occasions with one and the same manipulanda. Apples are sometimes red but they are also sometimes yellow. And one and the same discriminanda will on different occasions be used as signs of different manipulanda. Brown is sometimes coupled with and used as a sign of chocolate but at other times it is coupled with and used as a sign of, say, a negro skin. Similarly, the relations between manipulanda and utilitanda may be equally *equivocal* (*mehrdeutig*). Thus, for example, the run-through-ableness of a maze-alley does probably in somewhat more than 50 per cent of the time have the utilitanda character of getting the organism on towards some further place. But it by no means always has that character, as witness the case of blinds, whose very definition is that they do not thus get an organism on.[11]

A completely adequate diagram of the individual behavior-object and of these its three aspects would have to allow for such internal equivocalities. It would have to be built up, that is, on somewhat the same plan as Figure 1.4 which we shall come to in the next section.[12]

Finally, before passing on to the next section, we would like here also to point out that just the

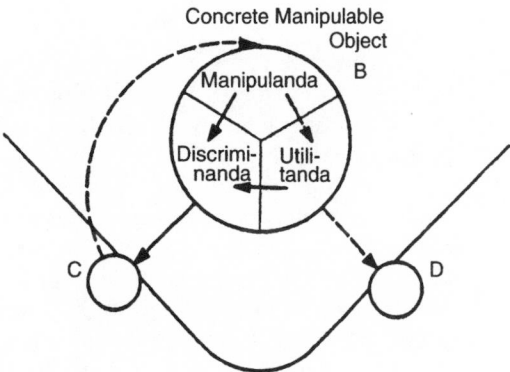

FIGURE 1.3 Aspects within the single behavior-object.

reverse of the general types of situation allowed for by Figures 1.2 and 1.3 also occur. That is, not only are there cases in which the chain between *c* and *d* must be depicted as lengthened, but there are also cases in which this chain is to be conceived as shortened—with fewer, or no, intermediate steps. Thus, in sufficiently primitive, or young, organisms the appropriate diagram would seem to be one in which the arrows in Figure 1.1 are contracted into a single one running directly from *d* to *c*. That is, in such cases response to cue, manipulation of means and achievement of the goal telescope into but one single process.

For example, Charlotte Bühler and her co-workers Ripin and Hetzer (**31**) and Rubinow and Frankl (**32**) have followed the development of the feeding responses in infants. The very youngest infants responded to the actual touch of the nipple only. But gradually with increasing age the babies began to respond with sucking movements to the laying on of the bib, then later to the approach of any sort of a pointed object. Until finally at about eight months they responded to the presence of a nipple plus a white fluid and to that only. Only at this last stage would the introduction into our diagram of the independent intermediate *hantierbarer Körper b* as in Fig. 1.1 seem to be needed or appropriate.

We will turn now in the next section to an expansion of Fig. 1.1 to allow for the sorts of complication which arise upon the introduction of non-univocalities between means-objects and goals and between cues and means-objects.

IV

Figure 1.1 presented the situation for the organism upon an assumption of univocal couplings of means-Gegenstand to cue-Gegenstand and of means-Gegenstand to goal-Gegenstand. But such an assumption is in reality never realized. The whole uncertainty of knowledge and behavior arises just out of such *equivocality* (*Mehrdeutigkeit*) in the causal surroundings.

Consider for a moment the nature of the causal connections in the physical world independent of organisms. We observe that, whenever any individual event occurs, a more or less extended complex of many independent part causes must have been existentially operative. Further,

any specific type of an event will on different occasions and in different places have different causes, or more exactly speaking, different total complexes of part causes. And also, vice versa, any given type of an event will itself operate as a part cause on different occasions and in different places for the production of different final total events. The causal interweavings of unit events among one another are thus, in both directions, equivocal. But some of these connections will be more probable than others.[13]

Exactly this same sort of causal equivocality must be applied, now, to the sets of causal chains— those between goals and means and between cues and Gegenstände—in which we are specifically interested. In order, however, not to overcomplicate the discussion we shall consider only a limited number of the actual possibilities.

Let us examine, first, the right-hand side of Fig. 1.4. It will be observed that we have depicted one positive goal and several negative goals.[14]

Further, we have shown only four main types of means-object relative to such goals. These four are to be designated as: *good, ambivalent, indifferent, and bad* (*gutes, ambivalentes, indifferentes, schlechtes Mittel*).

The "good" means-object may be conceived as one which, if manipulated, will tend to lead in a relatively high percentage of instances (say up to 95 per cent;[15] heavy arrow) to the positive goal and in only a relatively small number of instances (say 15 per cent; thin arrow) to a negative goal. An "ambivalent" means-object is to be conceived as a type which will lead with a relatively high probability (*i.e.* with high frequency) to the positive goal but one which may also lead with a relatively high probability to one or more negative goals. An "indifferent" means-object is to be defined as one which will lead with but very little probability, *i.e.* frequency, either to the positive goal or to a negative goal. And, finally, a "bad" means-object is one which will lead with high probability to the negative goal and with but little probability to the positive goal. Finally, we would throw out the suggestion that the "ambivalent" types of means and the "bad" types of means are in some situations (especially, if the negative goals are very intense) to be grouped together under one head and labelled "dangers." For both types will trend to lead with high frequency (heavy arrows) to negative goals.

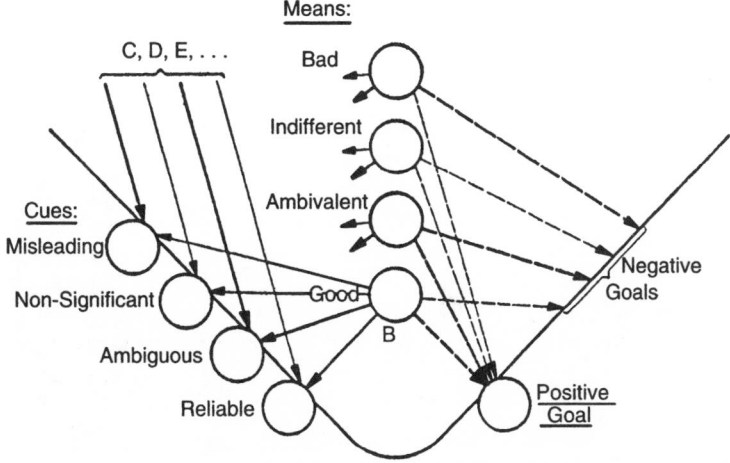

FIGURE 1.4 Four types of goal-means relation; four types of means-cue relation.

Turn now to the left-hand side of the diagram. We observe at once a similar analogous lack of univocality. But again in order not to overcomplicate the figure we have depicted only four main types of cue relative to the one "good" means-object, B. These four types of cue we have called "reliable" (*verlässlich*), "ambiguous" (*zweideutig*), "non-significant" (*bedeutungsarm*), and "misleading" (*irreführend*). The first type is to be conceived as capable of being caused with great frequency by "other objects" such as C, D, E, etc. The second, or "ambiguous" cue is to be conceived as a type caused with greater frequency by both the given object and other objects. The third, or "non-significant" type of cue, is to be conceived as caused with little frequency by either the given object or other specific objects. And, finally, the fourth or "misleading" type is to be conceived as one which may be caused with little frequency by the given object and with great frequency by other objects. Again, we would throw out the suggestion that the ambiguous and the misleading cues may for some individuals and under some conditions constitute a rather special common group to be designated as "hazardous." For both types of cue present a high degree of probability of leading the individual astray, *i.e.* of having been caused by other objects, C, D, E, etc. instead of the to-be-sought for good means-object B. (Hazardous cues

would thus be analogous to "dangerous" means-objects).

Considering now both sides of the diagram it appears at once that the psychological success of an organism will depend (i) upon its ability to pick out "good" means-objects for reaching the positive goal and (ii) upon its ability to select the reliable cues for this good means-object. An organism will be successful in so far as it can do both.

But let us indicate the real significance and experimental fruitfulness of these classifications of means and cues by turning to some concrete examples.

V

Let us illustrate, first, the right-hand side of the diagram. We may take a case of learning in rats.

Imagine a maze and let us suppose it somewhat unusual in type in that it has choice-points of the two sorts shown in Figs. 1.5A and 1.5B. Suppose, that is, that each choice-point has four alleys, instead of the usual two, issuing from it. Two of these always point south and two north. Further, one alley in each pair is always lighted and the other dark, and one has an electrified grill and the other no such grill. Further, in the cases of the 5A choice-points both the two south-pointing alleys will lead on, whereas both the two

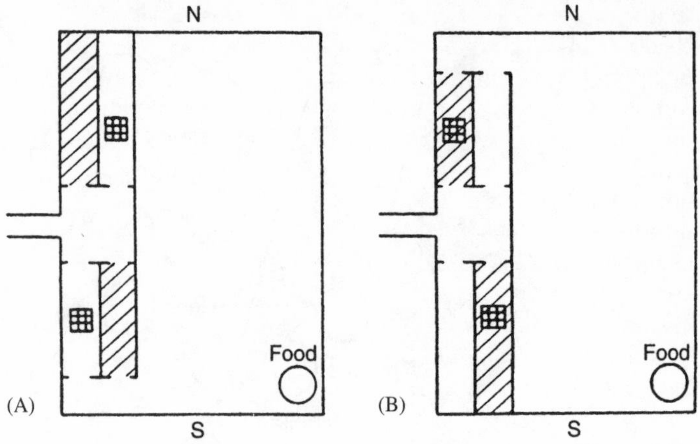

FIGURE 1.5 Schematic maze for the purpose of illustrating the four basic types of means-object.

north-pointing alleys will be blinds. Also in the 5A type of choice-point both the lighted alleys will have electric shocks and the dark alleys will have no shocks. In the cases of the 5B choice-points, on the other hand, everything will be just reversed; the north-pointing alleys will lead on and the dark alleys will provide the shocks.

Consider, now, a particular maze in which most of the choice-points are of the 5A type and only a few are of the 5B type. We see at once that in such a maze, the south-pointing dark alleys are "good"; for they will lead with a high degree of frequency to the positive goal food, (*i.e.* heavy broken arrow from good means to positive goal as shown on the right-hand side of Fig. 1.4) and with practically no frequency to either of the negative goals (electric shock) or undue exertion (*i.e.* blinds). (See thin broken arrow.) The south-pointing lighted alleys will be "ambivalent"; for they will lead with a high degree of frequency both to the positive goal, food, heavy broken arrow, and to the negative goal, electric shock (also heavy broken arrow). The north-pointing dark alleys will be "indifferent"; for they will lead with little frequency to the positive goal food (thin broken arrow) and with practically no frequency to the worse of the two negative goals—electric shock, also thin broken arrow. And the north-pointing lighted alleys will be "bad"; for they will lead with little probability to the positive goal, food (thin broken arrow) and with high probability (heavy broken arrow) to both the negative goals, electric shock and blind.

The interesting experimental question is: how will the rats behave in such a maze? Will they pick the "good" alleys and avoid the "ambivalent" the "indifferent" and the "bad"? Obviously the answer will depend upon the nature of their innate propensities, their previous experiences and their stage of learning in this particular maze.

Suppose that all the rats to be used in the experiment have an innate propensity to choose dark alleys rather than light. And suppose, also, that this innate propensity has been reënforced by specific preceding training in a discrimination-box where light alleys always led to electric shock. Suppose, in short, that the rats bring to such a maze a strong "hypothesis," based partly on innate endowment and partly on previous experiences, to the effect that dark alleys, as such, have a greater probability of leading to good consequences than do lighted alleys.

And let us likewise suppose that these to-be-used rats have also all had a preliminary feeding-period in the southeast corner of the room—that is, in the actual spot where the food-box in the maze proper is placed. Also, let us suppose this corner of the room to be in some way distinctly characterized, by virtue, perhaps, of the visual features on the ceiling, or because of odors coming from it, or in some other way. Let us suppose, in short, that the rats also bring a second "hypothesis" to the effect that food lies southward and that south-pointing alleys should, as such, be better than north-pointing alleys.

Rats bringing the above hypotheses and presented to the above sort of a maze should, right from the beginning, and without the need of any new learning, behave relatively "correctly"—*i.e.*, they should at once choose the "good" dark south-pointing alleys most frequently and the "bad" lighted north-pointing alleys least frequently. And presumably they should choose the "ambivalent" lighted south-pointing alleys and the "indifferent" dark north-pointing alleys with some sort of in-between frequencies. It is to be noted, however, there are as yet in the literature no experiments which give exact information as to the two latter sorts of possibility. We do not know, for example, whether the rats will show a greater preference (or lack of preference) for the "indifferent" dark north-pointing alleys, which have only a small probability of being either very good or very bad, or for the "ambivalent" lighted south-pointing alleys which have quite a high probability of being very good but also a high probability of being very bad. The possibility and desirability of further experimentation on such a point as this at once suggests itself. And such future experimentation might well prove extraordinarily suggestive. It might even prove a way of differentiating emotional dispositions. Thus, for example, the rat who tended to prefer "indifferent" means to "ambivalent" ones might perhaps be defined as "cautious," whereas the one who tended to prefer "ambivalent" means to "indifferent" ones could perhaps be designated as "courageous" or "dare-devilish." And, granting such definitions, then, such a set-up would also allow us to investigate the effects of such factors as degrees of hunger, or varying degrees of having been "blocked" (in Lewin's sense) and the like, upon such emotional states. Indeed, a whole array of possibilities of this general sort for future research suggest themselves.

Or, again, we may turn, now, to the consideration of other types of experiment. These would be experiments in which the total maze would not, as above, agree with the rats' initial hypotheses but in which the rats would have to acquire a new hypothesis (i.e. to learn). Two sub-types of case present themselves. On the one hand, there would be the type of experiment in which the detailed hypotheses which the rats brought with them were definitely wrong. And, on the other hand, there would be the type of experiment in which the animals brought no detailed hypotheses but merely a very general hypothesis which expressed itself as an initial readiness to explore equally all alleys. (N.B. This latter would be the perfect pure case of trial and error learning.)

To illustrate the former type, let us imagine a situation similar to that previously described save that the actual maze connections would be arranged just oppositely. That is, imagine a maze in which the great majority of choice-points will be like that in Fig. 1.5B and only a few like that in Fig. 1.5A. To such a maze the rats, with their innate propensities and previous experience just as before will bring absolutely wrong hypotheses. What will they do? Obviously they will learn. That is, although they will begin by selecting the objectively "bad" alleys and avoiding the "objectively" good alleys, soon they will begin to correct these initial selections and to acquire the necessary new hypotheses.[16] But the specifically new and interesting question, which experimentation will be needed to answer, is in what order will the old hypotheses—i.e., the old order of selection of blinds, drop out? What will be the intervening phases of relative preference for the different types of alley through which the animals will pass? Again a whole series of new experiments suggests itself.

Consider now the second sub-type of experiment—that in which the rat brings no specific hypotheses as to north-pointingness nor as to lightedness or darkness, but exhibits merely an initial equal readiness for all four types of alleys, i.e., what we may call the "pure" case of so-called trial and error. What will be the order of learning in such a case? Will the rats drop out of the "bad" alleys first, and then the "ambivalent" and then the "indifferent"? Or will they follow some other order? Again important further experiments are needed.[17]

The above must suffice to illustrate the significance, experimentally, of a classification of means-objects based on the probability-relations between such means-objects and goals. We will turn, now, in the next section to illustrations of the experimental significance of the analogous classification of cues, that is, to illustrations of the left-hand side of Fig. 1.4.

VI

We may imagine a case in which the "good" means-object in the particular instance must possess the property (Gegenstand) of lying at a certain specific spatial distance from the organism. That is, the organism, if it is to be successful, must be able to select correctly the "reliable" visual cues for *third-dimensional depths*. It must be able to distinguish between such "reliable" cues and those which instead are merely "ambiguous," "non-significant," or even "misleading."

As perhaps the best example of *reliable* cues for the visual perception of the third dimension we may take (for organisms with binocular vision) *bi-retinal disparity*. Differences of third-dimensional depth in the environment are projected differently into the two eyes. And the extent and nature of these differences is utilized by the organism as a cue for the perception of distance. But, although such bi-retinal differences do usually stand in almost univocal correspondence with actual differences of distance (relative to the point of fixation), this is by no means always the case. For by means of a stereoscope one can also provoke, as a result of pictures which are really flat, just these same bi-retinal differences. In this latter case the flat pictures produce bi-retinal effects which "normally" are produced only by real differences of third-dimensional depth. But such instances are obviously artificial and exceptional and have but a low degree of "general" probability. They are none the less possible and this possibility is cared for in Fig. 1.4 by the faint causal line debouching into reliable cues from "other possible objects" C, D, E. . . .

It is interesting to note, further, that the fact that a stereoscope is able to arouse impressions of the third dimension means that the perceptual system as such continues to adhere quite blindly to the hypothesis that bi-retinal disparity is necessarily a cue for third-dimensional depth. And the perceptual system does thus adhere to this hypothesis even when the presence of the stereoscope is an added item among the perceptual data. The perceptual apparatus is, in other words, by itself relatively short-sighted and superficial. It is incapable, at least without specific training, of separating out the case where bi-retinal disparity occurs by itself unaccompanied by a stereoscope from that in which there is the added perceptual data coming from the stereoscope. The perceptual apparatus is incapable of reacting to the former case as indicating with a high probability real third dimension and to the latter as indicating with high probability mere flat pictures. For such a prompt differentiation the superior and more fundamentally accurate processes of discursive thought appear to be required.

Again, let us also note that just the reverse sort of situation can also occur. Bi-retinal disparity cannot only be artificially produced (as by a stereoscope) but it can also be artificially destroyed. Consider, for example, the case in which a scene is observed not directly but in the finder of a camera. In this sort of set-up the effect upon the two retinas is that coming from a flat plane. There is no bi-retinal disparity although there are real differences of third-dimensional depth. In other words, bi-retinal disparity can not only have other causes than real depth in the environment, but real depth can under special, although "normally" improbable, conditions fail to produce bi-retinal disparity. Thus, even for this example of a very *reliable* type of cue, there still obtains some degree of equivocality in both directions,—in the directions both from Gegenstand as cause to cue as effect and from cue as effect to Gegenstand as cause.

Let us consider next an example of *ambiguous* cues for third-dimensional depth. Ambiguous cues we have defined as ones which though also frequently induced by the given type of Gegenstand are of less certain value in that they can likewise frequently result from other Gegenstände than the one in question. An especially good example of such cues relative to third-dimensional distances is *perspective*. Let us explicate. Many objects—especially those common in civilized environments—tend to be right-angled, or to be bounded by parallel lines, or to occur in rows made up of individual items all of equal size. Consider, for example, such objects as: streets, sidewalks, house façades, single windows and rows of windows, corridors, rooms, pieces of furniture and the like. Such single objects or series of objects are, however, very often presented to the organism at an angle, that is, not as face on but as stretching off into a third dimension. Thus it happens that distorted angles and distorted size relations (converging lines and trapezoidal forms, etc.) result with great frequency from differences of third-dimensional depth and the perceptual apparatus comes to use these distorted forms as distance criteria. Much oftener, however, than was true for bi-retinal disparity these distance criteria of "distorted forms" can also result from other causes than actual third-dimensional depth. Such forms can also be produced with great ease artificially—as for example, by a mere pair of carelessly drawn converging lines. And, likewise, there actually exist in the world many objects whose surfaces are really trapezoidal, diamond-shaped and the like. So that these latter objects even when face on also produce "distorted" images. Indeed many of the familiar optical illusions are cases in which just such "distortions" in actually flat surfaces are responded to as meaning stretching-off into the third dimension.

To return now to Fig. 1.4 we find this equivocality whereby distorted images can be produced very frequently either by really right-angled objects, rows of equal objects, objects with parallel boundaries stretching off into the distance, on the one hand, or by really distorted objects and artificial objects, on the other, allowed for by the forking of the causal lines which debouch into "ambiguous" cues. And the two branches of this fork are both drawn with heavy lines. That is, in terms of our example, the cue of distorted retinal images may result with about equal and relatively great probabilities either from true stretchings-off into the third dimension, on the one hand, or from actually distorted objects or from mere drawings, on the other.

In other words, a pure reliance upon perspective as a depth criterion necessarily leads to many mistakes (illusions). All the cases where appearances of depth are produced solely by drawings fall into this group. Consider, for example, Fig. 1.6. The row of three angles appears quite strikingly as a chain of three mountains really equal in size but extending back into the third dimension. But it is to be noted that when these curves do thus appear, it means that the perceptual apparatus has over-generalized. For in nature there is no very great tendency for rows of mountains equal in size to stretch away from one as so often happens for windows, trees and the like. In fact, the most frequent tendency in nature would seem to be for the nearer mountains (seen as they usu-

ally are from the plain) to be actually the smaller. Or, again, consider the other part of Fig. 1.6. If the two adjacent parallelograms are seen as an open book the perceptual apparatus has again over-generalized. For it has assumed that these angles (and perhaps all angles of this kind) are in nature really right angles. In a word, too great a reliance upon the ambiguous cues of perspective always means laziness and over-generalization on the part of the perceptual apparatus.

Let us consider, now, an example of *non-significant* cues for third-dimensional distances. A relatively good instance is that of *number of intermediate objects*. It appears that the more such intermediate objects there are between an observer and the main object, the further off the latter tends to appear. And in actual nature there is of course some probability that a longer distance will in truth be filled with more intermediate entities than a shorter distance. But there is also some probability that more intermediate objects may mean (result from) something other than greater distance. Intermediate objects will often lie so that the eye cannot detect them. And in any case, it is obvious that in nature there is no such constant relationship between number of intermediate objects and distance as there tends to be between bi-retinal disparity and distance. The cue of number of intermediate objects is then a good example of a relatively *non-significant* cue. (See again Fig. 1.4.)

Turn now to *misleading* cues. A relatively good example was found in the work of Holaday on the Konstanz-phenomenon in the perception of size (**19**, p. 454). In this investigation it so happened that in the main experiment, while working with certain definite distances, the left-hand one of the two objects to be compared (as to size) was at some definitely nearer distance than the other. As a result, it came out that when, in a subsidiary experiment under conditions of poor

 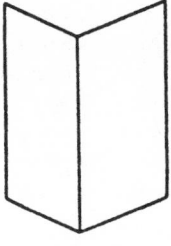

FIGURE 1.6 Failures of perception due to the persistent functions of hypotheses appropriate only in cases of real perspective.

visibility, the left-hand object was now really the farther away, the subject, because of his preceding training, with the same general range of distances, continued to see it, the left-hand object, as nearer. In other words, the effect of the preceding training in the main experiment perseverated and made the leftness of the given object (under conditions of poor visibility) into a cue for nearerness. Analogous results appeared also in the work of Eissler (**10**, p. 259) on the effect of turning forms out of the frontal parallel plane. Such perseverations (with resulting misleading cues) likewise seem to be frequent and well-known in experiments on weight perception. [See also Izzet, (**20**, p. 316), Brunswik, (**2**, p. 120).]

To sum up for this section, we would emphasize then that, in addition to its task of choosing correct means-objects, the organism has also that of developing an adequate reception system which will tend to select reliable cues, rather than ambiguous, non-significant or misleading ones. And its task is to do this even when all the different kinds of cues are present and competing with one another. The investigation of the degree and manner in which the perceptual system can or cannot do this as well as of its capacity for learning obviously sets the stage for many important further experimental investigations.[18]

VII

In the two preceding sections we have presented examples to illustrate experimentally the different classes of means-objects and cues. And we have seen that these classes are defined by the respective strengths of the causal probability lines between such types of means-objects and the plus and minus goals and between the former and types of cues. Any type of means-object has certain specific probabilities (given the causal structure of the particular environment) of serving as a frequent means for reaching the desired positive goal and it also has certain specific probabilities of leading rather to one or more of the negative goals. Similarly, any given type of cue has (given the causal structure of the environment) specific, respective, probabilities of having been caused by such and such a Gegenstand or of having been caused by such and such other Gegenstände.

The organism's task is thus, as we have seen, always that of picking out the means-objects and the cues which have the high probability-lines (in the given case) of leading to the required goals and to the appropriate means-Gegenstände. But the next point and the one which we especially wish to bring to the fore in this section, lies in the further fact that the values of these probability-lines are not fixed once and forever for all environments. A means-object, such as a dark alley, which is "good"—*i.e.*, has a strong probability of not leading to the negative goal of injury—in an environment of "free nature" may be "bad"—*i.e.*, have a strong probability of leading to a negative goal such, say, as that of an electric shock—in the special environment of a particular animal laboratory. Similarly, a cue such as bi-retinal disparity, which has a strong probability of having been caused by a true third-dimensional depth in the ordinary environment of hill and dale may have a very small probability of having been so caused in the more special environment of a psychological laboratory which frequently includes, as it does, stereoscopes and other "artificial" devices in front of the eyes.

It appears, however, that an organism usually tends to bring with it to any given new environment a set of already prepared hypotheses. These hypotheses result from its innate make-up and from its previous experiences of "normal" average environments? That is, it will bring with it expectations, based on heredity and early experience that certain types of means-object tend most frequently to serve as causes (routes) to positive goals and that other types tend most frequently as routes to negative goals. And, similarly, it brings hereditarily and from early experience a propensity to expect types of sensory data as having been most frequently caused by certain types of Gegenstände and as having been infrequently caused by such and such other types of Gegenstände. But the particular actual environmental set-up may not correspond to the "normal" average environment. God, or the experimenter, may have introduced rather unique and special causal corrections. In such special cases the organism must adjust itself to the new differentiating features and revamp its hypotheses accordingly.

For example, we have supposed that rats, by virtue of innate endowment or of their previous general experience of "normal" spatial environments, tend to bring with them to any maze the hypothesis that south-pointing alleys have, as means-objects, a very great probability of leading towards the south side of the room. But in a given particular maze it may have been established by the experimenter that, contrary to such "normal" probability, the south-pointing alleys shall, in this special case, have a greater probability of leading to the north side of the room and, *vice versa*, that the north-pointing alleys shall in this instance have a greater probability of leading to the south side of the room. It appears therefore that, if the rats are finally to be successful in this particular maze, they must be able to discover further identifying features which differentiate this maze from the "normal" one. And they must attach their new hypotheses to these further features. If they can do this, then when such further features are present, they will react to the south-pointing alleys as having the higher probability of leading north and to the north-pointing as having the higher probability of leading south. And only when such special further features are absent will they revert to the more general hypotheses — suitable for "normal" mazes and "normal" environments in general, — that south-pointing ways have the higher probabilities of reaching the south and that north-pointing ways have the higher probabilities of getting to the north.

Or, similarly, we may suppose that a binocular organism tends (on the basis of innate endowment and early childhood experience) to bring to the perception of the third dimension an hypothesis to the effect that "normally" bi-retinal disparity, as a cue, had a high probability of having been caused by (and, therefore, of meaning) third dimensional depth. But, in the very special laboratory environments which include stereoscopes, bi-retinal disparity often has a low probability of having been caused by real third-dimensional depth and may become by itself a misleading cue therefore. The binocular perceptual apparatus must, in such a case, correct its initial hypothesis, which was only appropriate for "normal" environments, by including, if it can, within its cue-system the further features as to the presence or absence of a stereoscope. But this, as we saw above, the perceptual system by itself seems unable to do. The organism to be successful must in this situation resort to that more elaborate apparatus which we call discur-

sive thought. That is, in this example the further specifications of the hypotheses needed by the organism for successful immediate adaptations require the cooperation of something more than the purely perceptual apparatus.

Or consider the reverse sort of case. A normally relatively bad means-object for getting to the south side of the room is, as we have said, a north-pointing alley. But under the special "arbitrary" conditions set up by a particular experimenter this round-about route may become a very good means-object for getting there. It appears, indeed, from experiments by Gilhousen[19] that rats which are overtrained on such round-about routes in a special set-up may become so "fixated" on the north-pointing round-about route that they will persist for a long time continuing to try to take it even after it is no longer the correct route. In other words, they can become so overtrained for the special case that when later the special conditions of that case no longer obtain they are unable to drop this special hypothesis.

Similarly, a normally very misleading cue for any specific third-dimensional nearness such, say, as the cue of "being the left-hand one" of two objects, can, as we have seen, under the very special conditions of a particular experiment become a relatively good "reliable" cue. Further, it appeared, however, that the perceptual system can become so overtrained for this special case that when later the requisite special conditions are no longer present the individual may (if the visibility conditions are poor) continue to see the left-hand object as at a certain distance even though it is no longer so. The perceptual apparatus in such a case has also become, by overtraining, so-to-speak "fixated" on lefthandedness as the appropriate and sufficient cue for a certain distance. But if the individual is, under other more "normal" conditions to behave correctly, his perceptual apparatus must be able to abandon this over-fixated hypothesis. The persistence of the latter is an evidence that the organism has become, so-to-speak, lazy and has dropped out some of the essential features of its original "normal" cue system.

To sum up, we may say in general that in the selection both of the means-objects which have high probabilities and of the cues which have high probabilities the organism responds in the form of hypotheses. These hypotheses it brings with it from innate endowment and from previous experience. These hypotheses tend to be correct for "normal" average environments. When, however, the probabilities in the particular environment are not those of a "normal" or average environment, then the organism, if it is not to go under, must acquire new hypotheses. Further, it appears that this new environment may differ from the "normal" either by being more general, or by being more specific, or by being equally, but differently, specific. And still further it appears that in any of these three types of cases the new hypotheses, which must be achieved, require the organism to take into its cue-system and into its selection of means-objects further identifying features. Learning, whether in the perceptual system or in the means-end system, is just such an acquiring of new hypotheses. But, and this is biologically the most important point, such new hypotheses should be attached to the specific identifying features of the particular situations to which they are appropriate. The organism should, that is, become docile to a very developed and subtle system of sensory cues, — in a way which allows it, for example, to respond differently to one and the same part-cue of bi-retinal disparity according to whether or not the further part-cues presented by a stereoscope are or are not so present.[20] And, similarly, it must also be docile to a very wide and subtle set of means-object differentiations. It must be able, for example, to distinguish the particular north-pointing maze-alley in some particular maze which as such leads south from other ordinary north-pointing alleys which are "normal" and lead north.

Thus the wholly successful organism would be one which brings, innately, normal averagely "good" means-end hypotheses and normal averagely "reliable" perceptual hypotheses; but which can immediately modify these innate hypotheses to suit the special conditions of a special environment; which can note and include in its cue-system and in its means-end-system the presence of the further identifying features of these special environments. But further, such an organism must also, if it is to be completely successful, be equally able at once to drop out such new hypotheses when the special features as to cue or means are no longer present.

In the case of ordinary trial and error learning (whether perceptual or means-end) the new features are noted and the new hypotheses acquired only under the hard task-master of actual bitter behavior. In the case of "insight" learning the new features are noted and the requisite new hypotheses are evoked as a result of innate endowment and general experience before they have ever actually specifically—behaviorally—been put to the test. In the case of unmodifiable instinct the new features are never noted and the new hypotheses never acquired; the organism continues to behave in the old fashion and goes under. In the case of motivational and emotional inadequacies the organism is either overhasty or overlazy in making observations of the new cue-features and the new means-features and in developing the requisite new more adequate hypotheses.

Indeed, we would like to throw out here, as a final word, the suggestion that all the problems of psychology—not only those of visual perception and of learning—but all the more general problems of instinct, insight, learning, intelligence, motivation, personality and emotion all center around this one general feature of the given organism's abilities and tendencies for adjusting to these actual causal textures, — these actual probabilities as to causal couplings.

VIII

In conclusion, we would summarize as follows:

1. The environment of an organism has the character of a complex *causal texture* (*Kausalgefüge* in which certain objects may function as the *local representatives* (*die Stellvertreter*) of other objects; these latter to be known as the *entities represented* (*die Vertretenen*).

2. This function of local representation has, however, two subvarieties.

(*a*) On the one hand, objects or situations may function as local representatives of others in that they provide (with the cooperation of the organism) *means-objects* (*Mittelgegenstände*) to the others; these latter to be known as the *goals* (*Zielgegenstände*).

(*b*) On the other hand, objects or events may also function as local representatives for others in that, being themselves caused by such other objects or events, they serve as cues (*Anzeichen*) for the latter. These latter in their turn would then be known as the *Gegenstände* relative to such cues.

3. The simplest paradigm involving these two kinds of local representation will be one in which an organism is presented with a single *behavior-object* (*hantierbarer Körper*). This behavior-object is to be conceived as lying "in between" the *need-goal side* (*Bedarf-Erfolg-Seite*) and the reception-reaction-side of the organism. And, as so lying, it may function causally in two ways:

(*a*) This object can (with the cooperation of the organism) function as the means-object for the reaching of some goal.

(*b*) This object can also send out causal trains which may be picked up as cues by the reception-reaction-side of the organism. These cues will then function to represent the Gegenstände which make up the object.

4. These resulting cues, considered as a reactional event, may be said anticipatively to "*lasso*" (*lasso-principle, i.e., sign-gestalt*) the present causal complex on the basis of past causal complexes. In other words, such cue-Gegenstände will be responded to as presenting then and there an actual instance of the given type of means-Gegenstand and as also presenting (transitively) through this means-Gegenstand the possibility of such and such a final goal-Gegenstand.

5. But such a paradigm with only one behavior-object between goal and cues is for some types of situation too simple and for others too complex.

(*a*) In many actual situations there may be more than one successive means-object and more than one successive cue-object. But such cases, although the picture must be complicated to allow for them, do not introduce anything new in principle.

(*b*) It also appears that such a single intervening behavior-object (Gegenstand-complex) may have three, somewhat independently variable and distinguishable, aspects. These are to be designated as its *discriminanda*, its *manipulanda* and its *utilitanda*. These further complicate the picture but they do not demand anything fundamentally new in principle.

(*c*) Finally, there are other types of situation, obtaining for very young or for very primitive organisms, in which there are no distinct intervening Gegenstände, as such, between cues and goals. The whole picture must in such cases be conceived as telescoped.

6. It appears now, further, that the causal couplings between goal and means or between the latter and cue (or between different aspects within any one of these) are seldom, if ever, *univocal* (*eindeutig*). For it appears that any given type of goal will be capable of being causally reached by more than one type of means-object. And, vice-versa, any given type of means-object will be capable of leading to more than one type of goal. Similarly, any given type of means-object can cause more than one kind of sensory cue and any one type of cue can be caused by more than one type of means-object.

7. Such *equivocality* (*Mehrdeutigkeit*) brings it about that the organism has to venture hypotheses as to what the given means-object will "most probably" lead to in the way of goals or as to what type of means-Gegenstand the given cues have with "most probability" been caused by. (Such hypotheses are always capable of purely objective definition.)

8. Further analyses of the actual types of probability-relation which may obtain suggest preliminary, and it would seem experimentally fruitful, classifications of means-objects into the four types: good, *ambivalent, indifferent and bad* (*gutes, ambivalentes, indifferentes and schlechtes Mittel*) and of cues into the four types: *reliable, ambiguous, non-significant and misleading* (*verlässliches, zweideutiges, bedeutungsarmes* and *irreführendes Anzeichen*).

9. It appears that the organism's task in any given case is to correct whatever hypotheses it brings with it to fit the real probabilities of the actually presented set-up.

10. The organism brings hypotheses based on innate endowment and previous experience which tend to be suitable to the probability-relations of "normal" environments. But in any actual given environment these "normal" probability-relations may not hold.

11. If, therefore, it is to be successful, the organism must eventually develop both cue-systems and means-object systems which are, at one and the same time, both wide and inclusive and yet full of very fine discriminations.

12. Finally, it appears that the study of the organism's abilities and propensities in the development and operation of such cue-systems and mean-end systems and resultant hypotheses involves not only the problems of perception

and of means-end learning, but also those of instinct, memory, insight, intellect, emotion—in short, perhaps, all the problems of psychology.

NOTES

This article was written during a relatively long stay of the one author, Tolman, in Vienna. A somewhat different version under the title *"Das Lebewesen im Kausalgefüge seiner Umgebung"* will, it is hoped, appear later in German. The authors have sought throughout to bring their two sets of terminologies into correspondence. The parallel German terms are presented here in parentheses.

1. For the term "texture" as well as for advice on various other English terms we wish to express special indebtedness to Professor S. C. Pepper. (See also **29**.)

2. The first modern psychologist to suggest the universal importance of this principle of "representation"—the scholastic *"aliquid stat pro aliquo"*—for *all* psychological phenomena was Karl Bühler (**7**). He has emphasized in particular the "sign" function of local representatives in their different forms, *i.e.* as *"signals"* for action and as *"Anzeichen"* in reception. He has made an especially important analysis of the sign function of *"symbols"* in his psychology of speech (**8**).

For another modern emphasis on the sign-function in perception and thought see Ogden and Richards (**26**).

3. The word *"Gegenstand"* has been employed by Brunswik (**2**) and will herein be further employed to designate, not complete environmental objects or bodies in their concrete totalities, but single object-characters abstracted from such total bodies. Such abstracted characters are conceived and defined in completely objective fashion. They are discovered and identified by processes of measurement and computation as these latter are carried out either by physics or by the more ordinary procedures of practical life. And it appears thus that in any single total *behavior-object* (*Korper,* *"Ding"*) there intersect numerous simple *Gegenstände*, such, for example, as: size, form, reflection-coefficient for light waves (*i.e.* physical "color"), hardness, weight, density, volume, chemical characteristics, etc. All these properties might at different occasions (in different life-contexts) become in different manner biologically important, or, to use the concept of Karl Bühler, become in different manner *"abstractively relevant."* From this standpoint the properties of a means-object, characterized previously by Tolman as *discriminanda, manipulanda, utilitanda,* are to be conceived as groups of *Gegenstände*, which are different with respect to their abstract relevancy for the organism. (Cf. **26**, Chapter III.)

Further, because of its generality and abstractness this word *Gegenstand* can be used not only for the properties of *means*-objects but also for the *cue*-properties of peripheral stimulation-processes (*e.g.*, intensity, form, or size of the projection of an object at the retina, the visual angle, etc.) as well as for such internal events or states as goal-satiation, and the like,—in short for everything, which can be defined in terms of physics (or geometry, etc.) and which is therefore capable of objective measurement.

4. It should also be noted that of the two of us it was primarily Brunswik (**2**, pp. 29 *f.*) who previously emphasized the importance of the feature of equivocality (*Mehrdeutigkeit*) in the environmental causal couplings. This sort of *Mehrdeutigkeit* is, of course, not to be confused with the possibility of a subjective *"Gestalt-mehrdeutigkeit,"* *i.e.*, with the fact—first emphasized by Benussi—that one and the same stimulus-configuration may on different occasions be responded to by quite different perceptual impressions.

5. This use of the term "hypothesis" in a purely *objective* sense was first made by Krechevsky (**23**) and has since also received the approval of Claparède (**9**). The objective ear-mark for such hypotheses lies in the appearance of systematic rather than chance distributions of behavior.

6. For all the various possibilities in this sort of situation see Kardos (**21**).

7. Previously (**33, 34**) Tolman used the term "sign-gestalt-expectation" for the organic event and the term sign-gestalt for the objective environmental complex corresponding (in the case of correct behavior) to this organic event. Here, however, it seems simpler for the term sign-gestalt-expectation to be omitted and to use the term sign-gestalt for the organic event alone. The environmental entity or entities (with reference to which the organic event—the sign-gestalt—occurs) are, as we are emphasizing throughout this article, to be conceived and described as simply some area within a total environmental causal texture. Such an area will contain as its most essential feature strands of "local representation."

8. It should be pointed out that one of the important features of the type of psychology here being argued for is that it demands and makes possible a characterization of the fundamental capacities of the organism in terms of the types of object and goal which the given organism is capable of thus "intentionally attaining." It is this feature which Brunswik had in mind when he called his a *"Gegenstand-psychology"* (*"Psychologie vom Gegenstand her."*), that is, a psychology from the standpoint of the organism's ability intentionally to attain Gegenstände. This type of an objective psychology is outlined theoretically in (**2**) and (**3**).

An article in English concerning the main experimental results and the fundamental concepts is also in preparation.

For another somewhat related treatment of the interconnection of the organism with its environment see the "Umweltlehre" of Uexküll (36).

9. If the child were able to reach the chocolate himself, the *adbc* part of Figure 2 would suffice. The whole situation would in fact reduce again to that represented in Figure 1.

10. An example for this latter would be paper currency which, at least in former times, served both as a cue for and a means to gold.

11. The terms discriminanda and manipulanda have already previously been used by Tolman (33, 34). The term utilitanda is here, however, now suggested to designate what previously (see especially 34) were called "means-relations."

12. This is perhaps also the place to point out that within the organism there will also be equivocalities as to goals. Professor Charlotte Bühler has pointed this out to us. It leads to such questions as the operation of such fictive goals positive or negative as general "expansion" or general "restriction" of life. [Cf. Charlotte Bühler (6) which with varying degrees of equivocality may perhaps control the more immediate direct goals. See in this connection also the distinction between superordinate and subordinate goals in Tolman, (33) pp. 28 *f.*]

13. Concerning the nature of the causal structure of the world in general, see, H. Reichenbach (30) and H. Bergmann (1).

14. The concept of negative goals is to be conceived here as including not only actually injurious consequences such as real physical injury but also cases which involve, merely, undue expenditures of time or energy in the reaching of positive goals.

15. The fact that we have chosen examples of percentages which total more than 100 is to allow for the fact that often one and the same type of means-object is capable of leading simultaneously both to the positive and to the negative goals.

16. The definition of learning as essentially the correction of old hypotheses and the formation of new ones has already previously been suggested by Tolman and Krechevsky (35).

17. The experiments in the literature which seem already to have made a beginning attack upon such problems as those suggested in this section are those of Hamilton (17a), Kuo (25) and Patrick (27, 28).

18. Some beginnings in this direction were in fact contained in the investigations of Holaday (19), Eissler (10) and Izzet (20). For still more recent investigations in the same direction see likewise Brunswik (2).

19. Gilhousen (13, 14). For other experiments on overtraining and fixation see also Hamilton and Ellis (15, 16), Krechevsky and Honzik (23), Hamilton and Krechevsky (17) Elliott (11) and Everall (12). Indeed, it would seem that what Köhler (24) has designated as "bad" errors (as distinct from "good" errors) are also of the nature of what we are here calling "fixations" resulting from overtraining.

20. Or to take, perhaps, a better example for this case of becoming docile to a very developed and subtle system of sensory cues, it appears that this is just what has happened in the case of the so-called Konstanzphenomenon in the perception of size, color and the like — thus, for example, to take the case of size-perception, it appears that the organism has developed an extraordinary ability and propensity to perceive, as intentionally attained Gegenstand, the "real" size of an object independently of enormous differences in the size of the visual angle which this object presents to the eye when at different distances away. But this means simply that the organism has come to include in its cue system visual angle plus one or more reliable distance criteria. Every type of perceptual *"Ding-konstanz"* depends in fact upon just such a mutual working together of a variety of cues (*e.g.*, direct retinal effects of size, color, etc.; distance criteria; direction criteria; illumination criteria, etc.) Cf. in this connection the discussion of Brunswik and Kardos (4) of the "Zweifaktorenansatz" of K. Bühler and the considerations concerning the equivocality of single stimuli by Heider (18) and also by Brunswik and Kardos (4).

REFERENCES

1. Bergmann, H. Der Kampf um das Kausalgesetz in der jüngsten Physik. Braunschweig: Vieweg, 1929.

2. Brunswik, E. Wahrnehmung und Gegenstandswelt, Grundlegung einer Psychologie vom Gegenstand her. Leipzig und Wien: Deuticke, 1934.

3. Brunswik, E. Psychologie vom Gegenstand her. Eighth Internat. Congress of Philosophy. Prague: Orbis, 1934.

4. Brunswik, E., and Kardos, L. Das Duplizitätsprinzip in der Theorie der Farbenwahrnehmung. *Zsch. f. Psychol.*, 1929, III, 307–320.

5. Bühler, Charlotte. Kindheit und Jugend (Genese des Bewusstseins) 3rd edition. Leipzig: Hirzel, 1931.

6. Bühler, Charlotte. Der menschliche Lebenslauf als psychologisches Problem. Leipzig: Hirzel, 1933.

7. Bühler, Karl. Die Krise der Psychologie, 2nd edition. Jena: G. Fischer, 1929.

8. Bühler, Karl. Sprachtheorie: Die Darstellungsfunktion der Sprache. Jena: G. Fischer, 1934.

9. Claparède, E. La genèse de l'hypothèse. Arch. de Psychol. 1934, 24, 1–155.

10. Eissler, K. Die Gestaltkonstanz der Sehdinge. No. 3 of: Untersuchungen über Wahrnehmungsgegenstände, edited by E. Brunswik. Arch. f. d. ges. Psychol. 1933, 88, 487–550.

11. Elliott, M. H. The effect of hunger on variability of performance. Amer. J. Psychol., 1934, 46, 107–112.

12. Everall, Eleanor. Perseveration in the rat. J. Comp. Psychol., in press.

13. Gilhousen, H. C. An investigation of "insight" in rats. Science, 1931, 73, 711–712.

14. Gilhousen, H. C. Fixation of excess distance patterns in the white rat. J. Comp. Psychol., 1933, 16, 1–24.

15. Hamilton, J. A. and Ellis, W. D. Behavior constancy in rats. J. Genet. Psychol., 1933, 42, 120–139.

16. Hamilton, J. A. and Ellis, W. D. Persistence and behavior constancy. J. Genet. Psychol., 1933, 42, 140–153.

17. Hamilton, J. A. and Krechevsky, I. Studies in the effect of shock upon behavior plasticity in the rat. J. Comp. Psychol., 1933, 16, 237–254.

17a. Hamilton, G. V. A study of perseverance reactions in primates and rodents. Behav. Monog., 1916, 3, no. 2.

18. Heider, F. Die Leistung des Wahrnehmungssystems. Zsch. f. Psychol., 1930, 114, 371–394.

19. Holaday, B. E. Die Grössenkonstanz der Sehdinge. No. 2 of Unters. üb. Wahrnehmungsgegenstände, ed. E. Brunswik. Arch. f. d. ges. Psychol., 1934, 88, 419–486.

20. Izzet, T. Gewicht und Dichte als Gegenstände der Wahrnehmung. No. 6 of Unters. üb. Wahrnehmungsgegenstände, ed. E. Brunswik, Arch. f. d. ges. Psychol., 1934, 91, 305–318.

21. Kardos, L. Ding und Schatten: Eine experimentelle Untersuchung über die Grundlagen des Farbensehens. Zsch. f. Psychol., Ergänzungsband 23, 1934.

22. Krechevsky, I. "Hypotheses" versus "chance" in the pre-solution period in sensory discrimination learning. Univ. Calif. Publ. Psychol., 1932, 6, 27–44.

23. Krechevsky, I. and Honzik, C. H. Fixation in the rat. Univ. Calif. Publ. Psychol., 1932, 6, 13–26.

24. Köhler, W. The mentality of apes. New York: Harcourt Brace, 1925.

26. Kuo, Z. Y. The nature of unsuccessful acts and their order of elimination. J. Comp. Psychol., 1922, 2, 1–27.

26. Odgen, C. K. and Richards, I. A. The meaning of meaning. New York: Harcourt Brace, 1925. Especially chapter 3.

27. Patrick, J. R. Studies in rational behavior and emotional excitement: I. Rational behavior in human subjects. J. Comp. Psychol., 1934, 18, 1–22.

28. Patrick, J. R. Studies in rational behavior and emotional excitement: II. The effect of emotional excitement on rational behavior in human subjects. J. Comp. Psychol., 1934, 18, 153–196.

29. Pepper, S. C. The conceptual framework of Tolman's purposive behaviorism. Psychol. Rev., 1934, 41, 108–133.

30. Reichenbach, H. Die Kausalstruktur der Welt und der Unterschied von Vergangenheit und Zukunft. Bayerischer Akademiebericht, 1925.

31. Ripin, R. und Hetzer, H. Frühestes Lernen des Säuglings in der Ernährungssituation. Zsch. f. Psychol., 1930, 118.

32. Rubinow, O. und Frankl, L. Die erste Dingauffassung beim Säugling: Reaktionen auf Wahrnehmung der Flasche. Mit Einleitung und Schluss von Ch. Bühler. Zsch. f. Psychol., 1934, 133, 1–71.

33. Tolman, E. C. Purposive behavior in animals and men. New York: Century Co., 1932.

34. Tolman, E. C. Gestalt and sign-gestalt. Psychol. Rev., 1933, 40, 391–411.

35. Tolman, E. C. and Krechevsky, I. Means-end-readiness and hypothesis—a contribution to comparative psychology. Psychol. Rev., 1933, 40, 60–70.

36. Uexküll, J. V. Umwelt und Innenwelt der Tiere. Berlin: 1909.

[MS. received August 30, 1934]

2

Psychology as a Science of Objective Relations [1937]

 COMMENT

Introducing a New Psychology from Vienna
Kenneth R. Hammond

Brunswik's introduction of his work to an audience at the University of California at Berkeley in 1936, shortly after he arrived in the United States for the first time as a visitor to the psychology department, tells us much about Brunswik the professor, as well as much about Brunswik the psychologist and the theme of his life's work. The introduction came in a lecture titled "Psychology as a Science of Objective Relations" to the Cosmos Club at the university, delivered, I am sure, in his then undiluted, and very heavy, German accent. Although I am uncertain about the nature of the Cosmos Club, I take it to have been a group of faculty members and other intellectuals, eager to be enlightened by a visiting professor of psychology from Vienna. If so, they were in for a surprise.

Instead of Freudianisms, the audience would encounter such Brunswikian sentences as the following: "In problems of reception (i.e., perception and thinking) as well as of action, psychology in terms of objects would turn out to be a physical and biological science, being concerned in particular with all kinds of fairly well-established (i.e., fairly univocal), far-reaching, interruptable causal couplings between the classes of reactions on the one hand, and the corresponding classes of releasing, or effected, 'attained' types of (environmental) constants or events on the other." What could that incomprehensible—by any standard—sentence possibly have meant to the members of the Cosmos Club listening to it in 1936?

That sentence may have been incomprehensible, but it tells us much about Egon Brunswik the man; it demonstrates the presence of a lifelong feature of his personality; he never underestimated the intellectual ability of his audience, nor would he compromise his ideas by watering them down. As a student in his graduate course some ten years later, I can testify that this particular Brunswikian feature had by no means diminished. And it persisted in his writing, as anyone who has read any of his work can testify. He put all of his heart and soul in every intellectual endeavor—his lectures, his written work, even his conversations with students. No detail was too small to be allowed to stand unexamined, uncriticized, and bereft of its proper place in the history, theories, and methods of psychology. On every occasion, he set out to deliver what he believed to be the full story, and nothing less. I am mindful of his course lectures, which always began with what was intended to be a brief résumé of the previous lecture. To the consternation of his students, however, the résumés frequently were not completed and, Brunswik being Brunswik, had to be completed at the next lecture, which, of course, led to a new summary to be completed, thus producing a course that had a tendency to go backward in time! Not so easy to grasp.

But the study of Brunswik's work pays off in a grand way. Yes, there will be the incomprehensible sentence; yes, there will be the elucidation that doesn't elucidate; but further study often makes the mysteries disappear, and then, the reader is grateful for the widening of horizons and the understanding gained. The reader becomes not only an enlightened student of psychology who has encountered a challenging new psychological theory, but also one who has met a comprehensive view of life that was itself, in the mid 1940s, revolutionary, and that remains revolutionary today. For one like myself, who had the privilege of watching the unfolding of his work, from that lecture to the Cosmos Club to the present struggle to find its place in the quagmire of contemporary psychology, his work offers an astounding series of events. Some of those revolutionary ideas, ignored, ridiculed, or denigrated when he presented them, have now become commonplace, have been absorbed (often incorrectly) into current jargon without attribution, and are thus taken for granted today. He was, no doubt, a man before his time, and as is often the case with such men, he was often misunderstood and poorly described.

The foremost idea in Brunswik's mind, and the one that guided all his efforts, was the organism's achievement of stable relationships with environment, especially as that was represented in the achievement of perceptual constancy. This concept refers to the fact that we (and other animals) are not slaves of single, isolated stimuli impinging on our retinas, our tympanic membranes, and other surfaces of our bodies. Rather, the wide variety of these numerous, uncertain, fallible data we receive from the outside world enables us to see, for example, that a person is six feet tall, even though her projected size and other stimuli on our retina change drastically as she moves about in our field of vision. Thus, despite all the changes in the stimuli impinging on our retina as she moves near and far, her perceived size remains constant, in accordance with her actual physical size.

This empirical phenomenon was described in 1936 at the Cosmos Club in this straightforward sentence: "A body of a distinct size may be represented in different ways: either by a certain small retinal projection connected with a stimulus-cue for a certain large distance or by a certain large projection connected with a cue for a certain smaller distance" (Brunswik 1937, p. 230). There is, in short, no fixed "stimulus-response" relation in visual or other forms of perception. This feature of perception—virtually infallible accuracy despite changes in fallible data—is the foundation for Brunswik's description of the way life on this planet has "come to terms" (a favorite Brunswikian phrase) with its environment; the fundamen-

tal importance of this phenomenon never left his mind. Nor, I believe, should it leave ours.

It is the lack of rigid stimulus-response relations and the flexibility of the use of information from the environment that make perceptual constancy possible. Nor are constancy phenomena limited to the perception of size; they appear in the perception of shape, color, and other visual phenomena as well as in other perceptual modalities such as hearing, touch, and weight. What Brunswik wanted this audience—and all future audiences—to see was that the idea of a simple behaviorism, of a stimulus-response psychology, was beneath the potential capacity of human beings (and other organisms). He wanted us to see that *Homo sapiens* has the capacity to respond to different stimuli in the same way, and to the same stimuli in a different way, and thus, that we are marvelously equipped to cope effectively with a highly differentiated—that is, textured—changing environment in a manner no stimulus-response-bound organism ever could. In short, the stimulus-response psychology that was dominating American psychology in his day was badly conceived and should be brought to an end. And it could be brought to an end without resorting to the mysteries of phenomenology, Gestalt psychology, or other approaches that could not become a science of objective relations. Finding a constant relation between a person's estimates of the size of an object despite (or, better, because) of variation of stimuli on the retina was a turning point, particularly since this phenomenon is found in the other perceptual modalities. And this phenomenon would serve as a model for Brunswik's view of the interaction between the organism and the environment.

This was not all the members of the Cosmos Club would have to learn from Brunswik. He wanted to make certain that they understood that it was a marvelous organism he was describing, one that normally took many uncertain, "imperfect"—that is, fallible—bits of information (cues) and organized them into a highly accurate perception of a single object, over a wide variety of circumstances. And he wanted to make certain that they saw the significance of this capability for survival in an imperfect natural environment. This admiring view of the organism was not only new in itself but also flew in the face of what appeared—and appears—to be the persistent goal of psychology, what many apparently believe to be its raison d'être, namely, the constant parade of the faults, foibles, and general cognitive incompetence of human beings.

Recall that in 1936, the members of the Cosmos Club would have been steeped in Freudian psychology, which put us at the mercy of our experiences as three-year-olds, in the bathroom and in our parents' boudoir, making us a victims of battles between mysterious unseen forces that would unerringly direct our futures in terms of the "psychopathology of everyday life." Psychopathology would provide the distortions of reality that we create, pursue, and become immersed in. But this professor of psychology from Vienna was not telling them about human beings who were hopeless, hapless victims of their childhood experiences and forces beyond their control; rather, he was describing exceedingly well-adapted organisms that had evolved in a harmonious and successful relation with their environment. And, he argued, it was understanding that process that should be the main business of a scientific psychology.

It's doubtful, of course, that many in the audience left Brunswik's lecture in revolt against Freud to become enthusiastic supporters of Brunswik's views; indeed, his claims for cognitively competent human beings would not begin to receive even modest support for decades, and then only after an uphill battle. Psychology would focus on human error, on the negative, long after Freud was given up. Although it took a more empirically oriented, scientifically respectable form, the emphasis on incompetence maintained its command over research directions for decades after Freud had been set aside. (See Hammond, 1996c, for the manner in which this struggle has worked out in modern cognitive psychology; see also Gigerenzer, Chapter 44, this volume.)

Brunswik's positive view of the cognitive competence of human beings and other organisms does not mean that he had a romantic vision of cognitive functioning, or that he overvalued the intuitive component of cognition. Quite the contrary; although he praised the power of intuitive perception that enable *Homo sapiens* to achieve perceptual constancy, which he declared to be of "extreme biological importance to the organism, since otherwise no orderly and self-consistent 'world' of remote manipulable 'independents'

could be established," he pointed out that this ability was derived from "an autonomous but more primitive function" than "verbalized measurement and computation" (1937, p. 257). Yet, "the difference [between intuition and analysis] seems to be merely one of degree. As has been shown by experiment, the perceptual system is—as compared . . . with discursive methods of knowledge—relatively inertial, stereotyped, superficial, confused, unanalytical, and sometimes narrow in its admission of and its ways of evaluating cues" (1937, p. 257).

Two points should be observed from that statement: Note that Brunswik asserted that, first the difference between intuition and analysis is "merely one of degree," and second, intuition is indeed a "primitive" form of cognition. That the difference between intuition and analysis is "merely one of degree" is reflected in what is now called cognitive continuum theory, a theory so named because it is based precisely on the premise that there is a continuum, not a dichotomy, between intuition and analysis. Although a newcomer to Brunswik might assume that this ground-breaking idea is offered only in this fragment of a sentence, the idea of a continuum appears throughout his work (see especially, Brunswik, 1956b). It would be hard to overestimate the importance of this concept, in terms both of breaking with centuries-old tradition and of opening new possibilities for research.

Brunswik, in short, admitted of no mystery in and assigned no supernatural power to intuition; experiments would show in detail the assets and liabilities of this form of cognition, at once so valuable as a biological resource and yet representing "the primitive, and in some sense blind, or 'stupid,' layer of our cognitive system." (He often offered the perception of distance from a flat surface in the stereopticon as an example of "stupidity"; no matter how often one is shown the flat pictures, one still sees the objects in the pictures as located in a distant field.) The positive life-enhancing features of intuition—actually unconscious utilization of fallible data—were a consequence of being an organism selected by a natural environment that required such cognitive activity. And all of this was to be discovered within a science of objective relations.

REPRINT

Psychology as a Science of Objective Relations

Egon Brunswik

I

There is sufficient evidence from more recent experiments in psychology that equal retinal stimulus-elements do not lead to equal experiences and reactions except under certain rather specific conditions. An unsophisticated observer will find himself surprised to be able to cover with his own finger a person entering the door of his living room. When the finger is moved to the right or left, thus doing away with the precise retinal coincidence with the person, the observer will soon become unable to recognize intuitively the actual retinal stimulus equality of the two distant things. This usually holds even for the case when he is making every inner effort towards an antagonistic, analytic perceptual attitude of the type which is used by painters or draughtsmen in order to represent the environmental situation in a similar way as it would project itself on a photographic plate or on a retina.

Instead of this, the unconstrained observer will find it easy and natural to perceive and to compare bodies satisfactorily with respect to their own measurable physical sizes, regardless of all changes in distance or spatial orientation. For a somewhat developed human being, an approaching visitor will not grow from a tiny fingerlike dwarf up to an immense giant, but will, within certain limits, quite fairly retain a constant apparent size. This "body-size constancy" (despite changes of distance and therefore of retinal stimulus-sizes) is under normal conditions a fairly reliable, deep-rooted, well-established, broadly supported habit of the perceptual system. It also holds almost equally well for objects not as familiar in their bodily characteristics and even under conditions of reduced clearness in spatial organization.

Reprinted from *Philosophy of Science* (1937), 4, 227–260 by permission of University of Chicago Press.

Perceptual constancy is not limited to the type of physical property ("object") called "body-size." In connection with changes in special orientation, even the shape of a body will be radically distorted in its retinal representation; for instance, a circle in oblique orientation will project itself as an ellipse. Despite this it usually will still appear in the "Gestalt" of a circle and the projective distortion will ordinarily not even be noticed. Furthermore, a piece of chalk placed in shadow may send equal or even less intense light-stimulation into the eye than does a piece of coal which lies beside it in direct sunshine. And yet under a normal, clear survey of the situation, the chalk will appear white and the coal black, corresponding to their invariant physical color-properties of high vs. low reflectivity. Quite similar effects to size-, Gestalt- and color-constancy have been found to exist in the field of audition, where the apparent loudness of a sound-source remains approximately constant even if the distance — and therefore also the intensity of the sound-wave which arrives at the ear-drum — is subject to considerable changes, etc.

In each of these cases the perceptual system proved itself able to establish, in a fairly approximate way, a constant, i.e. a one-to-one coupling between physical characteristics of distant bodies, on the one hand, and its own perceptual or motor reactions, on the other.[1] At the same time it succeeded in making itself independent from the varying relations of these distant bodies to the observer (e.g. distance) or to other objects (e.g. the sources of illumination). This effect is of extreme biological importance to the organism, since otherwise no orderly and self-consistent "world" of remote manipulable "independents"[2] could be established; the physical and topographical constants of the environment would be completely lost in the random variations of their "proximal" stimulus-representations.[3] No "things" (as, e.g., comrades, the enemy, food, tools) could be recognized as identical, when looked at under changed circumstances, since all their characteristics may have changed their actual projective values.

From the standpoint of an observing physicist or behaviorist, the stimulus-projections of the bodies on the retina belong to the effect-pattern which is sent from all parts of the total environmental situation to the stimulus-surface of the observing organism. Since this total effect-pattern is the only source for a correct orientation and reaction of that organism, the couplings which could be headed under the concept of "thing-constancy" must be mediated by it. In searching for characteristics of the total stimulus pattern which would be able to represent bodily characteristics in a fairly unambiguous way (e.g., body-sizes regardless of distance) we find certain sets of combinations of projective sizes, on the one hand, with distance cues (such as binocular disparity, perspective distortion of right angles, etc.), on the other. A body of a distinct size may be represented in different ways: either by a certain small retinal projection connected with a stimulus-cue for a certain large distance or by a certain large projection connected with a cue for a certain smaller distance. The same holds for the representation of the physical color of a body by combinations of the varying intensities of its projective retinal stimulus-value with cues for the corresponding actual conditions of illumination. The need for such a twofold (at least) stimulus-basis for the causal mediation of every kind of thing-constancy was pointed out by Bühler in his "duplicity-principle."[4]

An organism which has established a system of reactions which appear to depend in a fairly constant manner on body-characteristics as such, regardless of their actual retinal projections, has proved therefore two abilities: (1) to make use of indirect stimulus effects of bodies as cues or signs indicating their presence, (2) to integrate distinct stimulus-elements into unified functional wholes which act as a single unitary basis for further reactional effects. Both statements follow from a purely objective, physicalistic analysis of the type of achievement or success involved in the facts of thing-constancy. Since the first statement refers to the notion of meaningful representation by signs and the second to the totalitarian *Gestalt* principle, this way of functioning is best comprehended in the proposition of Tolman, that the intercourse of the organism with its environment takes place in the formation of "sign-Gestalten."[5]

The way in which this effect is attained may be compared with the functioning of a collecting lens. The single central ray arriving at a particular point does not allow any inference as to the distance of the point wherefrom it is starting. A possibility for such an inference will not become granted unless other partial-effects of the situation—that is, for our present case, the marginal rays—will be brought, by the collecting lens, from their original divergent status into convergence and finally to intersection. From a knowledge of the point of intersection and the distance, curvature and material of the lens, a fairly unambiguous statement regarding the location of the radiating point can be obtained.

An analogous general way of functioning is true for the case of perceptual thing-constancy. As has been pointed out, the gross characteristics of the direct retinal projections of the physical bodies in question are, *per se*, unable to represent in a satisfactorily unambiguous manner their sizes, forms, colors (reflectivities) etc. Certain particular further traits of the effect-pattern which reaches the retina, indicating distance, illumination, etc., have to be included in order to accomplish this task. These "cues for the circumstances" (*Umstandskriterien*) play, therefore, the rôle of the marginal rays in the case of the lens. The lens itself is represented in our more generalized case by the eye together with the optical sector of the nervous system. Corresponding with the more complex nature of the task, even the integrative action has to be spread out into more complex and extended patterns. The lens of the eye, which is involved in this system of procedures, is but a part of this bringing together of differently spread-out and randomly diverging effects of the situation which is to be mastered in regard to its behaviorally important physical traits.

The couplings established in thing-constancy, therefore, appear to be a particular complex case of a causal relationship. The characteristics of the bodies in the distant environment, on the one hand, and the final (perceptual or motor) reactions, on the other, are connected with each other by a texture of causal chains first diverging and then brought to a new convergence and to intersection at the point of reaction. Such a mechanism of "*multiple mediation*" may grant a one-to-one correspondence between object and reaction for all the variety of circumstances under which the object can be perceived.

The most important trait of this one-to-one causal relationship seems to be that, at certain mediating cross-sections of the causal texture mentioned, no single event will participate in it. Size-constancy, for instance, means that, e.g., an 8-cm. body will, under a great variety of conditions, always (approximately) be responded to as an 8-cm. body, that is, be recognized as such. There is a certain set of correct "8-cm. responses" given in all cases where an 8-cm. body is present. But nevertheless the direct retinal stimulus, which is an element of the mediating causal texture, will vary within a wide range corresponding to the actual distance of the body.

Along with the variability of the retinal projection and indirectly proportional to it, the corresponding stimulus-cues indicating the distance of the body will also vary.

Besides this variation which compensates for the variation of the direct retinal image another kind of variability of the distance-cues will be noticed, which may be even more interesting from the standpoint of the sign rôle which the proximal stimuli have to play in mediating the environment to the organism. One and the same distance may be represented once by a certain amount of binocular disparity, another time (or even simultaneously) by a certain amount of perspective distortion of bodies of right-angular form, etc. Organisms have learned to use a large variety of cues in a *vicarious* manner, especially where a certain life-important type of fact is functionally difficult to attain, i.e., where simple, always present, and unambiguous cues are not available. The cues thus belonging to one "*cue-family*" may have nothing in common among themselves, *per se*, i.e., in their intrinsic, geometrical properties. They may be connected by nothing except their indicating value for a more or less probable common cause which is remote from the stimulus-surface of the organism.[6] The formation of such an "or-collection" (*Oder-Verbindung*) of coordinate cues (or cue-configurations) cooperating and substituting for each other in releasing identical behavioral consequences without being similar among themselves, seems to me to constitute an objective *operational criterion for the fact that these stimuli have received "meaning"* for the organism by being admitted as signs for something else.[7]

To characterize these important features of multiple and variable causal mediation, we may call the constant far-reaching couplings between objects and reactions "interruptable." There are two focal (or modal) regions, or kinds of events—objects and reactions—, and the spatial and temporary gap between them appears to be in some sense over-bridged by their constant coupling, since at the mediating layer of retinal stimulation (and of primary physiological excitation) none of the types of single cues do correspond with either of these classes of events. But nevertheless the whole process can be completely understood in terms of a certain type of physical process, as symbolized by the case of the collecting lens.[8]

There is, of course, one common abstract feature in the total stimulus configuration which is actually mediating body-size to the organism: a certain mathematical function (product) of the visual angle, as indicated by the retinal size, on the one hand, and the distance, as indicated by the particular nature of the distance-cues available, on the other. If we should not be able to find such a common trait, which would be—within the limits of the reliability of the cue-elements in question—in a one-to-one relationship to the attained type of object, "body-size," the whole achievement would remain miraculous. There is no discontinuity in this sense. But, taken as concrete events, there is a large variety of functionally discriminable mediating cue-configurations, as compared with the undifferentiable equality within the field of the releasing remote object-property, on the one hand, and within the behavioral output, on the other. In this sense, the strain of univocality between object and reaction is indeed interrupted.[9]

Psychology deals with the abilities of organisms to establish intercourse in a successful way with the surrounding world, in reception (cognition) as well as in action. It seems, now, that a most essential description of (receptive) abilities could be given by differentiating as clearly as possible the types of physical properties ("objects") to which the organism is able to react in a fairly undisturbable, univocal manner, or which, in short, he is able to "*attain*." Let us return again to our example of size-perception. There the alternative would be whether, as a decisive type of object influences a reaction, we should have to consider the retinal stimulus in its own size-properties or the body far away which lies "behind" it as its partial cause and is represented by the stimulus to the organism. The problem would be, in short, whether an organism "sees" the retina or the remote environmental bodies.

We find an objective basis for deciding questions of that kind in constancy-research. Since the findings in higher animals did not afford a constant coupling between retinal projective size and reaction, but a rather satisfactory one between body-size and reaction, we may call body-size (and not retinal size) the attained object of reception. In the same way, under normal conditions, not the stimulus-intensity of arriving light-rays, but the reflectivity of body-surfaces would have to be called the attained object of color-reception, and likewise note the intensity of the received, but of the emitted sound the object of a normal auditory reaction, etc. This way of experimenting upon and describing an individual's abilities by *projecting the reactions upon their focal conditions,* or upon the environmental end-terms of the (cognitive) couplings, we may call *"psychology in terms of objects"* (Psychologie vom Gegenstand her).[10]

As can be shown, this method would not be limited in its application to the psychology of reception, but could be extended equally well to the psychology of overt action. In the former case the causal chains entering the organism are followed systematically backward until they reach types of causes which prove themselves to be, at least in "normal" cases, the most essential focal causes for the outcoming reaction; whereas in the latter case the causal chains set into action by some movements of the organism would have to be followed in a great number of different cases and under systematically varying conditions in forward direction in order to find out the common ends into which they converge (unless they are disturbed by "extraordinary" conditions). In studying action problems, psychology in terms of objects would specify a discipline which would operate in terms of success.

In problems of reception (i.e. perception and thinking) as well as of action, psychology in terms of objects would turn out to be a physical and biological natural science, being concerned in particular with all kinds of fairly well-established (i.e. fairly univocal), far-reaching, interruptable causal couplings between the classes of reactions on the one hand, and the corresponding classes of releasing, or effected, "attained" types of (en-

vironmental) constants or events on the other. *This—rather than the intrinsic properties of behavior as such—seems to me the primary topic of psychology, which thus appears to be defined by a formal criterion, as a certain particular type of objective correlation.*

The essentials of all response or behavior would in this way be projected upon the total manifoldness of the physical environment, segregating from it the particular "world" of the individual (or of one of its sub-functions, as, e.g., perception) as a part of the intellectually constructed world of a highly sophisticated human physicist. This would be "his world," the *"Umwelt"* (to borrow this term from Uexküll) for which he was able to establish fairly reliable cues and means, and which he thus mastered in cognition or in action (or in both at the same time).

This reacted-to world could be detected and described in a purely objective fashion. In fact, constancy research can be and has been undertaken equally well with animals as with human beings and has shown up highly developed achievements of thing-constancy in some of them. The general method may, in the representative case, be guided by the following frame: (1) a search for all equalities in the field of reactions, (2) a registration of all traits of the corresponding environmental situations, and (3) a finding out of those traits among them which are equal when reactions are equal. This is, in short, the method of reactional equalities, or of equivalent situations.[11] The particular emphasis from the standpoint of psychology in terms of objects lies on step (2), requiring a *satisfactorily abstract and differentiated conceptual system of possible objects* (see below).

Furthermore, constancy research is not limited to the organism's environment. As the work of physiologists like Cannon shows, even the "wisdom of the body" may be expressed in terms of its established constants, as e.g. in terms of the physiological regularities of temperature, blood-composition, etc., which all appear to be kept in a high degree invariant independently of a great number of randomly varying circumstances.

Thus the topic of psychology in terms of objects would be all kinds of "constant" couplings— kept fairly undisturbed from interfering "lateral" causal chains—between separate layers of the environment and of the organism, or within the organism itself, or even within the environment;

all of them would, in fact, require the integrative functioning of an organism or of one of its tools (as e.g., machines or collecting lenses).

Let us compare, in short, psychology in terms of objects with some of the outstanding traditional forms of psychological investigation: the early behavioristic research and the traditional type of psychophysics.

Leaving out of consideration some generalities not sufficiently emphasized to become effective in research or in detailed conceptual systematization, in both of these fields a rather undifferentiated stimulus-reaction scheme was used, which did not even sufficiently keep in mind the distinction between proximal stimuli and distant things or between reaction and its distant results. Since, e.g., in size-comparison experiments both bodies—the standard and the variable—were put carefully at the same distance from the observer and in the same surrounding, no decision could be made regarding our alternative mentioned above, namely whether retinal size (visual angle) or body-size is the actual object of perception. The outcome of this type of psychophysical experiment was, therefore, not much more than data about thresholds, i.e. the mere sensual acuity under certain very favorable but specified and artificial conditions, and not of the avoidance (or non-avoidance) of gross errors impending under the disturbing and misleading conditions essential to the random variability of practical daily-life situations. The *kind* of object actually mastered can not be disclosed unless the disordered variations of the proximal stimulus representations of the environmental entities have received a proper place in experimental research. On the contrary full emphasis is given to the neglected questions of the disturbances involved in these variations, in constancy research, where objects set up at different distances, indifferent orientations, surroundings, etc., are to be compared intuitively.

In a way analogous to psychophysics, the early behaviorism and physiological psychology seemed to become overconcerned with the mere mediation-problems of sensory, nervous and muscular action as such, and therefore lost contact with the decisive more remote focal causes and effects of these actions which have to be searched for in regions of the environment spatially or temporally distant from the organism in its present status.[12] Psychology appeared to be almost limited

to events in the organism itself or on its surface, whereas the anchor-points of life lying outside the skin did not enjoy an equal amount of analytical care.

Psychology in terms of objects, on the other hand, tries to apply some method which could be called *object-critical* (*gegenstandskritisch*): the type of object really attained in reception or action is ascertained by the application of objective operations and described in its precise conceptual distinction, involving a widespread conceptual differentiation of the older comprehensive notion of the "stimulus." The *"what-problems"* of objects attained are put in the first row and the *"how-problems"* of mediation admitted only in so far in psychology as they throw light upon what-problems.

II

The psychological problems treated in section I were apt to be formulated in an objective, behavioristic fashion. As organism was supposed to be studied in its causal relationships to the environment by a neutral observer in the same way as any physical problem would have been treated. If the proposition is true that we were concerned with a scheme for the most fundamental problems in psychology, we must be able to answer the question as to what bearing these considerations may have to that field which for a long time has been considered the central or even the only one in psychology: consciousness.

The problem of perception in the traditional type of psychology-psychology of consciousness—is usually stated in terms of anti-theses like the following: consciousness vs. reality; appearance vs. existence; subjectivity vs. objectivity; realm of immediately experienced introspected phenomenal qualities vs. realm of constructively inferred physical quantities; etc. In those terms the facts of thing-constancy at once appear in a fashion more familiar to common sense: a complete perceptual constancy would simply mean that a real 8-cm. body under all varying circumstances always succeeds in appearing in the apparent size of 8 cm., or a white chalk under all illumination conditions as white, etc., or, in short, that bodies would appear always in the same way as they really are, and that always what seems to be equal, is equal and vice versa. These formulations seem

at first to touch many problems and differentiations usually treated in philosophy and not in an
empirical science. But since our considerations
in the previous chapter have shown us that an
objective formulation of the constancy problem
does not involve any metaphysical complications,
we may be still hopeful that even the introspective
version of our problem might be formulated in
a way which is, and which will even look, philosophically neutral.

As a basis for physical statements not all kinds
of observations are equally admitted. As Schlick[13]
has especially emphasized, a certain type of observation plays an outstanding rôle as a basis of
physical judgments: the observation of complete
spatio-temporal coincidences. All kinds of *measurements* rely upon this highly specialized type
of observation.[14] The main outstanding feature of
this type of observation is an ideal self-consistency
(non-variability) of the data, which makes it possible to build up out of them a "world" which is
free of contradictions. However, no philosophical
distinction between an ordinary and such a selected type of perception could be made. Physics
and any "typographical" description of the world
are, primarily, a constructive outgrowth of a set
of measurements. For the introspecting psychologist there is no need to discuss any further questions as to an "independent reality" corresponding to this constructed physical world. He may
for his own empirical purposes stop at this point.
The problem of perception, therefore, would appear as a comparison of the results of the more
ordinary, carefree and everyday-life observation—
called perception in a narrower sense of the
word—on the one hand, with the outcome of
a critically selected special set of observations
followed by processes of explicit discursive intellectual and conceptual construction—i.e. the
"physical" world of measurement and computation—on the other hand. Thing-constancy, then,
could be formulated as a good correspondence
between intuitive judgment and measurement of
the characteristics of the environmental bodies,
regardless of the varying circumstances under
which the intuitive judgments occur.

In a formal sense the observer of a complete
coincidence underlying the operation of measurement is an observer of a relational datum, in
particular of an equality. No "qualitative" statement is involved. It is this trait which yields to
physics its "objectivity," that is the highest possi-

ble degree of self-consistency and unambiguous social communicability. This standard was
adopted for psychology in section I, referring
to the "method of reactional equalities." "Con-
sciousness-psychology" may equally well fulfill
this ideal. *Excluding all direct metaphorical reference to conscious "contents" we may restrict to the
subject's report to equalities among his intuitive
contents,[15] and yet get hold of the most subtle
phenomenal differentiations, or qualities, by "projecting" them upon the corresponding "objects attained" and thus representing them in environmental terms. This can be done by means of an
analysis of the releasing situations involved—thus
leading, in the end, to a fully appropriate analytical treatment of totalitarian problems.*

As an outstanding trait of these reactional
equalities there remains their reduced self-consistency and high variability in terms of their objects
attained. This may be ultimately due to the fact
that, like under variable atmospheric conditions,
there is a steady interference with all sorts of
coinciding outer and inner inequalities. For example, surfaces perceptually recognized to possess a certain well-known "color" (reflectivity) will
be different from each other in space and time,
will stay under different illumination, in different
surroundings, have different areas, etc., and thus
never remain quite untouched in their appearance.[16] But, likewise as is true for the mind, this
would not involve an obstacle to an exact treatment. Spatio-temporal point-coincidences as a
selected basis for physics is a simultaneous equality of two elements in *all* possible respects. That
is the trait which makes it especially outstanding.

Both versions of our problem, the behavioristic
as well as the introspective, appear to be in an
equal way *philosophically neutral*, or non-meta-
physical, since no change in the universe of discourse or general categorical system involved is
necessary. The introspective version need not
transcend the "realm of consciousness," since the
problem may be kept restricted to intuitive, set
off against sophisticated conscious data. The behavioristic version, on the other hand, will play,
in principle, within the frame of these sophisticated, constructive data alone, confronting measured reactions of an organism with measured
properties of its surroundings. These two versions
may be considered ultimately synonymous, or
tautological, thus giving but two different aspects
of one and the same empirical problem.

An interesting and promising statement concerning the subject-matter of psychology was made by Brentano.[17] He considered it essential for anything psychic "to have an object": the subjective contents of perception do "mean" something, which is distinguishable from them, as their object; so, for instance, my impressions of the table are pointing toward the real table. When we love, hate or fear, we love, hate or fear something; and so on for all conscious contents. This relation of the given contents to certain objects has been called "intentionality." Thus the real table would be the "intentional object" of the corresponding perceptual content.

Having in this way started a fruitful point of view, Brentano in some other respects failed to meet the decisive empirical questions, as formulated in the constancy problem. He was troubled by something he called different ontological status or "way of existence" (*Seinsweise*) of content and object, the former being subjective and phenomenal, the latter objective and real. Therefore, he hesitated to call intentionality (or "meaning") a genuine relation, since a relation may not link together entities which in some essential respect are incomparable. Meaning or intentionality should, according to Brentano, rather be called something (quasi-relational *"ein Relativliches"*), and in any case has to be considered as a relationship of its own original type, which by no means could be analysed with regard to its properties or be reduced to any other type of relation. Many other philosophers have followed Brentano in this point.

Brentano entitled his main work "Psychologie vom empirischen Standpunkt," but his notion of what is empirical—not very dissimilar from that of other "act-psychologists" and "phenomenologists" (like Meinong or Husserl)—was a quite introspective one: the actual object of any "act," or of its "content," has to be found by an immanent phenomenological analysis of this content itself. What the object of my perception is, may be read from this conscious phenomenon itself. It seems to me that this definition of the concept of "object" is a good example of what has been called "unnecessary duplication" of the world into phenomenon and reality. If the object of a perception is completely clear from an analysis of that content which is considered merely to represent it, there is no forceful reason to separate these two entities at all. Corresponding to

his (partially) wrong beginning Brentano's work lost itself in a kind of dogmatic phenomenalism which did not yield useful empirical results.

As may be seen from the former considerations, the present writer would agree with Brentano in defining the subject-matter of psychology by the *bipolar, diadic concept of intentionality*. But we would maintain a further step of development of this concept beyond act-psychology, abandoning the immanent-phenomenalistic trait in its definition. In order to get in touch with exact work in psychology, an *objective re-definition of intentionality and an indirect method of detecting the actual object* of any content has already been outlined above. For the sake of convenience, the couplings found in constancy-research would be called "intentional," indicating the life-sustaining effects of their establishment and their functional pointing towards something present in the environment.[18] Instead of the older notion of an "intentional *in*-existence" of the "intentional object" in the (conscious) response we might, then, better talk of an "intentional *co*-existence" of the object attained with the response.

In order to discriminate from Brentano's *"intentional objects,"* those types of physical objects for which perceptual constancy holds should be called "intentionally attained" objects. Psychology in terms of objects would, then, as far as problems of cognition are concerned, not be a description of the terminal limits of the "intentional causal couplings," i.e. of the organism's reactions (contents), in terms of properties of their own or of their "immanent intentional objects," but a description of the initial limits of these couplings, i.e. of the organism's actual cognitive achievements, in terms of the *"objects intentionally attained."* (To indicate an effort made towards the attainment of an object this object may be called *"intended."*)

The statement about the nature of the actual object of any reacting organism or observer (subject) could not any longer be made by the subject himself on the basis of an immanent introspective analysis of his actual content as such, but would be made by the experimenter—or at least by the subject in a changed rôle with additional empirical measurement support—on the basis of the outcome of an experiment, and therefore would gain objectivity. In cases where, by means of these indirect methods, equal reactions (or phenomena) should be found to correspond with equalities in certain (retinal) stimulus-values, these proximal stimuli would have to be called the intentionally attained object of perception; whereas, if reactional equalities should correspond to equalities of the distant bodies these bodies (or their abstract physical characteristics) would be called intentionally obtained objects. In fact, the outcome of such an object-critical analysis could be repeated, and therefore would have to be acknowledged, by everybody, just like the outcome of any other physical experiment.[19]

The revised operational definition of intentionality as an objective diadic relationship between individual and environment would also abolish its irreducibility and make it capable of a logical analysis in terms of the general relational theory as outlined by Whitehead and Russell.[20] According to our previous analysis of the couplings involved (see section I), the ideally perfect intentional relation would possess the character of a one-to-one (i.e. reversibly univocal), interruptable (i.e. multiply and variably mediated) causal relationship.

Furthermore, the intentional relationship shows some similarity with the marital relationship between husband and wife. Though this relationship is in both directions univocal—since each husband may have only one wife and each wife only one husband—it is yet "*asymmetrical*": the wife of the husband is not the husband of the wife. This attaches to the relationship a certain direction. In the same way it will hold for an intentional coupling—at least so long as it proves to be an ideal one—that, e.g., an 8-cm. stick will under all conditions look like 8 cm. long and anything that looks like 8 cm. long will also be found in measurement to have this particular length. But nevertheless reaction and object are not interchangeable, their relation possesses a certain direction, it is "asymmetrical."[21]

Finally, the objectively defined intentional causal coupling—besides being diadic, reversibly univocal, "interruptable" and asymmetric—would possess a certain kind of *transitivity*. For, all objects staying in a univocal relationship to a type of object which is intentionally attained could be considered even themselves as intentionally attained. This feature would become especially important in all kinds of "understanding" of representation of facts by the means of language or any type of "expression." The logical

traits mentioned yield a complete analytical conceptual reduction of the operationally re-defined concept of "intentionality."

III

Constancy-research, or the investigation of intentional couplings, is concerned with practical achievements of living beings. Therefore, it may not be expected to find as ideal results as have been assumed in the previous chapters. In fact, empirical investigations showed certain characteristic deviations from univocality which need for their precise representation a further differentiation of the conceptual system of objects in order to make possible a description of the achieved relationships in terms of their object-ends.

A simple size-constancy experiment is the following. A cube of 8 cm. height is set up in front of the observer at 1 m. distance. At 6 m. distance a variable series of cubes can be presented. Under usual everyday circumstances, in the average, not an 8 cm. but an 8½ cm. cube will be found to be the apparent equivalent to the standard 8 cm. cube in front. This can be considered as a slight, but nevertheless noticeable, influence of the diminished visual angle under which the cube far away is projected on the retina.

On the other hand, the objective projective equivalent of the standard cube in the plane of the comparison series would be a 48 cm. cube. But under usual conditions (excluding the case of retinal coincidence as mentioned above) even in the case of a strong effort toward an antagonistic analytic ("pictorial") attitude, an observer, not especially trained, will fall far short of attaining this value. Let us assume—in accordance with experimental findings—that the apparent projective equivalent will lie around 12 cm. In terms of an achievement analysis, this result indicates the inability of the perceptual system to get away in a satisfactory degree from its deep-rooted habit of bodysize-constancy; the deviation of the apparent value (12) from the true (48) has to be accounted for, again, as a mutual interference of the two different viewpoints of comparison: body size and projective size.

What perception really attains in both cases is a kind of compromise between two different types of "objects." In no case is the gross perceptual efficiency following an all-or-none principle in terms of relationships to environmental entities. But in the former case the attainment of the "intended" type of object is obviously much closer to the aspiration than in the latter, since 8½ is nearer to 8 than is 12 to 48.

An exact quantification, in terms of objects, of the *"degree" of bodysize-constancy* in both cases can easily be afforded by introducing a new scale which has its zero point at the value where not even a slight deviation away from a correct retinal comparison—which is, from a biological standpoint, a cheap but "bad" truth—towards size constancy would be realized, that is, in our example, at 48 cm. The point of unity, or of a "100% constancy," would, in our example, correspond with 8 cm.[22] For different reasons, not to be discussed here, the scale has to be subdivided in a logarithmic manner. According to a simply "constancy-ratio,"[23] the location of 8½ and 12 on this scale would then be computed as .96 and .76 respectively indicating a remarkably high body-size-constancy in the former case, guided by an intentional attitude towards it, and a respectable remainder in the latter case, where the individual made an opposite intentional effort.

A similar general way of response, but usually with less high degrees of constancy, has been found in the field of color constancy as well as in gestalt-constancy. The apparent size of the moon also follows the same principle of perceptual compromise. It has been found, furthermore, that the attainment of both types of objects—body-properties as well as retinal stimulus values—will increase slowly but steadily with repeated performance of the task, thus increasing the shift-span between the achievements of the two antagonistic perceptual attitudes (or modes or evaluation of the stimulus-configuration) in question.

The problem of perceptual constancy is not limited to alternatives of "independent" body-properties vs. projective stimulation properties. It can be generalized and transferred to perceptual "confrontations" and various other kinds of objects.

Let us take, e.g., a standard body weighing 15 grams and compare it with a set of comparison bodies of varying weight but each of them of equal volume, which might be twice the volume of the standard. Among this comparison series, therefore, the 15 gram object will be equal in weight to the standard, but different in density, whereas the 30 gram object will be equal to it in density and not equal in weight. The question put before the perceptual system is quite analogous to the alternatives discussed above. Perception has to decide whether it will acknowledge the type of equality holding between the standard and the 15 gram comparison-object; then we would have to draw the conclusion that "weight" was its intentionally attained object. Or perception may decide for a reactional recognition of the type of equality holding between the standard and the 30 gram object; then "density" has been the object of perception.

As could already be expected from the outcome of the other types of constancy experiments, perception even in the case of the new alternative—weight vs. density—does not yield responses which could be called "clean" (or all-or-none) in terms of the object attained. Neither weight- nor density-constancy has been found ideal under the conditions under which the experiment was performed. As has been found by Izzet, *l.c.*, in average, instead of the 15 gram object, the 17 gram object has been chosen as apparent weight-equivalent; and instead of the 30 gram, the 21 gram object as apparent density equivalent. Therefore, the same type of interference as above could be found again between different kinds of physical objects even in weight- and density-perception, showing a weight-constancy of about .80 and a density-constancy of about .50.[24]

It may again be pointed out that a traditional psychophysical weight-threshold experiment would not allow such a decision as to the kind of object actually perceived, since volumes would all be kept equal, and therefore the objective weight- and density-equivalents would coincide. It would leave open the question of "what" we perceive and give merely an account of the precision of perception as a measuring device under certain especially favorable conditions.

What should properly be called the intentionally attained object in cases like those mentioned, where neither the one nor the other correct *"pole"* of intention, i.e. no perfect constancy, is attained? An answer from the standpoint of an either-or would be: none; but this would not seem very reasonable, considering the clear-cut nature of the empirical results. The right proposition to make seems to be the following: In cases of interference or compromise of two (or more) different kinds of possible viewpoints of comparison, let us call an *"in-between object"* (*Zwischengegenstand*) the object of perception, as determined quantitatively by the constancy-ratio mentioned above.

The concept of an in-between object might at first seem paradoxical from the standpoint of the usual system of objects. In physics something may be either a weight or a density, in geometry either a length or an area, etc., but never a hybrid between two or more of these essentially different and in some way incompatible entities of different geometrical or physical dimension. But we are easily able to find analogies from the field of mathematics. The introduction of the complex numbers $(a + bi)$—where $i = \sqrt{-1}$—is filling up the empty field between the two orthogonal axes constituted by the scales of the real numbers on the one hand and the imaginary on the other, in the same way, as the logical constructs of the in-between objects do with the open gaps within the discrete system of the sharply distinct abstract types of objects, used in physics and geometry, into a continuous system of objects. These constructs are in no fundamental way different from the constructs used in other sciences. And they are also not mere products of speculative fancy, but means for a convenient quantitative representation of the essentials in the results of an empirical psychology, and therefore an outgrowth of a real scientific need.[25] In fact, they are nothing but a short means of expression of the finding that the type of perceptual response in question is a function of more than one of the variables as they are conceptualized in the current system of physics and geometry.[26]

By an extension of the conditions varied, the reaction has been proved in certain fields to be a function of more than two types of objects, as, e.g., in the case of a comparison of volumes in different forms, or in cases when the numbers of groups of dots, coins, or stamps are to be judged intuitively. In this latter case the size and even the value of the elements will influence the apparent number.

Precise statements as to the minimum number of abstract physical factors ("objects") which have to be considered to participate in the in-between object attained in any particular type of perception will, it is hoped, be available by some application of the mathematical methods used in factor-analysis. The aim would be a *generalized "multipolar,"* or *"multidimensional," psychophys-* ics, which would enable us to register the structure of the world as attained by the organism in an exact quantitative inventory.[27]

After an introspective analysis, Katz[28] distinguished two main "modes of appearance" of colors. Either a color looks compact and substantial, as belonging to a solid thing, in which case it appears sharply localized (e.g. at the surface of a paper), or it appears somewhat unreal, a mere sensational "color matter" without reference to a thing, with a spongy texture and not definitely localized in its distance. The colors as seen in a spectroscope, or the color of a hole in a screen, would appear in this latter way. The first mode of appearance is called "surface-color," the second "film-color."

The appearance of a surface-color would, when applied to Brentano's idea of intentionality, indicate that the (color of the) solid body remote in space is our intentional object. A film-color would represent the case in which no "thing" is supposed to be our object, and which, therefore, sometimes has been called the case of a "non-intentional" experience or of "mere sensation." The vagueness and indistinctness of the phenomenological method of determining the object of perception shows itself, among others, first in the fact that no precisely communicable treatment and no detailed quantification is possible in that kind of analysis.

Similar distinctions to those of Katz were made by Holaday (*l.c.*) and by Eissler (*l.c.*) as to the appearance of sizes and forms: under clear conditions they will appear "thingish" (*dinghaft*), under unfavorable ones in a more ghostlike and essenceless, merely *"figural"* way. Independently of that type of analysis, the main task of transferring of the procedure of object-finding into an objective plane was achieved by conducting constancy-experiments. Having done this, a correlation was found between the "thingish" mode of appearance and high degrees of thing-constancy, on the one hand, and the "figural" appearance and lower degrees of thing-constancy, on the other. But nevertheless the correspondence, as far as it could be ascertained at all, did not seem to be a very close one, showing that immediately experienced intentionality is a rather unreliable indicator for the goodness of perceptual achievement of a type of object in question.

IV

Let us, finally, turn to some applications of the psychology in terms of objects to current, more general questions. It is a frequently repeated statement that the distinction between "immediate experience" and "reality" is an undue duplication of the word. The duality in question is supposed to be merely one of representation. All datum might be described either immediately in terms of qualities or mediatively in quantitative terms. So, e.g., for "red" a certain range of wave-lengths could be substituted, for "experienced weight" the outcome of a weight-measurement, for "visual space" physical space, etc.[29] Both "languages"—it is supposed—can be easily translated into each other and indicate the same thing.

From the standpoint of constancy research, the following objection could be made against this statement. A projection of the immediately given world upon the scientific system of objects does not show a complete parallelism. The representation of the intuitive qualities within the abstract world of objects comes to lie in the empty spaces between the "clean" objects of physics and geometry. Therefore the lines coordinating the two aggregates in question to each other do not show a parallel and unambiguous texture but a complex entanglement. Therefore it is not "the same" (or "nothing but") that is represented once in qualitative and then in quantitative terms, when we describe e.g. the Eddingtonian table once as apparently so and so big, rectangular and black, and then in the abstract measurement terms of physics. As was pointed out above, the intentionally attained object of apparent body-size is not the measured body size, but an "in-between object" between it and retinal size; and the same holds for apparent vs. measured form, color, area, volume, weight, number, etc.

Under this aspect the "duplication" of the world into an "immediately given" and a reflectively constructed one does not seem any more undue or unnecessary, since their confrontation turned out to be a sincere empirical question, which in each particular case can be decided by experiment. It is true that intuitive perception gives a portrayal of the physical world, but this portrayal is in a certain way imperfect, not completely isomorphic; an investigation of this incompleteness is the very task of psychology.

Therefore, the "intentional," psycho-physical problem which we are dealing with can not be considered to be a mere pseudo-problem, an outgrowth of mere conceptual confusion. From the point of view of an achievement-analysis, the intuitive and discursive approach to the world do not have the same objects, and all their differences, as well as all differences in qualities, can, ultimately, be expressed in terms of their differences in objects attained. And though these differences are often minute and subtle, they will never fundamentally disappear. They give sufficient support for the type of "dualism" suggested. This dualism at the same time lost all its philosophical disturbances, since at no point of our underlying psychological consideration was any metaphysical question involved. It became a dualism of quick, carefree, stereotyped, intuitive experience vs. a critically selected and logically treated experience. The absolute gap between these two layers disappeared, but the difference became the more clear in quantitative terms of objects. This dualism may be considered to be the harmless and necessary heir of at least some aspects of the historical, unnecessarily troublesome dualism of "mind and body" or however else it has been formulated. It does away with the naive presupposition widely accepted by common sense that each experiential datum refers to but one of the scientifically conceptualized variables of the stimulation-process.

Let us turn to a second point of consideration. Empirical philosophy made much effort in order to find an "*indubitable*" basis of facts. A regress to the phenomena as given in completely naive immediate experience was suggested. Mach considered the mass of sensational elements as primary, Russell the more unitary "aspects" of things. These aspects have been considered to change with the position of the observer toward them. The thing itself would be a sort of collection of all of its different aspects.

From the standpoint of constancy research, it may be objected that both Mach and Russell were still not naive enough in their description of the immediately given. According to the experimental findings, a "thing" practically does not change its appearance with changes in distance, orientation, or illumination, etc., or at least by far not in the same degree as its proximal stimulus-representation does. A table remains, just in its most naive and immediate appearance, under all conditions the same phenomenally identical table as ever; its backside or its weight is phenomenally as present as its frontside or its color, no matter whether these phenomena correspond to "truth" (measurement) or not.

The incorrectness committed by Mach and Russell obviously has its causes in an incomplete elimination of functional considerations from phenomenal description (a widespread source of confusion, sharply criticized by Koffka); this was meant above by using the term: incomplete naïveté. In a way similar to their contemporary psychology they did, in essence, unduly overemphasize and absolutize "the skin," i.e. the structure of and the stimulating events on the retina and other stimulation-surfaces. The notion of the sensational elements of Mach cannot belie its descent from the punctiform mosaic structure of the sense-receptors in the retina or other parts of the body. And the "aspects" of Russell correspond to the direct projective patterns reaching the stimulus-surface. The main difference between Mach and Russell is that Russell had in some sense been infiltrated with a totalitarian Gestalt point of view, whereas Mach—though as an empirical scientist himself one of the initiators of the Gestalt movement and of constancy research—remained a psychological atomist in his principal theoretical ideas.

Psychology in terms of objects (which goes, in some respect, a further step beyond the old elementistic sensation psychology as well as beyond Gestaltpsychology) has to stress even more than it has been done before, the relativity of the concept of the immediately given (or the indubitable). Through more or less arbitrary shifts in attitude, a great variety of experiences can become phenomenally indubitable and primary. This was shown in detail by several experimental studies. Mach's famous unique juvenile experience of the world as being "genuinely" nothing but a mosaic of color, taste and smell, is a type of experience which never will happen except in a very extraordinary kind of analytical attitude.

From the standpoint of an achievement-analysis of the organism, in last essence, no fundamental distinction can be drawn between "immediate" and "discursified" responses. From this functional viewpoint it would not even be true that the physical world contains inference, whereas the phenomenal not. The facts of thing-constancy—which of course are deeply concerned with the immediately given—could never

be accounted for in functional terms without the assumption, most fundamental in psychology, that stimuli of various kinds are used as indicators for something else which causally lies "behind" them (cf. our operational criterion of meaning given above).

The formation of such quasi-"hypotheses" within the perceptual system has been studied repeatedly. Stratton was the first to make perception relearn the use of retinal images by turning them upside down through the application of certain lenses in front of the eyes. In recent experiments, the acquirement of artificial new cues by the perceptual system has been studied. Fieandt, in a study which is to appear soon (l.c.), succeeded in training perception to use in an intuitive way certain otherwise meaningless stimuli—e.g. even the ringing of a buzzer—as cues indicating the illumination-conditions, in particular a certain area of shadow carefully hidden from the somewhat narrow system of well-established perceptual shadow-cues. In consequence the introduction of this stimulus was followed by a quite immediately given apparent brightening of a certain shadowed disc, establishing its color constancy.[30]

But, nevertheless, all these training effects did not appear in the same sudden and radical way as discursive information would have affected our intellectual knowledge. On the contrary, they needed long-repeated training, and grew up but slowly and incompletely. The brightening effects of the newly established shadow-cues did not seem to be affected by the introduction or the lack of any direct "conscious" recognition of the particular stimulus as an indicator for the fact that the disc is shadowed. Similar (relative) functional isolation of perception from abstract knowledge is familiar from many of the well-known "illusions."

The same relative independence from discursive knowledge, and indication for the same more mechanical way of learning, was found in experiments with coins and stamps, where the influence of "value" upon the apparent number did not exceed a certain degree unless a sufficiently deep-rooted "underground" familiarity with the objects as bearers of value was established, even if this rôle was discursively well-known to the subject. On the other hand, these experiments showed that even "unsensual" and "conventional" traits like monetary value may enter the system of perceptual intuition.

In a merely functional sense, therefore, intuitive perception seems to be a somewhat autonomous but more primitive cognitive function (or sub-personality) working in principally the same "constructive" (inductive and—by the means of "transfer"-mechanisms—also deductive) way as the critical instances of verbalized measurement and computation do. The difference seems to be merely one of degree. As also has been shown by experiment, the perceptual system is—as compared, in a functional sense, with discoursive methods of knowledge—relatively inertial, stereotyped, superficial, confused, unanalytical, and sometimes narrow in its admission of and its ways of evaluating cues. The biologically required quickness of functioning and the mechanization involved make the contents of perception look more immediate in their appearance than the final outcomes of explicit operations do. In the same way as there is a primitive layer of our action system—the instinctlike "Id" of psychoanalysis—, the perceptual system is representing the primitive and in some sense blind, or "stupid," layer of our cognitive system. Perception, like the Id, does not "know" explicitly about its (stimulus-) motives and about the load of past experience functionally involved in each of its acts. There is no "sensual" layer or type of datum except functionally speaking. The functionally direct (e.g., the retinal size) may seem phenomenally most unnatural to realize, whereas the phenomenally simplest may be functionally most complex.

It is a merit of the totalitarian ("molar" instead of "molecular") behavioristic school represented by Tolman that purposive consciousness-terms like "expectation" or "hypothesis" (Krechevsky) have been redefined in objective, analytic terms. As was pointed out above, in this way of description of perception vs. physical measurement-approach, both appear to be fundamentally equal in their way of inductive functioning and not more than gradually different with respect to the correctness or "dullness" of their hypotheses, or the reliability and cleanness of intentional attainment of objects.

The possibility may not be excluded of attaining perceptually through sufficient training even types of objects which are mediated very indirectly, that is by very long and complex chains of causes and inference. A highly mechanized physicist may one day reach a point which in some sense could be considered to be a phenomenally immediate perception of remotely inferred constructs like an atom, or of the fulfillment of any conceptual requirement by a certain fact (as, e.g., of constancy of acceleration). This is to emphasize again, in a drastic way, the functional uselessness of the concept of the immediately given. With sufficient mechanization and in proper attitude, any abstract construct may become as accessible and "*anschaulich*" as any of our natural intuitive perceptions. From the standpoint of an instantaneous phenomenal analysis, constructs like atoms, then, would become as indubitable, or as dubitable, as the most "sensual" perception could be. The mediating events, formerly explicitly given, would become lost in their new rôle of mere mediation. And, in most cases, perception would also become able to shift arbitrarily between the two (or more) established ways of focalization, the old and the new. This lability, too, makes it clear that no epistemological (metaphysical) distinction could be successfully based upon the vague and variable phenomenological (introspective) distinction between a (supposedly indubitable) immediate given and a (supposedly dubitable) derived construct.

As a last problem we may touch in short the problem of partition (*Schnitt*) between observer (subject) and observed object as it has been raised in recent publications in physics.[31] According to the current view, the boundary between the observer and his object can be arbitrarily displaced.

Considering first a single perceptual act, we would state that no freedom is given at all as to the interpretation of the partition between subject and object, since this layer will be univocally dictated by the findings of constancy-research upon this act. In the case of a complete thing-constancy the partition is placed at the body far away, and the light rays have to be considered to belong to the observer. The same would hold also in the case of a stick touching and correctly mediating the surface qualities of a distant body, whereas at the same time the hand holding the "probe" is completely extinguished in its phenomenal representation. In the opposite case of a complete projective stimulus-constancy, the light rays arriving at the retina or the stick would become the object observed. And in the usual case of an incomplete compromise-solution, the partition would lie—conceptually, but not spatially—in-between the proximal stimulus and the distant body.

Regarding secondly the perceptual system as a whole, however, some arbitrariness in the layer of partition is given by the fact that, by a shift in attitude, the type of object of perception can be changed. But, as it has been pointed out above, this shift-span has its certain narrowly circumscribed limits; so, e.g., no complete shift may be expected along the scale between size-constancy and retinal comparison.

These two criticisms do not touch the correct statement in the theory of partition that a physicist with his set-up of scientific tools and his abstract methods of measurement and computation has a much higher degree of freedom in focalizing and shifting partition than has the more habitual, stereotyped and inertial system of intuitive perception. But even in this case a subsequent description would be predetermined as to the "object" of the procedure by the nature and success of the technical and conceptual operations involved.

In conclusion: the primary subject-matter of psychology is defined by a formal criterion as the objective pattern of couplings which an organism, in its causal intercourse with the environment, was able to focalize in a fairly "constant" way upon more or less remote (life-sustaining) types of "objects," despite the disturbing variability (multiplicity and ambiguity) of the single mediating stimulus-cues and means. Psychology is, therefore, a science of the relations achievements at the command of the organism, of well established far-reaching (cognitive or effective) success — quantifiable in terms of its "objects attained" —, rather than of mediation processes, as such. (In short, psychology is a science in terms of "what" rather than of "how.") Troublesome older "philosophical" problems, or pseudo-problems, — like dualism, meaning, intentionality, subjectivity, totality, immediate given — appear, within this system of a "psychology in terms of objects," in a revised, objectified form; they develop into problems of analytical psychological experimentation and conceptual reduction by an operational shift in their definition, thus disclosing the soundness of feeling underlying the original insufficient statement of these complex problems.

NOTES

This article was read, with minor changes, before the Cosmos Club of the University of California, at Berkeley, April 1936.

It is a short outline of some of the more general considerations made in the author's "*Wahrnehmung und Gegenstandswelt — Grundlegung einer Psychologie vom Gegenstand her*" (Leipzig, Deuticke, 1934).

A more extended presentation of the connected experimental research will be found in a series of studies edited by the present writer under the general title "*Untersuchungen über Wahrnehmungsgegenstände.*" Until now the following titles have appeared:

I. E. Brunswik, Die Zugänglichkeit von Gegenständen für die Wahrnehmung und ihre quantitative Bestimmung, *Archiv für die ges. Psychol.*, 1933, **88**, 377–418.

II. B. E. Holaday, Die Grössenkonstanz der Sehdinge bei Variation der inneren und äusseren Wahrnehmungsbedingungen, *ibid.*, 419–486.

III. K. Eissler, Die Gestaltkonstanz der Sehdinge, *ibid.*, 487–550.

IV. S. Klimpfinger, Über den Einfluss von intentionaler Einstellung und Übung auf die Gestaltkonstanz, *ibid.*, 551–598.

V. S. Klimpfinger, Die Entwicklung der Gestaltkonstanz vom Kind zum Erwachsenen, *ibid.*, 599–628.

VI. T. Izzet, Gewicht und Dichte als Gegenstände der Wahrnehmung, *Archiv f. d. ges. Psychol.*, 1934, **91**, 305–318.

VII. K. v. Fieandt, Dressurversuche an der Farbenwahrnehmung, *Archiv f. d. ges. Psychol.*, 1936, **97**, 1–30.

In English, a very brief sketch emphasizing the empirical aspects has been given under the title "Psychology in Terms of Objects" (*Proceedings, Anniversary, University of Southern California*, Los Angeles, 1936, 122–126). Furthermore, some points are brought out in a joint article of E. C. Tolman and the present writer, "The organism and the causal texture of the environment," *Psychol. Rev.*, 1935, **42**, 43–77.

1. It is essential to connect, in any case, the use of the term "constancy," as it became customary in psychology, with a further clear conceptual determination of the type of abstract (measured or computed) type of physical property or "object" (*Gegenstand*) for which the "constant" coupling to a certain type of reaction is successfully established.

Gestalt psychology, in its successful fight against the "*constancy-hypothesis*" (which has been an unrecognized premise of the old associationism), emphasized that there is no one-to-one correlation between retinal ("proximal") stimulation-elements and perceptual reactions. The same negative statement of an absence of a "retinal-size constancy" was the topic of our first introductory paragraph. This is far from being in contradiction to the positive statement of a body-size constancy. In fact, abandonment of the "constancy-hypothesis" even cleans away for finding that other physical something—body-size—which does stay in a (fairly good) one-to-one relationship to the reaction and thus easily presenting the environmental terms which gives proper sense and meaning to the establishment of the reaction.

2. The term "independent" was used by E. C. Tolman ("Psychology versus Immediate Experience," *Philos. of Science*, 1935, **2**, 356–380) in order to indicate types of objects whose definition does not include a reference to a relationship of an environmental entity to the organism.

3. The term "proximal stimulus" was used by K. Koffka ("Principles of Gestalt Psychology," New York, Harcourt Brace, 1935), in order to discriminate the stimulating event arriving at the sense organ from the "distant" body. For the sake of brevity we use the term "stimulus" always in the sense of proximal stimulus or even of primary psychological excitation, whereas the remote manipulable cause of the stimulation will be called "body" or "body property." Both, stimulus as well as body property, are types of physical entities or "objects."

4. *Cf.* K. Bühler, *Die Erscheinungsweisen der Farben*, Jena, Fischer, 1922, and E. Brunswik und L. Kardos, Das Duplizitätsprinzip in der Theorie der Farbenwahrnehmung, *Zeitschr. F. Psychol.*, 1929, **111**, 307–320.

5. *Cf.* E. C. Tolman, *Purposive Behavior in Animals and Men*, New York, Century, 1932.

6. According to their objective probability cues may be graded on a scale of "reliability." No cue, of course, is perfectly reliable, i.e. inimitable and therefore univocal in its indicative value. One may think of a stereoscope counterfeiting a cue of such high reliability, as binocular disparity is.

7. It has been shown by Holaday (*l.c.*) that binocular disparity is able by itself to sustain a high degree of size-constancy, whereas its elimination (by closing one eye) becomes almost ineffective in cases in which the full normal variety of other possible distance-cues is available. A similar and very perfect "substitutability" of tactual and visual cues for the volume of a body has been found by Izzet (*l.c.*) in experiments on weight-constancy.

The cognitive concept of the "or-collection" building up a "cue-family" has its parallel, on the action-side, in the concept of the "habit-family-hierarchy" of C. L. Hull ("The concept of the habit-family hierarchy and maze learning," *Psychol. Rev.*, 1934, **41**, 33–54). The term "hierarchy" is—in both cases—apt to indicate the differences in "goodness" or "reliability" of cues or means respectively. W. S. Hunter ("The psycho-

logical study of behavior," *Psychol. Rev.*, 1932, **39**, 1–24) made the fact of "vicarious functioning" a central point in the distinction between psychology and physiology.

8. The only question remaining open for a physical explanation is as to how natural or artificial tools (or organismic "institutions") like collecting lenses, or the even more complex organismic systems functioning in a similar integrative way, might have developed at all. This general genetic question of living organization belongs to the field of theoretical biology and the psychologist does not need to be concerned with it, since his problems are centered more around actual achievement and functioning.

9. Multiple mediation—i.e. checking as much as possible all variations in the situational circumstances—is one way of rendering "far-reaching" couplings undisturbed by interfering conditions of causation. Another practice would be that of keeping all conditions of observation actually as constant and insulated as possible and let no uncontrolled "lateral" causal chains interfere. This latter would be the procedure usually followed by physical as well as by the traditional psychophysical experimentation, and also by man-made machinery, as e.g. electrical transmission of a message. Here the univocality remains obvious along the whole chain of mediation. This second procedure is in general the more reliable one, but also the more round-about way as far as the single case is concerned.

10. Our emphasis upon the "object attained" may be considered as a kind of *long-sectional figure-ground treatment* of psychological research following the stimulating causal chains backwards in search for their actual "meaning" (see above), i.e. for those types of object within the environmental system upon which the reaction became focalized. The relationship of the "object attained" to "mediation" is a complement to the more cross-sectional relationship between figure and ground as emphasized in Gestalt psychology. Ground as well as mediation are both characterized as being present as stimuli but remaining lost amidst the "things" which they are "framing." *Cf.* also F. Heider, "Ding und Medium," *Symposium*, 1927, 1.

11. *Cf.* also H. Klüver, "*Behavior Mechanisms in Monkeys*," Chicago 1933. Some of the work of Lashley follows the same principle.

12. Even G. F. Skinner ("The Concept of Reflex in the Description of Behavior," *J. Gen. Psychol.*, 1931, **5**, 427–458), though maintaining that "psychologists had better give up the nervous system and confine their attention to the end-terms, does apologize for doing so in pointing toward the greater immediacy of observation of these end-terms and the reduced tempta-

tion for insecure speculation. We do not find it a matter of embarrassment, but rather one of positive emphasis, to go even further in psychology and restrain—as far as at least one term of the correlations in question is concerned—completely from the organismic events as such in favor of the initial (or terminal) environmental limits or focal systems as connected with one of the organism's activities.

13. *Cf.* M. Schlick, *Allgemeine Erkenntnislehre*, Berlin, Springer, 1925.

14. As it has been pointed out above, coincidence may be used sometimes as a help to attain explicitly in perception a certain kind of object which otherwise would not be represented by a conscious dictum, e.g. the retinal stimulus-sizes.

15. The author, *l.c.*, tried to show that even the mere *naming* of the apparent equality in question in conceptual terms—i.e. by indicating whether it is an equality of apparent size, or color, or weight, or density, etc.—is, in principle, omitted from "psychology in terms of objects."

Not only the actual attainment but even the types of intentional effort or "attitude" toward attaining certain "intended" objects may be disclosed by objective methods (in fact, by analyzing the statistical distribution of judgments with regard to the number of modes).

16. I agree with H. L. Hollingworth ("Experimental studies in judgment," *Arch. Psychol.*, 1913, **29**), who proposes, in accordance with Wells, to use variability as an objective quantitative index of "subjectivity" of judgment. (I would not, however, as Hollingworth does, rely upon a ratio of personal vs. group consistency, but keep the definition free from its "social" element and emphasize the more general point of non-attainment, or variable attainment, of a type of object.)

17. F. Brentano, *Psychologie vom empirischen Standpunkt*, Leipzig, 1874.

18. Thus the new concept of intentionality seems to be closely related to what Tolman meant in defining in objective terms the "purposive" character of behavior.

19. For a concrete example of the difference between the phenomenological and the object-critical method of object-finding see section III.

20. B. Russell, *Introduction to Mathematical Philosophy*, New York, Macmillan, 1919.

21. The intentional relation thereby might be defined as positive either in the direction from the object as initial term to the reaction as terminal limit—following the direction of the causal chains—, or in the opposite direction, from the reaction to the object as end-term. This latter would be more in accordance with the character of the perceptual reaction as a preparation to overt action towards the body in question as a manipulable means-object, and would also follow the direction of the immediately experienced "meaning" or conscious intentionality of the Brentano-type.

22. This scale could equally well also have its ends mutually exchanged.

23. *Cf.* E. Brunswik, Zur Entwicklung der Albedo-wahrnehmung, *Zeitschr. f. Psychol.*, 1928, **109**, 40–115, and *l.c.* The degree of failure with respect to body-size is indicated by deviations either below or above 100.—*Cf.* also R. H. Thouless, Phenomenal Regression to the "Real" Object, I, *Brit. J. Psychol.*, 1931, **21**, 339–359.

24. In a quite analogous way, in experiments with figures, interferences have been found between area and length of the edges, etc. (see below).

Some of these interferences, especially those occurring in the field of the original type of constancy research (as size-constancy, etc.), may be satisfactorily accounted for *in terms of the causal texture of the environment in its relationships to the organism*. Perceptual cues for remote objects always remain ambiguous, and therefore perception is forced to co-include in its basis for reaction a large number of more or less indirect and unreliable cues which in some cases may stay in but a very low correlation to the type of object which they are admitted to indicate. (This would hold, e.g., for retinal size *per se*, when taken as indicating body size. Indeed, the characteristic odd admixtures found in the results of size-constancy experiments may be represented as functions of the product retinal size times indicated distance [i.e. body-size], on the one hand, and of retinal size, *per se*, on the other.) As has been pointed out in the author's article "Psychology in Terms of Objects" (*l.c.*), the effect of such a general way of functioning is a decrease in the probability of exceedingly large perceptual errors.

For some other types of perceptual compromises an explanation *in terms of the technicalities of the sense-organs* at the command of the perceptual system might be found, by studying physiologically their structure and the way of their functioning. This seems to be especially true for pitch and loudness which both turned out to be joint functions frequency and energy of the sound. *Cf.* S. S. Stevens, "The relation of pitch to intensity," *J. Acoust. Soc. Amer.*, 1935, **6**, 150–154, and E. G. Boring, "The Relation of the Attributes of Sensation to the Dimensions of the Stimulus," *Philos. of Science*, 1935, **2**, 236–245.

25. Some relationships could also be found with the manivalued logics, in which the absolute alternative of true and false is given up in favor of a continuous scale between these two cases as mere extremes.

26. It could be objected that a presentation of psychological results in terms of functional dependence

of the reaction on various stimulus-factors would be as short and less confusing than to talk in terms of "in-between objects." The reason why we believe it more profitable, however, to make this terminological distinction is the following. Strict functional dependence would have to be expressed in terms of proximal stimulation. We would prefer, instead, to *express the (functional) relationship in terms of the remote significate*, instead of using the signifying stimulus, in all cases in which the operational criterion of meaning given in section I is fulfilled. This would necessarily introduce a certain ambiguity. But it may be still considered more favorable to do so from the standpoint of illuminating the essential cue-rôle of the stimuli in establishing the organism's ability to master its environment.

Let us consider an example. For a most direct functional analysis apparent size would be simply one or another function of retinal size and distance-cues, and the case of a perfect constancy would not be especially emphasized as against cases of incomplete achievement. In terms of "objects attained," however, the response would appear to be a "function" of body-size alone (i.e., in strict functional terms, of retinal size times indicated distance) in the case of a perfect achievement, and of body size and projective size, *per se*, in the case of an incomplete achievement. In the latter case retinal size would enter the function twice in different rôles, once as a constituent of body-size, then *"per se"* (see the note above).

A further complication for a functional analysis in terms of retinal stimulation seems to be that all equipotential members of a cue-family (see above), e.g. all stimuli and stimulus-configurations indicating distance, would have to be enumerated explicitly in terms of intrinsic properties of their own instead of simply being comprehensible in terms of their common "significate," as "distance-cues." By using the "object"-terminology the particular kind of environmental-func-

tional direction of interest in stating the dependences found could be indicated at once.

27. Since the ways of mediation will always determine the achievement, the highly abstracted type of object-critical analysis as outlined above would lead, ultimately, to a statement of all psychologically relevant types of "how"-problems and -findings in terms of "what," i.e. of objects attained.

28. D. Katz, *The World of Color*, London, P. Kegan, 1935.

29. As our examples show, we are dealing here with the "psycho-*physical*," not with the "psycho-*physiological*" relationship.

30. It has been found that even *ambiguous cues* (i.e. those of a reliability of their actual indicative value lower than 1) will be conditioned, though the response seems to retain a higher degree of tentativeness (reduced strength). In a recent unpublished study of the present author, conducted in order to throw further light upon this problem, rats were confronted with objectively ambiguous situations, possessing various degrees of probability of success or of punishment ("danger"). Even relatively small differences in probability were discriminated by these animals (whose functioning is, in fact, not very dissimilar to the relatively primitive cognitive system, called perception). As the writer hopes to be able to show later in detail, an evaluation of even some of the slightest correlations between possible cues (symptoms) and more remote traits seems to be true for perception, especially in making accessible the character-traits of other persons in social intercourse. Reactions to mere probability have also been found by Thorndike in some of his recent learning experiments.

31. See the discussion of the problem by V. F. Lenzen, "The interaction of subject and object in observation," Second internat. congress for the unity of science, Kopenhagen 1936.

Organismic Achievement and Environmental Probability [1943]

COMMENT
On Center Stage
Kenneth R. Hammond

Five years after the lecture at the Cosmos Club, Brunswik got his big chance. There would be a panel to which Brunswik would be invited as one of three speakers; the other two would be Hull and Lewin, two of the three most important psychologists of the time, who represented sharply opposing views. By all expectations, Tolman, not Brunswik, would have been the third speaker on this panel, inasmuch as the sharp rivalry among these three was the most prominent topic in academic psychology. Why Brunswik appeared instead of Tolman I do not know. But I know that Tolman was not a contentious person and probably did not look forward to this panel with much enthusiasm. I also have a hunch that Tolman saw that if Brunswik appeared in his place, Brunswik would have a great opportunity to make his case. Be that as it may, Brunswik appeared on the panel. I like to think that Tolman saw that if Brunswik could stand up to Hull and Lewin on this panel, his reputation would be made; he would immediately be a contender. And stand up he did, and he was indeed a contender from that point on.

Brunswik spoke with confidence. He laid out his theoretical and methodological agenda in a straightforward manner. He began by describing what he was interested in, and what psychology should be interested in, and why. He said the focal point of interest should be "the better than chance [relationships] existing between, and due to, an organism and variables in its physical envi-

ronment." That is, psychology should focus on understanding the great compatibility between organism and environment. Noting that there were two aspects to this, the (incoming) perceptual side and the (outgoing) side of overt behavioral effects, his central point was that there was ambiguity in all of this; there are "probable partial causes" and "probable partial effects." Survival in these circumstances "is possible only if the organism is able to establish compensatory balance in the face of comparative chaos within the physical environment" (Brunswik, 1943, p. 257). That phrase, "chaos within the physical environment," is critical to Brunswikian theory and method, and absolutely foreign to his copanelists, who took the stability of the environment for granted. Despite the overstatement implied in the word *chaos*, Brunswik intended to suggest that the natural environment, or at least the natural environment in which hominids and *Homo sapiens* evolved, was an environment that offered many "probable partial causes" and many "probable partial effects." Thus, it was a somewhat unpredictable environment. And because that environment selected those hominids who were able, by virtue of their lucky genetic endowment, to "establish stable interrelationships with [their] environment" by being able to establish "compensatory balance in the face of comparative chaos within [their] physical environment," we are here today, and it is the task of behavioral scientists to discover how that "compensatory balance" is achieved. And one way to do that is to start paying attention to "one of the comparatively neglected tasks of a molar environmental psychology" (the reader should take note here; this is probably the first time the words *environmental psychology* were used) and "to find out the extent to which environmental hierarchies of probabilities of object-cue as well as of means-end relationships do find a counterpart in similar hierarchies of evaluation by the organism" (Brunswik, 1943, p. 259).

Readers who are familiar with the expansion of Brunswik's work from 1964 forward will recognize that quantitative methods for accomplishing part of this goal—finding out the extent to which cue-object probabilities—that is, the ecological validities of cues (as he would later say) find a counterpart in the manner in which the organism makes use of the cues—were developed in terms of the lens model equation (see Hursch, Hammond, & Hursch, 1964; Tucker, 1964; see also Stewart, Chapter 27, this volume). Nevertheless, strange as it may seem, the full answer to the question about the extent to which the means-end probabilities in the environment are matched by the organism's evaluation of them remains to be systematically examined. (But see the fascinating experiments carried out by Garcia, 1990, who, while a graduate student at Berkeley, discovered that there are certain types of cues that are utterly foreign to a rat's environment and to which the rat cannot be conditioned at all.)

Acceptance (or denial) of these assertions will make a difference in your behavior as a scientist in the field of psychology. If you accept them, you pay a heavy price, for you will then join Brunswik in the belief "that the probability character of the causal (partial cause-and-effect) relationships in the environment calls for a fundamental, all-inclusive shift in our methodological ideology regarding psychology" (Brunswik, 1943, p. 261). That sentence in that panel was, of course, a bombshell. For Brunswik was not simply calling for new and different ways of running rats in different kinds of mazes, or a different way of calculating IQ scores, or any change of that order. No, he wanted a "fundamental, all-inclusive shift in our methodological ideology." Note that word *ideology*. That in itself was enough to raise the hackles of not only his copanelists but 99 percent of his audience. Use of that word meant that Brunswik was accusing them of employing an ideology to control the rules of experimentation.

Real scientists don't do that! They are coldly logical, not ideological. And no one doubted that Brunswik chose his words carefully. Therefore, the use of that word established a distance between Brunswik's views and those of Hull and Lewin—and many generations of future experimental psychologists—that is still hard to overcome.

No doubt there is compelling logic in the idea of holding certain factors constant and varying only the one of interest, particularly in applied research such as evaluating the effect of one fertilizer against another, or of one drug against another. That logic is clear and its empirical efficacy is well-tested—for applied research into simple questions. That is not the issue. The issue is this: Is this the appropriate logic of experimentation for the study of the behavior of organisms in a chaotic—that is, multicue—probabilistic environment? Brunswik's answer, of course, was no. And he called for an "all-inclusive shift" to what he later called "representative design" that would include such features. But that led to another issue: By asserting that a different theory of behavior required a different methodology, he was implying that method is not independent of theory, as we are ordinarily led to believe. Thus, Brunswik was putting forward a theory of the relation between organism and environment and demanding that psychology make an "all-inclusive shift in its methodological ideology" to accommodate that theory. (Modern psychology still does not grasp that argument—indeed, hardly addresses it, as may be seen from the misuses of the term *ecological validity*; see Introduction.) The price psychology was paying—and still pays—for its "methodological ideology" was "the limitation of stimulus-response psychology to narrow-spanning problems of artificially isolated proximal or peripheral technicalities of mediation which are not representative of the larger patterns of life" (Brunswik, 1943, p. 262).

Another shocker was in store for Hull and Lewin when Brunswik called for the use of correlational statistics—anathema to experimentalists—and trumped that by asserting that in addition "one would . . . have to insist on representative sampling of situations or tests, just as in the field of individual differences one has to insist on the representative sampling of individuals from a population to ascertain at least some kind of generality for the result. Proper sampling of subjects is thus replaced by proper sampling of objects or objectives." And "this would mean a randomization of tasks, a sampling of tests carefully drawn from the universe of the requirements a person happens to face in his commerce with the physical or social environment, as the defining class" (1943, p. 263). (For a current application of this remarkable methodological innovation and its effect on current conclusions, see Juslin, Chapter 36, of this volume.) Those arguments were surely revolutionary; they stood conventional methodology on its head. All three panelists would surely be surprised to find that Brunswik's revolutionary argument is now standard procedure in many studies carried out by researchers who took Brunswik at his word regarding the proper task of psychology. For example, in the several studies by Thomas Stewart and others (see Stewart, Chapter 27, this volume) on meteorological forecasting, it is storms that are the "objects" sampled, not meteorologists; in the studies of medical clinical judgments by Robert Wigton and others (see Wigton, Chapter 30, this volume), it is diseases that are the "objects" sampled, not doctors; in studies of highway engineering judgments by Hammond and others (see Hammond, Hamm, Grassia, & Pearson, 1987), highways are the "objects" that are sampled, not engineers. Specifically, it is the statistical properties of the objects presented in the task—the means, standard deviations, and so on of the distributions of the objects—and the statistical properties of the response systems evoked that are detailed, not merely the statistical

properties of the sample population. In short, the several hundreds of articles on learning under uncertainty (known as *multiple cue probability learning*; see Holzworth, Chapter 25, this volume) and the several hundreds of articles on judgment of an empirical criterion under uncertainty (known as *correspondence competence*; see Cooksey, 1996b) would not have been undertaken if it had not been for Brunswik's revolutionary assertions during that panel in 1941, and if the researchers had not had the courage to defy tradition in order to carry them out. The contributions of those studies may be found in Brehmer and Joyce (1988) and more recently in Cooksey (1996b). (See also the chapters in Part III of this volume for further examples.)

Because that sampling logic is utterly the reverse of what mainstream psychologists would demand of an experiment, they utterly rejected what Brunswik offered them without engaging his argument. Thus, they rejected the methodology that would allow them to establish generality over conditions, a problem that still plagues psychology. In what must be seen as desperation, many have hi-jacked the Brunswikians' concept of *ecological validity*, thus confusing the situation further (see Chapter 1, this volume).

This article, then, is one of the most important Brunswik ever wrote. It was delivered on a most auspicious occasion in 1941, written in beautiful style and clarity of expression, and his major thoughts are contained in it.

 REPRINT

Organismic Achievement and Environmental Probability

Egon Brunswik

I

The term 'achievement' will be used here as a generic term for the relationships better than chance existing between, and due to, an organism and variables in its physical environment. By physical environment we mean the 'geographical' surroundings as well as the stages along the 'historic' axis of the organism, that is to say, its past and future. Relatively stable relationships between organism and environment are among the descriptive features of the patterns found in observing life and behavior. Thus the recognition

Reprinted from *Psychological Review* (1943), 50, 255–272.

of such functional units need not, and will not, involve us in explanatory problems such as the alternative of mechanism vs. teleology.

Organismic achievement may extend in two main directions; (1) specificity regarding certain stimulus variables as antecedents or causes of reactions, and (2) specificity regarding certain results of organismic reaction. Examples for the former may be taken from the field of perception, for the latter, from the field of overt behavioral effects.

In the establishment of any kind of achievement one may distinguish two phases: (1) the portions of the causal chains within the physical environment, and (2) the portions of the causal chains within the organism. We will discuss the environmental portions first. In each case, variables not located at (that is to say, not defined in terms of) the boundary between organism and environment will be used as examples in order to make explicit the characteristic entanglements within the causal texture of the regions in question. As far as the environment is concerned, one will have to start from the so-called 'distal' stimulus- or effect-variables as reference points and study their relationships to the proximal (or boundary-) variables.

On the perception side, an example of a distal variable is the distance of objects. Causal chains determined by distance will, on their way into the organism, exert certain proximal effects, or criteria, upon the sensory surface of the organism. The most important feature of the general relationship between distal and proximal stimulus variables is its lack of univocality.

Firstly, there is ambiguity in the direction from cause to effect. Inventories of possible 'cues for third-dimensional distance' have been compiled from the beginnings of psychological inquiry. Current textbooks list something like ten depth criteria, such as binocular parallax, convergence of the eye axes, accommodation, linear and angular perspective, interception of far objects by near objects, atmospheric effects, number of in-between objects, vertical position. The list could be extended considerably further. The necessity for becoming so involved derives from the fact that none of these proximal variables can be considered to be *the* distance cue in the sense of an effect which would be present without exception whenever the distal condition should obtain. Some of the cues will more often, others less

often, be present, depending on circumstances, and occasionally all of them may be cut off (so that the fact of a certain distance relationship must remain unrecognized by the organism in question).

Secondly, there also is ambiguity in the reverse direction, that is to say, from effect to cause. A certain proximal stimulus feature, such as binocular parallax, may ordinarily be due to differences in depth, but it could occasionally as well be caused by an artificial setup of two flat pictures in a stereoscope. Or, the characteristic trapezoidal shape of retinal images constituting the depth criterion of perspective may frequently be due to distortion of rectangular objects seen under an angle, *i.e.*, extending into the third dimension; but it may also be due to an actual trapezoidal object in a frontal position with all of its points at the same distance from the eye.

On the environmental portion of the effect side, the relationships between objects and cues are replaced, in a symmetrical fashion, by the relationships between means and ends, or between proximal actions or habits and distal results. Examples showing the ambiguity of these relationships in both causal directions could easily be given in analogous fashion to the ones discussed above for the perception side.

Generally speaking, both the object-cue and the means-end relationship are relations between probable partial causes and probable partial effects. Thereby the entire universe of the living conditions of the organism or species in question might well be taken as a 'reference class' defining a 'population' of situations. Then there is a good chance that distance as a distal variable will cause distance cues, and that the so-called distance cues have been actually caused by distance, but it will by no means be necessarily so. We use the term 'partial' (cause or effect) since the members of the causal chain are in every particular instance determined by a large number of other relevant conditions. Cues as well as means can be ranked into 'hierarchies' in accordance with the degree of probability by which they are linked, in both causal directions, to the respective distal variables, and classified accordingly as 'good,' 'misleading,' etc. (13).

This brings us to the second point, the contributions of the organism. Survival and its subunits, which may be defined as the establishment of stable interrelationships with the environment, are possible only if the organism is able to establish compensatory balance in the face of comparative chaos within the physical environment. Ambiguity of cues and means relative to the vitally relevant objects and results must find its counterpart in an ambiguity and flexibility of the proximal-peripheral mediating processes in the organism. This pattern contrasts somewhat with the relatively specific focussing of vital processes upon the central-organismic and the distal-environmental variables. Thus each class of behavioral achievement may be represented, when telescoped into a composite picture covering extended periods of time, by a bundle of light rays passing through a convex lens from one focus to another, with a scattering of the causal chains in the mediating layers. Most objective psychologists who have made efforts to find a formal criterion by which behavior could be delimited from non-behavior have in various forms resorted to something amounting to such a lens analogy. Examples are Tolman's "persistence and docility of activity relative to some end" (12) as a criterion for purposiveness of behavior, Hunter's emphasis upon 'vicarious functioning' in defining the subject matter of a behavioristic psychology, Hull's emphasis upon such patterns as the 'habit family hierarchy' (6), some considerations put forward by Heider (5), and generally the concept of 'equivalence' or of 'equipotentiality' of stimuli and of acts.

The point I should like to emphasize especially in this connection is the necessary imperfection, inflicted upon achievements—as relations between classes—by the ambiguity in the causal texture of the environment, which remains apparent as long as single variables, that is partial causes and partial effects, are considered under otherwise not specifically controlled conditions. Because of this environmental ambiguity, no matter how smoothly the organismic instruments and mechanisms may function, relationships cannot be foolproof, at least as far as those connecting with the vitally relevant more remote distal regions of the environment are concerned. This intrinsic lack of perfection, that is of univocality, will on the whole be the greater the more wide-spanning the relationships involved are. The only way in which perfection could be secured would be by control over all the remaining conditions which could possibly become relevant in the given case. This however is something the react-

ing organism cannot do for lack of time if not for other more serious reasons—and thus something which the psychologist who wishes to catch and rationally to reconstruct organismic adjustment at large, with all of its faults and fallacies, should also not do. All a finite, sub-divine individual can do when acting is—to use a term of Reichenbach (11)—to make a posit, or wager. The best he can do is to compromise between cues so that his posit approaches the 'best bet' on the basis of all the probabilities, or past relative frequencies, of relevant interrelationships lumped together.

One of the comparatively neglected tasks of a molar environmental psychology is to find out the extent to which environmental hierarchies of probabilities of object-cue as well as of means-end relationships do find a counterpart in similar hierarchies of evaluation by the organism. This would mean that the environmental probabilities be first ascertained for all of the cues or means involved, with, say, the 'normal' life conditions of the organism taken as the defining reference class. This part of the research would be strictly environmental and preparatory in character and would not involve any reference to organismic reaction.[1] Very little has thus far been done in the direction of such an environmental analysis.

The most conspicuous exception is a certain knowledge we have about the so called 'physiognomic' relationships between certain mental states or abilities in our fellow-men, and their external physical characteristics. Such studies have, however, been undertaken primarily because of an interest centering in questions of the expressiveness of human beings viewed as subjects rather than because of an interest in some other subject's social environment and the problems confronting such a subject in his approach to objects of social perception. In effect, however, they have given us some information to be utilized for our purpose. The present writer has selected one of the few ascertained relationships found between ability and physique, namely the correlation of intelligence with height and with weight. To be sure, these correlations are extremely low, about .15, but this is all to the good, since many of the cues probably in use in perception are of such a low order of validity, including some of the lesser members of what may be called, in analogy to Hull's habit-family-hierarchy, the 'cue-family-hierarchy' of the distance criteria listed on page 256. Social perceptual reactions to schematized drawings of human figures as well as to photographs which had been magnified, reduced, and distorted in height and width turned out to be more favorable with respect to apparent intelligence and other apparent personality characteristics in the case of taller and broader body builds (2, 14). There thus may be intuitive responsiveness to social environmental correlations as low as .15 (though other possibilities of an explanation of the reactions, such as, *e.g.*, a psychoanalytic one, would have yet to be tested). Furthermore, there are indications that height and weight contribute only little to the impressions made, when compared with other factors such as the face, etc. Such a finding, if verified, would be in line with what should be expected on the ground of a perceptual compromise principle, since cues of low validity would then have to be given little weight by the organism in establishing the best bet.

The writer is attempting an analysis of the environmental validities of the distance cues, present, absent, and misleading or contradictory, in a set of pictures selected from magazines by a group of subjects and thus probably fairly representative of interesting life situations. The hierarchy thus established in a preliminary way appeared to be on the whole in fair agreement with what can be inferred from results of experimental studies about the subjective weight of distance cues which had been made to conflict artificially in stimulus configurations presented through the stereoscope.

On the whole, only scattered recognition has been given to the fact that object-cue and means-end relationships do not hold with the certainty obtained in the nomothetic study of the so-called laws of nature, but are rather of the character of probability relationships. This deficiency is most clearly reflected in the psychology of learning which has proceeded almost exclusively along a dialectically dichotomized all-or-none pattern of 'correct vs. incorrect,' 'right vs. wrong.' Situations in which food can be found always to the right and never to the left, or always behind a black door and never behind a white one, are not representative of the structure of the environment, but are based on an idealized black-white dramatization of the world, somewhat in a Hollywood style. They are thus not sound as experimental devices from the standpoint of a psychology which wishes to learn, above all other things, something about

behavior under conditions representative of actual life. In an effort to imitate experimentally the tangled causal texture of the environment more closely than is customary, the writer tested a variety of ambiguous environmental means-end relationships, using rats as subjects (1). The rate of learning (which may be taken as an index of organismic weight given to the means or cue in question) was found to vary with the probability, that is to say, with the combination of relative frequencies, of the intraenvironmental relationships tested.

II

I have expanded on this subject to such an extent because I believe that the probability character of the causal (partial cause-and-effect) relationships in the environment calls for a fundamental, all-inclusive shift in our methodological ideology regarding psychology. To be sure, in the field of wide-spanning relationships of a predominantly historic-genetic type, such as of heredity and of individual differences in general, this shift occurred at the time of Galton and his followers who established correlation statistics as a particularly suitable means of quantitatively expressing ambiguous probability relationships. The relationships existing between organism and geographic environment at large will have to be approached in basically the same way. In any wide-spanning correlation, be it of historic or of geographic reference, there are a great many relevant variables and specific control is lacking for all of them except the two (or few), whose relationship is under specific consideration. Such a deliberate neglect of specific control of relevant variables is the most fundamental negative characteristic of the 'molar' approach. Not more than generalized control by which membership is established in a broader class (including care for proper sampling) is exerted over the remaining relevant variables. For example, in comparing parents' intelligence with children's intelligence, not more than the most general features of the upbringing of the children such as health, normality, etc., are taken into consideration, instrumental detail is neglected. The situation is quite similar, though not quite so drastic, when we become interested in how well, in a practical achievement sense, we can estimate distal variables such as distance, or sizes and physical colors of objects, under all the varying circumstances of distance, surroundings, illumination, etc. (perceptual constancies). What the experimentalist is used to calling 'isolation of a variable' is in all these cases incomplete to a quite shocking extent. No univocality, no relationship resembling a 'law' in the traditional strict sense of the word can be uncovered under such circumstances.

The present paper thus represents an attempt to show that psychology, as long as it wishes to deal with the vitally relevant molar aspects of adjustment and achievement, has to become statistical throughout, instead of being statistical where it seems hopeless to be otherwise, and cherishing the nomothetic ideals of traditional experimental psychology as far as relationships between geographic stimulus variables and response variables are concerned. The price which has to be paid for such a double standard is the limitation of stimulus-response psychology to narrow-spanning problems of artificially isolated proximal or peripheral technicalities of mediation which are not representative of the larger patterns of life.

In particular, the extension of the principles of such an instrument as correlation statistics from individual differences to stimulus-response relationships involves, firstly, that instead of correlating two variables (e.g., different test performances), paired by being drawn from the same sample of individuals characterized in their structure and functioning only as members of a general reference population, one would have to correlate two variables (namely, a set of stimulus values and a set of response values) paired by being drawn from the same sample of situations or tests, characterized merely as belonging to the class, or 'population,' of living conditions of a particular individual (or category or species). In short, individuals are replaced by situations or tasks (which is to be distinguished from the mere exchange of the role of individuals for tests as in Stephenson's 'inverted' correlation technique). The achievement of a single subject, or even of a single subject in a certain particular attitude, could then be represented by a correlation coefficient based on a variety of test situations involving the stimulus variable in question.

To make the analogy complete, one would, secondly, have to insist on representative sampling of situations or tests, just as in the field of individual differences one has to insist on the representative sampling of individuals from a population to ascertain at least some kind of generality for the result. Proper sampling of subjects is thus replaced by proper sampling of objects or objectives. For general adjustment this would mean a randomization of tasks, a sampling of tests carefully drawn from the universe of the requirements a person happens to face in his commerce with the physical or social environment, as the defining class. For adjustment to, or cognitive attainment of, a single stimulus variable, such as distance, one would have to secure perceptual estimates of distance in a set of situations representative of all the situations and conditions in life which require judgment of, or adjustment to, distance. For each subject, this particular type of perceptual achievement could be represented by the correlation coefficient between measured distances and estimated distances. The more molecular pattern of traditional laboratory experimentation could thus be rounded out to include its molar counterpart, that is an achievement analysis deliberately neglecting the details, even if these details should be relevant in connection with one or the other member of the family of processes mediating this achievement.

An example of the application of the correlation technique to a stimulus response problem can be found in studies on social perceptual achievement, e.g., when intelligence is to be judged from photographs. Since the typical research of this kind the photographs are not analyzed with respect to their geometric characteristics, the investigation bridges over the mediating layers altogether, in contrast to the purely intra-environmental problems of physiognomies discussed above. It is characteristic of the traditional attitude of psychology that in these studies the sampling problem of social objects has rarely been given due consideration, both regarding sufficient number of social objects as well as the representative character of the sample. And this in spite of the fact that we usually find a sufficient and representative sample of subjects or judges.

On the whole, social perceptual problems have been rooted in the applied disciplines which have not come in too close a contact with the ideology of the 'exact' experimental laboratory psychology and thus have been more openminded to statistics from the beginning. As a methodological demonstration rather than with the purpose of fact finding, the present author has recently undertaken a study in perceptual size constancy in which the correlation technique was applied to a traditional academic stimulus-response problem. Proper sampling was attempted, and an effort was made to throw some light upon the traditional mediation problems of proximal stimulation, besides approaching the achievement problem (3). Purposely, one subject only was used. The person was interrupted frequently during her normal daily activities and asked to estimate the size of the object she just happened to be looking at. Measurements of the object-sizes, which were the distal stimulus variable under consideration, and of their distances from the subject were also taken in each case. These measurements made it possible to compute the relative sizes of the retinal images as well which constituted the most outstanding feature of the mediating proximal stimulus patterns. Estimates of size were found to correlate with object measurements much more closely (between .95 and almost 1.00, depending on method of evaluation, with naive perceptual attitude) than with retinal stimulus size (between .2 and .7). This result indicates the selective focussing of the organism's response on the distal rather than the proximal variable. In contrast to most experimental studies this result possesses a certain generality with regard to normal life conditions. It furthermore suggests that focussing of psychology upon the proximal and peripheral layer is not the most fruitful thing to do and may lead to an out-of-focus, sterile type of research.

In short, the notion will have to be revised that, while the psychology of individual differences deals with correlations (at least *de facto*), experimental psychology of the stimulus response type deals with, or should strive toward, the uncovering of 'laws' in the strict sense of the word. As Mises (9) has pointed out, law finding and the molecular, microscopic approach are inseparably tied together. In a strict sense, the laws of nature have to be formulated as differential equations, yielding a relationship of the variables in question within an infinitesimally small spatio-temporal region. Their customary macroscopic form is the result of a mathematical integration over time or space, an extension which tacitly implies a number of assumptions about the intervening conditions. Such conditions may be controlled in a sufficiently specific manner in an experiment in which either the possibilities of interference are limited (such as in an optical experiment) and can easily be surveyed, or where the span between the independent and the dependent variable is relatively small in space and time. In this sense the laws of nature are not extremely general, but extremely specific.

III

The tie between the nomothetic and the microscopic attitude is reflected not only in traditional experimental psychology, but also in those more recent endeavors which stress law finding in psychology. The two most outstanding of these attempts are represented by Lewin and Hull.

I agree with Lewin when he makes it clear that there is no place for statistics in a strictly nomothetic, or, as he calls it, systematic discipline (8). In fact, not even averages from a large number of cases or repeated observations are in order. Indeed, those psychologists who have accepted the ideology of accumulated observation have already deviated from the strictly nomothetic path. If all the relevant conditions are known, or rather if all disturbing influences are eliminated, only one observation is needed to ascertain a general law once and forever. Lewin calls this the technique of the 'pure case' and refers to Galileo's study of falling bodies as an example. In an attempt to apply his principles, Lewin has, however, paid the price of an 'encapsulation' of his psychology, at least insofar as theoretical structure is concerned, into what may be called the central layer of the personality. The 'field' within which Lewin is able to predict, in the strict sense of the word, is the person in his life space. But the life space is not to be confused with geographic environment of physical stimuli, nor with actually achieved results in the environment. It is post-perceptual, and pre-behavioral. It represents a cross section in time; yet, in spite of its cross-sectional—or, rather, actualistic—character, it is not considered static (as seems to be, for example, Titchener's old structuralism) but rather dynamic since events are defined as starting points for action. Whether or not, and in which way, action is carried out seems, however, a matter of secondary importance to Lewin. Thus no criterion for directedness of action which would be comparable to, say, Tolman's objective criteria for purposiveness of behavior, are explicitly worked out, and predictions can thus in a strict sense of the word not be tested. Furthermore, Lewin's interest in preparation for action rather than action itself is reflected in his criticism of the use of the concept of achievement, and of the 'historic-geographic' conception of psychology in general, as contrasted with the systematic, nomothetic. All this is only another aspect of what has probably led to his rejection of statistical methods. (It is understood, I hope, that I am referring to the fundamental core and texture of Lewin's theoretical work only and not to his practices which represent a healthy synthesis of his theorizing and the established ways of checking on results.)

Encapsulation into the central layer, with dynamics leading out of it, may be the least harmful of all the limitations which possibly could be imposed upon psychology: It may actually mean concentration upon the most essential phase in the entire process of life and of its ramifications. It may be the thing psychology has always been really after throughout its history. And there also is a 'dynamic' quality not only in the sense of reaching back to the object (as Brentano and James dreamed of) or forward to the goal (as Lewin undertakes to do) but also in the sense of giving full recognition to cross-sectional interaction within a large whole, the central system. In his topological psychology, furthermore, Lewin has probably developed the most adequate conceptual tool for dealing with the central layer (which Brentano did not). Yet it is for this methodological perfection that he has paid the price of encapsulation, in that he has furnished but one reference point for all extrinsic dynamics and omitted checks on extra-systematic reference points and thus prevented the actual realization of a truly dynamic outlook.[2]

I should also like to refer to Hull's mathematico-deductive theory of rote learning, as a highly formalized systematic attempt in present day psychology (7). In spirit, the material used goes back to one of the classics of experimental psychology, namely to Ebbinghaus' studies of mechanical memory and thus to a rather elementaristic body of facts. Again the degree of nomothetic perfection which has been reached (though along a quite different line from that of Lewin) appears to be accompanied by a loss of inclusiveness or broadness of content. It is in concepts like that of the habit family hierarchy that Hull has reached the greatest approximation to fundamental structures of life, a fact which is compensated for by the use of a less highly developed systematic apparatus in this latter case.

Somewhat related though much more bound to traditional modes of thought is a large group of psychologists, represented, for example, by Pratt (10), in whose opinion psychology cannot become truly scientific before it has resolved itself into more 'basic' disciplines such as physiology. The basic character of physiology is apparently given by the greater chances of dealing with laws in the strict sense, due to a more molecular character in the approach. Yet, as Woodworth (15) has pointed out, we have to realize that psychology is not a 'fundamental' discipline in this sense of the word.

What seems to be at the bottom of these tendencies is a certain halo effect regarding the concept of exactitude. The principle of methodological physicalism which defines the unity of the sciences should be understood to postulate intersubjective univocality of observation and of communication, not less, but also not more. This univocality is ascertained by the employment of measurement and of mathematical means of communication including such tools as topology. When Watson became the first great exponent of objectivity in psychology, the ideal of exactitude was pressed considerably beyond the purely methodological aspects of physicalism.

Thus, firstly, a point was made about the mechanistic character of psychology as contrasted with vitalistic notions. However, as Carnap has since emphasized, unity of method does not imply unity of laws (4). Molar behaviorists of the present day, such as Tolman, have thus ceased worrying about the problem of explanatory teleology, for which psychology anyway does not seem to be the competent forum, nor capable of furnishing relevant material.[3]

A second, less conceptualized and thus more dangerous bias is based on the confusion between univocality of observation and communication, on the one hand, and the univocality of prediction. It is the latter which leads to the insistence upon law-finding in psychology. Thus, in addition to the mechanistic bias, we have the nomothetic bias. From the standpoint of methodological physicalism, however, a correlation coefficient is just as exact, that is to say, just as public and palpable in its meaning as a law. And it has, it should be kept in mind, considerably more generality, and thus possibilities of prediction, than has an isolated single event such as those studied, in extreme instances, by historians and geographers. And, in a sense, it has even more generality than the 'general' laws of nature which are observed under such meticulously specified conditions.

Another element seems to enter here which may best be characterized by what Lewin (8) has called Aristotelian, as contrasted with Galilean, modes of thought (which, however, he himself has apparently failed to avoid in the instance to be referred to here). According to a certain tradition, sciences fall into two categories, nomothetic, or law finding, and idiographic, or referring to individual events. It seems as if psychology would here and there still maintain an Aristotelian, that is to say, an all-or-none attitude toward this dichotomy; if we cannot have the general law, then let us escape into singularity! In a formal sense, however, imperfect correlations fill in the gap between law and isolated fact. Laws allow prediction with certainty, statistics (correlations) predictions with probability,[4] isolated facts allow no prediction at all (unless reference to laws or correlations is tacitly brought in such as in geography where a certain constancy of the crust of the earth is assumed, or in clinical psychology, where a certain consistency of character is anticipated).

The acceptance of ambiguity of prediction as a legitimate and general feature of psychological results will probably meet with the same resistance which logicians had to face when they proceeded from a dichotomous true-false alternative to multi-valued logic, or which empirical scientists had to face when developing out of theological and metaphysical stages into the positive stage.[5]

Yet, in establishing the methodological unity of science, it will become increasingly important to emphasize thematic differences. Only when diversity of topic and specific method within unity of general method is fully recognized will we be capable of carrying over the full richness of the psychological problems inherited from introspectionism and other preparatory stages into a thoroughly objectified system. Among the primary obstacles to be removed seem to be the confusions surrounding the concept of exactitude, resulting in its over-expansion. There must be recognition

of the fact that there can be no truly molar psychology dealing with the physical relationships of the organism with its environment unless it gives up the nomothetic ideal in favor of a thoroughly statistical conception.[6] In turn, the topical unity of psychology within the constitutional hierarchy of the sciences can be established by specifying, in terms of focal variables, width of span, etc., the kinds of probability relationships maintained between the organism and its environment which are to be included within the scope of psychology.

In the end, this may not even mean a permanent renunciation of at least gradual approximation toward univocality of prediction. Techniques such as multiple correlation or analysis of variance, which consist essentially of a combination of correlations, will increasingly make it possible to narrow down correlations, will increasingly make it possible to narrow down prediction so that we will at least in a practical sense, come closer and closer to the traditional scientific ideal, the isolation of variables and the establishment of general cause and effect relationships. If we are not to forget the teachings of Hume and John Stuart Mill, we must realize that there is nothing observed but concomitant variation—of greater or lesser relative frequency—and that all analysis of causal textures rests upon this foundation.[7]

NOTES

This article was an address given at the Symposium on Psychology and Scientific Method held as part of the Sixth International Congress for the Unity of Science, University of Chicago, September, 1941.

Some of the author's remarks in the discussion concerning the papers of Hull and Lewin, as well as some of the replies to criticisms of the present paper, appear as notes here. Some minor changes have been made in the paper itself and a list of references has been added.

1. In the sense defined in footnote 3, such a statistical analysis of intra-environmental correlations would be termed 'psychological ecology' whereas the organism's proper adjustment to such correlations, to be expressed in terms of achievement, would be 'ecological psychology.'

2. In expanding upon his 'principle of contemporaneity' (which, by the way, is characteristic of what the present writer has called 'encapsulation into the central layer') Professor Lewin made the statement that it was

obviously of no interest to the psychologist as a psychologist whether or not a rat in a maze would actually get to the food, or whether or not the experimenter was going to give the food, as long as only the rat would start out on its way (or enter the alley). My reply is, that whether or not the animal is actually going to get to food is exactly what we are interested in. Of course, not a single instance would have to count, but general probabilities of arriving at food and the organism's ability to pick up such general probabilities. In the course of the discussion Lewin suggested that the term 'ecology' might be useful in the statistics of the interaction between organism and environment—which, however, Lewin would not want to have included as part of psychology proper.

3. For this reason, correlations observed between organismic variables and certain results of organismic reaction ('ends') as well as certain proximal or distal stimulus variables (objects) should not be branded as entailing undue teleology. In reply to criticism raised by Professor Hull it might be said that statements about such correlations are 'teleological' only in a strictly descriptive and not in the customary explanatory, vitalistic sense. Such terms as 'functionalistic' or 'focal reference' seem to be suitable to characterize such teleologically neutral references to empirically observed relationships between the organism and foci in its environment.

4. In discussing this point, Professor Reichenbach referred to statistics as yielding 'probability laws.' I can see no objection against using the term 'law' in such a sense if only the departure from the nomothetic principle is made clear.

5. Giving up the nomothetic ideal meets with emotional resistance quite comparable to the one encountered when other positions of security and mastery had to be given up in the course of 'Copernican revolutions' such as the dominant position of the earth within the universe, of man within the animal kingdom, or of the Ego within the system of human motivation. Thus one of the two major reasons, listed by Jaensch (until his recent death the most prominent figure of officially sanctioned contemporary German psychology) for the rejection of Gestalt psychology is the fact that Gestalt psychologists particularly emphasize ambiguity in perception, which is considered to be a frightening reflection of their own morbid psychic disposition.

6. It is in the difference in the use of statistics that we discover why psychology is not just simply "physics of the organism in its environment." The difference exists in spite of the recent emphasis upon the statistical nature of some of the most important sections of physics. It lies in the fact that non-univocality is in physics primarily confined to the 'microscopic' realm and appears to be eliminated, by the sheer weight of large numbers, as long as we remain within phenomena of a macroscopic order. On the other hand, psychology is thoroughly infiltrated with statistics even in the macroscopic sphere, and in fact the more so the more macroscopic, or 'molar,' its problems become. It was indeed for the quantitative expression of one of the most wide-spanning types of relationships, that of inheritance, from generation to generation, of physical and mental characteristics, that correlation statistics were first introduced into the sciences of life. The reason for this introduction of statistics is that relationships on the whole tend to become less foolproof the wider the stretch, in terms of spatio-temporal regions, over which they appear to be maintained.

7. In an attempt to show that the relationship of the positions of the three speakers of the meeting was complementary rather than contradictory, the author tried to relate them to well-established disciplines. In visualizing the organism and the organism in its physical (geographical) environment, Lewin's approach seems to be confined to the life center of the organism which may be compared to the study of law and general policy of intra-governmental function in a society. There is indeed lawfulness and consistency within such a system, yet splendid isolation unless contact with other regions is maintained through information, on the one hand, and the executive arm, on the other. Of those external relationships, Hull seems primarily concerned with engineering problems, especially in his attempt to find basic elements such as conditioning to which more complex units could be reduced. Molar behaviorism, in its turn, with its concentration upon vitally relevant if remote historic or geographic variables such as maintenance schedule, time required to reach food, etc., appears in the position of the economist (and hence the term ecological psychology, mentioned above, seems not inappropriate for this kind of approach). An important difference, though one of secondary order, between the type of molar approach represented by Tolman and that proposed by the present writer is that the former seems to put much additional emphasis upon inferences regarding the intra-organismic 'intervening variables' (which brings him close to Lewin), *e.g.*, a hunger drive as inferred from maintenance schedule; whereas the latter would tend, at least in principle, to discard for the moment intervening variables wherever they are not directly accessible. By representing an organism's or species' achievement system in terms of attained objects and results, such a psychology would in a sense be *without* the organism (i.e., would neglect all but a few focal details of organismic structure and intra-

organismic processes), yet would let us know much *about* the organism (*i.e.*, its relationships to the environment, in both cognition and action). By exerting actual measurement control mostly about stimuli and results, *i.e.*, about historic or geographic variables, and about central variables only where a direct physiological approach is possible, such a psychology would be the direct counterpart to that represented by Lewin. Namely, it would not be post-perceptual and pre-behavioral, but rather perceptual and behavioral. But in the end, it seems that none of the various aspects just discussed can be dispensed with in a completely rounded-out system of psychology.

REFERENCES

1. Brunswik, E. Probability as a determiner of rat behavior. *J. Exp. Psychol.*, 1939, **25**, 175–197.
2. ———. Perceptual characteristics of schematized human figures. *Psychol. Bull.*, 1939, **36**, 553.
3. ———. Size-constancy in life situations. *Psychol. Bull.*, 1941, **38**, 611–612.. (See also a forthcoming issue of *Psychol. Monogr.*)
4. Carnap, R. Logical foundations of the unity of science. *Encyclop. of Unified Science*, 1938, **1**, No. 1, 42–62.
5. Heider, F. Environmental determinants in psychological theories. *Psychol. Rev.*, 1939, **46**, 383–410.
6. Hull, C. L. The concept of the habit family hierarchy and maze learning. *Psychol. Rev.*, 1934, **41**, 33–54, 134–142.
7. ———, et al. *Mathematico-deductive theory of rote learning*. Inst. of Human Relations, Yale University, 1940. Pp. xii and 329.
8. Lewin, K. *Dynamic theory of personality*. New York: McGraw-Hill, 1935. Pp. ix and 286.
9. Mises, R. v. *Probability, statistics and truth*. New York: Macmillan, 1939. Pp. xvi and 323.
10. Pratt, C. C. *The logic of modern psychology*. New York: Macmillan, 1939. Pp. xvi and 185.
11. Reichenbach, H. *Experience and prediction*. Chicago: Univ. of Chicago Press, 1938. Pp. 410.
12. Tolman, E. C. *Purposive behavior in animals and men*. New York: Century, 1932. Pp. xiv and 463.
13. ———, Brunswik, E. The organism and the causal texture of the environment. *Psychol. Rev.*, 1935, **42**, 43–77.
14. Wallace, R. P. Apparent personality traits from photographs varied in bodily proportions. *Psychol. Bull.*, 1941, **38**, 744–745.
15. Woodworth, R. S. Dynamic psychology. —*Psychologies of 1925* (ed. by C. Murchison). Pp. 111–126.

Distal Focussing of Perception: Size Constancy in a Representative Sample of Situations [1944]

 COMMENT

Representative Design in Action in the Middle of the Twentieth Century
Kenneth R. Hammond

This is the most important methodological paper that Brunswik ever wrote. It did not contain any new theoretical ideas of importance, but without it, there never would have been a clear-cut, obvious demonstration of what he meant by "representative design" and how it should be carried out. Up to this point, he had never provided a full-scale explication and empirical application of representative design, at least in his papers in English. Despite the lack of such a demonstration, he had made much of this idea, the formation of which was evident in his days in Vienna, and he made much of it in the 1941 symposium with Hull and Lewin. So, one might say, this was Brunswik's answer to "put up or shut up," as the American vernacular would have it. And in this publication he certainly "put up," for he laid out the concept of representative design and its operational meaning in full detail.

But even with this very clear explication and demonstration, the idea of representative design had no effect on the "true believers" in experimental psychology, or on those who write textbooks in statistics for psychology students. Regrettably, it sailed right by the research community; it received only twenty-five citations in the first twenty years after publication and only four or five in the two decades after that. Nor did it have any discernible effect on perception psycholo-

gists, with the possible exception of Gibson, who acknowledged it only to deny its theoretical base. Yet, it has had a definite effect on students of judgment and decision making, who have followed other aspects of Brunswik's contributions. And there has been a strange by-product; there has been a strong tendency among psychologists in the field of judgment and decision making, as well as social psychology, to demand representative design; the oddity is that those who demand it don't know what it is that they are demanding. The psychologists who ask for psychological studies to possess *ecological validity* (a theoretical term introduced by Brunswik that does not mean representative design) seem to be indicating that they wish that psychological studies offered more realistic representations of the environment that their subjects live in. (This is often referred to as the *real world.*) The cry for "ecological validity" clearly is a demand for research that is not restricted to the conditions demanded by what Brunswik called "artificial, systematic design" that is at the basis of analysis of variance statistical models, the standard method demanded by psychological journals. Thus, although it cannot be claimed that Brunswik's "distal focussing" article produced this belated interest in the behavior of organisms in their natural habitat (I doubt that any of those who use the term ecological validity in the incorrect sense ever read this or any other Brunswikian article), one can see that this is another sense in which Brunswik was a man ahead of his time, and still is. For he laid out in this article exactly what would need to be done to achieve the ability to generalize the results of a study to an organisms' natural habitat, that is, beyond the confines of a laboratory.

To illustrate his point that conclusions about the efficacy of an organism's behavior require the inclusion of conditions representative of an organisms' natural habitat, Brunswik began this

study of visual perception of size constancy in 1943. He enlisted the aid of a graduate student who was to be his only subject. In order to meet the requirements of representative design, the subject made perceptual judgments over 174 situations that were representative samples of her natural habitat—the environs of the University of California at Berkeley. The article explains in detail just how that was accomplished, as well as demonstrating our excellent ability to achieve size constancy over a wide range of conditions.

  REPRINT

Distal Focussing of Perception: Size Constancy in a Representative Sample of Situations

Egon Brunswik

Acknowledgment

The subject upon whom our results are chiefly based was Miss Johanna R. Goldsmith, a graduate student in Psychology at the University of California. Dr. Herbert Bauer, after having served as an additional control subject in each of the situations spontaneously selected and responded to by the subject, changed over to his role as a non-interfering "experimenter" by making the necessary objective measurements of the situations in question.

After the entire survey was concluded, both subject and experimenter participated in the evaluation of the results. Among the team of students which helped with statistical tabulations and computations the author is especially indebted to Miss Virginia Gailbraith, Mr. Bernard Davis, and Miss Edith Bernhard.

Prof. Edward C. Tolman has been kind enough to read the manuscript in a thankless effort to improve upon its English.

Reprinted from *Psychological Monographs* (1944), 56(254), 1–49.

Chapter I. Introduction: Situational vs. Populational Generality

In a preceding article (5) the use of correlation coefficients was substituted for the "constancy ratio" (earlier developed by the present writer 3, 4, 46) as a method for measuring size constancy. The type of perceptual achievement called "size constancy" may be said to constitute an evidence of the good focussing of the perceptual system on the independent objective character of physical objects as contrasted with its poor focussing on the projections, per se, of the objects upon the retina of a subject. Correspondingly, in this preceding study, subjective estimates of size yielded high correlations with the "distal" stimulus variable to be perceived[1]—namely, "measured bodily size of objects"—and low correlations with the "proximal" stimulus variable—namely "visual angle", i.e. "projective", "photographic" or "retinal" size (cf. Chapter V).

This preceding study was carried out in a laboratory setup in which an array of arbitrarily selected sizes and distances was presented to eight subjects. The estimates given by the different subjects were averaged together, as if they had been those from a single subject. The "individuals" for computing the correlations were thus not the subjects but the different situations. And the "tests", or paired variables, which were correlated were the various types of physical size measurement—distal and proximal size—representing the stimuli or causes, on the one hand, and the size estimates (given by the one average subject) as the responses, on the other. On account of the arbitrariness and comparatively well controlled, singular character of the setup, this previous study is to be classed, however, as having been fundamentally of an "experimental" rather than of a "statistical" nature in spite of the fact that correlation coefficients were employed to represent the closeness of a stimulus-response relationship.

One of the most crucial difficulties of the experimental approach arises in connection with the question of the generality of the results. The use of the outcome of a certain more or less arbitrary experiment in predicting results in related but not identical situations is one of the "backdoors" through which premature generalization is likely to slip in unnoticed. Systematic variation of conditions, introduced in order to check up on the generality of an obtained stimulus-response pattern has been the ordinary remedy for this difficulty. Being "systematic," such a variation is in practice limited to the modification of conditions along a single or a few dimensions of the given setup, such as that of size, of distance, or of tonal frequency.[2]

The conception inherent in functionalism that psychology is the science dealing with the adjustment of organisms to the environment in which they actually live suggest the need of testing any obtained stimulus-response relationship in such a way that the habitat of the individual, group, or species is represented with all of its variables, and that the specific values of these variables are kept in accordance with the frequencies in which they actually happen to be distributed. As, say, in a survey of public opinion individuals must be selected so that the sample is representative of the reactions of the population as a whole, so in a study of perceptual achievement situations or tasks should be selected in such a way that the resulting sample is representative of the actual demands of the whole environment made upon the organism with respect to the actual stimulus variable under consideration

(e.g. the variable of size of physical objects).[3] In comparison with the traditional domain of statistical methods, the field of inter- and intra-individual differences, relatively little systematic attention has been paid to this problem of the "situational generality" of experimental results, i.e., of generality with respect to the conditions of the stimulus- and response-situation, as contrasted with what may be called the "populational generality" of the individual differences studies. (Depending on the emphasis desired, such terms as "environmental generality", "circumstantial (or conditional, mediational) generality", and the like may represent more accurately what has been, somewhat hesitatingly, designated above as "situational generality".)

To be sure, specific control over the various mediating or circumstantial variables in the situation will, under the conditions just postulated, have to be given up in favor of generalized control within certain rather wide class limits. This means the abandonment of one of the fundamental policies of the experimental procedure in favor of a type of control characteristic, rather, of the typical statistical approach. In the conceptual isolation of a distal variable a natural flexibility of proximal mediation is indeed one of the most important requirements.

The present paper is an extension of the previous one (5) in that, in the study of size constancy, the correlation technique has again been used—along with measures of errors—, but in addition an attempt toward proper sampling of stimulus-response situations has also been made.[4] The application of fundamental policies of statistics has thus been rounded out. A relationship between organism and environment traditionally studied in the laboratory has been treated by a statistical survey in order to obtain greater closeness to life. Correspondingly, and in fact on account of the mere probability relationship between proximal stimuli, or cues, and the vitally more relevant distal objects, and of the resulting ambiguities in the evaluation of the proximal stimulus patterns on the part of the perceptual system of the organism, only imperfect correlations can be expected to hold between environmental variables and responses (cf. 7, 44).

The primary purpose of this study has been to give a methodological demonstration of the evaluation of responses to a random sample of test-situations. The specific problem of the perception of size has been used merely as an example. And, in accordance with this same primary purpose, the present study has in its main line been based upon the reactions of one subject only.

The subject, a graduate student in psychology, was interrupted at irregular intervals during the course of her daily activities, in various outdoor as well as indoor situations, and asked to indicate which linear extension happened to be most conspicuous to her at the moment. Though the sample of situations thus obtained may not be perfectly representative of "life", there is no doubt that it is more representative and variegated with regard to size, distance, proportion, color, surrounding pattern of objects, and other characteristics than any laboratory design could hope to be.

In each of these "life" situations, the subject had to give intuitive perceptual estimates of: (1) object size, (2) projective size (visual angle) and (3) distance. Since these estimates were supposed to be representative of uncritical perception only, the subject was then asked to repeat, in each situation, the first two estimates, but with critical judgment superimposed ("betting attitudes"). There was thus, a total of five estimates.

In order to obtain a second set of data for purposes of comparison (since this could be secured with little extra effort) the experimenter, who accompanied the subject, was also asked to go through the same series of estimates, independently of the subject, previous to his making the required geographic measurements of the stimulus variables in question.[5]

There were no restrictions on the free use of the cues and sensory facilities which ordinarily mediate the intuitive impressions of size. An analysis, proceeding after the pattern of this study, of the role of particular mediating sensory instruments or groups of instruments in the establishment of the perceptual constancies would have to be carried out by an artificial modification or elimination of specific sensory capacities and an observation of the resultant effects in investigations otherwise comparable to the present one. In an experimental setup and with the use of the constancy ratio, such an artificially controlled study of size constancy has already been undertaken by Holaday (25).

Chapter II. Procedure

The present survey comprised a total of 180 situations; for 174, the data are complete. There were 19 experimental periods extending over four weeks, and separated from one another by intervals of from one hour to twelve days. In each period, from 5 to 23 situations were estimated. The time intervals between the situations were controlled by the experimenter in such a way that they varied randomly in length extending over not less than five and not more than sixteen minutes between successive sets of observations by the subject. The time required for each judgment was not specifically recorded but has been estimated not to have exceeded a few seconds in each case, with the more natural attitudes taking, on the whole, the least time.

The surroundings in which the survey was made included scenes on the street and campus, in the laboratory, at the desk, at home, and in the kitchen. An attempt was made to cover recreation and study, daytime and evening (including periods of artificial lighting) under conditions and in proportions representative of the daily routine.

The instructions given follow. The notations used throughout this paper for the various types of estimates are indicated in brackets.

"During the course of the experiment, please follow your daily routine as closely as possible. Each time a signal is given to you, notice the object, or group of objects, or empty space, which at the moment stands out as the prominent 'figure' in your visual field. Of that object, select the straight linear extension upon which you are most inclined to concentrate at the moment, no matter what the direction of this extension may be. (In case you have been looking at an empty space, this extension may well be a distance between two objects.)

"In the order given below, the following five attitudes should be taken in succession, and your judgment of size given in terms of the units of measurement most convenient to you.[6] Do not proceed to the next attitude before having registered your judgment on the prepared sheet. Do not move before having completed all five judgments.

"(1) *Naive perceptual attitude* [b]: Give your estimates on the basis of your first impression of the sizes of the objects in question. You should consider the sizes of the 'things' as seen in the ordinary attitude of daily life (not projective sizes relative to your location). Do not let yourself be influenced by your abstract knowledge about, or memory of, the sizes of the objects in question, or of optics, etc.[7]

"(2) *Analytical perceptual attitude* [*p*]: Try to perceptually analyze or to disintegrate the scene, in the way a painter would have to see it in order to be able to draw a perspectively correct picture—in other words, try to estimate visual angles, or the relative sizes of the projections of the objects as they could be measured on your retina or on a photograph with the camera set up where you are standing. Relate your judgment to an imaginary meter stick in a frontal plane at one meter distance from the eye.[8] As in attitude (1), however, you should rely exclusively on perceptual appearance after the field has become reorganized in the fashion described.

"(3) *Realistic betting attitude* [*b'*]: As in (1), concentrate upon 'things'. This time, however, critically superimpose upon perception all abstract knowledge available to you. Take the attitude you would have, if you were to bet upon the sizes in question to the best of your knowledge.

"(4) *Analytical betting attitude* [*p'*]: As in (2), try to compare retinal (projective) sizes, again in relation to an imaginary meter stick at one meter distance. This time, however, take a betting attitude analogous to (3).

"(5) *Perception of distance* [*d*]: Perceptually judge your distance from the object, on the basis of your first impression, in analogy to attitude (1)."

The experimenter's main function (aside from serving as a control subject) was to control the time intervals between situations, to record the general type of the object or situation responded to by the subject, and to measure physical sizes and distances of the extensions designated by the subject, or to secure a basis for their trigonometric computation.

Physical projective size was easily ascertained by dividing physical bodily size by physical distance (in meters). Bodily size was similarly ascertained if distance and projective size only could be physically determined. In like manner calcula-

tions were made for distance. In some cases the objective data had to be ascertained by consulting a map, or by inquiry, such as in the case of some of the larger distances or of signs erected on the top of a building, and the like. In eight cases of body size and in one case of a distance (out of our total of 174 complete situations) the exact measurements could not be obtained, and carefully scrutinized estimates had to be substituted.

Chapter III. Distribution and "Ecological" Interrelations of Geographic Variables

Figure 4.1 shows, for the situations selected by the subject, the environmental, 'geographic' data only, namely the distribution of the physical object sizes (bodily extensions, B), physical projective sizes (P) and physical distances (D) as measured, computed or otherwise objectively ascertained by the experimenter. For reasons of convenience, of the Weber law, etc. (see below), all data are plotted logarithmically,[9] with the use of .5 as the class interval. The limits of the intervals are at 1 mm. (corresponding to a logarithm of zero), 3.16 mm. (corresponding to a logarithm of .5), 10 mm., 31.6 mm., 100 mm., etc. For more precise references see Figure 4.2.

The logarithms of the 174 bodily extensions for which the data are complete are fairly normally distributed, as shown by the dotted line in the left graph of Figure 4.1. The extensions which have been omitted from the original 180 for reasons of incompleteness of the data are large (such as, e.g., the height of a flying airplane which could not be objectively ascertained) and thus, if presented, would have added to the upper end of the distribution.

The further considerations in this paper are not, however, based on the entire material, but on a sample of 93 situations which remain after all the extensions tilted into the third dimension, and thus distorted (fore-shortened) on the retina, have been eliminated. In this remaining standard group of 93 situations, data are complete for all items. By definition, this final sample comprises the frontal objects, i.e. the extensions which are oriented perpendicularly, or approximately perpendicularly, to the line of regard of the subject. The present study thus is limited to problems of size constancy proper (involving variations in the

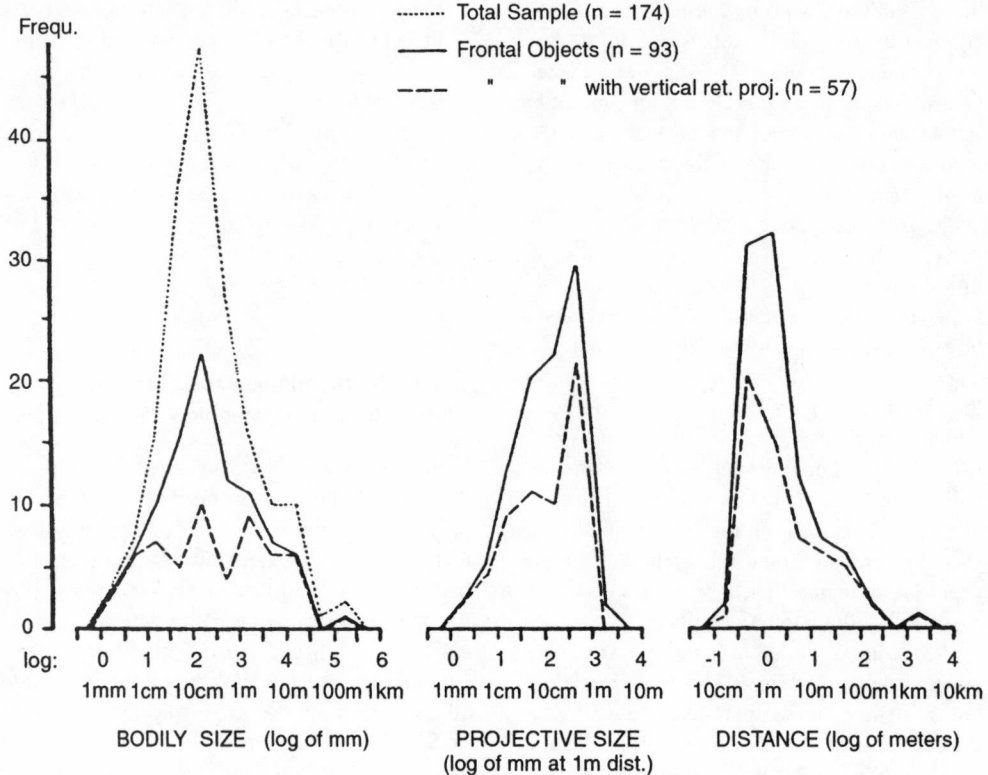

FIGURE 4.1 Frequency distribution of the logarithms of the geographic variables of bodily size, projective size and distance, characterizing the sample of extensions spontaneously responded to by our subject.

distance of objects) and excludes problems traditionally classified under "form-constancy", or estimates from situations involving rotation into the third dimension. (An analysis of the size-constancy of tilted objects, based on the total sample of 174 situations, might be presented in a further publication.)

The phrase 'perpendicular to the line of regard' which defines the extensions included in the frontal group, refers primarily to cases in which the perpendicular from the eye strikes the object somewhere near the middle and in which the visual angle is not too large so that the ends of the object are not too much distorted on the retina. Of the 57 upright frontal objects, for example, 44 fulfill the former requirement in a relatively strict sense (24 of the latter being approximately vertical and 20 being seen by looking

downward, as in reading a book). In the remaining 13 cases it is one of the ends of the objects which is seen perpendicularly, the position of the entire object thus being only approximately frontal. As can be inferred from Figure 4.2, the largest visual angles in our frontal group are about 45°, which corresponds to a projective size of one meter at one meter distance, or a tangent of 1. Situations such as the height of a house seen from a very short distance have been excluded from the frontal group though the lower portion of the house was in frontal position.

Regardless of the exact details of position, for all extensions classified as frontal, projective size (P) was computed by simply dividing bodily size (B) by perpendicular distance (D), i.e. by subtracting their logarithms, thus using the tangent of the visual angle in each case. Due to this standardization of procedure, errors up to a little

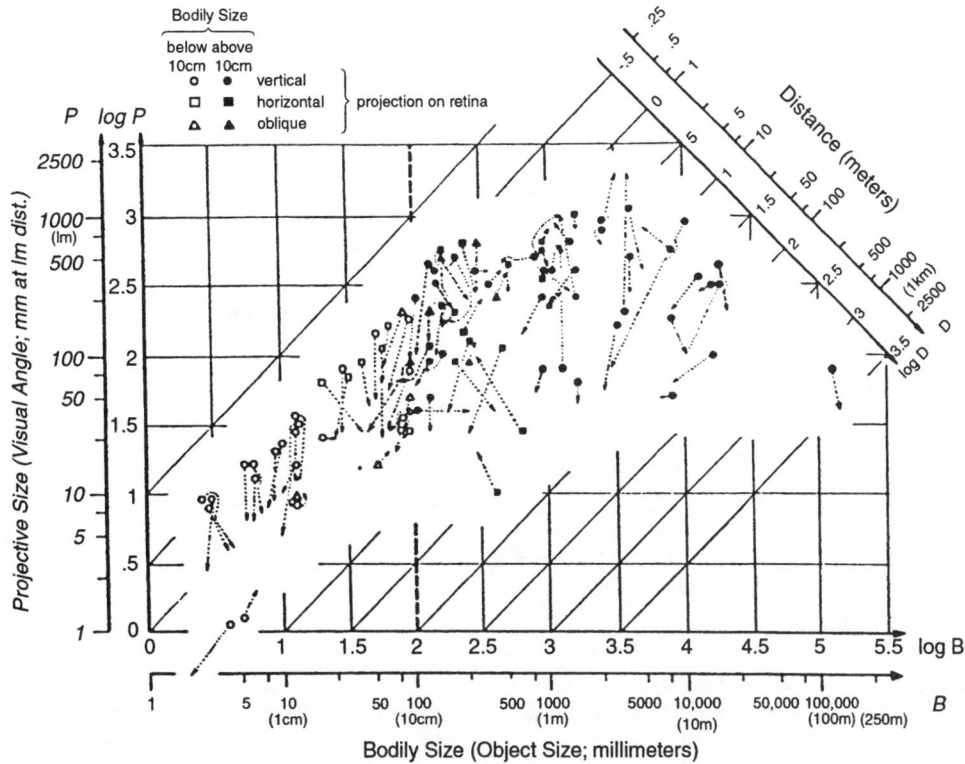

FIGURE 4.2 The 93 frontal extensions plotted in a field defined by the three functionally interdependent geographic variables of bodily size, projective size, and distance. The symbols (solid and outline squares, circles and triangles) are placed at the
intersection of the three mathematically interrelated measurements (B, P and D) characterizing each object or situation geographically. The arrow-head connected with
each symbol is based upon the respective pair of estimates of bodily size and projective size (b and p) used as coordinates. (This point does not necessarily coincide with
the explicitly estimated distance, d, which is not represented in this scheme; see Chapter VI.)

more than 15% are possible in the physical determination of the projective size of the objects
which were only approximately frontal.

In inferring retinal proportions from projective
size as computed above, a further source of error
is introduced by the absence of a perfectly frontal
orientation of the marginal portions of the 'frontal' objects (or of their projections on a frontal
plane) which are seen under a comparatively
large angle. In our frontal group, however, this increase (which is defined as the difference between the length of the arc and the tangent of
the visual angle) can never exceed somewhat
more than 20% (.08 logarithmic units).

Even when combined, the maximum error
possible as a result of the simplification of the
procedure in finding retinal size is still small
when compared with the variability of projective
sizes since the largest of our retinal extensions is
1,000 times as large as the smallest. In terms of
the logarithmic scale, the error could in no case
exceed .15, or 1/20 of the total logarithmic scatter
of projective sizes which covers the range from
about 0 to about 3. (The figure .15 corresponds
to an antilogarithm of 1.4 which is the factor accounting for an increase of 40%.) This potential
maximum also is less than half of the average of
the absolute logarithmic errors committed by the

subject in perceptually estimating projective sizes, namely .34 (see below, Table 4.1).

As shown by the solid line in the left graph of Figure 4.1, the 93 frontal extensions also are distributed approximately normally, when plotted logarithmically. This fact may be taken as an indication (though not a definite assurance) that our sample is representative. It may also be taken as a further justification for our policy of using logarithms in representing magnitudes. Bodily sizes range from a few mm. to more than 100 meters. Most frequent are sizes between 10 and about 30 cm., corresponding to the interval of logarithms of mm. between 2 and 2.5. The broken line refers to the 57 'uprights' of the 93 frontal objects. These 'upright' objects were projected approximately onto a vertical section through the optic center of the eye (i.e., along the intersection of the retina and the median plane). This would be the case for many vertical objects, letters seen when reading a book, and the like.

The middle diagram shows the distribution of projective sizes computed by dividing bodily size (in mm.) by perpendicular distance (in meters). Thus projective size is here defined as the extension, in mm., which is actually cut out by the light rays approaching the subjects, on a plane parallel to the subject's fovea at one meter distance from the eye (an arbitrary reference distance). Sizes on the retina itself are roughly proportional to these projective sizes so that the two concepts may in first approximation be used interchangeably, as was done above. The solid line refers to the 93 frontal objects. The distribution is skewed to the left, showing that the most frequent projective sizes are about 30 cm. to 1 meter. These also tend to be the maximal projective sizes. This modal interval corresponds to visual angles averaging around 35°. Some of the visual angles are, however, as small as 4 to 10 minutes of arc; and there is a gradual transition between the two extremes. The broken line again represents the 57 upright projective sizes. No computations were made for the relative sizes of the retinal representations of the extensions tilted into the third dimension.

Distances range all the way from 10 inches up to about a mile. They are shown in the right-hand graph of Figure 4.1 in which logarithms of meters are used as abscissae. The most frequent distances are between about 30 cm., the ordinary reading distance, and, some 3 meters. The distributions are positively skewed both for the entire group of frontal objects and for the group of 'upright' objects only. Again, no curve has been drawn for the total group. Many of the tilted extensions were in themselves so large and extended so far into the third dimension that it would have been difficult to assign to them any precise distances from the subject.

In Figure 4.2, the small circles, squares and triangles may be discussed first, disregarding for the moment the arrows connected with them. These symbols still deal with the purely physical aspects of the sample selected by the subject

TABLE 4.1 Focussing of perception upon distal rather than proximal stimuli (size constancy).

Attitudes	Subject				Experimenter			
	Means of algebraic deviations ("Constant Error")		Means of absolute errors (Variability)		Means of algebraic deviations ("Constant Error")		Means of absolute errors (Variability)	
	for B	for P	for B	for P	for B	for P	for B	for P
	$CE \pm Sigma_{CE}$	$CE \pm Sigma_{CE}$			$CE \pm Sigma_{CE}$	$CE \pm Sigma_{CE}$		
Uncritical perceptual (b and p, respectively)	−.035 ± .015	−.208 ± .038	.117	.339	+.020 ± .011	−.131 ± .040	.079	.325
"Betting" (b' and p', resp.)	−.011 ± .010	−.234 ± .041	.080	.366	−.003 ± .010	−.188 ± .039	.078	.344

This is here illustrated by logarithmic constant errors and their sigmas as well as average absolute errors, with respect to bodily size and projective size, for subject and experimenter, in uncritical perceptual attitudes and in "betting" attitudes, for all 93 frontal extensions.

and show the relationships between geographic bodily object size, B (horizontal axis of diagram); geographic projective size P (vertical axis of diagram); and geographic distance, D (shown at upper right of figure, and pointing downward). The three geographic variables can be represented in a two-dimensional field since they are, in a functional, mathematical sense, strictly interdependent, as defined by the equation $P = B/D$, or $\log P = \log B - \log D$. (P in its turn is equal to the tangent of the visual angle under which the object is seen, provided that both B and D are expressed in terms of the same unit.) Logarithms were again used throughout in plotting each of the 93 frontal situations. Of the total of 93 symbols the circles represent the 57 approximately upright frontal extensions, the squares, the 25 approximately horizontal frontal extensions, and the triangles, the remaining 11 oblique frontal extensions. Outline symbols refer to extensions smaller than 10 cm., solid ones to those of 10 cm. or over (see below).

The smallest extensions were mostly heights of printed or typed letters; the largest were heights of buildings, church towers, flag masts, trees, or hills. The uppermost square represents the length of a wall, the lowest, the width of a chimney. Examples of other frontal extensions are: length or width of matches, ashtrays, cups, bottles and other utensils, household goods, instruments, chess figures, books, furniture, windows, street signs, pavement squares, posters, etc. Empty distances such as the height of a room, or the distance between shelves, etc., were almost absent among the frontal objects, but comparatively frequent among the tilted ones which are not included in this presentation.

Most conspicuous general feature in Figure 4.2 is the fact that geographic bodily size, B, and geographic projective size or visual angle, P, are statistically correlated. The Pearson coefficient, from the data grouped in logarithmic intervals of .5 as indicated by the pattern of cells, and corrected for grouping, is $r_{BP} = .70$ for the entire frontal sample of 93. This correlation may be called an "ecological" one since it deals with a purely internal relationship between geographic variables relevant to an organism within the habitat of that organism (including the boundary between the organism and its surroundings), rather than with a relationship between a habitat variable and a response variable as is the case for the relationships discussed in subsequent chapters of this monograph.[10] The intrinsic imperfection of ecological relationships (7) finds its expression in the fact that r_{BP} is not 1.

This relationship is, however, due primarily to the fact that sizes smaller than 10 cm. are in daily life ordinarily all looked at from the same most favorable distance of about 30 cm. (see Fig. 4.2). This leads to a close tie between bodily size and retinal size within this size range.[11] The relationship also assumes a slightly curvilinear trend. The correlation disappears almost completely when only sizes above 10 cm. are considered. They are cut off in Figure 4.2 by the broken vertical line, and also represented by solid as contrasted to outline symbols. The correlation between B and P for this group of 59 objects is only .14. If the selection of objects to attend to in three-dimensional space, made by our subject is representative, there is, then, in an unbiased distribution of those objects which are all larger than 10 cm., a not much greater likelihood for large objects to cast large retinal images than for small objects to cast large retinal images, and vice versa. In other words, increase in the size of objects above 10 cm. is usually compensated for by an increase in distance. The visual angles thus remain of about the same orders of magnitude for stimuli coming from objects of all different sizes and at all the various distances.

This independent variability—in a statistical sense—of B and P for sizes above 10 cm. (which is quite compatible with the functional or causal relationship existing between these two and distance) will be a valuable feature in our subsequent efforts to isolate for study the focalization of the subject's response on the distal stimulus, B, from focalization of her response on the proximal stimulus, P.

As can be seen from a further inspection of Figure 4.2, there also is a marked positive relationship between B and D; the coefficients are .77 for the total frontal sample and .88 for the objects larger than 10 cm. This is a direct expression of the propensity of the subject to concentrate upon larger objects when looking at larger distances, or vice versa.

Projective size, on the other hand, shows almost perfect independent variability—in a statistical, ecological sense again—from distance (.08), with the relationship becoming slightly negative

(−.34) for object larger than 10 cm.[12] There is thus, if our sample of situations is representative, only a slight chance of successfully predicting distance from the visual angle of the objects of attention in the natural habitat of a present day intellectual, since a certain retinal size is about as often due to a comparatively small object at a small distance as to a comparatively large object at a large distance.

Chapter IV. Correctness of Perceptual Responses in Terms of Error

The dotted arrows extending from each symbol in Figure 4.2 are based on the first two types of estimates (verbal responses) given by the subject in each situation, b and p. As has been explained above, b refers to the "immediate", or intuitive, perceptual impression of bodily magnitude elicited by the object, p to the intuitive impression of projective values or photographic size obtained as a result of shifting toward the analytic attitude.[13] Each arrowhead is located at the point of our diagram combining the two estimates for the object in question, and using the same axes as for B and P, respectively. Each arrowhead thus represents, for the physical stimulus situation (an object of size B at the distance D possessing the projective value P) to which it is attached, the corresponding set of perceptual responses or "appearances", b and p (but, on account of perceptual inconsistencies, not necessarily of d, see Chapter VI). Length and direction of the arrows, or rather of their horizontal and vertical components, indicate magnitude and direction of errors of judgment in logarithmic terms.

(A) Perceptual: Size-constancy vs. "Constancy Hypothesis"

It becomes quite clear from a mere visual inspection of Figure 4.2 that arrows on the whole extend vertically more than horizontally, indicating greater errors for projective size than for bodily size. This is one of the several ways of expressing the establishment of "size constancy" and the comparative neglect of the retinal size relationships, per se, by the perceptual system. If the "constancy hypothesis" inherent in traditional structuralism (presupposing a strict one-to-one relationship between proximal stimulus element

and "sensation", cf., 31) were true, errors with respect to projective size should be small.

Computation of the average lengths of the two orthogonal components of the arrows has confirmed these findings quantitatively. Various kinds of averages of errors made in the purely perceptual attitudes with respect to B and P are presented in the first row of Table 4.1, the errors being defined as log b − log B, and log p − log P, respectively. The averages thus actually represent the logarithms of the geometric means of the ratios, between the raw estimates and the corresponding raw measurements, b/B and p/P, respectively.

The averages with the signs of the errors taken into consideration may, for the sake of brevity, be labelled "constant errors" (CE) though this term has thus far been applied primarily to cases in which at least part of the disturbing features causing the error has been systematically stabilized or specifically controlled for the entire experimental series. Sigmas (standard errors) of the constant errors are also given.

For our subject, the algebraic error for bodily size B is on the average −.035 in terms of our logarithmic scale. This value corresponds to an underestimation of B of about 7%. The constant error for projective size P, −.208, is about six times as large, corresponding to an underestimation of P by about 38%. For the experimenter in his role as a control subject the constant error with respect to P is seven times that for B, but the sign of the latter is positive and its amount, corresponding to an overestimation by only about 5%, is slightly under twice its own standard error. The significance of the difference between constant errors for B and for P, to be derived from the attached sigmas, is characterized by a critical ratio of 4.2 for the subject, and of 3.7 for the experimenter when the sign of the constant error is taken into consideration and of 2.7 when only the absolute magnitudes of the constant errors are compared.

Fractionated constant errors and their sigmas shown in Table 4.2 indicate a high level of significance for the difference between constant errors for B and P as far as objects within reach of the hand are concerned, with a critical ratio of 9 for the subject and of 14 for the experimenter for frontal extensions at distances less than one meter.

TABLE 4.2 Tendency toward comparative underestimation of distant objects as represented by logarithmic constant errors and their sigmas for objects at different distances.

		No. of objects	Ave. log D (m.)	Ave. log B (mm.)	Subject's Constant Errors		Experimenter's Constant Errors	
					for B $CE \pm Sigma_{CE}$	for P $CE \pm Sigma_{CE}$	for B $CE \pm Sigma_{CE}$	for P $CE \pm Sigma_{CE}$
	Distance							
Grouping of 93 objects not equated for B	Lesss than 1 m. (log below 0)	34	−.36	1.54	+.000 ± .019	−.430 ± .042	+.023 ± .014	−.416 ± .029
	1 m. to 3.16 m. (log from 0 to .5)	31	.26	2.39	−.015 ± .026	−.121 ± .050	+.025 ± .016	−.062 ± .037
	3.16 m. and more (log = .5 and more)	28	1.21	3.31	−.099 ± .034	−.034 ± .088	+.009 ± .031	+.132 ± .081
Same, equated for B	Comparatively near	46	.04	2.37	−.022 ± .012	−.294 ± .063	+.018 ± .014	−.235 ± .052
	Comparatively far	47	.59	2.38	−.044 ± .020	−.122 ± .052	+.022 ± .015	−.024 ± .053
B from 10 cm. to 10 m. (52 objects)	Less than 2 m. (log below .30103)	24	−.11	2.42	−.008 ± .021	−.207 ± .045	+.022 ± .010	−.166 ± .043
	2 m. and more (log = .30103 and more)	28	.83	3.01	−.014 ± .030	+.022 ± .075	+.013 ± .022	+.074 ± .093

The upper part of the table shows the results when the 93 frontal extensions are grouped into three distinct distance categories not equated for B. In the middle part of the 93 objects are regrouped in such a way that the geometric means for B are approximately the same in each of two distance groups. In the lower part a middle range of sizes is split into two distinct distance categories.

Measures of variability about the correct physical values may generally be more adequate than are constant errors in dealing with problems such as ours. To the right of the constant errors and their sigmas in Table 4.1, averages of errors, with the signs of the errors disregarded, are shown for B as well as for P. They are defined as averages of the 93 | log b − log B |, and of the 93 | log p − log P |, respectively.

These means of absolute errors (crude average errors) are measures of the variability of the estimates about the actual geographic values, or about an error of zero. Again, the values of P are considerably larger than those for B, in fact, about three times as large in the case of the subject and about four times in the case of the experimenter; the largeness of the difference is, however, in part due to the large constant error found for P.

Fractionated sigmas in Table 4.2 point in the same direction, the values for P being about two to five times as large as the corresponding values for B in the various distance categories.

As can be seen from Figure 4.2, the longest single horizontal component of an arrow extends over a little more than one cell, representing the height of a column of 10½ meters at a distance of 11 meters which had been estimated by the subject to be 2.9 meters high. In the same situation, the subject has also committed her largest error regarding projective size, represented by a vertical arrow-component about twice as long as the horizontal one, extending over more than two cells, i.e. one entire logarithmic unit; more precisely, projective size has in this exceptional case been estimated to be only about ½₂ of its actual value.

(B) Uncritical Perceptual Attitudes vs. Rationally Controlled Judgments

In the second row of Table 4.1 are shown, for subject and experimenter, results with the two types of "betting attitudes," b′ and p′, in analogy to the upper row which refers to the two intuitive perceptual attitudes. Reactions to B are in general more precise (i.e. errors are closer to zero) in the betting attitude than in the uncritical attitude. The significance of this improvement is, however, not established when the figures are compared item by item. For the experimenter, the constant error reaches the low of −.003 with a sigma of .010.

For P the opposite is true, and the tendency

toward an increase of constant error and variability is consistent for all the four comparisons that can be made.[14]

One of the principal difficulties in an investigation like the present is the question of whether the estimates given are based on genuinely perceptual, intuitive responses or whether they are merely reflections of more or less explicitly intellectual processes, including memory for numbers, etc. If this question is phrased in the usual introspective manner no decisive answer can be given to it, since no introspective alternative can be settled in an exact way as long as it has not been redefined in terms of objective criteria.[15] The above comparison of the so-called naive perceptual attitude with the betting attitude may nevertheless be taken as an occasion for the following rather casual remarks regarding the perceptual nature of the responses upon which this study is based.

According to the reports of both subject and experimenter none of the extensions estimated happened to be explicitly known to them in quantitative terms as a result of previous measurement or communication; consequently, the impression gained in the momentary situation had to be employed in each case. Familiarity with the objects, based on manipulation, as well as practical familiarity with the size of nearby objects, was of course given in many instances. This, however, is true in most cases of everyday perception, and the elimination of the factor of manipulatory familiarity would have seriously violated the principle of representative sampling of situations which was set forth in the beginning of this paper.

A more objective criterion as to whether or not judgment is determined by memory for numbers may be obtained by comparing the frequency of instances in which judgment of size is perfectly correct with that of those in which it is not. In the former instances, provided that they are more frequent than chance, one may suspect abstract knowledge to have slipped in unnoticed. In Figure 4.2, these cases are represented by the perfectly vertical arrows, indicating that measurement of B and judgment b were in perfect numerical agreement. There are 9 such cases for the subject, out of a total of 93; the corresponding figure for the experimenter (not represented in the graph) is 11. This proportion is rather low

in view of the fact that some of the measurements involved were taken to one significant digit only, and that exact correspondence did never occur in cases in which either measurement or naive perceptual estimate had been carried to more than two digits. Thus the tendency of the perceptual estimates toward round numbers (see footnote 13), in connection with the high degree of general correctness of judgments of bodily size, sufficiently accounts for the fact that the above-reported approximately ten percent perfectly correct responses were given. Unless one wishes to bring into the picture the possible significance, for our estimates, of abstract knowledge that is only approximately correct, there is thus no need to assume inroads of the higher cognitive functions upon perception as far as the naive realistic attitude is concerned.

A further corroboration of the relative autonomy of the system determining estimates of the type b, on the one hand, and of rational knowledge, on the other, may be gathered by comparing the perfectly correct responses given in attitude b with those given in the rationally infiltrated betting attitude b'. There is relatively little overlapping between the two. Of the 14 perfectly correct judgments given in attitude b' by the subject (16 for the experimenter), only 3 (experimenter, 6) are among those 9 (experimenter, 11) for which responses were correct in attitude b.

The scarcity of explicit knowledge of bodily sizes is further indicated by the fact that in all of our material there is only one case in which judgment is correct for a measurement which was taken to 3 significant digits. The diagonal of a panel, measuring 108 cm., was estimated to be 108 cm. by the experimenter in the betting attitude, b'. This extension might have been incidentally measured by the experimenter at a previous occasion without his explicitly remembering it.

(C) Compromise Tendency between Distal and Proximal Focussing

Comparing objects at small distances (upper left diagonal of Figure 4.2) with objects at larger distances (lower right-hand part of diagram), it will be noted that there is an increase in the frequency and degree of left-pointingness of the arrows, indicating a stronger tendency toward underestimation of bodily size for objects at greater distances.

This tendency is graphically not quite as clear as the one discussed under (A), yet it is also found to be significant after computation. The upper part of Table 4.2 shows constant errors and their sigmas, the objects being divided into three distance categories with approximately equal numbers of cases in each category. For the subject, there is no constant error when the 34 object-sizes at distances less than one meter are taken together. There is, on the average, a slight underestimation of the 31 objects in the next higher distance category, and considerable underestimation for the 28 objects at about three meters or more. The latter amounts to a geometric mean of algebraic errors of more than 20% (corresponding to the antilogarithm of −.099 which is .796, or about 20% below 1). The difference of the two extreme groups is significant at the 1% level of confidence. The experimenter shows a similar tendency, though considerably less clearly. For him the slight overestimation of objects decreases with increasing distance.

As should be expected, we find, corresponding to the underestimation of far object-sizes, that projective sizes are estimated higher (or underestimated to a lesser degree) when the objects causing the image are at a greater distance and thus possess a comparatively large bodily extension than when they are near at hand. Table 4.2 shows significant trends of this sort for both the subject and the experimenter.

The finding of the comparative overestimation of bodily sizes of near, and of projective sizes of far objects may be subjected to the argument that the cause of underestimation is to be sought in the largeness rather than in the sheer distance of far objects. The existence of a positive correlation between D and B has been mentioned above and is also directly evident from Figure 4.2. It is also shown by the increase of average B with the increase of distance in Table 4.2 (upper part of the column showing average log B). To meet this argument, the 93 standard frontal objects were regrouped, for each class interval of B, into a less-distant and a more-distant portion (if possible, equal numbers in the two portions) so that in the end the two resulting groups of 46 comparatively near and of 47 comparatively far objects were as closely equated with regard to B as possible. The result of this rearrangement is shown in the middle part of Table 4.2. In spite of the fact that the logarithmic averages for distance are still different by .55 logarithmic units (the near group averaging around 1 meter and the far around 4 meters, corresponding to .04 and .59), average B shows only a difference of .01 for the two groups. The responses show a trend that is similar to that discussed for the upper part of the table, though, as was to be expected on account of the decrease in differences in distance, less clearly and well below the level of significance as far as errors with respect to B are concerned. There is even a small, insignificant reversal in the case of the experimenter.

In order to eliminate the relative closeness of the average distances for the two groups of objects distinguished in the middle part of Table 4.2, and yet to avoid differences in size as much as possible, a third way of grouping was introduced using objects in a middle size range only, but applying a clearcut distance criterion as in the first type of grouping. The 52 objects between 10 cm. and 10 meters in size were divided into two approximately equal groups comprising distances above and distances under two meters. Results are shown in the lower, third part of Table 4.2. The difference in average distance between the two groups is now .94 (covering the interval from about 80 cm. to about 7 meters) instead of .55 as in the middle part of the table. Average bodily size is different for the two groups, though by no means as drastically as in the upper three rows of the table. The trend in the results in each case confirms the previous conclusions, though again below the level of significance.

Thus previous assertions regarding imperfection of the constancy mechanism in the direction of a slight overestimation of near and underestimation of far objects seem, on the whole, to be corroborated rather than contradicted. In other words, our results point toward a slight interference on the part of retinal size, per se, with the focussing of the perceptual system on the distal variable, bodily size (as mediated by retinal size in conjunction, of course, with a number of other proximal stimulus features, such as distance cues).[16] The generality of these experimental findings has sometimes been questioned but is now supported by our present sample of situations which is more representative of normal perception at large than were the situations involved in the previous laboratory experiments. Significance is reached, however, only when bodily sizes are permitted to be scattered over the various distances in an unconstrained fashion, distance as a variable then not being freed from its natural ties with bodily size. In view of the fact that this study is dealing with a statistical survey rather than an experiment we need not, however, be too much concerned with this lack of isolation of the two variables.

(D) Overestimating the Vertical?

Another previous statement of experimental psychology, although it does not belong to constancy research proper, may now be discussed briefly as a supplement. It is the so-called "vertical illusion". Unlike the findings of constancy research, this illusion, consisting in an overestimation of the upright as contrasted to the horizontal, seems, on the basis of our results, not to be generalizable beyond the limits of those experimental conditions under which it has thus far been studied.

In fact, when errors for the twenty-five horizontal objects (represented by squares in Figure 8.2) are algebraically averaged and compared with those for the 57 upright objects (represented by circles), an opposite tendency—toward comparative underestimation of the upright—is found, though below the level of significance. As is shown in Table 4.3, average estimates b, measured in terms of correct sizes B, are higher for the horizontal than for the vertical (−.021 vs. −.046); the difference is, however, not quite as large as its standard error. An analogous trend is

found in the experimenter's results: there is a decrease in his general tendency toward overestimation when we proceed from the horizontal to the upright extensions, but again the difference (.041 vs. .008) is not significant, the critical ratio being only 1.4.

Similar results are obtained when the 25 horizontal objects are compared with those 25 of the 57 upright objects which correspond most closely in distance and magnitude to the horizontal ones. As can be seen from the left part of Table 4.3 the two groups of 25 objects match very closely with regard to average D as well as with regard to average B. Again for both subject and experimenter estimates are comparatively lower for the upright than for the horizontal (in terms of algebraic deviations from the physical values), but again the difference hardly reaches its own sigma.

For comparison, the corresponding data on the 11 oblique extensions are also given in Table 4.3. On account of the small number of cases, however, no comment is made.

Since experiments of the traditional psychophysical type suffer from a lack of independence—in a statistical sense—and thus of isolation of distal and proximal variables, due to the stability of the mediating conditions (such as distance) under which the experiment is set up, it seems appropriate to check the vertical illusion not only in terms of B but also in terms of P. As shown in Table 4.3, the constant errors of the subject are nearly equal for all the comparisons to be made, whereas the experimenter shows, in

TABLE 4.3 Data pertinent to the problem of the "vertical illusion."

Direction in visual field	Number objects	Ave. Log D (m.)	Ave. log B (mm.)	Subject's Constant Errors		Experimenter's Constant Errors	
				for B	for P	for B	for P
				$CE \pm Sigma_{CE}$	$CE \pm Sigma_{CE}$	$CE \pm Sigma_{CE}$	$Ce \pm Sigma_{CE}$
Horizontal	all 25	.15	2.36	−.021 ± .030	−.218 ± .089	+.041 ± .021	−.092 ± .084
Upright	all 57	.41	2.43	−.046 ± .020	−.203 ± .039	+.008 ± .013	−.126 ± .050
	corresp. 25	.17	2.35	−.054 ± .023	−.215 ± .072	+.014 ± .014	−.178 ± .058
Oblique	all 11	.06	2.16	+.007 ± .048	−.191 ± .069	+.026 ± .016	−.245 ± .078

Logarithmic constant errors in estimating horizontal and vertical extensions support neither the distal nor the proximal interpretation of the vertical illusion.

conformity with the trends noted for B in both subject and experimenter, a slight and not significant tendency to under-rate the upright more than the horizontal.

The vertical illusion is thus counter-indicated, or at least not positively confirmed, by our representative sample of extensions and situations, whether it be conceived as referring to distal or proximal size as the crucial stimulus-variable.

(E) "Situational Generality" of the Weber Law for Length Discrimination

However, a more positive light is thrown by our data upon another classic of experimental psychology, the Weber law. When applied to the type of approach set forth in the present paper, the Weber law would lead us to expect that errors of judgment should on the average be the same for large and for small sizes, under the presupposition that the same logarithmic way of representation of errors is chosen which is used throughout this paper. In that case, numerical values of errors would, when taken from a sufficiently large sample of objects estimated, be in proportion to the size of the object judged which is what, in essence, is called for by the Weber law.

In a first type of approach to this problem, the 93 situations were divided into two groups, one containing relatively large, the other relatively small objects. An effort was thereby made to equate the two groups for distance in a manner analogous to that shown in, and discussed in connection with, the middle pair of rows in Table 4.2, the difference being that the two groups compared are here equated for D instead of for B. The purpose of this stipulation was to exclude the size-constancy aspect of the problem altogether. In this form the problem is approached in as good accord with the classical psychophysical tradition as is possible, i.e. with distance differences eliminated. There remains as a new feature only the sampling of objects and distances from natural situations which enables us to test the generality of the Weber law in terms of the conditions prevailing in everyday life.

In particular, the following procedure was adopted in segregating the two groups of extensions. Within each of the nine distance categories resulting from a subdivision of the D-scale in steps of .5 logarithmic units, as shown by the oblique lines in Figure 8.2, objects were divided according to their bodily size into two groups as nearly equal in number as possible. There was a further stipulation requesting that at the same time the total average of the distances of all the objects classified, within their distance categories, as "small", should be as nearly equal to that of the "large" objects as possible. To fulfill this second desideratum the two groups had to be made slightly unequal in number. There were 45 objects in the "small" as contrasted to 48 in the "large" group, due to the fact that in the next to the lowest distance category it was decided to have 15 "small" vs. 17 "large" objects so that the effect upon the D-averages of the one extremely large and distant object in our total distribution (see Figure 4.2) could be offset.

The results of this procedure are shown in Table 4.4. As can be seen from the third column, the logarithmic average distance is in fact very similar for the two groups. One of the consequences of this fact is that the distinction between B and P which is so important whenever questions of size constancy are involved need not be particularly kept in mind since whatever holds for B will under these circumstances hold approximately for the variable P as well. As is further shown in Table 4.4, the B-averages are at the same time more than sufficiently different for the two groups, though of course not quite as different as would be the case if the stipulation of equating the distance averages had not been made. In fact, the difference of almost 1.00 logarithmic unit existing between the logarithmic B-averages of the two groups indicates that our "large" objects are on the whole almost ten times as large as those in the corresponding group of "small" objects.

The remaining portions of Table 4.4 show averages of errors, computed logarithmically, and with the signs discarded, i.e. averages of $|\log b - \log B|$, for both subject and experimenter. The values computed for the "small" and the "large" groups are as nearly equal as could be expected. This holds for both subject and experimenter. The existing small differences are far from significant as can be seen from the attached measures of variability. It may thus be said that, as far as the specific manner in which the Weber law has been interpreted and applied here is concerned, its "generality" seems to be confirmed in the most satisfactory way.

TABLE 4.4 Data pertinent to the confirmation of the Weber law for length discrimination.

Object sizes	No. of objects	Ave. log B (mm)	Ave. log D (m)	Means of absolute errors $\|log^b - log\ B\|$	
				Subject Mean ± $Sigma_{Mean}$	Experimenter Mean ± $Sigma_{Mean}$
Small	45	1.87	.60	.118 ± .015	.081 ± .012
Large	48	2.84	.61	.117 ± .004	.075 ± .011

A second type of evaluation of our material pertinent to the Weber law may be briefly discussed in addition to the one already presented. Laying aside any regard for distance, and thus for projective size, objects have been classified into three categories according to their bodily size. The "small" group comprises the 34 objects smaller than 10 cm., the "medium" group the 34 objects between 10 cm. and 1 meter, and the "large" group, 25 objects larger than 1 meter. Average distances are of course quite different for the three groups (in fact, about 10 times as large for the "large" as for the "medium" group). In its general form this approach is analogous to that shown in the uppermost group of three rows in Table 4.2. In effect, it allows for all the natural concomitant variation of the distance with the size of those objects upon which our attention happens to become focused. This approach thus does not concern the Weber law in its traditional sense, but rather a broadened conception of the Weber law resulting from its combination with the "law" of thing constancy.

For the "small" and "medium" groups of objects averages of logarithmic absolute errors were again found to be very similar, for both subject and experimenter. There was, however, some increase as we proceeded to the "large" group. (To save space, the data are not shown in detail.)

Whether or not the latter fact may be taken as an indication, however indirect, for the generality of what has been called the "breakdown of the Weber law at the extremes" shall not be further discussed here. May it suffice to say that a similar procedure to that just outlined for B has also been followed through for P and for D, dividing them in three categories regardless of the other two variables concerned. For distance, results were found to be very similar to those reported for B. "Small" distances (under 1 m.) and "medium" distances (from 1 to 3.16 m.) showed about the same average amount of (logarithmic, relative) errors, with means of .058 and .059, respectively, for the subject, and of .053 and .050, respectively, for the experimenter. In contrast to this, errors are significantly larger for distances greater than about 3 m., namely .144 for the subject and .094 for the experimenter.

Chapter V. Coefficients of Correlation of Distal and Proximal Size with Perceptual Estimates

We proceed now to a presentation of the correspondence between measured variables and perceptual estimates in terms of correlation. As contrasted with measures of error, such as the constant error, used in the preceding section to represent perceptual achievement, the correlation coefficient possesses the major disadvantage of being limited to the representation of the degree of preservation of order, when the manifold of measured sizes is compared with the manifold of estimated sizes. This limitation is in contrast with the full representation of numerical correspondence between the objective and subjective scales which is offered, for example, by the constancy ratio, or by the measures of error. Nevertheless, from a biological (functionalistic) point of view such preservation of order may in itself be of value to the organism and hence worthy of notice by psychology.

Figure 4.3 shows the results rearranged in such a way that the relationships between physical (geographical) data and the subject's estimates can be expressed by correlation coefficients. The physical variables appear along the abscissae. In

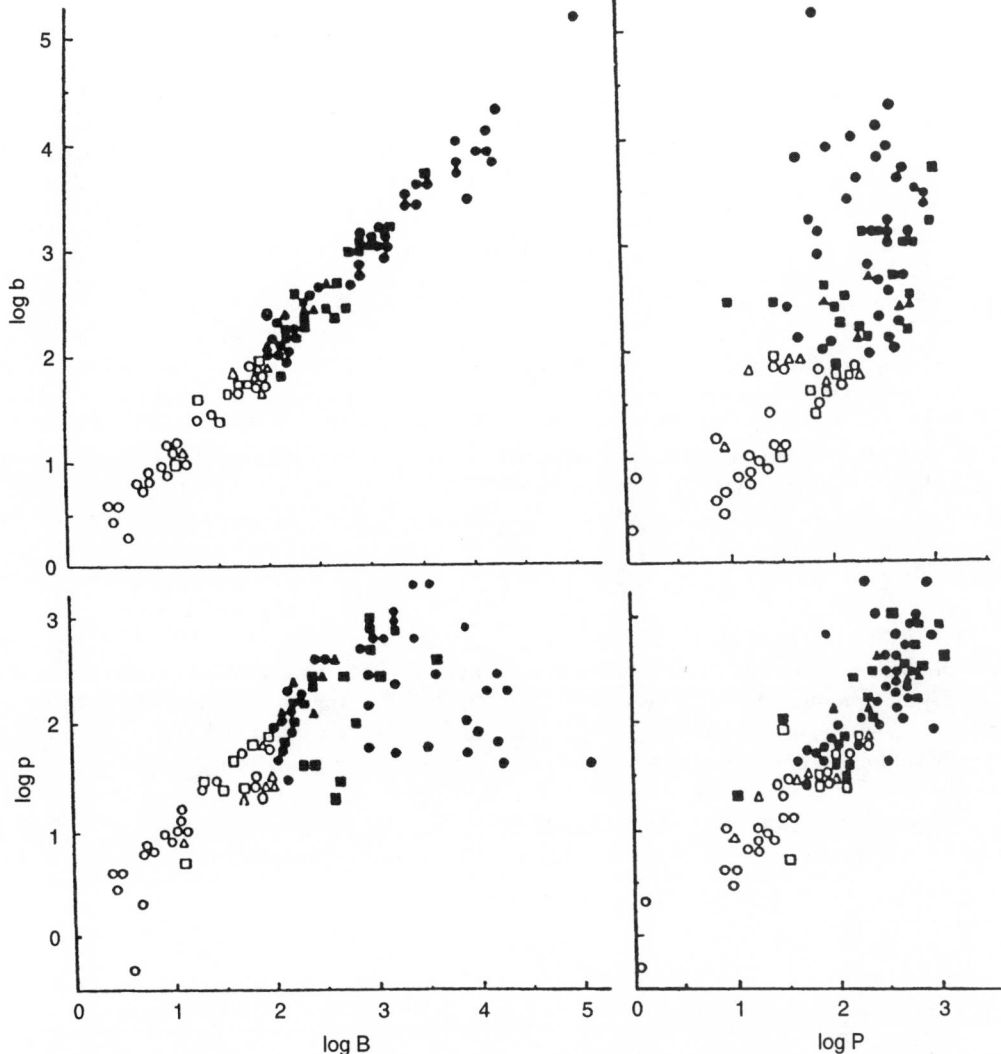

FIGURE 4.3 Scatter diagrams for the correlation between geographic variables B and P, and estimates b and p as given by the subject. (As in Figure 4.2, solid symbols refer to objects greater than 10 cm, outline symbols to objects smaller than 10 cm.)

the two left-hand figures these abscissae represent the logarithms of B, and in the two right-hand figures, the logarithms of P. (Distances are disregarded in both cases.) The subject's responses are represented along the vertical axes, whereby the two upper diagrams refer to estimates of bodily size, which thus have been named b, and the

lower diagrams to those intending to get at projective size, which thus have been named p.

Highest correlations should be expected where corresponding, or "homonymous," geographic and response data are brought together, that is, in the upper left diagram combining B and b and the lower right quadrant combining P and p. The relationship is indeed closer for these two quadrants than for the remaining two "heteronymous" ones which refer to how good the subject was in estimating bodily size when she wanted to estimate projective size (comparison of B and p, lower left), and vice versa (comparison of P and b, upper right).

It is also obvious that within the two homonymous quadrants by far the better agreement, i.e. the closer adherence to the diagonal of the figure, is found in the upper left figure which combines B and b. This is just another expression of the goodness of perceptual size constancy, as contrasted with a comparative lack of perceptual focalization upon the proximal sensory stimulus, even when such an attainment of, or constant relationship to, the variable P is purposely sought (by shifting toward an analytic destruction of the natural, habitual attitude of perception which is directed toward bodily things) as is done in attitude p.

Numerically, the correlation between B and b, or the degree of perceptual size constancy is, for our subject, represented by a Pearson r, corrected for grouping, of $r_{BP} = .99$[17] (Table 4.5, left part; the arrangement of the coefficients corresponds to the arrangement of the four scatter diagrams in Figure 8.3.) Due to the enormous variability along both axes such a high correlation is quite compatible even with the occasional grave errors of judgment which we have noted above. For the remaining quadrants the correlations are still relatively high, namely $r_{Pp} = .85$ for the lower right, and $r_{Bp} = .72$ and $r_{Pb} = .73$ for the two heteronymous quadrants. The latter two figures do not, however, mean very much, since, as was pointed out in connection with Figure 4.2, the two geographic variables, B and P, are correlated almost as high (.701) as are these two pairs of heteronymous variables.

An elimination of this obscuring feature was attempted in the following two ways: restriction to sizes above 10 cm., and the use of partial correlation.

The result of the former method can be intuited from Figure 4.3 directly by discarding the outline symbols and considering the solid ones only. As was reported above, for this sample of 59 objects the purely geographic, or ecological relation between B and P drops from .70 to .14 (cf. also Figure 4.2), and thus the two variables may, as a first approximation, be treated as independently variable. The correlation then is still as high as .95, instead of the previous .99 (cf. Table 4.5, right part), for the upper left diagram in Figure 4.3. This again represents size constancy. But the correlation drops from .85 to .57 for the lower right quadrant (this quadrant repre-

TABLE 4.5 Focussing of perception upon distal rather than upon proximal stimuli (size-constancy).

r, corrected for grouping, between	For the 93 frontal objects		Net relationships after partialling out		For the 59 frontal objects larger than 10 cm.	
	($r_{BP} = .70$ to be considered)				($r_{BP} = .14$ to be considered)	
	B	P	B	P	B	P
b	.99	.73	.98	.40	.95	.21
p	.72	.85	.32	.70	.08	.57

This is here illustrated by homonymous and heteronymous correlations of the geographic variables, bodily size and projective size (B and P), with uncritical perceptual estimates (b and p) given by the subject, based on the 93 frontal extensions, with r_{BP} left in (first part of table), as well as eliminated by partial correlation (second part) and by exclusion of small objects from the sample of extensions (third part).

sents perceptual attainment of relative retinal size when an effort is made to do so), and to a mere .08 and .21 for the remaining two heteronymous quadrants. The corresponding values for the 36 upright extensions out of the 59 extensions larger than 10 cm. (not shown in the Table) reveal the general trend even more clearly: they are, in the same order as above, .97, .53, .00 and .05, with an ecological correlation between B and P of only .06. For this sample, r_{bp} (i.e. the correlation between the two main types of estimates) has also been computed and was found to be −.25, indicating the statistical independence of the two types of judgments.

The coefficients in the right part of Table 4.5 show, more clearly than those presented to the left, the paramount role of the perceptual constancy of object sizes. With a considerable drop in precision, projective or angular size, per se, is also attained perceptually to some extent, if the proper shift in attitude is taken; whereas heteronymous combinations show only a negligible amount of perceptual achievement.[18]

In the middle part of Table 4.5, the net relationships are shown after partialling out P and B, respectively. The partial coefficients are in magnitude between the corresponding values to the left and to the right, and thus show a similar general pattern, confirming the conclusions drawn above.

In the previous publication (5) mentioned at the beginning of this article which also used the correlation coefficient as a means of expressing size constancy, an arbitrary selection of 15 cubes ranging from 5 to 7 cm. in size and placed at distances from 2 to 10 m. was used in a laboratory setup. The geographic relationship between B and P corresponded to a correlation r_{BP} of .10 and was thus similar to our 14 obtained here for sizes above 10 cm. The results calculated from averages of the estimates of eight observers, given in the natural b-attitude only, were in good agreement with those shown in the first line of the right part of our present Table 4.5, namely .97 instead of the present .95 and .26 instead of the present .21. The closeness of the numerical values should, however, be considered rather incidental, since the coefficients would no doubt have been quite different if other sizes or distances had been chosen for the experiment.

Correlation coefficients for both the uncritical perceptual attitudes and the betting attitudes have also been computed, for both subject and experimenter, using the 57 upright frontal extensions as a sample. Results summarized in terms of correlation coefficients are very similar for subject and experimenter though different errors were usually made in each single situation (see also Tables 4.1, 4.2 and 4.3). This is in line with the expectation, reasonably to be made on the basis of common observation, of the generality, from individual to individual, of the general scheme of perceptual focussing described above, though quantitatively the agreement may often be found to be less close. Results with the betting attitude show, in agreement with our previous findings (Table 4.1), on the whole a slight tendency toward improvement as far as the homonymous coefficients are concerned, and a corresponding slight lowering of the heteronymous coefficients. In particular, $r_{Bb} = .99$[19] and $r_{Bb'} = 1.00$ corrected for grouping and rounded, for both subject and experimenter. For the corresponding combinations of P with p coefficients are .87 and .90, for the subject and the experimenter, and with p', .89 and .87, respectively. Thus the tendency toward an improvement with a shift toward the betting attitude is with respect to P true only for the subject. Heteronymous correlations are again close to the geographic or "ecological" correlation r_{BP} which for the 57 upright objects is equal to .75.

Chapter VI. Estimates of Distance and the Question of the Internal Consistency of the Perceptual System

The correspondence between the uncritical distance estimates d and measured or computed geographic distances D is represented, in terms of error, in the first row of Table 8.6, in a way analogous to Table 4.1 where the same was done for bodily size and projective size. Logarithmic constant errors with respect to distance compare favorably even with those with respect to bodily size, being about the amount of the latter for the subject and about half of this amount for the experimenter in his role as a control subject. This discrepancy, however, was not significant. The constant error itself is not significant for the exper-

TABLE 4.6 Comparisons between geographic and explicit as well as implicit behavioral distances, for the 93 frontal extensions.

		Subject		Experimenter	
	Deviations	Algebraic Means $CE \pm Sigma_{CE}$	Absolute Means (Variability)	Algebraic Means $CE \pm Sigma_{CE}$	Absolute Means (Variability)
Behavioral vs. geographic distances	$\log d - \log D$	$-.030 \pm .012$	.114	$+.009 \pm .010$	.077
	$\log d_{bp} - \log D$	$+.153 \pm .033$	.278	$+.155 \pm .038$	.319
Implicit behavioral vs. explicitly estimated be-behavioral distances	$\log d_b - \log d$	$-.011 \pm .017$	.131	$+.005 \pm .010$	.139
	$\log d_p - \log d$	$+.201 \pm .037$	.328	$+.141 \pm .040$	.329
	$\log d_{bp} - \log d$	$+.178 \pm .034$	.298	$+.149 \pm .037$	.309

imenter, being not quite equal to its standard error. Absolute errors shown in Tables 4.6 and 4.1 are, however, sizeable and almost exactly the same for distance and for bodily size.[20]

By far the greatest single discrepancy between D and d for the subject holds in the case of a house of 14 meters height for which the geographic distance of 36 meters was estimated to be 12 meters, i.e. one third of its actual value. The maximum error of the experimenter is in logarithmic terms about the same, but in the opposite direction: a chimney of 42 cm. width at a distance of 39 meters was estimated to be at a distance more than three times as large, namely at 120 meters.

Correlations (again corrected for grouping) between D and d are likewise as high, if not higher, than those between B and b, namely .99 in the case of the subject and 1.00 (rounded) in the case of the experimenter, for the 57 upright frontal extensions. For comparison see the figures quoted at the end of Chapter V.

An interesting side issue is the question of the agreement between the actual distance estimate and the distance which appears to have been "registered" or "taken into consideration," in a functionalistic or organismic (not, or not necessarily, also in an introspective) sense, when the size judgment was established on the basis of the mediating proximal stimulus pattern. In the field of Gestalt- (form-) constancy as well as of size constancy, in a sizeable proportion of instances (about twenty in one of the three studies quoted below) a relatively high degree of perceptual con-

stancy has been found in spite of a complete negation, in an explicit perceptual sense, of the existing—and implicitly registered—difference in spatial orientation or distance, respectively, between standard and variable stimulus (18, p. 538 ff.; 30, p. 626 f.; 25, p. 458 ff.). This seemingly paradoxical result points toward a considerable amount of internal inconsistency within the perceptual system. Koffka (31, p. 229 f.) has questioned this result on account of the alleged scarcity of evidence and for reasons derived from his theories in a manner which seems, however, not quite convincing to the present writer.

The present study is not capable of furnishing, in itself, conclusive evidence on this point, primarily because the clearcut case of the non-recognition of a difference in distance is not given in our study since direct comparisons of situations have not been made by the subject. Indirectly, however, there is some evidence available.

The case can best be illustrated by referring to Figure 4.2. As far as the geographic data represented by the various types of symbols are concerned, there is strict consistency. Though three axes have been drawn, one for B, one for P, and one for D, each object is characterized by one point only, due to the univocal interdependence of the three variables as mathematical functions of one another in the physical universe.

No such internal consistency could, however, be found for the tips of the arrows connected with each of the large symbols. As will be recalled, the location of these arrowheads was determined by using the two subjective estimates, b and p, as coordinates. Each point so determined automatically refers to a certain distance when related to the third axis. This distance, "implicit" in the combination of judgments b and p, and thus to be labelled d_{bp}, does, however, only exceptionally coincide with the line, perpendicular to the D axis, which would represent the verbalized, "explicit" ("conscious") distance estimate, d, given by the subject in the given situation.

In other words, only exceptionally do we find that the distance which apparently has been underlying the act of judging an object to be so and so large and at the same time to produce a projective value of such and such magnitude, does correspond to the distance estimate as actually phrased by the subject. In most cases these two types of distance, d_{bp} and d, which are both organismic or "behavioral" distances—i.e., implicit or explicit responses to distance on the part of the perceptual system—, are nonetheless different.

In Figure 4.2, this could have been represented by adding a second arrow to the first, which would have to extend from the head of the arrow parallel to the D axis in one direction or the other until it reached the line representing the explicit distance judgment. Greater length of this arrow would represent a higher degree of internal inconsistency of perception.

An alternative way of representation would consist in constructing the two points corresponding to a combination of b and d, and p and d, in addition to the already existing point, b,p. The resulting triangle could also be used to represent perceptual inconsistency. In case of perfect internal consistency in judging the three variables the three points would coincide in one as does the combination of the three physical variables. Only in the case of internal consistency combined with external correctness of all the estimates, however, would this one point also coincide with the point representing the combination of geographic measurements.

The second row of Table 8.6 shows the average discrepancies between the type of implicit distance d_{bp} introduced above and geographic distance. Thereby, d_{bp} is defined as log b − log p (which is equivalent to the logarithm of b/p). It is evident that this implicit type of constant error by far exceeds the constant error computed from explicit d. The difference is highly significant. Variability about the correct value has likewise increased.

This fact is interesting to note, but it does not yet refer to our problem proper, namely the discrepancy between implicit and explicit behavioral distance. A comparison of this type is made in the lower part of Table 4.6. Actually three kinds of implicit distance are used there and contrasted with explicit distance. The last of the three is d_{bp} as defined above; the first two are what might be called fractionated implicit distances; d_b is defined as log b − log P, or, in other words, the distance which appears to have been taken into consideration, in a functionalistic sense, in establishing the judgment on bodily size, the other constituent of which is the relative size of the physical retinal stimulus; and d_p is defined as log B − log p, or in other words, as the distance which appears to have been taken into consideration, in a functionalistic sense, in establishing the judgments on projective size in an attempt to get away from the habitual perceptual attitude to implicitly construct bodily size from relative retinal size in conjunction with peripheral cues for distance. (Thus d_p actually relates to the undoing of a step which in itself presupposes some kind of reference to distance of the general kind represented by d_b.)

As can be seen from Table 4.6, the distance estimates implicit in the judgment b, namely d_b, do not differ very much from explicitly estimated distance. There is however a considerable discrepancy when d_p is compared with d. Obviously, thus, quite different behavioral distances must have been eliminated in the natural concentration of the subject on b, in establishing p, than those which are explicit in d. The last row in Table 4.6, referring to implicit distance d_{bp} combined from the judgments b and p, shows a picture quite similar to that obtained for d_p. In this row, the answer is given to the question put forward above as to the average length of the additional arrows which could be introduced in Figure 4.2. Since large discrepancies occur in all three of those instances in which p appears in the subscript, and in those instances only, it may well be said that the chief contributor to the internal inconsistency of distal perception must be sought in the inability of the perceptual system to discard the established distance cues, rather than in an inability to use them in a fairly consistent manner.

In comparing the second and fifth rows of Table 4.6 it appears that compound implicit distance, d_{bp}, shows about as much average deviation (algebraic as well as absolute) from geographic D as it does from explicitly estimated d. Both discrepancies are multiples of the one found in the first row between explicit and geographic distance. There is thus a considerable amount of external discordance with the corresponding physical variable along with the internal inconsistency with other data within the perceptual system.

In further illustration of the inconsistency of distance perception, reference may now be made briefly to the greatest single discrepancies between implicit and explicit distance. We may begin with the case which shows the least amount of deviation, namely the comparison between d_b and d. For the subject, the absolute maximum of the discrepancies is represented by a difference of +.47 of the logarithmic scale, or about as much as the distance between two of the oblique lines extending from the upper right to the lower left of Figure 4.2. It is the case, mentioned previously in Chapter IV, of the height of a column of 10.5 meters at a geographic distance of 11 meters which according to the resulting projective size, 955 mm., and the bodily size erroneously assigned to it by the subject, of 2.9 meters, should have been seen at a distance of $d_b = 3.03$ m. whereas explicitly estimated distance d happened to be much more nearly correct, namely 9 m. For the experimenter, the maximum discrepancy is even more drastic, namely +.94 logarithmic units, corresponding to not much less than the full length of a diagonal of one of the cells, or two distance-class-intervals, in Figure 4.2.

Discrepancies between implicit distances in which p appears as a subscript and explicit distance are correspondingly larger; they run up to −1.16 for the subject, in the same situation as above; the distance of the column to be derived from its actual size, 10.5 m., and the estimate of its projective size, 8 cm. (instead of the correct value of 95.5 cm.) would have had to be $d_p = 131$ m. instead of the explicitly estimated 9 m. (The implicit distance to be derived for this situation by combining the two estimates, b = 2.9 m. and p = .08 m., is $d_{bp} = 36$ m.) For the experimenter, the absolute maximum of a discrepancy between d_p and d is represented by the value +1.24.

Though, in an indirect way, the internal inconsistency of the perceptual system seems on the whole to be corroborated by our results, a few qualifying remarks should, however, be appended. To be sure, data on self consistency (reliability) of explicit as well as implicit functional distances would be needed in addition to our data in order to make the proof complete. Such data could be obtained, for example, by letting the subject repeat distance judgments for the same series of situations at another time. This has not however been done in this study. The good agreement between d and D shown in the first row of Table 4.6 might be taken as a hint that reliabilities would probably be good. Furthermore, one would have to consider the fact that a certain time interval and a number of shifts in attitude were interposed between the judgments b and p on the one hand, and d, on the other, which certainly did not make for greater consistency.

All evidence for internal inconsistency of the perceptual system is in support of what may be called the "autonomy" of the perceptual system as contrasted to the more explicitly rationalized approaches to reality such as measurement and computation which bear the marks of logical consistency. In the hierarchy of mental functions, perception appears to be among the more "primitive"; internal contradiction being one of the main defining characteristics of such primitiveness (4).

Chapter VII. Application of the Constancy Ratio to Our Material

The constancy ratio referred to in the introduction may be adapted to our material primarily in two ways. Since the constancy formula is based on a direct "behavioral" (subjective) equality of two objects at different distances (in the typical case of a "Standard" and a "Variable") some adjustments will have to be made to the formula for both ways in which we may apply it. To simplify the discussion, estimates of the type b (naive realistic perception) will be considered only, though all considerations would apply *mutatis mutandis* equally well to judgments of the type p or to the two kinds of betting attitudes.

(1) The first and simpler method will deal with

single estimates b and arbitrarily assume that they have been made with reference to an imaginary series of objects at a fixed distance, say, for the sake of simplicity, at one meter, as in the case of the p-judgments.

Taking the isolated square symbol in the lower middle portion of Figure 4.2, representing the width of a chimney, as an example, it may then be said that its true bodily size B of 420 mm. has been estimated to be like that of an object of b = 300 mm. (as indicated by the arrowhead) at our fictitious reference distance of one meter, whereby the physical size of its projection upon a frontal plane at the same distance, P, was computed to be 10.8 mm. The constancy ratio[21] is then

$$c = \frac{\log b - \log P}{\log B - \log P} = \frac{\log 300 - \log 10.8}{\log 420 - \log 10.8} = \frac{2.477 - 1.033}{2.623 - 1.033} = .91,$$

indicating the underestimation of this relatively distant object (the geographic distance is 39 m.) in terms of approximation to the constancy ratio of 1.00 which would indicate perfect perceptual achievement in this respect.

Constancy ratios could in this way be computed for each of our 93 situations. Other arbitrary reference distances could be chosen instead of 1 m., in which case the P-values would have to be multiplied by the new reference distance. In order to keep constancy ratios comparable with one another, the same reference distance would, however, have to be used throughout.

"Over-constancy" (i.e. values of the constancy ratio greater than 1) will result whenever objects further away than the reference distance are overestimated or objects closer than the reference distances are underestimated in size. It is apparent that there would be a considerable number of such cases whatever the arbitrary reference distance might be. The choice of the reference distance would, however, unduly affect the way in which results would be represented, for each particular object, in terms of the constancy ratio.

A further inadequacy lies in the fact that for objects at distances close to the reference distance the constancy ratios would be disproportionately sensitive to errors of estimation due to the fact that P in these cases would be nearly equal to B.

(2) In view of these shortcomings a procedure seems to be more adequate which would consider two objects at a time and thus do away with the necessity of assuming an imaginary Variable at an arbitrary reference distance. One may look for objects at different distances which have been estimated to be of the same size and compare their B's and P's. The only assumption to be made is that the objects would also have been estimated as equal with regard to b had the two situations been viewed in close succession instead of having been judged at widely different times in terms of a common abstract scale.

The procedure to be followed would consist in selecting pairs of situations for which the arrowheads lie on the same vertical and which thus are equal-appearing with respect to bodily size. Either one of the two objects may then be treated as the Standard or the Variable without effect upon the result provided that the logarithmic form of the constancy ratio is chosen (cf. 4, p. 67 f.), the geographic distance of the Variable to be used as reference distance for the projective values. Let whichever of the two objects is treated as the Standard be characterized by B, P, D, and the Variable by B', P', D'. Since, by hypothesis, the Standard looks, with respect to bodily size, like the Variable B', B takes the role of b in the constancy ratio as given above. The value of B in the formula remains unchanged, but for P the projective value relative to the distance of the Variable, that is PD', must be substituted for P. Thus

$$c = \frac{\log B' - \log PD'}{\log B - \log PD'}$$

which may be further transformed, by substitution of B'/P' for D', into

$$c = \frac{\log P' - \log P}{\log P' - \log P + \log B - \log B'}$$

This ratio will be 1 whenever there is no objective discrepancy between the bodily sizes B and B' which, by hypothesis, have been judged as equal.

For our previous example as the Standard, a reference case would be given by the triangular symbol in the middle of Figure 4.2 with a short arrow pointing upward in such a way that its head is on the same vertical line as the head of the arrow of the Standard. For this extension, the size of a bag, B' is 260 mm. and P' is 92.8 mm.

According to the above formula, c is found to be .82 for this particular combination of objects.

A case of over-constancy is given when, instead of the triangle, the square symbol closest to the Standard and with its arrowhead again along the same vertical as that of the Standard is used as the Variable. This is due to the fact that the new Variable, being at a closer distance than the Standard, is nevertheless underestimated to a larger degree than the standard. For this Variable, the length of a street sign, B′ is 700 mm. and P′ is 31.3 mm., resulting in a c of 1.9. The unusually high overconstancy value of the ratio is in part due to the relatively small difference in distance between the two objects which makes for exaggerated sensitivity of the constancy ratio as has already been pointed out above.

In a genuine sense, this technique applies only to combinations of objects with equal b estimates. Further assumptions would make it possible to include pairs with unequal b as well. The subject's total performance in size constancy could then be represented by, say, the mean and the sigma of the constancy ratios for all possible combinations of the 93 situations. Quite aside from the laboriousness of such a procedure, the reader will have noted the reasons for which the correlation coefficients and even the constant error seem to be preferable for many purposes as means of representing the total achievement in a sampling study such as the present one.

Chapter VIII. Discussion of Results: "Statistics" versus "Experiment" in Stimulus-Response Analysis

As will be recalled from Chapter I, the present study combines the use of two basic features of the practice of investigation that has developed especially with the growth of the biological and social sciences and has become known under the term "statistical". The first is the correlation coefficient as a measure of perceptual size constancy introduced in a previous publication (5). The second is new with this study. It is an attempt to secure a representative sample of task situations from which the paired values of the stimulus- and response-variables to be correlated with one another could be drawn. The present study thus can be used for a juxtaposition of the traditional experimental "style" or pattern of investigation

and a relatively new approach to stimulus-response problems which is more in keeping with the spirit of statistics in all of its ramifications and implicit connotations. Given the choice of any single criterion to distinguish "statistics" from "experiment", the present writer would vouch for the second of the above mentioned features, "representativeness", as contrasted with the "systematic" character of the experimental approach.

To be sure, there are elements of the statistical pattern in nearly every actually performed psychological experiment. These elements involve, however, usually only one of the two groups of components determining the response studied, namely, the factors in the responding organism expressed in terms of inter- and intra-individual differences. In contrast to this, the present study endeavors to extend these same statistical principles to the other group of independent variables, namely the realm of those stimuli which are to be studied—in the further course of the investigation—as possible factors in the causal ancestry of the responses in question.

It is to be noted that correlating stimuli with responses in a representative population of situations is a departure, from the customary procedure of correlating tests in a population of individuals, which is of a different, more radical kind than the "inverted" correlational technique (Stephenson, 41). In this latter technique there is a mere exchange of the role of individuals and tests by correlating persons on a sample of tests instead of tests in a sample of persons.

(A) Representativeness vs. Systematic Design of Variables, Variation, Covariation

The idea of representative sampling, when transferred from the study of individual differences to the study of the responses of an organism to its environment may be applied, firstly, to the choice of the variables to be studied for their ability to elicit specific responses in the organism, secondly, to the manner of variation (range and distribution within this range) of these variables, especially of those to be classified as "independent", and thirdly, to the manner in which such variables are allowed to covary (to vary concomitantly) with other variables in the field.

In the traditional experimental approach all three of these aspects of research procedure are handled arbitrarily, and mostly in a "systematic" fashion. Variables are often taken from the inventory of dimensions established in physics which does not consider typical organism-environment problems. The distribution of values usually follows an arbitrary range often dictated by the convenience of the experimenter, and within this range is mostly of a rectangular type with, say, an equal number of presentations of stimuli for each of a number of evenly spaced intervals.

Covariation with other variables is eliminated as much as possible. Probably the most characteristic policy of the classical experimental systematic approach is the "rule of one variable" (46), or what Lewin calls the technique of the "pure case" (32, p. 25). In its simplest form it takes its start from the ideal of eliminating covariation from the environmental variables by keeping all conditions constant (or at least under control) except for one independent variable, and to study concomitant variation in the dependent variable.

It has often been overlooked that in thus artificially untying the natural relationships between the so-called independent variable and many other variables in the field, this independent variable is artificially made to covary in strict unison with some of the remaining variables. The independent variable has thus not really been isolated. On the contrary, it becomes confounded with these remaining variables in an inseparable cluster.

An example is the classical psychophysical approach to length discrimination as represented, e.g., by the Galton bar experiment. The two halves of the bar to be compared are at the same distance. The fact that distance is kept constant leads, however, to a perfect tie of distal and proximal size (B and P in our study). Whenever the two bodily lengths are objectively equal they are at the same time projected in equal length upon the retina. A judgment of equality given in this situation yields no objective criterion by which it could be decided which one of the two variables—if any—is the crucial stimulus upon which the response is focused, ideally or at least approximately. At best there may be an introspective criterion—such as Brentano's awareness of intentional reference to the object—but this cannot be unconditionally trusted in any analysis of perceptual achievement (see 4, 25). Neither do the major results of classical psychophysical studies, threshold values, give any answer to such questions of selective focussing or stabilization of stimulus-response relationships. Results of such studies thus possess extremely limited generalizability.

As is pointed out by the present writer elsewhere (7, p. 265, and also in a paper now being prepared) the "experimental" and the "nomothetic", i.e. law-finding, policy are inseparably tied to one another and to the "molecular" or "microscopic", low-level-of-complexity type of approach (see also 35, 38). The "laws" uncovered by pure case experiments are in a sense not the most general, but, on the contrary, the most specific type of result to be found in the sciences. (This holds to a considerable extent even if an effort is made to combine such laws with one, another or in a multiple-variable design considering "interaction" within certain limits.) Concentration of scientific effort upon the search for absolute laws thus represents one of the fallacies in the ideology of the exact sciences, at least as far as their more "molar" (43) purposes are concerned. To a good measure, this is due to the unrecognized ties between variables, tacitly slipping in with the experimental technique.

In experiments on perceptual size constancy, distance and thus projective size, are made somewhat independent of bodily size. They are therefore experiments of a "critical" kind, setting up one variable against another instead of throwing them together in one cluster. Yet, since in an experiment all variations are systematic, there is a definite set or matrix of combinations of the various values of the variables leading to what might be termed "artificially interlocked" covariation. Examples for this are not only experimental studies of the more traditional type, such as that of Holaday (25), but also the author's previous correlational study (5). The latter is an experimental-statistical hybrid, but still fundamentally on the experimental side, if representativeness is taken as the major criterion. So also are most other multidimensional and correlational approaches including the multiple-variable design of experiments using the analysis of variance technique (20, 16, 17). It must be remembered that this latter quasi-statistical technique imposes restrictions upon the range—and thus upon the freedom and representativeness—of variation and upon covariance which are definitely on the rigid, systematic side, such as the necessity to pair each value of each factor or dimension with each value of every other variable under consideration.

One of the best goals for which orthodox experiments can be, and have been, properly used is the ascertainment of such minimum, or all-or-none, facts as the presence, at least under some conditions, and thus the possibility, of a certain mechanism. One such mechanism is the elimination of a variation of distance from the perception of object size in perceptual size constancy. Generally we find in this category the question of the contributingness, or else the non-contributingness, of a certain factor to an explicit response. Questions of degree of compromise and relative weight, of competing influences, of proper balance or unbalance of contrast and assimilation in compensatory mechanisms, which become so important in perceptual research, however, seem especially unsuited for the experimental approach at least if the molar aspects of adjustment to the actual environment rather than the more academic questions of mediational technicalities are in the foreground of interest. Stated in this form they represent more the ecological, or the historic-geographic, high-level-of-complexity, than the systematic type of question in the sense of Lewin (32, 33) which makes it understandable why they can be answered satisfactorily only statistically and not experimentally.

In line with statistical, and in contrast to systematic, experimental procedure, in the present study interference with the independent stimulus conditions has been cut to a minimum. Not more than the first of the above aspects, the bare choice of the variables—as distinguished from the manner of their variation and covariation—has been planned in advance and brought under active control. That is, the size of the bodily objects, B, their distance from the subject, D, and the angular size under which they project upon the retina, P, have been made to play, alternatively and in combination, the role of independent variables, whereas their variability and covariability was random and merely under passive, observational control by what hardly was an "experimenter".

The choice of these variables, though technically arbitrary, seems nevertheless justifiable from the standpoint of representativeness by the fact that they are generally recognized as highly im-

portant for the orientation of any higher organism in the world in which he lives.

Our concentration upon these variables is not only reflected but in a sense almost constituted by the fact that the experimenter was asked to measure them rather than others, such as, e.g., the color of the objects, the pattern of their surroundings, the distance cues available in each situation, etc. The latter variables are left to vary freely within wide limits of "normalcy" relative to the world we live in. Except for such rather casual "class control" their specific values remain unknown, though potentially knowable and utilizable, throughout our investigation (see Section D of this chapter).

Like the independent variables, the dependent variables b, b′, p, p′, d, were also selected by an advance decision. An attempt was made to have the subject (and the experimenter in his role as a control subject, preceding his topographical survey of the objective stimulus values in each situation chosen by the subject) supply them by taking the respective attitudes. As well as seemed possible, it was undertaken to show through an objective analysis of the results that the responses of the type b, p, and d, were of a genuinely perceptual rather than of a rational kind (see Chapter IV B).

In spite of this technical arbitrariness in selecting the dependent variables, it may again be argued that they are fairly representative of perceptual activities of human beings. There can be no doubt that this is true for the attitude toward bodily size and distance which are among the most relevant features of manipulation and locomotion. For projective size there is at least the practical situation of perspectively correct drawing or painting. Furthermore, taking this attitude is the most urgent concession that can be made to the traditional mediational type of research which is so much interested in questions such as to how well we are capable of responding, explicitly, to stimulus features at the "skin" if we do our best to concentrate on these sensory, proximal aspects of the situation ("constancy hypothesis", see Chapter IV A and Koffka, 31).

The fact that the response variables do not vary, or covary, in any ideally "systematic" way, but are characterized by smoothly rounded distributions and non-perfect correlations with one another and with the independent variables is a trivial one. In fact, this is true for both statistics and experiment. In the former technique both independent and dependent variables do vary and covary representatively, whereas in an experiment the independent variables—or at least the environmental variables among them—are made to vary systematically. But there always is representative variation and covariation with the independent variables on the part of the dependent variables, limited, of course, in the case of an experiment, by the specificities introduced through the artificial character of the variations and covariations in the field of the independent variables. Especially the results of a psychological experiment thus introduce an element of the statistical approach—reflecting the representatively varying and covarying personality variables referred to above—into the experimental procedure.

(B) Ecological Analysis: Distal Objects vs. Mediating Proximal Projections

The second aspect of the independent variables, B, D, P, namely their manner of variation, is left to the spontaneity of the subject and hence can be considered symptomatic of the environment as responded to by the subject rather than of the environment as dictated by an autocratic experimenter. The unsystematic, more or less normal distribution curves characterizing ranges of variation and frequencies for the three variables, as shown in Fig. 4.1 (Chapter III), are indeed part of the result of our investigation rather than of any advance design as would be the case in any orthodox experimental study.

The same policy of non-interference has been followed as far as the relationships of these variables among one another and with the remaining variables in the field are concerned. Thus, not only the manner of variation of B, D, and P, but also their covariation, is part of the result of our study rather than of a preconceived plan.

Representative covariation of a number of independent stimulus variables as introduced in the present study into the investigation of the perception of size shows neither perfect untying (correlations of zero)—and a corresponding perfect tying (perfect correlations)—of the various

pairings of the geographic variables B, D, and P, as would be the case in classical psychophysics (see Section A). Nor does it lead to interlocked systematic combination, as would be the case in laboratory experiments on the constancies, but rather to the unsystematic, casual covariation as shown by the symbols in Fig. 4.2 (Chapter III). Their distribution closely resembles those found in typical individual differences scattergrams. The "ecological" correlation coefficient between bodily sizes, B, and their retinal projections, P, is .70 for the entire sample of 93 frontal extensions.

This correlation shrinks, however, to .14 when extensions smaller than 10 cm. (constituting the chief domain of near vision) are left out. Here we have another of those cases cherished by philosophers of statistics in which there is practically complete "statistical" independence in spite of the presence of an unquestionable causal relationship—in any sense in which this term has ever been accepted—between B as cause and P as effect in each of the individual historic-geographic situations. This causal relationship is further underscored by the equation $P = B/D$, expressing strict functional (mathematical) interdependence of the three variables which exists whenever these variables are conceived in an idealized geometric scheme based upon the laws of physical optics. The statistical independence of B and P, which is of course quite compatible with their causal relatedness, is of great help when it comes to the analysis of perceptual achievement and of the focalization of the responses (Chapter V).

Another means of elimination of the ecological correlation of .70 between B and P in the treatment of the results has been partial correlation. Used judiciously, this technique may become an equivalent of the experimental policy of holding conditions constant in the study of stimulus-response relationships as it has always been, of practical necessity, in the study of individual differences. In fact, it may even be regarded as an improvement upon the experimental technique insofar as the attempted isolation of variables is not real but exists only within the abstractions of computation. In experiments of the classical psychophysical type in which the attempt at an isolation—futile as it may be—actively interferes with conditions by artificially rendering correlations to be either zero or perfect, there is no way of satisfactorily isolating B and P by means of the correlation technique, or by any other means, for that matter.

As discussed in Chapter III, the perfect mathematical interrelation existing within the three-fold group of B, P, and D, is borne out by partial correlations of either 1.00 or −1.00. Such a perfect covariation, at least in abstraction, is a feature quite unheard of in the field of organismic variables studied in terms of individual differences. But it would be quite common in an ecological analysis of the type of variables with which the physicist is primarily concerned.

It is evident that in size constancy research both systematic and representative covariation of stimulus variables remain possible, depending upon the outlook and aims of the investigator. There are, however, types of research for which it would be very difficult to use systematic covariation. Probably the most striking example is social perception, such as the intuitive estimation of leadership or intelligence of human beings from their physical appearance, or from photographs. Since in this case not only the reacting subjects but also the stimulus-objects are persons, individual differences and stimulus-response psychology are here found in curious intersection. Such "neighboring" variables as the patterns surrounding physical objects estimated for their size, or the shape and color of these objects, as well as "mediating" variables such as their retinal projections can be handled or kept constant in a fairly authoritarian way by any experimenter. But it seems nearly impossible to secure a group of social perceptual objects of varying intelligence yet, say, constant (or else ideally covariant) leadership qualities (a neighboring variable), or of constant (or else ideally covariant) height, length of nose, color of skin, or any other characteristic of the external physique which may participate in the mediation of the inner personality to the observer. Thus research in social perception (such as, e.g., 14) could not even attempt to "isolate" its crucial stimulus variables however fallacious such an isolation may be in the last analysis. Workers in the field of social perception were from the beginning forced to use stimulus material imbued with natural variation and covariation just as were the early students of heredity who established the correlation technique. The same type of natural variation and covariation is deliberately sought for in

this study for a type of material that has thus far always been approached in a systematic fashion.

It should be made clear, however, that the present writer advocates the use of representative stimulus samples and relationships not only where this becomes inevitable, or as a playful demonstration, but rather as a matter of positive scientific principle. We are today witnessing a convergence of the traditional academic and the applied and social branches of psychology, and thus of experiment and statistics. This is a step on the way to greater methodological unity within a more perfectly integrated science of psychology. It may, then, be well to point towards such recent topics of research as social perception which categorically call for a full-blown statistical pattern with all of its explicit or implicit ingredients complete.

(C) Analysis of Perceptual Achievement (Focussing of Responses)

Perceptual achievement is here defined as the relationship, established by the organism, between a natural class of responses and a class of stimuli, or, in short, as representative stimulus-response covariation.[22] With the independent and dependent variables chosen as they were, the major alternative is between the distal stimulus variable, bodily size, B, and its major mediating proximal stimulus variable, projective size, P, as the focus of perceptual organization.

Both the analysis of errors and of variability (Chapter IV) and the analysis in terms of correlation coefficients (Chapter V) clearly point toward a preponderance of B-reference over P-reference of perceptual responses, with a compromise tendency between the two references. In terms of correlation coefficients, undisturbed perceptual size constancy (i.e., size constancy in the natural, naïve realistic attitude, b) is in the high nineties, even if the ecological covariability of .70 between B and P is eliminated, either by the exclusion of small objects from the total sample of 93 frontal extensions, or by partial correlation (.95 and .98, respectively: see Table 5 and Figure 3). The high coefficients in spite of the presence of occasional large errors of judgment are due in part to the unusual variability of B extending over a range of 5 powers of 10, the largest object being about 100,000 times the size of the smallest (see Figures

4.1 and 4.2). The mediating variable under investigation, projective size, is attained to a much lesser extent (.57 and .70, respectively).

These results are nothing but a confirmation of a long emphasized tenet, that of the "approximate size constancy of phenomenal things" (angenäherte Grössenkonstanz der Sehdinge) emphasized since the days of Helmholtz and Hering and approached experimentally by a series of investigators, most recently by Holaday (25, see also 2). The generality of such matters as the degree of approximation to an ideal constancy, or of the compromise principle, with the normal life conditions of a civilized human being as the "reference class" (population of situations), could, however, not have been ascertained by casual observation or in any laboratory experiment but only by the securing of a representative sample of the reference class as was attempted in the present study.

It is an encouraging sign for the apparently not too unrepresentative choice of laboratory situations in at least some of the traditional experiments on size constancy that the general trend and proportion of results is quite similar to those of the present study. In this sense, the major results of our study may seem commonplace. A checkup of this kind is, however, a methodological requirement whenever the soundness, in a representative sense, of the premises of an experimental design is to be put to test.

On the basis of the results of Beryl and of Holaday on size constancy (after recomputation on a logarithmic basis) and of Mohrmann (36) on loudness constancy when the distance of a sound source is varied, the present writer (4, p. 70) concluded that logarithmic constancy ratios in problems involving changes of distance, and conducted under conditions only moderately curtailed with respect to the intuitive surveyability of the spatial arrangement, tends to be in the .90-ies for the natural attitude (directed towards bodily size, or intensity of sound at the source, respectively) and somewhere in the broader range around the middle of the constancy scale for a reduction attitude (directed towards projective size, or intensity of sound at the ear, respectively; see 4, p. 53). It is of course not possible to compare the numerical values of constancy ratios directly with our error scores, their variabilities, or with correlation coefficients. But the greater closeness of b to B than of p to P, as well as the compromise

character of both b and p between the poles B and P is nevertheless evident.

Furthermore, there is excellent agreement, with the numerical values directly comparable, between the present study and the previous correlational study of the present writer (5), even though the latter was still conducted under arbitrary laboratory conditions (see Chapter V).

Thus it may be concluded that distal rather than proximal focusing upon magnitude existed in our subject.

To be sure, the inter-individual rather than the situational generality of this result has not been scrutinized in our study, but its assumption seems highly reasonable because of the representativeness of our subject, the very close correspondence between her results and those of the experimenter in his role as a control subject, and because of the general agreement, within rather broad limits of variability, to be sure, of the results of a variety of subjects in the experimental studies on size constancy such as those just mentioned.

> The close numerical correspondence of the results of the two subjects is shown in Chapters IV and V in a variety of ways. The only major difference lies in the fact that the subject tends generally to underestimate sizes whereas the experimenter as a control subject tends to slight overestimation. This difference refers, however, to a rather absolute aspect of constant error which has little to do with the perceptual constancies.
>
> An important part of our results has, to be sure, not been checked by any control subject. It is the automatic selection, on the part of the subject, of the stimuli to be responded to, for which an ecological analysis has been made in Chapter III. With respect to this selection, the experimenter functioned in his major role as objective surveyor of the situations involved. At the moment at which the subject was stopped to start a new series of estimates, the experimenter did not know at which objects the subject was looking so that the experimenter may be assumed not to have interfered with the selection of the objects.

To the present writer the fact of distal rather than proximal focusing of responses seems of great general importance in psychology. It is by virtue of the relatively stable physical properties of solid objects as well as of their approximately stable representation in the perceptual response system of the organism that this organism becomes oriented in an organized, fairly predictable "world". Classical psychophysics is incapable of furnishing information about the degree to which such mastery has been attained. For, whereas a high threshold for length may lead to an increase of errors by a few per cent of a standard, this same standard would be over- or under-estimated a hundred- or thousand-fold if there were no constancy mechanism to stabilize our relationship to the object world. In this sense the classical policy is indeed penny-wise, pound-foolish.

In line with the importance, to the organism, of a stabilized object reference in perception, traces of this mechanism appear already in babies (8, 15) and high constancies are found in higher animals (31, 46). Piaget, in some of his more recent publications, has increasingly emphasized the importance of "conservation", i.e., the perceptual or conceptual discovery of more and more constancies in the environment—of such variables as number, volume, physical energy, etc., which tend to persist under a variety of changes in other aspects of the situation—as one of the fundamental principles in the development of the child. And in a similar vein, though with important material differences, Claude Bernard and Cannon (13, see also 21) have pointed out how another stabilization mechanism, "homeostasis"—establishing a constancy of the "internal" environment, e.g., of blood temperature—makes us free to live in a widely expanded world.

There is an intrinsic limitation to the degree of perfection of such mechanisms, however. No external constancies can ever become fool-proof. This is due to the probability character, i.e., the intrinsically non-perfect validity, in a statistical sense, of all the cues and means utilized in approaching the world of objects in perception and in action (see 7, 44). Representative stimulus-response covariation, i.e., the relations between the organism and the more remote distal environment, have of necessity to remain probability functions of greater or lesser approximation to ideal perfection. This is quite clearly borne out by our results. In this sense, the present study is nothing but an elaboration on William James' (29) statement that "perception is of definite and probable things".

Emphasis upon stabilization mechanisms such as the perceptual constancies seems part of a general "functionalistic" program in psychology, as foreshadowed by James and adopted by American Functionalism, though not actually carried out at that time on an adequate level of complexity that would include the aspect of stabilization. The general outlook of functionalism stems from Darwin and his emphasis upon practical adjustment to the environment in a struggle for existence. Thus, as has recently also been emphasized by Boring (2, especially Chapters 7 and 8), the study of perceptual constancies is part of a truly biological approach although it is, per se, quite detached from physiological.

In Chapter IV C, the compromise tendency between distal and proximal focussing has been pointed out by means of an analysis of the changing direction of the arrows indicating errors of judgment in Figure 4.2 as we pass from one part of the diagram to another. To further illustrate this point, it would have been possible to compute "heteronymous" error scores to be defined as log b − log P, and log p − log B, respectively (in contrast to the "homonymous" ones presented in Table 4.1, log b − log B, and log p − log P, respectively), but it was considered sufficient to present the analysis in Table 4.2 instead. The scattergrams and tables in Chapter V illustrate the compromise principle in terms of correlation rather than of error scores.

The question of the perceptual compromise between object size and retinal size has actually been the starting point of the present investigation. When in seminar discussions it was questioned whether there actually is such a compromise tendency or whether, if all estimates of size of objects at various distances were taken together, there might not be the same tendency for over- and under-estimation in nearby as in far away objects (in which case constancy ratios would average 1.00 rather than, say, .95, if all situations were considered), the present writer found that he had no answer. To be sure, it had been emphasized since Hering that the "interpretation in depth of the retinal image is not perfect and stops halfway between the flat retinal image and the bodily reality", and ever since experimental results have pointed in the same direction. But it was clear that no experiment but only a representative statistical survey of the type undertaken in the present study could really settle possible doubts and objections.

In order to understand better the nature of the compromise tendency between bodily size and visual angle one may point to the ecological correlations between projective size, and bodily size as well as especially distance (see Chapter III). We may limit our consideration to sizes larger than 10 cm, thus excluding most of our material involving near vision for which standard distance cues are plentiful and for which relationships of a character opposite to those which hold for the larger sizes and distances seem to hold. When we do so, the correlation between P and D is −.34. In this sense, projective size possesses objective validity—of a rather low and barely significant degree, at least—with respect to the distance of the objects that were under observation. Projective size thus has to be considered as one of the members of the "cue family hierarchy" of distance criteria, although certainly as one of the less distinguished in this family of, say fifteen or so members. Since we have reason to assume that each of these members carries a certain weight in the automatic evaluation of distance on the part of the perceptual system of the organism— modest as the power of a single cue of low validity may be in a given situation—, a large retinal image then will contribute to the impression of small distance and thus of a relatively large bodily size. This is exactly what is indicated by the compromise principle which thus can be reduced to the mechanism of interaction and vicarious functioning of distance cues, at least as far as the distance ranges not too close to the observer are concerned. (As a short cut in this argument one may point to the corresponding direct correlation between P and B of .14 or of .70 for the total sample.)

The possibility of an artificial, experimental establishment of new cues for distance, and for illumination in color constancy experiments, has been demonstrated or discussed by Holaday (25) and Fieandt (19). Considering the apparently very unstable character of these cues, and the rapidity with which they are extinguished, it seems reasonable to assume that new cues, highly valid as they may be within the limits of an experimental series, have similar reaction potentials as have cues of low validity but of longer standing (high statistical reliability).

The generality of the fact that the analytic attitude improves the relationship with projective size is most clearly confirmed in Table 4.5, showing the correlation coefficients between stimulus variables and response variables.

In contrast to the confirmations of previous assertions listed, the following claim of perceptual constancy experiments has however not, or at least not consistently, been verified in the present study. The present writer, interpreting results of Holaday and others, concluded that a shift from purely perceptual to corresponding betting attitudes would approximately cut errors with respect to both the distal and the proximal stimulus variable in half (4, p. 99f.). The present study has, however, shown a consistent improvement only for bodily size, whereas there was a deterioration for projective size in the majority of the pertinent comparisons made (see Chapters IV and V).

The situational generality of claims of previous perception experiments in fields other than the constancies have likewise been partly confirmed, partly not supported in an analysis of our material. There was a confirmation of the Weber law when freely interpreted by applying it to errors in natural situations which are far above threshold in terms of the standards of classical psychophysics (Chapter IV E).

No support, and even a slight counter-indication below the level of significance, was given to the vertical illusion (Chapter IV D)[23]. This fact does not strike the present writer as a surprise. There was not much exact research on the vertical illusion in the history of psychology, and the easygoingness with which this alleged phenomenon is illustrated in the literature sometimes borders on the shocking. For example, in Luckiesh' well-known book on visual illusions, published in 1922 (34), the only figures illustrating this illusion are a vertical which halves a horizontal to which it is perpendicular, and the familiar drawing of a silk hat. In both cases there are abundant sources of illusion outside of verticality vs. horizontality, such as the number of parts into which a figural unit is subdivided, proportion factors introduced by the presence of rectangular areas, curvature, cues for three-dimensionality, and the like. Even such more respectable examples as the square that looks too high when presented upright can hardly be taken for granted as a representative case.

In fact, in a study like the present which endeavors to be representative and as close to life as an academic problem could ever hope to come, one would not even want to deal with verticality as an isolated feature, not to speak of verticality when tied to other factors in a non-representative fashion. The present results rather refer to verticality as found in natural ecological association with other stimulus factors whatever these factors or the strengths of their correlation with verticality happen to be. (This does, of course, not exclude that there may be no such ecological associations.) In this sense, and in this sense only, do we question the vertical illusion.

There are numerous other instances in experimental psychology in which non-representative experiments have been overgeneralized even to the extent of being made anchors of an entire theoretical outlook or school point of view. An outstanding example is the wellknown Gottschaldt experiment, discussed and illustrated in most text books (e.g., 31, 46), which has been undertaken with the idea in mind to test the influence of past experience upon the organization of perception. The largely negative outcome of the Gottschaldt experiment can, however, in the opinion of the present writer, not be used as evidence of any generality against the experience hypothesis and in favor of a more genuinely Gestalt hypothesis of perception, since it uses geometric line patterns quite unrepresentative of the majority of stimulus configurations encountered by perceiving organisms. Rorschach ink blots, to quote just one outstanding example, are certainly more representative, though somewhat out of line in another direction, and they certainly unearth a host of empirically meaningful tendencies and assimilations to familiar objects in the subjects which respond to them.

It is not always easy to achieve representativeness, and some of the attempts to do so may be imbued with fallacies of their own. An example from the field of social perception close at hand to the present writer's work is the following. In collaboration with Reiter, the present writer (10) attempted to investigate a group of factors influencing the physiognomic qualities of human

faces, using schematized faces in which height of forehead, distance between the eyes, height of the nose, and position of the mouth were varied systematically in an interlocked multiple-variable combine. In an attempt to check upon these results, Samuels (39) succeeded, obviously not without difficulties, in selecting from college yearbooks, so that the age and sex of the individuals, as well as the pose and size of the photographs, were uniform, "human faces which matched the . . . drawings very closely in all the controlled variables". As can be easily seen from an inspection of Figure 4.2 in the article by Samuels, there remain quite a number of uncontrolled variables such as hair, ears, shape of the mouth, circumference of the face, etc. This in itself would of course not be a disadvantage if numerous representatives for each combination of traits could have been found. Since Samuels had only one representative for each combination, chance no doubt acted in the direction of emphasizing incidentals. The decrease in the degree of confirmation of Brunswik and Reiter's results when Samuels shifted from a plain repetition of these experiments (88% confirmation) to the photographs (63% confirmation) can thus not be construed as an argument against their generality.

As was pointed out by the present writer in a previous article (7), it is one of the curiosities of psychological methodology that the sampling problem of individuals has been so crudely neglected for a long time whenever individuals played the unusual role of stimuli rather than the traditional one of reacting organisms, as is true in the judging of intelligence or personality from photographs or first appearances. It is one of the purposes of the present study to help remove double standards of this sort.

Some findings of the present writer on the dependence of apparent intelligence upon height and breadth of schematized human figures were confirmed by Wallace (45) on what might be considered a satisfactorily representative basis, by using a magnification, reduction and distortion technique on photographs of actual persons which circumvents some of Samuels' pitfalls.

It seems generally possible, and practically often very desirable, to include certain elements of the experimental pattern of research into representative studies of stimulus-response relationships in order to get rid of disturbances introduced by some variables which the experimenter has reason to regard as insignificant or which he may on other grounds wish to exclude from the scope of the examination. Such selective exclusion is exemplified in the perception psychology of size by Holaday's (25) fractionated elimination, one by one, of distance cues under maintenance of the remainder of those naturally available. This policy is, however, to be sharply distinguished from the more atomistic and thus more harmful policy of the nineteenth century type of experimentation which preferred to have just one factor, such as, say, binocular disparity, present at a time, under the exclusion of all the others.

(D) Possibility of an Analysis of Mediating Cues and of Contributingness

It is in keeping with the fundamentally practical outlook of Functionalism that wide-spanning stimulus-response relationships, such as those between physical or social objects and responses should be approached under comparative neglect of the variables which causally mediate this relationship. In this sense our study, when stripped to a minimum, would above all include measurements of bodily size, and may omit measurement of distance and objective ascertainment of projective size.

Such a procedure would be analogous to those numerous studies in social perception in which personality traits, such as intelligence, were to be guessed from photographs whereby only the tested IQ-s and the estimates of intelligence on the part of the reacting subjects were specifically known, whereas the geometric features of the face and body as represented on the photographs were not considered in the evaluation nor even measured, but only kept within rather wide limits of normalcy ("class control" rather than "specific control"). Attainment or non-attainment of the one independent variable in question can then be expressed, say, by correlation coefficients (see Woodworth, 46, p. 251).[24]

In this sense, consideration of projective size in our study is a concession to the traditional molecular approach, undertaken primarily to refute the "constancy hypothesis" inherent in traditional Structuralism. More positively, it represents an attempt to demonstrate methodologically the present-day convergence of the traditional academic interests concentrating chiefly upon the "how" problems of mediational "explanation", with the applied line of development concentrating on the "what" of practical adjustment of a wide-spanning, molar kind. The result is a type of study in three "layers": distal focus, mediating proximal stimulus, final response.

The best parallel in the field of social perception seems to be the study by Cleeton and Knight (14) in which measures of face and body build (bodily distal variables of the first order' which here play the role of the relatively proximal mediating layer) were related to both the objective personality (distal layer of the second order) establishing the ecological correlations of "expression", and to the intuitive perceptual estimates of personality (final response), establishing the "impression" values of the cues mediating social perception. The over-all correlation between objective personality and estimates, representing "social perceptual achievement", is the one feature which this study has in common with the one-independent-variable approaches to social perception just referred to.

It goes without saying that mediation problems are by no means exhausted by the consideration of just one mediating variable, P, important as this variable may seem in the business of conveying the distal variable to the organism. As has been pointed out above, the correlation between B and P is none too good, certainly not as good as that between B and b which is mediated by P. In other words, the mediating variable P is unstable within the framework of the over-all relationship Bb which is relatively stable. Such an effect is possible only if the variability of P is compensated for by other mediating variables. These are, in our case, the cue family hierarchy of distance criteria.

In short, mediation of distal variables to the organism's response system is not only "variable", it also is "multiple". The entire mechanism is comparable, in a figurative sense, to light rays passing in a divergent bundle from one focus through a collecting lens and eventually converging in another focus (4, p. 96f.; 7, p. 258). The establishment of the constancies is thus "difficult" in an objective, functional sense referring to the complexity of its engineering, although it seems the easiest, most natural thing to the introspecting subject. To the latter mediating details have a way to "submerge", i.e., to remain implicit, in their mediating role. The necessity for a "duplicity"—encompassing direct projection and the cues indicating situational "circumstances"—in the mediation of the perceptual constancies was first clearly expressed by Bühler (12, see also 9). As a more general principle, the importance of "stimulus patterning" in connection with the idea of a "calculus of adaptive probability" was recently emphasized by Hull (28, p. 374ff.).

A complete understanding of mediation would require measurement of distance cues along with direct retinal projections of objects, thus increasing the number of independent variables considerably. The fact of distal focussing in perception implies that certain combinations of projective values and values of distance cues—the latter further complicated by "vicarious functioning" of the members of this cue family hierarchy—would show relationships with the distal stimulus B as well as with the final response b which would be at least as good as the over-all perceptual correlation linking B and b. Thus distal focussing is far from being magic; it is just a somewhat more complex causal relationship between B as a probable part cause and b as a probable part effect (see 7).

In the present study, the absence of even a passive, merely registering control of distance cues is matched by the freedom given to the subject to use those cues in a natural way to their best advantage.

The only restriction imposed upon another aspect of mediation—the somatic, physiological mechanisms involved—was not to move away from the point of observation as long as the estimates had not been concluded, and to keep the objects, if not fixated, in the focus of attention, otherwise reacting normally.

Appreciable interference with organismic variables was limited to the more ultimate aspect of mediation which emerges with the establishment of some of the dependent variables. This is the taking of attitudes toward perceptual reorganization, as well as exclusion or inclusion of the rational superstructure which is normally superimposed upon perception whenever it comes to decisions of a "betting" type in the practical life of normal human adults.

Naturally, all the neglected aspects could have been included had we been interested in a more thorough mediational analysis. Correlation coefficients would then have expressed perceptual achievement under elimination of, say, the distance cues present in binocular vision, or under conditions of dark adaptation, the influence of alcohol, etc.

In Chapter VI, an angle of mediation somewhat different from those just mentioned was demonstrated, namely that of the internal inconsistency of the perceptual system which is part of its relative autonomy of functioning when compared with the intellectual approach to reality. This was done by comparing the explicitly judged distances d with the distance-responses implicit in judgments of bodily size and of projective size. It was concluded that the chief contributor to the internal inconsistency of distal perception must be sought in the inability of the perceptual system to discard the established distance cues, rather than in an ability to use them in a fairly consistent manner.

An aspect somewhat related to problems of mediation proper is that of the influence upon the response, or the "contributingness", of such "neighboring" variables as the pattern of surrounding objects, the color of the object, etc. The term "neighboring" may be used for these variables to characterize the fact that they are not direct links in the causal chains mediating the focal variable, magnitude, to the organism, as are retinal projection or distance cues.

By measurements taken of neighboring variables, a large number of traditional problems of experimental psychology, e.g., the Müller-Lyer illusion, the influence of color upon apparent magnitude, etc., could be dealt with on an equal footing with some of the other side issues approached in the present study, such as the vertical illusion. It is one of the advantages of a sampling study of stimulus-response relationships that the original material contains a large amount of implicit information and practically inexhaustible possibilities for the analysis of mediation and of the contributingness of neighboring variables if only the proper measurements be taken. In fact, it seems that nearly all problems of this type in perception could be approached by using the same sample of situations, measured and evaluated in their response-eliciting capacity in a variety of ways.

In the end, a factor analysis, not of personality variables, but rather of the stimulus variables determining a system of responses, could be undertaken. Such a factor analysis of the focal and contributing dimensions in the environment would establish a description of the reacting organism in terms of the stability of its rapport with the various stimulus variables, distal or otherwise, in short, "in terms of objects" (4, 7).

> In the field of social perception, which has served as an example to illustrate many of our points of discussion, such phenomena as the "halo effect" would correspond to what we have called contributingness.

On the other hand, a study like the present one has the disadvantage of considerable clumsiness when compared with some of the simple laboratory tests or experiments. The present writer feels, however, that the advantages gained by at least a shortcut form of approach of the present type—perhaps one not even involving the computation of correlation coefficients—has its definite advantages over the use of standard experiments for purposes of testing. For example, the two-rod type of experiment in the form widely used in the testing of depth perception is certainly not representative of depth discrimination under conditions in which the monocular natural cues are not being cut out as much as they usually are in this test. As was shown by Holaday (25), binocular cues will add little to the efficiency of depth perception under such circumstances. Nor is the two-rod test representative of discrimination at greater distances. Generally, the scope and selection of tasks to constitute a representative test battery in the study of individual differences in abilities, hitherto largely left to common sense speculation, will have to be further scrutinized, at least to match the scrutiny which has become routine in the selection of the individuals to which the tests are given. Furthermore, whenever clinical statements concerning "loss of category" (Goldstein, 22), "social blindness" (Ch. Bühler, 11), and the like—referring to problems of focussing on certain more or less "abstract" environmental variables, and generally to selective alertness in the evaluation of stimulus patterns—are made, the only proper checkup seems to be in terms of a representative investigation. Such an investigation may be conducted on a larger or on a smaller scale, but it would basically have to follow the principle of natural sampling of task-situations, and it would most probably surpass in number and variety of observations the often quite casual material brought forward in support of the original claims.

Chapter IX. Summary and Conclusions

A "natural" sample of frontal "extensions" of various sizes and at various distances was secured by inducing, at random intervals, a student of psychology to designate whatever objects (extensions) she happened to be looking at at the moment.

The 93 extensions thus obtained from one subject were found to be normally distributed when the logarithms of their measured bodily sizes were plotted. Further, the "ecological" correlation between two of the "geographic" stimulus-variables characterizing each of the 93 situations, namely the bodily sizes of these extensions and the sizes of their representations on the retina of the subject (i.e. visual angle or "projective" size), was found to be far from perfect though positive when all size ranges were included. A natural flexibility of "proximal" (retinal) mediation—which is a necessary condition in the definition of each "distal" stimulus variable such as bodily size—was thus assured. The remaining mediating circumstances—such as especially the presence or absence of the various "distance cues"—as well as the mechanisms used by the subject (with the exception of mental attitude) in each situation were not specifically ascertained or interfered with in each case although on principle the method employed in this study would permit of such an extension of mediational analysis.

One of the principal significances of the present study, as the writer sees it, is that a traditional laboratory problem has thus been approached after the fashion of a statistical survey rather than of an "experiment". Stimulus situations have not been selected arbitrarily and controlled rigidly, but rather much in the same "representative" way as individuals are selected from a "population" in a typical study of individual differences. Generality of a stimulus-response relationship from one sample of situations or conditions to another ("situational generality" of a result) thus takes the place of what may be called the populational generality of the finding of investigations in which the correlated variables are tests paired by being given to the same sample of individuals. On the other hand, this situational generality is, at least on principle, limited to—and characteristic of— the one subject or attitude for which the survey has been undertaken.

The responses consisted in numerical estimates of each of the extensions given by the subject in a series of five more or less natural attitudes. These responses were quantitatively compared with the geographic data. Traditional measures of error of judgment such as the constant error were used along with the favorite tool of the statistical survey, the correlation coefficient, to characterize the various possible types of stimulus-response connections. (A comparison has also been made between these methods and the "constancy ratio" previously used as the quantitative expression of the perfection of perceptual thing-constancy.)

The results demonstrate again what is known as "perceptual size-constancy", namely the natural focussing of the perceptual system upon the distal stimulus variable "bodily size" and its comparative inability to respond to even such an outstanding mediating proximal stimulus-feature as the retinal proportions, even when an effort is made to do so. There was good agreement between the results obtained from the subject and those obtained from the experimenter who had served as a control subject prior to his making the necessary stimulus measurements in each of the 93 situations.

The situational generality of some of the more specific findings of previous laboratory research on the constancies, such as the comparative overestimation of near objects (perceptual compromise between distal and proximal focussing), and the improvement of estimates after shifting from purely perceptual to critically controlled ("betting") attitudes was also demonstrated by our subject, the latter, however, only for estimates of bodily size.

Overestimation of the vertical as compared with horizontal extensions was not, however, found in our data. Another side-line from traditional experimental psychology was likewise followed up, namely, the Weber law in its application to length-discrimination. The situational generality of this psychological principle was well confirmed by our data.

A certain amount of internal inconsistency within the perceptual system was revealed by the fact that "explicitly judged" distances varied considerably from various types of "implicit behavioral" distances as computed by combining the estimates of bodily size and projective size, and the true geographic measures. This inconsistency supports the writer's previously suggested interpretation of perception as a primitive and relatively autonomous function within the total cognitive system of the human being.

In conclusion, the writer would like to point out that the network of abilities characteristic of a certain organism—of a given species, age, state of mind, temporary physiological condition, or in command of a particular set of mediational cues and sensory instruments—might thus eventually be mapped out in terms of the intimacy, or safeguardedness (situational generality), of the rapport set up by the organism with the various vitally relevant issues in the nearer or more remote, physical or social regions of the geographic or historic environment ("psychology in terms of objects"). In essence, this implies a "biological" (as contrasted to a merely "physiological") attitude or program of research as it is inherent in psychology since the establishment of American Functionalism. The variables involved are thereby properly isolated in spite of—or rather because of—the absence of artificial control over the remaining circumstances. The selective focussing of organismic activity, may it be overt behavioral or covert perceptual, can thus be properly represented. The recognition of these achievements of living beings as probability functions with an intrinsically limited degree of perfection (due to the ecological ambiguity of cues if not to more intrinsically organismic imperfections as well) implies the convergence of the experimental and the statistical techniques in approaching problems of the stimulus-response type.

NOTES

1. The term "distal," borrowed from Heider and the Gestalt psychologists (cf. 5, 31), designates the more or less distant environmental features defined without reference to the boundary of an organism. It is thus employed whenever the relative independence of an organism's response from variations in the mediating "proximal" variables, such as the size of the retinal images, is to be emphasized.

2. See the recent interesting discussions of such variations by Spence (40) and Hull (26).

3. A more complete recognition of the principle of randomization of tasks would imply that not even the selection of the stimulus variable itself should be left to the arbitrariness of the experimenter. Instead of being limited to one or a few physical dimensions, a perfectly balanced study of perception (or of any other function) would cover representatives of a large number of simple or complex stimulus variables in proportion to the demands for mastery of these variables in the life of the individual or type or species in question.

4. An abstract of a preliminary report on some aspects of this study is given in (6).

5. Both subject and experimenter have normal vision.

6. Both subject and experimenter were brought up in the use of the metric system in daily life. This was an advantage for the purposes of the present survey.

7. Regarding the question of whether or not the subject was actually able to let herself be guided by perceptual intuition rather than by knowledge, see Chapter IV B.

8. That is to say, the judgment should refer to the extension, apparently cut out on an imaginary frontal plane at one meter distance, by the lightrays issuing from the object into the eye (but, of course, without the use of instruments such as a pencil held in front of the eye).

Illustrations and demonstrations of this kind were presented until it was assured that both subject and experimenter thoroughly understood the meaning of the instructions.

9. All of our quantitative results are in terms of this particular type of measure.

10. Some authors, for example Lewin, would probably prefer to use the term "ecological" to characterize relationship between organism and geographic environment. Since the Greek word *oikos* means home or homeland, and since no term is available to designate an analysis of intra-environmental physical relationships relevant, in an objective sense, to an organism living in its home region, the present writer suggests the use of the term as indicated above.

11. r_{BP} for the 34 objects smaller than 10 cm. is .73. Considering the decrease in variability of B (and also of P) effected by the limitation to small sizes, this coefficient means more than a direct comparison with the one obtained for the entire frontal group would suggest.

12. By partialling out D, P, and B, respectively, from the six coefficients mentioned in the text, partial correlations of 1 are obtained between B and P and between B and D, and of −1 between P and D. This fact is due to the perfect dependent variability—in a functional sense—of the three physical variables discussed.

13. A tendency to give round numbers is revealed by the fact that estimates are often given in terms of one-place numbers and rarely ever, except for distance judgments, involve more than two significant digits (not counting zero unless followed by a digit other than zero). This tendency is likely to increase errors; no further analysis of such effects is, however, undertaken in this study. Effects of practice have likewise not been especially analyzed. Considering the problems emphasized in this study they have, if present, probably not affected the general pattern of the results a great deal.

14. In the study on size constancy by Holaday (25, p. 462), rational control was found on the average to result in greater correctness with respect to the "intended" variable, whether this variable be bodily size or projective size, without, however, fully compensating for the trends found in the purely intuitive approaches. Deviations of the constancy ratios from the ideal values 100 and 0, respectively, were being cut approximately in half.

A similar improvement was found in an as yet unpublished study by Marianne Müller (37) on the Müller-Lyer illusion dealing with the problem of the perceptual compromise between length and area. Six different attitudes were to be taken, some of them concentrating on length, others on area and on esthetic balance. The sixteen subjects showed on the average a 28% constant error with respect to length in the whole-perceiving attitude toward length. The corresponding betting attitude (the only betting attitude employed) yielded a constant error of only 16%, a figure which is also better than that obtained when an analytic perceptual attitude toward length was taken, 22%.

In the study of Mohrmann on loudness constancy (36, p. 184) the transition from the purely perceptual to the betting attitude resulted in confusion and deterioration of performance rather than in an improvement.

15. In an attempt to overcome this difficulty, the present writer suggested a revision of the distinction between intuitive perception and rational approach to reality—and in fact, between various attitudes in general—in terms of a statistical analysis of the types and distributions of errors committed, that is, by an objective analysis of achievement rather than by direct introspection (4). No systematic use of such a procedure can, however, be attempted here. Indications of what might be called the relative autonomy of the perceptual system have been pointed out repeatedly by the present author.

16. An alternative expression for this would be to say that a "compromise object" (*Zwischengegenstand*) between bodily size and angular size is to be considered as the "intentionally attained" type of physical object or variable (4).

17. More precisely, this coefficient is .969 uncorrected, and .988 corrected for grouping.

18. This is in contrast to previous interpretations suggested by the present writer in consequence of the use of the constancy ratio as a measure of perceptual achievement. In that case the lack of perfect attainment of one of the two variables (or "poles of intention") in question appears automatically as an effect of the other, in a way which seems not quite justified in view of the present discussion.

19. More precisely, this value is .988 for the subject and .989 for the experimenter. For the subject, this coefficient has also been computed from the un-grouped logarithms of B and b. In good agreement with the upper figure, which is corrected for grouping, it was found to be slightly more than .99.

20. Distances estimated at random as a pastime by an expedition of astronomers in the Pacific revealed a wide range of estimates in each situation, with their averages, however, being close to the true values (1, p. 128). This is in line with our findings on intra-individual dispersions of errors from situation to situation.

21. The symbols used in this study are different from those of previous publications (3, 5, 46), but are readily translatable into those of the previous studies.

22. The correctness (or incorrectness, say, illusory or hallucinatory character) of a single response does not in itself constitute proof of an "achievement" in perception as defined here (or of its absence), just as a single coincidence, say, of high intelligence with high forehead, would not be accepted as proof of an existing correlation.

23. The material for an analysis of the Weber Law is implicit in the data necessary for the analysis of the constancies. Orientation in space is, however, one of the side-aspects of the situations involved. The experimenter had been asked to register it, in first approximation, along with the data essential for the analysis of the constancies, since horizontal vs. vertical orientation was considered a good example for possible "neighboring contributors" (see Section D of this chapter) in the estimation of size.

24. The fact that results of such studies, at least in the case of the judging of permanent personality features such as, especially, intelligence, are very discouraging must seem rather incidental. It can probably be explained by pointing to the absence of sufficiently valid cues. The constancies of such external properties of physical objects as size are very successfully established by the perceiving organism, obviously because of the larger number of relatively valid distance cues.

REFERENCES

1. Abbot, C. G. *The Earth and the Stars.* 1925.
2. Boring, E. G. *Sensation and Perception in the History of Experimental Psychology.* New York: Appleton-Century, 1942.
3. Brunswik, E. Zur Entwicklung der Albedowahrnehmung. Z. *Psychol.*, 1928, *109*, 40–115.
4. Brunswik, E. *Wahrnehmung und Gegenstandswelt.* Vienna and Leipzig, 1934.
5. Brunswik, E. Thing constancy as measured by correlation coefficients. *Psychol. Rev.*, 1940, *47*, 69–78.
6. Brunswik, E. Perceptual size-constancy in life situations. *Psychol. Bull.*, 1941, *38*, 611 f. (See also Psychol. Bull. 1940, 37, 585 f.)
7. Brunswik, E. Organismic achievement and environmental probability. Symposium on Psychology and Scientific Method, Sixth International Congress for the Unity of Science, University of Chicago, 1941. *Psychol. Rev.*, 1943, *50*, 255–272.
8. Brunswik, E. and Cruikshank, R. M. Perceptual size-constancy in early infancy, *Psychol. Bull.*, 1937, *34*, 713–714.
9. Brunswik, E. and Kardos, L. Das Duplizitätsprinzip in der Theorie der Farbenwahrnehmung, Z. *Psychol.*, 1929, *111*, 307–320.
10. Brunswik, E. and Reiter, L. Eindruckscharaktere schematisierter Gesichter, Z. *Psychol.*, 1937, *142*, 67–134.
11. Bühler, Ch. The social behavior of the child. In: C. Murchison, *Handbook of Child Psychology*, Clark University Press, 1931.
12. Bühler, K. *Die Erscheinungsweisen der Farben*, Handb. der Psychol. I/1, Jena: Fischer, 1922.
13. Cannon, W. B. *The Wisdom of the Body*, New York: Norton, 1932.
14. Cleeton, G. U. and Knight, F. B. Validity of character judgments based on external criteria, *J. appl. Psychol.*, 1924, *8*, 215–231.
15. Cruikshank, R. M. The development of visual size constancy in early infancy, *J. genet. Psychol.*, 1941, *58*, 327–351.
16. Crutchfield, R. S. Efficient factorial design and analysis of variance, illustrated in psychological experimentation, *J. Psychol.*, 1938, *5*, 339–346.
17. Crutchfield, R. S. and Tolman, E. C. Multiple-variable design for experiments involving interaction of behavior, *Psychol. Rev.*, 1940, *47*, 38–42.

18. Eissler, K. Die Gestaltkonstanz der Sehdinge (No. 3 of Untersuchungen über Wahrnehmungsgegenstände, ed. by E. Brunswik). *Arch. ges. Psychol.*, 1933, 88, 487–550.
19. Fieandt, K. v. Dressurversuche an der Farbenwahrnehmung (No. 7 of Untersuchungen über Wahrnehmungsgegenstände, ed. by E. Brunswik). *Arch. ges. Psychol.*, 1936, 96, 467–495.
20. Fisher, R. A. *Design of Experiments*, Edinburgh: Oliver & Boyd, 1937.
21. Fletcher, J. M. Homeostasis as an explanatory principle in psychology, *Psychol. Rev.*, 1942, 49, 80–87.
22. Goldstein, K. *The Organism.* New York: Amer. Book Co., 1939.
23. Heider, F. Environmental determinants in psychological theories, *Psychol. Rev.*, 1939, 46, 383–410.
24. Hering, E. *Grundzüge der Lehre vom Lichtsinn*, 1905 etc.
25. Holaday, B. E. Die Grössenkonstanz der Sehdinge (No. 2 of Untersuchungen über Wahrnehmungsgegenstände, ed. by E. Brunswik). *Arch. ges. Psychol.*, 1933, 88, 419–486.
26. Hull, C. L. The problem of stimulus equivalence in behavior theory. *Psychol. Rev.*, 1939, 46, 9–30.
27. Hull, C. L. The problem of intervening variables in molar behavior theory, Symposium on Psychology and Scientific Method, Sixth International Congress for Unity of Science, University of Chicago, 1941. *Psychol. Rev.*, 1943, 50, 273–291.
28. Hull, C. L. *Principles of Behavior*, New York: Appleton-Century, 1943.
29. James, W. *Principles of Psychology*, New York: Holt, 1890.
30. Klimpfinger, S. Die Entwicklung der Gestaltkonstanz (No. 5 of Untersuchungen über Wahrnehmungsgegenstände, ed. by E. Brunswik). *Arch. ges. Psychol.*, 1933, 88, 599–628.
31. Koffka, K. *Principles of Gestalt Psychology*, New York: Harcourt Brace, 1935.
32. Lewin, K. *Dynamic Theory of Personality.* New York: McGraw-Hill, 1935.
33. Lewin, K. Defining the 'field at a given time'. Symposium on Psychology and Scientific Method, Sixth International Congress for the Unity of Science, University of Chicago, 1941. *Psychol. Rev.*, 1943, 50, 292–310.
34. Luckiesh, M. *Visual Illusions*, New York: Van Nostrand, 1922.
35. Mises, R. v. *Probability, Statistics, and Truth*, New York: Macmillan, 1939.
36. Mohrmann, K. Lautheitskonstanz im Entfernungswechsel. *Z. Psychol.*, 1939, 145, 145–199.
37. Müller, M. Länge und Fläche als Faktoren in der Müller Lyer'schen Täuschung. University of Vienna Doctoral Dissertation (1935).
38. Pearson, K. *The Grammar of Science.* First ed., 1892 (Popular edition, London: Dent, 1937).
39. Samuels, M. Judgments of faces, *Character & Pers.*, 1939, 8, 18–27.
40. Spence, K. W. The differential responses in animals to stimuli varying within a single dimension. *Psychol. Rev.*, 1937, 44, 430–444.
41. Stephenson, W. Correlating persons instead of tests. *Character and Pers.*, 1935, 4, 17–24.
42. Thouless, R. H. Phenomenal regression to the 'real' object. *Brit. J. Psychol.*, 1931, 21, 339–359.
43. Tolman, E. C. *Purposive Behavior in Animals and Men.* New York: Century, 1932.
44. Tolman, E. C. and Brunswik, E. The organism and the causal texture of the environment. *Psychol. Rev.*, 1935, 42, 43–77.
45. Wallace, R. P. Apparent personality traits from photographs varied in bodily proportions. *Psychol. Bull.*, 1941, 38, 744–745.
46. Woodworth, R. S. *Experimental Psychology*, New York: Holt, 1938.

Points of View: Components of Psychological Theorizing [1946]

 COMMENT

Brunswik as Philosopher of Science
Kenneth R. Hammond

Although Brunswik did not develop his own theoretical viewpoint to any significant degree in "Points of View," we include it in this section because it contains his views about psychological theories in a way that explains the demands he placed on his own work. In this museum-like piece he put forward a framework for analyzing theories in terms of their "Explicitness of Theorizing, Intersubjectivity, and Formalization" (1946b, p. 524) and further divided theories in terms of their "degree of quantification, technical verbalization, colloquial verbalization, and unverbalized, implicit, theorizing." A second major classification is in terms of the "regional reference" of the variables or concepts in the theory. (The "regions" Brunswik referred to he described in detail later in his 1956 book, still a decade away, but even the 1946 descriptions are well worth the reader's consideration; see Part II of this volume). At this point "regional reference" simply refers to a distinction between "peripheralism" (by which he meant the behaviorists' "implicit belief that what is important in life and behavior of an organism can be found and identified at its surface") and a functionalistic, central-distal region that he found to be "significant of the convergent trends in present day psychology" (1946b, p. 527). He was prescient; that shift from peripheralism to an emphasis on a central-distal functionalism later came to define the essence of the cognitive revolution of the 1960s.

No one talks like that anymore. Such issues are rarely addressed, and as a result, the relative desirability of these or other features of theorizing have not been made explicit. Nor have they been applied to current theories of cognition. There is almost no consideration of the nature of current theorizing within the field of judgment and decision making. Although there may be critiques of definitions of terms, such as *probability*, few are interested in or prepared to make metatheoretical critiques of existing theories. Even the term *intuition*, which many researchers have devoted their lives to denigrating as a useful cognitive activity, has received scant theoretical consideration, or even serious definition.

There seems to be implicit agreement that quantification and technical verbalization are good, but we also seem to like colloquial verbalization (e.g., "the endowment effect")—it lends an air of reality. I admit to having done the same with one of Brunswik's central concepts; in my book *Human Judgment and Social Policy* (Hammond, 1996c), I substituted the colloquial term *indicator* for *cue* for the reason that I wanted the reader to see the ubiquity of the use of "cues" in our culture, where they appear in technical as well as colloquial communication as "indicators." We have hundreds of indicators that appear, and are used, in all walks of life, and I wanted the reader to become aware of how often we make judgments based on "indicators" of only partial validity. Brunswik used the psychologists' term, *cue*, because he was talking about perception to perception psychologists, and they knew what that meant. I turned to *colloquial verbalization* in order to communicate more effectively to an audience of nonpsychologists.

Although we have all been taught to try to avoid unverbalized, implicit theorizing, the search for lawfulness seems to have been given up in favor of discovering "effects" (with the possible exception of Kahneman & Tversky's 1979 prospect theory). The matter of regional reference is of great importance and must rank among Brunswik's greatest contribution. We—Brunswikians included—remain casual about describing and differentiating among the specific properties of the displays of information. This article may well deepen our awareness of the fact that tasks as well as people have "regional" properties—surface and depth—that are analogous to proximal and central regions in people. That differentiation between the surface and depth of tasks or objects requires us to think about what difference that distinction makes. That is, to distinguish between surface and depth of tasks encourages us to theorize about and empirically analyze the various relations between the surface and depth properties of tasks and objects. It is easy to see the importance of this distinction in the case of social perception; here, the surface of the organism to be judged for, say, friendliness is primarily the person's face; it is the "display" that conveys the information about the depth variable, friendliness. Friendliness is the intended variable to be achieved (or "attained") by the judge. In more technical circumstances, the display may be the display of information on the screen of a monitoring or tracking system, and the variable to be achieved may be the position or direction of a friend or foe. In such cases, we can ask what is the most effective manner in which the surface properties of the task (the display) should convey information about the depth variable (e.g., location of the object) and thus most effectively aid the judge, or tracking person, to most accurately track the object (see Adelman, Henderson, & Miller, Chapter 38, this volume; see also Hammond, Hamm, Grassia, & Pearson, 1987, for a detailed empirical examination of this topic).

In addition, Brunswik employed a third category, "level of complexity and closeness to fact," to distinguish among theories and theorists. Although he applied these categories to theorists of another day, most of the discussion is about the categories themselves, and thus, the reader can apply them to current theories or points of view. Indeed, it would be a valuable undertaking to describe current research programs in the field of judgment and decision making in these categories.

It can be done. For example, I have taken the judgment theories that follow from the Gestalt tradition (e.g., the "heuristics and biases " research program) and contrasted them with the research program that follows from the functionalist tradition. This produced what I claim to be a clarification of goals and methods that shows that the two research programs are not competitive but complementary and should be used in conjunction with one another, rather than in competition with one another (Hammond, 1996c). Admittedly such modern integrative efforts are seldom met with more approval than were Brunswik's integrative efforts some fifty years ago. Nevertheless, younger scholars, not blinded by personal ambition, are apt to take advantage of the research developments such integrative efforts provide, and therefore, there is room for optimism about clarifying our points of view, which was clearly Brunswik's intention in presenting "Points of View" in 1946.

REPRINT

Points of View: Components of Psychological Theorizing

Egon Brunswik

As in other disciplines, theoretical contemplation and organization in psychology serve primarily two purposes: to prepare as well as to interconnect observations which otherwise would be, or appear to be, unrelated or incidental. In this endeavor, carefully defined or elucidated *concepts* are combined to form *hypotheses*, *postulates*, or *laws*—depending upon the degree of tentativeness and of empirical confirmation—and these in turn are woven into *theories* of greater or lesser comprehensiveness.

Most of the major theoretical efforts in the psychology of the past climaxed by developing into backbones of *schools* or *systems*. Such a development hinges upon claims of universal applicability of the underlying theoretical principles and leads to their expansion over wide areas of psychology. This process is frequently characterized by an emotional investment that in itself seems sufficient explanation for the strong assertive emphasis usually associated with schools. Theory then becomes a powerful propagandistic policy making agent directing future research activities over and above its original synoptic function.

The chief difficulty of schools lies in the fact that they usually are inseparably entwined with the specific character of the *field* of research in which their major theories or principles were originally developed, and that none of the principles suggested has so far positively proved its worth in carrying the full explanatory load imposed upon it by its exponents. Attempts to generally subsume the functioning of behavior under the phenomenon of conditioning (as in classical behaviorism), or under the phenomenon of closure of perceptual patterns (as in Gestalt psychology), may serve as illustrations. The maturing psychology of the present tends somewhat to de-glamorize the youthful enthusiasm, singleness of purpose, and the search for ultimates inherent in the founding of all-inclusive schools, leaving room for a multiplicity of quasi-basic principles and thus paving the way for an integration of schools into a unified family of parallel fields and functional principles.

Contemporary schools of psychology. Among the numerous major and minor trends, the following stand out most clearly at the beginning of the twentieth century: *functionalism* (Dewey, Angell, Carr) and *behaviorism* (Watson) as the major American movements, with distinct roots in England (Darwin) and Russia (Pavlov, Bekhterev), respectively; and *Gestalt psychology* (configurationism; Wertheimer, Köhler, Koffka) and *psychoanalysis* (Freud), originally in Continental Europe, but now likewise chiefly represented in America, and thus contributing to the present day convergence of all schools into a more solidified common enterprise.

All these schools have been described as revolts against the ruling psychological school of the nineteenth century, *structuralism* (Wundt, Titchener), some of them objecting primarily against its subjectivism ("introspectionism"), others against its bit-by-bit approach as represented primarily by such "atomistic" concepts as sensation and association.

The chief aim of behaviorism is to establish a psychology exclusively on the basis of "objective"—external or physiological—observation undertaken in the manner of the physicist. Thus psychology would be freed from the uncertainties of introspective observation, or subjective, "private" experience, which was the traditional method of psychology up to the end of the nineteenth century. A sizable number of more specific concepts or theories, such as those of the conditioned reflex, of the preponderance of environment and learning over heredity and maturation, etc., are more or less incidental, yet important characteristics of behaviorism.

Reprinted from *Encyclopedia of Psychology* (pp. 523–537), P. L. Harriman (ed.), Philosophical Library, 1946, by arrangement with Carol Publishing Group.

The chief aim of Gestalt psychology—somewhat anticipated by structuralism's major nineteenth century rivals, *act-psychology* (Brentano) and the psychology of William James—is to expand the scope of investigation, especially also of introspection, so as to embrace the meaningful units of experience ("phenomenology") or of behavior in their entirety, so that getting lost in insignificant detail and losing sight of the dynamic "field" context may be avoided.

At present there is a trend to weld these two basic tendencies in modern psychological development, the one toward objectivity and the other toward an adequate level of complexity, into a unified, new psychology. Conceptually most articulate among the many manifestations of such a convergence is *molar behaviorism* (Tolman) which endeavors to avoid the "molecular" inclinations of classical behaviorism as well as the lingering preoccupation with introspection of the gestaltists, incorporating at the same time features of functionalism.

Whereas both behaviorism and Gestalt psychology are in the "academic," experimental-theoretical tradition, functionalism and psychoanalysis stress problems of adjustment and thus try to encompass close-to-life features of behavior and their practical implications. The former specifies primarily in the tradition of evolutionary utilitarianism and expands in the direction of applied and comparative psychology, whereas the latter is in close touch with the outlook of psychotherapy.

In an effort to systematically classify theories and schools, the following three categories will best serve as guiding aspects: (A) their clarity as given by the degree of "formalization," (B) their frame of reference in terms of concentration upon variables in certain areas, or "regions," of observation and/or of inference, and (C) their "level of complexity" and its adequacy or inadequacy in the general framework of psychology.

(A) *Explicitness of theorizing. Intersubjectivity and Formalization.* The standards of "objectivity" for direct observation have repeatedly been stated to consist in "intersubjectivity," "lack of ambiguity," etc., and are best exemplified by the operation of pointer-reading and other cases of observation of spatio-temporal point coincidences. Similarly, in theory construction it seems to be possible to work with a system of symbols, or a "language," which is completely clear, i.e.,

which for all persons concerned, and for each person at different times, leads to identical results once the premises have been unambiguously stated and accepted. In such a case, one may speak of the "public" character, or the inter- and intrapersonal univocality, of construction and communication. The content of theorizing may be brought into the open and made precise to various degrees. The following major instances may be distinguished.

(1) Highest internal consistency of the kind described is achieved through the use of mathematics or, to an even greater extent, of symbolic logic. In this case one may speak of *formalized theorizing*. The farthest advance in this direction so far is Hull's "hypothetico-deductive" theory of rote learning in which the classical schema of association by spatial or temporal contiguity—to which the behavioristic schema of conditioning is conceptually related—is used to establish a system of postulates and derived theorems in the fashion of axiomatic geometry, to be checked against reality by experiments and revised if necessary.

Contrary to widespread belief, quantification is not an essential requirement in the establishment of utmost rigor in the above defined sense. In consequence, along with symbolic logic, such other purely relational, non-metric branches of mathematics as topology have also been used in the formalization of psychology, primarily by Lewin. Existing vaguenesses in topological psychology are mainly due to the insufficiency of the rules for the reality testing of hypotheses or predictions rather than weaknesses in the texture of the theory itself.—In statistics, an example of a non-metric yet mathematical procedure is ranking.

On the other hand, the frequently encountered merely programmatic employment of mathematical symbolism, such as in expressing, say, performance as a "function" of both stimulus and motivation—$P = f(S,M)$—will give only the external semblance of formalization unless the concepts entering the statement have been rigorously defined. And it will, aside from this, remain without much value unless the functional relationship has been stated with some degree of specificity.

(2) In a second, somewhat less rigorous, case, to be called *technical verbalization*, either more or less artificial terms, such as conditioning, are introduced, or common terms are vested with a

new meaning by more or less arbitrary redefinition. The major emphasis is in this case usually on the definition of concepts, whereas theory construction and derivations are mostly of shorter breath than in formalized theorizing. Definitions themselves are often in terms of common language elucidation (as is, by the way, often enough the case with such so called "undefined concepts" as, e.g., "syllable exposure," "reaction," "stimulus trace" in Hull's formalized theorizing). Yet, a great deal of precision may be obtained by this technique especially when the terms are taken from the "thing language" (Carnap). There seems less danger of losing sight of meaningful content in the process of theorizing, such as often seems to accompany exalted rigor.

Examples from physics of technical redefinition are the intramural usage of "work," "clock," etc. In psychology, technical verbalization can be found at its best in molar behaviorism, especially in such fundamental instances as Tolman's "operational redefinition" of "purposive behavior" as "persistence through trial and error, and docility, relative to some end." As in the case of the concept of "work" in physics, the psychological concept of purposiveness is thus stripped of its introspectionistic and finalistic (vitalistic) connotations. At the same time a descriptive criterion is given for the testing or verification of any statement made about the presence or absence of purpose in the new, behavioristic, sense, in any instance involved. Furthermore, the fundamental principle of "vicarious functioning" is incorporated into one of the most basic, if not the most basic, notions in psychology. (This principle, by the way, has also been introduced by Hull in his earlier work on the "habit-family-hierarchy" but fell into oblivion after he turned to the more molecular enterprise of formalization.)

Yet, as in such common instances of technical verbalization as law making by legislative bodies, there is seldom enough precision to render interpretation unnecessary. One of the few notable possible exceptions to this is Krechevsky's behavioristic redefinition, so far primarily applied to animals, of a "hypothesis" as a sequence of choices that is different from a chance sequence. Statistical criteria of significance might be applied to ascertain such a difference. Furthermore, there are few even among those introducing a redefinition who are able to keep the new technical meaning constantly in mind without slipping back into other technical or colloquial meanings of the term. (The use of subscripts to designate technical usages of terms has sometimes been suggested but so far seldom been carried through consistently in conventional write-ups.)

On the other hand, the hidden connotations and the accumulated apperceptive mass of terms loaded with tradition may often establish ties of meaning that will in the end greatly stimulate thought over and above the purely technical machinery to which proceedings otherwise might become limited. Although more mature disciplines may be able to afford to renounce such intuitive sources of progress, psychology in its present stage, with but few of its inherent problems explicitly stated, may do better not to dispense with this important life line. Thus for the sake of historical continuity operational redefinition of traditionally mentalistic terms may often be preferable to the coining of altogether artificial terms.

(3) The use of terms directly borrowed without redefinition from the vocabulary of every day life, to be termed *colloquial verbalization*, plays a decreasing role in modern psychological thought. Not long ago, however, a technique often employed in philosophy, that of attempting to "clarify" (rather than redefine) the meaning of a common term has been widely employed in introspectionism, e.g., in deciding whether sensations were "intentional"—i.e., pointing to an object outside themselves—or merely static contents of the mind, whether "orange" was a composite or a simple sensation, what was "immediately given" in experience and what was "mediate," whether or not there was such a process as "imageless thought," etc. Intuitions concerning the essence of language, of insight, or of a rejected minority group, fall in the same category.

Excursion on *level of abstraction.*—An aspect of special interest in this context is the development of what may be called the level of abstraction of concepts employed in psychological theorizing. The issue may be exemplified in the history of physics by the shift of the theory of the elements from concrete substances of daily observation, such as water or fire, to the highly abstract, often hardly visualizable constructs of electrons or wave fields. With the usual lag of many hundreds or even thousands of years, psychological theories have labored along the same path. For example, the "faculties" underlying the "phrenology" of Gall more than a hundred years ago are nothing but hypostasized daily activities, such as hope, speech, calculation, or imitation. In neo-facultative modern factor analysis, as developed especially by Spearman and Thurstone, the factors are the end product of a fully formalized system of derivation from test results and their statistical correlations. These factors emerge as purely mathematical constructs, and it is often very difficult to "name" them, i.e., to relate them to directly observable activities or even abstract features of such activities.

The theory of psychoanalysis which deals with the subject of motivation, a topic even more complex and subtle than that of physiognomics or intellectual abilities directly subsumable under the "reality-principle," has just recently started on this road of emancipation from the concrete. In its beginnings at the end of the last century, first one of the major of the directly experienced as well as outwardly manifested instincts, sex, was assigned a basic role by its founder, Freud. When Adler substituted the drive for mastery and social prestige as an alternative basis for reduction of a wide variety of observed strivings (including certain aspects of sex), it seemed like a revival of the water vs. fire alternative in ancient Greek natural philosophy. Very soon, however, it was made clear that the term "sex" was to be used in a redefined, broadened sense whereby the term "genital" was to take over the narrower function of what was colloquially called "sexual." The concept of "libido," especially emphasized by Jung, and designating a generalized vital urge, is an example of an artificially imposed term that at the same time led further away into abstractness. (In spite of such and other important differences, the schools of Adler, of Jung, and of others differ primarily in content or technique rather than in basic theoretical texture from that of Freud and are therefore not especially considered in the present article.) It seems quite likely that in the future all concrete concepts used in preliminary theorizing on personality dynamics will give way to truly formalized constructs in the fashion of modern factor analysis. It may be expected that in the course of such a development many of the misunderstandings and endless controversies, as well as a good deal of the emotional resistance that so often arises against revolutionary statements made in terms of the common language vocabulary, will be mellowed and will eventually

disappear. Needless to say that observational exactitude and statistical caution are apt to increase in parallel with the adoption of objective criteria in theorizing and a formalized set of concepts and assumptions.

(4) This side remark on level of abstraction leads us back from the primary emphasis on concepts characteristic of the various stages of informal verbalization to problems of the assertive content of theorizing. Due to the flexibility of the meaning of common terms, hidden assumptions or prejudices are apt to slip in unnoticed. In this case we have *unverbalized, implicit, theorizing*. In the development of psychology accusations of the presence of such "tacit presuppositions" play quite a prominent role in the struggle of new against older schools. Probably the best known instance is that of the "constancy hypothesis" which, according to Gestalt psychology, is tacitly inherent in many of the policies or specific assumptions of structuralism. According to this supposed hypothesis each isolated stimulus element impinging upon the sensory surface of an organism will—at least within each specific sense department—at first elicit an effect in consciousness that is univocally correlated to the character of the stimulus, e.g., a large retinal image the impression of largeness in strict proportion to the size of the area stimulated.

Inadequacy in the treatment of the pre-conscious, physiological interaction and organization of the perceptual field, such as of the tendency towards "good" figure, or of the perceptual thing-constancies—establishing correctness of judgment about, say, object size regardless of distance rather than about the size of the peripheral retinal projection—has been held against the constancy hypothesis. It is being pointed out that its roots lie in the confusion of the actually observed "phenomenal" experience with the mosaic-like "functional" anatomy of the peripheral sensorium, leading to a false molecularism in introspective as well as eventually also in functional psychology. If all this had been made explicit, it is said, such an assumption would never have been made in earnest. Implicit hypotheses thus apparently may be much more harmful than explicit ones, quite aside from the element of irrational or wishful thinking that may enter into them.

(B) *Regional reference*. It seems that implicit theorizing has its best chance whenever explicit theorizing is programmatically discouraged. The best example is early behaviorism with its overt hostility to theory, rationalized as a wish to limit psychology to "fact" and thus to avoid the discord contained in traditional informal, speculative, "medieval" theorizing. Not only has this attitude been very short lived, giving way to elaborate formalized theorizing, but—what is more—an analysis of the research policies of classical behaviorism reveals the presence of an unusual number of unverbalized biases, which make a good case for Goethe's statement that "any fact is in itself theory." One of the most important of the prejudices inherent in behaviorism is its *peripheralism*, which may be rationally reconstructed as the implicit belief that what is important in the life and behavior of an organism can be found and identified at its surface—apparently because of the fact that that is the portion which is most conveniently observable—thus rendering theoretical construction of what Tolman has called "intervening variables" unnecessary. A long series of frustrations marks Watson's search for "the" organ of learning, first among the organs of the sensory, then of the motor periphery. Only the hard way, by experiment, and in the course of the resulting reorientation toward a molar behaviorism by Tolman and by Lashley is the "generality" of animal learning, the vicarious functioning of sensory as well as of motor cues or departments, and with it the *central* basis of orientation and the prime importance of the brain, being made clear.

By the same token, and in line with the spirit of functionalism, the actually achieved environmental end-results of a behavioral unit (e.g., the actual reaching of food) becomes one of the most important focal regions of observation. Result-variables of this kind are a special case of what recently is sometimes called a *distal* variable (Heider, Brunswik). It may then be said that the peripheral, sensory-motor unit of the glandular or muscular reflex is in both Tolman and Hull (in the latter only in his pre-formalization phase) being overshadowed by a central-distal outlook.

From the concept of implicit theorizing it is only a short step to a discussion of such major movements in psychology which, in spite of the employment of often very high powered theoretical procedures, are characterized by the absence of that aggressive or propagandistic superstructure which would make them schools in the tradi-

tional sense of the word. Yet, by virtue of a relocation of the focal regions of interest, as well as of other changes in basic research policies, some of them are as revolutionary as their more vocal competitors, or even more so; such movements may thus well be called "implicit schools." In line with a general reluctance to indulge in open theorizing—a kind of intellectual puritanism—implicit schools are found most prominently in America. The functionalism of the turn of the century has often been said not to be a system in the customary sense; yet this is due not so much to a lack of explicitness but rather to the fact that functionalism embraces a variety of heterogeneous movements which had joined forces against structuralism. Truly implicit schools have not even gone to the trouble of finding a label for themselves which would characterize them as an "-ism." Identifiable merely by the names of their most outstanding representatives, the following three stand out within academic psychology: Lashley, Thurstone, Murray. Along with such explicit theorists as Tolman, Hull, or Lewin, they have probably exerted the strongest influence in the current reorganization of actual psychological research policies, at least in America which is at present the center of psychological work.

It is significant of the *convergent trends in present day psychology* that, with all of the existing differences, the work of the leading psychologists just mentioned, possibly with partial reservations in the case of Hull and of Lewin, can be subsumed under the above formula of a shift from peripheral to a more *functionalistic, central-distal* emphasis.

In the case of Lashley, the emphasis on the central region which Tolman introduces by inferring "intervening variables" such as "purposes," "hypotheses," etc., in new, operationally redefined versions, is found in such observational directness as to be acceptable without ambivalence even to the traditional behaviorist. The only direct approach to the central region is the physiological. It is through experimental brain-lesions in rats in the case of Lashley. This approach is radically different from the sensory technology, or the sensory-motor reflexology, of the structuralists, or of the early behaviorists, respectively. The genuinely psychological character of this work is given by the fact that, just as in the case of Tolman, the central variables—such as extent of cortical lesion—are linked to, or correlated with, the reaching of a certain characteristic end state, such as the arrival in the food compartment of a complex maze.

Lewin's foothold in the region of behavioral results is somewhat doubtful as far as his theoretical system is concerned; all his real emphasis centers on inferences concerning, and the intrinsic lawfulness of, the central region, per se. The Lewinian "life space," which refers to the internal setting of the stage for action after perception has taken place, is conceived as a dynamic "field" rather than a conscious reality. This is an important step toward objectivism, although it has been pointed out that much of Lewin's rather casual technique of inferring the life space may in fact be "phenomenological" in the introspectionistic sense. As is conscious experience, the life space, being segmented into macroscopic units, is ideally describable in terms of a non-metric topology (see above) and Lewin is to be credited with the fact that he is the first and so far the only major psychologist to attempt the use of this happily non-quantitative yet mathematical instrument. Given the limitation of scope inherent in this comparative encapsulation into the central layer—which has definitely to be considered a molecular feature—it may be relatively simple for Lewin to develop psychological laws, especially if supported by a somewhat unscrutinized side glance at overt behavior as a testing ground for the predictions made.

Whereas Lewin, with his primary emphasis on central field dynamics, reveals his direct descendance from Gestalt psychology most clearly, both Lashley and Tolman may be looked upon as those most evenly balancing behaviorism and Gestalt psychology into a new synthesis of these two major schools. Likewise, it is in Tolman and Lashley that the functionalistic component, represented by utilitarian result-emphasis; becomes most prominent. Hull's espousal of intervening variables and of the concept of molar behavior may help to illustrate his tendencies toward, and emphasis on, central processes.

Thurstone's functionalistic leanings on behavioral results are revealed by his start from test scores. In counterdistinction to most other testers, however, he does not consider the mathematical evaluation of such results in terms of correlation or factor analysis merely as a more economical description within the distal layer. By ostentatiously adopting the much scorned tradition-

loaded term "faculty" as an alternate to the neutral term "factor," he clearly puts the emphasis on the central layer of abilities and dispositions. And by the strict formalization of the rules of inference of the central factors from the distal test-scores he sets an unparalleled example of exactitude in the theoretical establishment of intervening variables. For this reason, as well as probably for the minimum display of an explicit school-superstructure, Thurstone shares with Lashley the probably least ambivalent acceptance of his particular style of work in spite of the fact that Thurstone freely indulges in theorizing of an inferential kind.

Whereas up to this point the synthesis was of behaviorism with functionalism or with Gestalt psychology or both, Murray may be considered as the academic psychologist who has gone farthest toward an integration with psychoanalysis. The emphasis on the central which he shares with all the other contemporaries listed, takes in him the form of an emphasis on "needs." As in psychoanalysis, the center of gravity is thus placed on forces of motivation assumed to be relatively stable whereas in Tolman and Lewin it is more the fluid, short-range changes of motivation that absorb most of the interest, and in Thurstone it is primarily the cognitive rather than the motivational side of the relatively permanent pattern of dispositions that absorbs the bulk of attention. The shift from the peripheral to the distal variables is reflected in Murray's emphasis on the "effects" of behavior rather than the "actones" which constitute behavior when viewed as it issues from in organism. As is psychoanalysis, Murray's system of needs and its environmental conditions as well as consequences is one of the least formalized and thus most severely criticized. As does psychoanalysis, however, it probably contains the seeds for a system more comprehensive in scope than are those based more exclusively on the academic tradition, exemplifying once more the inverse relationship that exists—at least during the adolescent period of a science—between methodological perfection, on the one hand, and adequate complexity, on the other.

Generally, the most fundamental regional difference between academic psychology and psychoanalysis is the former's preoccupation with *"geographic"* environmental relationships, the well-known stimulus-response schema, whether the stimulus be "proximal" (peripheral) or "distal" (including the social). In contrast to this, psycho-analysis endeavors primarily to discover relationships of present motivation to certain focal regions along the *"historical"* axis, mostly the remote past, including especially early childhood. Recent academic emphasis on motivation as an experimental variable (Tolman and others), on "operant" (spontaneous) as contrasted with "respondent" behavior (Skinner) will in the end help to close a gap that should be recognized as one of divergent interest in wide open spaces rather than as one of conflicting views on a crowded common battleground of research.

(C) *Level of complexity and closeness to fact.* After discussing primarily some of the formal aspects of theorizing, such as explicitness, the aspect of the material content of a theory was brought into the picture so far primarily under the heading of differences in regional emphasis among the various schools. Other aspects of content are primarily those of scope, or level of complexity (molar vs. molecular outlook) and certain allied methodological problems (such as primarily experiment and "law" vs. statistics). These aspects can conveniently be called to attention in close connection with still another formal aspect of theorizing, namely that of the relationship of theory to the factual reality of observation. This shall be done here under the heading of "closeness to fact" of a theory. The following major instances will be distinguished: (1) surface theories, maintaining the observational level of complexity, and (2) dynamic (explanatory) theories of both the (a) subordinate, mediational and (b) the superordinate, functional type, characterizing a more macroscopic and a more microscopic level than that of the original sequence or co-existence of observations.

Some theories are close to what is customarily called a pure "description" of fact. The simplest way of describing facts is by *enumeration*. In this case, however, facts remain unrelated to one another and no predictions can thus be derived from them. Therefore, this approach is often considered to be outside of what is usually understood to constitute "science"; and it does not contain any element of theory, although a formalized "language" may be necessary to establish it.

(1) Theory begins with synopsis. But it is only in idealized cases, exemplified, say, in geometry, that description can truly be said not to go beyond the fact. A good illustration is the description of

a circle or any other line by an equation, as is done in analytic geometry, instead of by an enumeration of all of its points. But whereas in geometry the number of points is infinite, in any empirical science only a finite and often very limited number of points is available. Synoptic description in this case becomes the fitting of an idealized continuum of points to a discontinuous series of points. In accepting the fitted curve as an alternative description one thus already transgresses the facts available; the points "interpolated" between the existing data, as well as especially those "extrapolated" beyond the ends of the observed series of points, contain an element of prediction, stated in terms of what amounts to a "law," which definitely oversteps the boundaries of a purely synoptic alternative to simple enumeration. Yet, when compared to other instances of theorizing, curve fitting stands out as singularly non-interpretative and lacking in dynamic implications, unless of course the character of the curve is taken as a starting point for further considerations, comparisons and reductions. Thus "phenotypical approach," or "phenomenological theory" (the term here not in its introspectionistic meaning), "empirical theory," "descriptive theory," or *surface theory* would seem to be appropriate labels for synoptic description.

Most outstanding examples of curve fitting in psychology can be found in the experimental psychology of learning and of forgetting (with the logarithmic curve as a favorite), as well as in other more strictly developmental fields. The most comprehensive approach of this kind was recently undertaken by Woodrow in an attempt to find a "generalized quantitative law" for a wide variety of fields in psychology including learning, psychophysics (as an alternative to the earliest genuinely psychological quantitative law formulated, the Weber-Fechner law), the development of intelligence, and others. In combining two hypothetical factors, one for the ceiling inherent in all human performance, the other representing what might crudely be labeled sensitivity, Woodrow went somewhat beyond a mere synopsis, in the direction of underlying dynamics, but he himself regards his attempt as a surface theory. Being an exponential function with a large number of parameters which vary from application to application—in contradistinction to the "universal" physical constants, such as the speed of light, which remain the same in a wide variety of contexts—Woodrow's formula can be fitted to an extremely wide range of curve shapes, thus reducing the value of synopsis which would seem to lie in comparative specificity. There can be no doubt, however, that this kind of theorizing has a place and a future in psychology.

Another frequently used instance of synoptic description is the correlation coefficient and related measures of concomitant variation of variables. As are the mathematical functions mentioned above, correlation coefficients are abbreviated, comprehensive—although not complete— descriptions of sets of points in space, in this case determined by the frequencies over the cells of a two-dimensional scatter diagram. Contrary to frequent, often tacit misuses in practice, a correlation coefficient does not indicate direct causal relatedness of the two variables in question and is therefore just another instance of a theoretical construct to be subsumed under surface theorizing.

(2) Whenever the genotypical, conditional-genetic approach involving generalized "nomothetic" (i.e., law-asserting) statements about cause and effect is involved one may speak of *dynamic theories*. More broadly, the term may also be applied to assumptions about individual, "idiographic," cause-and-effect sequences without reference to lawfulness. Although most textbooks explicitly warn against confounding observed correlation with causation, few rules are given for the methodical determination of cause and effect sequences. There can be no doubt, however, that in the end all such statements are based upon the observation or application of some kind of empirical correlation. Two major ways seem to be open: (a) by the use of statistics, gathering and combining observed correlations with only imperfect control over remaining relevant conditions, along pathways prepared by partial and multiple correlation or related techniques; none of these techniques have, however, yet been developed to an inclusiveness which would guarantee causal analysis of a foolproof nature. Or (b) by the use of the classical type of experiment, rigidly controlling all relevant conditions and observing concomitant variations of the one (or few) remaining ones. Most of the laws formulated in physics, and some stated regularities in psychology have been established in this latter fashion. In the field of personality and individual differences, however, only limited controls are possible and

statistical methods, including the above mentioned factor analysis, have been more successful. Many statements of causation in this and other fields have been left to informal or even unverbalized theorizing often labelled "intuition," "understanding," and the like, which upon being made explicit would most likely reveal their character as a statistical theory, though most likely lacking in sufficient scrutiny with respect to sampling, separation of issues, etc.

There is a close relationship between dynamic theories and what is customarily called *explanation* of a fact or an observed regularity. To remove any semblance of a fundamental cleavage, explanation has sometimes been called "added description," in the typical case through reference to generalized evidence stated in the form of a sometimes more, sometimes less rigorously established law or regularity. There are two major usages of the term "explanation" in psychology.

(a) Most specifically, it is applied to a tracing of a chain of cause and effect through many, and in the ideal case through all, the intermediate stages that lie between the originally observed coexistence or succession of facts. Quite frequently observation of such intermediate stages is impossible and systematic principles of a lower level of complexity, but usually of higher generality, often called micro-laws, are called upon to substitute for historic-geographic observation on the spot.

In colloquial terms, such tracings attempt an answer to the question "How does it work?" and the assumptions adopted, idiographic or nomothetic, may therefore be called "how-theories," "technological theories," "microtheories" or, preferably, *mediation theories*.

Generalized mediation theories play an outstanding role in psychology, and can be found in their purest form in the theories of vision and audition developed ever since the middle of the last century by Helmholtz and others. They are based on observations of gross correlation between such stimulus variables as wave length of light or sound, on the one hand, and of psychological response qualities such as sensations of color and tone and their attributes, such as hues, subjective pitch and loudness, etc., on the other. Unresolved alternatives, such as those existing among the resonance theory, the telephone theory, and the volley theory of the functioning of the ear and the auditory nerve, occupy the interest of psychologists up to the present. Their counterparts in the field of vision have, without being completely settled, already faded from the attention of psychologists into the domain of a more molecular discipline, physiology. Many other mediation problems may ultimately become relegated to such more "fundamental" sciences.

Mediation theories of much broader scope have recently been developed to explain features of behavior which themselves span considerably wider gaps than those existing between proximal stimuli and peripheral excitations or central sensations. The most outstanding example is Hull's theory of behavior, a sequel to his work in formalized theorizing mentioned earlier in this report. Hull tries to fill the gap between the geographical stimulus-environment existing at a certain moment, on the one hand, and the accomplished behavior act, on the other, with a chain of inferred links, combining the Pavlovian schema of conditioning with the Thorndikean principle of reinforcement through the law of effect (satisfaction of drive). This schema, emphasizing past experience (or past behavior) as has English associationism and later structuralism, is, however, only one of two major alternatives. The opposite theory is one of internal field dynamics, more specifically, of the closure or completion of incomplete patterns—which include unsolved "problems" along with the originally studied incomplete geometrical patterns which perceptually tend to become "better," more regular, symmetrical, simple, in short, "prägnant"—through the intrinsic laws governing the interplay of forces within the "closed system" of the organism. Various forms of such a theory have been proposed by Gestalt psychology and related movements, such as the Würzburg school of Külpe, Bühler and Selz. The association and completion theories have in common that they are phrased in terms of intervening variables, and sometimes even in quasi-physiological terms, by the use of such "unobservables" as excitatory or inhibitory potential, brain field, etc., and only indirectly in terms of the environment. It is for this encapsulation within the organism that both of these theories have to be classified as mediational. (The same holds, by the way, for the highly mathematized theories of Rashevsky and his collaborators.)

There remains, however, an important difference that characterizes the association theory as more "molecular" in comparison with the completion theory. In the interpretation of the Gestaltists the association theory, being patterned after the model of the reflex arc, or of a telephone switchboard system, is a "machine theory," whereas the completion theory is dynamic in a more genuine sense of the word by its emphasis on free interaction of energy within large areas of the nervous system. The basic conception of "mass" functioning of the nervous system as developed by the modern behaviorist, Lashley, or by the biologist, Paul Weiss, is in accord with such a field interpretation. Under this aspect Lashley, along with Tolman, has to be classified as a molar behaviorist whereas Hull retains some characteristics of molecular behaviorism in spite of an attempt to introduce several specific molar features into his behavior theory, such as "stimulus patterning," "behavioral oscillation," etc.

(b) Given an observed macroscopic causal correlation of two variables, one may, as an alternative to mediational theorizing, attempt to see their connectedness as embedded within an even broader causal texture. In want of a fully established term one may label efforts of this kind *functional theories*. Comparing the two approaches in terms of analogies all of which are somewhat inadequate, mediational theorizing may be said to correspond to mathematical interpolation, functional theorizing to extrapolation, or the relationship may be said to be similar to the one of technology to economics, or to the one of tactics to strategy in military science. And whereas the mediationist's primary question was said to be "how?" the functionalist may be said—with certain specifications—to ask "why?"

Broadest term under which behavioral activity may be subsumed as a part-function is " survival." Handed down from Darwin, it is extensively used by modern formalizers of behaviorism such as Hull, revealing functionalistic leanings, even where specific theory tends toward the mediational by stressing the (quasi-) physiological as contrasted to the more broadly "biological" aspects of adjustment. Such somewhat unorthodox appendages to early behaviorism as Thorn law of effect, or the recent emphasis on "instrumental" vs. "classical" conditioning reveal present trends toward functionalism within behaviorism. To an even greater extent this is true of such concepts as Tolman's operationally redefined "purpose" (see above), or the "wishes" and "needs" of psychoanalysis or of Murray, especially when stress is also placed upon a satisfying condition in the physical or social environment. The essential step in this respect is the introduction of the actually accomplished behavioral results as remote and sometimes purely environmental distal variables, along with those of a physiological or stimulus nature.

Generally, a functionalistic theory can be considered the viewing of an event as suspended between two "foci" for which a correlation has been established previously. One of the clearest examples is given when a specific habit, say, the running of a rat through a door, is seen as a part, or as one of many possible over-all manifestations, within the framework of a habit-family-hierarchy (to come back to the term of Hull). The antecedent or initial focus of such a complex behavioral unit may be a state of physiological need, the consequent or terminal focus may be the actual arriving at the place where food can be found. In between lie the variety of habits, means, or instruments through which the correlation of initial and terminal focus is being mediated at various occasions, in "vicarious functioning" of the various instruments.

The most controversial feature of functionalistic theories is the relating of an instrument to the terminal focus so that its role as an "instrument" becomes "response inferred" (the term by Spence). More concretely, this would be the case if it were stated that a rat runs through a gate "because it wants to get to the food" or that a person leaves town "because he wants to get away from his parents." Such formulations have been severely objected to because of the teleological associations connected with them in the history of psychology. But actually, as becomes especially clear in Tolman's redefinition of "purpose," such a formulation need not mean anything but the purely descriptive reference to the fact that running through a gate has in the past frequently been observed to result in an arriving at food, and that running through the gate has at the same time been observed to be one in a series of events in which the animal proved to be "persistent and docile through trial and error," with the reaching of food being the crucial condition for quiescence.

It is a question of terminology as to how far reference to a "wish" or "purpose" in terms of a terminal focus can be considered "explanation." It would certainly be accepted as such in conversational language. Most of the theories in

psychoanalysis are of this type, not to speak of such entire disciplines as economics, in which automobiles may be considered to run because there is a demand for transportation (functionalistic macro-theory) rather than because they contain cylinders, gasoline, wheels, etc., in proper arrangement (mediational micro-theory). Psychologists brought up in the tradition of the exact molecular natural sciences may be reluctant to accept a why-theory, or they may at least request a "whence"-theory (referring to initial focus, or cause), if not a how-theory, in preference to a "whither"-theory of the kind just described (referring to a terminal focus, or probable effect).

Reluctance in this respect may only partly be due to the teleological nature of functional theories; another strong reason seems to be given by the fact that the more wide spanning a correlation, the less it is apt to reach the univocality usually requested of a "law." Examples for this may be taken from correlation statistics ever since its inception (Galton, Pearson), with its early preoccupation with problems of heredity of physical or mental characteristics, or from psychoanalytic theories asserting that adult behavior in many instances may be explained as a substitute or symbolic fulfillment of wishes thwarted in early childhood. No more than statistical correlations could at best be obtained between initial and terminal focus of such patterns, with most of the intervening variables beyond the reach of controls other than those by broad class-membership (e.g., "normal" environment or physical development).

Still more fundamentally: Such controls should not even be applied if it were possible to do so since the maintenance of relatively stable long-distance relations in spite of variable mediation seems to be one of the major characteristics of life. So much so that various forms of stabilization models have been laid down—often by behaviorists concerned with the delimitation of the field of psychology as a whole—as the chief objective criterion of behavior vs. non-behavior. This is already quite explicit in such classical-behavioristic analogies as A. P. Weiss's raindrop-analogy or Hunter's principle of vicarious functioning, and it is furthermore inherent in Tolman's above mentioned definition of purpose (with a predecessor in McDougall); Hull's habit-family-hierarchy, Lashley's equipotentiality of brain areas, Murray's irrelevance of actones, Freud's symbolism and other mechanisms such as displacement, sublimation, etc., likewise belong here. Analogous "lens-models" (Brunswik) have been suggested in the psychology of perception (thing-constancies). Even in physiology, stabilization mechanisms, such as the principle of homeostasis (constancy of the internal milieu, e.g., of blood temperature, in spite of changes of external conditions, activity, etc.) as emphasized by Cannon play an outstanding role.

Explanation or not, terminal reference as theory in the sense of "added description" can hardly be objected to if it is made clear that the realm of previously observed fact is not bring transgressed and that a mediational explanation is not bring attempted except possibly as a probability statement.

A special mediation problem: *mechanism vs. vitalism.*—A problem sharply to be distinguished from those discussed so far is terminal reference as an absolute "ultimate," i.e., as an explanatory principle sui generis. Ever since Aristotle's entelechies the vitalistic notion of a "final" causality superimposed upon physical causality has remained an issue in psychology. The alternative to vitalism is mechanism, i.e., the assumption that all facts of life, including goal-strivingness as a descriptive phenomenon, can in the end be reduced to, or subsumed under, ordinary physical laws. Actually, this problem is not a functional but a mediational one. In order to decide empirically the mechanism-vitalism alternative one would have to go into extremely minute detail of the mechanism of heredity, restitution, or regeneration, or of the physiological happenings at the time of choice between alternative behaviors. It would involve a checking upon conservation of energy of extremely minute quantities. It is thus that the problem has recently become entangled with those of the quantum physics of the atom, whereby some theorists have attempted to reintroduce the vitalistic principle of freedom of will through the indeterminacy or alleged statistical, unpredictable nature of the processes within the atom. Any possible settlement of the mechanismvitalism problem is utterly beneath the order of magnitude of the processes with which even the most molecular psychologist is concerned. Regardless of whether one violently espouses mechanism, as was done by Watson, or vitalism, as was done by McDougall, the decision was dogmatic; more recent thinkers such as Tolman therefore do not refer to this problem at all, appar-

ently considering it permanently shelved as far as psychology is concerned (although they privately may believe in an ultimate resolution of macroscopic behavior patterns into processes predictable in a physical manner). Logical positivists, such as Carnap, explicitly declare the problem of the unity of physical and biological *laws* an empirical question not to be solved dogmatically or by speculation, and unsolved so far; the unity of *method* of observation and theory construction within the realm of all the sciences being the only requirement to be fulfilled in establishing an objective psychology ("methodological physicalism").

Theories about Theories and Research Policies in Psychology.—The above discussion leads us to the various arguments that can be found throughout the psychological literature in judging the value or adequacy of certain fundamental assumptions or basic policies adopted by individuals and schools in psychology. Some of these issues have been brought up before in this report, such as the problem of objectivity, formalization, or operational redefinition. Other theories about theories deal with genetic problems of the history of science.

An outstanding recent example is Lewin's distinction of Aristotelian and Galileian modes of thought in psychology, somewhat similar to Comte's distinction of the theological and metaphysical vs. the positive stage in the development of science in general. The Aristotelian mode of thought is taken as a representative of the older philosophical or speculative approach and is most characteristically manifested by a tendency toward the setting up of "dichotomies," i.e., of absolute rather than relative distinctions between opposites, such as mind and matter, learning and insight, mechanism and vitalism, nomothetic and idiographic disciplines, etc. Galileian modes, according to Lewin, lead to the transformation of such notions into truly scientific ones, the replacement of differences in kind by differences of degree, a general adoption of quantitative methods and a discovery and emphasis upon lawfulness. In consequence, theories should be, and are in practice, judged not only in terms of their direct merit, but also more indirectly, in terms of their genetic level which in a general way may allow us to anticipate their adequacy.

To the present reviewer, the discussion about the status of laws in psychology seems of particular importance. In fact, he is inclined to advocate the replacement of the classical experiment, with its emphasis upon the discovery of strict laws, by a more statistical procedure even in stimulus-response psychology as the only practicable way to establish an exact, yet molar objective psychology. Imperfect correlation or probability laws would then take the place of unequivocal laws, although the latter most likely "exist" and can be discovered at the expense of adequate complexity.

Another issue of similar, methodological nature is the relative weight to be assigned to the idiographic, case-descriptive, "clinical" approach as contrasted with the nomothetic, more generally law-finding (which in this alternative would include the statistical). This is a reiteration, on a more advanced and formalized plane, of the old controversy as to whether psychology in its basic orientation is a natural science dealing with generalities, or a "cultural" science (*Geisteswissenschaft*) dealing with singularities, or at least with "individuals" that have to be intuitively "understood" in terms of some—possibly self-consistent, i.e., idiographically "lawful"—personal "styles of life" peculiar to them alone.

Theoretical issues of this type may appear to stand isolated at times, yet the answers given to them form the nucleus of the fundamental philosophies of science crystallized in the various psychological systems or schools.

EGON BRUNSWIK

BIBLIOGRAPHICAL NOTES

Only references to publications in, or translations into, English are included here. Sources for the most recent movements in academic psychology are given in somewhat greater detail, since they occupy the limelight of recent discussion and since only scant comprehensive treatments or adequate up to date bibliographical selections have appeared after the early thirties. An effort has been made to select in each case the most concise presentations available, among them quite often presidential addresses of the American Psychological Association, so that the reader may be enabled to make the best use of his time and energy in his endeavor to obtain a full view of the issues involved in modern psychological theorizing.

(1) *Original sources on schools and movements.*— The two major historical forms of nineteenth century introspectionistic psychology are most outstandingly represented in American psychological literature by

Wundt's pupil, E. B. Titchener, in his posthumously published presentation and belated defense of structuralism, *Systematic Psychology, Prolegomena* (Macmillan, 1929), and by W. James, in his chronologically much earlier but in spirit more modern *Principles of Psychology* (2 vols., Holt, 1890) which shows some common elements with Brentano's act-psychology but in certain ways also foreshadows most of the later "crisis" schools, including American functionalism, behaviorism, Gestalt psychology, and even psychoanalysis.

These major movements are in their original form most clearly represented in J. R. Angell's presidential address, "The province of functional psychology" (*Psychol. Review* 1907, 14), in J. B. Watson's third and latest book, *Behaviorism* (Norton, 1924), K. Koffka's *Principles of Gestalt Psychology* (Harcourt-Brace, 1935), and S. Freud's *Introductory Lectures on Psychoanalysis* (Allen & Unwin, 1922, originally 1917), the latter to be augmented by such indexed and glossaried *General Selections* from his works as the one edited by J. Rickman (Hogarth Press, 1937).

The formalized, physiological-behavioristic theorizing centering about learning problems reaches a climax in two books by C. L. Hull (the first in collaboration with several other authors), *Mathematico-Deductive Theory of Rote Learning* (Yale Univ. Press, 1940), and *Principles of Behavior* (Appleton-Century, 1943). Especially the latter has, in the years immediately following its publication, elicited an unprecedented amount of critical reviewing, discussion and counter-discussion, such as in the *Psychol. Bulletin* (Koch, Ritchie; on math-ded. theory: Hilgard and others), the *Journ. of Genetic Psychol.* (Leeper, Welch), the *Amer. Journ. of Psychol.* (Skinner).

More important from the standpoint of the development of a molar approach is some of the last of Hull's writing of his period preceding formalization, especially three articles on "The concept of the habit-family hierarchy" and related schemata (*Psychol. Review*, 1934–35, 41, 42).—Less well known among psychologists, but no less important in the field of formalized quasi-physiological theorizing in psychology at large, and gradually working up to such complex topics as esthetic appreciation of forms, Gestalt problems, the perceptual thing-constancies, etc., are N. Rashevsky's *Mathematical Biophysics* and *Advances and Applications of Math. Biology* (Univ. of Chicago Press, 1938 and 1940, resp.), followed by A. S. Householder and H. D. Landahl, *Math. Biophysics of the Central Nervous System* (Math. Bioph. Monogr., No. 1, 1941), and largely based on, and augmented by, numerous papers in *Bulletin of Math, Biophysics* (beginning 1939).—A less technical type of formalization of learning theory is attempted in B. F. Skinner, *The Behavior of Organisms*

(Appleton-Century, 1938). For a general discussion of learning theories see E. R. Hilgard and D. G. Marquis, *Conditioning and Learning* (Appleton-Century, 1940).

Molar behaviorism of a non-vitalistic, operational kind representing a convergence with both functionalism and Gestalt psychology is first conceived by E. C. Tolman in his *Purposive Behavior in Animals and Men* (Appleton-Century, 1932), as well as in "Psychology vs. immediate experience" (*Philos. of Science*, 1935, 2) and a series of articles, many of them in the *Psychol. Review*, including one in collaboration with E. Brunswik on "The organism and the causal texture of the environment" (1935, 42), and the presidential address, "The determiners of behavior at a choice point" (1938, 45). One of the most outstanding operational redefinitions of an originally introspectionistic concept may be found in I. Krechevsky, "Hypotheses in Rats" (*Psychol. Review*, 1932, 39). An excellent presentation of the experimental evidence forcing the shift from Watson's peripheral to Tolman's central behaviorism, together with illustrations of the methodological changes involved, is given in R. S. Woodworth, *Experimental Psychology* (Holt. 1938, first half of Chapter 6).—Still closer to Gestalt psychology than Tolman is K. Lewin, *Dynamic Theory of Personality*, and *Principles of Topological Psychology* (McGraw-Hill, 1935 and 1936, resp.), continued in his still more technical *Conceptual Repres. and Meas. of Psychol. Forces* (Contrib. to Psychol. Theory, No. 4, 1938), and in "Formalization and progress in psychology" (Univ. of Iowa Stud. in Child Welfare, 1940, 16–3).—Going beyond Gestalt psychology in the direction of an objective functionalism as does molar behaviorism, but centering about the perceptual thing-constancies rather than about the means-end problems which constitute their mirror image on the overt behavioral side, is E. Brunswik, in a summary of his book whose title is best translated as "Psychology in Terms of Objects" (1934): "Psychology as a science of objective relations" (*Philos. of Science*, 1937, 4; some serious errata corr. 1938, 5).

The best source for H. E. Murray's synthesis of certain elements of modern psychology and of psychoanalysis are the first two chapters of his *Explorations in Personality* (in collaboration with numerous other authors of the Harvard Psychological Clinic; Oxford Univ. Press, 1938). The ambiguous character of the need-to-effect relationship involved is stressed in E. Frenkel-Brunswik, *Motivation and Behavior* (Genetic Psychol. Monographs, 1942).

Only scant theoretical utterances are available in the case of such "implicit" school-leaders as Lashley and Thurstone. The former's "Basic neural mechanisms in behavior" (*Psychol. Review*, 1930, 37), and the latter's non-technical "The vectors of mind" (*Psychol. Review*, 1934, 41)—both presidential addresses—, as well as Thurstone's defense, against Anastasi and others, of his factors as the operational revival of the old "faculties" in "Shifty and mathematical components" (both authors in *Psychol. Bulletin* 1938, 35; see also 1940, 37), may be consulted to advantage.

(II) *Texts on schools, and other comprehensive treatments.*—The period up to the close of the era of divergent schools of psychology, i.e., roughly up to 1930, has found its terminal expression in a number of comprehensive books. Among these probably the most widely used is E. Heidbreder, *Seven Psychologies* (Appleton-Century, 1933), a clear and well proportioned presentation of the major systems on a relatively elementary level, and with an adequate selection of references to original sources up to that period which may serve as a first guide to those interested in the semi-historical literature on systems of psychology. Of similar intent but of somewhat lesser inclusiveness is R. S. Woodworth, *Contemporary Schools of Psychology* (Ronald Press, 1931). With a historical slant, and organized more about fields than schools proper, is G. Murphy, *Historical Introduction to Modern Psychology* (Harcourt-Brace, 3rd ed., 1932), with an appendix by H. Klüver on such exclusively continental movements as "intuitionism." For similar reasons, R. Müller-Freienfels' somewhat unwieldy *Evolution of Modern Psychology* (Yale Univ. Press, 1935), may also be recommended, although with reservations. First hand summaries of a considerable number of schools by their originators or by close collaborators were assembled by C. Murchison in *Psychologies of 1925*, and *of 1930* (Clark Univ. Press), among many others of such sometimes otherwise not easily accessible but important authors or movements as Sander's brand of configurationism (the Leipzig group), Russian "objective psychology" and "reflexology" in both the Pavlov and the Bekhterev versions, and Janet's and Adler's sub-varieties of psychoanalysis.

Comprehensive presentations of the developments in psychological theorizing since the early thirties are at this writing available only in the form of short articles of necessarily limited usefulness, and even these are few and far between. Almost without exception, these papers also reflect the current general trend toward a higher level of abstraction in the presentation or discussion of schools or theoretical issues. E. Brunswik, "The conceptual focus of some psychological systems" (first publ. 1939, reprinted in *Twentieth Century Psychology*, ed. by P. L. Harriman, Philos. Library, 1946) uses a considerably oversimplified, schematic presentation of the various schools in terms of regions and patterns of their research emphasis. A fundamentally similar purpose, but even more stressing systematic issues rather than schools, underlies the penetrating study by F. Heider, "Environmental determinants in psychological theories" (*Psychol. Review*, 1939, 46). The merits of J. R. Kantor, "Current trends in psychological theory" (*Psychol. Bulletin*, 1941, 38), are somewhat obscured by the author's going off the main line of current discussions. A unique survey of the changing points of view implicit in the psychological research since the closing decades of the nineteenth century is given in G. W. Allport's presidential address, "The psychologist's frame of reference" (*Psychol. Bulletin*, 1940, 37). This analysis based on careful study of the content of articles in the leading psychological periodicals may well anticipate a future development toward an objectified and statistical treatment of the history and trend of psychological ideas.

(III) *Systematic discussion.* — The recent emphasis on discussion centering about fundamental problems and basic methodological issues inherent in the founding of schools, rather than about these schools as the unifying centers themselves, is represented in such books as C. C. Pratt, *The Logic of Modern Psychology* (Macmillan, 1939), and C. R. Griffith, *Principles of Systematic Psychology* (Univ. of Illinois Press, 1943). Both these ambitious undertakings fall, however, somewhat short of their mark. The latter contains the most nearly complete list of references in theoretical psychology, at least as far as the recent American literature appearing as books or in the routine theoretical periodicals, including the philosophy of science relevant to psychology, is concerned, giving more than 1500 titles. E. G. Boring's most recent historical treatise *Sensation and Perception in the History of Exp. Psychology* (Appleton-Century, 1942), presents material or discussion relevant to systematic problems and schools of psychology (in Chapters 1, 2, 7, and 8).

In the periodical literature, the following two issues seem to emerge as rallying points in the modern type of methodological theorizing: (1) objectivity in its broadest sense, the problem of being "exact" — or "scientific" — in psychology, which is at the root of behaviorism and is most recently reflected by the discussion on operationism in psychology, and (2) the problem of keeping on an adequate level of complexity, i.e., sufficiently rich and close to life in context, scope, and content, "molar" rather than "molecular," as represented by the various programmatic trends inherent in Gestalt psychology, psychoanalysis, as well as in a good part of functionalism. Symposia have recently been devoted to each of these two basic issues.

(1) A "Symposium on Operationism" (*Psychol. Review*, 1945, 52, No. 5), with Boring, Bridgman, Feigl (shifting toward the problem of the level and generality of laws, and of explanation), Israel, Pratt and Skinner

as contributors, climaxes a development of interest in "methodological positivism" that found its first comprehensive presentation in American psychological literature in S. S. Stevens's frequently quoted article on "Psychology and the science of science" (*Psychol. Bulletin*, 1939, 36) and has since achieved major proportions. It is closely related to the trends toward methodological integration of the physical with the biological and social sciences in terms of observation as well as of logical formalization advocated directly or indirectly by such contributors to the *Internat. Encyclopedia of Unified Science* (Univ. of Chicago Press, beginning 1938) as Carnap, Morris, Dewey, Russell, Woodger, Reichenbach, Brunswik and Ness. Among the numerous isolated articles on related problems we mention only two of the most outstanding and best known: G. Bergmann and K. W. Spence, "Operationism and theory in psychology" (*Psychol. Review*, 1941, 48), and the latter author's "The nature of theory construction in contemporary psychology" (*Psychol. Review*, 1944, 51).

(2) In a "Symposium on Psychology and Scientific Method" (University of Chicago, 1941; publ. in No. 3 of *Psychol. Review*, 1943, 50), Brunswik, Hull, and Lewin discuss what seems more recently to crystallize as the nucleus of the problem of adequate complexity, namely the formal criteria of behavior, the alternative of classical laws vs. statistical probability laws, and the status of the "intervening variables" as well as of the "field" concept in psychological theorizing. The classical desire to encompass psychological phenomena by one or a few fundamental laws climaxes in H. Woodrow's presidential address, "The problem of general quantitative laws in psychology" (*Psychol. Bulletin*, 1942, 39). The closely related more purely methodological alternative of classical "pure case" experiment vs. a more representative type of experiment in the study of stimulus-response correlations is answered in favor of the latter in E. Brunswik, *Distal Focussing of Perception* (Psychol. Monographs, No. 254, 1944). Indirect support for the probability conception of psychological research may be gained from such authors as the physicist, R. v. Mises, in his *Probabililty, Statistics and Truth* (Macmillan, 1939).

The relationship — methodological or otherwise — of academic psychology as a whole to psychoanalysis is discussed by both sides in a "Symposium on Psychoanalysis as Seen by Analyzed Psychologists" (inaugurated by G. W. Allport, in *Journ. of Abnormal and Social Psychol.*, 1940, 35). Among the eleven participants, Boring, Sachs, Landis, J. F. Brown, Murray, Frenkel-Brunswik, and Alexander (in an afterthought) represent major psychological movements or emphasize the theoretical rather than the biographical, practical, or generally the content aspect of the controversy. See also K. Lewin, "Psychoanalysis and topological psychology" (*Bull. Menninger Clinic*, 1937, 1). The widespread current trend of psychoanalysts toward emphasis on the "ego" with its "reality principle" has first been made an issue in Anna Freud, *The Ego and the Mechanisms of Defense* (London, 1937). Related to this is a stress on the actual cultural and social environment in the formation of character or neurosis by such relatively independent contemporary psychoanalysts as Horney, Fromm, Kardiner. The books of these authors as well as such comprehensive surveys as *Psychoanalysis Today* (ed. by S. Lorand, Int. Univ. Press, 1944) show the increasing convergence of psychoanalysis with the traditionally "situational" (rather than "historical" and "depth"-psychological) emphasis of academic, stimulus-response psychology. That this convergence is also a methodological one is exemplified by the purpose implicit in R. R. Sears, *Survey of Objective Studies of Psychoanal. Concepts* (Soc. Science Research Council Monogr., No. 51, 1943). Another monograph in the same series, G. W. Allport, *The Use of Personal Documents in Psychol. Science* (No. 49, 1942), shows the new methodological awareness for the "idiographic" or "clinical" approach as a whole of which psychoanalysis is but one of several possible manifestations.

6

Remarks on Functionalism
in Perception [1949]

 COMMENT
Thinking about Error and Errors about Thinking
Kenneth R. Hammond

This brief discussion paper was written in the context of what in 1949 and 1950 was a "hot topic," the relation between personality and perception. To oversimplify: Does our personality literally determine what we see? This question became central to many prominent psychologists of the immediate post–World War II period and was given a name, the New Look in perception. It was an exciting time, not only because it appeared that psychology was going to change its theory and research, but also because it appeared that the New Look was going to close the gap between "tough-minded" experimental psychologists and "tender-minded" personality psychologists. Each would gain, it was thought; the experimentalists would show that all their hard, narrow scientific work had broad meaning after all; the personality psychologists would show that their fuzzy concepts could be demonstrated in the lab by the experimentalists and, therefore, were not so fuzzy after all. As Jerome Bruner and David Krech (anchors of the then Harvard-Berkeley axis), who edited the volume in which the papers appeared, put it, "The editors feel that the papers embodied in this volume represent an important step forward in psychology. The approach represented serves to make the clinician aware of the potentialities of the laboratory—not only in its rigor but its flexibility. The experimentalist, for his part, is made to realize anew that his subjects have personalities and aspirations and anxieties, that they live in society and that all these facts influ-

ence in critical ways their behavior" (p. vii; Bruner & Krech, 1949/1950).

Were they right in their enthusiasm and optimism? Opinions will differ. But the New Look had a rather short life, and one can hardly argue in this time of a badly splintered psychology that the gap between experimentalists and personality has disappeared. This outcome might have surprised most of the authors but would hardly have surprised Brunswik, for his was one chapter that bucked the trend that Bruner and Krech so optimistically anticipated.

What was the "trend"? It was a trend toward an emphasis on error in perception, a trend that Brunswik was entirely familiar with because of his European background, which would have made him very familiar with Gestalt psychology and its emphasis on illusion and error. But the theme of Brunswik's theory and research was entirely in the opposite direction, and he delicately made this clear in this chapter. He didn't want to confront his colleagues with the charge that they were on the wrong track, so he broadened the topic for them, and the reader of this volume will benefit.

The reader of this volume may well experience a certain sense of *déjà vu*, however, for the topic of error in judgment has been a highly visible one for the past three decades in the field of judgment and decision making. The approach (known as *heuristic and biases*) taken by Daniel Kahneman and Amos Tversky has been not only

123

to focus on error in human judgment, but also to argue boldly that error is where the focus should be, an argument met with equal boldness by the Brunswikian psychologist Gerd Gigerenzer. The source of error in Kahneman and Tversky's view is not personality, but cognition itself. It might be an overstatement to say that human error has been always been an obsession of psychologists, but it would not be hard to make the case for that view.

There are two reasons for the importance of this piece by Brunswik: One is his treatment of the topic of error; the other is that it offers an early exposition of his concept of ecological validity. With regard to the first, not only are we are treated to his general review of the critical matter of error, but it is here that he introduced his own work on error, in which he demonstrated the differences in the distributions of error in perceptual and analytical cognition. This is a great contribution that has been ignored by cognitive psychologists of all varieties. Researchers have been so eager to demonstrate error in intuitive perception and judgment that they have overlooked altogether errors in analytical cognition. No one has drawn the contrast better than Brunswik: "The 'stupidity' of perception thus is by no means to be construed to mean maladaptiveness; as we all know, life has survived on relative stupidity from time immemorial, and if threatened in its existence it is so by malfunctioning of the intellect rather than by malfunctioning of perception" (1956b, pp. 92–93). Further:

> Considering all the pros and cons of achievement, the balance sheet of perception versus thinking may thus seem seriously upset against thinking, unquestioned favorite of a culture of rational enlightenment as the latter has been. . . . So long as we accept . . . vicariousness as the foremost objective criterion of behavioral purposiveness, perception must appear as the more truly behavior-like function when compared with deductive reasoning with its machine-like, precariously one-tracked, tight-rope modes of procedure.
> The constantly looming catastrophes of the intellect would be found more often to develop into catastrophes of action were it not for the mellowing effect of the darker, more feeling-like and thus more dramatically convincing primordial layers of cognitive adjustment. (1949, p. 93)

This passage, so reminiscent of the battles between the rational and romance philosophers of the eighteenth century, has an important message for judgment and decision researchers of the twenty-first, particularly those who would dare to advise the managers of public affairs, including ministers of defense: Be careful of your enthusiasm for rational analytical procedures and solutions; when correct, they are valuable; when wrong they will be "terribly wrong," a phrase used by Robert McNamara to describe his analytically derived judgments about the conduct of the war in Vietnam.

The Absorption and Distortion of "Ecological Validity"

If the first feature of importance in this article has been largely ignored, the second feature, the introduction of the concept of *ecological validity*, has been grasped all too enthusiastically and, regrettably, distorted altogether. Curiously, this distortion comes about in the attempt to achieve the representative design of experiments advocated by Brunswik (see especially his 1943 paper, Chapter 3, this volume). In what follows, I present only a few central examples of this absorption and distortion organized in terms of usage by well-known psychologists.

In a "Retrospective Review" of the six volumes edited by Sigmund Koch that summed up the progress of psychology (published 1959–1963), Michael Wertheimer (1998) not only reminded psychologists of this monumental work but specifically called attention to "the profound overall conclusion of the entire study, [which] was that psychology must 'work itself free from a dependence on simplistic theories of correct scientific conduct'" (p. 9). That was the essence of Brunswik's conclusion made fifty years earlier; he would urge that "simplistic theories of correct scientific conduct"—in his words, "the systematic design of experiments"—be replaced by the representative design of experiments. But the concept of representativeness was lost when James Jenkins (and others) mistakenly substituted the concept of ecological validity.

James Jenkins

Roughly a decade after the Koch volumes appeared, James Jenkins (1974), then president of the Division of Experimental Psychology, would declare in his presidential address, in front of an audience to whom the message would be anathema, that "it is true . . . that a whole theory of an experiment can be elaborated without contributing in an important way to the science because the situation is artificial and non-representative. . . . In short, contextualism stresses relating one's laboratory problems to the ecologically valid problems of everyday life" (p. 794). Jenkins, an outstanding experimentalist himself, should have received a medal for his courage in telling his audience the last thing they would want to hear, that their "artificial" and "non-representative" laboratory methods were flawed in the most fundamental way. Unsurprisingly, his message fell on deaf ears, as did Koch's. But Jenkins would not be the last to confuse the concept of ecological validity with the representative design of experiments.

Jonathan Koehler

Some twenty years later, Koehler (1996) asked, "The base rate fallacy; does it exist?" He answered his question by saying that "we have been oversold on the base rate fallacy in probabilistic judgment" (meaning that the experimental results have been overgeneralized). And much like Jenkins two decades earlier, he emphasized the need for a "more ecologically valid" research program as a remedy. In short, Koehler reported as fact exactly what Jenkins and Koch had warned their constituents about, namely, overgeneralization of results from laboratory experiments. Koehler seems to want to be a Brunswikian, for he used a Brunswikian concept—albeit inappropriately—to remedy the situation. He asked for "a more ecologically valid research program" when what he really meant—and wanted—was a more "representative" design of experiments. In short, Koehler wanted to be a Brunswikian but didn't know how to manage it.

He was not alone. His article drew commentaries from forty contributors. The term *ecological validity* was used on forty-six occasions (!) by sixteen of the forty commentators. (Only one usage was correct.) Koehler's article thus demonstrates three circumstances: (1) By 1996, the limitations of traditional laboratory methods had become more visible; (2) there was now a clear demand for a methodology that would allow generalization; and (3) many psychologists were attempting to remedy matters through the absorption and misuse of the concept of *ecological validity*, when they should have been referring to the Brunswikian concept of *representative design*.

Leda Cosmides and John Tooby

A further recent example of the pursuit of generality pursued through representative design that is tied to the corruption of the concept of *ecological validity* can be found in Cosmides and Tooby (1996). These well-known evolutionary psychologists sharply denied the conclusions drawn by Tversky and Kahneman regarding the general incompetence of "people's" judgments under uncertainty; they stated "We show that correct Bayesian reasoning can be elicited in 76% of subjects—indeed 92% in the most ecologically valid condition—simply by expressing the problem in frequentist terms" (p. 1). What Cosmides and Tooby meant by "the most ecologically valid condition" they left unexplained, but their usage is instructive in two ways: First, it shows us that by 1996, two established psychologists would assume that their readers would know what they meant by use of the term *ecologically valid*, and that no further explanation would be necessary. This not only indicates that the corruption of this term was widespread, but also shows their strong desire for generalizability. It shows us that they were justifying their conclusion, which falsifies the one drawn by Tversky and Kahneman, by claiming greater generality. They backed this claim by asserting greater, or better, representation of some larger, or different, set of conditions in their experiment than those used by Tversky and Kaheman, namely, relative frequencies rather than probabilities. But their claim rests upon nothing more than the borrowed—and misused—concept of *ecological validity*. No awareness of the work of Brunswik (or anyone else) on the matter of ecological validity or generalization is indicated.

Tooby and Cosmides's justification of their claim for overthrowing results obtained by Tversky and Kahneman lies in their asserting greater ecological validity (undefined) for their conditions. But Dawes (1996, p. 20) saw it differently. He objected to Koehler's request for a "more ecologically valid research program" of research because we may already have "too much ecological validity"! Thus, we see demands for both more and less ecological validity, although there is no explanation in any case of what exactly it is that is being demanded.

Roger Shepard and James Gibson

Perhaps the most surprising absorption of the concept of ecological validity occurs in the work of Shepard (e.g., 1994). Shepard is renowned for his outstanding, mathematically sophisticated theory of perception and his elegant laboratory experiments. His work may be said to be in direct opposition to that of the ecological approaches taken by Brunswik and Gibson. In 1984, Shepard attempted a rapprochement with what he called Gibson's "ecological optics," however. What is of interest to us is the curious manner in which both Gibson and Shepard absorb the concepts of representativeness and ecological validity; both utterly confused the meaning of these two terms. For example, here is Shepard in 1984 quoting Gibson: "Gibson . . . suggest[ed] that performance in a tachistoscopic experiment . . . is 'a mere laboratory curiosity, *unrepresentative* (italics mine) of day-to-day activity'" (pp. 426–427). Note that when Gibson used the word *unrepresentative*, he was using it as Brunswik would (perhaps a result of having spent a year with Brunswik) to deny the value of the use of tachistoscopic method. His denigration of that method as a "mere laboratory curiosity" is another way of expressing what Jenkins (1974) meant when he said, "It is true . . . that a whole theory of an experiment can be elaborated without contributing in an important way to the science because the situation is artificial and non-representative" (p. 794).

But then Shepard (1984) used the term *ecological validity* (not *representativeness*) to turn the tables on Gibson: He argued that it was precisely that "laboratory curiosity," that "ecologically invalid environment," that was used by "animal behaviorists [to discover] that animals have internalized the invariant period of the earth's rotation" (p. 442) and thereby made an important finding! Shepard thus defended the use of the "ecologically invalid" tachistoscope because it produced a useful result, a discovery not otherwise obtainable.

We cite this episode because it illustrates four points: (1) Even psychologists of the stature of Gibson and Shepard absorbed Brunswikian concepts relating to (2) generalization to explain and (3) disagree about (4) the most fundamental as-

pect of their work. Both men sought generalization; both saw the ultimate value of their work in its generalization; but they disagreed over whether the result is a useless "laboratory curiosity" or a great discovery, and in the context of their discussion, there is no way to resolve the disagreement. How can this be explained to those who must decide on funding psychological research?

Shepard returned to the question of representativeness ten years later in his striking article titled "Perceptual-Cognitive Universals as Reflections of the World" (1994), in which he carried out his theme of discovering invariant relations between the structure of the world and the mind. Again, however, we see his fundamental interest in representing the natural world in his theory, but not in his experiments. The phenomenon of apparent motion had his attention, and he asked "Why, for example, does one experience a single object moving back and forth at all, rather than experience what is actually being physically presented in the laboratory—namely, two visual stimuli going on and off separately?" (p. 4). He answered: "It is simply more *probable* in our world (italics mine) that an enduring object abruptly moved from one position to a nearby position than that one object suddenly ceased to exist and, at exactly the same instant, a separate but similar object just as suddenly materialized in another position" (p. 4). Had Shepard suddenly become a "closet Brunswikian"? Any student of Brunswik will recognize that sentence as one that might have been uttered by Brunswik, for it offers a perfect Brunswikian explanation of apparent movement; it refers to the relative frequency of events in a natural world. For example, here is Brunswik placing the organism in a probabilistic world: "So long as the organism does not develop, or fails in a given context to utilize completely, the powers of a full-fledged physicist observer and analyst, his environment remains for all practical purposes a semierratic medium; it is no more than probabilistically predictable (Brunswik, Chapter 17, this volume).

Textbook Absorptions and Distortions

Nothing defines the absorption of a concept into the mainstream of psychology more clearly than its appearance in a textbook. Textbooks legitimize, for students must rely on textbook definitions for authenticity. They will quote them in their term papers, and even if the textbook definition is wrong, it will die a lingering death. And by 1989, a definition of *ecological validity* had indeed found its way into *Cognition* (Matlin, 1989), a textbook widely used for an introduction to cognitive psychology. In the second edition, she stated "One of the most common complaints in recent years concerns the issue of ecological validity," which she defined in this way: "Ecological validity means that the results obtained in research should also hold true in 'real life'" (p. 8; a fourth edition in 1997 repeats essentially the same definition). Her corruption of this central Brunswikian concept illustrates two points emphasized in this chapter. The first is the widespread concern about generalization of results, and the second is the misguided, unwitting absorption of Brunswikian terms into the mainstream. Thus, when Matlin asserted (without attribution to a source) that "one of the most common complaints in recent years concerns the issue of ecological validity," she supported my

observation above that it is the matter of generalization from the laboratory to circumstances outside the laboratory that is of great concern to psychologists today. And when Matlin went on to define ecological validity as if it were intended to mean that laboratory results "should also hold true in 'real life,'" she wanted it to mean generalization but reduced it to absolute nonsense, for there is no such definable thing as "real life." In fairness to Matlin, as will be shown below, it is the cognitive psychologists in the field of memory who seem to have begun this confusion. Indeed, it is they who are struggling to find which method of research—traditional laboratory style or attention to "real life"—will provide the road to truth.

In short, this little-known article by Brunswik contains material of considerable significance to modern psychology. It provides his view of the nature of error in a far more sophisticated manner than is currently the case, and it introduces the concept of *ecological validity*, currently absorbed in a distorted fashion by prominent psychologists and textbook writers.

 REPRINT

Discussion: Remarks on Functionalism in Perception

Egon Brunswik

The type of functionalist thinking espoused by Bruner and Postman (4) may serve as an occasion for a more general discussion of perceptual functionalism and its relation to formalism.

Veridical vs. Subjectivistic Aspects of Perception

One may readily agree with Bruner and Postman's identification of formalism and Gestalt psychology. Perhaps some of the Gestaltists will not like this, but I cannot help but see the long-range core of Gestalt psychology to be the law of

Reprinted from *Journal of Personality* (1949), 18, 56–65, by permission of Blackwell Publishers.

prägnanz, of which in turn the principle of closure is but a special case. While closure is without doubt all important in creative problem solving, it does by the same token interfere with what Bruner and Postman have aptly designated as the "veridical" aspects of perception. Retouching of form may beautify the world, and it may be helpful in other ways; at the same time it is inaccurate, and it cannot in and by itself reconstruct environmental realities. Tendency toward geometric regularity and good form does not in essence go beyond the tradition of the study of subjectivistic illusion as inaugurated in the Graz school of the 1890's. The dynamic interaction in a closed brain field which is assumed to underlie the tendency toward prägnanz amounts to a kind of self-sufficient encapsulation of the perceptual system. Its inherent formalism[1] constitutes a scientific analogy to philosophical rationalism and apriorism. The Kantian heritage in Gestalt psychology has been acknowledged especially by Metzger, one of the leading orthodox second-generation Gestaltists (19, pp. ix, xvi).

The established concept of functionalism, on the other hand, includes some aspects of perception other than Gestalt which Bruner and Postman seem to be inclined to subsume under formalism. I shall first discuss the veridical functions of perception. They may be stratified into three major subdivisions, in accordance with the depth level of cognitive attainment.[2] Most narrowly confined of the three is classical psychophysics, including peripheral, sensory-neural technology. Since this type of approach concentrates on relations with the "proximal" stimulus impact, it does not reach the biologically most relevant layer of manipulable physical and social objects. It is thus comparatively insignificant from a functionalistic point of view, except indirectly.[3]

Probabilistic Functionalism in the Study of Thing Constancy

Next are the perceptual thing-constancies. On the European continent, this topic was as much a major fashion of the between-the-wars period as, say, conditioning in this country. In the field of color, it was set up in a style all of its own by David Katz, Bühler, Gelb, and others. Thing-constancy research concentrates on measurable correlations between distal stimulus variables and organismic responses. These correlations are eminently relevant to orientation in the environment and thus to adjustment in the most specifically functionalistic, that is, utilitarian sense of the term.

Contrary to a widespread notion, thing-constancy is neither historically nor conceptually a part of Gestalt psychology. Emphasis on "framework" and other formalistic schemes of balance and equilibration, typical of the Gestalt psychological handling of the constancy problem, can be shown to be inadequate in dealing with the distal relationships involved; this also includes the adaptation-level theory of Helson (referred to by Bruner and Postman). Even a thinker as personally close and as sympathetic to the Gestalt

point of view as Fritz Heider has stressed the fact that Gestalt psychology is not properly concerned with "distal" object relationships (13).

A resolution of the inherent difficulties can be effected only by proper recognition of the role of "cues" in perception. Although this is essentially a semantic concept, it has a symmetrical counterpart on the overt behavior side in the concept of "means" as stressed especially in Tolman's purposive behaviorism. In emphasizing the important role played by assemblies of vicarious, mutually interchangeable cues — in independent parallelism to Hull's simultaneously developed emphasis on "habit-family-hierarchies" in overt behavior (15) — the present writer (5)[4] seems to have placed himself not only beyond, but in opposition to established Gestalt doctrine. In reviewing my book, Metzger declared the revival of the emphasis on cues a return to an outmoded atomism, intellectualism, and associationism. Among those more sympathetic, Boring (2) has aptly characterized this revival as a "modern equivalent" of Helmholtz's doctrine of unconscious inference, apparently hinting at the existence of important differences along with the obvious similarities.

In trying to nail down the changes effected between the corresponding stages of what must be considered a spiral-like recurrence of analogous principles on different levels of methodological scrutiny,[5] I should like to refer to a recent paper (9) in which I tried to demonstrate a discrepancy between perception and thinking proper in strictly functional terms. The traditional method of introspection combined with plausibility arguments was replaced by a differential analysis of the statistical distribution of errors. A task in size constancy was presented, in as nearly identical versions as possible, once to direct perceptual observation, once as an arithmetical reasoning problem. Perception proper was in our example characterized by a compact and fairly normal distribution of accuracy, with relatively few perfect answers but also few drastic errors. The explicitly intellectual approach, on the other hand, yielded in our example a considerable proportion of "on-the-dot" correct responses; these were accompanied, however, by isolated bars of very crude errors representing typical confusions with potential alternate tasks, as well as by erratically scattered, sometimes way-off and bizarre mistakes. The latter facts point toward a danger-ous one-track quality which may well turn out to be inherent in much of explicit reasoning. In our example, at least, thinking was found to use one or a few relatively foolproof cues in a crudely machine-like system of switches. The more im-plicit "logic" of perceptual quasi-inference, on the other hand, must here, as in many other instances, be seen as characterized by compro-mises between a large number of rather insuffi-cient yet stereotyped cues. This injects an ele-ment of comparative "stupidity" into perceptual intuition which, from a biological point of view, is made up only in part by the quickness of the responses established in this manner.

The error statistics on which this demonstra-tion of functional difference, and thus of the sepa-rate identity and the comparative autonomy of perception and explicit reasoning, is based is part of a more general policy of objective achieve-ment analysis which has been developed in the study of the thing-constancies. It is by pointing to this behavioristic feature of modern perception research that we can best become aware of the long way we have come from the introspective act-psychology of Brentano and of other early European and American functionalists. In act-psychology the "object" is not defined by measur-able variables in the environment but possesses a rather dubious ontological status in a no man's land essentially derived from introspection. It thus has no adjustment relevance and does not directly contribute to functionalism as we under-stand it today.[6] The same holds for the "pheno-menological" interest which stands at the begin-ning of the study of color constancy. It must be stressed, however, that act-psychology and phe-nomenology are important, and perhaps indis-pensable, preliminaries to molar research of the objective kind.

Again, there is an analogy between my own suggestion to replace Brentano's and James's in-trospectionistic "intentionality" by "intentional attainment" as operationally defined through ex-perimental data in thing-constancy in combina-tion with the mathematical theory of relations, and the redefinitions of such terms as "purpose" or "hypothesis," by Tolman and by Krech, in the framework of operational behaviorism.[7] In conceiving of the interest in higher mental func-tions in general as the product of a "tender" frame of mind, one may perhaps say that act-psychol-ogy has dealt with the tender in a tender way, whereas we methodological positivists try to deal with the tender in a "tough" way. In a nutshell, this combination is perhaps the crux, and at the same time the great challenge, of modern psy-chology in general.

Since the establishment of veridical distal en-vironment relations is contingent upon the trust-worthiness, or statistical validity, of cue-to-object relationships, and since this "ecological" validity is in turn essentially limited by the erratic nature of the environment, attainment of distal variables can never be better than probable. Environment-oriented objective functionalism thus is necessar-ily "probabilistic functionalism" (5, 7, 8, pp. 47 ff., 54). The limited validity of perceptual cues must also be considered the basic reason for the principle of perceptual compromise, known since the days of Hering, and more recently quantified by such devices as the constancy ratio (5). If single cues lack in trustworthiness, there must be com-promise between many of them to assure as high object-attainment as possible.

The fact that new cues can be incorporated into the perceptual system in an almost condition-ing-like manner has been demonstrated by Fieandt (11), while successful learning of probabilistic cues was demonstrated by myself and by others (6, 18). All such acquisition involves contiguity association. While Köhler, and now again Wal-lach in his symposium paper (23), stressed the importance of memory traces within a Gestalt psychology which is in other respects not always favorable to recognition of past experience, we must note that the further argument in Wallach's paper involves primarily the principle of similarity rather than its historical rival, contiguity. Ehren-fels's famous criterion of transposition, later es-poused in Köhler's theory of physical Gestalten, stresses the generality of form-perception and is thus likewise based on the similarity principle, which in turn is one of the oldest and most con-cise expressions of internalistic formalism in psy-chology. Study of the thing-constancies, on the other hand, has led, in the manner pointed out above, to recognition of specific and docile com-merce with the environment through sensory cues, much in the tradition of English empiricism and associationism, both preparatory movements to functionalism in the utilitarian sense.

Social Perception and Representative Experimental Design

Broadest and most inclusive of the veridical perceptions is given by social perception. As understood here, this term does not refer to the influence of social factors on perception at large, but rather to the attainment of what may be called covert-distal traits of personality and intelligence in other people by way of, say, intuitive snap judgements. Whereas classical psychophysics and the overt-distal multidimensional psychophysics of the thing-constancies have gradually emerged in European academic tradition, the study of social perceptual achievement has been pioneered chiefly by personnel experts in the framework of American applied psychology, after the first war, and generally is in the direct tradition of the objectively and practically oriented wing of American functionalism.

The fact that social perceptual attainment is notoriously meager must not detract from its inherent intent. On the contrary, it may help in stressing the probabilistic, rather than strictly "nomothetic," character of studies dealing with complex textures of interwoven factors in the physical or social environment. By the same token, the study of social perception brings home in a most natural way the necessity of representative design of experiments as the methodological counterpart of probabilistic functionalism (8).

Perception, Motivation, Personality

Let me now turn to the type of functionalism on which Bruner and Postman have concentrated in their paper. It is not utilitarian in the same cognitive sense of the word as are the two branches of distal veridical functionalism just discussed. In stressing the contribution of the organism, more than that of the stimulus configuration, to perception, it shares in the emphasis on non-veridical illusions so characteristic of Gestalt psychology. Since, however, the sources of illusion are now some motivational forces rather than the comparatively trivial disturbances issuing from the stimulus configuration, the types of distortion involved may well be part of an adjustment mechanism of still broader scope than those studied in the

psychology of distally veridical perception. In some related cases, such as in the autokinetic phenomenon and perhaps in extreme cases of autism, the perceptions involved are almost without an external stimulus, and there is resemblance to the Gestalt studies of prägnanz under reduced stimulation.

Error, maladaptive as it is in a narrowly cognitive sense, is seen in its productive aspects in both motivational functionalism and in some applications of Gestalt thinking. But whereas the Gestalt point of view remains broadly cognitive in that it stresses "good" error in the course of coolly inventive creativity—by no means free of motivational strain to be sure—recent motivational functionalists seem to be more inclined to emphasize what may be called the "beneficial" role of distortive mechanisms in over-all clinical personality adjustment.

It may be well to note that the crucial step in studying the role of motivation is not the abstract recognition of its importance but the more purely methodological fact that motivation is made actually to vary in the experimental design rather than just being controlled as a constant. Watson knew that no rat would run a maze unless hungry or otherwise motivated; but it was the actual variation of degree of hunger as in the work of Tolman which opened up the study of motivation in behavior. Quite in analogy, the studies on the perception of number with Austrian stamps and Turkish coins (reported in my *Wahrnehmung und Gegenstandswelt* in 1934[8]), and the improved development of these experiments, with American and Canadian stamps, by Ansbacher (1), fall just short of a full-fledged consideration of motivational factors of perception. They stop with the attempt to establish the influence of "learned" values upon perception, with an eye primarily on familiarity. It is only by Bruner and Goodman (3) that varying strengths of motivation toward these values are introduced. While thus our group has established values, they have established the *need* of these values, as a factor in perception. True, that attitude has been varied and found to be influential in our experiments as it had been for some time in the study of thing-constancy proper; but aside from the fact that mere verbal instructions are weak substitutes for a kind of motivation built as much into the person as is Bruner and Goodman's rich-vs.-poor variable, our instructions have in most cases endeavored to shift the direction of perceptual intention from one cognitive variable to another rather than to modify the strength of intent toward one and the same variable.

It must be stressed, of course, that not all influence of motivation on cognition leads away from "truth." It value or need serve mainly as an emphasizer, say, in establishing figure-ground organization, the case is merely one of selection. In such cases of an influence of the value, say, of coins on their perception as found in our own studies or in those of Bruner and Goodman, however, there is actual distortion. On second thought, one may wonder how well the distinction between selection and distortion would stand up under conceptual scrutiny.

In the attempt to amalgamate motivational problems with those of perception it seems possible to go further than is the case in most studies of this kind. As has been pointed out by Else Frenkel-Brunswik (12) one may integrate the two aspects either in a "perception-centered" manner, that is, by adding a motivational factor, such as a need, fear, or reward as a further variable to the traditional core of perception psychology, or else one may borrow the basic categorial structure from personality dynamics. This latter procedure she calls the "personality-centered" integration of the psychology of motivation with that of perception. In her own case, ambiguity-tolerance is in this manner being derived from emotional ambivalence and the degree of its repression as conceived of in psychoanalysis, whereby her earlier work on mechanisms of self-deception plays the role of an added stimulus. It is easily understood that a development of this kind has little to do with the academic line of tradition leading from Gestalt ambiguity, as inaugurated by Benussi in the framework of the old Graz school, to the recent work on probability learning. In all of this latter development individual differences in rigidity vs. flexibility are consistently ignored, quite in the tradition of what Boring has called the psychology of the "generalized human mind" (even though in some instances the generalized human mind has become a generalized animal mind). Rather than being related in their origin, the two lines of development may join after each of them has established itself independently of the other.

Conclusion

This leaves us with a total of six distinct kinds of perception psychology, not counting the early, purely introspective so-called functionalism of the act-psychologists. Bruner and Postman thus have hit it on the dot in their nightmarish prophecy of a multifarious tower of Babel, and they have been obliged sooner than they may have anticipated. Actually, differences may be less drastic than meet the eye. The two oldest schools of thought, veridical classical psychophysics and non-veridical Gestalt psychology, are the least functionalistic of the six, although the creative aspects of Gestalt processes must definitely be vindicated in this respect. The remaining two veridical aspects of perception, thing-constancy and social perception, being distal in character, are genuinely functionalistic. They represent the sober objectivity of the reality principle, so much in vogue in modern dynamic ego-psychology though perhaps in temporary eclipse on its own side of the fence in this era of all manners of convergence and crosspassing. Furthermore, the probabilistic element inherent in distal perception implies a progressive outlook on research design. Both the distal and the motivational—that is, central—emphasis in perception psychology are new developments. Each in its own coldly cognitive or more hotly soul-searching way is a constructive protest against the sterility of peripheralism, whether that of nineteenth-century structuralism or that of the earlier stages of behaviorism.

NOTES

1. The onesided formalism of Gestalt psychology proper—that is, of the so called Berlin school centering about Wertheinier, Köhler, and Koffka—has also been noted by the leading experimentalist of the rival Leipzig group, Sander, in his far too little known summary of Gestalt research before the German Psychological Association in 1927. According to Sander, the "geometric-ornamental" tendencies on which the Berlin group concentrates represent but a relatively primitive phase of development, especially also in the "actualgenetic" emergence of single perceptual responses (20, pp. 65 ff.).

2. Concerning the concept of perceptual attainment, see 5. For a more recent exposition of the various peripheral-proximal and distal strata and the mecha-

nisms involved in the attainment of the latter, for a schematic outline of the corresponding historical sequence of structuralism (classical psychophysics), Gestalt psychology, and objective (probabilistic) functionalism as discussed in this paper, and for the reverberations of this shift upon experimental design, see 8, especially the summary presented in Fig. 7 (pp. 28.ff.), and Fig. 10; see also 10.

3. This should not detract from the fact that, as is being pointed out in this symposium by Klein and Schlesinger (16), threshold tests and related devices of classical psychophysics may have important diagnostic value in the framework of a differential—rather than more strictly functional—psychology (for this latter distinction, see 8).

4. For the relation to Hull just mentioned see (8), p. 48; for an illustration of the vicarious functioning of distance criteria in perception as demonstrated by Holaday, see p. 23.

5. For further elaboration, see 10.

6. It is for these all-important differences between the "subjectivistic" and the "objectivistic" approach that the "probabilistic functionalism" suggested by the present writer (see below) is not to be put in one class with act-psychology, as a prominent author seems to have recently implied (14, p. 261). Aside from similarity—in form, though not in content—to Tolman's, Lashley's, and Hull's brands of behaviorism (the last named in its more distinctly molar pre-axiomatic phase) as in part pointed out below, there is an affinity to Woodworth's more purely programmatic dynamic psychology, whereas the relationship to the introspectionistic phases of functionalism is no more than historical. See further 10.

7. See 5, 21, 17. For a mutual acknowledgment of the symmetrical relationship of thing constancy research and molar behaviorism, see 22; see also 10.

8. On pp. 140–150 of this book (5) there is a relatively detailed account of the otherwise unpublished work of I. Zuk-Kardos with stamps and of A. Fazil with coins.

REFERENCES

1. Ansbacher, H. Perception of number as affected by the monetary value of the objects. *Arch. Psychol.*, 1937, No. 215.

2. Boring, E. G. *Sensation and perception in the history of experimental psychology.* New York: Appleton-Century, 1942.

3. Bruner, J. S., and Goodman, C. C. Value and need as organizing factors in perception. *J. abnorm. soc. Psychol.*, 1947, 42, 33–44. (Also published in: T. M. Newcomb and E. L. Hartley (eds.). *Readings in social psychology.* New York: Holt. 1947.)

4. Bruner, J. S., and Postman, L. Perception, cognition and behavior. *J. Personal.*, 1949, 18, 14–31.

5. Brunswik, E. *Wahrnehmung und Gegenstandswelt.* Vienna: Deuticke, 1934. (For a summary of the theoretical aspects, see the same author's Psychology as a science of objective relations. *Philos. of Science*, 1937, 4, 227–260; errata corr. 1938, 5. 110.)

6. Brunswik, E. Das Induktionsprinzip in der Wahrnehmung. In H. Pieron and J. Meyerson (eds.), *lle congrès international de psychologie, 1937.* Paris: Alcan, 1938, 346 ff. (See also the forthcoming article by E. Brunswik and John L. Herma, Probability learning of cues in a perceptual weight illusion.)

7. Brunswik, E. Organismic achievement and environmental probability. (Part of: Brunswik, Hull, Lewin, *Symposium on psychology and scientific method.* University of Chicago, 1941.) *Psychol. Rev.*, 1943, 50, 255–272.

8. Brunswik, E. *Systematic and representative design of psychological experiments.* Univ. California Press, 1947.

9. Brunswik, E. Statistical separation of perception, thinking, and attitudes. (Abstract.) *Amer. Psychologist*, 1948, 3, 342. (A more detailed paper is in preparation.)

10. Brunswik, E. *Methodological foundations of psychology.* (To appear as No. 10 of R. Carnap and C. Morris (eds.), *Internat. encycl. of unified science.*) Univ. of Chicago Press, 1950.

11. Fieandt, K. v. Dressurversuche an der Farben-Wahrnehmung. (No. 7 of: *Untersuchungen über Wahrnehmungsgenenstande*, hersg. van E. Brunswik.) *Archiv für die ges. Psychol.*, 1936, 96, 467–495.

12. Frenkel-Brunswik, E. Intolerance of ambiguity as an emotional and perceptual personality variable. *J. Personal.*, 1949, 18, 108–143.

13. Heider, F. Environmental determinants in psychological theories. *Psychol. Rev.*, 1939, 46, 383–410.

14. Hilgard, E. R. *Theories of learning.* New York: Appleton-Century, 1940.

15. Hull, C. L. The concept of the habit-family-hierarchy and maze learning. *Psychol. Rev.*, 1934, 41, 33–54, 134–154.

16. Klein, G. S., and Schlesinger, H. Where is the perceiver in perceptual theory? *J. Personal.*, 1949, 18, 32–47.

17. Krechevsky, I. Hypotheses in rats. *Psychol. Rev.*, 1932, 39, 516–532.

18. Levin, M. M. Weight illusions induced by cues of low validity. (Abstract.) *Psychol. Bull.*, 1943, 40, 582.

19. Metzger, W. *Gesetze des Sehens*. Frankfurt: Kramer, 1936.

20. Sander, F. Experimentelle Ergebnisse der Gestaltphychologie. In E. Becher (ed.), *Bericht über den 10. Kongress für exp. Psychologie, 1927*. Jena: Fischer, 1928, 23–88.

21. Tolman, E. C. *Purposive behavior in animals and men*. New York: Century, 1932.

22. Tolman, E. C., and Brunswik, E. The organism and the causal texture of the environment. *Psychol. Rev.*, 1935, 42, 43–77.

23. Wallach, H. Some considerations concerning the relation between perception and cognition. *J. Personal.*, 1949, 18, 6–13.

Representative Design and Probabilistic Theory in a Functional Psychology [1955]

In Defense of Probabilistic Functionalism: A Reply [1955]

COMMENT
Explaining to the Nobility
Kenneth R. Hammond

In July 1955, a strange event at the University of California at Berkeley marked the further development of the Brunswik story. A panel of scholars was assembled to criticize the work of one of their contemporaries, and a large audience assembled to hear them do it. At this conference of the Unity of Science Institute, Brunswik would put forward a summary of his views, a panel of his peers (the psychologists Ernest Hilgard, David Krech, and Leon Postman and the philosopher Herbert Feigl) would criticize them, and then he would offer a rebuttal. That was not the only event at this meeting, but it was a major event among this group of philosophers of science.

Members of the audience found Brunswik holding forth on "Representative Design and Probabilistic Theory in a Functional Psychology," in which he explained virtually all of his main ideas. The panel then criticized his presentation, and Brunswik replied to them ("In Defense of Probabilistic Functionalism: A Reply"). These papers, then, are essential reading for students of Brunswikian psychology. For by 1955, Brunswik's theoretical argument had become rounded out, his methodological critique sharpened, and its place in the history of psychology defined. These papers allow us to see how it all stands up to criticism by his peers.

There are two points that appear in his presentation to which the reader should be alerted. Both concern the matter of generalization of results, a topic that still defies solution by conventional methods of experimental design. First, Brunswik tackled the problem of generalization from the orthogonal designs on which rest the bulk of the publications of academic, scientific psychologists. He showed that the very efforts to make the conclusions from the experiment firm are those that defeat the possibility of generalization beyond the laboratory conditions that produced them. His use of the example of the "bird flying over the green field" is particularly helpful. Second, he showed that he did not intend "representative design" to be restricted to a demand for representation of the "real world" (a meaningless concept) but intended it to refer to the extent to which the statistical properties of the laboratory task represent the statistical properties of the situation to which the results are to be generalized. In short, the same logic that is used to justify generalization over a subject population should be used to justify generalization over the task situation. (See Juslin, Chapter 36, this volume, for a compelling example of the consequences of the failure to do this.)

This paper, and its defense, is so comprehensive and yet so detailed that, although it does not appear at the beginning of the collection, it might well be read first. All the major ideas are here,

put forward for an audience for which Brunswik had the greatest admiration.

 REPRINT

Representative Design and Probabilistic Theory in a Functional Psychology

Egon Brunswik

The movement in psychology most directly concerned with the challenge of unification with the exact sciences is behaviorism. At the present time, two major factions are discerned within behaviorism. One, represented chiefly by Hull (26), tries to elaborate classical behaviorism into a tightly woven, formalized system of strict laws about intraorganismic processes in the nomothetic tradition of physics. The other, inaugurated chiefly by Tolman and his program of molar or "purposive" behaviorism (47), attempts to deal with behavior "relative to some end" and thus to restructure behaviorism in the tradition of the utilitarianism of Darwin and of early American functionalism.

It may be argued that nomothetic behaviorism overexpands physicalism beyond the necessary observational and procedural core and includes unessential borrowings from the specific thema of physics. A functionally oriented objective psychology, on the other hand, dealing as it does with organism-environment relationships at the more complex level of adjustment, may be seen as falling in line with a more searching interpretation of the historical mission of psychology. The present paper concentrates on summarizing and expanding earlier contentions (2, 7, 8, 48) to the effect that the environment to which the organism must adjust presents itself as semierratic and that therefore all functional psychology is inherently probabilistic, demands a "representative" research design of its own, and leads to a special

type of high-complexity, descriptive theory.[1] This program provides not only the necessary thematic diversification from the classical natural sciences but also leads to the long overdue internal unification of psychology.

We will develop our arguments first with the use of an example involving behavior as a "constant function" of a characteristic end state, and then in reference to the functionalism of the perceptual constancies where progress along methodological lines is somewhat further advanced.

Systematic Designs and the Study of Distal Achievement

Behavior as Constant Function

One of the earlier functional behaviorists, Holt, suggested that the movements of an individual be defined in terms of "that object, situation, process . . . of which his behavior is a constant function. . . . So in behavior, the flock of birds is not with any accuracy, flying over the green field; it is, more essentially, flying southward" (24, pp. 161–166). This statement, rather paradigmatic of functionalist modes of thought, involves selective description. The preferred hypothesis contains reference to a remote end (south); or, in the words of Heider (21), it sets "distal determination" over "proximal determination," that is, in our case, over description on terms of momentary position (green field).

In defending his seemingly teleological attitude Holt points to the emphasis some positivist

Symposium on the Probability Approach in Psychology
Reprinted from *Psychological Review* (1955), 62, 193–217.

physicists—we may think primarily of Mach—place on the relatively descriptive study of "functional relationships"; these may connect events over space or time regardless of the traditional tracing of causal chains in near-action.

Tied Variables: Functionally Irrelevant Generalizations

Holt's problem of constant function involves generalization. One of the most time-honored traditions in experimentally testing generalizability demands that one, or perhaps a few, conditions be varied in a planful manner decided upon by the experimenter while all others are held constant. The purpose is to assure isolation of the so-called independent variable. For their arbitrary orderliness and confinement such designs may be called "systematic."

For example, we may move the birds backward along the line of their flight, say, to position I in Fig. 7.1. The birds may persist in their original direction and in this sense show generality of behavior. But it is easily seen that this experiment is irrelevant to Holt's chosen alternative. The two directions, "southward" (solid arrow) and "over the green field" (broken arrow) coincide; allowing for all possible types of response, the two variables involved—south vs. non-south, and green-field vs. non-green-field—are perfectly correlated and thus inseparable so far as the available evidence is concerned. This constitutes artificially induced perfect confounding, and may be labeled "tied-variables" design or, in short, tied design.

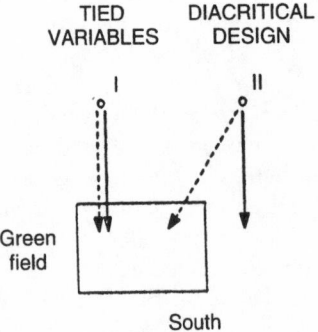

FIGURE 7.1 Systematic designs in the study of behavior constancy (applied to an example from Holt 24).

Responder replication, that is, repetition with new individuals or with the original individuals at other occasions, is likewise irrelevant to Holt's alternative, regardless of the interindividual or intraindividual consistencies that may be observed. This must be pointed out in view of a rather deeply ingrained trend in psychology of throwing the entire problem of generalization and of statistical significance onto the responder rather than onto the situation (7, pp. 36 ff.; further drastic evidence to this effect, unearthed by Hammond [18, 19], will be referred to in the section on clinical application).

Diacritical Confrontation: Splitting of Tied Clusters vs. Isolation of Variables

The real testing of Holt's preferred south hypothesis does not even begin until adherence of behavior to the southward direction is made situationally incompatible with adherence to the green field. This could be achieved, say, by moving the birds sideways to position II in Fig. 7.1. The two arrows issuing from the new starting point are now divergent rather than parallel. The responder is placed at the crossroads and forced to take sides. The previously tied situational factors are now "confronted" (2); we may speak of this variant of systematic design as "diacritical" design.

We soon discover that southwardness is still tied to such factors as the general areas of start, temperature and other climatic conditions, topographical landmarks, magnetic cues, and so forth; and so is the greenness of the field to its squareness or size. What we have accomplished in diacritical design is to separate or "split" one original encompassing cluster into two subclusters of tied variables; but we have not really "isolated" our variable as it may have seemed at first glance, and therefore are not yet entitled to speak of its attainment as a constant function.

Perception as Constant Function

A concrete perceptual problem comparable to Holt's problem of the constancy of southward flight is that of size constancy. The alternative here is between invariance of the response relative to the measured (or computed) sizes of the stimulus impact at the retina (or at a parallel photographic screen) as the proximal variable, which we will call P, and invariance relative to the measured sizes of physical bodies underlying this impact as the distal variable, B. Size constancy involves the predominant focusing of the response on B.

Classical Psychophysics as Pseudounivariate Design

With distances variant as they are in daily life, there is a certain degree of statistical independence between B and P despite the existing causal nexus between them. During the classical phase of psychophysics, however—still strongly in evidence today—the implicit design policy was artificially to tie the distal and proximal variables. For size this is achieved by holding the distance from the observer constant. A good example is the Galton bar. The task is molded closely after ordinary physical length measurement except that the lines are laid up length-wise rather than being superimposed. This creates a tied-variables design which is comparable to case I in Fig. 7.1. Note that the tying of the two variables is the direct result of a celebrated device of systematic design, the holding constant of a third variable (in our case, distance).

This design may also be cast into the form of a table of presence, or scattergram. Figure 7.2 presents the major systematic designs in their minimal form, assuming only two levels of strength for each of the situational variables. In the case of the classical tied-variable design the two variables are perfectly correlated. All entries lie along a diagonal. Photographic size (assumed to be plotted vertically as in Fig. 7.3) is always large when bodily size (plotted horizontally) is large, and vice versa. And judgments correct (or incorrect) concerning one of these variables are automatically correct (or incorrect) concerning the other, just as Holt's birds, by flying south from position I, automatically must fly over the green field. The classical design therefore precludes decision as to whether the response focuses on proximal (photographic) or distal (bodily) size; nor

does it allow the conclusion that the response focuses on either, for that matter.

In the classical phase, the tying of variables was done inadvertently and in considerable naiveté as to the interpretational consequences involved. Since only the bar was directly manipulated and only one scale was read in doing so, the impression prevailed that there was only one independent variable. The notion of univariate design was somewhat obliquely reinforced by the tendency to confine the concept of stimulus to the proximal stimulus variable that had been arranged to vary in unison with the bar. The possibility of varying degrees of dependent variability within the design itself was thus ignored and no provision was made to state the relationships explicitly, so much so that the term "dependent variable" could become synonymous with the organism's eventual responses. Since classical design purports to be univariate yet fails to isolate the distal from the proximal variable, it may be called "pseudounivariate" design, and in our particular example may be specified as proximo-distally neutral design.

Thing Constancy Research as a Form of Multidimensional Psychophysics: Factorial Design

The diacritical confrontation of distal and proximal size is achieved by removing one side of the bar to a different distance from the observer, say, a smaller one. This has an effect on design analogous to the moving of the birds from position I to position II in Fig. 7.1. It is now incompatible for the two lengths to be equal bodily and photographically at the same time. The new combination of a relatively small bodily size with a relatively large photographic size injected into the design is plotted in the upper left corner of the center chart in Fig. 7.2. The forking or parting of the ways which is characteristic of diacritical confrontation may be visualized by assuming the near object to be the Standard and the far one

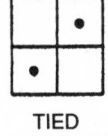

TIED VARIABLES

DIACRITICAL DESIGN

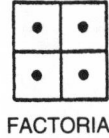

FACTORIAL DESIGN

FIGURE 7.2 Minimal scattergrams of systematic designs. Repeatable in k dimensions.

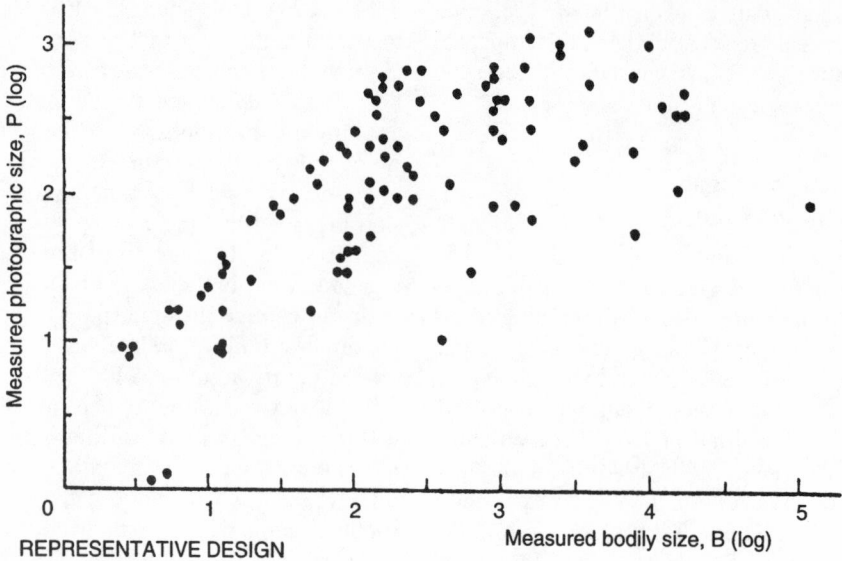

FIGURE 7.3 Scattergram of an example of representative design used in the study
of size constancy (adapted from Brunswik, 6, 7). Analogously in *x* dimensions.

the Comparison, the latter being left to vary along
the diagonal.

By projecting the Standard two ways, along
a horizontal and along a vertical line, to their
respective intersections with the diagonal representing the Comparison series, we obtain two
points of objective equality (or POE, formed in
analogy to Woodworth's PSE for point of subjective equality [see 7, 53]). One represents the variable *P* and the other *B* in the experiment. By
contrast, in a classical experiment the Standard
coincides with a point on the diagonal and thus
the two POE's merge in one point, further supporting the erroneous impression of univariate
design of which we have spoken above.

The relative allegiance of the response to *B* or
P, or the degree of perceptual "compromise,"
may be ascertained by inserting added values between (or beyond) the two ideal "poles of intention" (2) along the diagonal (7, p. 17, Fig. 7.4).
The constancy ratio (called Brunswik-ratio by
Woodworth) is a simple device to project the obtained PSE's onto the span between the two pole
POE's.

Note that the Comparison in psychophysical
experiments has often been called *the* "Variable,"
so that not only classical psychophysics but even
our present diacritical experiment may give the

superficial impression of unidimensionality, in
spite of the fact that the presence of two POE's
clearly marks it as a case of multidimensional psychophysics. In this sense we may say that while
classical design is pseudo-unidimensional, diacritical design is crypto-multidimensional.

By adding a fourth point, diacritical design
becomes the well-known factorial design (14),
also shown in Fig. 7.2. In essence, this is no
more than adding a mirror image to diacritical
design, with added advantages accruing by virtue
of the increased symmetry. Some of the Vienna
constancy experiments have employed such a
double diacritical design (2, pp. 167 ff.) but they
will not be discussed here.

Variate Packages and the Indefinite Regress of Systematic Design

Diacritical confrontation or factorial design may
be carried to several dimensions. Their number
is, or at least should be, known to the experimenter; it may be designated by *k*.

In analogy to what we have said about Holt's
example of bird migration, all results remain contingent upon the ties existing within the more or
less incidental situational instance from which
systematic variation has taken its start. If we use

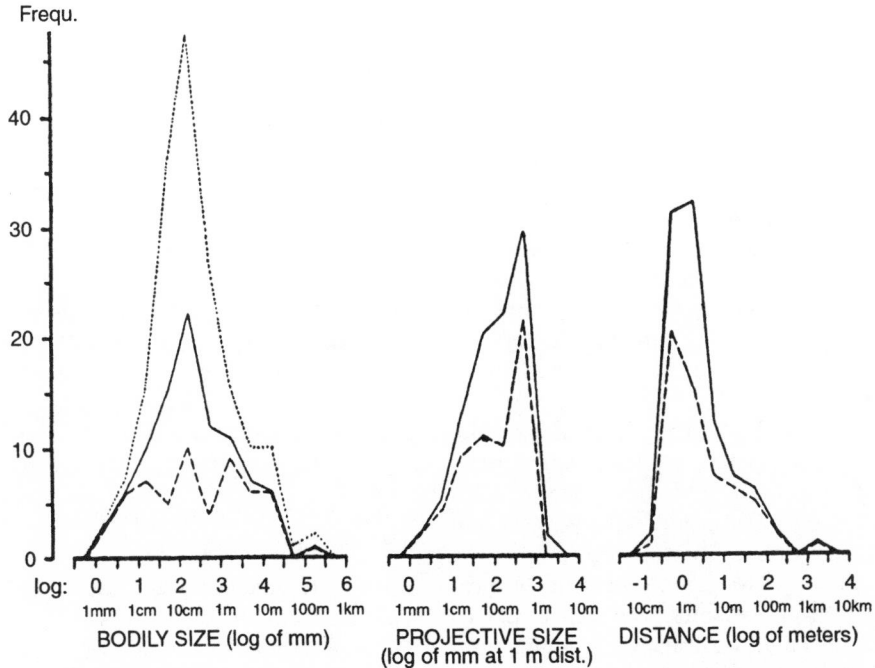

FIGURE 7.4 Frequency distributions of three ecological variables for the representative design shown in Fig. 7.3 (solid curves; the dotted curve includes tilted objects and the broken curves refer to a subsample of vertical objects, both not discussed here). (From Brunswik, 1944)

the term "variate" for the specific values along the various variable dimensions, each concrete situation may be regarded as a "variate package." Originally, each of the particulars or variates in the package has equal claim for being singled out in the description, and one or a few factorial separations remove but little of this indeterminacy. Complete "systematic" isolation of one variable as the crucial factor would involve diacritical confrontation with a very large, and in fact indefinite, number of originally tied situational variables.

Representative Design in the Study of Distal Achievement

From a purely formal point of view the systematic confrontations would have to include the indirect cues for size and distance on which the mechanism of constancy must depend. But it is evident that setting the distal variable against its own instrumentalities would cut out the ground from under the very function whose constancy is to be put to test. Tolman (47) has stressed that all behavior requires the presence of means or "behavior supports." He has also pointed out that the only admissible operational criterion for the testing of "purpose" is the observation of the actual reaching of the end, at least in part of the behavior instances in the class under consideration. But reaching the south or any other distal goal, be it behavioral or perceptual, can obviously become a more or less stabilized function only if the flight of the birds is allowed to take adequate advantage of the natural resources of orientation and locomotion, much as such man-made stabilizers as gun sights must be tested under conditions of practical use.

Ecology and Situational Instance

Constant psychological function thus is intrinsically limited, or probabilistic, rather than "universal." Flying southward, being right about object sizes, or any other gross or "molar" behavioral or perceptual function can never attain the status of an ironclad and universally applicable so-called "strict" law in the sense in which these laws were idolized in the classical phase of the natural sciences. The basic aim of our initial quotation from Holt requires delimitation of a more specified universe within which the animal is set to operate. This is in line with the "syntactic requiredness" (22) to define all probability in terms of a corresponding reference class or universe. In line with biological usage we will call this universe "ecology." An ecology is defined as the natural-cultural habitat of an individual or group, but is otherwise free of contamination by the system of specific responses. Rather, the ecology is the objective, external potential offered to the organism for survival and its subordinate needs. Nourishment value of foods, as it exists prior to and regardless of its recognition or consumption by the responder, is an example of an ecological variable or set of variables; object size and its system of cues enters via its relevance for manipulation or orientation.

Since the responder merely acts like a catalyst in the definition of the ecology, the ecological environment is not to be confused with Lewin's psychological environment or "life space" which is defined as the reflection of a situation within the response system (see 5).

Situational instances in an ecology are analogous to individuals in a population of responders. Both may be considered as sets of more or less incidental variate packages. The difference is that instances can be taken apart and created at the spur of the moment while individuals usually cannot. But, as we have come to see, a program of functional research demands that they too be left as they come. We must resist the temptation of the systematic experimentalist to interfere, and must introduce a laissez-faire policy for the ecology.

Representative Sampling of Situations

As we cannot possibly hope to encompass the entire population of individuals in research, but must sample representatively, we must sample instances in the study of functional achievement. Taking the cue from differential psychology, we may transfer the entire formal statistical instrumentarium developed in the study of personality to functional problems as a new content. This will

assure, to any desired degree of approximation, a balanced view of psychological function as it comes about by a synopsis of performance under comfortable conditions, manageable vicissitudes, and a due proportion of risks or well-nigh insurmountable odds.

In terms of experimental design there results a combination of constraint and license in which the experimenter is in no more than supervisory control over the adequacy of sampling. There will be a limited range and a characteristic distribution of conditions and condition combinations. If in this manner psychological experiments take on the character of statistical surveys, we may speak of "representative design" (7).

A Representative Design in Perceptual Size Constancy

Since in representative design the accent is on sampling from an ecology and on the generalizability of functional constancies to this ecology, rather than on sampling and generalizability in reference to a responder population, it was deemed advantageous for demonstration purposes to confine a pilot survey of perceptual size constancy to a single subject. Using n for the number of responders and N for the size of the situation sample we thus had $n = 1$ subject, a graduate student in psychology; there were $N = 93$ object situations (6; 7, pp. 41 ff.). The objects were sampled, in a reasonably random manner, from the sizes that became "figure" to the subject in her daily routine, in package with their natural setting and accompaniment of depth cues.

Ecological Validity and Dependent Variability within the Design: Textural Ecology

As in all representative design, the design in itself has the character of a result, even though this result concerns the ecology only and is no more than the precondition of psychological investigation proper. The design obtained for our size constancy survey is shown in Fig. 7.3. The two major distal and proximal stimulus variables are plotted logarithmically, B in terms of millimeters, and P in terms of millimeters at an assumed projection distance of 1 meter.

The manner of covariation, defining what we have called dependent variability within the design, may in first approximation be expressed by a correlation coefficient. In our case the Pearson r between the logarithms of B and P is .70. This coefficient estimates the cue potential of the proximal variable P relative to the distal variable B in the given ecology, in analogy to the way the validity of a test relative to a personality trait may be ascertained for a population of responders. A correlation between ecological variables, one of which is capable of standing in this manner as a probability cue for the other, may thus be labeled "ecological validity." The study of ecological validities, being bivariate correlational, defines what we may call a structural or textural ecology, in contradistinction to the emphasis on unidimensional distribution (of temperature, precipitation, size of population centers, etc.) which is more typical of biological and a part of cultural ecology.

Our particular coefficient indicates that large retinal impacts are somewhat more likely to be caused by relatively large objects, regardless of distance. Considerable as this relationship may seem, it is, as we shall see in a moment, trifling in comparison with the final achievement of the constancy mechanism. This gain becomes possible only by an additional utilization of distance cues. For some of the less valid of the commonly listed perceptual depth criteria, such as vertical position, subdivision of space, and brightness, Seidner has found moderate ecological validities ranging to about .4 (report on preliminary data in 7, pp. 47 ff.). It is easily seen that not even the so-called primary depth cues, such as binocular disparity, are foolproof in our ecology. For example, binocular disparity is present in the stereoscope, yet depth is absent in the underlying reality; in viewing reality through a camera, on the other hand, binocular disparity is absent while depth is present in the chain of causal ancestry.

In our present example the analysis was not carried to an explicit treatment of depth criteria and other context factors. With the use of photographs, such as those Seidner had available for his analysis of depth cues, a great variety of them could be analyzed in a single enterprise. In fact, Fig. 3 must be seen as combining but two out of a practically unknown number, x, variables. Since covariation must be allowed to take its natural course, the different juxtapositions would of course not look exactly alike, as they do in factorial design, but would merely be analogous, forming in the end an x-dimensional space in which all factors could be considered simultaneously.

Quite aside from the avoidance of the pitfalls of systematic design—in which all factors held constant are lost for the investigation, and the resultant tied-variable clusters only lead to confusion—representative design, while cumbersome and laborious, is thus potentially a very economical technique.

> Projections of the frequencies in Fig. 7.3 upon the main axes are shown in Fig. 7.4. Our sample, restricted to sizes not tilted into the third dimension and thus by-passing the problem of shape constancy, is represented by the solid curves. It is reassuring to find the distribution for B fairly normal. (The third graph shows the distribution for distance as related to a dependent distance axis that may be imagined to run across the upper right-hand part of Fig. 7.3 under 45°, forming a triangle with the main axes; the crowding of both small and intermediate objects along the 10-inch limit of near vision leads to skewed distribution and is the chief source of the curvilinearity that may be observed in Fig. 7.3.)

Functional Validity (Achievement)

We now turn to covariation between the distal stimulus and the response variable which will define perception in its approximation to "constant function" as understood by Holt. Figure 7.5, left, shows the stimulus-response scattergram for the logarithms of the perceptual estimates, b (so labeled because they were given in the natural, naive-realistic attitude toward bodily size, B) as plotted against the logarithms of B. The entries cling fairly close to the diagonal, much more closely than the major cue variable, P, was found to cling to B in Fig. 7.3. Appraising the maximum errors committed in the particular estimates, however, we find that some entries deviate as much as one-half of a power of 10 from the diagonal, corresponding to about three- to four-fold over- or underestimation of the length in question.

A generic summary description of the degree of perfection of size constancy may again be sought in the correlation coefficient. This represents what may be called the "functional validity" (7) or "achievement" (*Leistung, 2; for definition see 5, p. 255*) of the class of responses, b, relative to the distal stimulus variable, B. For the total

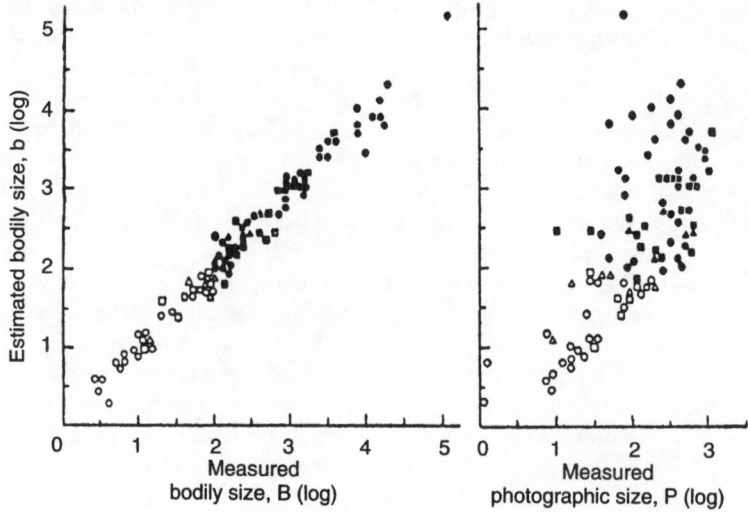

FIGURE 7.5 Scattergrams of perceptual achievement (functional validity) for a subject responding to the representative design shown in Fig. 7.3. (Open symbols are used here to designate objects smaller than 10 cm., see below; the differences in shape are irrelevant in the present context.) (Adapted from Brunswik, 1944, 1947.)

sample of 93 situations this correlation is close to .99 (more accurately, .987 when computed from ungrouped logarithms with three significant places [see 7, p. 44]), in spite of the occasional sizable errors referred to above.

By contrast, the functional validity of b relative to photographic size, P (Fig. 5, right), is only .73; in addition, this is quite close to the purely ecological association of B and P, .70, so that little independent focusing of b on P is indicated. Perceptual restructuring toward photographic size (painter's attitude, p) raises the correlation of the response with P no more than to .85. Other attitudes, deliberately inviting intellectually controlled judgment ("betting") and thus the "stimulus error," will not be discussed here, nor shall we go into the question as to whether or not the estimates b and p are purely perceptual.

Ecological Replication and Ecological Significance of Differences

The analogy to the statistics of individual differences may be carried still further. We may consider each new chance selection of items like those in Fig. 7.3 as an "ecological replication" of

the original sample. In representative design the traditional quest for repetition under "identical" external conditions ceases to be legitimate. Instead, we must seek comparable conditions as drawn from a common universe, just as in differential psychology there is no repetition in the strict sense when other or even the same individuals are used.

Problems of the ecological significance of differences in the statistical sense may be raised, and handled, accordingly. The size of the sample to be used in computation is now given by the number of situations, N, rather than by the number of subjects, n. In this sense the ecological generalizability of distal rather than proximal focusing, in the area of size constancy with distance variant, has been established for our one subject; and even the more crucial in a wide array of relatively moderate ecological validity coefficients of depth cues, referred to above from the material of Seidner, have been found significantly above zero.

In the strict, technical sense, our representative survey of size constancy is completely void of interindividual generalizability. An approach to responder generality was made by using the recorder as a second subject; his distal functional validity was .993, quite close to the .987 for our subject. Furthermore, Dukes (12) has independently obtained a correlation of .991 for a six-year-old boy, using a different sample (N = 67) and a somewhat different technique.

It may well be that in many contexts individuals in a population are more homogeneous or stereotyped than are situations in an ecology, and that the ascertainment of ecological generality may be a more challenging task than that of responder-populational generality. Harvey needed only one person to demonstrate the circulation of the blood, and Ebbinghaus needed only himself as a subject to lay the foundation for much of modern learning theory, ecologically narrow as this theory may be.

To complete our analogies between responder-populational and ecological generalization problems, we may set physical size measurement and intuitive or critical estimates of size in analogy to a battery of tests given, not to n persons, but to N situations of the environment. Each type of observation or attitude represents one of these tests. The problem of the degree of "objectivity" of various classes of observation, and thus of certain scientific approaches, can then be handled statistically in terms of their inter- or intraindividual "observational reliability" as tests, in which a sample of situations has taken the place of a sample of persons (see 7, p. 33 and 8, pp. 11 f.).

Representative Separation and Mathematical Isolation of Variables

It will be remembered that under systematic design a true isolation of variables can be achieved only by a virtually infinite series of diacritical confrontations or factorial designs piled upon one another. Representative design, while not laying claim to full isolation, separates variables to the extent to which they are separated in the particular ecology but no further, and does not tolerate any artificial perfect tyings (or untyings) between variables. Variables may thus be said to be "representatively separated." From a systematic point of view, a good deal of spuriousness remains built into the textures studied under this policy, samples as these textures

are of an ecology that likewise is complexly textured. Representative design is not afraid of this spuriousness; in fact, it welcomes it for the sake of the behavior supports it allows in the execution of the functional approach.

The challenge of further isolation must be met by after-the-fact, mathematical means, as in the study of individual differences. For example, we may use partial correlation as a mathematical means of holding constant a certain variable. Partialing out P from our above correlation between b and B (and thus in effect reducing the ecological validity of P from .70 to 0) still yields a functional validity as high as .98; whereas factually eliminating the sizes under 10 cm. in Fig. 7.3—to the right of log $B = 2$—and thus reducing the ecological validity of P from .70 to .14 in a quasi-systematic move, reduces the functional validity to .95 (see also 7, Fig. 7.9 and the accompanying text).

It must also be noted that, in contradistinction to systematic design, the process of analysis may be stopped at any point, falling back on the nonreductive aim of functional research, together with the assurance that the unresolved part of the associations is safely within the fold of the ecology to which the investigation has been geared from the beginning.

Systematic Experiments with Representative Features

We now turn to certain experimental policies, some of them common, which may be considered transitory between systematic and representative design. Representative features may be injected in otherwise systematic designs in a variety of ways.

Quasi-representative Choice of Variables and of Their Variation or Covariation

Some measure of representativeness may be achieved by the choice of variables with particular life relevance, such as "value," as a factor in constant function. Since ecology embraces cultural norms held valid by the law enforcement policies of a society, along with those connected with physical law or geographical contingency, monetary value becomes a challenge to perceptual attainment on a par with other object properties.

Cognitive considerations of this kind, rather than the emotive or motivational aspects of value, per se, prompted the study of what could be called perceptual value constancy. In experiments concerning the apparent numerosity of stamps and of coins, Zuk-Kardos and Fazil (reported in 2, pp. 140–150) as well as Ansbacher (referred to in 7) found number constancy with value variant and value constancy with number variant fairly high, although tainted with compromise between the two variables.

Another quasi-representative step is to gear the manner of variation or of covariation between variables to the general scheme of natural conditions in a planfully controlled way, as when the association between a certain cue or means and the object or reward is made probabilistic rather than absolute (4, 10).

Experiments Centered about an Exemplary Instance: Successive Omission vs. Successive Accumulation of Cues

A certain effort toward representativeness is discernible whenever a "lifelike" situation is taken as the starting point of the experiment. In the field of size perception such experiments are likely to abandon, at least in some of their phases, the chin rests, darkrooms, screens with small openings, alleys of edges without thickness, or other laboratory paraphernalia in vogue during the late nineteenth century. This liberalization owes much to David Katz (29) and his work in another area of perceptual constancy—color constancy with illumination variant. For size constancy, a study by Holaday (23; see also 7, p. 23), and the studies by Holway and Boring (25, by Gibson (16) and to some extent one by Joynson (28) have proceeded by essentially the same functional scheme.

In each case there is what we may call a core or "exemplar" situation—somewhat arbitrarily chosen, to be sure—which contains a fairly natural array of cues. Superimposed upon this core is a greater or lesser number of systematic variations so that the design is still fundamentally systematic in its ramifications. The systematic part usually effects what may be called "successive omission" from the originally unknown, or at least not fully scrutinized, array of cues, while the more

nearly classical approach tends to eliminate all natural cues, then building up from nothing in a technique of "successive accumulation" (7, pp. 22 ff.).

By and large the functional studies of size constancy have borne out Hering's old assumption of "approximate size-constancy" according to which more distant objects tend to be slightly underestimated (although not nearly as much as would correspond to the shrinkage of their photographic size). But it is significant, from the methodological point of view, that in some of the studies the most favorable cue conditions yielded on the average slight over-rather than undercompensation for distance ("overconstancy"), and that the over-all level of "compromise" varies considerably from study to study. In addition, laboratory experiments inadvertently employing certain atypical contexts or backgrounds will yield drastically different results, not to speak of essentially traditional experiments that programmatically employ grossly distortive configurations, like the situations recently created by Ames (27).

Under the aspect of representative design, all these systematic experiments must be viewed as ecological single cases of "instances" with artificial elaboration that leaves a large portion of the core elements untouched. Each of these experiments is indisputable in its results, but at the same time is of unscrutinized ecological generalizability. The variate packages constituting these experiments or experimental settings may be projected somewhere in the x-dimensional manifold of representative design which we have exemplified for two dimensions in Fig. 7.3. Each imaginary point, or small, orderly group of points, in such a space represents a potential systematic experiment. Mostly there is little technical basis for telling whether a given experiment is an ecological normal, located in the midst of a crowd of natural instances, or whether it is more like a bearded lady at the fringes of reality, or perhaps like a mere homunculus of the laboratory out in the blank.

As a matter of principle, individual sample situations, no matter how lifelike, cannot answer the functional problem as to the degree of perceptual constancy, even though by the use of responder replication or by systematic variation their results may become generalizable in certain directions and standardized for testing purposes.

Only representative design can answer this problem. By a set of analyses not reflected in the figures of the present paper, the ecological generalizability of the principle of perceptual compromise, or of "approximate" size constancy as originally suggested by Hering, has been established for our subject along with the broader principle of distal rather than proximal focusing.

Canvassing as Accidental Quota Sampling of the Ecology

In still other cases an entire array of individual systematic experiments may appear to be laid out after quasi-representative principles, so as to cover the ecology or the mediational pathways by a vaguely conceived "one of a kind" rule. This tacit sampling procedure forms a counterpart to what polling statisticians might describe as a most rudimentary form of stratified, "quota" or proportionate sampling and is usually of the highly erratic type sometimes labeled "accidental" in statistics. We will speak of this primitive type of coverage of the ecology as "canvassing."

In the field of the perceptual constancies, the attempted extension of basic principles, such as that of distal focusing or of compromise, from size to shape to color constancy, is an example of canvassing. A cross-departmental extension to "loudness constancy" with distance of sound source variant was undertaken by Mohrmann (37), yielding generally similar results. Kinesthetic experiments with falling bodies, with and without the aid of visual cues, have established the functioning of a perceptual "weight constancy," with speed (and thus with kinetic energy) variant (2, pp. 161 f.). The above-cited experiments on value constancy further augment the picture of canvassing of the perceptual constancies.

Truncated Factorial Design and an Impasse in the Analysis of Variance

The basic intent of representative design is toward design proper; that is, it concerns the employment of a statistical selection device for the stimulus sample; only secondarily is it concerned with statistics as a procedure of evaluation. Its relevance to analysis of variance is thus indirect, and derives solely from the fact that this evaluation

technique is an adjunct to factorial design, conceived in its shadow and thus wrought with its inherent inadequacies.

At first glance factorial design may appear ideal, since all plots are filled, while in representative design normally only part of the plots is filled; representative designs would thus seem readily extractable from factorial designs if anyone should wish to extract them, but not vice versa. The first catch is, however, that some of the intercombinations of variates may be incompatible in nature or otherwise grossly unrealistic.

An example is furnished by a study of the perceptual impression values of schematized faces by Brunswik and Reiter (2, 11; for a summary and discussion see 7, pp. 40 f.). In effect, this was an early factorial design, with a $3 \times 3 \times 3 \times 3 \times 3$ layout (Fig. 7.6). Fortunately for our argument, we were naive enough to depart from the complete array of intercombinations so far as two of the five "facial" variables chosen are concerned. The inadvertently unorthodox part is the truncated treatment of the "nose," as plotted in Fig. 7.7. Two opposite corners are left empty so that there are only seven noses instead of nine, making for a total of $3 \times 3 \times 3 \times 7 = 189$ facial schemata. The result is an oblique relationship in the artificial ecology of the design which is not unlike the representative ecological correlation shown in Fig. 7.3 for size constancy, even though with a strange orderly tint that bespeaks the systematic origin of the stimulus distribution.

The reason for the departure from strict orderliness of the design was given by the desire—still somewhat vague at the time—to achieve better representativeness. One of the desiderata was to make the schemata look as "facelike" as feasible; the omission of two of the nine possible noses was prompted by their unusually bizarre and ridiculous appearance which threatened to spoil the seriousness of an already precarious attitude on the part of the subjects. In many other psychological contexts certain intercombinations may be unrealistic or disruptive in similar or in some other ways.

Like the design, our original evaluation was makeshift. Years later the main effects and some of the first-order interactions were found significant in terms of analysis of variance as applied to the 189 original impressions of intelligence (composite from 10 adult subjects), although this

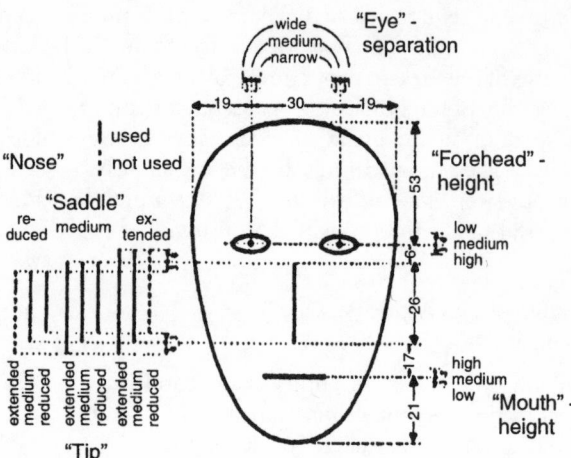

FIGURE 7.6 Five-factorial schematized face (adapted from Brunswik and Reiter, 11).

of course implies little concerning the ecological generalizability to live faces. For our schemata it appeared that impressions of intelligence are aided primarily by high or medium forehead, medium mouth, and medium nose.

In the analysis of the impression value of the "nose" the omission of the two cells necessitated—as my statistician colleagues, Drs. Rheem F. Jarrett and Robert Rollin, informed me—the employment of such *ad hoc* procedures as the "missing plot" or the "unequal numbers in cells" technique (30, pp. 220 ff.). These techniques are not only artificial and rather uncommon; what is more, they involve the somewhat hypocritical pretense that part of the data was lost, or at least that the material is not quite as it ought to be. Under representative design, involving as it does variate packages in many more dimensions than factorial design could handle practically, oblique distributions are not only legitimate but will in most cases be dictated by nature or by

culture, and thus be mandatory. Evaluation techniques will have to be fitted to the materials that may be obtained under such design, rather than vice versa.

Major Varieties of Psychological Theorizing

We now turn to the implications of our above considerations for psychological theory. Three types of psychological theorizing will be discussed: (*a*) theory as the ratiomorphic explication of probabilistic functional—notably distal—achievement and of its strategy: (*b*) theory as the customary nomothetic and more or less molecular reduction of function; and (*c*) theory as comparative methodology, both within psychology and between psychology and the other sciences.

Theory as a Ratiomorphic Model of Functional Achievement and Its Strategy: Focusing and Vicarious Mediation

The representative study of distal constant function, as reported above, is schematically described in Fig. 7.8. The wide-arching functional validity coefficient constitutes a generalized statement of the organism's perfection in the attainment of a given distal variable; it falls under the concept of "descriptive theory" by virtue of its generality alone. In addition, an inventory or mapping of the full array of outpost variables attained by an individual or species, as well as of

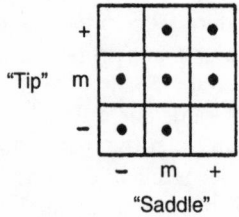

FIGURE 7.7 Truncated treatment of two out of the five variables shown in Fig. 7.6.

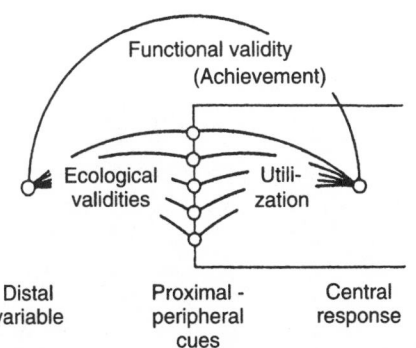

FIGURE 7.8 The lens model as applied to perceptual constancy (adapted from Brunswik, 1952).

the degree of such focusing ("psychology in terms of objects," 2, 3), promises to lead to further generalizations concerning preferential focusing on distal vs. proximal variables at large, concerning the relationship between life relevance and distality, and concerning related biological-functional problems.

As is further indicated in Fig. 7.8, the overall functional arc may be broken down into an extrasystemic and an intrasystemic constituent, called respectively, ecological validity and utilization. The general pattern of the mediational strategy of the organism is predicted upon the limited ecological validity or trustworthiness of cues which we have observed earlier in this paper. This forces a probabilistic strategy upon the organism. To improve its bet, it must accumulate and combine cues. Thus we arrive at a better understanding of the principle of mutual substitutability, or "vicarious functioning," of means (or cues) for each other which Hunter, Tolman (47, ch. i), and most other behaviorists looking for a structural criterion have incorporated in their basic definitions of behavior or purpose (see 8, ch. ii). Hence the lens-like model in Fig. 7.8, which may be taken to represent the basic unit of psychological functioning. No matter how much the attainment is improved, however, distal function remains inherently probabilistic.

In the light of this model all "constant," or rather, quasi-constant function, be it "intuitive" or explicit, can be explicated as a statistical reasoning process remindful of Helmholtz's "unconscious inference," albeit without its introspection-

istic and perfectionistic overtones. Forming a Latin-Greek hybrid, we may speak of this as a "ratiomorphic" theory of achievement (9).

One of the most important aspects of such a theory concerns the relationship between ecological validity and utilization. Ideally, cues should be utilized in accordance with their validity. But here we must inject, among other things to be brought up later in this paper, the element of "cost" to the organism, just as we must ask for the cost of an automobile along with its efficiency in budgeting our expenditures. Functional theory here takes on certain features of economic theory.

Theory as Nomothetic Reduction

We have left the discussion of the systematic approach, in favor of that of representative design, at the point where the former was about to embark on a diacritical confrontation of constant function with its own cues or other mediating instrumentalities. This type of confrontation has been practiced extensively in psychology, notably in its more classical phases. In the founding period of behaviorism, Watson and Lashley (50) set out to transport homing birds in closed cages over distances sometimes far outside their natural range. Others have since used anesthetics, faradic cages, or rotation on a phonograph turntable in the dark throughout the journey (45). The artificially distortive laboratory experiments on the perception of size and distance to which we have referred above as preceding, and in part paralleling, the quasi-representative and representative studies of the last quarter century fall in the same category.

The objective of this type of behavior or perception study is to trace performance step by step to identifiable processes, cues, or tracks of mediation; in the end they are to be "reduced" to the "laws" of one of the more microscopic, more "fundamental" disciplines, notably physiology. Traditionally, many psychologists have seen in such a reductive explanation of behavior the major task of psychological theory. The nomothetic behaviorism of Hull and of his sympathizers, mentioned at the beginning of this paper, reveals its reductionist aim most clearly in the use of a "physiologizing" terminology.

To the study of distal function and of its grand strategy the reductive approach adds the study of tactics; to the study of achievement and of its macromediation, both of which fall within the province of functional-representative design, it adds the study of micromediation, which falls in the province of nomothetic-systematic design. The functional approach has its place mainly in the appraisal of the interplay and relative contribution or weight of factors in the adjustment to a given ecology, while the reductive approach reveals the technological details of the machinery that brings about such adjustment.

Theory as Comparative Methodology: Observational Unity and Thematic Diversity of Science

The injection of physiology into the discussion brings us to a branch of psychological theory which overlaps with the philosophy of science and is best labeled comparative methodology of science. One of the major concerns of such a science of science, or metatheory, is with the basic unity of the sciences. In present-day psychological discussion this problem is subsumed mainly under the watchword "operationism." Here it is often forgotten that the basic requirement for scientific exactitude is a relatively modest one, and in a certain sense a more commonplace one than anticipated. It involves no more than the inter- and intrasubjective univocality of observation and communication which is sometimes called "methodological physicalism" (8), but should better be specified as observational or procedural physicalism; but it does not include the univocality of prediction which is the major *raison d'être* of the nomothetic approach (5).

We may therefore take the position that in the end the unity of science is better served by allowing the reaffirmation or elaboration of this unity to be superseded by a working out of the thematic diversity of the sciences within the minimum common platform. This diversity of themata involves both the aim of the different disciplines and the designs capable of serving these aims.

Thematic Physicalism and the Nomothetic-Reductionist-Systematic Syndrome

The different explicit and implicit trends toward the unification of science which have dominated the last half century have been under the spell of a somewhat stereotyped image of physics. The thematic element in this cliché may be explicated as the emphasis on the "general," and notably on the strict, univocal regularities or laws which possess universal applicability; this is also known as the nomothetic approach. Universality of law presupposes homogeneity of the universe; hence it matters little where and when and over how large an area a phenomenon is studied. Experimental design may thus safely be left to the convenience and liking of the experimenter and thus become systematic. And, as Mises (36) has pointed out in discussing probabilism in physics, macrolaws have their origin in differential equations, that is, in principles conceived for minute space-time splinters. The triad of nomothetic aim, microreductionist procedure, and systematic design which we have come to recognize as a syndrome in traditional psychology thus is revealed as an emulation of a pattern indigenous to the specific thema of physics.

As has been pointed out in greater detail elsewhere (8, sec. 9), the basically elementistic character of physical law is not obviated by, and has little to do with, the empirical fact of a probabilistic microstructure in thermodynamics or within the atom. Nor must such structures be seen as related to, or in any way supporting, our arguments for the probability approach in psychology; functional psychology is macroprobabilistic in that the identity of the individual case is maintained (as in a scattergram) while it is lost in the physical macrolaw which for ordinary practical purposes is absolute.

General vs. Particular: Physical Law, Geographic Fact, Ecological Correlation

The first to warn against the overestimation of the general over the particular in science was Windelband (52). In a somewhat stilted application to personality and to the humanities, he was led to suggest the well-known distinction between nomothetic and idiographic disciplines. Unfortunately, the latter term encompasses both the low-brow, strictly enumerative approach to historic-geographic fact seen in isolation, and the extremely high-brow emphasis on the "unique" lawfulness of the individual or culture; more properly, the latter case should therefore be labelled the "idionomothetic" approach.

Within the natural sciences, an example of the purely enumerative approach is given by those branches of geography that deal with topographical mapping. The fact that no application of the general physical laws is possible without the constants, parameters and boundary conditions furnished by geographic types of information is frequently neglected in theoretical discussion. Except at the level of control ordinarily accessible only to the physicist observer, these constants are not available (at least not fully so) to the responding organism. Hence the chains from select distal to proximal to central variables in perception are chains of (probable) partial, rather than of total, causation. The universal lawfulness of the world is of limited comfort to the perceiver or behaver not in a position to apply these laws, and he therefore must rely largely on whatever snitches of particular or semigeneralized information he may be able to assemble. This is what we meant earlier in this paper by the assertion that ordinarily organisms must behave as if in a semierratic ecology.

With data from our representative size-constancy survey described above the relation between physical law and ecological correlation is illustrated in Table 7.1. The first row of ecological validities has been introduced above in discussing Fig. 7.3, and the remaining two pairs are added here from our material. Partial correlations derived from either of the two columns of three coefficients yield (in as close approximation as may be expected) the perfect positive or negative correlations listed in the third column of figures. These in turn reflect the well-known proportionality law, given still further to the right. Since derivation is possible from all alternate ecologies (as exemplified by our sample of 93 vs. the sub-

sample of 59 situations mentioned earlier), it is evident that textural ecology adds valuable probabilistic information to the vastly distilled relational information incorporated in the universal laws of physics. Essentially this is information abstracted and summarized from the geographies that make up the ecology, and is information of the type finite organisms may best be able to absorb in learning, notably in probability discrimination with partial reinforcement.

It is for the same reasons that the laws of triangulation, which underlie the binocular depth mechanism and which only recently have once more been the starting point for nomothetic treatment of this mechanism (32; see also 17), are of somewhat academic interest so far as the actual perceiver is concerned. And for similar reasons we stressed, earlier in this paper, the limited validity of this mechanism within our cultural ecology, in which the perceiver is routinely exposed to optical instruments as well as to flat pictures as substitute means of access to three-dimensional reality.

Nonfunctionalistic (Intraorganismic) Uses of Probability in Psychology

It will be remembered that in our molar-functional view of organism-environment interplay, uncertainty is a feature of the relationships between the organism and the distal environment, to wit, of proximal-distal relationships in the case of ecological validity and of central-distal relationships in the case of functional validity; uncertainty is not seen as a necessary feature of intraorganismic processes. In a certain sense this is perhaps in reversal of a tradition which has seen nothing but law in the environment, but was

TABLE 7.1 Textural Ecology and Physics (Adapted from Brunswik 7, Fig. 10)

Variables Correlated	Ecological Validities		Nomothetic Approach		
	Full Sample (N = 93)	Sizes over 10 cm. (N = 59)	Partial Correlation		Law of Physical Optics
			Variable "Held Constant"	Coefficient Obtained	
B × P	.70	.14	D	1.00	
B × D	.77	.88	P	1.00	B = PD
D × P	.08	−.34	B	−1.00	

indeterministic or vitalistic so far as the reacting organism is concerned.

Some recent movements have viewed processes within the organism from the probability point of view. While probabilistic functionalism is inherently intersystemic, their approach is intrasystemic. We have no quarrel with them except that we must make it clear that they are confined to problem conceptions which are oversimplified from the standpoint of molar functional psychology, encapsulated as they are within the boundaries of the organism.

Intraregional statistical approaches in psychology may be classified under three major headings: central, peripheral, and peripheral-central. An example of a central statistical theory is the study of "random nervous nets" as developed in the framework of mathematical biophysics by McCulloch and Pitts (33), later in collaboration with Landahl (31). Concern is not with "this" neurone synapsing on "that" one, but rather with "gross" distribution of tendencies and probabilities associated with points or regions in the net. This statistical "rather than deterministic" biophysics was used by Rashevsky (39) as an underpinning for his fundamental equations of mathematical biophysics much in the manner in which the kinetic theory of gases serves as a reductive support to thermodynamics. Rapoport and Shimbel (38, 42) have extended the theory to the dynamics of social interaction.

An application of probability to a peripheral problem is given by the "statistical behavioristics" of Miller and Frick (35). The exposition is encapsulated within the single region of overt responses. The study of "stochastic" (i.e., to a certain extent predictable) word sequences in common English which has come in vogue recently is more or less bodily transferred to an analysis of human "courses of action"—which are related to the "strategies" in the playing of games (49)—and of the "dependent probabilities" resulting from the fact that the preceding occurrence of a response does not always return the system to the original state. Here the only cue considered is given by the preceding time series of events of the same kind. This procedure is not indigenous nor particularly congenial to the thematic content of psychology. Rather, it is somewhat mechanically transplanted from those segments of cybernetics in which unidimensional sequential distribution and correlation are pre-

dominant (51)—another instance of falling for ready-made gadgets, even though at a more elevated level.

Skinner's (43) concept of "probability of response" may likewise be classified under the heading of peripheral encapsulation, the term being no more than a fanciful expression for (relative) frequency of response as one of the traditional scores in learning experiments involving the motor output.

The "statistical learning theory" of Estes (13) is an example of a peripheral-central theory, or perhaps of a peripheral-peripheral theory crossing through the entire organism from input to output. Based as it is on evidence from systematic experiments, there is reason to doubt that the "behavior samples" and "statistical samples of environmental events" which are linked by the theory are even tacitly envisaged as representative samples.

Rudimentary Emergence of the Concept of Cue in Cybernetics and the Theory of Telecommunication

Outside of psychology, and within movements which in some of their more obvious aspects have become templates for most of the intraorganismic probabilism just cited, a first step in the direction of the bivariate type of correlation analysis which is covered by the concept of ecological validity is made by Wiener (51) in his analysis of double time series. Such series are, as Wiener points out, most conspicuous in economico-sociological and meteorologico-geophysical applications, since in both instances the relative lead of one time series with respect to another may well give much more information concerning the past of the second than of its own. For example, on account of the general eastward movement of the weather, Chicago weather may be more important in the forecasting of Boston weather than Boston weather itself. It will be noted that even here the comparison stays within the same kind or physical denomination ("weather"); in such cases comparisons or correlations are not yet genuinely bivariate as are those between proximal cues and objects, or between means and goal attainments.

A more direct exposition of those mathematical principles of communication which are of particular relevance to the understanding of focusing by vicarious functioning as it occurs in psychological mechanisms has been given by

Shannon and Weaver (41). In terms of the vocabulary of the special brand of telecommunication engineering involving semicontrolled media, to which the theory has been geared, perceptual cues and behavioral means are like "signals" in "coded messages." The mediating channels are contaminated with interferences or constraints of their own. The result is equivocation. It is then "not in general possible to reconstruct the message with certainty by any operation on the signal." Shannon's diagram showing the fanning out of "reasonable causes" (messages, inputs) for a given "high probability received signal" or effect, and of "reasonable effects" (signals, outputs) from a given "high probability message" or cause in a channel, bears formal resemblance to the equivocal types of coupling between intra- and extraorganismic regions to which this writer called attention twenty years ago (2, Fig. 7.2) and which can also be read into our diagram of the lens model in Fig. 7.8.

Whenever the "capacity" of a channel is less than the richness of variability of the source from which it accepts messages, the channel is "overloaded." Then it is

> impossible to devise codes which reduce the error frequency as low as one may please. . . . However clever one is with the coding process, it will always be true that after the signal is received there remains some undesirable (noise) uncertainty about what the message was (41, p. 111).

We may add that, in quite the same manner, the crux of organismic adjustment obviously lies in the fact that distal perceptual and behavioral mediation must, by the nature of things, in the general case rely on overloaded channels, with the ensuing limited dependability of all achievement mechanism. And we may note that at least part of the trouble lies with the overloading and noise in the external rather than the internal medium.

Shannon and Weaver point to one means by which the chances of error can be decreased, however. This is "redundancy," as exemplified by, but by no means restricted to, verbal repetitiveness. When there is noise there is some real advantage in not using a coding process that eliminates all the redundancy, for the remaining redundancy helps combat the uncertainty of trans-

mission. The reader will recognize that the vicarious functioning of cues and of means—functional patterns we came to acknowledge as the backbone of stabilized achievement—may be viewed as special cases of receiving or sending messages through redundant, even though not literally repetitive, channels. The probability of error, given by the variety of possible causes or effects that could result in, or be produced by, the type of event in question, can thus be minimized; this is the case in the gain of the overall functional validity (.99) over the ecological validity of the major retinal cue (.70) in our representative survey of size constancy referred to above, in which the organism acts as an intuitive statistician.[3]

A suggestion of extending the theory of communication to multivariate patterns of mediation has recently been made by McGill (34). It is hoped that this will open up the full scope of vicarious functioning to formal treatment.

Clinical and Related Aspects of Representative Design

There are several ways in which representative design has become involved with social and clinical psychology. Two of them deal with sampling aspects exclusively, and another two concern both design and the functional theory of the vicarious functioning of cues.

Representative Sampling of Persons in the Role of Objects

The case in which not only the responding subjects but also the stimulus objects are persons furnishes perhaps the most obvious demonstration of the necessity for representative design. It is for this symmetry of subject and object that such media as the social perception of personality from photographs seem to offer the best chance of convincing the designer that there must be a sizable N of social objects alongside the customary sizable n of subjects (judges). Yet a survey of the respective literature revealed that, apparently by force of a somewhat thoughtless, content-bound tradition, the object N is on the whole pitifully inadequate in comparison with the subject n, with fallacies of generalization ensuing (7, ch. vi and p. 38).

Hammond has been especially astute in exposing comparable lapses in the logic of design and of evaluation in other areas of social psychology (18) and in clinical psychology, notable in the study of the effect of the sex or personality of the examiner upon Rorschach and other projective test results (19)—even on the part of standard texts in psychological statistics. It turned out that it was a surprisingly widespread practice to apply only one (responder-populational) test of significance using n, and to tacitly consider this test to cover ecological generality in the same breath.

Representative Sampling of Stimulus Configurations as Test Situations

Concerning representativeness as to the purely physical stimulus configurations used in testing, test designers have so far not pressed beyond the stage designated as canvassing, earlier in this paper. At best, tests were either picked to reflect roughly the current distribution of systematic laboratory experimentation—in particularly fortunate cases, such as in Thurstone's factorial study of perception (46), with an emphasis on more recent and more complex types of experimental problems—or there was an informal effort to assemble a battery of "close-to-life" situations. If the tests were selected from a pool of existing tests the term "sampling" was occasionally applied, but it was usually forgotten that sampling from an artifact, even when this sampling itself should be random, merely perpetuates earlier bias (7, pp. 50 f.).

Similar considerations apply to the customary so-called sampling of behavior, of acts, or of traits from a trait universe (including the construction of adjective check lists), so long as the respective universes or sampling procedures are but informally scrutinized.[4] The degree of representativeness is in each of these cases determined not by the most but by the least representative step in the chain of defining the universe and of drawing the sample. Since trait sampling concerns the responder rather than the ecology, and hence is not part of representative design proper, this is added here merely parenthetically.

From a technical point of view it is not sufficient to have one close-to-life test, or even many of them. As we have pointed out in the main part of this paper, there must be balanced coverage of life. A mere multitude of situations may be designated as M tests, reserving N for the size of truly representative ecological samples. (M is chosen as the letter preceding N, or as the first letter in *many*; the capital letter is used in slight departure from the practice suggested earlier [7, pp. 34 f.]). Only for the true N can technical tests of ecological significance as envisaged in representative design be applied.

Such stimulus configurations as the Rorschach inkblots are biased variate packages, in the sense of the word as defined earlier in this paper. They invite what Sander (40) has called "realistically-meaningful" (*sinnhaft-bedeutungsvoll*) or "onto-tropic" tendencies, in contradistinction to the "geometric-ornamental" or "eidotropic" tendencies (toward *Prägnanz* or "good form," such as abstract circles, squares, or other purely geometric formations) as described by the gestalt psychologists proper. Since these ontotropic tendencies are considered to represent a higher developmental stage than the formalistic eidotropic tendencies, both in ontogenesis and in the "actualgenesis" of the instantaneous perceptual experience, a more genuine sampling of stimulus patterns and the setting up of more representative evaluation categories may become diagnostically valuable.

Allowance of Vicarious Functioning as a Representative Feature in Test Construction

As we have seen, one of the most important principles of functional theory is that of vicarious functioning. Its earliest recognition stems not from academic psychology but from one of the theoretical antecedents of clinical psychology, psychoanalysis. Under the direct influence of psychoanalysis, Frenkel-Brunswik (15) has developed the study of "alternative manifestations" of the latent dynamic structure of needs on a statistical basis, using multiple correlation with overt behavior elements; the way to the rational reconstruction of clinical intuition which is asked for in another line of Vienna tradition, logical empiricism, was thus opened. The relationships that may or may not exist with Lazarsfeld's subsequent theory of "latent structure" (44) will not be discussed here.

In my own work the attention to vicarious functioning has concentrated on perception rather than on behavioral expression (and, within perception, on physical objects or on the more static traits of social objects), and the implications of vicariousness upon representative design have been developed through this medium (7, ch. v, vi, viii; for more general discussion see 8, ch. ii). In his contribution to the present symposium Hammond (20) has expanded this to demand allowance of multiple mediation patterns for, and an attendant multiple cue analysis of, clinical judgment by recourse to the requirements of representative design.

Ecological Validity and Utilization of Clinical Cues

A problem ensuing from the work of Frenkel-Brunswik and of Hammond, just cited, is the question about the extent to which the ecological validity of the potential cues available to clinical intuition is duplicated by the weight given these cues in their utilization on the part of the responding clinician. Hammond and his collaborators at Colorado (20), and, independently, Smedslund at Oslo (in an as yet unpublished study), have recently found cases of gross discrepancy in this respect, involving both the ignoring or even the reversal of valid cues and the overutilization of cues of low validity.

Pitfalls of Systematic Design in Biological Application

As we have seen, representative design is especially indispensable whenever the relative contribution of different variables in a functional context is the subject of investigation. But it must not be forgotten that any systematic experiment, regardless of how oddly conceived it may be, represents at least one actual or potential ecological instance, and in this sense is a bit of reality; in addition, as we have seen, it may be the only means of obtaining knowledge in the reductive context of science.

Impressive as are the achievements of reductive experimentation in the biological sciences, the dangers resulting from the tying of variables and from other characteristics of nonrepresentative designs have rarely been completely avoided. The history of science furnishes ample evidence of harmful effects of systematic design upon practice or theoretical outlook. As a layman, one may think of hygiene in medicine with its dramatic changes between the complete neglect and the excesses of aseptic or antiseptic policies; the boiling of milk and devitaminization; anemia and the eating of liver, and so forth. All of these practices appear as playballs of variables arbitrarily selected for study, which thus acquire undue prominence and throw the picture of the interplay of factors out of balance; and the shortcuts involved in the ecological overgeneralization of results may be even more serious. The biochemist or nutritionist who shuns eggs but is a chain smoker, and the cancer specialist who does the opposite, are too familiar examples to require elaboration.

Systematic Design in Cliché Literature

We may also regard the "world" of popular novels and movies as an artificial, cultural subecology. Its outstanding feature is the presence of clichés; these include both personality stereotypes and plot formulas. Clichés are similar to experiments using systematic design. Factors that show some degree of independent variability in real life are artificially tied. Old-fashioned opera plots or soap melodramas that "drip with generosity" share with cowboy movies what David Hume would have called "inseparable" associations of noble character, overpowering strength, fairness, courage, youth, final success, and so forth, or of their opposites. The cliché is a "worn" case or incident, by no means impossible or nonexistent but made prominent out of all proportion to its frequency, and to the detriment of all other types of incident. Like the systematic design of experiments, it superimposes artificial "laws" upon an ecology which it thereby depletes.

In the case of the systematic experiment it is these artificial laws in the design which, as we have suggested, are at least in part responsible for the often striking lawfulness of the results. At this point the suspicion arises that the didactic role which systematic experimentation obviously plays in the mental economy of the scientist, by virtue of the simplicity and order it both requires in the design and furnishes in the result, may outweigh the fact-finding competence of systematically designed experiments. Certainly the more drastically simplified forms of art of which we have spoken, and which are so similar in pattern to the systematic experiment, are clearly didactic rather than informative in any realistic sense; we do not go to the movies to find out about life or to form a scientifically airtight theory about personality, in spite of the fact that movies may sometimes be helpful in temporarily smoothing the perplexities of life.

The main function both of art and of systematic experimentation, then, is to shake and mold us by exaggeration and extreme correlation or absence of correlation. But exaggeration is distortion, and this distortion must in science eventually be resolved by allowing the more palatable systematic design to mature into, and to be superseded by, the more truthful representative design.

Conclusion: Unity of Science and Unity of Psychology

Our considerations in comparative methodology have brought into focus the thematic diversification that is possible within the over-all unity of exact, observationally physicalistic science. They may facilitate the cheerful relinquishment of the overheated nomothetic bias under which the development of psychology has long suffered and which is making the establishment of a molar-functional psychology an uphill battle. Acceptance of the probabilistic conception, both for the propaedeutic study of ecology and for the functional analysis of perceptual or behavioral achievement, not only sets normative psychology on the right track; it also united it methodologically with differential psychology, thus lending ideological support to the inherently statistical character they both share, and making a virtue of this often bemoaned necessity.

Psychology thus acquires the distinctive, well-circumscribed internal unity and coherence which we have long searched for, and the reality of which many of us have doubted. This unity emerges, as does perhaps all good unity of—and in—science, as one of methodology or grand design. In both of its major aspects, representative design and functional theory, it centers about probabilistic texture and the ways of its exploitation by the organism. The fact that organismic achievement and its reconstruction in psychology are characterized by certain similarities with predictive procedures in economics, meteorology, and especially in the study of telecommunication through uncontrolled, noisy external media,

should help to bring into focus the family of sciences in its entirety. Such a focusing should help to set in proper perspective our traditional thematic dependence on, or need for succorance from, a select few of the older disciplines which may have appeared particularly glamorous, especially physiology and physics.

NOTES

The series of papers by Egon Brunswik and by Leo Postman, and of the following discussion papers by Ernest R. Hilgard, David Krech, Herbert Feigl, and Egon Brunswik, are adapted from the first part of a symposium held, under the same title and under the chairmanship of Edward C. Tolman, at the *Berkeley Conference for the Unity of Science*, University of California, July 1953.

A contribution by Kenneth R. Hammond to a second, more practically oriented part of the original symposium will appear in the next issue of this journal (20).

The Institute for the Unity of Science in Boston, which sponsored the conference, has contributed approximately one-half the publication cost of these papers.

The present paper has been considerably expanded beyond the original exposition read at the symposium of which it was part. However, care was taken not to alter the substance of the argument on which the subsequent paper by Postman and the ensuing discussion are based.

1. The expansions beyond the earlier publications listed concern mainly the use of a behavioral example at the beginning of the paper; the brief consideration of such semirepresentative policies as "canvassing"; certain comparisons with factorial design and the analysis of variance, as well as with nonfunctionalistic uses of probability in psychology; and a discussion of actual and potential applications to the clinical-social area and to related domains.

2. The present statistical application of redundancy is not to be confused with one recently suggested by Attneave (1). In his case the concern is with the exploitation (extrapolation) of *strict* law as it holds over limited stretches of space (or time), say, along part of the contour of an ink bottle. In an earlier context, this writer has spoken of such regularities of limited scope as "local laws" (*Lokalgesetze*, 2, pp. 209, 212). By virtue of their strictness their treatment falls under our above-mentioned heading of an idionomothetic approach; its only relation to the probabilistic approach lies in the fact that the area to which a local law is limited may

be considered as a subecology, and that the organism may have to proceed by basically similar mechanisms to ascertain either of the two types of limited regularities, the strict or the probabilistic.

3. Guttman states, seemingly without being much concerned about the underlying problem, that "the processes of sampling people and of sampling items are not at all identical; random sampling, stratified or not, is used for the first, but is not applicable to item construction" (44, p. 54).

REFERENCES

1. Attneave, F. Some informational aspects of visual perception. *Psychol. Rev.*, 1954, **61**, 183–193.

2. Brunswik, E. *Wahrnehmung und Gegenstandswelt*. Vienna: Deuticke, 1934.

3. Brunswik, E. Psychology as a science of 227–260. (Errata corrected 1938, **5**, 110.)

4. Brunswik, E. Probability as a determiner of rat behavior. *J. exp. Psychol.*, 1939, **25**, 175–197.

5. Brunswik, E. Organismic achievement and environmental probability. *Psychol. Rev.*, 1943, **50**, 255–272.

6. Brunswik, E. Distal focussing of perception: size-constancy in a representative sample of situations. *Psychol. Monogr.*, 1944, **56**, No. 1 (Whole No. 254).

7. Brunswik, E. *Systematic and representative design of psychological experiments*. Berkeley: Univer. of California Press, 1947. (Also in J. Neyman [Ed.], *Berkeley symposium on mathematical statistics and probability*. Berkeley: Univer. of California Press, 1949.)

8. Brunswik, E. *The conceptual framework of psychology*. Chicago: Univer. of Chicago Press, 1952. (*Int. Encycl. unified Sci.*, Vol. I, No. 10.)

9. Brunswik, E. "Rationmorphic" models of perception and thinking. In N. Mailloux (Ed.), *Proc. 14th Int. Congr. Psychol.*, Montreal, 1954, in press.

10. Brunswik, E., & Herma, H. Probability learning of perceptual cues in the establishment of a weight illusion. *J. exp. Psychol.*, 1951, **41**, 281–290.

11. Brunswik, E., & Reiter, L. Eindrucks-Charaktere schematisierter Gesichter. *Z. Psychol.*, 1937, **142**, 67–134.

12. Dukes, W. F. Ecological representativeness in studying perceptual size-constancy in childhood. *Amer. J. Psychol.*, 1951, **64**, 87–93.

13. Estes, W. K. Toward a statistical theory of learning. *Psychol. Rev.*, 1950, **57**, 94–107.

14. Fisher, R. A. *Design of experiments*. Edinburgh: Oliver & Boyd, 1935.

15. Frenkel-Brunswik, Else. Motivation and behavior. *Genet. Psychol. Monogr.*, 1942, **26**, 131–265.

16. Gibson, J. J. Motion picture testing and research. Washington, D. C.: U. S. Government Printing Office, 1947. (*AAF Aviat. Psychol. Program Res. Rep.* No. 7.)

17. Graham, C. H. Visual perception. In S. S. Stevens (Ed.), *Handbook of experimental psychology*. New York: Wiley, 1951. Pp. 868–920.

18. Hammond, K. R. Subject and object sampling: a note. *Psychol. Bull.*, 1948, **45**, 530–533.

19. Hammond, K. R. Representative vs. systematic design in clinical psychology. *Psychol. Bull.*, 1954, **51**, 150–159.

20. Hammond, K. R. Probabilistic functioning and the clinical method. *Psychol. Rev.*, in press.

21. Heider, F. Environmental determinants in psychological theories. *Psychol. Rev.*, 1939, **46**, 383–410.

22. Hempel, C. G. *Fundamentals of concept formation in empirical science*. Chicago: Univer. of Chicago Press, 1952. (*Int. Encycl. unified Sci.*, Vol. II, No. 7.)

23. Holaday, B. E. Die Grössenkonstanz der Sehdinge. *Arch. ges. Psychol.*, 1933, **88**, 419–486.

24. Holt, E. B. *The Freudian wish*. New York: Holt, 1915.

25. Holway, A. H., & Boring, E. G. Determinants of apparent visual size with distance variant. *Amer. J. Psychol.*, 1941, **54**, 21–37.

26. Hull, C. L. *Principles of behavior: an introduction to behavior theory*. New York: D. Appleton-Century, 1943.

27. Ittelson, W. H. *The Ames demonstrations in perception*. Princeton: Princeton Univer. Press, 1952.

28. Joynson, R. B. The problem of size and distance. *Quart. J. exp. Psychol.*, 1949, **1**, 119–135.

29. Katz, D. *The world of colour*. (Trans. by R. B. McLeod from the 2nd German Ed. [1930].) London: Kegan Paul, 1935. (First German edition, 1911.)

30. Kendall, M. G. *Advanced theory of statistics*. Vol. II. (3rd Ed.) New York: Hafner, 1951.

31. Landahl, H. D., McCulloch, W. S., & Pitts, W. A statistical consequence of the logical calculus of nervous nets. *Bull. math. Biophysics*, 1943, **5**, 135–137.

32. Luneburg, R. K. *Mathematical analysis of binocular vision*. Princeton: Princeton Univer. Press, 1947.

33. McCulloch, W. S., & Pitts, W. A logical calculus of the ideas immanent in nervous activity. *Bull. math. Biophysics*, 1943, **5**, 115–133.

34. McGill, W. J. Multivariate transmission of information and its relation to analysis of variance. *Hum. Fact. Operat. Res. Lab.*, 1953, Rep. No. 32.

35. Miller, G. A., & Frick, F. C. Statistical behavioristics and sequences of responses. *Psychol. Rev.*, 1949, **56**, 311–324.

36. Mises, R. v. *Probability, statistics and truth.* New York: Macmillan, 1939.

37. Mohrmann, K. Lautheitskonstanz im Entfernungswechsel. *Z. Psychol.*, 1939, **145**, 145–199.

38. Rapoport, A. Cycle distributions in random nets. *Bull. math. Biophysics*, 1948, **10**, 145–157.

39. Rashevsky, N. *Mathematical biophysics.* (Rev. Ed.) Chicago: Univer. of Chicago Press, 1948.

40. Sander, F. Experimentelle Ergebnisse der Gestaltpsychologie. *10th Kongr. exp. Psychol.*, Bonn, 1928, 23–88.

41. Shannon, C. E., & Weaver, W. *Mathematical theory of communication.* Urbana: Univer. of Illinois Press, 1949.

42. Shimbel, A., & Rapoport, A. Statistical approach to the theory of the nervous system. *Bull. math. Biophysics*, 1948, **10**, 41–55.

43. Skinner, B. F. The experimental analysis of behavior. In *Proc. 13th Int. Congr. Psychol., 1951.* Stockholm: Lagerström, 1952, Pp. 62–91. (Also in *Amer. Psychologist*, 1953, 8, 69–78.)

44. Stouffer, S. A., *et al. Measurement and prediction.* Princeton: Princeton Univer. Press, 1950.

45. Thomson, A. L. *Bird migration.* (Rev. Ed.) London: Witherby, 1942.

46. Thurstone, L. L. *A factorial study of perception.* Chicago: Univer. of Chicago Press, 1944.

47. Tolman, E. C. *Purposive behavior in animals and men.* New York: Century, 1932.

48. Tolman, E. C., & Brunswik, E. The organism and the causal texture of the environment. *Psychol. Rev.*, 1935, **42**, 43–77.

49. Von Neumann, J., & Morgenstern, O. *Theory of games and economic behavior.* (2nd Ed.) Princeton: Princeton Univer. Press, 1947.

50. Watson, J. B., & Lashley, K. S. *Homing and related activities of birds.* Washington: Carnegie Institution, 1915.

51. Wiener, N. *Extrapolation, interpolation, and smoothing of stationary time series.* New York: Wiley, 1949.

52. Windelband, W. *Geschichte und Naturwissenschaft.* Strassburg: Heitz, 1894.

53. Woodworth, R. S. *Experimental psychology.* New York: Holt, 1938. (2nd Ed., with H. Schlosberg, New York: Holt, 1954.)

 REPRINT

In Defense of Probabilistic Functionalism: A Reply

Egon Brunswik

There are two aspects of probabilistic functionalism: representative design and functional theory (11). Let me consider the arguments concerning theory first.

1. As a starting point, let me take exception to the use of the term "uniformity point of view" in contradistinction to "probability point of view" and also to the identification of the former with

Symposium on the Probability Approach in Psychology
Reprinted from *Psychological Review* (1955), 62, 236–242.

the nomothetic approach with which Postman's cogent analysis (27) begins. Uniformity is a matter of reality, or of beliefs about reality, while the search for laws is a matter of what to admit to representation out of that reality. I suspect that one of the main sources of confusing the existential with the representational in the present context is the otherwise splendid book of readings on contemporary psychological theory by Marx (24) in which papers by Hull (20) and by myself (5) were rechristened and juxtaposed under the above labels by the editor. These papers had originally been part of a symposium in which Lewin (23), for once, joined forces with Hull if only in common defense of the nomothetic point of view against my own plea for probabilism.

The term "uniformity point of view," which I myself have never used, erroneously suggests that being a probabilist excludes the belief in uniformity, perhaps in the way in which some of the quantum physicists—or in quite another way the vitalists—do not believe in uniformity. The allegation which Hull made in the same vein at the beginning of his paper, asserting that I do not believe in the "existence" of laws applicable to behavior, is thus based on a misunderstanding. The same holds for the present remarks of Krech (22). Contrary to what he imputes, I *do* believe that "God does *not* gamble"; I fully realize that the impasse of quantum physics is irrelevant to our case, uncertainty being for all practical purposes wiped out at the level of physical macro-laws—which are still microlaws to us psychologists—and that vitalism is mere dogma.

But the crucial point is that while God may not gamble, animals and humans do, and that they cannot help but to gamble in an ecology that is of essence only partly accessible to their foresight. And although an infinite and omniscient intellect could operate by law and ratiocination alone, as a psychologist even such a being would have to follow the methodological postulate of behavior-research isomorphism (10, p. 25) and operate at the probabilistic level of discourse. As in geography or textural ecology, this does not entail the negation of law; it merely entails relinquishing attention to law within certain contexts. As these disciplines do not go "beyond" law, we do not either; and as they are sciences, so is probabilistic psychology.

As we all recognize, I presume, not only the legitimacy but also the necessity of the strictly descriptive or statistical disciplines in addition to the nomothetic sciences, it would seem that Krech's as well as Feigl's (15) tendency to relegate the definition of the basic thema of a science to personal preference and taste amounts to a shrinking away from the tasks and obligations inherent in the scientific potential of reality. Each level of parsimony and of generalization, from the most disjointedly enumerative description to the most universal of laws, entails a challenge of its own. As there must be a balance of occupations in a society so that all the potential

demands are filled, so in science at large there must be an equitable distribution among the variety of potential themata. Insistence on reduction as a universal goal of science can only result in blighted spots on the landmap of scientific enterprise. Rather than excommunicating functional psychology from the sciences, advocates of this exclusive form of reductionism—be it persons or groups or even entire phases of the history of our science—are embarking on a self-excommunication from psychology.

Probabilistic functionalism is not, in turn, hostile to reduction. It merely places correlational achievement mapping of generalized functional arcs at the top of a hierarchical pyramid (10, ch. ii); this is followed by the macro-mediational analysis of vicarious attainment strategy. As to the third level in this pyramid, the reductive study of micro-mediational tactics, I agree with Professor Hilgard (19) that this and the entire nomothetic approach should not be "replaced" by the probabilistic approach of the two top levels, although I would like to place reductionism in a marginal position to psychology unless it is executed in firm contact with the two functional aims. In order to reduce, we must know what to reduce. We must reduce "from above," that is, starting from such high-complexity functional units as the lens model. Bertalanffy (1, 2) has in effect done so when he attempted a reductive explanation of "equifinality" in terms of Prigogine's new open-system thermodynamics (see also 10, pp. 42 f.). Most of the "laws" that play a part, say, in learning theory were gathered at a surface level of complexity, and either in oblivion of, or in but casual or mysterious contact with, the more broadly functional contexts in which they are embedded.

The nomothetic-reductionist-systematic type of approach has in the past been overstressed at the expense of the probabilistic-functional-representative approach, notwithstanding all the epoch-making discoveries to which Hilgard had referred. We have had all of the former and nothing of the latter for too long. Now we must balance psychology in the molar and molecular realm.

In contrast with most previous movements in psychology, probabilistic functionalism thus does not exclude anything; rather, its scope is encompassing enough to allow us to envisage a system to end all systems.

2. We have recently been admonished by Koch (21) to expand the use of the label "theory" be-

yond the nomothetic endeavors in the narrower sense. What Koch, and probably Feigl in the present symposium, mean by "meta-theory" is theory about theorizing, perhaps including matters of differential thema and design as subsumable under the label of comparative methodology.

But it seems to me that the liberalization of our notions of theory must go still further. We must include within the scope of theory proper the substantive part of functional considerations also, involving primarily the structure of the lens model as a ratiomorphic explication of achievement rather than merely its reduction to physiology or physics. This model involves focal points, areas of unspecificity, mechanisms of substitution, and other devices of multiple mediation. When Feigl demands generality of a theory, the lens model has it: in fact, the very essence of generalized achievement is incorporated within it, and it can be transferred from perception to action and other psychological functions. It even may be used for "explanation" in the sense of subsuming a single act under a generalized "wish," ascertained by the probabilistic application of operational criteria of "purposiveness" such as those of Tolman (see 29, ch. i). The lens model also has productivity: predictions concerning the efficiency and foolproofness of functional attainment, concerning performance in other areas or dimensions of the ecology, and so forth, may be "derived" from it, and the probabilistic character of these derivations should not detract from the potential rigor and objectivity of the procedures involved.

In other words, we must restore the term "model" to its original meaning, as in speaking of a model of San Francisco Bay water currents, or of the models of medieval technologists. In speaking of "models," many psychologists have come to confine themselves to what essentially amounts to mathematical curve fitting in the tradition of strictly nomothetic theorizing; as we have seen, however, this not only is a labor of Sisyphus but also a labor the fruits of which may be blown over like a hosue of cards when representative design is applied.

Professor Feigl's reluctance to part with the cherished technical meaning of the term "theory" is, to be sure, reinforced by the majority trend in recent psychological "theory construction." But we must insist that the opening up of probabilistic vistas requires some flexibility, some of the "posi-tivism, not negativism" which he himself has preached in other contexts (13) but which, as it must seem from his remarks, he has not always exercized when the challenge was to recognize the growth potential of the psychological thema. This technical meaning of theory, incorporated as it is in Feigl's hierarchy of "levels of explanation," which stretches from strict description through surface laws to low-order and high-order theory (14), reveals only too clearly its origin in the situation in physics with its reduction of, say, the low-order theory of planetary motion by Kepler to the higher-order theory of gravitation by Newton and eventually to the theory of Einstein. Trying to enforce this content-bound schema on another domain is but one more instance of thematic physicalism. Like all automatic transfer of content-alien scaffoldings, it can only result in obscuring the indigenous thema and theoretical structure of the host discipline.

That the question of the applicability of the term "theory" cannot be dismissed as a mere matter of terminology became clear to me when I was asked, at Gustav Bergmann's instigation, to write a note on one of the less well-known papers by Hammond, one in which the situation created in psychology by representative design was set in analogy to that in relativity physics, with special reference to the fact that in both cases regularities hitherto considered universal turn out to be contingent upon a limited ecology (18). Bergmann saw a difficulty in the fact that it was a "design" that was juxtaposed to a "theory." In my reply to this argument (9) I pointed out that the methodology of representative design was inseparable from an inherent theory, and that this theory had been made sufficiently explicit in the original publication (7) under the more modest label of "generalization." The same policy has in part been followed in my main contribution to the present symposium (11).

3. If I understand correctly, Krech agrees with the general thesis that the nomothetic and the microscopic approach go together, while Postman does not. The latter correctly points to Skinner as a psychologist who is nomothetic yet nonmediational. But micromediationism, reductionism, or physiologism are but a few of many possible forms of being atomistic. Another is the encapsulation within the boundaries of the organism, of which

Skinner is equally guilty with Hull, and which is the price paid for some success along nomothetic lines.

It also must be held against Postman that only if our aim is microexplanation or nomothesis at large must we depart in our investigation from the conditions which we intend to explain. The same holds with respect to what Feigl has pointed out in referring to Nagel's telling objection that explanations of teleology cannot in themselves be teleological. The aim of functional psychology is indeed like that of applied psychology, as Postman correctly imputes; or perhaps it goes even further than applied psychology, which has employed systematic design against its own best interests.

4. And now to Hilgard's penetrating argument on representative design as it affects our sampling study of size constancy (6). His suggestion of reading the names of the objects to a blindfolded subject and obtaining estimates of size on this basis will be followed through. Let me venture a guess as to the outcome. In our ecology the functional achievement correlations will be still high, although appreciably lower than in the original study with its unhampered use of the common direct cues. But it is not true that with the use of words we are necessarily overstepping the boundaries of perception in an uncontrollable way, as Hilgard seems to imply. On the contrary, perception must be seen as a cross-departmentally unitary function, and words or other auditory cues are as legitimate a part of the potential mediating cue family hierarchy as are the visual—and in fact the tactile-kinesthetic—cues. Since object names had to be used by the subject of the original study in her communication with the recorder in the course of the observations, Hilgard's suggested design falls more in the category of impoverished rather than in that of shifted cue situations. Under fully representative design, it would be a violation of basic policy *not* to include name cues and the analysis of their effects, rather than the contrary as Hilgard seems to assume.[1]

One must not forget that, ideally, representative design would require huge, concerted group projects, involving as it does a practically limitless number of variables, but that at the same time its rewards in after-the-fact evaluation could be equally widely ramified. In the pilot study under discussion (6) only a select few of these evaluation possibilities were exploited, and the entire problem syndrome of cue participation was left in the dark save for the indirect ascertainment, via the sampling of the objects, of a reasonable degree of representativeness. Since, in principle, under representative design all variables are allowed to vary and none are held constant artificially, their role can be ascertained after the fact. For the same reason, there is a gain rather than a loss of information, contrary to what Postman seems to fear. And we may add that partial correlation, on which Hilgard has expressed reservations, is just one example out of many possible mathematical ways open to, or to be developed by, the statistician for this after-the-fact analysis.

Our earlier prediction of the outcome of Hilgard's suggested naming experiment had to be specified to our ecology. Another ecology is conceivable in which the common objects sampled, such as books, windows, trees, hills, and so forth would be so univocally standardized that, given proper perceptual learning, the name could be utilized as a foolproof cue to size. Hilgard's variant of our design would in this case yield perfect correlation, while visual cues could merely upset this achievement. With such a change in ecology the trend of results would thus be reversed, much as in Hilgard's example from Sears and Whiting there was a trend reversal which likewise could be subsumed under representative design.

> I should like to add parenthetically that this latter example seems to me to involve primarily a responder-populational variable—weaning age and its range—and only secondarily an ecological impasse; but since both such types of universes should be treated alike and sampled under representative design, this difference is fundamentally beside the point here.

5. A similar expansiveness applies to the case of Postman's concern lest motivational bias be excluded from representative design. Representative design merely complements and completes the existing ways in which the necessity of representative sampling has been recognized, so that in the end such sampling will extend over all psychologically relevant variables.

This does not imply, however, that the concept of functional research should be equally broadly conceived. Postman is correct in assuming that the "veridicality" of perception is the major issue in the study of its functional validity, and that our brand of functionalism is not directly and not primarily concerned with need variables or the structure of the need system. Only insofar as needs or values help the cause of, or interfere with, veridicality—and this may be the case either in "perception" or in "judgment," as Postman[2] correctly remarks—do they become part of the functionalist's direct concern. Even interference may be functionally constructive, such as when needs serve as emphasizers of the size or of some other attribute of a life-relevant object. Furthermore, as we have said (11), values form part of the system of natural-cultural "laws" and as such in themselves become objectives of cool, veridical attainment; it is primarily for this reason, and not because of their entanglement with the world of needs, that we incorporated them in our earlier perceptual constancy program (4). And we may add that all these variables are as much a potential part of an isolating statistical analysis as are Hilgard's word cues.

It is only when it comes to delving into the need structures themselves, their variability and their etiology, as is the case, say, in Bruner and Goodman's comparison of the effect of values on rich vs. poor subjects (3), or in Postman, Bruner, and McGinnies' development of such dynamic aspects as "perceptual defense" (28), that the wisdom of applying the label of functionalism may be doubted. This must be made explicit, especially in view of a somewhat unfortunate current trend toward an overexpansion of the concept of functionalism, by Osgood (23, pp. 294 f.) and by others, according to which all such need considerations would be seen as an outgrowth of the functionalist tradition. Bruner and Postman can themselves not be entirely absolved of having contributed to this trend (for further discussion see 8). In genuinely functional analysis needs appear as mere background elements, only as necessary for all utilitarian considerations—that is, essentially as constant parameters rather than as actual variables or as systems of interdependent variables—the latter being exemplified by Frenkel-Brunswik's "personality-centered" approach to perception (17).

Let me conclude with a consideration of Postman's plea of the *status quo*. As has been pointed out repeatedly in this symposium, much depends on definition. Therefore, if it is being recognized that representative design and the resulting functional theory are a going and a growing concern, while systematic design and the nomothetic approach are about to level off and to reach the point of diminishing returns—if, in other words, the *status quo* is conceived not in a static but in a dynamic manner—then I too am heartily in favor of this *status quo*. And when I hear the acknowledgment, as I think I have by Postman and by Hilgard in the present discourse, that systematic design is a preliminary and an eyeopener to the attack on a larger, representative scale, then I am confident that this *status quo* will indeed be a dynamic one.

The peaceful coexistence of which Postman speaks may even be turned into a situation in which the probabilistic approach begins to repay the debt it owes to the reductionist vanguard. In discussing Hilgard's argument on representative design we have come across the problem of perceptual learning. The presence of such learning must be assumed on the broadest possible basis if perception is to be adjustment to an ecology. It is for this reason that an experimental study of the acquired utilization of artificial illumination cues in perceptual color constancy was made part of our Vienna program; the finding was that such acquisition is possible to a certain extent but that perceptual learning requires slow "stamping in" and is surprisingly autonomous of explicit intellectual awareness (Fieandt, 16).

Even purely ecological surveys may become fruitful for the theory of perception and learning. This writer and Kamiya (12) have demonstrated (with the use of $N = 892$ separations between adjacent parallel lines in a roughly "proportionate" sample of shots from a current motion picture) that the long-recognized gestalt factor of "proximity" possesses a certain modest ($r = .12$) but statistically significant ecological validity as an indicator of mechanical object unity. Its utilization as an organizing principle for perceptual "figures" is thus a probabilistically adjustive mechanism. The realization of this fact may help to open the door for a possible "reduction" of the hitherto unabsorbed gestalt dynamics into learning theory. The latter may thus eventually become universalized under the associationist-functionalist aspect, much as Newton's theory has incorporated both terrestrial gravitation laws and Kepler's laws of planetary motion within a common higher-order theory.

NOTES

1. As this goes to press I have before me an as yet unpublished, independently conceived study by R. C. Bolles and D. E. Bailey in which a representative sample of $N = 54$ familiar objects was presented to $n = 5$ adult subjects first nonvisually by naming or brief verbal description, and then visually. The authors have kindly given me permission to quote from their results. Nonvisual estimates were almost as accurate ($r = .988$) as visual estimates ($r = .994$), and in fact considerably more accurate than this writer would have guessed offhand. Yet the difference between the two achievements was found to be statistically significant (using the ecological N of 54, as is called for under representative design); in addition, the errors under the two conditions correlated to a relatively moderate extent only. The cue systems involved in the two performances thus seem to a considerable extent nonoverlapping, perhaps having less in common than I conjectured when I suggested above that the verbal situations were merely impoverishments of the full perceptual situations.

2. *Note by Leo Postman:* As I have tried to show elsewhere (26), the phenomena originally interpreted as perceptual defense can be adequately accounted for in terms of (*a*) principles of associative learning and (*b*) variables governing Ss' performance in the experimental situation. On these grounds the relevance of such phenomena to functionalist analysis in the narrower sense specified by Brunswik may be defended.

REFERENCES

1. Bertalanffy, L. v. The theory of open systems in physics and biology. *Science,* 1950, **3**, 23–29.
2. Bertalanffy, L. v. Theoretical models in biology and psychology. *J. Pers.,* 1951, **20**, 24–38.
3. Bruner, J. S., & Goodman, C. C. Value and need as organizing factors in perception. *J. Abnorm. Soc. Psychol.,* 1947, **42**, 33–44.
4. Brunswik, E. *Wahrnehmung und Gegenstandswelt.* Vienna: Deuticke, 1934.
5. Brunswik, E. Organismic achievement and environmental probability. *Psychol. Rev.,* 1943, **50**, 255–272. (Also in Marx, **24**).
6. Brunswik, E. Distal focussing of perception: size-constancy in a representative sample of situations. *Psychol. Monogr.,* 1944, **56**, No. 1 (Whole No. 254).
7. Brunswik, E. *Systematic and representative design of psychological experiments.* Berkeley: Univer. of California Press, 1947. (Also in J. Neyman [Ed.], *Berkeley symposium on mathematical statistics and probability.* Berkeley: Univer. of California Press, 1949.)
8. Brunswik, E. Remarks on functionalism in perception. *J. Pers.,* 1949, **18**, 56–65.
9. Brunswik, E. Note on Hammond's analogy between "relativity and representativeness." *Phil. Sci.,* 1951, **18**, 212–217.
10. Brunswik, E. *The conceptual framework of psychology.* Chicago: Univer. of Chicago Press, 1952. (*Int. Encycl. Unified Sci.,* Vol. I, No. 10.)
11. Brunswik, E. Representative design and probabilistic theory in a functional psychology. *Psychol. Rev.,* 1955, **62**, 193–217.
12. Brunswik, E., & Kamiya, J. Ecological cue-validity of 'proximity' and of other Gestalt factors. *Amer. J. Psychol.,* 1953, **66**, 20–32.
13. Feigl, H. Logical empiricism. In D. Runes (Ed.), *Twentieth century philosophy.* New York: Philosophical Library, 1943. (Also in H. Feigl & W. Sellars [Eds.], *Readings in philosophical analysis.* New York: Appleton-Century-Crofts, 1949. Pp. 3–26.)
14. Feigl, H. Rejoinders and second thoughts (Symposium on operationism). *Psychol. Rev.,* 1945, **52**, 284–288. (Also as: Some remarks on the meaning of scientific explanation. In H. Feigl & W. Sellars [Eds.], *Readings in philosophical analysis.* New York: Appleton-Century-Crofts, 1949. Pp. 510–514.)
15. Feigl, H. Functionalism, psychological theory, and the uniting sciences: some discussion remarks. *Psychol. Rev.* 1955, **62**, 232–235.
16. Fieandt, K. v. Dressurversuche an der Farbenwahrnehmung. *Arch. ges. Psychol.,* 1936, **96**, 467–495.
17. Frenkel-Brunswik, Else. Intolerance of ambiguity as an emotional and perceptual personality variable. *J. Pers.,* 1949, **18**, 108–143.
18. Hammond, K. R. Relativity and representativeness. *Phil. Sci.,* 1951, **18**, 208–211.
19. Hilgard, E. R. Discussion of probabilistic functionalism. *Psychol. Rev.,* 1955, **62**, 226–228.
20. Hull, C. L. The problem of intervening variables in molar behavior theory. *Psychol. Rev.,* 1943, **50**, 273–291. (Also in Marx, **24**.)
21. Koch, S. Theoretical psychology, 1950: an overview. *Psychol. Rev.,* 1951, **58**, 295–301.
22. Krech, D. Discussion: theory and reductionism. *Psychol. Rev.,* 1955, **62**, 229–231.
23. Lewin, K. Defining the "field at a given time." *Psychol. Rev.,* 1943, **50**, 292–310. (Also in Marx, **24**.)
24. Marx, M. H. *Psychological theory: contemporary readings.* New York: Macmillan, 1951.
25. Osgood, C. E. *Method and theory in experimen-*

tal psychology. New York: Oxford Univer. Press, 1953.

26. Postman, L. On the problem of perceptual defense. *Psychol. Rev.,* 1953, **60,** 298–306.

27. Postman, L. The probability approach and nomothetic theory. *Psychol. Rev.,* 1955, **62,** 218–225.

28. Postman, L., Bruner, J. S., & McGinnies, E. Personal values as selective factors in perception. *J. abnorm. soc. Psychol.* 1948, **43,** 142–154.

29. Tolman, E. C. *Purposive behavior in animals and men.* New York: Century, 1932.

[Manuscript for this symposium received August 17, 1954]

PART II

EXPLICATIONS

Iconoclasm at Work

A.

Demonstrations of a New Methodology

Representative Design

8

Probability Learning of Perceptual Cues in the Establishment of a Weight Illusion [1951]

 COMMENT
Probability Learning or Partial Reinforcement?
Mats Bjorkman

The study by Brunswik and Herma (B and H in the following) was an "early systematic effort" to investigate probability learning of perceptual cues in "an artificial miniature environment" that is representative of natural conditions (p. 170). *Representativeness* implies that cues should be given validities similar to those obtaining in the natural environment. How low are the ecological validities that can be discriminated by the organism? How rapidly does the organism adapt to the probabilistic structure of the environment? Does probability learning reach a final level at which it stabilizes? These were questions of primary interest to B and H, as in Brunswik's (1939c) early study of probability learning of instrumental acts.

Characteristics of the Experiments

The arrangement of the experiments was quite simple, in principle. Two objects were lifted simultaneously, one in each hand. The objects were dichotomized in heavy (500 g or 200 g) and light (100 g). Heavy and light objects were distributed differently for the two hands. Thus, lateral position was a cue to weight. The objects were made in two colors with a fixed relationship between position (hand) and color, that is, complete confounding of the cue variables. This was done "in order to reinforce the position cue in immediate perception yet at the same time to

introduce an additional factor that may prove confusing to explicit penetration of the design by the S" (p. 171). A cycle of trials from the main experiment is shown in Table 8.1. The proportion heavy to light was 2 : 1 for Hand A and 1 : 2 for Hand B. Expressed as a correlation coefficient, lateral position had an ecological validity of .33. In other experiments of the study, the ecological validities were .6 and 1.0.

Table 8.1 illustrates that three types of trials occurred during a block of trials. *Positive* trials represented the majority trend, that is, "heavy" for Hand A and "light" for Hand B. *Negative* trials, which were rare, contributed to the opposite trend. *Balanced* trials, finally, functioned as test trials in which the two weights were equal. The participant was told "that after some but not all of the presentations, he would be asked which of the two objects appeared heavier at the first moment of lifting. Immediate impression was to be expressed as a snap judgment" (p. 173–174).

Now, because of a phenomenon called *successive weight contrast* (or *weight expectancy illusion*) the discriminative "snap judgment" will be affected by weight impressions prior to the test trial: "Lifting of a relatively heavy weight is found to elicit an underestimation of weight in subsequent trials, and vice versa for light weights" (p. 171). Positive trials reinforced the contrast phenomenon because they *induced overestimation in the hand for which light objects dominated and under-*

167

estimation in the hand dominated by heavy objects. The rare negative trials had the opposite effect and tended to weaken weight contrast. Balanced trials could be expected to be "neutral" because they tended to induce overestimation, or underestimation, for both hands.

Successive weight contrast was the dependent variable of interest: "A case of contrast as defined in this paper is given when of the two objectively equal (or approximate) weights of a balanced trial, in its function as a test trial, the one presented on the side with generally lesser frequency of heavy objects is judged as the heavier of the pair" (p. 174). The focus is on the relationship between percentage of contrast judgments and previous experience of different kinds of trials: "A 50 percent contrast-effect represents chance response. Any significant rise above chance, although indicating the establishment of a perceptual 'illusion,' at the same time shows that probability learning is effective; it thus represents the over-all 'correct' response from a learning point of view" (p. 174–175).

Probability Learning and Partial Reinforcement

The authors asserted that the establishment of weight contrast "shows that probability learning is effective." Probability learning here differed from what this notion refers to today. The participants were not required to *infer* "heavy" or "light" on the basis of lateral position, as one would have expected had the task been a case of cue probability learning, but to *discriminate* between objects of equal weight. If the purpose of the experiments had been to study cue probability learning, the dominating response would have been the opposite to weight contrast.

It is not the uncertain relation between lateral position and light/heavy objects that matters for weight contrast. The efficient factor is *the relative frequency of positive trials.* As a consequence, the notion of ecological validity—that is, the correlation between lateral position and heavy/light objects—is psychologically irrelevant, although ecological validity and relative frequency of positive trials are closely related.

That B and H's use of the term *probability learning* is confusing to a present-day reader has to do with the fact that they made no distinction between probability learning and partial rein-

forcement. To B and H, ambiguous versus unequivocal cue-event relationships were identical to partial versus continuous reinforcement. This is evident already in the introductory paragraph, where they explained their purpose of "setting up an artificial miniature environment in which the relationship between cue and referent variable is probabilistic rather than absolute, that is, in which reinforcement is 'partial' . . . rather than of the conventional unequivocal kind." In their descriptions of the experiments, B and H reported ecological validities (.33, .6, and 1.0) and at the same time referred to reinforcement in the form of positive trials. Wordings (p. 172–173) such as "reinforcement ratio," "a straight series of eighteen positive reinforcing trials" (conventional training), and "a single reinforcement trial" (one-trial learning) express the fact that it is the positive trials that induce contrast responses. Since the proportion of positive, reinforcing, trials is the independent variable of interest, it is obvious that *partial reinforcement* would have been a more adequate term than *probability learning.*

These comments, of course, are made in hindsight. However, a reading of B and H's paper may be facilitated if, for a moment, one forgets modern connotations of probability learning and reads the paper with a view to partial reinforcement.

Results

Main Experiment

In the main experiment, training consisted of eight basic cycles (see Table 8.1), half of them in reverse order. This makes a total of seventy-two trials given without interruption. The order of the cycles was such that four test trials in a row occurred at trials 26–29 and 44–47. The learning curve averaged for each test trial over thirty-six participants is shown in the bottom part of Figure 8.2. Data from a replication of the first eighteen trials with a new set of thirty-six participants are reported in Table 8.2. The agreement between the two sets of data seems fairly good, indicating a satisfactory reliability.

The learning curve in Figure 8.1 rises rapidly from about 50 percent for the two balanced trials that initiated the training series to a first peak at Trial 11. During continued training, there is no sign of a stabilization at an asymptotic level.

Rather, "there is a somewhat paradoxical gradual decline to a final value in the neighborhood of 65 percent in the face of continuing trend reinforcement" (p. 175).

It should come as no surprise that it was the positive trials that produced the contrast effect: "Each of the minor upswings which may be noted follows upon a sequence of positive, trend supporting presentations which is interrupted by no more than scattered balanced trials and is free of negative trials" (p. 175). Balanced trials, however, tended to extinguish the illusion: "The deepest depressions, on the other hand, are found at the only two trials which conclude an accumulation of as many as four balanced presentations in a row (actually the most trend-weakening ecological evidence in the entire series). These trials are twenty-nine and forty-seven" (p. 175). That positive trials reinforced and balanced trials extinguished the weight illusion is precisely what one should expect. These results follow from the fact that the illusion is the accumulated result of previous trials, some strengthening, others weakening the illusion.

Higher Reinforcement Ratios

An increase of the heavy to light ratio to $4:1$ increased the percentage of contrast responses above the level it had for the ratio $2:1$. "Conventional training," corresponding to the ratio $1:0$, was investigated by a series of eighteen positive trials followed by four test trials. The contrast effect was complete for the first two test trials and dropped to 65 percent for the last two, confirming both the contrast-inducing effect of positive trials and the rapid extinction during balanced trials.

One-Trial Learning

The idea of testing the possibility of one-trial learning in a context of probability learning is somewhat peculiar. Obviously, one cannot learn a cue-event correlation in a single trial. Nevertheless, the one-trial condition is interesting because it may illuminate further the impact of positive trials. A single positive trial was followed by two balanced trials. The contrast score was 87.5 percent for the first test trial and 75 percent for the second. Although these figures were based on only twelve participants, they "suggest quick es-

tablishment of the characteristic response" (p. 176). A single trial is obviously sufficient to induce a preparedness of the sensory system to make discriminations that are biased in the direction of weight contrast.

Awareness of the Cue Weight Relation

After completion of the short series of eighteen trials, the participants were asked the following question: "In your opinion, which objects were on the average heavier, the green or the red?" and then a similar question concerning " . . . the right or the left?" The result, reported in Table 8.3, shows that only about 20 percent of the participants were aware of the cue-criterion relationship between position (or color) and weight. The majority of the answers were based on recollection of the responses on test trials, which were contrast responses in the majority of the cases. B and H discussed this finding with reference to two learning processes going on concurrently. The one was explicit and "seems in our case to be determined chiefly by the overtly verbalized contrast illusion predominant in the test trials with their objective balance of weights" (p. 177). The other was assumed to occur because "the existence of our perceptual contrast effect reveals the acquisition, on a more primordial level, of a concurrent implicit quasiexpectancy in the correct direction" (p. 178).

To the reviewer, it is hard to understand that the existence of weight contrast would imply two concurrent learning processes, the one explicit and conscious, the other implicit. First, the weight illusion is not something that is learned, in the ordinary sense of the word. Rather, it is a consequence of *a temporary preparation of the sensory system*, accomplished by positive trials. Second, as the experiments were designed, there was no reason to pay attention to the cue weight relation. The participants' task was to make discriminative judgments at the test trials, and in doing this, they had to rely on the immediate impression of *heaviness*. Lateral position, and hence the cue weight relation, was irrelevant for the immediate, "snap judgment." It should come as no surprise, then, that it was the responses during test trials that were recollected. The results in Table 8.3 are consistent with other results in the B and H paper, showing that reinforcement by positive trials makes the sensory system biased in the direction of weight contrast.

Summary

It has been argued above that the experimental design used by B and H should be viewed as a case of partial reinforcement rather than cue probability learning. Reinforcement was varied over a wide range with respect to both number of positive trials and their relative frequency. A consistent finding was that the weight illusion is established rapidly and extinguishes rapidly. The weight illusion is a short-lived perceptual phenomenon, which appears under certain experimental conditions, like those used by B and H.

A further finding, which intrigued B and H, was that the contrast responses, after having reached an early maximum, declined under continued reinforcement. The authors speculated that this "paradoxical" decline might be characteristic of learning with less than 100 percent reinforcement. The reviewer, however, is more willing to agree with their guess that "the paradoxical decline of our probability learning curve is wholly or in part an artifact of our use of an illusion as the test of learning; as is well known from texts in experimental psychology, some illusions have been shown to decline through practice" (p. 177). Rapid acquisition, rapid extinction, and fading out during practice were the main findings concerning the weight illusion.

However, the importance of B and H's paper is not primarily the experimental results as such. The fact that it represents an early effort (the experiments were conducted in Vienna in 1937) to construct a task that mirrored important aspects of the natural environment is far more significant. Two features are typical of this Brunswikian endeavor toward *representativeness*. First, B and H avoided the conventional "first-training-and-then-test" arrangement of the experiments. Test trials were inserted "quasi-randomly" among positive and negative trials. Second, three types of trials (positive, negative, and balanced) with contradictory impact were used to represent the ambiguity that often characterizes the natural environment. The significance of the paper is that it made irregularity and ambiguity the object of empirical study.

   REPRINT

Probability Learning of Perceptual Cues in the Establishment of a Weight Illusion

Egon Brunswik and Hans Herma

The trustworthiness of the sensory cues used by the perceptual system in establishing orientation in the environment is in general of a strikingly limited nature (1, 5). The dependability of cues may be defined as the statistical relationship between two environmental variables, as an "ecological validity" (5, 6). The intuitive utilization of

Reprinted from *Journal of Experimental Psychology* (1951), 41, 281–290.

at least some cues of an ecological validity of possibly as low as .1 to .3 by the perceptual system seems suggested by some recent studies in social perception (4, 6, 21). If the study of the acquisition of perceptual cues is to be "representative" of natural conditions, the experimental design will have to duplicate the low dependability of the ecological relationships involved (see 6, chap. X). This can be done by setting up an artificial miniature environment in which the relationship between cue and referent variable is probabilistic rather than absolute, that is, in which reinforcement is "partial" (13) rather than of the conventional unequivocal kind.

The present paper describes an early systematic effort in this direction. The experiments were conducted 14 years ago at the University of Vienna.[1] In the meantime the study was repeated, with improvements, by Levin (14, 15). In certain respects, these studies parallel in the field of perception an investigation of probability learning in rats conducted at the University of California in the spring of 1936, and published three years later (3).

Experimental Design

Medium

The response used in our study as a test of perceptual learning was the well-known so-called "weight expectancy illusion" described by Müller and Schumann (16), Steffens (18), and Myers (17). In this illusion, lifting of a relatively heavy weight is found to elicit an underestimation of weight in subsequent trials, and vice versa for light weights. The phenomenon may also be described as a successive weight contrast. Its high sensitivity made it seem the ideal medium for our study. Under this illusion, there is a dual determination of each weight perception, one by the anticipatory cue and one by the subsequent direct impact.

In our case, the problem was restated as one of differential response in simultaneous lifting of pairs, and a probabilistic design was employed to induce the contrast effect. The major cue-variable was defined by two discrete lateral positions, presentation to right vs. left hand. In order to reinforce the position cue in immediate perception, yet at the same time to introduce an additional factor that may prove confusing to explicit penetration of the design by the S, objects were made in two colors. For each S, there was a fixed relationship of position (hand) and color, that is, the two cue-variables were confounded with each other, or artificially "tied" (6), except for two special experimental series not carried beyond the exploratory stage; for the sake of brevity, we will describe our experiments in terms of position throughout this report. The significate or referent variable, weight, was also handled in a dichoto-

mous manner by being limited to two discrete and markedly different levels of strength, to be called "heavy" and "light."

Objects

The objects used in lifting were of three types. Objects in group I consisted of wooden blocks of 10 cm. height with a square base of 4 cm. by 4 cm. Since it seemed possible that the excess finger pressure required in lifting the blocks could interfere with the contrast effect, objects in groups II and III were given the shape of a flower pot 6 cm. in height, 4 cm. at the base, and 7 cm. at the top, that could be suspended from the fingertips. The objects were drilled and some of them evenly filled with lead to adjust for weight. They were lacquered to prevent identification by visual inhomogeneities. The standard "light" and "heavy" weights were 100 and 200 gm. for the blocks and 100 and 500 gm. for the pots, with duplicate sets in red and green.

In order to loosen up the Ss' impressions of equality in the test trials, the green standards in groups I and II were replaced in the test trials by two "approximates" slightly above and below the respective standard and alternating with each other from one test trial to the next to neutralize the deviations over the series. The deviations were 10 per cent up and down (in terms of the lesser weight) in group I, and 20 per cent in group II. For group III, only standard weights were used.

Experimental Series

Over-all relative frequencies of position-weight combinations were made complementary to each other on the two sides, but their sequences were kept independent of each other and were quasi-random. In our training sequences each trial is defined by a quasi-incidental pairing of two individual position-weight combinations. If on both sides the majority trend of reinforcement for the respective side happens to prevail, we speak of a positive (+) pair. The relatively rare pairings of minority combinations constitute negative (−) trials. Pairings of a majority with a minority combination will be called balanced (0); in this case, presentations on the two sides are either both "heavy" or both "light." These units of the training sequence offer a sensitive medium for whatever weight illusion may be developing and thus

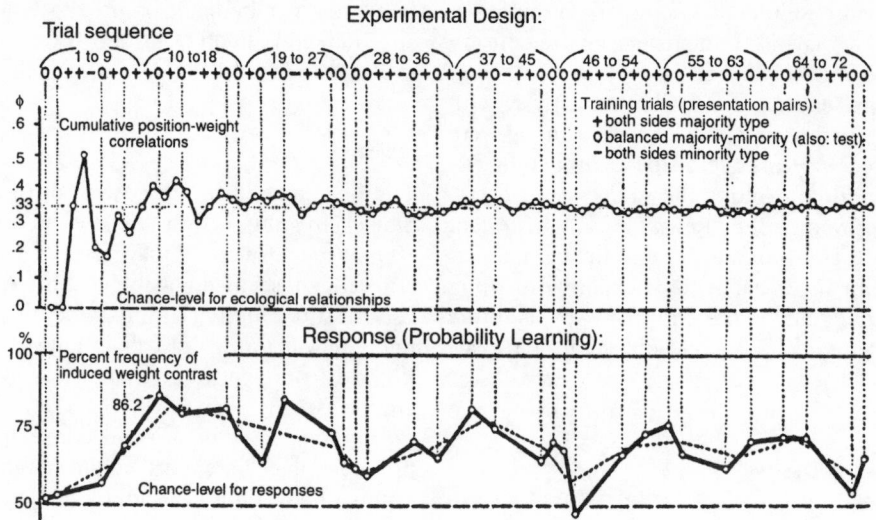

FIGURE 8.1 Design of main experiment with an artificial ecological association of
φ = .33, and probability learning in 36 S8. (Dotted vertical guide lines connect test trials in presentation sequence with corresponding per cent frequencies of illusion, passing between adjacent points of cumulative ecological correlation curve.)

were chosen to fulfill the added function of test trials.

In all, there were eight experimental series. Since in the above mentioned experiments with rats (3) a reinforcement ratio of 2 to 1 (67 per cent) had been found to be just below the threshold of probability learning, while 3 to 1 (75 per cent)

TABLE 8.1 Basic Cycle of Nine Trials in the Main Experiment

	Presentations		
Trial No.	Hand A	Hand B	Trial Type
1	Heavy	Heavy	Balanced (test)
2	Light	Light	Balanced (test)
3	Heavy	Light	Positive
4	Heavy	Light	Positive
5	Light	Heavy	Negative
6	Light	Light	Balanced (test)
7	Heavy	Light	Positive
8	Heavy	Heavy	Balanced (test)
9	Heavy	Light	Positive
Total	Heavy: 6	3	Positive: 4
	Light: 3	6	Balanced: 4
			Negative: 1

was distinctly above threshold, and since at the same time 2 to 1 (or φ = .33, see below) is of a similar order as the ecological validities of what appear to be the most dependable bodily cues in the natural social perception of human traits, this ratio was chosen for the position-weight associa-tion of our *main experiment*. The minimum by which the over-all frequency ratios on the two sides can be realized consists of $(2 + 1) \times (2 + 1) =$ 9 pairings. Of these, $2 \times 2 = 4$ are positive, $1 \times 1 =$ 1 pairing is negative, and $(2 \times 1) + (1 \times 2) = 4$ are balanced. The basic cycle chosen is shown in Table 8.1. In order to ascertain, for our group of Ss, the degree of approximation to complete absence of the illusion, i.e., to "chance" response, prior to the introduction of trials upsetting the hand-weight balance, we have compromised the principle of random sequence of trials to the point of having the first cycle begin with two balanced (and, thus, testing) trials. The total training series consisted of eight basic cycles, four of them in opposite order to increase random-like variety of sequence, and running into each other to form an uninterrupted training sequence of 72 trials (top of Fig. 8.1).

The center bottom portion of Table 8.1 repre-sents a four-fold table. Since the two variables,

position and weight, have been made dichotomous in the artificial ecological universe represented by our experimental design, the degree of
intimacy of their association may be described
in correlation terms by Pearson's mean square
contingency coefficient for two discrete variables, known as ϕ (phi) (9, p. 352 f.). For the main
experiment, this coefficient is .33. The accumulation of ecological evidence regarding hand-
weight correlation is shown graphically in the
middle part of Fig. 18.1. At the beginning there
is gross fluctuation after each new trial, but after
the conclusion of each cycle the coefficient is
always exactly .33. There is very close approximation to the over-all ratio after the second cycle.

For the full series of the main experiment 36
Ss were used, 12 each with object groups I, II,
and III. The sequences of substitute approximate
weights used with object groups I and II were
opposite to each other so that the results of each

individual test trial are strictly comparable with
the next for the total group of 36 Ss.

Since the first 18 trials (two cycles) of the main
experiment seemed the most crucial from the
point of view of results, they were duplicated
with a new set of 36 Ss (*short series*).

To study relearning, for group III of the short
series (12 Ss) the original 18 trials were followed
without interruption by a *reversal series* duplicating the original series with opposite sign for each
non-balanced presentation pair. This is shown at
the top of Fig. 8.2; the upper curve represents
the cumulative ecological position-weight association which swings down for the second 18 trials
as negative evidence accrues, ending at chance
level.

A *higher reinforcement ratio*, 4 to 1 (80 per
cent, $\phi = .6$), was employed in a further experiment. The minimum cycle, to which this series
was limited, consists of $(4 + 1) \times (4 + 1) = 25$ tri-

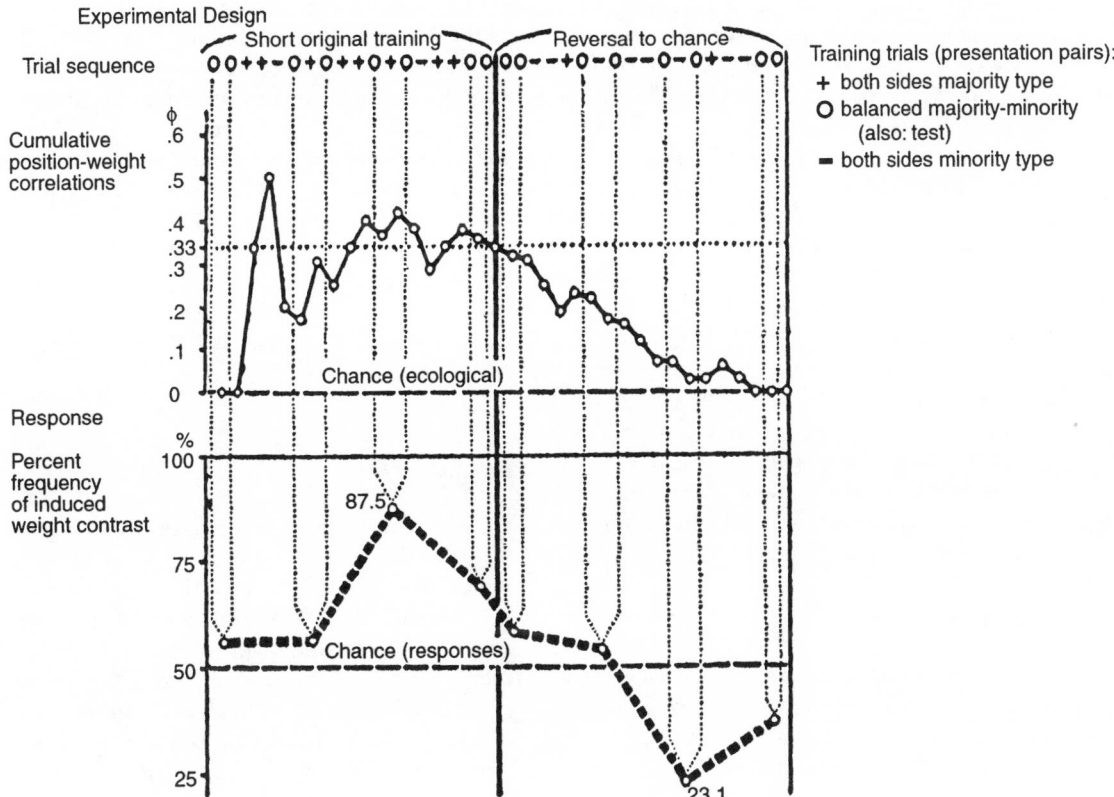

FIGURE 8.2 Reversal to ecological chance after short series, and probability learning-
relearning pattern, in 12 S8.

als, made up of $4 \times 4 = 16$ positively reinforcing pairs, $(4 \times 1) + (1 \times 4) = 8$ balanced pairs, and $1 \times 1 = 1$ pair of negative unbalance. Their quasi-random sequence (with the negative trial near the middle) was as follows:

$$00 + + + 0 + + 0 + + + + - + 0 + + 0 + + + + 00.$$

There were 12 Ss. Object group II was used; to offset the possible effect of the use of approximate weights, results of adjacent test trials were pooled in four pairs.

Conventional training, that is, perfect ecological correlation (100 per cent, $\phi = 1.00$) was studied by means of a straight series of 18 positive reinforcing trials, followed by four balanced test trials to get an idea of the extinction rate for our type of response and, thus, indirectly, of the pre-experimental trend of judgment in the present series; Ss and weights were as in the 4 to 1 series.

The possibility of a *one-trial* establishment of our contrast illusion was likewise studied, using 12 additional Ss. A single initial reinforcement trial was followed by two balanced trials.

Separation of the position from the color cue was undertaken in two special series. The number of Ss was 12 in each of them, using object group III. But in this case part of the Ss had participated in one of the earlier sessions. These series are therefore no more than exploratory. In the first, three positive reinforcing trials were followed by two balanced test trials in which the colors shifted position. In the second, there were 18 trials in which there was consistent (100 per cent) association of weight and color combined with an over-all neutrality of the position cue (50 per cent positive and 50 per cent negative position-weight reinforcements switching in quasi-random sequence). This was followed by four balanced test trials, with a continued switching of the position of the colors.

Subjects, Procedure, Instructions

The Ss were psychology students or other persons with some psychological background. Except for the two exploratory special position vs. color series, each of the Ss was allowed to participate in one experimental series only. In all experiments, for half of the Ss the preponderance of heavy over light weights was on the right side, and for half, on the left.

Experiments were performed individually. The S was seated comfortably in front of a screen placed on a table. Behind the screen sat E, arranging the stimulus objects for presentation. These were placed on a felt-covered, sound-absorbing tray that could be slid through an aperture in the lower part of the screen so as to come within easy reach of the S. The S was told that a series of pairs of objects similar to a sample pair now before him would be presented to hm for simultaneous lifting, and that after some but not all of the presentations, he would be asked which of the two objects appeared heavier at the first moment of lifting. Immediate impression was to be expressed as a snap judgment. The so-called third category, "equal" (including "undecided"), was permissible but was to be avoided as much as possible. The S was further instructed not to look while the objects were moved in and out of position. Upon a signal he was to turn his eyes downward so as just to be able to locate the objects without fixating them, the unexplained purpose of this being to prevent individual identification of the weights through minimal cues. He or she then was to grasp the objects with fingers pointing downward and lift them simultaneously and rapidly to a height of no more than a few inches, the right object with the right hand and the left object with the left, setting them back in place as quickly as possible, the entire lifting procedure to take no more than about 1 sec. This was then demonstrated by E taking the place of S. There were no preliminary trials. Each of the test trials was followed by the question: "At this trial, which one appeared heavier?"

Results

A case of contrast as defined in this paper is given when of the two objectively equal (or approximate) weights of a balanced trial, in its function as a test trial, the one presented on the side with generally lesser frequency of heavy objects is judged as the heavier of the pair; if it is judged lighter, we have an assimilation judgment. The over-all contrast-effect induced by the probability training is defined as the percentage of contrast judgments, including half of the equal judgments. A 50 per cent contrast-effect represents chance response. Any significant rise above chance, although indicating the establishment of a perceptual "illusion," at the same time shows that probability learning is effective; it thus represents the over-all "correct" response from a learning point of view.

Main Experiment and Short Series

While object groups I and especially II yielded a smaller total of equal judgments over the entire series, the over-all contrast effect as defined above is very close for the three groups (within about 2 per cent of each other). Results have thus been lumped together for the 36 Ss on each of the 32 balanced trials serving as test trials. They are shown in the bottom part of Fig. 8.1. The probability learning curve rises rapidly from near-chance to a maximum of 86.2 per cent. This maximum is reached at the fifth test trial, that is, the eleventh training trial. Afterwards, there is a somewhat paradoxical gradual decline to a final value in the neighborhood of 65 per cent in the face of continuing trend reinforcement. The general trend of the major and minor peaks, located at trials 11, 22, 38, 55, and perhaps also at trials 65 to 67, is one of consistent decline. The over-all trend is best shown by the thin broken line, a smoothed curve obtained by averaging the values on the first and second, then those on the third and fourth tests, and so forth.

Results of the short series are compared with those of the main series in Table 8.2. There is close correspondence of the general trend for the two sets; the eleventh trial marks the peak for both of them, and there is a consistent downward trend from then on. The upward swing is statistically significant, with a critical ratio of 4.5 between trials 1 and 11 for the entire group of 72 Ss. The paradoxical downward trend is likewise significant, with a critical ratio of 2.7 between

trials 11 and 18. The best-fitting linear slope for the entire material presented in Table 8.2 is 3.3 per cent on our scale per unit step from one of the eight test trials to the next ($r = .64$); this is significant at better than the .01 level. The nonlinearity of the trend is likewise significant at better than the .01 level ($\eta = .94$).

More detailed inspection of the probability learning curve of the main experiment reveals that a definite recency-effect appears to be superimposed upon the general shape of the curve. While the over-all initial rise followed by a slow downward trend is obvious from an inspection of the smoothed curve in Fig. 8.1, the actually obtained values as given by the heavy solid curve present a more uneven picture. Each of the minor upswings which may be noted follows upon a sequence of positive, trend-supporting presentations which is interrupted by no more than scattered balanced trials and is free of negative trials. The deepest depressions, on the other hand, are found at the only two trials which conclude an accumulation of as many as four balanced presentations in a row (actually the most trend-weakening ecological evidence in the entire series). These trials are 29 and 47.

Reversal Series

Results for this series, smoothed in the manner described above for the thin broken curve of the main experiment to eliminate incidental factors, are shown by the lower curve in Fig. 8.2. During the reversal period the curve drops far below the chance level, coming closer to chance again at the very end. Both this downward and paradoxical upward trend are quite symmetrical to the up and paradoxical down of the original training.

TABLE 8.2 Per Cent Frequency of Induced Contrast for the Two Initial Cycles of the Main Series and for the Short Series

	Test Trials							
Experiment	1	2	6	8	11	13	17	18
Main series (36 S_s)	51.4	52.8	57.0	69.5	86.2	80.5	82.0	73.6
Short series (36 S_s)	54.2	57.0	59.7	68.2	87.6	77.7	64.0	62.6
Totals (72 S_s)	52.8	54.9	58.4	68.9	86.9	79.1	73.0	68.1

Higher Reinforcement Ratio

Per cent frequencies of weight contrast, averaged for pairs of the eight test trials of this series in a manner similar to Fig. 8.2, are as follows: 42, 92, 84, 83. Since the number of Ss is small, it may be stated only tentatively that there again is an upward and subsequent downward trend, as familiar from the main experiment, although the rise is to a greater height despite the below-chance start of the curve, and the tapering-off is toward a higher level.

Conventional Training

For the first two of the four test trials following the 18 continuous positive trials of this series, the contrast effect was complete (100 per cent) for the 12 Ss employed; for the combined responses on the last two trials, the induced contrast dropped to 65 per cent, indicating a relatively strong effect of recency and a rapid rate of extinction.

One-Trial Learning

The contrast score after the single reinforcement was 87.5 per cent for the first and 75 per cent for the second of the balanced trials, each figure representing this time, to be sure, only one trial per S. These results suggest quick establishment of the characteristic response, although pre-experimental position tendencies, not testable in this particular case, may, of course, have considerably deviated from the ideal chance level of 50 per cent with such a small number of Ss.

Exploratory Position vs. Color Series

In the first of these two series, the contrast score on the first test trial was perfect (100 per cent) in terms of position in spite of the reversal of color; if color rather than position had been the more effective cue, the score should have been significantly under 50 per cent. On the second test trial the score fell to 75 per cent, indicating perhaps that there had been not too much pre-experimental bias in favor of the result on the first test trial.

The second exploratory position vs. color series, in which the training was carried by color alone while position was kept neutral, had no appreciable training effect. For both the first and second pairs of test trials the score was 46 per cent while it should be significantly above 50 per cent if color were picked up as a cue for weight.

Discussion

Long-range Trend of Probability Learning: Paradoxical Decline

Successful establishment of an extrinsic cue for weight, in spite of the fact that its over-all ecological validity is no better than 2 to 1, reveals superiority of sensitivity of probability learning in this particular case of human perception over the particular case of probability discrimination in rats studied by Brunswik (3). Over and above all the more obvious differences in problem and procedure that make a fair comparison well-nigh impossible, it must be stressed that the corresponding rat experiment guaranteed exploration of both sides only on those trials on which the first turn was to the unrewarded side and the animal had to "correct" itself by turning to the opposite side. In the present experiment information is always complete and even simultaneous on both sides. Furthermore, the training period was only one-third as long in the experiment with rats as it is in the present experiment. An experiment by Jarvik (12) has shown that low reinforcement ratios may yet produce learning after a prolonged latency period.

The fact that the initial upswing of the probability learning curve is followed by a tapering-off despite continued reinforcement is quite atypical of ordinary learning curves obtained with the standard 100 per cent reinforcement design, and has, therefore, been called "paradoxical" in describing the results. Apparently, probability learning has certain characteristics of its own. It may well be that the learning mechanism as a whole is characterized by a certain tendency toward an initial all-or-none response (3). If justification of a positive response is not complete in the further course of reinforcement, there apparently follows what purposive behaviorists like Tolman (20) may be inclined to consider a disappointment or disruption of (verbalized or unverbalized) expectancies. Such a type of reaction would imply an eventual settling on a compromise level of frequency, as observed in our material. This in-between solution would be somewhat of an analogy to the well-known compromise tendencies that spoil the accuracy of the perceptual constancies (1, 6). So long as we limit our consideration to the evidence presented here, however, the possibility cannot be excluded that the paradoxical decline of our probability learning curve is wholly or in part an artifact of our use of an illusion as the test of learning; as is well known from texts in experimental psychology, some illusions have been shown to decline through "practice."

From a purely descriptive point of view of our main experiment shows a fairly close agreement between the level of the final, near-horizontal stretch of the learning curve covering approximately the last three training cycles, within which an average induced contrast-effect of about 65 per cent is maintained, and the ecological frequency ratio of 2 to 1, or 67 per cent. A similar picture is given in our experiment with a 4 to 1 ratio. We would hesitate to assume, however, that a general principle underlies this correspondence, as appears to have been claimed by some authors, notably by Hilgard (10, p. 272), in his discussion of Brunswik's experiment with rats (3) and, perhaps, also by Grant and Hake (8).

Follow-up experiments by Levin (14,), in which the standardized random sequence of the basic cycle of our main experiment was systematically evened out by the use of a total of nine alternate types of cycles, each of them presented to a different group of Ss, further confirmed the characteristic shape of our probability learning curve with its initial upward swing followed by a gradual downward trend, although the peak was found to be somewhat delayed.[2]

In an experiment by Jarvik (11, 12), dealing with the differential anticipation of one of two alternatives in randomized word sequences, a reinforcement ratio of as low as 60 per cent vs. 40 per cent was found to be above the threshold of probability learning, although there was a considerable delay of the peak. There also were suggestions of ensuing decline, but they were far from being statistically significant.

Recency-Effect

The positive influence of recency in temporarily raising the learning effect was revealed by a detailed study of our main experiment. It is also evident in the dropping of the reversal training

curve *below* the chance level, in the effectiveness of short-term or one-trial reinforcement, and in the relative rapidity of extinction after extensive conventional absolute reinforcement; the latter is in line with Fieandt's (7) finding of rapid extinction in case of artificially established illumination cues in perceptual color constancy.

Jarvik (11, 12) has reported a shift from the positive to a negative recency-effect during continuous "runs" of positive reinforcements in probability series. There is no analogue to this in our results, indicating that the phenomenon may be specific to certain conditions, perhaps those favoring an analytical attitude toward the single response.

Learning and Awareness of What Is Being Learned

In order to throw light upon the relationship between the learning of a cue by the perceptual system and the explicit intellectual awareness of the cue on the part of S, 22 of the 24 Ss participating in those of the short series which were not followed by additional reversal training (groups I and II) were asked the following questions after completion of the experiment: "In your opinion, which objects were on the average heavier, the green or the red?" After answering this, the Ss were asked a similar question concerning " . . . the right or the left?" Those Ss who in this second case seemed uncertain as to whether they should refer to the judgments actually asked for by the E, or to their impressions in the total trials regardless of whether or not these impressions were overtly expressed, were told to refer to the latter.

Results are shown in Table 8.3. Conscious impressions in terms of right vs. left position seem in four-fifths of the cases in opposition to the correct. Explicitly conceptualized learning

TABLE 8.3 Frequency of Awareness of Relation of Cues to Weight

S's Report	Position Cue	Color Cue
Correctly aware of cue	4	5
Incorrectly aware of cue	16	14
Undecided about cue	2	3
Total	22	22

thus seems in our case to be determined chiefly by the overtly verbalized contrast illusion predominant in the test trials with their objective balance of weights, rather than by the objectively and undoubtedly also subjectively far more drastic opposite differences in the trials with positive (vs. negative) imbalance. Yet, the existence of our perceptual contrast effect reveals the acquisition, on a more primordial level, of a concurrent implicit quasi-expectancy in the correct direction. This case of learning with "submerged mediation" (1) is not only what Thorndike (19) and others have referred to as "learning without awareness of what is being learned"; it is learning *against* awareness of what is being learned. Restriction of verbalization to the test trials has made it possible for the two levels of learning to stand out more clearly against each other.

As is further shown in Table 8.3, the overt effect seems to hold about equally well for the other potential cue, color (14 vs. 5 cases). In part this may be due to the fact that, as was revealed by a further question to the Ss (results not shown in the table), four of them had become aware of the univocal relationship between position and color, and another 15 thought that such a relationship was maintained in the majority or in most of the trials; only three Ss claimed that there was no relationship between color and position.

Summary

Artificially established ecological associations of 2 to 1 (67 per cent, $\phi = .33$) and of 4 to 1 (80 per cent, $\phi = .60$) between position (right- vs. left-hand presentation) as a perceptual cue, and weight as the referent variable were found to be effective in inducing an illusion of weight contrast. The probability learning curve, after first rising rather rapidly, shows a subsequent slow but steady decline to a compromise position. The decline is "paradoxical" in view of continued reinforcement of the over-all association. This decline may be an intrinsic characteristic of probability learning or merely the result of our use of an illusion as the test of learning. A short-range positive recency-effect is superimposed upon the characteristic long-range trend.

Added experiments deal with reversal of training, one-trial learning, and an exploratory establishment of the position cue, rather than a confounded color cue, as the one chiefly utilized by the perceptual system in our experiment.

Under the conditions of our experiment, perceptual probability learning seems not only not to be based on, but to run counter to, what is being learned at the conscious level.

[Manuscript received April 14, 1950]

NOTES

1. A brief report of the study was given by Brunswik at the International Congress of Psychology in 1937 (2).

2. For a brief discussion of other aspects of Levin's study relevant to our problem, see Brunswik (6, p. 54).

REFERENCES

1. Brunswik, E. *Wahrnehmung und Gegenstandswelt.* Vienna: Deuticke, 1934.
2. Brunswik, E. Das Induktionsprinzip in der Wahrnehmung. In H. Piéron and J. Meyerson (Ed.), *Communications, 11th International Congress of Psychology, Paris, 1937.* Paris: Alcan, 1938. P. 346. (Abstract.)
3. Brunswik, E. Probability as a determiner of rat behavior. *J. exp. Psychol.,* 1939, 25, 175–197.
4. Brunswik, E. Perceptual characteristics of schematized human figures. *Psychol. Bull.,* 1939, 36, 553. (Abstract.)
5. Brunswik, E. Organismic achievement and environmental probability. *Psychol. Rev.,* 1943, 50, 255–272.
6. Brunswik, E. *Systematic and representative design of psychological experiments: with results in physical and social perception.* Berkeley: Univ. of California Press, 1947.
7. Fieandt, K. v. Dressurversuche an der Farbenwahrnehmung. *Arch. ges. Psychol.,* 1936, 96, 467–495.
8. Grant, D. A., and Hake, H. W. Acquisition and extinction of the Humphreys' verbal response with differing percentages of "reinforcement." *Amer. Psychologists,* 1949, 4, 226. (Abstract.)
9. Guilford, J. P. *Psychometric methods.* New York: McGraw-Hill, 1936.
10. Hilgard, E. R. *Theories of learning.* New York: Appleton-Century-Crofts, 1948.
11. Jarvik, M. E. Probability discrimination and the gambler's fallacy in guessing. *Amer. Psychologist,* 1946, 1, 453–454. (Abstract.)
12. Jarvik, M. E. Probability learning and a negative recency effect in the serial anticipation of alter-

native symbols. *J. exp. Psychol.*, 1951, **41**, 291–297. `

13. Jenkins, W. O., and Stanley, J. C. Partial reinforcement: A review and critique. *Psychol. Bull.*, 1950, **47**, 193–234.

14. Levin, M. M. Weight illusions induced by cues of low validity. *Psychol. Bull.*, 1943, **40**, 582. (Abstract.)

15. Levin, M. M. Inconsistent position cues in the establishment of perceptual illusions. Unpublished Doctor's dissertation, University of California, 1946.

16. Müller, G. E., and Schumann, E. Über die psychologischen Grundlagen der Vergleichung gehobener Gewichte. *Pflüg. Arch. ges. Physiol.*, 1889, **45**, 37–112.

17. Myers, C. S. A *text-book of experimental psychology*. New York: Longmans-Green, 1911.

18. Steffens, L. Über die motorische Einstellung. *Z. Psychol.*, 1900, **23**, 241–308.

19. Thorndike, E. L. *The fundamental of learning*. New York: Columbia Univ. Press, 1932.

20. Tolman, E. C. *Purposive behavior in animals and men*. New York: Appleton-Century, 1932.

21. Wallace, R. P. Apparent personality traits from photographs varied in bodily proportions. *Psychol. Bull.*, 1941, **38**, 744–745. (Abstract.)

9

Thing Constancy as Measured by Correlation Coefficients [1940]

 COMMENT

To Know an Experimenter

Elke M. Kurz and Ralph Hertwig

Whenever Brunswik researched perception, he simultaneously made psychological research itself an object of study. Brunswik was not a perception psychologist on the one hand and a philosopher of psychological methodology on the other; he was always both at the same time. This two-sided research agenda was his forte and his achievement; it constituted a challenge for his contemporaries, and it remains a challenge for us.

Common wisdom has it that "to know a man you should walk a mile in his shoes." We believe that it is equally true that "to know an experimenter you should replicate her study." For this reason we replicated the experimental study reported in the paper "Thing Constancy as Measured by Correlation Coefficients." This paper is crucial in Brunswik's work as it stands for the emigrant's attempt to relate his Viennese work to highly esteemed methodological tools of his new academic home. In this sense, this paper marks the transition between his Viennese past and his American future. Before we describe our replication of Brunswik's study, let us also appreciate his intellectual transition in relation to his biographical transition from Privatdozent at the University of Vienna to assistant professor at the University of California at Berkeley.

Constancies and Transitions

In August 1939, "Thing Constancy as Measured by Correlation Coefficients" arrived on the desk of Herbert S. Langfeld, then editor of *Psychological Review*, less than two years after its author had left Vienna and gone to Berkeley. How perceptual constancies can best be measured was a research question that accompanied Brunswik from his old to his new academic home. The term *thing constancy* is a literal translation from the German term *Dingkonstanz*. Thing constancy, or perceptual constancy, is our tendency to perceive size, color, shape, loudness, and other features of our surroundings as relatively constant despite changing projections on perceptual surfaces. Size constancy, for instance, entailed that "for a somewhat developed human being, an approaching visitor will not grow from a finger-like dwarf up to an immense giant, but will, within certain limits, quite fairly retain a constant apparent size" (Brunswik, 1937, p. 228). In Vienna, Brunswik had measured perceptual constancy of various sorts using a *constancy ratio*. This measure was of his own creation (Brunswik, 1928; for a definition, see p. 189, and also our Figure 9.2) and became subsequently known as the *Brunswik ratio* (e.g., Woodworth, 1938, p. 864).

At the University of California, Brunswik had an influential supporter, Edward Tolman. In a letter to the vice president and provost of the university dated December 2, 1937, Tolman wrote "that it would be not far short of a crime for the University to let him [Brunswik] go." They did not commit this crime, and Brunswik accepted a position there in 1938. Else Frenkel, a colleague at the Vienna Psychological Institute, came to the United States, and she and Brunswik were married that year. In other respects these were, of course, not happy times. Austria was annexed to Nazi Germany in 1938, and Adolph Hitler's plans of persecution, aggression, and war were painfully apparent. Brunswik also worried about his former advisers, Karl and Charlotte Bühler, who had been forced to emigrate (Ash, 1987). In a letter addressed to Walter Miles at Yale University, dated April 22, 1938, Brunswik inquired about the "chance to place them." In the same letter, he indicated that he was going to send "this same letter to a small number of other psychologists who [he thought] might be particularly interested in the Bühlers" (*Archives for the History of American Psychology*, Ms. #1134). These efforts to assist his mentors were not met with particular success.

In Berkeley, Brunswik (1937) prepared an English presentation of his Viennese research program. This program was a sophisticated continuation of Karl Bühler's theoretical positions. According to Bühler's duplicity principle, constancy phenomena were the result of at least a "two-fold stimulus-basis" (Brunswik, 1937, p. 111; see Doherty & Kurz, 1996). After 1937, this research program became subjected to a probabilistic "breeze." Brunswik participated, for instance, in a "statistical discussion group" with colleagues at the psychology department (p. 191, footnote 5). Eventually, in his paper of 1940, Brunswik introduced correlation statistics to his perception research, then he carefully weighted the pros and cons of his new and his old ways of measuring thing constancy.

Brunswik's paper of 1940 was in many ways just a beginning. The work that Brunswik carried out after his move to Berkeley reflects his process of immigration. In this process, "old" and "new" cultures are compared and evaluated in order to achieve an integration. Brunswik became an American citizen in 1943. Two years later, he participated in the first University of California Symposia on Mathematical Statistics and Probability, with a paper that was later, in 1947, published as "Systematic and Representative Design of Psychological Experiments" (and posthumously, in 1956, republished as Part I of his book *Perception and the Representative Design of Psychological Experiments*). This paper represented, as he phrased it, his "bringing to convergence European academic with Anglo-American statis-

tical tradition" (Brunswik, 1947, p. 56). Premonitions of this intellectual integration were already present in his paper of 1940 (p. 191), which ended with a statement that revealed his clear sense of direction: "The author's ultimate aim is to establish a multidimensional psychophysics which will include the distal environment within its scope."

Berlin "Replicates" Berkeley

Our original motive for replicating the study reported in "Thing Constancy as Measured by Correlation Coefficients" was to "walk in Brunswik's shoes." But to be honest, we also harbored some disbelief concerning an effect that we noticed in his data. To our surprise, participants' performance revealed consistent overestimation of physical size (compare the bs and es in Table 9.1, p. 187, where b stands for body size and e for average estimate). Would we find the same clear-cut overestimation effect with our replication?

We structure the presentation of our replication according to the rationale of present-day APA format. Brunswik's original paper, however, was organized differently; it consisted of three main sections numbered I, II, and III. The first gave a report of his laboratory study, including a rudimentary version of his later lens model (see Kurz & Tweney, 1997). In Part II, he analyzed and compared his new and his old measures of achievement, by and large coming out in favor of correlation. The third section was dedicated to the pragmatic aspects of his new tool, showing how his use deviated from the tool's more-or-less conventional use. We superimposed APA format on Brunswik's study in order to accentuate those aspects of Brunswik's practice that deviate from our present-day expectations. In our presentation, *Berkeley* signifies Brunswik's study of 1940, *Berlin* our replication of 1998.

Hypotheses

Berkeley

No explicit hypotheses were stated or formally tested. As indicated by the title of the paper, Brunswik's aim was measurement.

Berlin

Initially, we were surprised at the consistent overestimation of size reported by Brunswik. We would have expected some more-or-less random variation of the estimates around the body sizes of the cubes. We quickly figured out that such an overestimation effect was consistent with Brunswik's Viennese theory of in-between-objects. This theory postulated that estimated size lies in between body size and proximal size. (Note, that we use *projective size* and *proximal size* interchangeably.) It follows that size is overestimated whenever projective size is larger than body size, which was the case for all cubes in Brunswik's experiment (compare the *b*s and *p*s in Table 9.1, where *b* stands for body size and *p* for projective size). Projective size was larger because of the following considerations. For example, given a cube with an edge length of 70 mm at a distance of 10 m, its projective size measured in degrees of visual angle is equal to the projective size of a comparison cube of 84 mm at a distance of 12 m. Because the comparison series was at a larger distance from the observer than the cubes that had to be estimated, and because projective size was determined with respect to the distance of the comparison series it followed that projective size was larger than body size for all cubes. Brunswik's theory of in-between-objects made a clear prediction and was clearly corroborated by his results.

Method: Participants

Berkeley

"Eight students were used as observers, each of them running through the experiment only once" (p. 188). Brunswik averaged their estimates and then reported only the values averaged across the participants.

Berlin

Eight researchers from the ABC research group at the Max Planck Institute for Human Development were used as observers, each of them running through the experiment once. (The entire ABC group was rewarded with cake at coffee time when the results were presented.)

Materials

Berkeley

A set-up of 15 cubes made of natural hardwood, ranging from 50 to 70 mm, was presented to the observers at frontal planes of 2, 4, 6, 8 and 10 m distance, three cubes at each distance. The lateral distance between neighboring cubes was approximately 80 cm. In the rear of the room, at a distance of 12 m from the observer, a comparison series of 13 cubes ranging from 30 to 90 mm with step-intervals of 5 mm was set up. All objects were placed on tables of usual height. The observer was seated on a slightly elevated chair and so had a complete view of the set-up. The sizes and distances of the cubes are schematically represented in Table 1 (p. 187; a more elaborated version of Table 9.1 can be found in Brunswik, 1956b, p. 68).

The experimental arrangement of the cubes kept the correlation between distal stimuli (the *b*s) and proximal stimuli (the *p*s)—that is, between body sizes and projected sizes—at a low value and, as Brunswik (p. 188) remarked, "could, as *e.g.* for the purpose of a further demonstration, easily be brought down to zero."

Berlin

The only room spacious enough for this setup at the Max Planck Institute for Human Development was a large conference room. Given the distribution of windows in this room, its space was not evenly lit. We turned on all the lights and even brought in an additional lamp to approximate evenly distributed light conditions. (When setting up the experimental arrangement, it became apparent to us that this study could only have been conducted by a person who loved measurement.)

A participant in a pilot run pointed out that the comparison task was complicated by the necessity to count the cubes in the comparison series in order to name their respective number. We therefore numbered the comparison cubes on a banner mounted on the wall behind the comparison series.

Procedure

Berkeley

"The observer was asked to take a natural unconstrained attitude, and to match each of the 15 cubes with the comparison series. . . . The order of the judgments was systematically varied from observer to observer" (p. 188).

Berlin

For the instructions that would induce "a natural unconstrained attitude" we consulted Brunswik's paper of 1944 (p. 4, "naive perceptual attitude"). Before the participants entered the conference room, we showed them a schematic representation of the experimental arrangement, similar to the elaborated version of Table 9.1 shown in Brunswik (1956b, p. 68). With the instructions, we emphasized that physical size should be the basis for their judgment; we even showed two cubes of equal size during the instruction phase.

Each participant was asked to make fifteen judgments. The experimenter specified a particular cube in the array (e.g., third row, middle cube), and the participant answered by giving the number of the cube in the comparison series that matched the specified cube in physical size. The experimenter specified the cubes in random order; the order was different for each of the eight participants.

Results

Berkeley

The data in Brunswik's study of 1940 were the estimates of cube size as determined by participants' choice of corresponding comparison cubes. For each of the fifteen cubes, an average estimate, e (averaged across the eight participants), was reported in Brunswik's Table 9.1. In his Table 9.2, he presented the "correlations among distal stimuli, proximal stimuli, and perceptual responses" (p. 188). The correlation between proximal stimuli and perceptual responses was $r(ep) = .26$, whereas the "distal correlation, directly expressing far-reaching perceptual achievement" was as high as $r(eb) = .97$. Brunswik did not mention it explicitly, but size was consis-

tently overestimated in the averaged data he presented (see our Figure 9.2).

Berlin

Did we replicate Brunswik's findings? Yes and no. Yes, because we obtained nearly identical correlations: The correlation between proximal stimuli and perceptual responses, $r(ep)$, was .21, and the correlation between distal stimuli and perceptual responses, $r(eb)$, was .98. No, because we did not replicate the systematic overestimation effect he found. Rather, as the average estimates in Figure 9.1 show, we found (1) underestimation in three cases, (2) perfect calibration of the estimate in one case, and (3) in the remaining cases, merely slight overestimation. The interesting point here is not that our colleagues at the ABC group performed better than Brunswik's Berkeley participants but that the calculation of correlation coefficients is not sensitive to such substantial reduction in error.

A pattern of results similar to the one we obtained on the aggregate level was also observed on the level of the individual estimates. Out of a total of 120 estimates (eight participants estimating fifteen cubes) cube size was underestimated in twenty-eight cases, was accurately estimated in thirty-eight, and was overestimated in fifty-four cases. It should be added that the participants in Berlin overestimated cube size in no case by more than 15 mm or underestimated cube size by more than 10 mm, which corresponds to choosing three or two cubes, respectively, to the left or right of the matching cube in the comparison series. The data reported by Brunswik do not allow for a corresponding analysis on the level of individual estimates.

Why is there such a discrepancy between Brunswik's and our findings concerning the estimates' precision? Here, a study by Beverley E. Holaday may indicate a possible answer. Holaday was an American student at the University of Vienna in early 1930. It is interesting to note that Brunswik served as participant in Holaday's study, and he also edited Holaday's paper for the *Archiv für Psychologie*. Holaday (1933) manipulated multiple variables and combinations thereof and studied their impact on perceptual size constancy. He had no less than twenty-eight experimental conditions! Based on these results, Holaday established a rank order of experimental

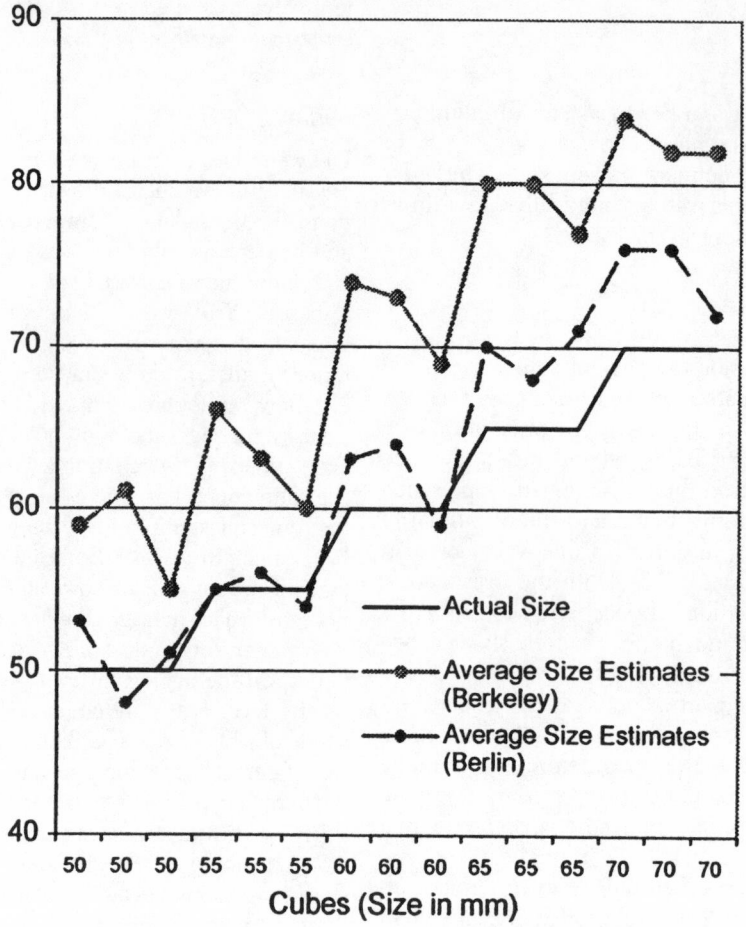

FIGURE 9.1 Average estimates of cube size obtained in Berkeley and Berlin. The cubes are ordered according to their actual size, and within each size category (e.g., 50 mm), the cubes are ordered according to their distance from the observer (starting with the nearest cube).

conditions according to a constancy ratio index. What is relevant to the discrepancy between Brunswik's and our findings is that the average value for the constancy ratio that we determined in our replication is about comparable to the value Holaday (1933) reported for "critical attitude," an attitude that Brunswik characterized as follows (1944, p. 4): "Take the attitude you would have, if you were to bet upon the sizes in question to the best of your knowledge." Brunswik repeatedly pointed out the importance of instructions in constancy research (e.g., Brunswik, 1947, p. 20). Although we attempted to induce a naïve

perceptual attitude via our instructions, we may have failed in the ecology of our lab, in which betting is part of the lab culture.

Discussion

Correlation Statistics

Brunswik's use of the correlation coefficient to measure achievement was unconventional—and was met by harsh resistance—because it divorced correlation statistics from the study of interindividual differences (Gigerenzer, 1987). The correlation coefficient first emerged from Francis Galton's studies of anthropometric data, more specifically, of interindividual differences in the relation between height and forearm length (Stigler, 1986). In psychology, correlation statistics remained pragmatically linked to the measurement of interindividual differences, to the point where psychology was split into two more-or-less unrelated disciplines, the "correlational" and the "experimental." In the late 1930s, Brunswik began to use the correlation coefficient for the quantification of perceptual achievement and mediation—in complete disregard of interindividual differences.

In his paper of 1940, Brunswik went so far as to average the estimates of eight participants and then to consider this average "as the result of one single experiment with *one observer only*" (p. 188, italics added; see above "Participants: Berkeley"). Brunswik removed—so to speak, with one stroke—variation between participants from consideration (a practice considered unacceptable today, although still frequently used). But note the context, Brunswik's intention was to liberate an established tool from its familiar context (the study of interindividual differences) and to make it serve a new purpose (the measurement of achievement).

Achievement

In 1940, Brunswik characterized his Viennese understanding of achievement as "the degree of perfection of *the constancy mechanism*" (p. 189, italics added). Achievement meant the degree to which the perceptual system was able to move its response from the proximal stimulus. Thus, achievement was relative only to the proximal stimulus, not—yet!—to the distal environment. This understanding of achievement was reflected by his constancy ratio. In the case of size perception, the ratio related the differences between estimated size and projected size and between body size and projected size. The third possible difference—namely, that between estimated size and body size (the errors)—had not been formally considered in his Viennese program (see Figure 9.2).

In Berkeley, achievement became measurable by a "distal correlation" (p. 188). Thus, the environment was no longer "distant" (p. 187) but

had become measurable in its relation to "the perceptual system—or the organism in general" (p. 191), and hence epistemologically closer. The relation between perceptual response and distal stimulus (the distal correlation r_{eb} in Figure 9.2) was now treated on a par with the relations of response and distal stimulus to the proximal stimulus (the correlations r_{ep} and r_{bp} in Figure 9.2).

However, as with the old measure, correlation did not take the *amount* of deviation of judged size from actual size—that is, of error—into account. This design feature of the correlation coefficient was nicely revealed in our replication of Brunswik's study. Although we replicated Brunswik's reported correlations almost identically, our participants were much better calibrated than his. Brunswik himself seems to have realized this limitation of correlation statistics. Already in his paper of 1941, he included systematic error analysis in his constancy research. Later, in his contribution to a Symposium on Personal and Social Factors in Perception held during the 1949 meeting of the *American Psychological Association* in Denver, he expanded his use of error analysis to distinguish perceptual and reasoning processes.

To Know an Experimenter . . .

While preparing our replication of Brunswik's (1940b) study, we sought answers to questions that we could not find answered in his paper. Among those questions was, for instance, whether we should correct for differences in body size of the observers by adjusting the height of the swivel chair on which the participants were sitting. Brunswik's paper shows nearly complete absence of such procedural concerns. We see two reasons for his "disregard." First of all, the paper of 1940 was not meant to be a research paper, in the sense of being a detailed report of a particular laboratory study of size perception (see Brunswik, 1940b, p. 190). Rather, the paper was a "sketchy beginning, with the purpose of demonstrating a general principle," namely, how correlation analysis "deals with both the distal and the proximal" (p. 190). Second, we believe that the absence of such concerns also reflects Brunswik's developing opposition to the "classical" ideal of experimental control.

Brunswik came to be convinced that the "classical experiment," which "has been handed down

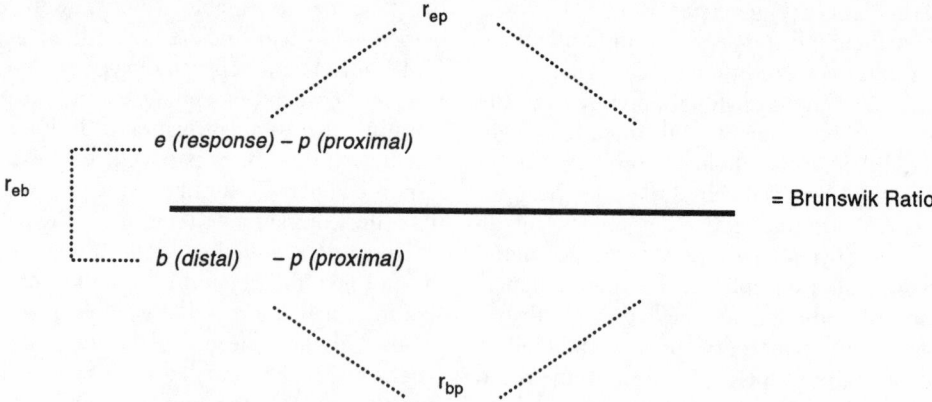

FIGURE 9.2 Correlations among distal stimuli, proximal stimuli, and perceptual response and how they map onto Brunswik ratio. In 1940, Brunswik used *e* to denote estimate, *p* to denote projected size, and *b* to denote body-size. He also refered to *e* as the perceptual response, to *p* as the proximal stimulus, and to *b* as the distal stimulus.

to us from such famous origins in physics as Galileo's study of the fundamental laws of falling bodies" (Brunswik, 1947, p. 8), was of limited utility to the experimentalist in psychology. For him, the "classical formula" in the context of psychological experimentation meant the following (1947, p. 9): "All relevant external conditions (and there are supposedly not too many) to be systematically controlled, all internal conditions to be treated quasi-systematically by computational elimination of random variability." Brunswik's opposition is nicely illustrated by the annotations that he made in his copy of Woodworth's (1938) *Experimental Psychology* (which, thanks to Kenneth Hammond, the Brunswik Society, and Ryan Tweney, will be preserved at the Archives for the History of American Psychology, Akron, Ohio). On page two of Woodworth's text Brunswik doubly underlined the phrase "he [the experimenter] holds all the conditions constant except for one" and commented in fine pencil "*imposs!*" (see for a reprint of this page with Brunswik's annotations Kurz and Tweney, 1997, p. 228). Consequently, Brunswik had also a low regard for the "autocratic

experimenter" (Brunswik, 1944, p. 35). And he fully endorsed the idea that "modern experiments on thing constancy are deliberately 'poorly controlled' with respect to cues, when viewed from the standpoint of the classical experimentalist" (Brunswik, 1947, p. 23).

We have come full circle. Brunswik was not a perception psychologist on the one hand and a philosopher of psychological methodology on the other—he always was both simultaneously. His study of 1940 introduced the distal environment into his perception research, and as a consequence, he had to rethink psychology's notion of the experiment. Crucial steps of Brunswik's rethinking of experimental methodology after 1940 may be traced in his paper "Distal Focussing of Perception: Size-Constancy in a Representative Sample of Situations" (1944). But here again, it may be the case that "to know an experimenter . . ."

NOTE

We wish to thank Gerd Gigerenzer, Wolfgang Hell, Laurence Fiddick, Martin Lages, and Anita Todd for their comments on earlier versions of this paper.

 REPRINT

Thing Constancy as Measured by Correlation Coefficients

Egon Brunswik

The term 'perceptual thing constancy' is applied wherever a certain type of perceptual response is found, under ordinary circumstances, to vary concomitantly with a certain kind of physical property of distant, or 'distal,'[1] environmental bodies (such as size, shape, reflectivity to light) rather than with the actual 'proximal' stimuli directly elicited by such distal properties, either on the retina or on some other receptor surface of the organism. The classical quantitative expression of co-variance between any pair of variables is the correlation coefficient. The present paper attempts to demonstrate, in a quite preliminary and non-technical fashion, the use of correlational analysis as a means of representation of the degree of perfection of perceptual thing constancy. As our example we have chosen, in the field of size-constancy, an experiment which was especially designed for the purpose.

I

A set-up of 15 cubes made of natural hardwood, ranging from 50 to 70 mm, was presented to the observer at frontal planes of 2, 4, 6, 8 and 10 m distance, three cubes at each distance. The lateral distance between neighboring cubes was approximately 80 cm. In the rear of the room, at a distance of 12 m from the observer, a comparison series of 13 cubes ranging from 30 to 90 mm with step-intervals of 5 mm was set up. All objects were placed on tables of usual height. The observer was seated on a slightly elevated chair and so had a complete view of the set-up. The sizes and distances of the cubes are schematically represented in Table 9.1. The measured size of the cubes which is the distal stimulus and is labeled **b** (body-size) is indicated in bold-faced type. As

Reprinted from *Psychological Review* (1940), 47, 69–78.

TABLE 9.1 Experimental Arrangement
(Raw scores in italics)

Distance from observer (meters)		Data on the cubes (in mm)		
12		Thirteen comparison objects with sizes ranging from 30 to 90 mm		
10	b	70	55	50
	e	82	60	55
	p	84	66	60
8	b	55	60	70
	e	63	69	82
	p	83	90	105
6	b	65	50	65
	e	80	61	77
	p	130	100	130
4	b	60	70	55
	e	73	84	66
	p	180	210	165
2	b	50	60	65
	e	59	74	80
	p	300	360	390
		Position of observer		

can be seen, there are three cubes each of 50, 55, 60, 65 and 70 mm height, randomly distributed over the whole field.[2]

The figure in ordinary print, placed in the third row of each group of figures, indicates in each case the proximal stimulus value, that is to say, the actual retinal or 'projective' size *p* of the cube in question, in terms of the comparison series as related to the actual position of the observer. For example, the left rear cube, size 70 mm and at a distance of 10 m, occupies the same space on the retina of the observer as would an 84 mm cube at the distance of the comparison series, 12 m. Similarly, the right front cube, size 65 mm, is projectively equal to a 390 mm cube at 12 m distance; and so on. The values indicated are only approximate since lateral distortion has not been taken into account. This latter, however, from the point of view of our purpose, is of minor importance.

The observer was asked to take a natural, naive and unconstrained attitude, and to match each of the 15 cubes with the comparison series. Eight students were used as observers, each of them running through the experiment only one. The order of the judgments was systematically varied from observer to observer. The italicized figures in the middle of each group of figures give the perceptual (verbal) responses, namely the average estimates, e. For the purpose of our paper they may as well be considered as the result of one single experiment with one observer only, since at no stage of our considerations will the matter of individual or of time differences be considered nor will the correlation technique be applied to these latter.

In each of our fifteen instances, e is in an intermediate or 'compromise' position between b and p, usually much closer to the former than to the latter. This way of reacting is typical of most constancy experiments performed under ordinary conditions, yielding what has been labeled the phenomenon of 'approximate size constancy.' We may express the degree of this approximation by computing correlation coefficients between the three sets of variables.[3] The result is given in Table 9.2.

Two of these three coefficients contain the response-variable, e. *They indicate that estimated size shows a much higher degree of concomitant variation with the size of the distal environmental bodies than with the size of their projections upon the retina though these latter, are essential in conveying body size to the organism.* The fact that r_{eb} is not unity, and r_{ep} not as low as r_{bp}, is an expression of the lack of perfection of the constancy mechanism, which gives p, per se, an exaggerated emphasis.

The third coefficient, r_{bp}, has nothing to do with the observer's response but is concerned rather with the purely external interrelationship between the size of the distal body and the size of its retinal stimulus representation. This coefficient is very low. Indeed, when taken by itself, p is a very 'unreliable' cue for the size of the body 'causing' p (cf. **5, 6, 19**). Due to the fact, however, that large objects placed at various distances will on the whole elicit somewhat larger retinal images than small objects at similar distances, the correlation is not quite as low as would seem to be desirable from the standpoint of an experiment such as ours, *i.e.*, it is not quite zero. Since this tendency in our case (as often in nature) is insignificant in comparison to the distorting influence of the difference in distance, r_{bp} is low enough to be discarded in a first approximation. By slight changes in the arrangement it could, as *e.g.* for the purposes of a further demonstration, easily be brought down to zero.

The fact that the distal correlation *eb*, directly expressing far-reaching perceptual achievement, is high whereas the two correlations containing the mediating proximal link p are low may, when taken by itself, seem paradoxical. The answer is, of course, that something has been left out of the picture, namely a group of proximal stimulus feature more or less correlated with the distance between object and observer which, duly brought together with p, will functionally explain the presence of a high correlation between e and b. The fact remains, however, that the proximal

---

TABLE 9.2 Correlations among Distal Stimuli, Proximal Stimuli, and Perceptual Responses

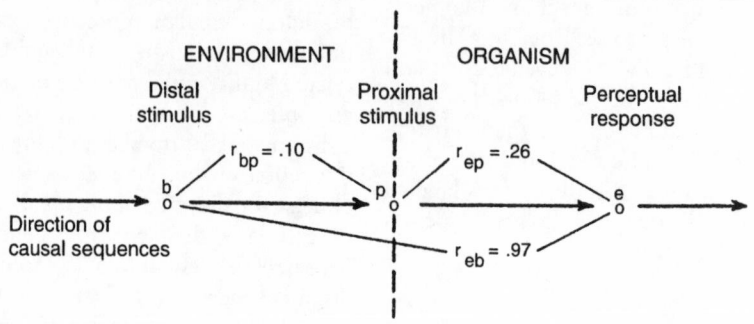

stimulus configuration mediating this correlation, or the constituents of this configuration, show a high degree of variability and flexibility, whereas e and b do not, and thus it is these latter which stand out as focal points of perceptual or organismic activity in general. It is these focal points, usually of vital importance, in the near or remote environment upon which a molar psychology should concentrate its efforts. A supplementary consideration of the general character and of the degree of the flexibility of mediation as expressed by low mediational correlations will help to complete the picture.

II

In recent years the degree of perfection of the constancy mechanism has repeatedly been represented by means of a constancy ratio, c, introduced by the author (3), whereby

$$c = \frac{e - p}{b - p}.$$

By the use of this formula, the degree of constancy can be computed for each of our cubes separately, yielding 15 c-values. They tend to be higher for the cubes near the observer than for those farther from him (for reasons which are of little bearing here). If computed from the logarithms of e, b and p instead of from the numerical values (*cf.* 17, p. 344; 4, p. 391), their average is .69.

The constancy ratio has several practical advantages. It is applicable, in principle, to any single pair of cubes set up at different distances and judged by an observer as equivalent with regard to apparent size. Furthermore, it expresses the constancy-achievement by one single index, c, relating e to both b and p at the same time. And it does so in such a way that the fixed values $c =$ o and $c = I$ always represent the same kinds of outstanding achievement, namely complete lack and complete perfection of perceptual constancy, respectively.

The correlational technique suggested above possesses none of the advantages. It requires a whole set of bodies of various sizes and at various distances (not to mention requirements regarding the frequency distributions of these sizes and distances). These objects have either to be ranked among each other, or matched to a common

scale, as was done in our experiment. The degree of achievement, or its contrary, deviation from the correct judgment in a certain direction, appears in distinctness only after a joint inspection of all three of the coefficients has been made, or only after some new index has been evolved. (In the simplest and crudest possible case, the latter could, for instance, be the difference between r_{eb} and r_{ep}, .71; which, by the way, in our particular case would be very similar to our average c-value, .69.)

On the other hand, as the author has pointed out previously (4, 5), the constancy ratio is too much bound up with certain rather incidental aspects of the experiment, such as the physical dimension in which the stimulus-situation is varied. It is of little use when the interplay of more than two variables is to be considered, and it does not isolate sharply the character even of these two variables (*cf.* 5, 1). It is not limited to values between the ideal poles 0 and 1. For example, values above 1 also indicate deviations from perfect constancy as do those below 1 though in a different direction. This shortcoming has been especially emphasized by Koffka (12, pp. 227, 234).

In contrast, the use of correlation techniques, though clumsier at first sight, is an approach of much more basic significance. It brings the constancy problem within the scope of the standard instrument developed to disentangle complex causal textures of whatever nature. It helps in the giving up of the exclusive search for strictly univocal correspondences, in psychophysics as well as in stimulus-response psychology in general, by rendering more legitimate the carrying over from the psychology of individual differences to these disciplines of what the author would like to call a 'deliberate lump-treatment' (7).

In doing so our approach goes beyond 'multidimensional psychophysics' of the merely proximal type, represented, for example, by the studies of Stevens (16, p. 70 *ff*; *cf.* also 20, p. 509), or Richardson (13). In this latter fairly recent type of research a perceptual response (such as the apparent loudness of a tone) has been studied as a function of more than one stimulus-variable (such as the frequency as well as the intensity of the underlying sound wave). Though the relationships found may justly be called complex and thus in a certain respect lacking univocality, yet the scope of such studies remains limited to the strictly lawful relationships which hold between a complex of proximal stimulus features and the response. Our aim, on the other hand, is to expand the investigation, regardless of the lack of a perfectly reliable representation of distal events in the proximal region, into the distal environment.

In so widening our scope, we are enabled to determine statistically the distal (along with the proximal) factors upon which the perceptual system has become fairly well focalized and which thus have become virtually the most effective determiners of the response. It is this type of far-reaching stimulus-response correlation which Holt (11, pp. 161 f.) and Hobhouse (9, p. 15) had in mind (cf. Heider, 8) and to which even earlier objective psychologists like Bechterev (2, p. 17) and Watson have occasionally referred, in an abstract way, and yet failed to deal with concretely, due to the difficulties caused by the lack of perfection inherent in such couplings.

This whole procedure should not be conceived as being limited to problems of perception, and to the use of correlation coefficients in the technical meaning of the term. Problems of overt behavior such as the obtaining of food by an animal are just as capable of quantitative correlational analysis of the relative importance of proximal and distal effects.

III

Our method differs from the most common use of the correlation coefficient in that the role of the individuals tested is taken over by the objects in the physical environment of a certain individual organism, and the role of the tests applied to the individuals is taken over by various (in our case three) kinds of manifestations, or effects, of these objects, namely size as measured by applying a meter-stick directly to the object (b), size of the effect of the object on the retina of the organism in question (p), and size as it is perceptually anticipated by that organism (e).

Thus our method has little in common with the modification of procedure suggested by Stephenson (15), who interchanged individuals and tests, and whose method thus, in contrast to ours, remained in the realm of individual differences.

Likewise, our method differs from the application of the correlation technique and of factor analysis to any combination of distal perceptual

tasks such as occurs in the studies of Thouless (18), Sheehan (14, pp. 52–56), and Hofstätter (10, pp. 27–33). There again the concern was with factors within the personality determining individual differences in perceptual achievement whereas the determining factors in our case are of an environmental nature.

As has been mentioned above, our method also transcends proximal multidimensional psychophysics, in that it includes the testing of distal determinants. It thus may become a tool for what might be called distal (and multidimensional) psychophysics.

In a certain way related to our approach are cases like that of Woodworth (20, p. 251) in which the emotions as expressed on a person's face have been correlated with judgments of these emotions given by a group of observers. The emotional state of another person is an environmental feature even a step farther distal than the size of a body. The chief difference when compared to our procedure lies in the fact that in the case just mentioned the distal stimulus only is considered, and the more proximal representations neglected. The same holds for cases in which the intelligence of a group of persons has been correlated with intelligence as judged from photographs of these persons.

Our procedure, on the other hand, deals with both the distal and the proximal, the achievemental and the mediational aspects. The outcome may lead to subordinating the latter to the former, but as far as the procedure is concerned both are taken into account and their relationship is examined.[4]

This article is no more than a sketchy beginning, with the purpose of demonstrating a general principle. All questions of detail and the further development of the statistical procedure such as the application of the analysis of variance, the isolation of the effective environmental factors, the fulfillment of the requirements for the application of the standardized correlational methods (such as normal distribution of the variables, etc.) and their possible modifications, the question of reliability of measures, etc., will have to be discussed in further publications of a more technical nature.[5]

Summary

An example has been given from the field of perceptual size constancy of the way in which correlational analysis may be helpful in determining quantitatively the degree to which the perceptual system—or the organism in general—is successful (under ordinary circumstances) in giving a specific response to, or in focalizing upon, a certain feature of the remote physical environment in spite of disturbances resulting from the incidental character of the proximal (retinal) stimuli mediating these distal environmental features. And it appears as characteristic of the constancy mechanism that high correlations of the response with distal factors may be accompanied by low correlations with the mediating proximal cues. The author's ultimate aim is to establish a multidimensional psychophysics which will include the distal environment within its scope.

NOTES

1. This term, recently adopted in this connection by Heider (8), is less open to misunderstanding than the term 'distant' which has too narrow spatial connotations.

2. Thus size constancy in this case might have been spuriously supported by 'central tendency' imposed by the comparison series. There is however sufficient evidence from other studies that this factor is not a decisive one.

3. Since our concern is only with demonstrating the principle, the numerical values given in Table 1 have been used in computing these correlations, instead of the probably more preferable logarithms of these values.

4. In a recent article (8), Heider has interpreted the author's conception of a 'psychology in terms of objects' as being limited to the distal aspects with exclusion of the proximal. Actually, this is not the case. Foci of correlations with organismic events will be recognized wherever they may be found, in the proximal as well as in the distal environment. Furthermore, even in the case of distal foci there is interest in the proximal aspects of mediation. This concern is best shown by the positive assertions made in this paper about the lowness of the correlations holding for a certain type of proximal events.

5. The author is being aided in this work by a statistical discussion group under Professor Tryon. Some of the special problems will be worked out in collaboration with Mr. Robert Gottsdanker.

REFERENCES

1. Ansbacher, H. Perception of number as affected by the monetary value of the objects. *Arch. Psychol.*, 1937, **215**, 1–88.
2. Bechterew, W. *La psychologie objective*. Paris: Alcan, 1913, iii and 478 pp.
3. Brunswik, E. Zur Entwicklung der Albedowahrnehmung. *Z. f. Psychol.*, 1928, **109**, 40–115.
4. ———. Die Zugänglichkeit von Gegenständen für die Wahrnehmung und ihre quantitative Bestimmung. *Arch. ges. Psychol.*, 1933, **88**, 377–418.
5. ———. *Wahrnehmung und Gegenstandswelt*. Leipzig, 1934, xi and 244 pp.
6. ———. Psychology as a science of objective relations. *Phil. Sci.*, 1937, **4**, 227–260 (for errata, see same journal, 1938, **5**, 110).
7. ———. The conceptual focus of some psychological systems. *J. Unified Science (Erkenntnis)*, 1939, **8**, 36–49.
8. Heider, F. Environmental determinants in psychological theories. *Psychol. Rev.*, 1939, **46**, 383–410.
9. Hobhouse, L. *Mind in evolution* (3rd ed.). London: Macmillan, 1926.
10. Hofstätter, P. R. Über die Schätzung von Gruppeneigenschaften. *Z. Psychol.*, 1939, **145**, 1–44.
11. Holt, E. B. *The Freudian wish*. New York: Henry Holt, 1915.
12. Koffka, K. *Principles of gestalt psychology*. New York: Harcourt Brace, 1935, xi and 720 pp.
13. Richardson, M. W. Multidimensional psychophysics. *Psychol. Bull.*, 1938, **35**, 659–660.
14. Sheehan, M. R. A study of individual consistency in phenomenal constancy. *Arch. Psychol.*, 1938, **222**, 1–95.
15. Stephenson, W. Correlating persons instead of tests. *Character and Personality*, 1935, **4**, 17–24.
16. Stevens, S. S., & Davis, H. *Hearing: its psychology and physiology*. New York: John Wiley, 1938.
17. Thouless, R. H. Phenomenal regression to the 'real' object. *Brit. J. Psychol.*, 1931, **21**, 339–359.
18. ———. Factor analysis in problems of perception. *Proc. Eleventh Internat. Congr. Psychol.*, Paris, 1937.
19. Tolman, E. C., & Brunswik, E. The organism and the causal texture of the environment. *Psychol. Rev.*, 1935, **42**, 43–77.
20. Woodworth, R. S. *Experimental psychology*. New York: Holt, 1938, xi and 889 pages.

[MS. received August, 1939]

10

Probability as a Determiner of Rat Behavior [1939]

 COMMENT

Demonstrations for Learning Psychologists: "While God May Not Gamble, Animals and Humans Do"
Michael E. Doherty

This is a commentary on Brunswik's 1939 paper "Probability as a Determiner of Rat Behavior." What a delicious paradox in that title! *Probability* as a *Determiner!* Did a sly smile cross Brunswik's countenance when, as he cast about for a title, he first juxtaposed the words *probability* and *determiner?* The goal of this commentary is to place that paper in the context of the times when it was written, to situate it in the wider context of Brunswik's comprehensive theory and method, and to reach outside his work to assess its place in the larger context of the study of behavior.

The Times

The experiments were done at Berkeley in 1936 and 1937. The time is worthy of note, as it was less that two decades after the disastrous Treaty of Versailles and the ensuing world-wracking Depression. It was at the beginning of the roiling up of World War II in Europe. And it was in the midst of an era during which the Zeitgeist in scientific psychology was characterized by a philosophy of science that has been called, only half in jest, physics envy. As the bitter reactions to Brunswik's probabilism clearly show, scientific psychology of the 1930s and 1940s was committed to the search for univocal, deterministic laws. It was more than a decade before information theory (see Shannon & Weaver, 1954) highlighted the irreducible uncertainty that is characteristic of

all communication, and before the implications of Thurstone's law of comparative judgment came to fruition in the theory of signal detectability (Swets, Tanner, & Birdsall, 1961), itself a model of decision making under uncertainty. These and other events of the 1950s shook the very foundations of the deterministic Zeitgeist. The cognitive revolution, a revolution quite congenial to probabilism, was yet three decades down the road when Brunswik was conceptualizing and running the subjects for the 1939 paper. Skinner's *Behavior of Organisms* (1938) was being written contemporaneously with "Probability as a Determiner" and appears as a footnote in Brunswik's paper.

A scant few years after the publication of the 1939 paper, Brunswik was moved to describe his experiment as a reaction against the typical learning experiment of the day, "in which food can be found always to the right and never to the left, or always behind a black door and never a behind a white one, [as] not representative of the structure of the environment, but . . . based on an idealized black-white dramatization of the world, somewhat in a Hollywood style" (Brunswik, 1943, p. 261). Truly a damning commentary on the times!

The Place of the 1939 Paper in Brunswik's Wider Theory

"Probability as a Determiner of Rat Behavior" is one of just two papers that Brunswik devoted to learning, the other being Brunswik and Herma (1951). The latter paper, though, focused on the process that dominated Brunswik's scientific work in the United States, perception. Even though the 1939 paper dealt with learning, many of the major ideas in Brunswik's mature theory of probabilistic functionalism are represented clearly in the paper. The very first sentence is "In the natural environment of a living being, cues, means or pathways to a goal are usually neither absolutely reliable nor absolutely wrong" (p. 195). Consider the implications of each phrase: "In the natural environment" conveys at the outset his commitment to explaining behavior in the world rather than being content to stay conceptually "encapsulated" in the laboratory. The sentence goes on, "of a living being." Brunswik's psychology is a psychology of organisms, not just human beings, and more fundamentally, as the first two phrases together imply, of organisms in their natural environments. Next comes "cues, means or pathways to a goal," which reflects Brunswik's conceptual focus not only on perception but also, stemming from his collaboration with Tolman, his growing attention to goal-directed action. The phrase "pathways to a goal" is a clear manifestation of Brunswik's commitment to a thoroughgoing functionalism. The final segment of the sentence, which says that the aforementioned features "are usually neither absolutely reliable nor absolutely wrong," is a ringing statement of probabilism.

The concepts of ecological entanglement of cues and of vicarious functioning are at the core of Brunswik's psychology, and the consequent need for representative design is at the core of his methodological prescription for a cumulative science of psychology. Ecological entanglement is represented clearly in Table 10.1, which shows that several formal aspects of the experiment were not orthogonal, a situation that was likely regarded by his contemporaries as showing the presence of confounding. Among the aspects of the experiment that were not orthogonal—quite deliberately so, of course—were the proportions of probabilities of reward on the two arms of a T-maze, the differences between the probabilities, the ratios of the probabilities, which of the two sides presented ambiguous information and whether the final point of each run was predetermined! Not having the statistical machinery of multiple regression at his command (although this paper reflects Brunswik's first use of correla-

tional statistics [Leary, 1987, 124]), Brunswik used exquisitely careful comparisons between the conditions to try to understand the relative influence of the entangled variables that he had manipulated. The statistical techniques he used, traditional critical ratios, were nomothetic in character, but the latter part of the paper has a distinct idiographic flavor, as he discusses the effects of individual rats with idiosyncratic biases, such as position habits. Ecological entanglement was carried to the limit in the "danger" part of the experiment, in which food reward and shock were *perfectly* correlated.

In discussing the results, Brunswik wrote that "the strength of response appears to follow rather a kind of compromise" of tendencies, an idea deeply entrenched in his thinking about perception, and a term closely related to the concept of vicarious functioning. Brunswik was exploring the use of different cues, even as those cues were causally contingent on the same environment, as physicalistically defined. Moreover, the concept of a hierarchy of cues, which is such an integral part of the mature lens model, was an essential part of Brunswik's interpretation of the results of that experiment. Witness "Discrimination seems, therefore, firstly, to increase with an increasing difference of probabilities, even when their ratio is held constant [and] Secondly, when the difference of probabilities is held constant, some indication is given that an influence is superimposed which is due to the varying ratio of probabilities, per se" (p. 200).

The Place of the 1939 Paper in Brunswik's Methodology

The above is not to imply that "Probability as a Determiner of Rat Behavior" could be represented as a textbook case of representative design. It was decidedly not, nor was it a systematic design. The design of the "Probability as a Determiner" experiment, executed in 1936, presented multiple, probabilistic cues, hence permitted vicarious functioning, but was in no way predicated upon an ecological survey, much less run in the rat's natural environment. Not until Brunswik's elegant 1944 psychological monograph *Distal Focussing of Perception: Size-Constancy in a Representative Sample of Situations* was there to be a demonstration of the power of a design that was representative in spirit, even if not fully in execution. The entanglement of the features manipulated in the environment, though, was a foreshadowing of the principles of the representative design of experiments, and, as noted above, of Brunswik's later extensive usage of correlational statistics.

The term *physics envy* was cast in an implicitly pejorative light above. Brunswik was uncompromising in his criticism of "thematic physicalism," which Postman and Tolman (1959) described as "the uncritical imitation of the (real or alleged) aims and procedures of physics" (p. 507). As this and all of Brunswik's empirical papers make abundantly clear, however, Brunswik was not a critic of methodological physicalism, which is simply "the acceptance of the criteria of objectivity in observation and communication" (Postman & Tolman, 1959, p. 507). "Probability as a Determiner" shows that Brunswik was as uncompromising in accepting the criteria of objectivity in observation and communication as he was of condemning an unthinking imitation of what his contemporaries understood as the physics of the day.

The Place of the 1939 Paper in Scientific Psychology

I would love to say that "Probability as a Determiner" had an immediate and powerful impact, but it did not. I see the paper as part of Brunswik's profound body of work, stunning in its depth and scope when all of the papers are read in a concentrated fashion, but far ahead of its time. That is one reason it was largely ignored. (Another likely reason was hinted at above; the world was about to be plunged into a cataclysm that absorbed the attention of psychologists as well as everyone else: World War II.) But what evidence suggests that it was largely ignored? Hammond (1966a) documents the hostile reaction of Brunswik's contemporaries, but the impact of a paper is better judged from citations in subsequent empirical papers, books, and reviews. The most logical place to look, so I thought, for a possible impact of a paper that was concerned with the learning of probabilistic information was the "probability learning" literature that exploded in the decades after World War II. I looked largely in vain. McGeoch (1942) did not mention Brunswik at all, and McGeoch and Irion (1952), who

summarized the probability learning literature up until the 1950s, mentioned the 1939 paper in a footnote. Kling and Riggs, in their 1971 revision of Woodworth and Schlossberg's (1954) book, in which fully thirty pages are devoted to probability learning, did not cite Brunswik at all, nor does his name appear in Bush and Estes's (1959) *Studies in Mathematical Learning Theory*. Estes's (1959) "The Statistical Approach to Learning Theory," in Sigmund Koch's multivolume assessment of psychology at midcentury, cited the 1939 paper as being "associated with the origin of the now popular term *probability learning*" (p. 410). Estes went on to note that Brunswik's results were "not obviously incompatible" with the predictions of his (Estes's) mathematical model, and that he had actually replicated Brunswik's study. But in Estes's 1975 multivolume *Handbook of Learning and Cognitive Processes*, Brunswik gets but one passing mention, that in reference to Tolman and Brunswik's (1935) "casual [*sic*] texture of the world" (p. 7).

But Brunswik's ideas did not die with him. Leary (1987), in a paper exploring the influence Brunswik had on the Zeitgeist of scientific psychology, noted that Brunswik was "unusually prescient about later developments in psychology," (p. 115) and that he "foresaw and advocated the emergence of probabilism, psychological ecology, perception and cognition as key areas of psychological interest, increased scrutiny of the validity and reliability of psychological knowledge, greater historical and philosophical awareness, and the recognition of the 'inextricable entanglement of theory and method'" (p. 137).

A more direct impact of "Probability as a Determiner" can be seen as what came to be known as *multiple cue probability learning* (MCPL) by Hammond in the United States and by Smedslund in Scandinavia. The MCPL paradigm has been instrumental in leading to new insights in a wide variety of areas, including the role of cognitive feedback in learning (Balzer, Doherty, & O'Connor, 1989; Doherty & Balzer, 1988), the effects of psychotherapeutic drugs on learning (Gillis, 1975; Hammond & Joyce, 1975), and the structure of interpersonal learning and conflict (Brehmer, 1980b). Numerous MCPL studies have been done on artificial tasks to investigate the effects of formal task properties, such as cue intercorrelation, cue variance, and consistency of cue labels with the cue distributions.

Brunswik's impact on the study of learning has been significant in the Bowling Green psychological laboratories. MCPL research directly investigating feedback effects include several doctoral dissertations. Steinmann (1974) investigated transfer of training in the MCPL paradigm and showed increasing judgmental consistency, but not increasing knowledge acquisition, as subjects shifted from problem to problem. Holzworth (1980) showed that learning proceeded apace whether the criterion information was presented before or after the cue information. In unpublished dissertations, Fero (1975) showed powerful cognitive feedback effects across the board with experienced ward personnel who were making judgments about men on a drug ward, but Clover (1979), in a field study, failed to find cognitive feedback effects with highly experienced U.S. Air Force personnel decision makers, who had made thousands of decisions of the sort that the intervention was aimed at influencing. A student of Kirk Smith unexpectedly found that passive observation led to better learning in MCPL tasks than did active sampling, at least in the presence of irrelevant information (Kamouri, 1986).

Many other Brunswikian studies, some of them MCPL studies, have been carried out in collaboration with graduate students. The MCPL studies include Holzworth and Doherty (1976), in which we manipulated the precision of the feedback subjects received and found that, in the ranges of precision studied, it did not make any

difference. Brookhouse, Guion, and Doherty (1986) isolated social desirability response bias as one source of the discrepancy between subjective and regression weights. Cue unreliability was the focus of York, Doherty, and Kamouri (1987) and O'Connor, Doherty, and Tweney, R. D. (1989) pursued the effects of different kinds of environmental error.

Balzer and his students followed the reviews of the cognitive feedback literature by Balzer, Doherty, and O'Connor (1989) and Doherty and Balzer (1988) with two MCPL studies. Balzer, Sulsky, Hammer, and Sumner (1992) investigated what components of cognitive feedback make a difference to learning, and Balzer et al. (1994) looked at the format of the feedback. And in dissertations, O'Connor (1990) and Hammer (1991) both pursued the role of task complexity in cognitive feedback research. (See Holzworth, this volume, for a description of the growth of MCPL studies.)

Why the litany? I opened this section by saying that "I would love to say that 'Probability as a Determiner' had an immediate and powerful impact, but it did not." Now I can close it by saying that "Probability as a Determiner" has indeed had a lasting and powerful impact.

NOTE

The author thanks Ryan Tweney for a careful critique of this commentary.

 REPRINT

Probability as a Determiner of Rat Behavior

Egon Brunswik

Introduction

In the natural environment of a living being, cues, means or pathways to a goal are usually neither absolutely reliable nor absolutely wrong. In most

Reprinted from *Journal of Experimental Psychology* (1939), 25, 175–197.

cases there is, objectively speaking, no perfect certainty that this or that will, or will not, lead to a certain end, but only a higher or lesser degree of probability (*cf.* Tolman and Brunswik, 9). The psychology of learning reflects only occasionally this trait of the environment (*e.g.* Thorndike, 6, 7).[1] Usually the connection between means and end is made by the experimenter to be what Hume or John Stuart Mill would call indissoluble or inseparable, one of the alternative behaviors being always rewarded and the other never.

The need to study ambiguity experimentally became especially urgent in the psychology of perception. The natural cues used by the perceptual system are, without exception, ambiguous in character. This, in its turn, leads to ambiguity of the response as well. As indicated in recent studies (1, 2), the perceptual system under certain conditions will learn to make use of new kinds of cues even if they do not prove to be highly reliable.

The present report deals with an attempt to study the learning response of organisms to ambiguous means to a certain end, within the field of overt action, in a way comparable to the studies in perception. Rats were used as subjects. A single choice situation was given. In a series of experimental conditions the relative frequency, or the degree of 'probability', of reward on the two sides was varied. The question was to what extent the animals would be able to learn to prefer the more frequently rewarded side to the less profitable one, or, in short, to distinguish a better chance of reward from a less good one. In the 'main experiments,' five different combinations of probability were used. In additional 'danger experiments' two of these combinations were repeated with punishment added in each instance of an unsuccessful choice. In both of these experiments the original training was reversed after a number of trials in order to study relearning of probabilities. A further group of special experiments was performed in order to throw light upon some particular problems to be discussed later.

The Experimental Procedure

The set-up consisted of a one-unit elevated T-maze. The paths on both sides were equal in length, namely 115 cm. The approach, from the starting point to the choice point, was 60 cm long. The breadth of the path was 4.5 cm, its height above the floor 80 cm. Before entering the food compartment, the animal had to pass a one-way door.

Wet food was used as a reward, and the same amount was given each day. In those cases in which no reward was given on one of the two sides (see below), the door to the food compartment at the end of the respective path was closed and the animal had to turn and go to the other

door. In each trial the animal finally obtained food. The food was evenly distributed over the various runs in such a quantity that no extra feeding was necessary. The weight of the animals was controlled over the period of the experiment, an attempt being made to keep it approximately constant. The training was preceded by a hunger period which was kept constant for all animals. No preliminary training was given.

In all of the main experiments the 'original' training consisted of 24 runs for each animal. Four trials were given on the first day, four on the second, eight on the third, and eight on the fourth. After the original training had been completed, 'reversed' training consisting of 16 more runs was given on the two following days with eight runs on each day. The length of the training periods was chosen after preliminary experiments had shown their suitableness.

In the main experiments five different training groups, or types, with 48 animals in each group were used. The first of these groups was trained in the usual, unambiguous all-or-none fashion, one side being always rewarded, the other side never. The objective chances for the animal to find food on side A as against the chances to find food on side B were, therefore, 100 percent to zero. Objectively speaking, the effect on either side was predictable with certainty. We may call this group the '100 : 0' group.

A second group found food on side A only in 3/4 of the cases, whereas side B was rewarded in the remaining 1/4 of the cases. These latter cases might be called the 'exceptional' cases, as contrasted to the regular ones. The objective chances of success were 75 percent to 25 percent on the respective sides. The second training group, therefore, shall be labeled '75 : 25.'

The exceptional cases were randomly distributed among the regular ones in an artificial chance order (see below). Let us call A the 'generally more profitable,' or, in short, the 'profitable' side. B might then be called the 'generally less profitable' or the 'unprofitable' side. Let us call each choice of the more profitable side a 'correct response' and each choice of the less profitable side an 'error.' The terms 'error' and 'unsuccessful choice' are therefore not used synonymously in this study due to the particular conditions of our experiment. In all of the exceptional cases the successful choice is an error; and the unsuccessful choice is a correct response since the generally better chance was preferred to the less good one.

A third group was treated in a way analogous to the second, with the only exception that the probability of reward on the two sides was 2/3 against 1/3. We call this group '67 : 33.'

The three above mentioned groups have in common the feature that for every run there is food on one and only one side. The two sides are complementary to each other and the ultimate end of each run is fully predetermined.

A further group found food on side A in all of the cases and, in addition to this, on side B in 1/2 of the cases. We call this group '100 : 50.' It differs from the remaining four groups insofar as the ultimate end of each run is not determined beforehand, since in half of the cases a choice of either side leads to food.

The last training group might be called '50 : 0,' food being given only on one of the sides in half of the cases. In the remaining half of the cases the animal found both doors closed. In such cases it had to return to the choice point once more, was picked up there by the experimenter and rewarded in a food box placed in a neutral position.

In Table 10.1 a survey of the five training conditions is given. The order of presentation is rearranged in such a fashion that a decreasing series is formed with regard to the difference and to the ratio of the probabilities of reward on the two sides, whereby for each step there is either a decrease in the former or in the latter, the remaining feature being held constant. (See also the graphical representation in Fig. 10.3.) Row 4 refers to the trait of absolute objective certainty vs. uncertainty which will be considered later.

In the reversed training period for each group the profitable side now was made unprofitable and vice versa. The proportion of the respective probabilities, however, was kept the same for each group as in the original training.

In order to study the effect of the kind of ambiguity produced by a repeated reversal of training, group 100 : 0 received additional training for six consecutive days after the main experiments had been concluded. On each day eight trials of the 100 : 0 type were given but the direction of the training was reversed each day as compared to the day before. On the thirteenth and last day of the total training period a single additional trial was given in order to get data corresponding to the initial trials of the preceding phrases.

Each group of 48 animals was divided into 4 sub-groups of 12 animals each. In each sub-group for one half of the animals the right side was made more profitable, for the other half the left. The experiments were conducted in four temporally different periods. In each period one sub-group out of every training group was run in order to secure the greatest possible technical homogeneity between the training groups. For the same purpose, the animals in the various groups were approximately matched with regard to age, sex, and ancestry. A total of four animals died during the course of the experiment. They were replaced by other animals added to the last of the corresponding sub-groups.

The sequence of the regular vs. the exceptional cases was varied from sub-group to sub-group in such a fashion that for each training group an equal distribution of the exceptional cases

TABLE 10.1 Survey of Training Conditions

Row						
(1)	Reward on profitable vs. unprofitable side in terms of percent of trials, indicating proportion of resp. probabilities	100 : 0	50 : 0	75 : 25	100 : 50	67 : 33
(2)	Difference of probabilities	100	50	50	50	33.3
(3)	Ratio of probabilities	Infinite	Infinite	3 : 1	2 : 1	2 : 1
(4)	On which side is training unambiguous?	Both	Unprofitable	None	Profitable	None
(5)	Is final point of each run predetermined?	Yes	Yes. (In half of the cases in extra compartment.)	Yes	No	Yes

was obtained. As an example, Table 10.2 shows the distribution of the rewarded cases among the non-rewarded on the unprofitable side for the four sub-groups of training group 75 : 25 during the first eight trials. In the following trials the sequences shown were interchanged among each other. Table 10.2 shows, furthermore, the analogous scheme for training type 100 : 50.

In addition to the main experiments two further experiments of the types 75 : 25 and 100 : 50 were conducted. They differed from the corresponding main experiments insofar as every unsuccessful attempt to reach food was punished by an electric shock. As suggested above we may call these experiments 'danger experiments,' since not only varying probabilities of success, but also of detriment were involved. A further difference between main experiments and danger experiments was the omission of the fourth day of the original training. This was done in order to maintain an approximately equal level for the results of the original training of the main experiments and of the danger experiments yielding an even start for relearning. The number of animals was, as in the main experiments, 48 in each group, subdivided into subgroups of 12. Thus the total number of animals used in the study was brought up to 336.

In the danger experiments, an electric grid of 30 centimeters length was placed in front of each of the doors and charged with 35 to 50 volts in every case in which the door behind it was closed. As in the main experiments, an animal which once had chosen his side had to proceed entirely up to the door and then attempt to open it. In those infrequent cases in which the animal attempted to turn after the first touch of the shock, he was forced back by the experimenter until he had tried to open the door.

For all of the conditions, the experiments with three of the sub-groups were performed in the spring of 1936, whereas the fourth sub-group was added in 1937. The study was conducted at the University of California in Berkeley. The author is indebted to a seminar-group under the direction of Prof. Edward C. Tolman for valuable suggestions and criticisms.

A number of preliminary experiments in which a somewhat different scheme of training and experimental technique was used, and in which the training for each animal was extended over a period of several months, will be reported in a separate publication.

Results and Discussion

Figure 10.1 shows the results of the main experiments for the five training groups. Let us consider first the original training. As a test for the rat's response we choose the results of the last eight trials. The quantitative data are given in Table 10.3. The averages and the sigma scores are computed from the number of 'errors,' that is, those cases in which each rat chose the generally less profitable side, during the last day of the original training. Row 3 shows the averages recomputed as percentage scores. In the remaining three rows

TABLE 10.2 Examples of the Artificial Chance Sequences of Non-rewarded and Rewarded Cases on the Less Profitable Side for the First Eight Runs (+ indicates food, − no food)

| | Training group 75 : 25 | | | | Training group 100 : 50 | | | |
| | Sub-groups | | | | Sub-groups | | | |
Run Number	I	II	III	IV	I	II	III	IV
1	−	−	−	+	−	+	+	−
2	+	−	−	−	+	−	+	−
3	−	+	−	−	−	+	−	+
4	−	−	+	−	−	+	+	−
5	−	−	+	−	+	−	−	+
6	−	+	−	−	−	+	−	+
7	+	−	−	−	+	−	+	−
8	−	−	−	+	+	−	−	+

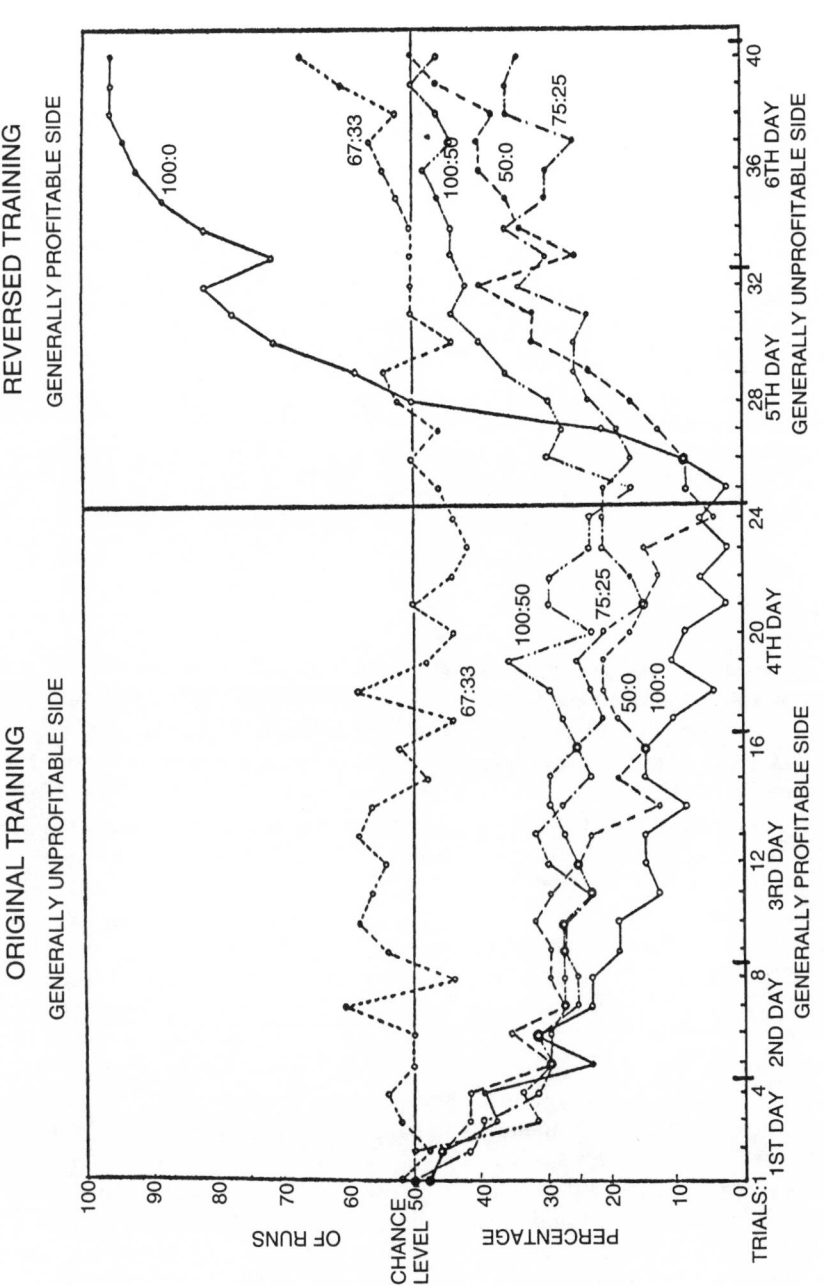

FIGURE 10.1 Results of main experiments.

TABLE 10.3 Main Experiments. Results of Original Training

Row	Training Groups in Terms of Probability of Reward	100 : 0	50 : 0	75 : 25	100 : 50	67 : 33
(1)	Average runs to unprofitable side in last 8 trials	.56	1.25	1.62	2.21	3.75
(2)	Sigma of average	.21	.30	.37	.44	.46
(3)	Percentage error scores computed from Row 1	7.0	15.6	20.2	27.6	46.9
(4)	CR with chance	16.7	9.2	6.5	4.0	.5
(5)	CR with training group 67 : 33	6.5	4.5	3.6	2.4	—
(6)	CR with training group 100 : 0	—	1.6	2.5	3.6	6.5

The first row shows the average number of times an animal chose the unprofitable side during the eight trials of the last day of the original training. In the second row the sigmas of these averages are given. In Row 3 the data given in Row 1 are expressed, in correspondence to Fig. 10.1, in terms of average percentages. The chance level is at 50 percent. In the remaining rows a list of some of the more important critical ratios is given.

of Table 10.3 a series of critical ratios to be discussed later is given.

(1) *Threshold of Probability and of Certainty.* Learning, that is discrimination of probabilities, takes place definitely for all of the groups except training type 67 : 33. According to Row 3 the deviations from chance level, that is from 50 percent, are as high as 22.4 even in the case of training type 100 : 50 which yields the smallest amount of learning after type 67 : 33. The CR's move within the range from 4.0 to 16.7 (Row 4). For training group 67 : 33, on the other hand, the deviation from chance is only 3.1 percent. As shown by the low CR of .5, this difference is negligible.

Let us compare training type 67 : 33 directly with the four remaining conditions. As is shown in Row 5, the first three differences are unquestionably above chance. Since, furthermore, according to Fisher (*cf.* 3, pp. 62 ff, 548), with a number of animals like ours CR's of 2.0 indicate 'significant' differences and CR's of 2.7 'very significant' ones, even the difference between conditions 100 : 50 and 67 : 33 with a CR of 2.4 can be called significant. As far as the training given is concerned, among all the conditions 75 : 25 seems to be particularly similar to 67 : 33. Considering the shortness of the training the number of 'exceptional' cases is 8 and 6 respectively, yielding a difference of only 2. Yet, as is shown by the CR of 3.6, in connection with the data con-

cerning the results of training group 67 : 33 mentioned above, condition 75 : 25 is definitely above, whereas 67 : 33 is below what might be called the 'threshold of probability' under the general conditions of our experiment.[2]

It was to be expected that the traditional unambiguous training type 100 : 0 would yield the best results. Indeed its error score of 7.0 percent is not far from 0. It is, as shown by the last row of Table 10.3, significantly different from the scores of all the other conditions except training group 50 : 0. The remaining conditions can, therefore, be called more or less definitely below the 'threshold of certainty' under the general conditions of our experiment. By saying this we mean that the response is clearly distinct from the response found in the case of an unambiguous training of the same length.

(2) *Influence of Probability Difference.* The rank order of scores follows exactly the order of training conditions as shown in Table 10.1 on the basis of a combined consideration of the order of the differences (Row 2) and of the ratios (Row 3) of the probabilities of success on the two sides of each of the probability discrimination problems.

Discrimination seems, therefore, firstly, to increase with an increasing difference of probabilities even when their ratio is held constant. As was mentioned above, training groups 100 : 50 and 67 : 33 react differently to a significant de-

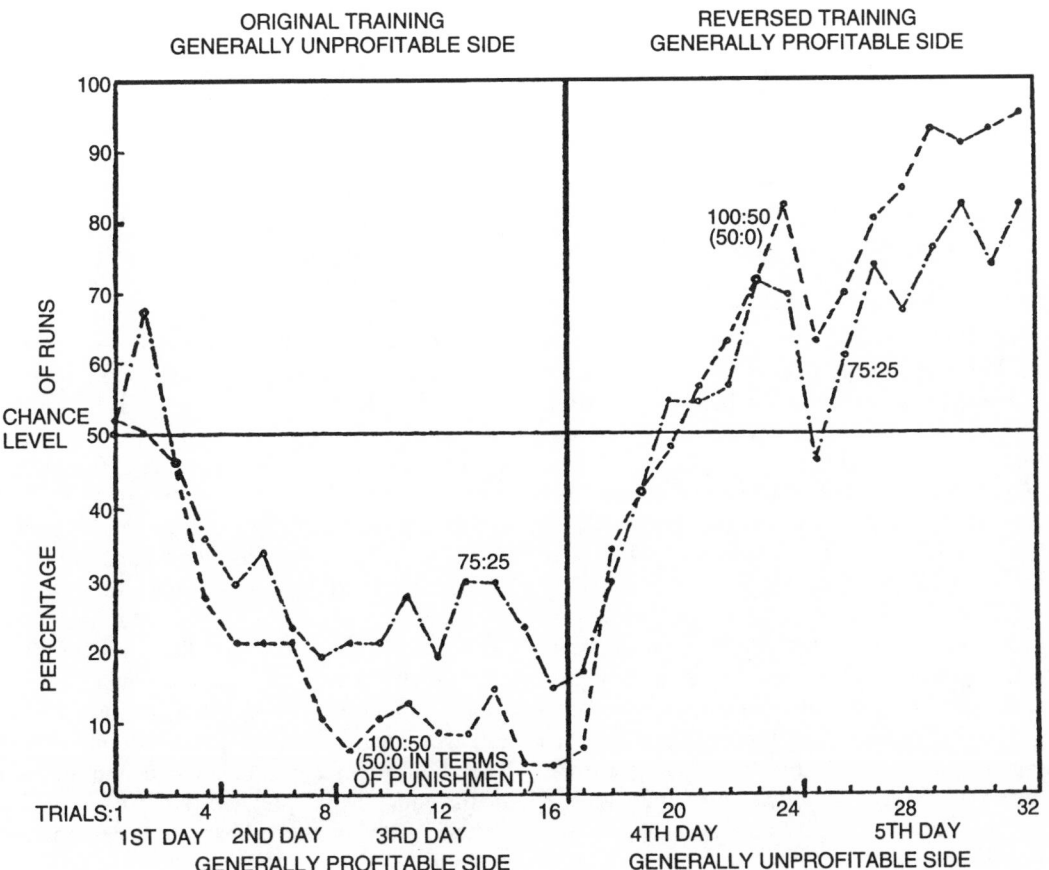

FIGURE 10.2 Results of danger experiments.

TABLE 10.4 Danger Experiments, Original Training

Row	Training groups in terms of probability of reward	75 : 25	100 : 50	
	Corresponding probability of punishment ...	25 : 75	0 : 50	
(1)	Average runs to unprofitable side in last 8 trials	1.81	.69	
(2)	Sigma of average	.31	.24	
(3)	Percentage error scores computed from Row 1	22.6	8.6	
(4)	CR with chance	7.1	13.8	
(5)	Corresponding percentage score of main experiment (third day)	26.0	100 : 50 26.5	50 : 0 22.6
(6)	CR of difference between danger score and main score	.5	2.9	2.5

Results given in analogy to Table 10.3. Row 5 shows the corresponding scores of the main experiment. Note that the comparison had to be made with the results not of the fourth but of the third day of the main experiment. Row 6 indicates the significance of the differences between the scores given in Row 3 and in Row 5.

gree though they both have the same probability ratio of 2 : 1 and differ from each other only by having probability differences of 50 versus 33.3. Though below significance, the difference between training groups 100 : 0 and 50 : 0, with probability differences of 100 and 50 respectively, shows markedly the same trend in spite of the fact that for both the ratio of probabilities is infinity.

(3) *Tendency toward Weber Law of Probability.* Secondly, when the difference of probabilities is held constant, some indication is given that an influence is superimposed which is due to the varying ratio of probabilities, per se. We have in mind the three conditions 50 : 0, 75 : 25, and 100 : 50. For all of them the probability difference is 50 whereas the probability ratio decreases from infinity to 3 : 1 and 2 : 1 respectively. The error scores in Table 10.3 increase from 15.6 to 20.2 and 27.6, that is, learning decreases slightly with decreasing ratio of probability. In our main experiment, however, this tendency is not quite significant. The CR of the difference between training groups 50 : 0 and 75 : 25 is only .8 and between training groups 75 : 25 and 100 : 50 only 1.0. Between 50 : 0 and 100 : 50, however, there is a CR of 1.8 which comes near to the value of 2.0 given by Fisher as the lower limit of significance for a number of subjects equal to ours. Taking the gradual increase of the scores of the three conditions as a whole, there is still more reason to believe that their sequence is not due to chance though no standardized statistical means were used to express this increase in significance quantitatively.

Further evidence for the influence of the probability ratio, per se, is given by the results of the 'danger' experiments, in which an electric shock in each case of an unsuccessful choice was applied. The data are given in Fig. 10.2 and Table 10.4 in a way similar to the main experiments. As follows from Rows 1 and 2 in Table 10.4, the CR of the difference between the two 'danger' conditions 75 : 25 and 100 : 50 is 2.9. This is more than the lower limit for 'very significant' (according to Fisher 2.7). It exceeds also by far the corresponding CR for the main experiments in spite of the fact that the main experiments had a longer training period. For further discussion *cf.* Sect. (5).

It is to be noted, furthermore, that the direction of the influence of the probability ratio upon

discriminative learning is reversed in the case of the 'danger experiments.' As was shown in the main experiments, learning is fairly likely to increase with the probability ratio, per se, of reward. However, it decreases markedly when an emphasis is put on the non-rewarded side by the introduction of punishment. Learning then increases with an increase of the probability ratio of punishment. Apparently the avoidance of punishment becomes a stronger motive as compared with the anxiousness of the animal to reach food as quickly as possible. If we consider not food, but rather punishment the 'stimulus' most active in the danger experiments, danger experiment 100 : 50 becomes representative of main experiment 50 : 0 rather than of main experiment 100 : 50; condition 75 : 25, however, does not change its formal character (*cf.* the top part of Table 10.4). If this aspect is considered, the reversal of results mentioned above disappears and the results of both the main experiments and the danger experiments can be expressed simultaneously in the following generalized way: Discrimination of probabilities tends to increase with the increase of the ratio of the probability of *emphasis*[3] on the two sides of the probability discrimination problem.

This statement bears a certain resemblance to the Weber Law as formulated in the psychophysics of sensation. Since the present study is to be considered a contribution to what might be called the 'psychophysics of probability' the above result could be interpreted as a tendency toward a 'Weber Law of probability.' It should be kept in mind, however, that the analogy cannot be stretched so far as to assert an independence of the learning effect from factors other than the probability ratio. As was shown above, the probability difference, per se, has an influence too, and this influence appears to be even more marked than that of the probability ratio. The strength of the response appears to follow rather a kind of compromise of the two tendencies exerted by probability difference, on the one hand, and probability ratio, on the other. This is, however, not an obstacle in the way of comparing our findings to those related to the Weber Law of traditional psychophysics, since some results of the psychophysics of sensation could similarly be interpreted as deviations from the Weber principle in the manner of a compromise with other factors such as stimulus difference, though the role of the ratio of the stimuli usually is much more marked than in our case.

A graphical representation of the conditions, and, of the results discussed in the last two sections, can be found in Fig. 10.3. Note how the curve of the original learning shows a continuous downward trend though this trend is accompanied merely by a fall of either the curve representing the probability differences or the curve representing the probability ratios but never of both at the same time. Note furthermore the correspondence in the directions of the curves for the main experiment and for the danger experiment where the training conditions for the latter are expressed, as suggested above, in terms of punishment and not of reward.

(4) 'Frequency' vs. 'Frequency-Configuration.' As implied in the statements of the foregoing paragraphs, our results can be understood only as reactions to the total pattern of frequencies of reward and non-reward on the two sides of the discrimination problem, of which 'probability difference' and 'probability ratio' are but single aspects. An attempt to explain the results in terms of isolated frequencies could not be generally justified. Though it might seem possible, for example, to look at the 50 : 0 curve as possessing half the acceleration of the 100 : 0 curve, for which the frequency of reward on the profitable side is twice as large as for condition 50 : 0, yet in other cases a similar consideration would fail. For example, conditions 100 : 0 and 100 : 50 possess the same amount of reward on the profitable side and yet the two curves are significantly different. Or: curve 67 : 33 has at the end of the original training not reached the level which was attained by curve 75 : 25 after 21 trials (that is, at the

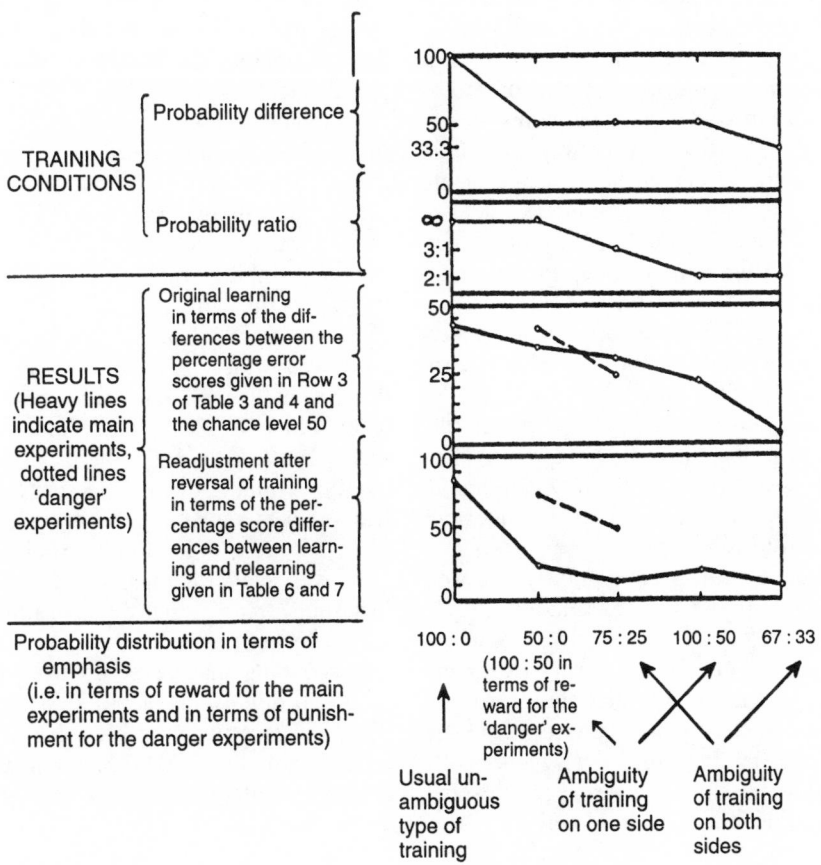

FIGURE 10.3 Graphical survey of training conditions and of results.

middle of the last day of the original training), in spite of the fact that under these conditions the absolute frequencies of reward on the profitable side are equal for the two conditions. In short, the traditional notion of 'frequency' (or of 'relative frequency') as a factor influencing learning has to be amplified to that of a 'frequency pattern,' of which isolated frequencies are but special aspects applicable under the limited conditions of a non-ambiguous training.

It goes without saying, however, that not only frequency, but also recency as an isolated factor could not account for our results, since in that case all curves would have to assume a strictly horizontal trend, due to the rectangular distribution of the 'exceptional' cases as outlined in Table 10.2 and the corresponding test. No special attention was given in this study to the effect of recency, per se.

(5) *Is 'Being without Exception' an Emphasizer?* Objective inseparability of good or bad means-end relationships is considered to be an important factor in human life. In such cases there is either a 100 percent or a 0 percent probability for a certain kind of happening. It is shown in Row 4 of Table 10.1, in what way our conditions differ with respect to the presence or absence of strict non-ambiguity on the two sides of our discrimination problem. The trait of certainty, or of 'being without exception,' is more frequently associated with the conditions represented on the left side of the table. These conditions, at the same time, are those for which learning is better. One might, therefore, try to ascribe discrimination not so much to the probability differences or probability ratios—represented in Row 2 and Row 3—but chiefly to nonambiguity versus ambiguity of training on one or both sides as represented in Row 4.

A more detailed inspection shows, however, that such an argument can be excluded. Firstly, conditions 75 : 25 and 67 : 33 both entirely lack 'certainty.' In each of these cases there are 'exceptions' from the rule on both sides of the discrimination problem. Nevertheless, the results of the two respective training groups are significantly different, as was outlined above. Secondly, considering security as such, condition 75 : 25 is worse off than its two neighbors, 50 : 0 and 100 : 50. There is, however, as Row 3 of Table 10.3 shows, not the slightest indication that any effect is superimposed on that of the variation of

the probability ratio among these three conditions. In Figure 10.3 this is indicated by the straight course of the middle part of the original learning curve connecting 50 : 0 with 100 : 50. We have to conclude, therefore, that for our material it is chiefly the high probability difference and the high probability ratio, and not lack of ambiguity on the particular sides of the discrimination problem, per se, which yields advantage to the discrimination problems on the left side of Table 10.1.

Concretely speaking, our results tend to indicate that, for instance, a probability discrimination 95 : 5 (having only one 'exceptional' case out of 20) would be almost as easy to learn for the rat as is 100 : 0. It seems to be a particular feature of the discursified aspects of human behavior to overemphasize the 'always' and the 'never,' that is, for example, to draw a sharp boundary line between the exceptionless validity of logical or physical 'laws,' on the one hand, and 'merely statistical' regularities or high probabilities of a less unambiguous and therefore much less principal character, on the other. This attitude, however, might be rather strange to an animal of a more primitive status of organization, like the rat, as it is likewise strange to the intuitive system of human perception or to the chief core of our human practical activities.

The possibility might not be excluded that in the case of the danger experiments the advantage of condition 50 : 0 (in terms of punishment) as compared with 75 : 25 is due not so much to the decrease of the probability ratio, per se, but rather to an influence of complete security from punishment on one side of training pattern 50 : 0. The question could not be decided quantitatively unless experiments under other conditions (e.g. 55 : 5, or 100 : 50, both in terms of punishment) were available for comparison. It should be kept in mind, however, that there was no indication of an effect of certainty, per se, in the case of the corresponding main experiments. To a certain extent all discussions of this kind become futile due to the fact that complete security always goes with extreme probability ratios and thus the two alternative interpretations become synonymous at least as far as the borderline types of training are concerned.

(6) *Relearning of Probabilities.* Let us turn now to the results of the reversed training (Table 10.5). As is shown in Fig. 10.1, by far the best result

TABLE 10.5 Results of Main Experiments at the End of
Reversed Training

Training Type	100 : 0	50 : 0	75 : 25	100 : 50	67 : 33
Average runs	7.12	3.04	2.52	3.67	4.50
Sigma of average	.18	.47	.51	.52	.47

Average number of runs per animal to formerly profitable, now unprofitable side, for the eight trials
on the second and last day of the reversed training

was obtained with training group 100 : 0. As pointed out above, the advantage of this condition as compared with some of the other training types was not very marked during the original training period. This holds especially with regard to condition 50 : 0, yielding with 100 : 0 a CR of not more than 1.6 for the last day of the original training (*cf.* Row 6 of Table 10.3). The last day of the reversed training shows a marked difference between these two conditions with a CR of 8.2 in spite of the fact that it had also to compensate for an opposite difference established in the original training. In the case of relearning, therefore, condition 50 : 0 seems to be definitely below the threshold of certainty (*cf.* above Sect. 1). Two probability patterns mastered with approximately equal success in learning might, therefore, be clearly differentiated in relearning. In addition to learning, relearning thus seems to be a sensitive instrument in testing probability discrimination.

The differences between the percentage error scores of the last day of the original training and those of the last day of the reversed training, as well as their CR's, are given in Table 10.6. There is, according to Fisher, a significant trend in the direction of extinction or relearning in all instances except training types 75 : 25 and 67 : 33. In the latter case, however, not even learning could be observed. The close resemblance between the difference scores and the CR's for train-

ing types 75 : 25 and 67 : 33 indicates that in this case two conditions, though significantly differentiated in learning, do not differentiate in relearning. The additional confusion introduced by the reversal of the probability pattern might be effective in bringing condition 75 : 25 down below the threshold of probability.

It should be noted, furthermore, that the two conditions 75 : 25 and 67 : 33 which are the worst off in relearning at the same time are characterized by 'ambiguity' of training on both sides of the discrimination problem. This might be an indication of the fact that at least in the case of relearning of probability patterns the feature of 'being without exception,' per se, could be helpful. This issue was discussed in the preceding section on original learning but answered negatively. As was suggested above, the amount of ambiguity added by the reversal of the training might be bearable in case of a fairly clear-cut pattern but might break down orientation in case of a high degree of ambiguity intrinsic to the probability pattern itself.

In Fig. 10.3 the differences mentioned can be seen graphically. Whereas the middle section of the curve for original learning is approximately a straight line, the relearning curve shows a dip at the point 75 : 25. Since the middle part of the probability difference curve is a straight line and the middle part of the probability ratio curve

TABLE 10.6 Relearning of Probabilities in the Main Experiments

Training Type	100 : 0	50 : 0	75 : 25	100 : 50	67 : 33
Difference of percentage score of original vs. reversed training	82.0	22.4	11.3	18.3	9.4
CR of this difference	23.4	3.2	1.4	2.1	1.1

The first row shows the amount of relearning (or unlearning), that is the difference of the average percentage
scores of the last eight trials of the original training as given in Table 10.4 and of the last eight trials of the
reversed training. The second row shows the critical ratio of this difference.

shows a continuous downward trend, the deepening mentioned might be due to the effect of the two-fold ambiguity of condition 75 : 25 superimposed on the effect of the probability ratio.

The results of the reversed 'danger' experiments are shown in Table 10.7 and Fig. 10.2. Relearning is significant for both conditions. As in the case of original learning, training type 100 : 50 (that is, 50 : 0 in terms of punishment) shows the better results. As can be seen from Fig. 10.3, on the whole, relearning is much better in the case of the danger experiments than in the case of the main experiments, though learning had been stopped at a point of approximate equality of the training effect. This might be due either to a greater efficiency of the danger set up, as such, or to the smaller amount of fixation of the original training due to a smaller amount of repetition. It seems plain, however, that the principle of emphasis as outlined above holds not only for learning but also for relearning.

(7) *Individual Patterns of Experience.* As an objection to our evaluation of the results it could be said that the probability patterns used in our training are defined in purely objective terms, that is, from the standpoint of the possibility of success and failure as arranged by the experimenter and not by the pattern of success and failure as experienced by the animal. This latter pattern might vary from animal to animal according to the individual choices made.

So, for instance, a rat trained after the scheme 100 : 50 might accidentally never choose the less profitable side '50' except when this side happens to be rewarded. Such an animal would be likely to become 'optimistic,' that is, to build up the hypothesis that whatever choice it makes would be successful. For this particular rat pattern 100 : 50 would actually be a pattern 100 : 100.

Though less likely than 100 : 50, even patterns 75 : 25 or 67 : 33 could thus become effective as patterns 100 : 100 if only the particular animal always would happen to choose the side rewarded in the respective trial. Other animals might equally well become thoroughly 'pessimistic' if they accidentally should choose the non-rewarded side in every single instance. In those cases the pattern would become, in the eyes of the rat, a 0 : 0 pattern. Numerous other varieties would be possible. In particular, there is a certain chance that some animals trained after the scheme 100 : 50 would experience exactly the same pattern as some animals trained after the scheme 75 : 25 or 67 : 33.

A special situation with regard to the patterns experienced is also given in those cases in which an animal becomes fixated on one of the two sides. Experience then is limited to this side except in those cases in which it is not rewarded and in which the animal therefore has to turn to the other side. Except for training type 50 : 0 this other side would then be experienced without exception as a success. Furthermore, for animals fixated on the correct side the training would become exactly alike under conditions 100 : 0 and 100 : 50.

To the objections raised the following reply is to be made. For all of the training types except 100 : 50 the position of the final goal of each run is predetermined and becomes known to the animal in every instance. The two sides are complementary and there is never food on both sides. It is only the additional amount of negative information given in the case of an unsuccessful choice which may vary from animal to animal. Furthermore, for all the training types except 100 : 50 and 100 : 0 each animal is forced to have experiences on both sides during the course of

TABLE 10.7 Results of Danger Experiments at the End of Reversed Training

	75 : 25	100 : 50
Training Type in Terms of Reward	75 : 25	100 : 50
Training Type in Terms of Punishment	25 : 75	0 : 50
Corresponding to Table 5		
Average runs	5.56	6.60
Sigma of average	.35	.28
Corresponding to Table 6		
Percentage difference original vs. reversed training	46.9	73.9
CR of this difference	8.0	16.0

Data given in analogy to Tables 10.5 and 10.6

the experiment and thus to give up strict fixation on one side. Finally, some of the instances mentioned are constructions of extreme cases whose practical occurrence seems obviously to be highly improbable.

In addition to these arguments, however, an empirical investigation concerning individual animals seemed to be desirable. Therefore a detailed analysis of the 24 trials of the original training of all the individual animals used in our study was performed out of which the following results should be emphasized.

As far as the interrelation of training groups 100 : 0 and 100 : 50 is concerned, there is fixation on the correct side throughout the whole course of the original training in 11 and 8 cases respectively. To the latter group (of 48) thereby 7 animals were added which were trained according to training plan 100 : 50 during the original training but had to be replaced because of an error committed by the experimenter during the reversed training period. In addition to the 8 animals fixated on the correct side there were 6 animals in group 100 : 50 which never found their choice of the less profitable side successful. There were, therefore, in group 100 : 50 14 animals out of 55 which received training which also would have been possible under condition 100 : 0. As a compensation, there were 6 animals of the 'optimistic' type in group 100 : 50 which found food on the less profitable side in every instance they chose it. Comparing the improvement from the first eight to the last eight trials of the original training for these 20 animals, representing incomplete or deviating types of experience, with the improvement of the remaining 35 animals of this group, we find rather similar scores, namely .91 and .75 respectively. In contrast to that the analogous score for the 48 animals in group 100 : 0 is 2.15, and it must be remembered that in this latter group there were 11 animals fixated on the correct side who therefore were unable to make any progress at all. This suggests that the deviating animals can well be included with the group representing, as a whole, training type 100 : 50.

In groups 75 : 25 and 67 : 33 there were 5 and 3 animals respectively who were fixated on the correct side and 1 and 2 animals respectively who were fixated on the incorrect side. As was said above, however, all of the 96 animals in these two groups were forced to have experiences on the other side of the discrimination problem in one-fourth to three-fourths of the cases. This feature marks them off from the animals fixated on the correct side in groups 100 : 0 and 100 : 50. Furthermore, there were no cases of 'optimism' or 'pessimism' suggested to the animals by the incidentals of their training history. In group 75 : 25, there were only 2 animals who experienced, out of the 24 trials, less than 6 failures (namely 4 and 5) and only 3 animals who experienced more than 16 failures (namely, 18, 18 and 19). Similarly, in group 67 : 33 there were only 2 animals experiencing less than 8 failures (namely 7 and 7) and no animals experiencing more than 16 failures. There were, furthermore, only 2 animals in group 75 : 25 and none in group 67 : 33 who did not experience at least 2 failures on the correct side in case they chose this side more than 8 times. And there were only 3 animals in group 75 : 25 and none in group 67 : 33 who did not experience at least one success on the incorrect side in case they chose this side more than 2 times. It can be concluded that the patterns of experiences made by the individual animals are to a considerable extent uniform within the respective group and conform fairly well with the intended training types. These groups may therefore be taken, as a whole, as true representatives of the respective probability patterns.

(8) *Repeated Reversals.* Figure 10.4 shows the results of the repeated reversal training of the training group 100 : 0. In contrast to Figs. 10.1 and 10.2 the results are expressed in absolute numbers of runs. Furthermore, in order to be able to compare graphically the successive periods, in each case of the reversal of training the curve is interrupted and drawn in such a way that the responses which were correct the foregoing day are now plotted as errors. An exception is made only for the first trial of each retraining period, where the result is plotted in terms of both the old and the new curve. The left part of the figure representing the main experiments is a repetition of the corresponding curve in Fig. 10.1.

In comparing the starting points of the consecutive curves as emphasized by small squares, a definite downward trend can be observed. The animals seem to learn that the direction of training might be alternated. A general distrust of the stability, or 'conservation,' of the particular distribution of success and failure seems to become established. At the same time there is an improvement from day to day of the success reached

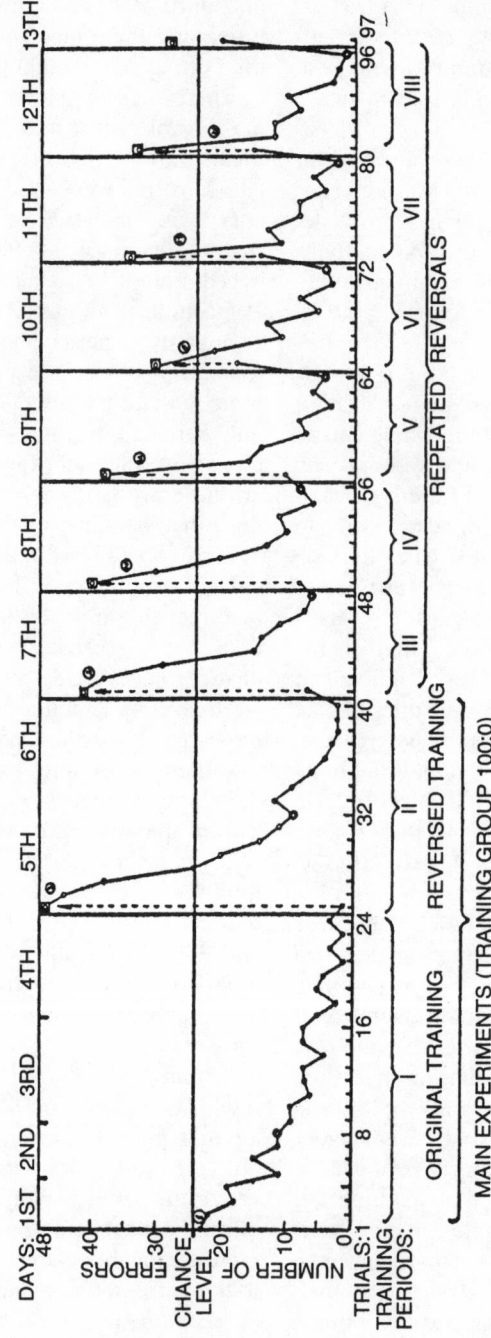

FIGURE 10.4 Results of repeated reversals.

at the end of each training period of 8 trials starting from the last reversals. This is indicated by the encircled points. Both these features together are expressed by the increasing upward trend of the last unit of each curve representing the transition from the last trial to the first trial of the succeeding reversed period.

The increasing adjustment to reversal of training also reveals itself in the fact that there is a tendency toward increasing steepness of the first link of each of the consecutive curves. In Fig. 10.4 the numbers inserted indicate the progress made from the first to the second trial of each phase. Taking the total training there is an increase from 1 on the first to 21 on the last day. It seems as if it would become possible, after having made the rats acquainted with the situation, to 'tell' them, by means of the first trial, in a way almost as generalized as is human language, which side they should choose during the day in question. The rats have 'learned to relearn,' or to respond to the first few trials of a day as a 'symbol' for the conditions during the trials to come. A discussion of former findings on this problem is given by Krechevsky (4) who reaches a conclusion similar to ours.

Summary

As a contribution to what might be called the 'psychophysics of probability,' five groups of 48 rats each were rewarded on the two sides of a choice situation different proportions of times ('main experiments'). A training of 24 trials failed to establish a discriminatory response in only one of the groups, for which the chances of reward on the two sides were 2/3 against 1/3 (group '67 : 33'). In contrast to that, groups '100 : 50,' '75 : 25' and '50 : 0' were significantly above the 'threshold of probability' in an increasing order. For the last of these groups, 50 : 0, the difference with control group '100 : 0' which represented the traditional unambiguous type of training dropped below significance ('threshold of certainty').

Discrimination increases with the difference of the probabilities of success on the two sides, a further influence being superimposed due to the ratio of probabilities (tendency toward a 'Weber law of probabilities'). Additional experiments of the type 75 : 25 and 100 : 50 introducing special punishment for each non-rewarded choice ('danger experiments') showed that the increase in discrimination goes with the increase of the ratio of the probability of 'emphasis' as given by punishment or by success, and not with the increase in the ratio of probability of success, per se.

Analyses of the factors of isolated frequencies of reward or non-reward, of recency, and of the training histories of individual animals did not impair the validity of our interpretations. The question as to the role of perfect inseparability of a means-end connection as an additional emphasizer could not be answered univocally as far as our animals were concerned.

After a reversal of the probability patterns for 16 consecutive trials, group 75 : 25 dropped below threshold, showing as little relearning (or extinction) as group 67 : 33. Likewise the readjustment shown by group 50 : 0 dropped far below that of 100 : 0.

Repeated reversal of training type 100 : 0 showed increasing promptness of adjustment.

NOTES

1. The usual case of an occurrence of 'exceptions' in training experiments is the insertion of test trials within a series of conditionings. Experiments of the type such as recently published by Skinner (5) in which only one out of a large number of trials was rewarded differ from ours insofar as the sequence of rewarded versus non-rewarded trials was not a chance order and that the animals were not faced with a discrimination problem between two different kinds of probability patterns.

2. Preliminary experiments of the present author on learning of ambiguous cues in perception (1) seem to indicate that under the conditions of these experiments, in contrast to the present findings, the perceptual system is able to learn cues even if their indicative value is as low as 67 : 33, yielding a tetrachoric correlation coefficient between the cue and the event indicated of not more than $r = .33$.

3. It has to be noted that in the present connection the term 'emphasis' is used in a somewhat different sense than in the study by Tolman, Bretnall and Hall (10) where it was introduced to designate the fact that it is easier to learn to go to an emphasizer than away from it.

REFERENCES

1. Brunswik, E., Das Induktionsprinzip in der Wahrnehmung, Communications, 11^e Congres Internat. de Psychologie, Paris 1937.

2. Fieandt, K. v., Dressurversuche an der Farbenwahrnehmung (No. 7 of: E. Brunswik, Untersuchungen über Wahrnehmungsgegenstände), *Arch. f. d. ges. Psychol.*, 1936, **96**, 467–495.

3. Guilford, J. P., *Psychometric Methods*, McGraw Hill, New York and London, 1936.

4. Krechevsky, I., Antagonistic visual discrimination habits in the white rat, *J. Comp. Psychol.*, 1932, **14**, 263–277.

5. Skinner, B. F., *The Behavior of Organisms*, D. Appleton-Century Co., New York and London, 1938.

6. Thorndike, E. L., *The Fundamentals of Learning*, Columbia University Press, New York 1932.

7. Thorndike, E. L., *The Psychology of Wants, Interests and Attitudes*, D. Appleton-Century Co., New York and London 1935.

8. Tolman, E. C., The determiners of behavior at a choice point, *Psychol. Rev.*, 1938, **45**, 1–41.

9. Tolman, E. C. and Brunswik, E., The organism and the causal texture of the environment, *Psychol. Rev.*, 1935, **42**, 43–77.

10. Tolman, E. C., Hall, C. S., and Bretnall, E. P., A disproof of the law of effect and a substitution of the laws of emphasis, motivation and disruption, *J. Exper. Psychol.*, 1932, **15**, 601–614.

[Manuscript received January 23, 1939]

11

Ecological Cue-Validity of "Proximity" and of Other Gestalt Factors [1953]

 COMMENT

Demonstrations for Gestalt Psychologists: Psychology without a Subject
Michael E. Doherty

One searches in vain in Brunswik and Kamiya's 1953 "Ecological Cue-Validity of 'Proximity' and of Other Gestalt Factors" for a description of the subjects. There were none. The reason is simple: A fundamental feature of Brunswik's thinking was that in order to understand the system we call the organism, we must first understand the system in which that organism has evolved and in which the organism is functioning. He regarded a study of the environment as a necessary antecedent—his word was "propaedeutic" (Brunswik, 1956b, p. 119)—to the understanding of the organism, and the paper by Brunswik and Kamiya illustrates beautifully an analysis of a particular environmental system. It is psychology without a subject.

Textural Ecology as a Propaedeutic to Functional Psychology

Brunswik's call for investigating the environment was not the usual hand waving; it was a principled, conceptually articulated call. He wrote at length of the causal texture of the ecology, meaning that the environment must be conceptualized not in physicalistic terms, but rather as a system composed of survival-related distal objects, a system that has a richly textured surface and that extends away from the organism in depth. These survival-related objects scatter their effects errati-cally in such a way that the surface, or "skin," of the environment presents itself to the organism coming to terms with that environment as an array of interrelated cues. Brunswik conceptualized the uncertain relationships among these cues and the relationships among the proximal cues and the distal objects as probabilistic, at least so as far as the organism could know. Hence, the argument went, to know the organism we must first know the environment.

What Did Brunswik and Kamiya Do?

In a nutshell, Brunswik and Kamiya selected six still photographs taken from a film and made careful measurements of "the proximity of similars," defined as parallel line pairings, in the pictures. Fully 892 such line pairings were assessed. In addition, Brunswik and Kamiya made categorical judgments of the distal realities depicted by the line pairings, thus enabling correlations between the proximities of the pairings and the categories of realities they represented. In the parlance of the lens model, Brunswik and Kamiya were describing the ecological side of the lens, and they were doing so explicitly in terms of the ecological validities of the cue of proximity for the various categories of the distal variable. They were assessing the ecological validities, or r_{ie} values, of what had until then been conceptualized as an innately given, autochthonous stimulus factor by the Gestalt psychologists.

Representativeness

The research reported in Brunswik and Kamiya exemplifies several fundamental features of representative design. The investigators used highly complex photographs, rich in meaningful detail, not the abstract, stylized stimuli of the Gestalt psychologists (see, e.g., Chapter 6 in Kohler, 1929), nor the bare, physicalistically defined stimuli typical of contemporaneous experimental psychologist. Furthermore, Brunswik and Kamiya did not fall into the easy trap that Brunswik (1956b, Chapter 7) called the double standard in the sampling of subjects and the sampling of objects. They sampled situations in that they not only used six photographs as stimulus materials but also made exhaustive measurements of multiple instances of parallel lines (what they referred to in the paper as "separations") in each.

But Brunswik and Kamiya's very words show that they realized that the sampling of photographs was not, in the full sense of the term, truly representative. They described the procedure as "a convenient approximation to situational representativeness" (p. 215). The degree to which the procedure was not fully representative was brought into sharp relief by Hochberg (1966).

Hochberg's Criticism

In a paper entitled "Representative Sampling and the Purposes of Perceptual Research: Pictures of the World and the World of Pictures," published in Hammond (1966b), Hochberg pointedly noted that "Brunswik has been sampling, not proximal stimuli, but a special class of distal objects, pictures" (italics in the original, p. 372). Hochberg made essentially two arguments to the effect that the procedures employed by Brunswik and Kamiya had fallen short of Brunswik's own standards for representative design.

First, Brunswik and Kamiya's ecological validities were based on static pictures. A fundamental feature of visual perception in our normal intercourse with the world, whether one accepts J. J. Gibson's version of ecological psychology, derives from the stimulation resulting from the motion of the observer, a source of stimulation impossible in picture perception.

Second, Hochberg questioned whether the photographs sampled were representative of any interesting population, asserting that the photographs had "no stateable relationship to the normal tridimensional world" (p. 372). The photographs were not randomly sampled; rather, "they were chosen by a cameraman from a population of possible camera positions, by an editor from a population of pictures submitted to him, and both of these 'human filters' were at some pains to eliminate those pictures that are confusing, misleading or unpleasing" (p. 373). They were then chosen by the magazine editors and, finally, by the investigators.

These criticisms are apposite and severe. In spite of them, the research without a subject by Brunswik and Kamiya stands as a serious and virtually unprecedented attempt to quantify ecologically relevant aspects of the environment. The measurement of the separations and the identification of the distal realities in Brunswik and Kamiya must have been tedious, painstaking work. The magnitude of a true ecological survey of even a delimited aspect of the visual world that would meet the rigorous standard of true representativeness that Brunswik espoused would be a daunting task, indeed. Hochberg, in the same paper, noted that a true ecological survey, critical though such a survey might be to two of the premier perceptual systems of the day, would be "incredibly expensive" and had not yet been accomplished.

How Was Brunswik and Kamiya's Research Received?

Like much of Brunswik's work, it was out of step with the times. The psychology of the day was largely either encapsulated within the organism or devoted to an empty organism. The stirrings of the cognitive revolution may have been felt, for the seeds had been sown by Hebb (1949) and others, but its birth was yet a few years away. The paper was not widely cited. It was treated in rather cursory fashion even in Postman and Tolman's (1959) presentation of Brunswik's probabilistic functionalism. It merited just a half sentence, and an ambiguous one at that, in Riesen's (1954) *Annual Review* article on vision. It was neither mentioned in Floyd Allport's (1955) *Theories of*

Perception and the Concept of Structure, nor did it find its way into J. J. Gibson's 1966 and 1979 books.

Unfortunately, the Brunswik and Kamiya paper in particular, and Brunswik's exhortations in general, concerning the need for ecological surveys have been, to this day, largely ignored.

Brunswik's Concern with Foundational Issues

Before leaving Brunswik and Kamiya, it should be noted that this paper reflects Brunswik's lifelong concern with foundational issues. The research reported in the paper was not just a demonstration of some technical aspect of the lens model. The paper was not about some photographs, nor was it about the assessment of some ecological validities that were really rather uninteresting in their own right. What was the paper, then, about? It was an indirect challenge to a fundamental idea of Gestalt psychology, the precept that the Gestalt principles of organization function as autochthonous factors *independently of the experience of the individual organism.* Brunswik and Kamiya claimed to have shown not that proximity is in fact a learned, probabilistic cue, but "that an objective basis for probability learning" is possible.

 REPRINT

Ecological Cue-Validity of "Proximity" and of Other Gestalt Factors

Egon Brunswik and Joe Kamiya

Gestalt psychologists have stressed the influence of certain stimulus-factors upon figural unity in perceptual organization. Prominent among these factors are 'proximity,' 'equality' (or 'similarity'), 'symmetry,' 'good continuation,' and 'closure' in the sense of the closedness of a line or pattern in the stimulus-configuration.[1]

According to orthodox Gestalt theory, the effectiveness of these factors rests on dynamic processes inherent in the brain field, rather than on accumulated past experience; while occasioned by respective characteristics of the stimulus-configuration which acts as a set of 'topographical' factors at the boundary of the system, the dynamics themselves are in the nature of 'physical Gestalten,' that is, of a spontaneous physiological 'self-distribution' built into the organism prior to, and as a condition for— rather than as a result of—learning.[2] For this reason

it is also said that the factors mentioned operate in an 'autochthonous' manner, that is, are indigenous to the organism so far as their organizational effect is concerned.

A more broadly functionalistic view of perception would suggest an alternative interpretation of the factors of perceptual organization which at the same time would be well in keeping with modern learning theory. According to this view these factors would be seen as guides to the life-relevant physical properties of the remote environmental objects, and thus as playing a part in adjustment; in more technical language, they would be conceived of as proximal 'cues' to the so-called distal bodily reality.

The possibility of such an interpretation hinges upon the 'ecological validity'[3] of these factors, that is, their objective trustworthiness as potential indicators of mechanical or other relatively essential or enduring characteristics of our manipulable surroundings. This problem is analogous to that of the 'physiognomic' or other external cues offered to the organism for potential utilization in social preception. Here we know,

Reprinted from *American Journal of Psychology* (1953), **66**, 20–32. Copyright 1953 by the Board of Trustees of the University of Illinois. Used with the permission of the University of Illinois Press.

for example, that height possesses statistically significant ecological validity with respect to intelligence; but we also know that this validity, which may be expressed in terms of a correlation coefficient, is of a very low order (perhaps 0.1 or 0.15). Thus the cue is a crudely 'probabilistic' one, and so would have to be any learning involved in its acquisition. Another analogy is with the so-called depth-cues in the perception of third-dimensional space, such as vertical position or subdivision of the field. For some of these cues, ecological validities somewhat higher than those typical of social perception, but still of definitely limited value, have been established by Seidner.[4]

Any study of ecological validity can be no more than propedeutic to psychology; concern is limited to a survey of statistical relations among variables as typical of the natural or cultural habitat of an individual or group while the question of the actual utilization of cues or of other aspects of organismic response is left untouched. In short, such studies deal with *potential* cues, not with cues actually employed. Yet ecological surveys are indispensable not only for an understanding and appraisal of responses but, as is especially true in our particular case, for general problems in psychological theorizing as well.

There can be no doubt that the ecological validity of the Gestalt factors, when seen as potential perceptual cues, could likewise be of no more than very limited value. In part perhaps for this reason, but certainly at least in part by virtue of their predilection for dynamic rather than learning-type explanations, Gestalt psychologists were prone to brush aside suggestions of 'generalized experience' as the possible source of the laws of perceptual organization. Thus they were pointing out that there are "in nature . . . *fully as many* obtuse and acute angles . . . [*e.g.* the branches of trees]" as there are right angles.[5] This statement was made to explain preference for rectangularity as a *prägnant* form of organization. Or they were pointing out that "my general experience is that, *as often as not*, similar members of a group are movable, and move, independently."[6] This in a broad presentation of similarity, proximity, and other organizational factors as allegedly autochthonous principles. In effect, statements of this kind atomize reality by playing down regularity in our surroundings or by asserting ecological zero-correlations.

Our aim is to take the guesswork out of the ascertainment of frequency relationships of the general kind hinted at in the above quotations. This is to make up for the resistance, intrinsic to Gestalt psychology, against extrapolations into 'causally remote strata' on the basis of probabilistic cue validity,[7] and against the 'cue' or 'sign' concept in perception in general.[8]

Present Study

The present study thus endeavors to extend the purely ecological type of analysis from physiognomic and depth cues to some of the Gestalt factors mentioned at the beginning of this paper.[9] In the main, we will concentrate on 'proximity',[10] with a side-glance at 'symmetry' and 'closedness.'[11] The problem is, then, whether these factors, when present in the proximal stimulus-configuration on the retina or in a picture, possess some objective indicative value as to the unities in the underlying distal physical reality. In other words, in tending, as we are said to do, to unite closely adjacent (or symmetrical, or closed) sets of elements of the stimulus-configuration into a common 'figure,' are our chances improved that the figural units seen will correspond to the stable mechanical units we are able to manipulate behaviorally? This question can be answered in the affirmative if there is a statistically significant correlation, however low, between the picture factors and the structure of the geographic reality depicted in the picture in such a way that closely adjacent (or symmetrical, or closed) pictural elements can be traced with greater frequency to a single mechanically coherent object, rather than to incidental configurations without lasting value or significance.

Materials

Our material thus must fulfill two conditions. First, it must be a representative sample of stimulus-configurations or situations and situational elements from a universe of conditions to which we are exposed.[12] Secondly—an automatic consequence of the fulfillment of the first requirement—the material must be classifiable both proximally, *i.e.* in terms of characteristics of the retinal projection or of a picture *per se*, and distally, *i.e.* in terms of an underlying geographical stratum merely represented but not actually present on the retina or in the picture.

In the gestalt psychologists early attempts to demonstrate the organizational effect of factors in the stimulus-configuration none of these requirements was fulfilled. With only scattered exceptions (such as the star clusters referred to in footnote 2), the stimuli considered are limited to standardized dots or simple lines; and these elements and patterns lack representational meaning, thus discouraging even the thought of an ecological analysis.

A convenient approximation to situational representativeness in the field of perception is the use of pictures from popular magazines. After some deliberation, we settled on a series of varied episodes from the current motion picture, "Kind Hearts and Coronets," as selected for reproduction in *Life* magazine.[13] There were seven situations, all of which we used; they are presented without omission of any part in Figs. 11.1 to 11.7. In the original, all reproductions are 4 in. wide; heights vary in proportion to those shown. As is to be expected, the description of detail in our figures falls considerably short of that in the magazine pictures. Our illustrations are merely to be taken as rough guides.

Definition and Classification of Proximity

The survey on proximity was based on all pairs of discernible adjacent parallel lines in the picture. As Koffka has lucidly explained, proximity is not to be understood as operating "between events of *any* kind"; proximity cannot be divorced from the other factors, it must be defined as "proximity of similars."[14] In our case the similarity was defined primarily as parallelism, and thus in terms of direction.

The criteria of selection of our sample were further specified as follows.

(1) The line-pairings had to be adjacent, that is, not separated by a third parallel. An example is, in Fig. 11.7, the separation between the boundaries of the tree trunk in the center (Item q); on the other hand, the separation between the left boundary of this tree and the left boundary of the tree at the extreme right (Item [s][15]) was not included because there was a third parallel between them.

(2) The two lines forming the pair had to be at least in part overlapping, that is, they had to share a common perpendicular. An example of a part-overlapping line-pairing included in our sample is, in Fig. 11.7, the separation between the inner boundaries of the two tree trunks mentioned above (Item r). Excluded was, for example in Fig. 11.5, the separation between the front edge of the box placed on the table between the two men and the lower edge of the picture partly visible in the extreme upper left corner (Item [n]); the two lines, although parallel, do not overlap.

(3) Near-parallel pairs with not more than 5° divergence were included in our sample. An example is, in Fig. 11.7, the separation between the center tree and the branch or tree extending upward in continuation of the profile of the man at left (Item p); the separation between the lines was in such cases defined as the approximate average distance.

(4) Curved or part-curved lines were also included when they could reasonably be called parallel. Included was, for example in Fig. 11.1, the visible part of the clerk's collar (Item c, which is at the same time an example for slight divergence); excluded was, for example in Fig. 11.4, the space between the brims of the straw hats of the woman obscuring the view of letters T and E in 'VOTES' and the woman standing in the left foreground of the picture (Item [j]).

Excluded were, furthermore, 'good' continuations of interrupted lines, the other part of which had already been considered. An example is, in Fig. 11.5, the picture frame after having been interrupted by the clock (Item [l]); only one side of the interrupted line pair was counted.

Excluded were, finally, all cases of distinctly poor photographic definition, for example, in Fig. 11.5 the frame of the picture at the top right (Item [m]).

In applying these stipulations, a total of 892 separations was obtained as our final sample. In terms of proximity as our potential cue-variable, the sample was divided into eight intervals in geometrical progression from the limen to 0.5 mm., 0.5 to 1 mm., 1 to 2 mm., 2 to 4 mm., and so forth, to 32 to 64 mm. Distribution and (geometric) means for the total sample are shown in the bottom part of Table 1. The mode is at the Interval No. 2, 0.5 to 1 mm. Grouping all separations to coincide with the geometric mean between the limits of their respective intervals,

FIGURE 11.1 to FIGURE 11.7

their geometric mean is 1.37 mm. Also shown is the mean and sigma in terms of class interval numbers, 2.95 and 1.54; since intervals progress in a geometrical scale so far as the measured values are concerned, 2.95 is in effect likewise a geometric mean.

It seemed possible that the perceptual system may come to utilize not picture-proximity as such, but rather separations as seen in three instead of two dimensions.[16] Since this argument invokes principles of perceptual size- and shape-constancy, it introduces a distal aspect into the classification; that is, however, an aspect quite different from our main, mechanical-distal referent variable of 'coherence.' To meet the present argument, the sub-sample of separations for which both lines seemed to lie at (approximately) the same depth, or in a common frontal parallel plane, was considered separately from the total sample. Data relating to this sub-sample are shown in the tables in parentheses beneath the main figures. Our N for this sub-sample is 483; note that mode and mean as well as over-all distribution are in close agreement with those of the full sample.

Distal Classification of Proximity in Terms of Mechanical Coherence

All classification in terms of distal variables, that is, of the realities depicted by the line-pairings, involves interpretation of picture content and thus implies a certain degree of uncertainty. In cases of doubt, which fortunately turned out to be fewer than anticipated, the two authors consulted with each other and, if necessary, with further observers unfamiliar with the purpose of the investigation.

The distal variable chosen as the referent variable in our analysis of possible signification of the cue variable may be labelled 'mechanical coherence.' The following schema of six discrete categories differentiating in terms of, or at least relevant to, mechanical coherence was arrived at after considerable trial and error and deliberation. The schema is exhaustive in that it makes it possible to place each of the 892 separations in one and only one category.

(1) Fully exposed mechanical units. This category comprises all separations in which both lines

of the pair represent mechanical boundaries of one and the same mechanically coherent object.

Examples are, in Fig. 11.1, the width of the crown of the hat worn by the man in the center (Item a), or, in Fig. 11.7, the vertical tree trunk in the background between the two men (Item q). Of all our categories this is the most frequently represented, encompassing a total of 334 items (163 of them representing pairs in a common frontal plane).

(2) Passages and overlapped recessions. Under this category are subsumed separations representing holes, gaps, passages, or spaces *between* mechanical units; these separations traverse over a depth or recession, with the background fill overlapped on both sides by other objects.

Examples are, in Fig. 1, the dark doorway (Item b), or, in Fig. 11.6, the curved dark background area between arch and lamp (Item o). In all, there are 171 (73) such items in our sample.

(3) One-sidedly covered mechanical units. These are separations in which one of the lines represents the mechanical boundary of one object, the other the mechanical boundary of another object overlapping the first.

Examples of such protruding object parts are, in Fig. 11.7, the bright lower part of the coat of the man at left extending beneath the right coat sleeve (Item t), or, in Fig. 11.1, the visible end of the white cuff on the clerk's left wrist (Item f). There are only 56 (21) items of this kind in our selection of pictures.

(4) Ornamental divisions. This category comprises separations defined by color inhomogeneities on a coherent surface, such as stripes or flat moldings, so long as they are not caused by light and shade distribution.

Examples are, in Fig. 11.2, the vertical stripes on the object behind the officer's right upper arm (Item g), or, in Fig. 11.4, some of the letters on the large sign in the center (Item k). There are 204 such items in our pictures. While in all other categories the frontal sub-group is considerably smaller than the full group, in this case it is only about 10% less (182). This is due in part to the fact that the parallel edges of stripes or moldings are frequently flat, and in part to their better definition in the picture in those cases in which they are located frontally.

(5) Shadow-bounded separations. This category defines separations for which one line of the pair is a shadow contour and the other represents

a mechanical boundary of the object *on which* the shadow is cast. Many items in this category do not represent shaded areas but rather normally illuminated areas "left over" after deduction of a shadow.

Examples are, in Fig. 11.3, the lighted expanse of the upper end of the ship's door above the head of the captain (Item i), or in Fig. 11.1, the separation between the edge of the panel in the lower right corner of the picture and the right contour of the umbrella shadow mentioned below (Item e). This is the least populous category, with a total of only 33 (13) items.

(6) *Shadows.* As defined for our purpose, this category is limited to separations between two shadow contours (penumbras), or between one shadow contour and a mechanical boundary of the object *casting* the shadow.

An example of the former, bilateral shadow is, in Fig. 11.1, the shadow cast by the umbrella handle on the panel of the cabinet in front (Item d); an example of the latter, unilateral shadow is, in Fig. 11.2, the shadow of the knife blade on the table in the lower righthand corner of the picture (Item h). There are 94 (31) items in this category.

It can be readily seen that our classification system has bearing on its purpose of differentiating between mechanically enduring and essential, and mechanically less essential or unessential cases. Category (1), comprising more than one third of our separations, represents mostly relatively stable spatial relations, invariant even under dislocation of the object; on the other hand, many of the passages and recessions of Category (2)—with the exception of such items as fixed doorways—will easily change at the flick of a hand, and so will one-sided overlappings of Category (3). Shadow distribution, Categories (5) and (6), is altogether dependent on changing conditions of illumination, and ornaments, Category (4), are likewise in themselves mostly misleading as to behavioral orientation. It must be noted for later discussion, however, that shadows, as defined under Category (6), especially when narrow, are frequently instrumental in bringing to prominence the mechanical boundaries of manipulable physical bodies (as witness the shadows that help establish the identity of the door mentioned above in connection with Item i of Fig. 11.3).

Ecological Validity of Proximity

Results of the ecological analysis of the proximity-coherence relationship are presented in our two tables. In the six center pairs of rows of Table 11.1, distributions and means are shown for the six categories in a manner described further above for the bottom row of totals. In Table 11.2, critical ratios between these means are shown for a series of cogent juxtapositions of Category (1) with the other categories, single and combined. The ecological relationships involved are summarily expressed by the point-biserial r. The two variables correlated are degree of proximity as the 'proximal' or picture variable, and mechanical coherence as dichotomized in any one of the juxtapositions just mentioned as the 'distal' or significate variable.

Results confirm the hypothesis we had from the start, to the effect that smaller separations, that is, greater proximity between adjacent parallels, tends to go with greater frequency of mechanical coherence in the distal reality underlying our pictures. This is revealed by the fact that the relatively incidental separations subsumed under Categories (2) to (5) show larger means than does mechanical unity Category (1); this is especially true so far as Categories (2) and (5) are concerned. In line with this, the point-biserial correlation between proximity, on the one hand, and the dichotomized variable of exposed mechanical unity Category (1) *vs.* passages and overlapped recessions Category (2), on the other, is positive; the specific value of r is 0.34 (0.37 for frontal separations). The critical ratio of the difference between the means for the two categories involved is 7.15 for an N of 505 lines pairings (5.53 for the 236 frontal items), and the relationship is thus statistically highly significant.[17] Expanding the second item in the dichotomy to a pooled category consisting of passages, overlapped recessions, and ornaments—Categories (2) and (4) combined—yields 0.20 (0.18); this is lower than the first figure(s) but still statistically highly significant.

The only incidental type of line-separation for which the mean is smaller than for mechanical units is 'shadows', as defined under Category (6). This indicates that in our sample shadows tend to be still narrower than exposed mechanical units. The proximal-distal correlation becomes signifi-

TABLE 11.1 Frequency Distributions of Line-Separations in a Representative Study of Proximity

| | Proximal cue-variable: 'Proximity' of adjacent parallels in the pictures | | | | | | | | | | | |
| Distal realities represented by line-separations | Class intervals of line-separations (in mm.) | | | | | | | | N | Interval | | Geom. mean (mm.) |
	<0.05	0.5–1	1–2	2–4	4–8	8–16	16–32	32–64		Mean	SD	
(1) Fully exposed mechanical units	57 (24)	126 (73)	67 (24)	43 (18)	29 (17)	10 (6)	2 (1)	0 (0)	334 (163)	2.70 (2.71)	1.34 (1.38)	1.15 (1.16)
(2) Passages, overlapped recessions	16 (7)	31 (7)	36 (17)	30 (15)	20 (10)	16 (7)	15 (7)	7 (3)	171 (73)	3.88 (4.07)	1.92 (1.87)	2.60 (2.97)
(3) One-sidedly covered mechanical units	4 (2)	18 (9)	14 (7)	9 (1)	7 (1)	4 (1)	0 (0)	0 (0)	56 (21)	3.16 (2.67)	1.37 (1.16)	1.58 (1.12)
(4) Ornaments (e.g. stripes, flat moldings), letters	14 (8)	87 (80)	54 (46)	16 (16)	33 (32)	0 (0)	0 (0)	0 (0)	204 (182)	2.84 (2.91)	1.18 (1.19)	1.27 (1.33)
(5) Shadow-bounded separations	0 (0)	4 (2)	9 (1)	10 (7)	7 (3)	2 (0)	1 (0)	0 (0)	33 (13)	3.91 (3.85)	1.21 (.93)	2.66 (2.55)
(6) Shadows	46 (13)	27 (10)	8 (5)	7 (2)	5 (0)	1 (1)	0 (0)	0 (0)	94 (31)	1.95 (2.00)	1.23 (1.16)	.68 (.71)
Totals	137 (54)	293 (181)	188 (100)	115 (59)	101 (63)	33 (15)	18 (8)	7 (3)	892 (483)	2.95 (2.97)	1.54 (1.53)	1.37 (1.38)

The top figures refer to the cases drawn from the over-all sample; the bottom figures (in parentheses) to those cases out of the total in which the two edges or contours represented by the lines may be assumed to be located in the same frontal plane.

TABLE 11.2 Ecological Validity Coefficients of the Factor of Proximity (Nearness) of Lines in the Pictures (as the Proximal Stimulus-Variable), and Various Juxtapositions of Mechanical Unity with Other Underlying Causes (as the Represented Distal Stimulus-Variable)

Correlations between proximity (nearness in line-separations in the picutres), and Category (1) vs:	N	r	CR
Category (2)	505 (236)*	.34 (.37)	7.15 (5.53)
Categories (2) and (4)	709 (418)	.20 (.18)	5.45 (3.54)
Categories (2)–(6)	892 (483)	.12 (.13)	4.00 (2.91)
Category (6)	428 (194)	−.22 (−.19)	5.10 (2.98)

*For explanation of figures within parentheses, see Table 11.1.

cantly negative in this case, −0.22 (−0.19). It must be kept in mind, however, that our material is based on situations with relatively artificial illumination; therefore, the pattern of shadows may be less representative of our normal surroundings than are other features of our sample, although common observation would seem to confirm that shadows are relatively frequently narrow.

A further pair of correlations shown in Table 11.2, 0.12 (0.13), is that linking proximity with exposed mechanical unity vs. a pooling of all other categories, including shadows. The low values obtained reflect the fact, just discussed, that shadows countermand the trend in the rest of the mechanically relatively incoherent separations. On account of the large N, 892 (483), even these low over-all figures are statistically significant; the ecological validity of the proximity factor as a cue for mechanical coherence thus remains unchallenged by inclusion of the special category, shadows, displaying a contrary trend.

Since, as referred to above, shadows help to bring out mechanical units in perceptual figure-ground organization, they may be pooled with this category rather than with the others. The coefficient obtained by such juxtaposition of Categories (1) and (6) vs. Categories (2), (3), (4) and (5)—not shown in Table 11.2—is 0.26 (0.21 for the frontal sub-sample), with a CR of 8.09 (4.77). This may be taken as an alternative, somewhat more liberal measure of the over-all ecological validity of the proximity cue.

Preliminary Analysis of Symmetry and Closedness

Much higher ecological validity than was obtained for proximity is foretold, by limited evidence, for the stimulus-factors of closedness and symmetry. Two proximal classifications were used in this context, both involving joint reference to these factors.

The first was a combined 'symmetry-closedness' factor. Only curved lines returning to their origin and showing symmetry about at least one axis were included in this class. A total of only 11 cases satisfying this criterion could be detected in our set of pictures. Most of them were in Fig. 11.5, for example, the outline of the bottle in the center (Item z), or the face of the clock in the right center background (Item x). All 11 items

signify object units; thus the obtained ecological validity would be perfect for this limited sample; but statistical significance is of course not established, and no such ideal value should be expected upon closer scrutiny.

Secondly, a separate 'symmetry-without-closedness' classification was defined by curved outlines not closed but involving at least a half-turn, that is, possessing at least one pair of parallel tangents touching the curve in opposite directions, and with the added stipulation that the part of the curve between the parallels be symmetrical. An example is, in Fig. 11.5, the rim of the fruit bowl at the left front (Item y); in this case the incompleteness is due to 'interception' by other objects blocking out part of the rim, thus establishing a valid instance of the familiar perceptual depth-cue. Another example is, in Fig. 11.1, the outer circumference of the hat (the width of which constituted Item a). Of the total of 10 cases in this group all but one signify object unity. The lone exception is, in Fig. 11.5, the bowl-shaped object between the head of the man at the right and the picture referred to above as Item [m]; the outline of its counterpart on the other side of the clock was too hazy in the picture to be eligible for out sample.

Discussion

As all studies aiming at representativeness, the present analysis may in a strict sense be applied only to the specific natural-cultural universe from which our sample is drawn. Although we have made no effort to define this universe in a formal way, it can probably be taken as a first approximation to the universe to which most of us are perceptually exposed.

The successful demonstration, within any framework stipulated, of the ecological validity of a gestalt-factor does not automatically imply the legitimacy of its interpretation as a learned cue. It merely shows that an objective basis for probability learning is offered the individual within the framework chosen. Since, however, all ecological validities represent a challenge to the organism for utilization, and since probably many cues are actually being utilized roughly in proportion to the degree of their validity,[18] our findings lend plausibility-support to the *reinterpretation of proximity as a cue acquired by generalized probability learning.* If this should become possible for other gestalt factors also, they all could be seen as externally imposed upon, rather than as innately intrinsic to, the processes in the brain; they would then appear as functionally useful rather than as whimsically 'autochthonous.' It goes without saying that such an interpretation would lose much of its cogency if it would turn out that proximity has similar organizing effects in individuals, groups, or species in whose habitat or culture it has no (or opposite) ecological validity.

Actual utilization of the proximity factor on the part of the perceptual response system, although doubtless present in the above-mentioned type of artificial examples brought forth by the gestalt psychologists,[19] would seem to require further study by means of more representatively selected stimulus-situations. This is especially true when the problem is the relative weight given to this factor by the organism in comparison with the other factors of organization. 'Crazy worlds' in the sense of universes with artificially reversed validities could also be constructed to which animals could be exposed from birth on and their perceptions studied.

It should be noted that in the company of the other acknowledged gestalt factors the factor of proximity plays somewhat the rôle of a stepchild. Proximity is brought in relation to 'association by contiguity,' for which it is said to furnish the perceptual underpinning allegedly indispensable in any learning; in turn, learning by space-time contiguity is notoriously minimized in gestalt psychology. Furthermore, and in line with this, proximity is seen as being at a disadvantage in the face of "parts which 'fit' each other, which jointly form a 'good curve.' [These] are more strongly unified than such as have no intrinsic relation and are linked by *mere* (italics ours) proximity. Such 'good continuation' distinguishes a meaningful text from a nonsense series; therefore the process corresponding to the apprehension of the meaningful material must be better organized than that corresponding to a nonsense series."[20] It is in part for reasons such as this that we intended to include a study of some of the more genuine gestalt factors, such as symmetry and closure, in our ecological program. Since our pictures, well suited as they were for proximity, yielded only a most meager sample for those other factors, we must leave these additional problems for further investigation.

Summary

In a selection of seven pictures of common perceptual situations, all the $N = 892$ separations between discernible adjacent parallels were classified as to the degree of their 'proximity' (nearness, smallness of line-separation) in the picture. They were also classified as to mechanical object coherence in the geography depicted. Point-biserial correlations describing the 'ecological validity' of proximity (the 'proximal' stimulus-variable) as a potential indicator of mechanical coherence (the 'distal' variable) range from 0.37 to 0.18 for various dichotomous juxtapositions of mechanical units and more incidental separations such as passages or ornaments, but excluding most shadows. Since shadows tend to be still narrower than coherent objects (r about -0.2), their inclusion lowers the validity coefficient to about 0.12; even this value is statistically significant in view of the largeness of the sample. High ecological validity is foretold, by limited and statistically not significant evidence ($N = 21$), for the further factors of 'symmetry,' with and without 'closedness.' The frequently emphasized perceptual organization effect of proximity (leaving the other gestalt factors for further investigation) may thus well be rooted in a generalized probability learning of its over-all ecological validity in the natural-cultural universe to which we are habitually exposed, rather than in an 'autochthonous' gestalt dynamics of the brain field.

NOTES

1. Following an analysis by G. E. Müller, the classic presentation is by Max Wertheimer, Untersuchungen zur Lehre von der Gestalt: II. *Psychol. Forschung*, 4, 1923, 301–350; abridged translation in W. D. Ellis, *A Source Book of Gestalt Psychology*, 1938, 71–81.

2. Wolfgang Köhler, *Gestalt Psychology*, 1947; esp. 107, 132 f. For the operation of the factor primarily under consideration in the present study, 'proximity,' a striking model from the physical chemistry of liquids (the diffusion phenomenon of 'cassinotaxis') is offered by Wolfgang Metzger, *Gesetze des Sehens*, 1936, 169; the example used is the frequently quoted case of the well-known perceptual organization of the star cluster, 'big dipper,' in accordance with the 'law' of proximity.

3. Egon Brunswik, *Systematic and Representative Design of Psychological Experiments*, Univ. of Calif. Syllabus No. 304, 1947; 30, 34 ff.

4. See Brunswik, *idem.*, 47–50.

5. Wertheimer, in Ellis, *op. cit.*, 87 (italics ours).

6. Köhler, *op. cit.*, 142 (italics ours).

7. Brunswik, *Wahrnehmung und Gegenstandswelt*, 1934, 112, 228. For an answer to Metzger's criticism of the cue concept as defined in this book see Brunswik, Remarks on functionalism in perception, *J. Personality*, 18, 1949, 56–65, esp. 58. For a broader recent discussion of the 'non-distal' orientation of Gestalt psychology see Brunswik, *The Conceptual Framework of Psychology*, 1952.

8. For Kurt Koffka's views see his *Principles of Gestalt Psychology*, 1935, 160 and elsewhere in the book. See further Metzger, *Psychologie*, 1941, 15–17; concerning the defense of the cue-concept see references in footnote 7.

9. A preliminary report was given by the writers, under the title "Ecological validity of Gestalt factors as perceptual cues," at the 1951 meetings of the Western Psychological Association (abstracted in *Amer. Psychol.*, 6, 1951, 496).

10. Also known as 'nearness' or 'adjacency' in the visual field, and not to be confused with the concept of proximal in contradistinction to distal in the regional definition of stimuli or responses.

11. The term is used here in contradistinction to 'closure;' this latter term we should like to see reserved for the tendency of the perceiver to close up gaps when responding to non-closed stimulus configurations.

12. Concerning the methodological requirement of 'representative design' and its application to psychological ecology see Brunswik, *op. cit.*, 1947, Chap. II, and VI to IX.

13. *Life*, June 19, 1950, 79–84. Reproduced by permission.

14. K. Koffka, *op. cit.*, 164–167.

15. Examples of items not included in the sample are placed in brackets [ ] here and in the figures.

16. This point was made in a seminar discussion by Mr. Gordon Bronson.

17. Since the standard error of the point-biserial r could not be found in any of a number of current advanced statistical texts, the critical ratio of the means was used as the only test of significance.

18. Brunswik, *op. cit.*, 1947, 41, 48 ff.

19. These examples have in part been incorporated into experiments on animals, such as those on birds by M. Hertz, Wahrnehmungspsychologische Untersuchungen am Eichelhäher, *Zsch. f. verge. Physiol.*, 7, 1928, 144–194; for discussion see Köhler, *op. cit.*, 142–149. In a second of two papers using rats, I. Krechevsky (An experimental investigation of the principle of proximity in the visual perception of the rat, *J. Exper. Psychol.*, 22, 1938, 497–523) has shown proximity to be effective, but only under certain motivational conditions. Concerning the purely cognitive aspects involved Koffka, *op. cit.*, 167, remarks, "How proximity and equality will work when no regular or simple pattern can be the result has not yet been investigated. In this, and in many other respects, our knowledge is still incomplete."

20. Koffka, *op. cit.*, 569.

[*Accepted for publication June 2, 1952.]

B.

Demonstrations of a
Comprehensive Theory

12

The Conceptual Framework of Psychology [1952]

⬥ COMMENT

Brunswik's *The Conceptual Framework of Psychology:* Then and Now

Ray W. Cooksey

Egon Brunswik, in his 1952 monograph *The Conceptual Framework of Psychology*, developed and articulated his integrated vision for psychology as a science. A strong argument can be made that, of all of Brunswik's later works, the 1952 monograph represented his crowning achievement simply because of its scope and intent (Bergmann, 1952, in his review of the monograph, observed that "intellectually, this is the equivalent of three books, or, to put it conservatively, of one well-sized book and two monographs of about one hundred pages each. . . . a distinguished piece of work by a distinguished author"; pp. 654–655). In this monograph, Brunswik critically and comprehensively evaluated the history, philosophy, methodology, and theory of psychology. No other psychologist to that date had had the vision or the courage (or, one could argue, the poor timing) to objectively and rigorously evaluate the entire discipline as a prelude to setting forth a new conceptualization that purported to address the argued shortcomings that had amassed over decades of psychological research. Brunswik's arguments threatened the very foundations and goals of psychology, as he intended, in order to stimulate deeper and more critical insights. He promulgated this threat at precisely the time when psychology was rapidly coalescing into two clear disciplines (see Cronbach, 1957) that had adopted fairly entrenched and opposed positions with respect to the interconnectedness between

psychological theory, methodology, and focal phenomena of interest (see Gigerenzer, 1987, 1994; Leary, 1987, for further discussions). In a very real sense, Brunswik's monograph was the concrete manifestation of one man's attempt to stimulate a scientific revolution (see Kuhn, 1970), effectively a unification of the two disciplines, on his own purely by reasoned argument backed by a prodigious knowledge of what had come before and an unshakeable belief in where the future lay. Brunswik's ideas were not well received, nor did they have their intended effect within his shortened lifetime. However, since the mid-1960s, there has been slow and steady erosion of resistance to his ideas as many of his arguments have been found to ring true (see Hammond, 1996b).

The most exciting thing about reviewing Brunswik's 1952 monograph today is the sense of history and knowledge that accompanied the complexity of thinking behind his ideas. As will be argued below, his ideas retain currency and have begun to be reflected in such guises as the increasing prevalence of triangulation in behavioral science research, growing acceptance of the validity and utility of both quantitative and qualitative data in theoretical conceptualizations, and the emergence of systems theory and complexity as modern conceptualizations for human behavior within specific environmental contexts (such as organizations, workstations, courtrooms and classrooms, public office, and private life). While many of these modern developments do not explicitly acknowledge the debt they may owe to Brunswik's ideas, his influence is detectable all the same.

Synopsis of Brunswik's 1952 Monograph

In 1952, Brunswik set out to establish a conceptual framework for psychology that was both objective and functional in its focus. Since it was not feasible to reprint the lengthy monograph in the present volume, it will prove useful to provide a brief overview of its structure and content. Brunswik's arguments in the monograph were developed through five distinct yet interrelated sections, culminating in his vision for modern psychology as an objective yet human science.

"Experience and the Emergence of the Objective Approach"

Brunswik's monograph began by tracing the historical development of psychology as a science from early subjective sensationist perspectives to more recent objective positivistic perspectives. This development paralleled the slow evolution of psychology, through the centuries, from a primarily philosophical introspectionist orientation to a natural science empirical orientation. In his historical retracing, Brunswik married considerations of both the content and the substance of psychology with the methods of research and theorizing used to focus inquiry about that content and substance. Thus, from the beginning, Brunswik showed that theory, behavior, and method were inextricably intertwined and therefore were to be taken as a unified package rather than as distinct strands of focus. His bold intention to attack the fundamental problem of psychology and its identity as a "science" is clearly shown in the following quote:

> On its way to becoming a science, psychology had to face certain requirements of procedural policy or general methodology. The issues involved fall into two major groups. One deals with the rigor of fact-finding, inference, and communication. In this respect, there must be methodological unity of psychology with the other sciences, especially physics. In contemporary psychological discussion this requirement is often expressed by saying that we must make psychology an "objective" or an "operational" discipline in the general manner attempted by behaviorism. . . . A second set of problems arises in connection with efforts not to lose sight of the specific tasks of psychology in the process of objectifying it but to establish exact study on an adequate level of complexity, sometimes called "molar" or "functional." The thematic identity of psychology can be, and can only be, established by the recognition and programmatic employment of specific research "designs" and aims relatively uncustomary in the other natural sciences. Such diversity is not only compatible with, but necessary within, the basic unity of the sciences. (p. 1)

In short, Brunswik argued that psychology must be both like and unlike the other natural sciences, but that this represented not a paradox, but a natural evolution for a science focused on behavior. He also alluded to the fact that, up to that time, psychology had not yet achieved a level of focus of adequate complexity. This was a point he made more forcefully later in the monograph when criticizing the overly simplistic approach to behavioral phenomena implicit in psychology's wholehearted adoption of the systematic decompositional approaches embodied in the statistical and experimental methodologies of Sir Ronald Fisher (and others).

"The Functional Unit of Behavior and the Level of Complexity of Psychological Research"

Brunswik began this section of his monograph by saying

> While differing in important points of elaboration, behaviorists have been rather unanimous in their definitions of the basic structural characteristics of behavior. These definitions contain all the necessary conceptual elements for making explicit the general characteristics of an approach necessary to establish objective psychology on an adequate level of complexity. But they have left to the general methodologist the actual drawing of conclusions concerning the design of a type of research that would match the pattern of behavior itself. (p. 16)

Here, Brunswik essentially asserted that behaviorist approaches to psychology had set the stage for an objective psychology but that these approaches merely provided the platform upon which a more appropriately complex psychology and method must be built. Brunswik then constructed, upon this basic platform, his lens model (see his original reproduced representation in Figure 12.1) as a useful representation for depicting key functional concepts such as achievement, vicarious mediation, and vicarious functioning in a way that more appropriately captured the complexity of the behavioral phenomena being studied. Achievement was characterized as the critical index of organismic adjustment to probabilistic environments.

Vicarious mediation (where proximal cues to distal events were only probabilistically related to those events) and vicarious functioning (where proximal cues were only probabilistically related to central processing within the organism in pursuit of successful achievement) were critical processes associated with adaptive achievement in complex environments. Brunswik argued that the methods used to study achievement needed to be similarly complex in conception and symmetric in focus (studying both the organism and its environment simultaneously seeking the "wide-arched dependencies" between them; p. 19). Brunswik argued that traditional statistical methods, with their focus on nomothetic generalization, systematic control over environmental variables, and subject-focused sampling methods, were insufficient for this task. He proposed a broadening of the methodological scope of psychology to encompass representative design, which afforded the same detail of attention to the objects in the environmental context of the organism when it was studied or observed as the traditional methods afforded for the actual organisms under study. This necessarily meant relaxing the fixation of psychologists on highly controlled environmental contexts, single variable manipulations, and orthogonal factorial experimental designs—a message that proved difficult for most psychologists of that time to hear (see Leary, 1987, for further discussion of this difficulty with Brunswik's message). It also meant that a more idiographic-statistical approach was called for which relied more heavily on probabilistic and correlational indicators. This approach was more congruent with individual differences/correlational psychology than with traditional experimental psychology in domains such as perception or

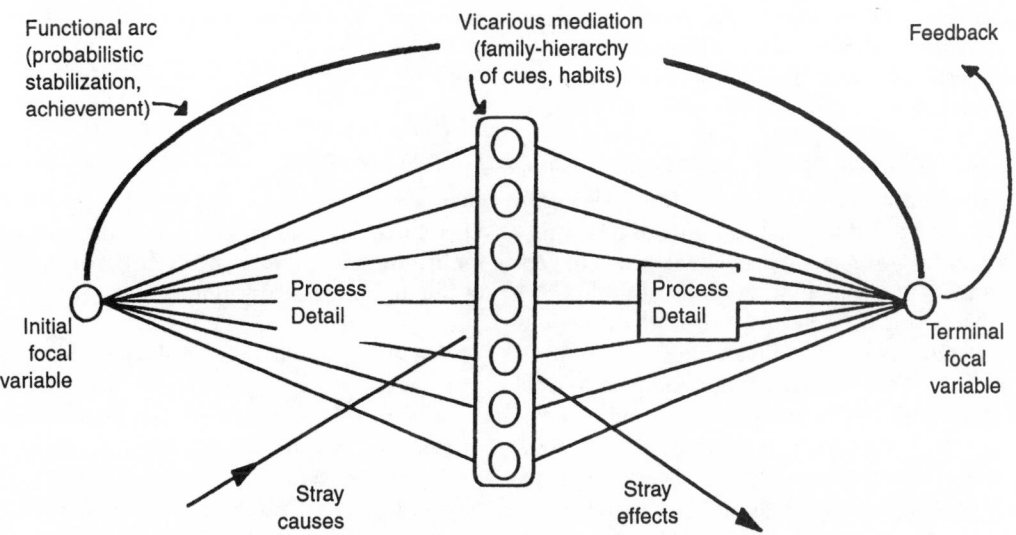

FIGURE 12.1 The lens model: Composite picture of the functional unit of behavior. In *The Conceptual Framework of Psychology* (p. 20), E. Brunswik, 1952, Chicago, IL: University of Chicago Press. Copyright 1952 by University of Chicago Press. Adapted with permission.

learning (recall the early reference to the "two disciplines of psychology" by Cronbach, 1957, and later in Cronbach, 1975).

"Misconceptions of Exactitude in Psychology"

Having argued that the lens model and its attendant concepts constituted the primary functional unit of behavior, Brunswik then proceeded to review historical misconceptions of exactitude in psychology as it tried to emulate the natural sciences, especially physics:

> For a while, psychology has tried to copy not only the basic methodological principles but also the specific thematic content of physics, thus nipping in the bud the establishment of somewhat more specific methodological directives outlined in Chapter II [of his monograph]. As Murchison has put it, psychology has tried to do *what* physics does rather than trying to do *as* physics does. The ensuing fallacies, or "biases," surrounding the concept of objectivity, operationalism, or scientific exactitude in psychology may be grouped in three major syndromes. These range from thematic physicalism proper to some more derived preconceptions, hesitations, and inhibitions. (p. 36)

In referring to thematic physicalism, Brunswik called into question the uncritical or "naïve" importing of the "molecular attitude" (focusing on elemental reductionism) and "nomothetic synthesis" (focusing on lawful generalizations) "biases" from physics (pp. 36–37). By modeling psychology so closely on physics, Brunswik essentially argued that method had unrealistically predetermined the focus of behavioral study. Instead, Brunswik proposed a more molar attitude (later embodied in the central-proximal-distal regions of reference) coupled with an idiographic-statistical approach which admitted to probabilistic relationships between an organism and its environment. In his words, "The unrealistically absolutized nomothetic-idiographic dichotomy is resolved on the common ground of the probability approach" (p. 38).

Brunswik then extended his argument to address various debates evident through the history of psychology. For example, he blurred the distinction between quantification and qualification (p. 39). He resolved the debate between emer-

gence and vitalism by reference to the molar attitude that established the correct level of analysis for psychological phenomena (p. 41). This argument was accompanied by an astonishingly accurate presaging of the modern push toward open systems theory and chaotic dynamics in behavioral systems, advocated early on by Ludwig von Bertalanffy and Ilya Prigogine, which Brunswik linked to his concept of "equifinality"; p. 42). Finally, Brunswik commented on the predominance of the law of parsimony as a criterion for theory choice by essentially arguing that parsimony could be taken too far if driven by the simplistic search for the mechanistic reductive explanations characteristic of the molecular attitude adopted from physics (p. 43).

Brunswik highlighted the illusory nature of a truly objective psychology, molded in the same pattern as physics, due to the inherently subjective nature of the phenomena it studied. Further he argued that while one might contemplate employing "objective" research methods where possible, there was still a role to be played by the more subjective phenomenological approaches, especially as a preliminary to formal theorizing and hypothesis testing. Implicit in this perspective was Brunswik's softening of the traditionally perceived hard distinction between, and polarized (and mutually hostile) attitudes toward, quantification in the natural sciences and qualification in the social sciences.

"Traditional Approach and Constructive Crises in Psychology"

In this section of his monograph, Brunswik elaborated three essential criteria that formed the basis for his structural history and evolutionary analysis of the discipline of psychology:

> The subsequent historical analysis will be in terms of the three basic aspects developed up to section 8 [of the monograph]: (1) objectivity; (2) molarity, involving both the functional arc and the width of vicarious mediation; and (3) regional reference, involving the distinction of central, peripheral-proximal and distal areas, both on the reception and on the effection side. (p. 50)

Here Brunswik considered the historical trends in psychological science as it moved from early sensory psychophysics, intentionalism, early functionalism, and psychoanalysis through to the emergence of Gestalt psychology and behaviorism. It is important that the reader visualize this developmental history of psychology, from meditative philosophy through to objective functional psychology, as Brunswik did (see Figure 12.2). It is through this visualization that Brunswik's perspective on the primacy of the functional arc and the lens model, embodied in the objective functional psychology diagram, is given concrete substance as well as historical emergence. (Elsewhere in this section of his monograph, Brunswik diagrammatically represented sensory psychology and Gestalt psychology as "part-objective" manifestations of experimental psychology [p. 53] and psychoanalysis/dynamic personality psychology as a depth psychology, which highlighted the key role that vicarious functioning played in behavior [p. 57].) Brunswik's entire purpose in this section of his monograph was to set the reader up for his inevitable conclusion, hammered home in the final section, that a probabilistic functional psychology represented the unique, yet broadly consistent with respect to the other natural sciences, identity and focus for twentieth-century psychological science.

"Convergence toward an Objective Functional Approach"

Brunswik brought his arguments full circle in the final section of his monograph by showing that an objective functional approach was possible and was the natural way for psychology to evolve as its own kind of human science. He showed how newer developments in psychology could be linked, at least partly, to this objective functional orientation. Thus, Brunswik showed how the distal-central regional reference could be seen to emerge, at least in some measure, within surprisingly diverse domains of psychology such as molar behaviorism (Tolman), dynamic personality theory (Murray, Frenkel-Brunswik), topological psychology (Lewin), learning theory (Estes and, to a lesser extent, Hull), factor analysis and mental testing (Spearman, Thurstone), mathematical biophysics (Rashevsky), cybernetics (Weiner), and communication theory (Shannon). However, none of these domains could be seen to instantiate the full measure of the perspective Brunswik was advocating, rather he saw these various developments as contributing incremen-

tally to the imperative of a full realization of his integrative view. To illustrate, consider Brunswik's final paragraph in the manuscript where, although focusing on communication theory, he implied that all of what he had reviewed with respect to recent (as of 1952) developments in psychology might contribute to the realization of his full perspective:

> Communication theory may well contribute to the efforts, stressed in the present paper, to determine the structural and functional properties of the unit of behavior in abstract terms. Such determination will in turn contribute toward an explicit recognition not only of the rules and restrictions but also of the licenses and liberties of the objective as well as of the molar approach. It will further contribute to the much-needed establishment of psychology as a discipline of distinctive, well-circumscribed internal coherence and formal unity of purpose within the more broadly unitary framework of science at large. (p. 92)

What Impact Did Brunswik's Monograph Have in His Time?

The specific impact of Brunswik's monograph is difficult to establish in the context of psychology in the 1950s. Part of the reason may be that the monograph compressed too many of his ideas using terse and precise language. The inherent difficulty of Brunswik's ideas, coupled with their apparent threat to the established and increasingly solidifying status quo in psychological theory and method, meant that encapsulating them in a single, very dense monograph was an unfortunate strategic decision on Brunswik's part. Evidence may be reflected in Brunswik's later spreading of his ideas with deeper explanations and illustrations through several outlets, some appearing posthumously, following the publication of the monograph (e.g., Brunswik, 1955c, 1956a, 1956b, 1957, 1959, 1963, 1966). Thus, while the 1952 monograph represented his crowning achievement in many ways and depicted the coalescence and convergent synergy of the strands of his thinking, it was perhaps exactly the wrong vehicle for conveying that thinking. Leary (1987) provided a very clear appraisal of why Brunswik's monograph failed to achieve its potential to impact the discipline when he said, "There is no

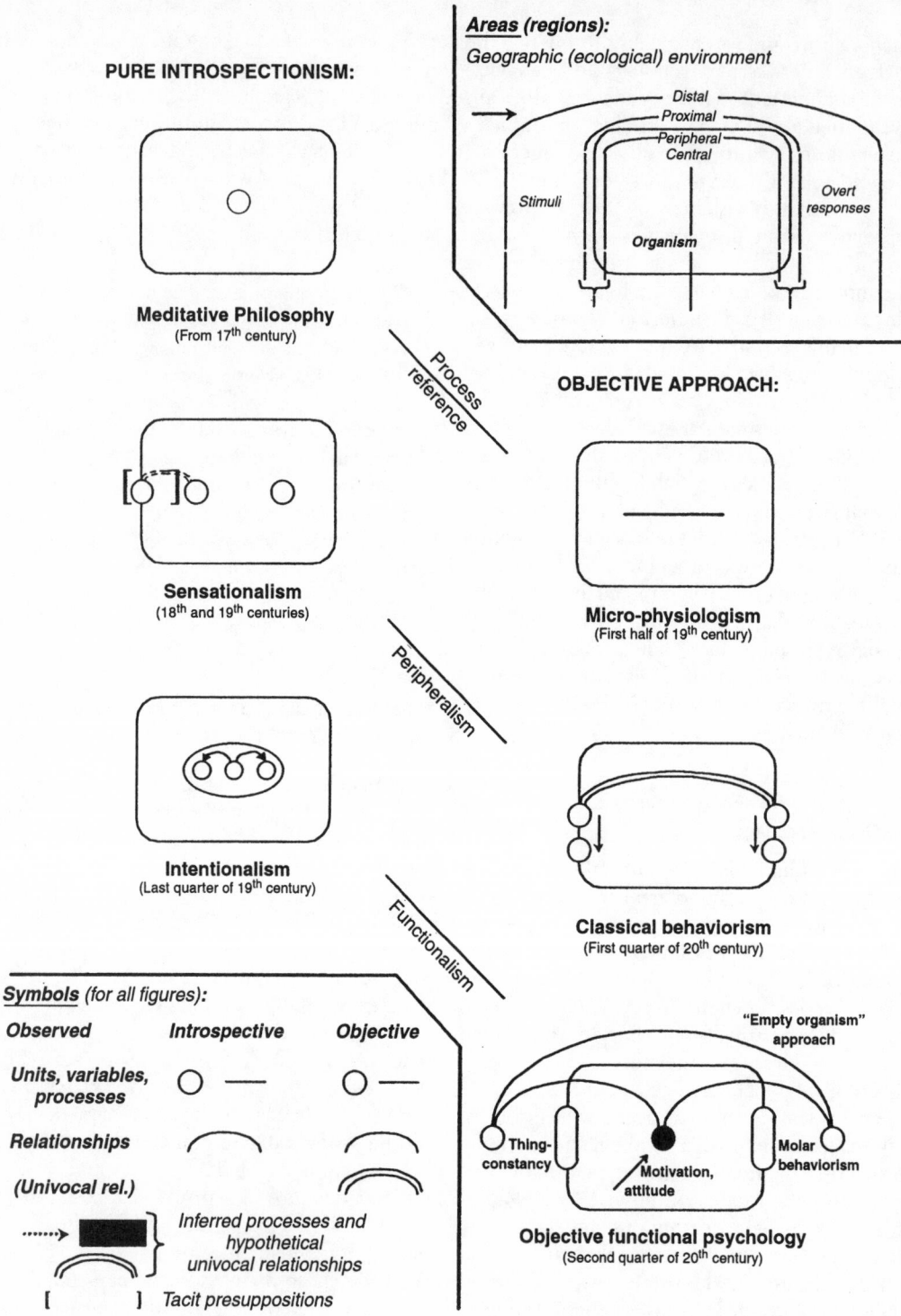

FIGURE 12.2 Major stages of introspective and objective psychology. In *The Conceptual Framework of Psychology* (p. 51), E. Brunswik, 1952, Chicago, IL: University of Chicago Press. Copyright 1952 by University of Chicago Press. Adapted with permission.

question that the style of Brunswik's communication—his uncompromising efforts to say things just right and just once—had a deleterious effect on the understanding of his message" (p. 136). In a further footnote to this point, Leary made an interesting observation about Brunswik's communication style as contradicting the very approach he was trying to establish:

> Ironically, Brunswik's excessively terse style violated his own theoretical understanding of the need for "redundancy" in communication. See the very last section of his *Conceptual Framework of Psychology*, entitled "Redundancy as an Antidote to Equivocation." Brunswik's contentions in this regard exemplify a basic principle of probabilistic functionalism: the more redundant the cues or means (stimuli, words, behavioral options) the greater the probability of accurate or appropriate achievement (perception, communication, goal attainment). (p. 142)

Only two specific reviews of the monograph have been identified (Bergmann, 1952; Hochberg, 1954), and both reflect a less-than-complete understanding of what Brunswik was really trying to accomplish, perhaps partly exacerbated by Brunswik's style, which as Bergmann (1952) stated was "overly parenthetical and allusive, his vocabulary formidably polysyllabic" (p. 654). It may be that the style issue prevented sufficient penetration into Brunswik's ideas for the reviewers to grapple with, for each review tended to focus on the surface rather than the depth of Brunswik's ideas. Further, Bergmann (1952) said, "I cannot help feeling that the way in which he [Brunswik] closely intertwines logical analysis with advocacy is most unfortunate" (p. 655). Thus, despite the power and logic of Brunswik's arguments, an unintended side effect was the creation of the perception that he was just pushing his own particular "special line of research" (Bergmann, 1952, p. 655). This interpretation led Bergmann to conclude that Brunswik's structural history of psychology was fatally flawed by this unintended side-effect: "But even structural history is a dangerous weapon in the hands of a man with a cause" (p. 656). Hochberg (1954), while concluding that Brunswik's monograph, "as a review of psychology's problems, . . . is imaginative and intriguing" (p. 386), nonetheless felt moved to say, "This reader feels some misgivings concerning how much of this survey [Brunswik's structural history] is relatively atheoretical *methodology* and how much is substantive (if implicit) theory" (p. 387). Julian Hochberg clearly missed the essential point that Brunswik was making, namely, that theory and method cannot be so cleanly disentangled (just as the complex nexus of proximal cues impinging upon an organism cannot be so cleanly disentangled). Theory and method imply and inform each other, and this was precisely what his structural history was trying to show. Leary (1987), thirty-five years after publication of the monograph, reflected this insight into Brunswik's message when he referred to Brunswik's "recognition of the 'inextricable entanglement' of theory and method" (p. 137).

The defensiveness evident in these two reviews of Brunswik's monograph (more in Bergmann's review than in Hochberg's) provided a near-impenetrable bulwark against the force of Brunswik's ideas, with the result that the ideas merely crashed against the walls, making little impression or lasting impact. Unfortunately, this trend would continue with respect to several other later works by Brunswik (many of which are reviewed in the present volume). The result was that his ideas never cracked the shell of resistance in mainstream psychology except in the clear case of the early work by Hammond (1954, 1955) and Smedslund (1955). Leary (1987) summarized the general impact of the Brunswik monograph by saying, "Although it contributed to his reputation, Brunswik's monograph did not convert many psychologists to his point of view" (p. 129).

It was not until the 1960s that Brunswik's ideas, many of which were embedded in the 1952 monograph, received a good airing in addition to some well-considered criticism. This airing took the form of an edited book (Hammond, 1966b), where several mainstream psychologists (e.g., Donald Campbell, Lee J. Cronbach, Roger Barker, Theodore Sarbin, and Jane Loevinger) exposed, perhaps for the first time, the fact that they had been influenced, however subtly, by at least some of Brunswik's ideas. The first chapter in this book, written by Hammond (1966a), presented the first down-to-earth account of Brunswik's systemic ideas, many of which were essential ingredients in Brunswik's 1952 monograph. The major selling point of Brunswik's ideas was the lens model analogy and the idiographic-statistical approach in the form of multiple regression analysis of human judgment (see the different presentations that emerged during the 1960s and 1970s: Dudycha & Naylor, 1966; Hoffman, 1960; Petrinovich, 1979; Slovic & Lichtenstein, 1971; Snow, 1968, 1974). Yet, outside the immediate influence of Hammond and his students and associates, with the notable exception of Petrinovich (1979) and Snow (1974), the concept of representative design tended to be a semi-invisible side dish, often only picked at, for the lens model/multiple regression main course. Brunswik in 1952, of course, perceived all of these developments as a single integrated system—a lesson that has perhaps only most recently begun to insinuate itself into the awareness of a wider range of researchers and theorists.

What Were Brunswik's Key Lessons for Behavioral Scientists in His Time?

Brunswik packaged a wealth of ideas and insights into his monograph, but certain ideas stand out as key lessons for psychologists and other behavioral scientists of the time. The most important of these ideas came as an inseparable conceptual "triplet" described in Part II of the monograph.

The Lens Model

The first component of the conceptual "triplet" was the concept of the lens model, which embodied a symmetric focus on organism and environment, the linking of organismic behavior and environmental objects/events through a functional arc, and the probabilistic representation of vicarious mediation in the environment and vicarious functioning within the organism. Brunswik used the lens model analogy as his conceptual device for moving psychology to a more appropriately complex behavioral focus:

A stabilized or relatively stabilized connection between focal variables taken as classes rather than as individual occurrences, as established through vicarious functioning either in perception or in overt behavior, may be characterized as an "accomplishment" or "achievement." . . . The term "function" will likewise in the main be used to characterize wide-arched dependencies of this kind, in contradistinction to the more micro-

scopic aspects of the "functioning" of physiological processes. Focal variables outside the organism may be called "functionally attained." . . . From a "molar" point of view, comprehensive patterns of this kind may be taken as the dynamically integrated and effective units of behavior. Organisms may in this sense be characterized as "stabilizers" of events or of relationships.

The total pattern involved, when viewed as a composite picture of numerous cases of individual mediation from initial to terminal focus bears resemblance to a bundle of rays scattering from a light-source and brought back to convergence in a distant second point by a convex lens. A generalized "lens model" for stabilized functional units is shown in Figure 1 [see Figure 12.1 here]. While correlation between the focal variables is assumed to be relatively high although in general not perfect . . . , those of each focus with the single elements or chains of mediation may be low. A semicircular arrow is appended in the figure to the terminal focus to indicate that lens patterns do not stand in isolation but are apt to reflect back upon the organism in a future state in what is now sometimes called a "feedback" loop . . . , such as when arriving at the food is followed by satiation and reinforcement of the preceding behavior. . . . Further lens patterns may be involved in this process. (pp. 19–20)

In two relatively short and admittedly very dense paragraphs, Brunswik established the key parameters of his lens model conceptualization, highlighted its probabilistic nature and the utility of correlation as the measure of uncertainty, showed how it can explain learning in organisms, and linked the model to more dynamic systems theories (very new stuff in 1952) through the incorporation of the feedback loop. The reader should note that the feedback loop aspect of Brunswik's lens model has been retained in modern-day renditions of the lens model only as a between-person process (as in the interpersonal learning and interpersonal conflict implementations of judgment analysis or social judgment theory; see Chapter 2 in Cooksey, 1996b). Feedback in the sense that Brunswik seems to mean it, within organisms, has been lost in modern-day implementations, although some attempts are now being made to build it back in (see, for example, Chapter 8 in Cooksey, 1996b, and work by Brehmer, 1996).

Representative Design

The second component in the "triplet" was the concept of representative design. Brunswik described representative design as the methodological imperative for appropriately simulating or sampling the ambiguous causal texture of the environment, and he juxtaposed it with mainstream systematic design that unrealistically disambiguated this causal texture:

> By extension of the principle of sampling from individuals to situations, representative design countermands a number of preconceived methodological notions of nomothetic experimentation, among them the "rule of one variable," i.e., the studying of one factor at a time. It further countermands the more general inclination to design experimental research in accordance with formalistic-"systematic" patterns which are too narrow to bring out the essentials of behavioral functioning although they may involve a shift to "multivariate" or to Fisher's "factorial" design. (p. 30)

Brunswik's lesson here was that systematic experimental design, whether focused on single or multiple factors, got one no closer to tapping into the fundamental behavioral unit described by the lens model. Psychology had bought into the sophisticated experimental science offered by statisticians without thinking about what it meant for investigating the behavioral phenomena of interest.

Idiographic-Statistical Approach

The third component in Brunswik's major "triplet" was the establishment of the idiographic-statistical approach to behavioral research, which emphasized situational sampling, in conjunction with representative design, within the environmental context of a single organism coupled with a statistical approach (linked by Brunswik to correlational statistics) to capturing the probabilistic nature of relationships between the distal, proximal, and central regions of reference:

> The distinction between natural and cultural sciences . . . is traditionally linked with that between the strictly nomothetic (and explanatory) approach which in principle claims absolute predictablity and the idiographic (case descriptive)

approach which, strictly speaking, does not know of predictability. Yet, "clinical" psychology with its emphasis on understanding the single case is possible only by the recognition of a certain self-consistency of the individual throughout shorter or longer stretches of his personal history on a probability basis, and with the tacit or explicit help of a more generalized study of individual differences and their interrelationships. Even the spatially unique topographic aggregates of geography show marked consistency in time and thus deal with "local" probability laws of a statistical nature rather than with bits of information strictly isolated from each other. Generally, in modern science, the unrealistically absolutized nomothetic-idiographic dichotomy is resolved on the common ground of the probability approach. (p. 38)

In the 1952 monograph, Brunswik went even further, later in his discussion, to reinforce a point he had made in some of his earlier work (e.g., Brunswik, 1943) that "it is no longer appropriate to investigate strict laws in psychology; their repudiation is a methodological or representational, not an ontological, statement" (p. 38), a perspective with which Hull (1943a) and Lewin (1943), among others, took great exception. It is perhaps easy to see why this idea would strike many psychologists as "heresy" since it went to the core of the "natural" science, logical positivist roots of the prevailing perspective. Compounding the problem was the fact that Brunswik seemed to be admitting that there was some value in more phenomenological subjectivist approaches to the study of behavior (where the idiographic perspective was valued and the nomothetic perspective generally uninteresting), an issue to be discussed further below.

Theory and Method

The second of Brunswik's major ideas was reflected in the very nature of his approach to setting out a structural history of psychology: the idea that psychological theory and method were inextricably intertwined. Indirectly, Brunswik was sending a warning to the psychologists of the time that there were many dangers hidden in the wholesale importation of methodology (highly controlled experimentation coupled with an asymmetric emphasis on subject sampling in ignorance of context and situation sampling) from other natural sciences and disciplines in the absence of any reasoned consideration of how those methods would both influence, and be influenced by, the very substance of the psychological discipline, namely, behavior in context. Indeed, Brunswik's 1952 message here was that psychology needed to define its own methods in full recognition of the appropriate goals for those methods as pathways for informing theory and understanding of behavior. The lens model provided just the vehicle for this message:

> In applying the lens model to psychological methodology, one may metaphorically paraphrase Spinoza's parallelistic credo and demand that the "order," or pattern, of research "ideas," or design, should be the same as the pattern of the "things" studied, which in our case is behavior. Research may be said to have reached an adequate, "functional," or "molar" level of complexity only if it parallels, and is thus capable of representing, behavior in all its essential features. We may call this the methodological postulate of behavior-research isomorphism. (p. 25)

One point of interest in Brunswik's arguments, virtually ignored by most, was that, while he explicitly pursued a more "objective" functional psychology in the context of acknowledging the inherent limits to that objectivity because of the very phenomena under study, he moved some distance toward embracing the utility of the more subjective or phenomenological social sciences — a very broad-minded leap for a psychologist in America at that time. Brunswik seemed to realize that keeping disparate philosophies of approach apart in the study of mind and behavior was counterproductive in the pursuit of a truly integrative behavioral science. Thus, it can be argued that Brunswik presaged the concept of at least certain forms of triangulation as a research strategy—a concept that Campbell and Fiske (1959) would later pick up, indirectly, in the form of their multitrait-multimethod matrix approach to construct validation, although not oriented toward the admissibility of subjectivist input. To illustrate, consider Brunswik's 1952 observations on the demise of introspectionism in psychology:

> A special case of relinquishing imperfect modes of approach regardless of their potential fruitful-

ness is given by the early behaviorists' over-all rejection of introspectionism, and of speculation and philosophy in general. Aside from the fact that the "private" character of conscious data is a relative rather than an absolute matter . . . and the line between science and non-science may therefore be difficult to draw, subjectivistic and introspective psychology is proving itself time and time again an inexhaustible nursery for the supply of novel problem patterns and for reorientation regarding the basic aims and outlook of psychology. (p. 45)

Brunswik's 1952 thinking in this regard can be further reinforced by noting his attitude toward quantification and qualification in psychology:

> Ever since Ewald Hering, however, phenomenologists have insisted that there is a "visual space" in which experience is organized; they and the gestalt psychologists have described the inhomogeneity and "anisotropy" of this perceptual, or "behavioral" space as compared with the physicist's space. Such recent investigators as S. S. Stevens have pointed to the surprising consistency and to what may be called the "transitivity" of such introspective operations as the bisecting or doubling of subjective auditory intervals. Facts of this kind tend to mellow the absoluteness of the quality-quantity dichotomy. . . . As pointed out by Russell . . . measurement and the use of numbers go beyond the essential requirements of the objective approach as defined by univocality of observation and of commmunication. Relational terms such as "between," "above," "ancestor," designating order in a series, is all that is required. The usefulness of such "comparative" or "topological" concepts has also been pointed out by Hempel and Oppenheim. (pp. 39–40)

Thus, Brunswik, despite favoring quantification as a route to objectification, was not averse to admitting that there may be elements of quality that should be factored into our understanding of behavioral systems. This is a viewpoint reflected in current debates on the role of quantitative versus qualitative data in behavioral research, a debate that researchers such as Jick (1979) resolved by appealing to their joint, mutually supportive utility in triangulated research methodology.

The Future for Psychology

Finally, Brunswik sought to anticipate where psychology was headed into the future and signaled that there were numerous new developments on the horizon that could be enriched by, as well as build on, the objective functional psychology he proposed. Many of these new developments were highlighted earlier (e.g., cybernetics, communication theory, dynamic personality psychology, topological psychology), and it was through these new connections that Brunswik (1952) sought to show that his objective functional psychology, as the natural evolutionary progression of centuries of psychology, had far wider implications than those that were more obvious for the domain of perception:

> During a third phase of modern psychology, beginning in the 1930s, there is a "convergence" of the predominantly Anglo-American tradition of empiricist rigor (behaviorism, pragmatistic emphasis on overt action, statistical scrutiny) with predominantly Continental stress on complexity and richness of scope. This convergence possesses all the earmarks of a genuine "synthesis" of the preceding divergent, mutually "antithetical" movements (to apply Hegel's notions of the dialectics of creative process). It is not an eclectic intercombination of selected fragments of existing schools; rather abstract methodological features are united for the first time in formations of striking novelty of style. . . . More specifically, recent developments in psychology emerge as a combination of a de-emphasis of the peripheral region and the establishment of a central-distal or at least a central frame of reference which takes cognizance of the predominantly central-distal focusing of behavior itself. (pp. 66–67)

What Are Brunswik's Key Lessons for Behavioral Scientists Now?

The central ideas in Brunswik's monograph have many important implications for today's behavioral scientists and are being reflected in various disciplines to a greater or lesser extent. Interestingly, the psychological domain where Brunswik did most of his critical empirical work,—namely, perception—is not one of the domains that now enjoy the influence of his ideas. First and foremost, Brunswik's concepts are most strongly reflected in research on human judgment and decision making, primarily because Hammond (1954, 1955) and one of his students (Todd, 1954) found the lens-model/representative-design/idiographic-statistical-approach "triplet" to be a useful approach to studying clinical decision making— the applied area of psychological diagnosis criticized heavily by Meehl (1954) for its overreliance on less than perfectly consistent human clinicians. Hursch, Hammond, and Hursch (1964) derived the lens model equation that brought Brunswik's view of the importance of multiple correlation as a tool for capturing vicarious functioning into a coherent methodological analysis system that operated at the idiographic level. These humble beginnings stimulated the increasing trend in studies citing Brunswik's influence summarized much later by Hammond (1996a, reprinted in this volume)—a trend that essentially mapped the growth in popularity and applicability of multiple cue probability learning (MCPL), social judgment theory (SJT; Hammond, Stewart, Brehmer, & Steinmann, 1975; see also the special issue of *Thinking and Reasoning* devoted to SJT and edited by Doherty, 1996), and, most recently, *Judgment Analysis* (Cooksey, 1996b).

More important, Brunswik's key ideas are now seen to be spreading into important new areas, even if his influence is not always directly acknowledged: naturalistic decision making (see Klein, Orasanu, Calderwood, & Zsambok, 1993; Zsambok & Klein, 1997); adaptive decision making (Payne, Bettman, & Johnson, 1993); human-computer interaction and ergonomics (Vicente, Christoffersen, & Pereklita, 1995); human resource management and organizational behavior (Cooksey & Gates, 1995); and public policy (Hammond, 1996c). In many areas reflecting Brunswik's influence, the key concept brought on board appears to be explicit acknowledgment of the importance of environmental influences on human behavior, whether couched in terms of the lens model or some other representational system. Representative design has been periodically revived as something worth doing, more recently by authors who had demonstrated no previous commitment to Brunswik's idea (e.g., Edwards, 1983). Unfortunately, however, Brunswik's original meaning for representative design, as characterized in his 1952 monograph, has frequently been distorted by some to mean "real-life" research or, worse, "ecologically valid" research—reflecting an essential misunderstanding of a key Brunswikian concept (see the discussion by Hammond, 1998, in his electronic essay on the Internet).

Brunswik's 1952 allusion to open systems theory, thermodynamics, and cybernetics in his monograph has produced recent fruit in the expanding present-day push for systems thinking and modeling to replace simplistic linear thinking and modeling processes (see, for example, Checkland, 1981; Senge, 1990; also see Cooksey, 1996a, for an extension of judgment analysis using nonlinear systems theory):

> As has been pointed out by Bertalanffy, the recent extension of thermodynamics from closed to open systems, advanced especially by Prigogine since 1946, has led to "fundamentally new principles" under which "self-regulation" and "equifinality" can be subsumed. Especially equifinality—given when the "final state may be reached from different initial conditions and in different ways" in the sense of our "terminal focusing"— has often been considered the main proof of vitalism. . . . Organisms have in the past erroneously been likened to closed systems with their tendency toward equilibrium; actually they are—as had already been pointed out by the biophysicist, Hill, in 1931—open systems in a relatively time-independent, quasi-stationary "steady state" maintained by a continuous flow of component materials. (p. 42)

This quote would not be out of place in many modern developments describing systems approaches to behavior, and it shows the extent to which Brunswik had thought about the implications of his lens model with its feedback loop.

Brunswik (1952) made another interesting statement deep in his monograph that presaged very recent developments in applying chaos and complexity theory to understanding human behavior and decision making (see, for example, Cooksey, 1996a; Cooksey & Gates, 1995; Cooksey, 2000):

> It must be stressed once more that the probability character of behavioral laws is not due primarily to limitations in the researcher and his means of approach but rather to imperfections in the potentialities of adjustment on the part of the behaving organism living in a semi-chaotic environ-

mental medium. In this sense, even an omniscient infinite intellect, when turning psychologist, would have to adopt a probabilistic approach. (p. 28)

Today, complexity theory (e.g., Bossomaier & Green, 1998; Waldrop, 1992) can be seen to connect with Brunswik's account if one essentially considers successful adaptation to circumstances by self-organizing systems as exhibiting Brunswikian "equifinality"—many paths to a goal, limits to predictability of such paths, and sensitivity to initial conditions. Brunswikian links to Darwin and evolutionary psychology are also evident (see Hammond, "How Probabilistic Functionalism Advances Evolutionary Psychology," this volume), being signaled by Brunswik in his (1952) monograph when discussing his lens model:

> The broadest context into which behavioral units may ultimately be fitted is "(probable) survival" as a descriptive fact of life. The concept of survival, established by Darwin, Tyler, and other biological and sociological functionalists of the nineteenth century, is extensively used by Hull in his recent formalization of classical behaviorist theory. . . . It may be added that even lenses in the literal sense of the word are, when taken as a class and as imbedded within a stabilization mechanism, to be found only within, or as products of, higher organisms. (p. 21)

Another lesson from Brunswik's monograph that is critical to keep in mind is the importance of not losing touch with the history and evolution of one's discipline, for this may provide the well-spring for new integrative insights into how to move forward while avoiding the pitfalls of the past. That Brunswik was able to do this at all in his monograph was an impressive display of intellectual prowess (even Bergmann, 1952, while taking issue with Brunswik's approach to structural history, said, "On the basis of the evidence presented, it is safe to say that few, if any, are better qualified than Brunswik to undertake this arduous task"; p. 656). That Brunswik was able to do it so thoroughly and in such an integrated and systemic fashion spoke of an intimate knowledge of where one has come from linked to where one is going (Hochberg, 1954, said, in a simultaneous compliment and criticism, "In short, this [the monograph] is an intriguing overview of psychological concepts and methodology from a strong, consistent [and hence necessarily selective and biased] theoretical position, and will serve as an excellent introduction to Brunswik's viewpoint for those with an adequate psychological background"; p. 388). In today's world of increasing research specialization, this integrative "seeing the forest as well as the trees" capacity, rare in any case, is rapidly becoming at risk of extinction. It is also one of the reasons that systems theories and systems thinking have evolved as essential tools for behavioral scientists (see Checkland, 1981; Churchman, 1971; Müller-Merbach, 1994). Brunswik, as evidenced in his *Conceptual Framework of Psychology*, was arguably the first systems theorist in psychology, but it has taken forty to fifty years of concerted efforts on his behalf for the discipline to fully appreciate what Brunswik offered.

13

Survival in a World of Probable Objects [1957]

 COMMENT

On Gibson's Review of Brunswik

Alex Kirlik

In a concluding passage of *On the Origin of Species* (1859/1966), Charles Darwin wrote:

> Although I am fully convinced of the truth of the views given in this volume . . . I by no means expect to convince experienced naturalists whose minds are stocked with a multitude of facts all viewed, during a long course of years, from a point of view directly opposite to mine. . . . But I look with confidence to the future—to young and rising naturalists, who will be able to view both sides of the question with impartiality. (p. 406)

Born just one year apart, Egon Brunswik and James J. Gibson were highly successful psychologists who were never very successful in convincing the bulk of their contemporaries of the truth or utility of their psychological systems. Both of these men put forth radical theoretical positions for their time and were marginalized during much of the most active portions of their careers for exactly this reason. But both have successfully influenced many "young and rising" psychologists, who have adopted their systems and in so doing have strongly shaped modern theory: Brunswik, in the psychology of judgment and decision making, and Gibson, in the psychology of perception and action.

Points of Contact

The most striking aspect of Gibson's review is its positive tone, in stark contrast to the many highly critical assessments of Brunswik's work offered by other contemporaries, such as Hull, Lewin, and Koehler (see Brunswik, 1955a, 1955b). Although one cannot help but wonder if some of the platitudes offered by Gibson (e.g., "His work is an object lesson in theoretical integrity," Gibson, 1957, p. 35) were sharpened by Brunswik's then recent death, the tenor and tone of the review are laudatory. Gibson clearly seems here to have seized on the rhetorical opportunity provided by the review format to indirectly advance many of his own views through the clever and selective use of Brunswik's voice. Consider this early passage:

> Brunswik never took refuge in the sterile theory of the private phenomenal world. He was too well aware that functional behavior demands veridical perception. Nor would he accept the Gestalt theory of a brain process which would spontaneously produce the correct object in phenomenal experience. (p. 245)

The economy of the rhetoric is masterful, for in one fell swoop Gibson indicted entire schools of then-dominant psychological and philosophical theorizing for their "sterile" idealism and "private" subjectivism. In lieu of the deftly chosen *spontaneously* in the final sentence Gibson might just as well have said *magically* without change of theoretical meaning and import. In these few words, Gibson even manages to offer his own radical, realist alternative as if it were an obvious and mundane fact: Brunswik was "*too well aware* that functional behavior demands veridical perception," a sentence designed to read as if the agreement of these two men settled the matter once and for all.

What most strongly united Brunswik and Gibson, and what set them apart from their contemporaries, was their focus on achievement, on veridical perception, on how it is even possible for behavior to be productive. "By rights," Gibson (1957) noted, "the animal should not have functional contact with the environment, and yet it does" (p. 245). Solving this puzzle was the task both Brunswik and Gibson set for themselves. While they differed in the details of how to approach the solution, they were united in taking achievement to be psychology's central problem, and thus united in their objection to the mainstream psychological theory of the day, which stood on an empirical foundation of optical illusion, sensory bias, and perceptual error, constructs suited more to passing judgment on behavior than to explaining it. Gibson once remarked that what was most wrong with psychology was that psychologists did not stand in proper awe of their subject matter. Both the content and the tone of his review testify that he did not include Brunswik in this criticism.

Both Brunswik and Gibson realized that if they took the central question of psychology to be understanding achievement, they could not find the answer to this question solely within the boundary of the skin. Achievement is always achievement *of* something, and this something cannot be defined without reference to the environment. In particular, what must be understood according to Brunswik and Gibson was how the organism attains a stable, functional relationship with the external world. Both the organism and its environment participate as equal partners in providing both the criteria and the resources for adaptation. And in describing the environment Brunswik and Gibson both realized that ontology must come before epistemology in psychology. The psychologist must describe and measure the environment of the organism before questions of how the organism comes to achieve knowledge of that environment can even be asked.

For this reason, Brunswik and Gibson both spent significant portions of their careers describing the ecology: the environment for perception, cognition, and action. The psychologist cannot not rely on the subjective impressions of laboratory participants or on his or her own introspections in describing the ecology. To do so would put the epistemological cart before the ontological horse, and the result would be a psychology ever confined to the head. Nor can psychologists turn to physics to do the job for them. Why should the obscure distinctions and dimensions best suited to modern theorizing about the inanimate world (e.g., heat versus temperature) be the same distinctions and dimensions most crucial for a biological creature to detect, measure, and respect (e.g., predator versus prey)?

Although Brunswik and Gibson both recognized the need for detailed ecological analysis and description, they parted company on exactly how to carry out this enterprise. The sharpest point of contention between them was ontological: What are the ecological primitives? What are the units of ecological analysis and measurement? Gibson alluded to his dissatisfaction with Brunswik's position on this point:

He accepted without criticisms the usual list of cues for the third dimension, referring as they do to the perception of a single object, and he conceived of the environment as a collection of single objects rather than as an array of adjoining surfaces. If the cues for depth, so conceived, are ill-defined or circularly defined, not cognate with one another and non-isolable, he was willing to accept this state of affairs without impatience, and to proceed as he could. (p. 245)

Gibson was obviously uncomfortable with Brunswik's choice of the single object as the ecological ontological primitive. He believed that this naive ontological decision ("accepted without criticisms") created an artificial epistemological problem: How could veridical perception, the backbone of functional behavior, rest on the shoulders of such "ill-defined" and "circularly defined" sources of information? Gibson's preference was to try to eliminate or simplify the epistemological problem using as a preemptive strike a more judicious choice of environmental primitives. In his criticism of Brunswik's distance perception experiment based on asking what the subject is "looking at," Gibson asked:

Now does this procedure genuinely represent the variable of size in the human habitat? A tendency for objects to be evenly *spaced* in the physical world would be missed by this sampling of the internal dimensions of single objects. The ordinary perceiver does not look at interspaces, although he sees them. Perhaps the regular spacing to be found in the structure of things is more important for perception than the variability in the sizes of things. The present reviewer is convinced that the environment is geometrically lawful, and not the reverse. (p. 246)

On this point Gibson and Brunswik had an honest and fundamental disagreement. For Brunswik (1955a), "God may not gamble, animals and humans do" (p. 236), while Gibson's realist position focused on the complete informativeness of stimulation.

A second point on which Gibson and Brunswik appeared to disagree concerns the proximal-distal distinction that serves as a foundation for Brunswikian theory and method. Gibson was known to be sharply critical of any distinction between proximal and distal stimulus information, as he believed it to be a false dichotomy directed toward solving a nonexistent problem. Gibson believed that psychologists had created an artificial problem (how the organism infers distal properties from proximal stimulation) by assuming a too finely grained unit of analysis in describing the so-called proximal stimulus. As a result, the organism was viewed as piecing together disparate proximal evidence to obtain distal information, where in Gibson's view the organism should be seen has having access to the molar, distal information directly within proximal stimulation.

Gibson thus argued for a collapse of the proximal-distal distinction. At first blush, Gibson's position would seem to stand as an outright rejection of Brunswikian theory and method, making so much, as it does, of proximal-distal relationships. However, an important point bears keeping in mind when comparing Brunswik and Gibson in this regard. Gibson never rejected the fundamental distinction between the environment of an organism and the information available to an organism about that environment. As evidence for this claim, one only needs to appreciate the crucial role that the term *specification* plays in Gibson's later writings, and in the modern Gibsonian literature as well. The organism is seen as picking up information that *specifies* environmental events, affordances, surfaces, and the like. For largely historical and rhetorical reasons, modern followers of Gibson prefer not to construe this distinction in terms of the proximal and the distal: Gibson's rejection of this theory-laden language allowed him to clearly articulate his radical position and still provides a touchstone for the Gibsonian approach. However, there is nothing that would keep one from applying Brunswikian theory and method to the analysis of the specification relations that play such an important role in modern Gibsonian theory. In fact, there may be good reasons to do so.

A Modern Analysis

Disagreement between Brunswik and Gibson crystallized around the issue of whether the organism's relation to the environment should be considered irreducibly probabilistic or fully informative. In addressing this problem in its modern light, it is useful to examine the progress of Brunswikian and Gibsonian theory and method since 1957. Brunswik's project has been taken up and advanced by a group of scientists focusing mainly on judgment and decision making, many of whom are contributors to this volume. Since Gibson's death in 1979, his project has been adopted and extended by a collection of scientists focusing instead on perception and action. Writing as one of the few members of both the Brunswik Society and the International Society for Ecological Psychology (ISEP), and as an occasional participant in both societies annual meetings, I think it is fair to say that communication and collaboration between members of these two groups is minimal. Each tradition largely searches where the comfortable lamplight of its prevailing theory is brightest: for Brunswikians, in probabilistic ecologies; for Gibsonians, in fully determined ones. A speaker at a Brunswik meeting presenting a graph showing a noisy regression fit to judgment data will always interpret the noise in terms of the lens model constructs *cognitive control* or *environmental predictability*. A speaker at an ISEP meeting discussing a regression fit to perceptual data will either avoid mention of the noise or else chalk it up to the technology of curve fitting and experimental error. Few experimental psychologists today are asking the high-level questions Brunswik and Gibson asked of each other.

One theorist who has considered the matter at sufficient altitude is James Cutting. According to Cutting (1986), for some aspects of perception, such as perceiving objects in depth, history is on the side of Gibson regarding the informativeness of stimulation:

Indeed, many cues to layout of depth are hardly subtle: They hammer home to the perceiver certain relations among objects in the visible world. They specify certain aspects of what is perceived, and they allow few, and at most times no, alternatives. (p. 41)

Gibson's ontological choice to describe the environment not in terms of everyday objects, but instead in terms of arrays of textured surfaces and the optical flow patterns that specify them to an ambulatory perceiver has resulted in the discovery of sources of information for depth much more informative than Brunswik's original cues. On this matter, Gibson's approach has indeed been successful in taking some of the mystery (for the scientist) and epistemic difficulty (for the perceiver) out of depth perception. Gibson's ontological choice has indeed uncovered some "invariants," or sophisticated types of information available to perception, that may not have been discovered by an approach more content to assume an irreducibly probabilistic ecology. But overall, how successful has the invariant discovery enterprise been? In Cutting's (1986) view:

> Unfortunately, there is no recourse other than to discover invariants one by one. It is a plodding, empirical, endeavor, and if all research efforts are gauged collectively, the invariants appear to be somewhat recalcitrant to discovery. Gibson turned his later efforts away from this type of empiricism and toward explicating the notion of affordances. (p. 243)

It is unclear whether Gibson turned away from the invariant discovery problem because of its difficulty or instead because he became more interested in the more molar problems of meaningful interaction with the world. What is certain, though, is that by the time of his 1979 book, *The Ecological Approach to Visual Perception*, Gibson's thinking had begun to take on a distinctly Brunswikian tone in at least one crucial respect: Compare Gibson's notion of affordances for meaningful action with Tolman and Brunswik's earlier (1935) *manipulanda* properties, such as grasp-ableness, pick-up-ableness, sit-on-ableness, and run-through-ableness (Tolman and Brunswik, 1935, p. 465).

A Modern Synthesis

Is the divide-and-conquer strategy underlying the now nearly independent Gibsonian and Bruns-

wikian research traditions adaptive? Or have these two local hill-climbing efforts merely delayed consideration of important questions about the global ecological landscape? The answer to both questions is probably a qualified yes. On the first point, it now seems as if some portion of the disagreement between Brunswik and Gibson can be resolved by noting that perhaps they were both right, but about different things. The fact that Gibsonian theory has proven most valuable for understanding dynamic visually guided action, while Brunswikian theory has proven most valuable for understanding judgment and decision making, may actually reflect a deep and important distinction between the functions cognition performs in these two different classes of tasks. What Brunswik and Gibson took to be a unitary phenomenon — perception of the external world — may not be such a unitary phenomenon after all.

It is now widely accepted in visual neuroscience that visual perception in the primate cerebral cortex is served by two largely independent streams of processing (Ungerleider and Mishkin, 1982; Goodale and Milner, 1992; Goodale, 1993). Originally described as the "what" and "where" systems by Ungerleider and Mishkin, the currently accepted distinction between these visual streams is in terms of "what" and "how" systems. The ventral stream of visual processing mediates the perception of enduring characteristics of objects and perceptual categorization, whereas the dorsal stream mediates the dynamic control of skilled actions directed toward environmental objects (Goodale, 1993). Consider Goodale and Milner's description of a patient, DF, with visual agnosia due primarily to damage to the ventral visual processing anatomy:

> Despite her profound inability to recognize the size, shape, and orientation of visual objects, DF showed strikingly accurate hand and finger movements directed at the very same objects. Thus, when she was presented with a pair of rectangular blocks of the same or different dimensions, she was unable to differentiate between them. When she was asked to indicate the width of a single block by means of her index finger and thumb, her matches bore no relationship to the dimensions of the object and showed considerable trial to trial variability. However, when she was asked simply to reach out and pick up the block, the aperture between her index finger and thumb changed systematically with the width of

the object, just as in normal subjects. (Goodale and Milner, 1992, p. 22)

Much if not most modern work in the Gibsonian perception and action tradition exhibits a clear preference for studying perceptually guided movement, rather than verbal report, in describing and evaluating the adaptivity of behavior (e.g., walking, reaching). On the other hand, modern Brunswikian judgment and decision research relies heavily on verbal responses. Neither Brunswik nor Gibson, of course, had access to data suggesting a "what" versus "how" distinction in visual processing. But armed with this knowledge, and with the benefit of hindsight, we can now see that perhaps both these theorists were essentially correct about fundamental aspects of behavior but overgeneralized their positions.

Reconsider Gibson's criticism of Brunswik's distance perception experiment using data created by asking at intermittent intervals what the subject was "looking at." Gibson made a telling comment in noting that "the ordinary perceiver does not look at interspaces, although he sees them." (p. 246) He (or she) of course "sees" them in that walking behavior, for example, is directed toward these interspaces. What neither Brunswik nor Gibson sufficiently appreciated was that participants in this experiment were performing two quite different and largely independent perceptual tasks: object naming and verbal distance esti-

mation, on the one hand, and perceptually guided locomotion, on the other.

In this light, the debate over whether information pertaining to interspaces is truly "more important for perception" than information about objects, as Gibson implied, might have made sense in 1957, when these two theorists had no reason to believe other than that they were arguing about the same thing. Today, we should know better. If the brain has special equipment devoted to both visually guided movement and object recognition and judgment, claims that one of these abilities is more "important" or "fundamental" than the other are distressing. Argument along these lines signals a retreat in psychology toward a comfortable willingness to pass judgment on behavior in lieu of doing the hard work of explaining it, a road neither Brunswik nor Gibson would have taken for himself.

Brunswik had an idea, representative design, a logic for ensuring that theoretical issues are decided to the greatest extent possible in psychology by empirical data, and thus minimally by a theorist's prejudices about which phenomena are most fundamental or important. But a logic is not enough; one also needs the motivation: The motivation to survey the global ecological landscape in a manner unbiased by the lamplight of current theory, to keep ontology before epistemology in psychology. And on this point, Gibson was surely right. "It is," as he put it in his review, "an onerous demand."

 COMMENT

On Gibson's Review of Brunswik and Kirlik's Review of Gibson

Ray W. Cooksey

J. J. Gibson reviewed Brunswik's (1956b) book in February 1957. In that review, Gibson showed that he, more so than many other psychologists of the time, had understood what Brunswik had to say about psychology and its methods in general, and about perception in particular. While Gibson may not have accepted all of

what Brunswik had to say (as shown by Kirlik, in this chapter), he nonetheless respected the integrity with which Brunswik expressed his ideas. The degree of discomfort induced by Brunswik's book cannot be underestimated and is captured most aptly in Gibson's (1957) own words:

This is, indeed, a profound and disturbing book. Brunswik realized, unlike most behaviorists, that the objects an animal can respond to are just as important for his behavior as are the responses he can make. He realized, unlike most sensory psychologists, that novel psychophysical methods are necessary—ones not confined to the narrow problems of so-called sensations. And he realized more than his contemporaries that the problems of perception, as of behavior, cannot be solved by setting up situations in the laboratory which are convenient for the experimenter but atypical for the individual. He asks us, the experimenters in psychology, to revamp our fundamental thinking and to adopt a consistent functionalism in which the organism survives—when it does—by adapting its behavior to a world of merely probable objects. It is an onerous demand. Brunswik imposed it first on his own thinking and showed how burdensome it can be. His work is an object lesson in theoretical integrity. (p. 246)

There are two essentially disturbing aspects to Brunswik's ideas flagged in this quote from Gibson: (1) the concept of a probabilistic ecology within which an organism operates and (2) the concept of representative design. It seems clear that Gibson himself had difficulty with these concepts, and his later work, as shown by Kirlik, did not implement these concepts in any fundamental way. Representative design is, almost by default, discarded as being too hard to consistently implement, and as Gibson noted, even Brunswik had difficulty implementing his own ideas consistently—the overwhelming tug of systematic design and its orientation to the isolation and disambiguation of cause and effect seems to have been almost irresistible.

Buried in Gibson's (1957) review is a lesson from Brunswik that must be taken to heart by all modern psychological researchers:

The experimenter has little or no basis for knowing in advance whether his experiment is representative or unrepresentative. It might seem to him lifelike, yet prove to be not so. The experimenter's only policy is to keep on experimenting so as to sample the world adequately. He must operate, if not in darkness, at least in theoretical twilight. To state the situation of psychology so bleakly takes courage. (p. 246)

The lesson here is that the best that representative design can do is increase our chances of studying individual behavior under conditions that adequately represent the environmental circumstances and events encountered by that individual. How much worse off are we, then, when we completely ignore the principles of representative design in favor of tight experimental control through systematic design? A generalizable psychology cannot be achieved, in Brunswik's view, without devoting appropriate attention, however difficult it may be to do, to the context in which an individual is situated when perceiving and behaving.

We have yet to achieve such unity in the discipline of human judgment and decision making as illustrated by the recent debate stimulated in the Hammond and Schneider (1997) conference symposium. The tension so aptly captured by Gibson in his review still exists. As Kirlik stated, "logic is not enough; one also needs motivation." We have had forty years or so of logical argument, first by Brunswik, then by a rather small group of researchers who were convinced by his arguments. For these people, the compelling logic of the arguments provided all the necessary motivation to produce research that attempted to meet the new demands. For the rest, even where Brunswik's arguments were well understood, the motivation to conform remained lacking. Momentum is growing, however, especially with modern-day pressures to consider research participants and sponsors as stakeholders in the research process itself. In this new context for knowledge acquisition, the knowledge that researchers produce must be seen as meaningful and useful in, and relevant to, wider contexts. This creates direct pressure to move outside the laboratory as Brunswik did early on and as social judgment theorists/judgment analysts later did (see, for example, Brehmer & Joyce, 1988; Cooksey, 1996b; Doherty, 1996; Hammond, Stewart, Brehmer, & Steinmann, 1975; Hammond, Rohrbaugh, Mumpower, & Adelman, 1977). The emergence of "naturalistic decision making" (Klein, Orasanu, Calderwood, & Zsambok, 1993; Zsambok & Klein, 1997) is a recent case in point. While their debt to Brunswik may not always be consistently acknowledged, they are clearly traveling on the trail that Brunswik blazed. In this case, the motivation is clear: lack of fit between what decision research is producing and the contexts in which decisions are actually made. Concomitant with this is an increasing emphasis on correspondence (or accuracy) in judgment research as opposed to the more traditional experimentally driven coherence emphasis (see Hammond, 1996b, for a discussion of this evolution). Finally, a renewed emphasis on general systems theory and its applicability to behavioral phenomena has stimulated the emergence of new conceptualizations that are broadly consistent with Brunswik's original arguments, taking account of both individual and environment (see, for example, Cooksey & Gates, 1995; Cooksey,

1996a, 2000) and using triangulated multimode research methodologies. Thus, what was an "onerous demand" in 1957 (having access to less sophisticated research technologies and methodologies) today has become a solvable problem having access to appropriate technological and methodological support tools. We no longer have any excuses not to travel down what Brunswik spent his life showing was arguably the most appropriate path for psychology to take in its epistemological pursuits. We are in a better position than ever to take an appropriately Brunswikian, complexified view of human behavior.

 REPRINT

Survival in a World of Probable Objects

James J. Gibson

The notion of *cues* for perception and behavior is widely used but seldom carefully examined by psychologists. Brunswik spent thirty years studying such cues, and he shows in this book the kind of psychology which can legitimately be founded on the cue-hypothesis. This is enough to make the volume an important work, but it also contains for good measure a general theory of perception, a specific theory of object-constancy, a survey of experiments on constancy, a critique of methods in perceptual research, a program for the reform of experimental method in psychology, and an effort to bridge the gap that exists between the logic of individual differences and the logic of the laboratory experiment. It is not an easy book to read, but Brunswik was not content to make it easy either by reducing the scope of his theory to a 'model' or by shirking intellectual difficulties. His style is formal and technical, but he wrote with conviction and enthusiasm.

Reprinted from *Contemporary Psychology* (1957), 2(2), 33–35. Review of Egon Brunswik (1956), *Perception and the Representative Design of Psychological Experiments* (Berkeley: University of California Press).

Born in Budapest, for ten years instructor in the University of Vienna, Brunswik was, until his death shortly before the publication of this volume, a professor at the University of California in Berkeley, a philosopher of science, a scholar in the best European tradition, and at the same time a whole-hearted convert to the ways of American psychology. His death unhappily makes us consider this volume a summing up of his views. His intention was, however, that it should be only the beginning of many new lines of thought.

Brunswik recognized that the problem of how we perceive objects, or how animals respond adaptively to objects, is fundamental to most of the other problems of psychology. On the assumption that sensory stimuli cannot specify objects but only some of their properties, the stimuli must be considered as *cues*. Perception and behavior are necessarily indirect functions of objects, for cues have only a limited validity as indicators of them. Even the most elaborate combination or cluster of sensory stimuli cannot specify an object for an animal—it can only make the object's existence highly probable. We cannot avoid the problem of determining the 'cue-value' of stimuli, but experimental evidence seems to show that cues are substitutable for one another, that they are interlocking and non-isolable and very troublesome to work with in combination. Brunswik faced this evidence squarely and followed out its implications to the end. All who take the cue-concept for granted should do the same.

Any theory of perception must also be a theory of thing-constancy. Brunswik's pioneering work on this problem in visual perception led him to the puzzle of how responses are determined by the distal stimulus (the object) as well as by the proximal stimulus (the retinal image), and to the "dilemma of whether we 'see' the retina or the outside world". The facts of the constancy experiments point to a distal 'focusing' of perception, but since the proximal stimulus is necessarily untrustworthy, this achievement of the organism must he accounted for. There has to be correction, compensation, and stabilization. Perception is based on insufficient evidence but, suprisingly, it is generally correct. By rights, the animal should not have functional contact with the environment, and yet it does.

In his struggle with this dilemma, Brunswik never took refuge in subjectivism or the sterile theory of the private phenomenal world. He was too well aware that functional behavior demands veridical perception. Nor would he accept, the Gestalt theory of a brain process which would spontaneously produce the correct object in phenomenal experience. Instead he was driven to consider the difficult position of supposing that both the perceptual process and the environment itself are *probabilistic*, that is to say, imperfectly lawful. This is not a comfortable theory; Brunswik himself could not rest comfortably in the lap of uncertainty. Nevertheless he disciplined himself to make a virtue of what he considered a necessity.

The perceptual system of the human observer can achieve either of two aims, the distal or the proximal. For the explanation of why it tends to achieve the object, under instructions to take a "naive-realistic" attitude, Brunswik could make the following suggestions.

(1) The system accumulates cues to the object more or less as a lens accumulates light-rays from an object, and it brings them to a single 'focus.'

(2) The system behaves like an 'intuitive statistician': it computes the probabilities of things in a three-dimensional environment by weighting and combining the cluster of cues.

(3) The system is not wholly rational but quasi-rational: it incorporates checks and balances which sacrifice precision for the minimizing of gross error.

(4) The system is similar to homeostasis in that it achieves a stabilization of perceptions and a stereotyping of phenomenal objects.

These suggestions do not constitute a theory of perception by the usual standards of scientific theory, but Brunswik was in doubt whether such standards should be applied in psychology. Perhaps psychology must remain "geared to uncertainty," at least for the present. All Brunswik could be sure of about perception was two things. First, that configurations in the field of view indicate objects in the world with a limited degree of trustworthiness. The 'ecological validity' of such cues can only be determined experimentally. Second, that these configurations come to mediate object-perception only because they offer the organism an *opportunity* for probability learning; the percept is always a wager. Thus uncertainty enters at *two* levels, not merely one: the configuration may or may not indicate an object, and the cue may or may not be utilized at its true indicative value.

Brunswik was not a sensory physiologist. He did not consider for himself the nature of sensory processes nor the problem of placing the dividing line between sensing and perceiving. What the bare impressions are — the raw materials for probability learning — he never attempted to say. He accepted without criticisms the usual list of cues for the third dimension, referring as they do to the perception of a single object, and he conceived of the environment as a collection of single objects rather than as an array of adjoining surfaces. If the cues for depth, so conceived, are ill-defined or circularly defined, not cognate with one another, and non-isolable, he was willing to accept this state of affairs without impatience, and to proceed as he could.

The implications of this theoretical position for experimental method are far-reaching and even, as Brunswik understood, revolutionary. It means that a *representative* rather than a *systematic* design should he used in future experiments, and to this experimental policy he devoted a full half of his book. Believing as he did that theory and method are inseparable, he considered that he could here make a lasting contribution to psychology.

The classical way of finding the cause of an effect is to be systematic, to isolate and control single variables one at a time. But this procedure will not do in the study of perception or behavior, where cues are multiple and interactive. So, to clarify this matter, Brunswik classified all the thing-constancy experiments in which he ever had a hand, plus some others. This survey, in itself, is useful. His classification, however, is in terms of variation and covariation of dimensions. His aim is a "multidimensional psychophysics." He wanted to know how much the results of an experiment can be *generalized*. One experiment on perception, he argued, may be "ecologically normal," that is to say, representative of a whole crowd of natural instances, while another experiment may apply only at the fringe of reality (to bearded ladies, for example) and its outcome will be quite misleading for the world in general.

With this statement we might all agree but Brunswik's position went beyond. He asserted that *the experimenter has little or no basis for knowing in advance whether his experiment is representative or unrepresentative*. It might seem to him lifelike, yet prove to be not so. The experiment's only policy is to keep on experimenting so as to sample the world adequately. He must operate, if not in darkness, at least in theoretical twilight. To state the situation of psychology so bleakly takes courage.

The experimenter can improve his chances of success by using representative design in his experiment. To do so he must first sample the environment, or habitat, of the individual he is testing. Consider Brunswik's procedure for sampling the environment in a size-constancy experiment. The experimenter follows a subject about in the course of an ordinary day's activity and asks, every few minutes, what the subject is *looking at*. The replies are recorded (along with the estimates of size). The physical size of the object is later measured (along with its distance from the subject). The distribution of sizes is taken to be a representative sample (and this can be correlated with the distribution of estimates). Now does this procedure genuinely represent the

variable of size in the human habitat? A tendency for objects to be evenly *spaced* in the physical world would be missed by this sampling of the internal dimensions of single objects. The ordinary observer does not look at interspaces, although he sees them. Perhaps the regular spacing to be found in the structure of things is more important for perception than the variability in the sizes of things. The present reviewer is convinced that the environment is geometrically lawful, not the reverse. Yet, in any case, Brunswik was correct in arguing that a sort of ecology for perception is necessary if we are ever to understand the process.

In his position Brunswik was bound to be impressed by the logic and way of thought appropriate to the study of individual differences. He admired the Anglo-American development of statistical reasoning. He came to believe that statistical procedures were not just makeshift substitutes for experimental control but the essence of psychological research and the core of psychological theory. The shift of emphasis toward probabilism would be difficult, no doubt, but necessary — so he was convinced.

This is, indeed, a profound and disturbing book. Brunswik realized, unlike most behaviorists, that the objects an animal can respond *to* are just as important for his behavior as are the responses he can make. He realized, unlike most sensory psychologists, that novel psychophysical methods are necessary — ones not confined to the narrow problems of so-called sensations. And he realized more than his contemporaries that the problems of perception, as of behavior, cannot be solved by setting up situations in the laboratory which are convenient for the experimenter but atypical for the individual. He asks us, the experimenters in psychology, to revamp our fundamental thinking and to adopt a consistent functionalism in which the organism survives — when it does — by adapting its behavior to a world of merely probable objects. It is an onerous demand. Brunswik, imposed it first on his own thinking and showed us how burdensome it can be. His work is an object lesson in theoretical integrity.

C.

Final Thoughts

14

"Ratiomorphic" Models of Perception and Thinking [1955]

 COMMENT

"Perception" versus "Thinking": Brunswikian Thought on Central Responses and Processes
William M. Goldstein and John H. Wright

Although it may behoove Socrates and minds of his stamp to acquire virtue through reason, the human race would have perished long ago if its preservation had depended only on the reasonings of its members.

(Jean-Jacques Rousseau, 1755/1964, p. 133)

The constantly looming catastrophes of the intellect would be found more often to develop into catastrophes of action were it not for the mellowing effect of the darker, more feeling-like and thus more dramatically convincing primordial layers of cognitive adjustment.

(Egon Brunswik, 1956b, p. 93)

The items reprinted in this volume by Brunswik (1955b), Leeper (1955) and Murphy (1955), are abstracts of papers presented at a symposium on "The Relation of the Person to His Environment," held in Montreal at the 1954 meetings of the International Congress of Psychology.[1] In his contribution, Brunswik reported some of his theoretical and empirical work on central psychological responses and processes, emphasizing (1) that flexible and rule-like strategies of integrating information could be distinguished by the distributions of judgments; (2) that "perception" and "thinking" might be found to correspond with these two strategies of integration; and (3) that "perception" and "thinking" could both be conceived of as special cases of a larger category of

processes he described as "ratiomorphic." We will discuss this work in four sections. First, we will consider how Brunswik's research on central processes might appear to conflict with his general disapproval of an "encapsulated" psychology that focuses exclusively on internal processes. We will show that despite some appearances to the contrary, Brunswik's mature framework was not hostile to studies of internal process if they were conducted "properly." Second, we will explicate Brunswik's conceptual distinction between the processing strategies, the logic behind his empirical method for distinguishing between them, and his reason for proposing an overarching category of ratiomorphic processes. Third, we will briefly review Brunswik's empirical and theoretical work on the strategies underlying, and the interactions between, "perception" and "thinking." Fourth, we will relate Brunswik's work to research that he influenced directly as a progenitor and that he anticipated as a precursor.

Brunswik and Central Processes?

Brunswik had a vision of and for psychology that comprised the nature of the field, its definitive problems, and its appropriate methodology. Moreover, that vision provided guidance in prioritizing research problems. To understand Brunswik's work on central processes, then, one must see how the topic was situated in the context of Brunswik's larger program. Elaborating this context is the burden of our first section. The task isn't entirely straightforward, however, because Brunswik appeared to display some ambivalence toward research on central processes. Others have noticed and attempted to account for his apparently conflicting statements about central processes (Leary, 1987; Leeper, 1966).[2] We cannot definitively reconcile these ostensible inconsistencies. Nevertheless, we believe that Brunswik's varying statements about central processes can be understood as reflecting shifts of emphasis within a larger unifying framework. In this section, we will try to show that central processes always had a place in Brunswik's theoretical framework, even if his explicit clarification of their place came rather late.

Functionalism

Brunswik (1957) considered the main business of psychology to be the study of "the interrelationships between organism and environment" (p. 5). Fully unpacking this deceptively simple remark is beyond the scope of this paper, but a key aspect of it provides the unity underlying Brunswik's varying statements about central processes. Specifically, Brunswik subscribed to *functionalism*, in (at least) two senses. First, Brunswik considered some organism-environment interrelationships to be of special importance, namely, those by which organisms become attuned to and manage to get things done (i.e., to "function") in their environments. This sense of functionalism has Darwinian overtones along with connections to the functionalist movement of American psychology in the early twentieth century. Although in itself this first sense of *functionalism* doesn't imply anything about mental states or central processes of the organism, Brunswik also had intellectual roots extending to a second functionalist movement, namely, the nineteenth-century European functionalism (also called *act psychology*) of Franz Brentano. Act psychology embraced the study of consciousness in a way that American functionalism did not. However, it meshed well enough with American functionalism in its portrayal of mental processes as active and purposeful, and in its insistence that mental states have the quality of being "about" something (e.g., about the outside world). That is, mental states are "intentional," in a technical sense of the term;

they point to or "intend toward" something outside themselves.

European functionalism, especially the "intentionality" of mental states, is reflected in Brunswik's emphasis on organisms' *distal* focusing. The things that organisms need to care about are remote from them in time and space. Yet they have direct access only to proximal/peripheral matters, that is, to the energy that impinges on their sensory surfaces and to the contractions of their muscles. Somehow, organisms must "extend" beyond their surfaces, operating through the mediating layer of the proximal and peripheral (1) to bring their (central) perceptions into line with (distal) stimuli, and (2) to bring about (distal) states of affairs that coincide with their (central) desires. Whether, how well, and how organisms succeed in coordinating distal and central matters might be thought of as the vicissitudes of (one sort of) intentionality, and it is one of the hallmarks of the Brunswikian framework that primacy is accorded to studying these issues. In this sense, then, a concern for central responses and processes was always present in Brunswik's approach.

A Psychology in Terms of Objects

When Brunswik put the two functionalisms together, however, and combined them with logical positivist and molar behaviorist ideas about the requirements of objectivity in science, he arrived at an approach to psychology in which matters of central response and process were submerged. Clearly, not all aspects of the distal environment can be coordinated reliably with central states and thereby "attained" or "achieved," for appearances can be deceiving and one can't always fulfill one's desires. But those types of physical properties ("objects") that an individual *can* "attain" in perception or action "would be 'his world,' the '*Umwelt*' . . . for which he was able to establish fairly reliable cues and means, and which he thus mastered in cognition or in action (or in both at the same time)" (1937, p. 236, italics in original). A functional psychology, according to Brunswik, would undertake to specify this "attainable" world. The procedure would involve grouping together those environments that elicited the same reaction in an individual, and searching for the physical invariants among these environments. (For example, if a two-pound stimulus elicited the same reaction independent of the size of the stimulus, then it is weight and not density that is being "attained.") Brunswik (1937) wrote, "This way of experimenting upon and describing an individual's abilities *by projecting the reactions upon their focal conditions*, or upon the environmental end-terms of the (cognitive) couplings, we may call '*psychology in terms of objects*'" (p. 235, italics in original).

Note that psychology in terms of objects depends on the organism's reactions (e.g., reports of central states) only insofar as they are required to group together the environments that elicit the same reactions. The physical properties that remain invariant among these environments are of primary interest. This is how the central responses as well as the processes became submerged. As Brunswik (1937) wrote, "The '*what-problems*' of objects attained are put in the first row and the '*how-problems*' of mediation admitted only in so far in psychology as they throw light upon what-problems" (p. 239, italics in original). Thus, "psychology is a science in terms of '*what*' rather than of '*how*'" (p. 260). These quotations emphasize that, in Brunswik's view, mediating processes (matters of "how") are subordinate to the organism's functional adjustment to the external environment (matters of "what"). In other remarks concerning similar issues, Brunswik emphasized the benefits of studying distal-to-distal relationships, while bypassing the central responses. For example:

[By contrast with Tolman, I (i.e., Brunswik)] would tend, at least in principle, to discard for the moment intervening variables wherever they are not directly accessible. By representing an organism's or species' achievement system in terms of attained objects and results, such a psychology would in a sense be *without* the organism (i.e., would neglect all but a few focal details of organismic structure and intra-organismic processes), yet would be *about* the organism (i.e., its relationship to the environment, in both cognition and action). (1943, p. 271; italics in original; see also 1952, pp. 71–73.)

A Tripartite Approach to Psychology: Achievement, Strategy, and Tactics

Despite Brunswik's statements about psychology in terms of objects, we saw above that his approach had always included some degree of concern for central responses and processes, even when it lay beneath the surface. In a paper published posthumously, Brunswik (1957) discussed a tripartite approach to perception (with a corresponding analysis for overt action) that was couched explicitly in terms of central-distal relationships, and that explicitly found a role for studies of "mediation" processes:

The full scope of the cognitive problem, at least so far as external perception is concerned, would then seem to involve a theater stretching all the way from the distal to the central layers. Its prime aspect would seem to be the over-all correspondence between a certain distal and a certain central variable, so that the former could be considered successfully mapped into the latter. This first aspect we call cognitive "achievement" or "attainment," or also "functional validity" of the final response relative to the distal focus.

The second aspect of the cognitive problem concerns the gross characteristics or macrostructure of the pattern of proximal and peripheral mediation between the distal and central foci. This is the problem of the grand strategy of mediation. . . .

A third aspect of the cognitive problem is given by the attempt to break down the cognitive process further into its component parts. It concerns the special technology of the machinery along each of the several possible tracks of mediation. It may therefore be labeled the problem of micromediation, or of mediational tactics. The special ways in which [a particular kind of] appearance, if any, may be established neurologically furnish an example of such a problem. (pp. 8–9)

In our view, this description of Brunswik's approach best captures the spirit of the framework. It exemplifies American functionalism, in that it emphasizes the successful adjustment of the organism to its external environment. It shows its European functionalist heritage, in that it inquires into the quality and processes of intentionality (understood here as the central-distal correspondence). Finally, it elaborates just what it means to admit how-problems "only in so far . . . as they throw light upon what-problems" (1937, p. 239). Specifically, it shows that Brunswik wanted studies of process to be guided "from

above" by an understanding of functional relationships. Thus, the study of achievement (concerning "what" is achieved and how well) should
guide and constrain the study of grand strategy
(concerning the conceptual "how-problems" of
determining the particular proximal cues used,
their relative weights, their vicarious intersubstitutability for one another, etc.). The study of
grand strategy, in turn, should guide and constrain the study of micromediational tactical "machinery" (which we understand to include both
internal physiology and external physical transmission of cues to the sensory surfaces). With this
hierarchical arrangement of research problems,
even studies of detailed internal processes are
conducted with the aim of explaining the organism's adjustment to its environment and so avoiding a solipsistic "encapsulation."

Reasoning as a Universal Behavior Model

Brunswik's mature framework may have included
a role for studies of central processes, but that
does not necessarily grant them high priority.
When and why did Brunswik decide to study such
"how-problems"? Brunswik's interest in matters of
central process actually began quite early.[3] His
contrary remark about "psychology without the
organism" (1943) came in a paper given at a
symposium held in 1941 at the Sixth International Congress for the Unity of Science, during
the period when Brunswik was emphasizing his
psychology in terms of objects. This remark apparently was added as a reply to Hull, who had
discerned the subtle reliance on central processes
and commented that Brunswik "seems at certain
moments at least to introduce perception as a
variable intervening between the physical stimulation of his subjects and their verbal responses"
(Hull, 1943a, p. 280). Leary (1987) suggested
that Brunswik's interest in central processes might
have been rekindled by this interchange with
Hull. In any case, Brunswik subsequently reintro-
duced central responses and processes as an explicit part of his theoretical and empirical work.

As Leary (1987) also noted, however, the main
controversy at the 1941 symposium concerned
Brunswik's call for psychology to become thoroughly probabilistic. The basis for Brunswik's
probabilism was widely misunderstood, and the
misguided criticisms of his position "were to

plague Brunswik in his remaining years" (Leary,
1987, p. 126; see also Gigerenzer, 1987). Although we can only speculate about Brunswik's
motives, we suspect that his post-1941 work on
central processes may have been prompted as
much by the need to expand on his probabilistic
approach as by the need to be more explicit about
the role of central processes. A reason for this
impression is that Brunswik's (1966) Montreal
symposium paper included several moves aimed
at explaining and extending his claims that proximal cues are inherently ambiguous and leave the
organism uncertain about distal states. In particular, the paper makes it clear that these claims are
meant to apply not only to "perception," narrowly
construed, but to "thinking" as well, in sum, to *all*
occasions when organisms make use of proximal
cues to derive conclusions about the distal environment.

Grand Strategies of Mediation

Rather than starting his analysis with a distinction
between "perception" and "thinking," Brunswik
began by discussing strategies for using proximal
cues. Specifically, he began with a tough case
that his critics were likely to consider a counterex-
ample to organisms' uncertainty: the case of a
physicist making a measurement or prediction via
physical law (e.g., range finding by triangulation).
Theoretically, the prediction can achieve perfect
accuracy, by integrating the proximal cues according to inflexibly patterned rules that "duplicate the environmental laws" (1966, p. 488).
Brunswik described such "machine-like interaction in a single-track net within the responding
system" as implementing a "'certainty-geared' interaction or strategy" (1966, p. 488). This strategy
involves the strict, rule-based manipulation of a
"relatively small number of basic cues" (1956b,
p. 92, italics deleted) and is exemplified by "syllo-
gistic reasoning" or "mathematical calculation"
(1966, p. 487).

Even the certainty-geared strategy, however,
cannot ordinarily guarantee perfect accuracy, because physical laws have preconditions. For example, the range-finding physicist has the advantage (or, more precisely, needs the advantage) of
"'control' of relevant environmental conditions"
(1955b, p. 256, this volume), for otherwise "the
absence or presence of optical inhomogeneities"
(1966, p. 487) can only be assumed at some risk.

Moreover, the implementation of the strategy can go awry, and doing so in a particular manner is the signature of this strategy: "The entire pattern of the reasoning solutions . . . resembles the switching of trains at a multiple junction, with each of the possible courses being well organized and of machine-like precision yet leading to drastically different destinations only one of which is acceptable in the light of the cognitive goal" (1956b, pp. 91–92). Thus, the certainty-geared strategy is potentially very accurate and consistent but tends to be fragile. It reveals itself by producing both "high precision and . . . erratic mistakes" (1966, p. 489), accurate estimates as well as absurdly inaccurate estimates—in sum, a very irregular discrete distribution of errors with a relatively large variance.

By contrast with the certainty-geared strategy, Brunswik also discussed a "probability-geared" or "uncertainty-geared" strategy that uses "multiple systems of mutually substitutable, or 'vicarious,' cues" (1966, p. 488) in a "check-and-balance system of . . . multiple-track mediation" (1966, p. 489). That is, rather than aspiring to the potential perfection of the certainty-geared strategy, the probability-geared strategy seeks to integrate "a whole family of cues of more or less limited trustworthiness" (1966, p. 488) after the fashion of a statistical prediction. The consistency and accuracy of the resulting judgments depend on the number, redundancy, and ecological validity of the integrated cues. Typically integrating a relatively large number of modest cues, the probability-geared strategy tends to be approximately accurate, fairly inconsistent, but also robust. Thus, it again reveals itself in its error distribution. It should produce few perfectly accurate estimates, many approximately accurate estimates, and thus a nearly continuous distribution of errors with a relatively small variance.

Ratiomorphism

However the certainty-geared and probability-geared strategies might align with thinking and perception, Brunswik saw advantages in recognizing both as falling "under the model of reasoning-type inferences" (1966, p. 490) for which he coined the overarching term of "ratiomorphism" (1966, p. 491). For "[o]nly by at least implicit recognition of this underlying commonality [between the strategies] are we enabled to proceed

to differentiation between relatively autonomous cognitive subsystems at the more molar level of strategy and of achievement" (1966, p. 491). That is, Brunswik opposed prejudging or defining or introspecting about the properties of "thinking" and "perception," as others had done.[4] Rather, as always, Brunswik advocated that researchers concentrate on the functional adjustment of the organism to its environment, and recognize that "[p]erception and thinking both serve the same task of the organism: to know its environment" (Brunswik, 1934b, translated in Hammond, 1966b, p. 530). By grouping together these "different forms of imperfect inferences regarding the environment" (1955b, p. 256, this volume), researchers could *investigate* "thinking" and "perception," by examining how environmental and task factors affected the error distributions that are the signatures of the "grand strategies" in use.

A Functional Differentiation between "Perception" and "Thinking"

A Demonstration Experiment

In his 1954 Montreal symposium paper, Brunswik illustrated such investigations and offered his thoughts about the alignment of certainty- and probability-geared strategies with "thinking" and "perception." As a demonstration, Brunswik summarized the error distributions obtained from two versions of a size estimation task: (1) a perceptual version, in which a display of the stimuli left "the normal array of distance cues . . . intact" (1956b, p. 91), and (2) a "thinking" version, in which "the question was made part of a[n] . . . examination, giving such numerical indications about the situation that the correct answer could be univocally ascertained" (1956b, p. 91). As expected, Brunswik found that the errors in the perceptual condition were regular, while the errors in the thinking condition were quite irregular.[5]

"Perception" and "Thinking"

Brunswik acknowledged that the tasks he employed in his demonstration were "rather obvious and certainly not representative of 'perception' versus 'thinking' at large" (1966, p. 489). Still, as a methodological illustration, the experiment helped to make "a beginning . . . toward an objective explication of the age old yet hitherto rather introspectionistic or speculative, and thus precarious distinction between these major sub-systems of cognition" (1966, p. 489). Brunswik then voiced his hypotheses regarding the processes underlying "perception" and "thinking." Specifically, "[w]hile we may . . . find perception fairly uniformly exhibiting the probability-geared strategy, 'thinking' in the customary sense of the term is without doubt much less homogeneous . . . [even though] there undoubtedly is a certain core province of thought or of the 'intellect' which is single-track in the manner of [the certainty-geared strategy]" (1966, p. 490).

Brunswik also acknowledged that the strategies could interact in complex ways, so that "the lines between thinking and the perception become vague and entangled" (1934b, translated in Hammond, 1966b, p. 530). Specifically, thinking can monitor perception and override it. For example, "thinking by means of reasoning and general knowledge may notice that the distance was underestimated, and it can correct the impression of the apparent size in the direction of a better intentional attainment of the intended object" (1934b, translated in Hammond, 1966, p. 528).

Brunswik as Progenitor and as Precursor

Judgment and decision researchers who have pursued Brunswik's distinction between certainty-geared and probability-geared strategies have tended to characterize the strategies as "analysis" and "intuition," respectively, and have undertaken to study the task conditions that elicit them, rather than asking how the strategies line up with "thinking" and "perception" as such.[6] Probably the best known project to extend the theoretical and empirical work of Brunswik in this direction is the Cognitive Continuum Theory (CCT) of Hammond and his colleagues (Hammond, Hamm, Grassia, & Pearson, 1987; see also Abernathy & Hamm, 1995; Hamm, 1988; Hammond, 1996c). CCT goes beyond Brunswik's consideration of interactions between strategies, rejecting any sharp dichotomy between analysis and intuition. Instead, it asserts that intuition and analysis constitute extreme modes of thought, and that a continuum of "quasi-rational" processes occupies the middle ground between them. Both surface and deep characteristics of the task environment are

hypothesized to influence the mode of processing that will be elicited, with repercussions for achievement. Interestingly, CCT shares Brunswik's doubts about the (often-presumed) superiority of analysis over intuition. Depending on the task conditions, CCT does not necessarily predict that analysis will optimize performance.

Other research has also supported and extended Brunswik's work. Ahl, Moore, and Dixon (1992), for example, asked subjects to predict the temperature of a container of liquid that results from mixing two containers of liquid of two different temperatures. They found that when subjects estimated the final temperature intuitively (i.e., perceptually), the errors of the estimates were distributed regularly about the correct answer. They also found that when the same subjects estimated the final temperature analytically (i.e., mathematically), the errors of the estimates were distributed quite irregularly, as predicted by Brunswik. Interestingly, Ahl et al. (1992) found a result that Brunswik did not predict: The error distribution for the analytic task depended on the order of the tasks. Specifically, performing the analytic task second made its distribution of errors narrower and more regular, which suggests that performing the intuitive task first helped subjects choose the right analytic strategy in their second task. This result suggests that thinking and perception may interact in a way that Brunswik did not anticipate.

Beyond the research that was influenced directly by Brunswik, his work on central processes can be regarded as anticipating subsequent conceptual and methodological developments. Conceptually, Brunswik refused to take "perception" and "thinking" at face value and insisted on analyzing them in terms of underlying processes of proximal cue integration (i.e., the probability-geared and certainty-geared strategies). Placing both strategies in the larger category of ratiomorphic processes, Brunswik argued that instead of trying to investigate "perception" and "thinking" as such, researchers should study perceptual and intellectual *tasks* in terms of the cognitive strategies they elicit. Brunswik's general interest in the adaptability of cognitive strategies to task conditions anticipated one of the dominant topics of research on judgment and decision making in the last several decades.

Methodologically, Brunswik recognized that the strategies underlying perception and thinking need not be studied by introspection, for some of their key properties are revealed by the patterns of errors. Moreover, Brunswik's use of error distributions to detect different cognitive strategies anticipated a similar analysis of patterns of inconsistency (albeit not "error" in the sense of inaccuracy) by later judgment and decision researchers. For example, Coombs (1958) and Tversky (1969) each used systematic violations of stochastic transitivity to test hypotheses about the cognitive processes underlying preferential choice.

Finally, Brunswik's characterization of the certainty-geared and probability-geared strategies as, respectively, rigidly rule-based and flexibly intuitive ways of integrating information, anticipated psychology's current interest in the nature of intuitive and analytic modes of thought by some thirty-five years. We have already mentioned Brunswik's influence on Hammond and his colleagues (Hammond et al., 1987) and on Ahl et al. (1992). In addition, Brunswik's distinction between rule-based and intuitive processes anticipated Langer's (1989) distinction between mindfulness and mindlessness, Epstein's (1994) distinction between cognitive and experiential systems, Reyna and Brainerd's (e.g., 1995) fuzzy-to-verbatim continuum, and Sloman's (1996) division of cognition into associative and rule-based systems, among others.

Conclusion

Brunswik's research on central processes needs to be put into the context of his larger body of work in order to be understood fully. The effort to do so is amply repaid with theoretical and methodological insights that shed light not only on Brunswik's thought, but also on current trends in psychological research.

NOTES

In the text of this comment, any citation that doesn't explicitly name the author is a reference work by Brunswik.

1. Gardner Murphy's paper was subsequently published in 1956 in the *British Journal of Psychology*. Brunswik's paper was made available by Robert Leeper for publication in Kenneth Hammond's edited volume on *The Psychology of Egon Brunswik* (1966b), where it appeared under the title "Reasoning as a Universal Behavior Model and a Functional Differentiation be-

tween 'Perception' and 'Thinking.'" An expanded version of Leeper's own paper was also published in Hammond's book (1966b). Some of Brunswik's further thoughts on central processes can be found in his 1956 book, *Perception and the Representative Design of Psychological Experiments* (see pp. 89–99).

2. Leeper (1966) suggested (1) that Brunswik's pronouncements sometimes may have exaggerated his true position as he attempted to redress an imbalance in the field, and (2) that Brunswik's own work on central processes was fully in keeping with the spirit of his larger theoretical framework. Specifically, Brunswik's own work was undertaken with methods that avoided the pitfalls of "encapsulation" and a narrow focus on "mere mediation." Leary (1987) emphasized the evolution of Brunswik's ideas over time and suggested that Brunswik may have reconsidered his position on central processes some time after a symposium held in 1941 (and published in *Psychological Review* in 1943).

3. Brunswik had conceived of the methodology for distinguishing between perception and thinking as early as 1937. In a footnote, Brunswik had written, "Not only the actual attainment but even the types of intentional effort or 'attitude' toward attaining certain 'intended' objects may be disclosed by objective methods (in fact, by analyzing the statistical distribution of judgments with regard to the number of modes)" (Brunswik, 1937, p. 241). Moreover, Brunswik discussed the distinction between perception and thinking (and hinted at the methodology for differentiating between them) as early as 1934. (See Hammond, 1966b, pp. 528–531, for an English translation of the relevant passage.)

4. For example, others have drawn the distinction between thinking and perception: (1) along epistemological lines (favoring perception or thought as the surer route to justified knowledge, according to one's empiricist or rationalist leanings); (2) along ontological lines (perception being of concrete things that exist externally while thought may be of abstract or nonexistent or even self-contradictory things); or (3) according to various qualities of subjective experience (perception being more "vivid" than thought, perceptual processes being unconscious and thought processes being occasionally or partially conscious, perceptual results manifesting themselves in nonverbal modes while thought processes manifest themselves primarily in verbal modes).

5. Brunswik had reported this experiment earlier, at the 1948 meetings of the Western Psychological Association (see 1948, for the abstract). Additional details, and the results of additional conditions that are not so straightforward (e.g., manipulations of "attitude"), can be found in Brunswik's book (1956b, pp. 89–99).

6. However, for continuing interest in the distinction between perception and cognitive processes, see, for example, Fodor (1983).

7. Coombs (1958) used certain patterns of violations to determine whether choice alternatives were compared to each other directly, or compared to each other in terms of their proximity to an ideal point. Tversky (1969) showed that violations of weak stochastic transitivity can be used to distinguish choices based on a holistic evaluation strategy from choices based on a dimensional evaluation strategy.

 REPRINT

"Ratiomorphic" Models of Perception and Thinking
Egon Brunswik

Bodies of information may be treated enumeratively, as in geography, or nomothetically, as in physics. Pending added geographic "control" of relevant environmental conditions, physical laws allow dependable prediction from a single cue for each constituent variable ("certainty-geared interaction").

Sampling of geographies from a circumscribed but otherwise uncontrolled natural-cultural habitat or "ecology" as the reference universe, acts as a vague substitute for direct control of the medium allowing "blind" probability learning of stereotyped regularities of limited statistical validity. Predictability in ecological textures may be improved by multiple systems of mutually substitutable, or "vicarious", cues, with resultant cue-rivalries and compromises ("probability-geared interaction").

The varieties of the utilization and/or distortion of these information potentials by a responding organism are best approached objectively by means of functional behaviorism rather than introspectively. By recognizing "perception" as predominantly probability-geared and "thinking" as predominantly certainty-geared, these presumed major sub-systems of the cognitive apparatus may be operationally redefined. A cognitive task approached once by typical intuitive perception and once by typical explicit ratiocination is used as a concrete illustration, and the persons' strategy is projected upon their achievement in establishing correct environmental relationships ("psychology in terms of objects"). For perception, multiple-track check-and-balance mediation is revealed by a relative paucity of on-the-dot precise responses counterbalanced by a relatively organic and compact distribution of errors free of gross absurdity. For ratiocination, single-track strategy proves highly vulnerable in practice; inadvertent task-substitutions and other derailment-type errors often reaching bizarre proportions belie the relatively large number of absolutely precise responses.

Perception and thinking thus emerge as different forms of imperfect inferences regarding the environment, subsumable to a common behavior model patterned upon reasoning ("ratiomorphic" reduction, if this Latin-Greek hybrid be permitted). Turning to cybernetics for further explanation, "thinking" resembles the standard use of calculating machines whereby the representational control of the input is tacitly entrusted to the extraneous human operator and single-track nets appear sufficient for the remaining, chiefly deductive leg of the construction process, with switching errors inside the machine as the major source of failure. Intuitive perception resembles inductive cybernetic "predictors", or, still better, telecommunication under partial ignorance of the extrasystemic medium for which "redundancy"—which is essentially vicarious mediation—is the only countermeasure.

Reprinted from *Acta Psychologica* (1955), 11, 108–109, with permission from Elsevier Science.

The rising importance of ratiomorphic models in the literature on mathematical biophysics, on the theory of emotion and motivation, and on clinical intuition is pointed out. At least for perception, gestalt psychology is interpreted as concentrating on, achievementally relatively neutral or even negative dynamisms ("pregnance"; illusions) which in spite of their potency within the intrasystemic field are but side-aspects of uncertainty-geared interaction, and as oblivious of the "associationistic" requirements imposed upon perception by the probabilistic character of its environment—extrapolative functions; furthermore, it may well be ratiocination rather than perception that produces the most erratic forms of sudden change or reversal. A somewhat indirect point of agreement with gestalt psychology is the vindication of the more primordial cognitive functions against the rationalist's overevaluation of the intellect.

 REPRINT

Complex Intermediate Processes between Situation and Response: Their Methodological Implications

Robert Leeper

In the same way that psychology has profited by developing technical concepts about experimental design, perhaps psychology likewise may profit from a more careful development of its "methodology of conceptualizing or explaining".

One means of understanding more clearly how this problem has been approached by different psychologists is to relate our discussion to the experiment which Brunswik's paper describes on perception vs. thinking.

In his own earlier papers, Brunswik has urged a methodology analogous to the perceptual approach in his experiment. He urged that we develop psychological laws in terms of correlations between representative sets of stimulus-situations and related behavior-products. He urged that we avoid studies trying to discover how situations produced results.

Except that the matter of representativeness often has been neglected, this approach actually has been used much more widely than Brunswik seemingly has realized. Innumerable studies of individual differences, industrial psychology, education, and sociology have been of this sort.

Reprinted from *Acta Psychologica* (1955), 11, 110–111, with permission from Elsevier Science.

Such studies usually have revealed low correlations between such distal factors, but possess some value anyway. For example, it is worthwhile to an insurance company to know that college professors have fewer automobile accidents than lawyers or ministers or vaudeville performers. However, the important task for psychology is not just the discovery of such rough means of prediction. More truly it is the development of those principles and means of measurement which will permit maximally precise predictions of the behavior and experience (a) of one individual as contrasted with another, and (b) of the same individual under different circumstances.

To achieve such precision, we must follow a method analogous to the "thinking" approach in Brunswik's experiment. To do this, if we are to use a broad range of experimental data, we must state relationships via factors and processes within the organism. As Brunswik's own experiment indicates, low distal-distal correlations occur because most of the determinants which will permit predictions lie *within* the organism in any given situation, rather than in the immediate objective situation.

This method of explaining by means of inferred factors has been used by Hull's group as well as by Gestaltists and others. Hullian thought, however, has not taken sufficiently into account the enormous complexity of these internal processes, their dynamic-organizational character, nor their frequent step-wise changes which result from the gradual, cumulative effects in some other parts of such complex systems. Evidence for these points comes from a number of as-yet unpublished studies on the "non-continuity phenomenon" in learning, and from published studies, on the "non-continuity phenomenon" in learning, and from published experiments by Saldanha and Bitterman, Witkin, Köhler, and others.

We constantly have the risk, when we try to use this "thinking" type of methodology, that we will overlook some crucial factors, base our principles on too miniature an area of research, or somehow over-rate the amount of real "explain-ing" that we have done. Thus, somewhat as Brunswik claims, probably Gestalt psychology has not made a sufficient attempt to explain the fidelity or veridicality of cognitive processes. On the other hand, it is not adequate to "explain" veridicality merely as Brunswik tends to do—by citing evidence that considerable fidelity exists. The things that account for fidelity must be understood, probably, in terms of a field theory developed, not only in a sense clearly defended by Murphy, but also in two related senses seen in Lewin and in Köhler and Tolman.

The type of approach earlier advocated by Brunswik cannot be a substitute for such more complex thinking. But, it should be a part of our method—as in his experiment—as a means of guarding against "brilliant absurd errors".

 REPRINT

The Boundaries between the Individual and His World

Gardner Murphy

The boundaries between person and world may be viewed in terms of physical, biological, psychological, and social science. All four suggest that boundaries call for clarification.

From Democritus to Schrödinger the physical view suggests that what is inside man is essentially like what is outside; he is a bit of the cosmos, duplicating it in substance, frequently also in structure. Cosmic environment permits momentary isolation of small portions of itself. L. L. Henderson has shown that in vital processes like respiration it is meaning less to define where the boundary lies.

Biological research nevertheless suggests that within an "open system", effective principles (e.g., homeostasis) may differ from those generally obtaining outside. We may avoid dualism of substance, yet provide dualism of function (C. D. Broad). Life exists precisely because within a protected area unique processes go on. It seems important to ascertain how far Henderson's conception of the *gentle gradient* holds good, how far the *sharp gradient* of homeostatic isolation prevails. Some philosophers (T. H. Huxley, B. Russell) assume paradoxically that while man is made of cosmic stuff, his values are irreconcilable with cosmic processes.

From the viewpoint of psychology, the gradient is ordinarily steep. Thus in cognition the person is conceived to apprehend what is fully external to himself. Yet psychology offers three other approaches. The Gestalt conception of inner structure reveals a parallel with the sharp gradient of homeostasis. Isomorphism represents inner structure as mirroring outer structure, not because man is (as with Hecht) at the mercy of the environment, but because his own dynamic is attuned to it.

Reprinted from *Acta Psychologica* (1955), 11, 111–113, with permission from Elsevier Science.

The second conception presupposes formal independence of the environment, combined with absolute dependence through give-and-take, the tennis game of acts and signals, the world of cybernetics, of Brunswik's navigation through a sea of uncertainties, Leeper's complex contacts with heterogeneous reality, Sears' dyadic functions—a world whose reality is *reciprocity*, not the events-within-the-person which our self-reliant grandparents knew.

The third conception goes even further. In the life-space of Lewin there is no fixed division of inner and outer, and in some types of field theory a unified world of person and environment yields a gradient as gentle as that of Henderson, with implications which encounter resistance proportional perhaps to our culturally ingrained conviction that there *must* be something utterly our own.

If we view this problem not "from outside", but from the standpoint of the experiencing person, some fragmentary evidence suggests several *different kinds* of gradients between self and non-self: evidence regarding the child's slow development of awareness of self and of others; evidence from psychiatry and anthropology regarding forms of experience ranging from sharply defined, pathologically distinct awareness of self to the opposite pole of depersonalization in which selfhood is lost. The psychology of India has explored such experiences, both empirically and conceptually.

No psychology aspiring to completeness can ignore them.

Another challenge is offered by experiments in parapsychology, in which distant randomized material has now been shown in a dozen laboratories to be accessible to cognition, in confirmation of hypotheses regarding variables likely to soften psychological barriers between perceiver and object. In S. G. Soal's work, for example, the minds of three persons interact in a unitary field.

Finally, social science emphasizes interdependence, "membership character" of person in group, making it sometimes operationally impossible to chop apart interpersonal totalities.

Perhaps we might conclude that some aspects of persons are relatively sharply bounded, others the reverse. Paradoxically we give heroic stature both to the supreme Whitman-like "individualist" and to him, like Gandhi, who is selfless in devotion to a social goal. In an era in which humanity can hardly expect to survive without fuller knowledge of the biosocial value of individualistic and social impulses, research is needed into the sources both of man's need to isolate himself and of his need to soften his individuality in the presences of his fellow men and of the sea and the stars; we need to understand how his culturally molded selfhood sometimes leads him to make the gradient much *less* steep, sometimes much *steeper*, than it is.

15

Perception and the Representative Design of Psychological Experiments [1956]

 **EDITORS' NOTE**

We have included the following excerpt from Brunswik's 1956 book because it shows us how he expanded his conceptual framework from perception to thinking. These are remarkable pages, for they include remarkable thoughts in remarkable language. By linking and distinguishing thinking and perception theoretically, he showed how he could accommodate both the analytical and the intuitive functions of cognition within a single framework. Moreover, he showed their relationship through the brilliant innovation of describing the different types of error produced by each cognitive function. Perception, he would argue, produces a normal distribution of errors, whereas analysis produces exactly correct answers together with widely dispersed errors (see Figure 15.1). In these pages, he further developed his ideas about compromise in intuitive functions and the "dangers in explicit logical operations," a thought that had occurred to few other psychologists, all too enamored of rationality. And finally, in beautiful prose so typical of Brunswik's writing, he uttered a revolutionary remark: "The balance sheet of perception versus thinking may thus seem seriously upset against thinking, unquestioned favorite of a culture of rational enlightenment as the latter has been." All this is iconclastic material that, although largely ignored by the psychologists of the twentieth century, should challenge and inspire the psychologists of the twenty-first century to advance our thinking about cognition.

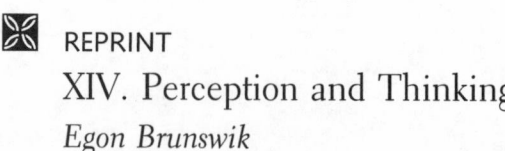 **REPRINT**

XIV. Perception and Thinking
Egon Brunswik

In this chapter we take temporary leave of questions of representative design and of its various

Reprinted from pages 89–93 of E. Brunswik (1956), *Perception and the Representative Design of Psychological Experiments* (Berkeley: University of California Press), by permission of University of California Press.

approximations in order to follow up some of the implications of our developmental scheme with respect to the general problem of the interrelationships between perception and the intellect proper. In this context we will also turn to the classification of perceptual attitudes and their relation to the so-called stimulus error.

1. Compromise vs. Pointed Distribution of Response

Perfect attainment of the distal pole in figure 31 is possible only if the laws of physics are being applied to all the situations in question. The particular law involved in the case of size constancy has been stated at the center of the left-hand side of figure 10 (p. 51). It is easily seen that it can be applied only if a series of relevant conditions in the external medium is known. Only then can the confirming cases of a cue be sifted from the infirming cases, and a single cue — say, for distance — will suffice where perception needs many. A foolproof ascertainment of distal variables thus requires not only knowledge of the law but also manipulation and locomotion; there is no time for such instrumentality in "instantaneous" perception, let alone the availability of the law. Only the measuring and computing physicist can be reasonably "certainty-geared;" intuitive perception must remain "uncertainty-geared." Since perception is not equipped with the necessary added information, its performance must depend on relatively superficial and stereotyped cues of limited ecological validity, preferably a multitude of them; attainment can never be ideal under such circumstances. Even if on the average attainment of the pole should be perfect, considerable variability would remain as a result of the intrinsically limited validity of perceptual cues for distance or bodily size.

The distinction between certainty-geared and uncertainty-geared functioning is one by definition. But its concrete use in distinguishing between thinking and perception should be illustrated at least by example. We have therefore constructed a task in size constancy in two corresponding versions, one involving a typical case of perception and the other a typical ease of arithmetic reasoning (for brief reports see Brunswik, 1948, 1954). In both cases 8 cm was the distally correct response (B) and 16 cm was the objective proximal equivalent (P). In the perceptual version a stimulus situation was actually presented in the laboratory, with the normal array of distance cues left intact. In the intellectual or "thinking" version the question was made part of a subsequent examination, giving such numerical indications about the situation that the correct answer could be univocally ascertained. Partially overlapping groups of undergraduates (n = 28

and 27, respectively) served as subjects. All had been previously given an explanation of the problem and had been informed of the major trend of results of experiments in perceptual size constancy.

Results of the perceptual version of the task (fig. 15.1, top) show the usual trend toward "approximate size constancy" (B-pole) tainted with the characteristic slight compromise tendency toward the opposite type of task, photographic correctness (P-pole). All responses (PSE's) fall in a compact and fairly normal frequency distribution, with the geometric mean at 8.95 cm. This corresponds to a logarithmic constancy ratio of .84. It is to be especially noted that, as is usually the case under ordinary conditions of a thing-constancy experiment, there is no particularly outstanding frequency of precisely correct answers.

For the reasoning approach (fig. 15.1, bottom), on the other hand, almost half of all the answers (13 out of 27) coincide with B and thus are on-the-dot correct. A second discrete bar — of more moderate height, to be sure — represents on-the-dot correctness relative to a second major potential task, one not actually asked of the subjects; this is the finding of the retinal equivalent (P). It demonstrates one of the typical pitfalls of reasoning, namely, the going off in the wrong direction by being right about something else.

It may thus be said that while, in our case at least, perception lingers in the twilight zone of compromise, thinking shows some of the pointedness alluded to at the right end of figure 31. The intellectual approach, using measurement and calculation, thus appears to fulfill the ultimate ends of perception in a way perception itself is incapable of doing. In humans the two levels of cognition coexist, mostly in peace, sometimes in conflict. As we have mentioned on page 22, Werner has spoken of perception and thinking as "analogous functions" serving the same cognitive purpose at different developmental levels. The regression in the perceptual constancy curve after adolescence which we have discussed in the preceding chapter may be accounted for by the fact that in adults the needs for supreme accuracy are best taken care of by measurement and calculation, and that a modest drop in intuitive perception may thus be well afforded.

All this does not mean, as we have seen, that thinking is without error. The second bar, at (P),

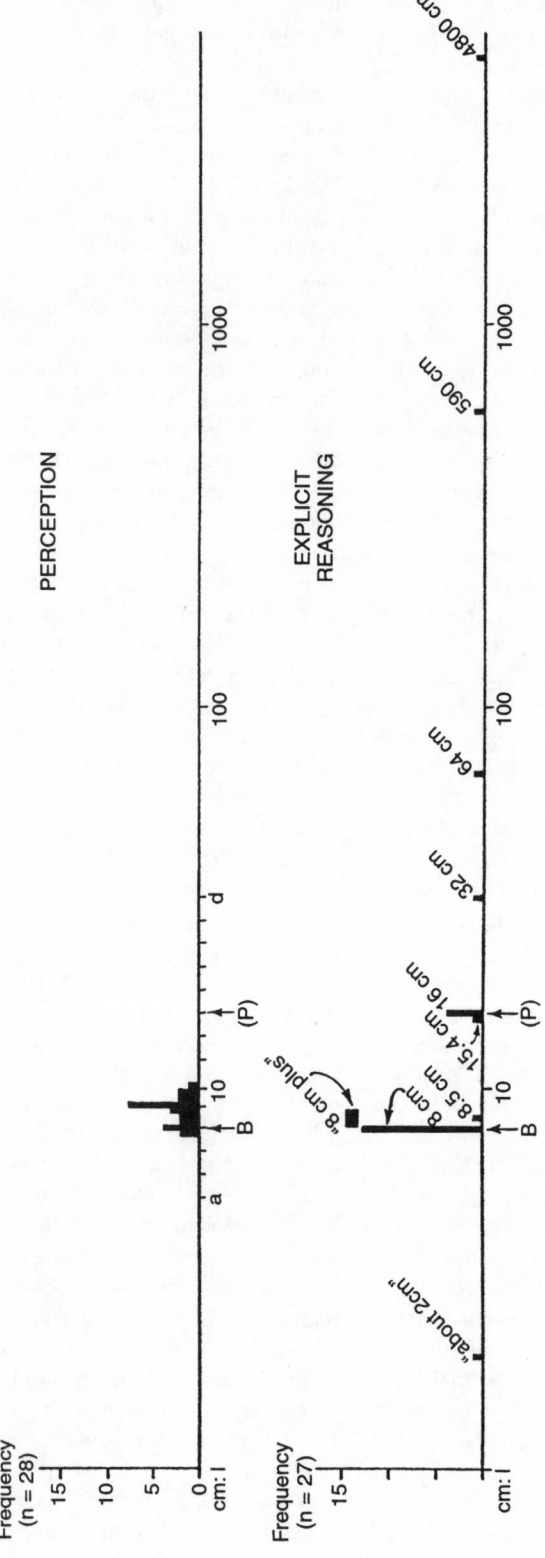

FIGURE 15.1 Distribution of accuracy and error in perception vs. thinking. (From data by Brunswik, 1948.)

represents error in terms of the task actually asked for. In fact, for all the answers given in the reasoning version of the task, the mean PSE (logarithmic) is 14.7 cm, which corresponds to a c-ratio of only .12; and the S.D. is more than ten times that obtained for the perceptual version.

The entire pattern of the reasoning solutions in figure 32 resembles the switching of trains at a multiple junction, with each of the possible courses being well organized and of machine-like precision yet leading to drastically different destinations only one of which is acceptable in the light of the cognitive goal. This pattern is illustrative of the dangers inherent in explicit logical operations. The relative ease of switching off at any one of a series of choice points in a basically linear, unidimensional, all-or-none series of relays is at least in part the result of the precise formulation, yet *relatively* small number of basic cues, involved in most typical reasoning tasks. The combination of channeled mediation, on the one hand, with precision or else grotesquely scattered error in the results, on the other, may well be symptomatic of what appears to be the pure case of explicit intellectual fact-finding.

On the other hand, as we have seen, intuitive perception must simultaneously integrate many different avenues of approach, or cues, Whereas distance is directly stated in the reasoning version, its perceptual "registering" must remain based on insufficient evidence, that is, on criteria none of which is foolproof or fully "ecologically valid." This of course makes for the task not being exactly the "same" in the two versions, but merely "analogous." It is the insufficiency of single cues which must be seen as responsible for the establishment in perception of "cue-family-hierarchies" (the phrase coined in analogy to Hull's "habit-family-hierarchy," see Brunswik, 1952, p. 19). For depth, such a series of cues is shown in figure 10. All of them must be seen as contributing to the result, often in competition with each other.

A further feature, often noted by introspectionists in search of a distinction between intuitive perception and thinking, is the flash-like speed of perceptual responses. It is a biologically very valuable feature, especially where life is constantly threatened by sudden danger or where chances of success depend on quick action. The almost instantaneous promptness of perception could hardly be achieved without the stereotypy and superficiality in the utilization of cues which

we have noted and which makes for a certain intrinsic "stupidity" of the perceptual apparatus (see Brunswik, 1934, pp. 119 f., 128, 223 ff.).

The various rivalries and compromises that characterize these dynamics of check and balance in perception must be seen as chiefly responsible for the above noted relative infrequency of precision. On the other hand, the organic multiplicity of factors entering the process constitutes an effective safeguard against drastic error. Even with extensive statistical sampling of size-distance combinations under life-like conditions as we have undertaken it in § VII/3, the over- or under-estimation as to bodily size was no more than three- or fourfold in the most extreme cases (see above, p. 47) and thus is ordinarily within the limits of ½ power of 10 when translated into the logarithmic terms of our figure; this contrasts with an order of magnitude of three powers of 10 for our extreme example of a reasoning error. Ordinary perceptual illusions are known seldom to exceed average values of forty per cent, and drastic fooling of perception is rare except under highly artificial conditions. As we must hold against recent criticism by Ittelson (1951), the "stupidity" of perception thus is by no means to be construed to mean maladaptiveness; as we all know, life has survived on relative stupidity from time immemorial, and if threatened in its existence it is so by malfunctioning of the intellect rather than by malfunctioning of perception.

Considering all the pros and cons of achievement, the balance sheet of perception versus thinking may thus seem seriously upset against thinking, unquestioned favorite of a culture of rational enlightenment as the latter has been. From the point of view of strategy, perception would likewise appear to have gained in stature by our realization of its inherent "vicarious functioning." So long as we accept, with Hunter (1928) and Tolman (1932), vicariousness as the foremost objective criterion of behavioral purposiveness, perception must appear as the more truly behavior-like function when compared with deductive reasoning with its machine-like, precariously one-tracked, tight-rope modes of procedure. The constantly looming catastrophes of the intellect would be found more often to develop into catastrophes of action were it not for the mellowing effect of the darker, more feeling-like and thus more dramatically convincing primordial layers of cognitive adjustment.

Ending on a note of caution, we should like to stress that the representativeness of our two versions of a common cognitive task is open to some doubt. Many specific conditions could be listed under which it is perception which is bizarre while it is thinking which is mellow and given to compromise. Aside from deductive considerations, only representative design could definitely prove us right or wrong in our conjecture that the juxtaposition which we have presented is more typical than its reverse.

As mostly in this book, however, our major aim is not content but the demonstration of methodological possibilities. In the present case this is the possibility of raising the distinction between psychological functions from the traditional introspectionistic to a more objective level by the use of a comparative statistical analysis of the strategy and of the achievement of cognitive functions in terms of error distribution.

16

Ontogenetic and Other Developmental Parallels to the History of Science [1959]

 COMMENT

Finding a Place in History: Some Reflections on a Talk Given by Egon Brunswik

Alexander J. Wearing

Was Egon Brunswik a genius? Even if he was, was he one who spoke to both his time and ours? That question concerned him, and it might also concern the historian of psychology who asks why some people and ideas prosper and inspire and others do not.[1] His contemporaries and students testify to the power and reach of Brunswik's mind, but when we leaf through the many books in the psychological canon,[2] it is uncommon to find a reference to him. In the typical author index, "Bruner, J.", is almost always followed by some one other than "Brunswik, E." Perhaps that is because he had his fifteen minutes of fame and is now of historical interest only?[3] His work may not even be of historical interest. Texts on the history of psychology also pass him by (see, e.g., Brennan, 1986; Hergenhahn, 1992; Hillner, 1984; Hunt, 1993; Leahey, 1987).

Yet it was to Brunswik that Bruner dedicated his premier book, a work that may be said to have inaugurated cognitive science. And his ideas still live! There is a learned society that bears his name. Far from being peopled by fringe dwellers and mossbacks, it consists of lively scientists at the cutting edge of their disciplines. Articles and books that reflect his influence are appearing in increasing numbers (see, e.g., Hammond, 1996c; Cooksey, 1996b). There are Brunswikian Web sites.[4] Is it possible that the orthodox are wrong, and that the stone the builders of psychology

rejected may become at least one of the chief cornerstones? Whatever the judgment of the text-writing arbiters, there are those who would answer yes and claim that the future is ours. Indeed, an alternative title for this book could have been *Vivat Brunswik*.

An Obscure Paper from a Far-Off Time?

To speak to this contradiction, we consider an obscure paper, "Ontogenetic and Other Developmental Parallels to the History of Science" (1959), presented by a still young Egon Brunswik to the History of Science Dinner Club at Berkeley in 1939. The ostensible focus of the paper is the recapitulative relationship between ontogeny (concerned with the origin and development of the individual) and phylogeny (the evolution of types[5]), an idea with a long history in psychology.[6] Brunswik began his talk, "It has been argued that in any natural development, higher order products must pass through a necessary sequence of more primitive, preliminary stages." (p. 271),[7] and he referred to "the famed biogenetic law, conceiving of ontogenesis as a recapitulation of phylogenesis" (p. 271).

Recapitulation is, however, only one of the themes woven into this address. One can also read Brunswik's paper for the light that it throws on his thinking about himself and his work, and on his place in psychology. Whether his was a passing reputation or whether his fame is more enduring is a matter we can now reflect on as we stand at the millennium.

Unlike those of his publications that are directed to readers in psychology, this paper tells us something of Brunswik himself, his intellectual "outsiderhood," and his need to provide a justification for his approach to psychology by giving his work legitimacy within the enterprise of science. As he observed, "It has been abundantly observed by students . . . of the history of science that novelty tends at first to be met by stunned and rather indiscriminate rejection" (p. 272). Strong words, but maybe heartfelt. As we know, in the end he believed that he had not succeeded in overcoming this perceived rejection by the gatekeepers of scientific psychology. Sixteen years[8] after giving this address, he took his own life.[9] We may ask whether a longing for mainstream legitimacy may have resulted in Brunswik, that adventurous thinker of new thoughts, being cautious in following the more provocative and perhaps more interesting implications of his ideas.

Binding Things Together: Brunswik's View of the World

How did Brunswik's path differ from that of his fellow experimental psychologists? A short answer may be that he put things together (what engineers do) rather than take them apart (a characteristic of the analytic scientist). In this paper, he explicitly bound together perception and thinking—and beyond that, intuitive[10] and analytic cognitive processes (Hammond, 1996c)—thus allowing *Homo Brunswikiens* as a whole person to both apprehend and interact with the environment,[11] reflecting his correspondence rather than coherence[12] view of the world.

Joining together what science has put asunder, Brunswik began by discussing the relationship between people and their environment. In the first part of his paper he argued that *there is a continuing interaction between external demands and internal functioning.* He asserted that the mark of science, analytic thinking, is also the highest form of human cognition. This explicitly normative position enabled him to justify the privileged status of human judgment in his view of the relationship between people and their environments.

Brunswik then made three claims that bear on the relationship between a person and his or her environment. The first is that there is a biological (and therefore invariant) hierarchy or a sequence of functions. For example, he wrote that perception must precede thought. The second claim is that, within the constraints of a fixed biological structure, a particular task induces its own hierarchy of functions. The nature of any one task gives relevant specific responses a high priority. Playing chess induces different responses from buying a house. Other less relevant responses must therefore receive a lower priority. In other words, not only does the organism stand in an interactive relationship to its environment, but the way in which its resources are mobilized depends on its "appreciation" (see, e.g., Endsley, 1995) of that environment. Moreover, albeit implicitly, Brunswik was talking not of aggregates, or a concatenation of processes, but of systemic organization ("each science . . . must grow like an organism"; p. 274).

The third aspect of our relationship to our environment (as Brunswik sees it) is that we construct models of, or inferences about, the world and use these models to interpret incoming information and then use this interpreted information to modify or adapt our model of the environment. Brunswik talked, for example, about "the almost instantaneous growth of perceptual actuality as we open our eyes to a new scene" (p. 272). This "almost instantaneous growth" presupposes a criterion model, or Brunswik alluded to the same idea when talking about the importance of "good errors" in the problem-solving behavior of Koehler's chimpanzees as they maneuvered a banana into their cage. Good errors lead in turn to the refining of a person's representation or model of the world. Before a representation can be refined, it must be testable in terms that a person can understand, at a level of usable molarity. In this paper, Brunswik saw people as enquiring scientists, not as puppets dancing to the movement of environmental strings.

As we can see, the logic of Brunswik's theoretical orientation points toward a "systems" view (see, e.g., Senge, 1990) of the organism and its environment. Why, having pointed the way, was he tentative in venturing along this path? Unlike his theory of perceptual achievement, which he was able to model with multiple regression, he had no means available to represent this more complex situation. As Gigerenzer (1996) pointed out, 1939 was before Brunswik conceived of people as intuitive statisticians. It was even before he had begun using correlations, which he then regarded as complex. Perhaps, as a consequence of what he saw as the limitation of the available mathematical models to capture the correspondence between what we would now call his cognitive model and the distal world, he pursued this "systems" line of thinking no further.

Using Recapitulation as a Justification

When the talk on which this article is based was given (1939), the notion that ontogeny recapitulates phylogeny was still current. Brunswik used this idea to make an argument that there is a parallel between the history of science and the development of children. Children learning to understand the physical world seem to recapitulate the development of science, especially physics.

That is, Brunswik used discernible developmental trends in the sciences, buttressed by the ontological evidence from studies of child development, to indicate the direction that he believed that psychological research must go as it became more "adult." In identifying this development, Brunswik seemed to take a Whig[13] view of history, with its belief that *Homo sapiens* has ascended rather than descended from the apes. He argued that by observing the developmental trajectory of children, it is possible to see the direction in which science is heading. From this observation, it is then possible to prescribe how psychology should be framing its theories and its empirical activity. In foretelling its phylogenetic destiny by saying not only where psychology was, but where it ought to go, Brunswik echoed the optimistic liberalism of the late nineteenth century, which saw *Homo sapiens* at the apex of evolution.[14] Thus, the doctrine of recapitulation provides a normative framework for evaluating one's own development as a scientist as well as that of others. Brunswik's view, albeit implicit, seems to be that a proper reading of the ontogenetic record should allow a scientist to determine the direction of phylogenetic evolution, and to use that information to position himself or herself in the mainstream of his or her discipline.

Brunswik in the Mainstream

These themes underlying Brunswik's research, and the metaphor of recapitulation, led him to make a key point: "So-called operational redefinitions of traditionally metaphysical or subjective concepts such as 'purpose' (by Tolman[15]), 'hypothesis' (notably in animals; by Krech), 'intentionality' (by this writer [Brunswik]), and so forth, which since 1930 have been *superseding* (italics added) John B. Watson's iconoclastic early behaviourism, must be seen as . . . constructive interpretation" (p. 274). Thus, Brunswik located his work firmly in the mainstream of empirical psychology and saw it as a further development from, rather than an alternative to, behaviorism, the orthodoxy of the day.

Having asserted that his work was in the mainstream, Brunswik went on to outline the central properties of cognition. Brunswik wrote that "educated adults, while freeing themselves from illusory entanglements so far as their thinking [is] concerned, can still be shown to fall for them in their direct perceptions" (p. 276). Even adults are still prone to perceptual illusions.

Egocentrism

Brunswik identified two further characteristics of thinking that are fundamental to his view of how a person relates to the world: egocentrism and level of abstraction. The development of science and the development of human beings are both marked by seeing the world independent of self, by what Freud called "retreating narcissism."[16] This is not a take-it-or-leave-it matter to which Brunswik was indifferent. It allows and enables the correspondence view of truth (Hammond, 1996). Concept formation, a sine qua non of thinking, moves over time from the subjective or egocentric to the objective, focusing on the attributes or cues of the objects themselves. This allows the establishment of the lens model (Cooksey, 1996b; Hammond, 1996c) as a proper representation of higher processes. Objects exist in the environment independent of the observer. They are known via cues (or indicators, or attributes) that have an objective relationship to the object, which relationship maybe known only approximately by the observer.

Abstraction

With regard to the second aspect of concept formation, abstraction, Brunswik's position was that "there can be little doubt that science proper tends to move at intermediate levels of abstraction" (p. 278). One must steer a course between specificity and abstraction, achieving a Goldilocks (just-right) balance. Brunswik wanted to conceive of the world as an entity with cues (or properties, or indicators), and he needed to be able to represent them in a *usable* form. To be in that form, they have to match human experience. The way in which the world is perceived is learned. Thinking operates on learned perceptual categories. Perception and thought must come together for a person to function. As it turns out, although Brunswik did not make the point in this paper, the problem of measuring the achievement of the Goldilocks standard is handled easily and gracefully by the lens model as it links subjective and objective reality. It was surely evident to Brunswik, and also evident (he presumably hoped) to his listeners, that his formulation placed him squarely *an der Spitze* of the phylogenetic development of psychology.

Modeling the Situation

It is still necessary for an empirical science, with a correspondence orientation, to be quantitative. The correlation coefficient is, of course, the key measure for the lens model, as it indexes the association between the organism and the objects in the environment, as well as the association between the objects themselves. When Brunswik gave his talk, he was at the beginning of his "correlational period." He had not yet come to see people as intuitive statisticians (Gigerenzer, 1996). Brunswik held fast to what he could measure and what he could model. Although his address is run through with the idea of representation of the world that includes the ideas of probability and causally linked entities, he lacked the tools to go further with these ideas.

Brunswik concluded his talk by saying that "psychology has . . . expanded from considera-

tions tied to the internal life . . . to a sensationist-peripheralist emphasis . . . and eventually to a stage in which the external reference to the inner state becomes the major issue" (p. 279). He continued that "there is a parallel development at a methodologically higher, more 'objective' level which . . . begins with the physiological psychology encapsulated within the body, progresses to classical behaviourism . . . with its . . . stimulus response approach, and so far has culminated in the more complex, more 'molar' forms . . . in which the long-range, or distal, external correlates or referents of observed or hypothesised central or brain processes are the major issue" (pp. 279). Brunswik was talking about a world in which there are entities in the environment, known by their cues or indicators, and linked to a representation in the mind.

He then came to the point (it may be argued) to which the paper is directed: "From the genetic point of view, both 'objectivity' (scientific exactitude) and 'molarity' (that is, adequate complexity of scope) are subsumable under the concept of difficult or late developmental level" (p. 279). That point in the narrative of scientific development was where Brunswik located himself. A properly correspondent, quantitative representative of the person in her or his environment is ontogenetically in the full flower of development and thus may be regarded as the culmination of phylogenetic evolution.

A New Way of Representing a Complex Brunswikian Environment

Brunswik's perceptual focus was on "achieving" a distal object. He realized that if perception is probabilistic, then the entire context of perception is important. Although he was not explicit, even in the paper under discussion, it is clear that his theory looks toward multiple observers and multiple objects, all potentially linked with one another. Constructing a theory that cannot be modeled is an enterprise without scientific fruit. In talking about the cognitive processes underlying perception, Brunswik was able to utilize the ideas of correlation and regression to make his theoretical ideas empirically tractable. He seems not to have had a means of representing the more complex systems toward which his theory inevitably pointed. Hence, the notion of organization is latent in this paper, as well as in others, waiting for the availability of mathematical procedures that could model the psychological processes.

In the 1970s came a new means of representing complex causal systems, structural equation modeling (see, e.g., Schumacker & Lomax, 1996; Hart & Wearing, in press). In terms of representing the Brunswikian world, it can be seen as an extension of multiple correlation and regression. In the 1980s, structural equation modeling became generally accessible, and the 1990s saw it being widely used in studies that involved complex causal relations among variables, mainly in education, and social and organizational psychology (see, e.g., Hart & Wearing, 1995, in press). Research workers in these areas know little of Brunswik, and those working in the Brunswikian tradition are experimentalists and do not usually work in field settings with large samples. Even so, structural equation modeling, more than most other procedures, is able to represent the conceptual richness of Brunswik's theorizing. At the same time, this procedure is rooted in observation; the models are empirical.

When we consider individuals as they look at the organization of which they are members, it is evident that we can represent the ways in which they will perceive their environment in terms that are Brunswikian. The entities and the relations between them are equivalent to the perceptual world surrounding a Brunswikian perceiver. If we ask members of an organization about their organization, they will see it in terms of probabilities and functional relationships between entities.

Let us consider a specific example. One of the most widely used means of undertaking diagnostic assessment of organizations is the use of employee opinion surveys (EOSs). These surveys ask, in effect, how employees perceive their organization. They ask for the respondents' judgments of aspects of the organization such as feedback, pay, working conditions, management, and stress and morale, to list just a few. These constructs are latent (not observed directly) but are reached through items that are specific and relatively concrete. Not only do the responses provide an image or a profile of the organization, but they also allow the calculation of the strength of the association between the aspects. The structural equation model can be thought of as a collection of regression equations, or as a sophisticated lens model.

Once we can envisage one way of capturing Brunswik's vision (theory is not quite the word), we can imagine a multitude of tools, ranging from the application of lattices to understanding networks to systems dynamics modeling (see, e.g., Senge, 1990), as well as structural equation modeling.

Extending Perception to Organizations

This paper suggests a natural extension of Brunswik's thinking, grounded as it is in experimental studies of perception, to social and organizational psychology. It shows Brunswik thinking in terms of empirically observed organic systems ("each science . . . must grow like an organism" (p. 274)), where an organism consists of a set of related variables interacting with one another.[17] At the same time, in introducing this idea of an interactive system, he was opening the door that leads from individual behavior to the idea of policy,[18] since action depends on thought, which in turn depends on apprehending the environment. Distinguishing between intuitive and analytic thinking and conceiving of the organism as interacting with a causally textured environment (for those preferring continuous functions) or networks (for those who like their representations discrete) lead one to think about Brunswik and social and organizational psychology. The relationship between molar[19] behavior and the environment in the context of probabilistic functionalism provides a potentially fruitful way of thinking about both social and organizational psychology.[20] Brunswik was concerned with a field or network (although he did not use that term) of interacting psychological variables that are meaningful to the person as perceiver and thinker. Indeed, in order to be psychologically meaningful, the "molarity" needs to reflect the level of analysis used by the members of the organization. The simple form of Brunswik's model has an observer achieving a distal object via a set of cues, although *indicator* (cf. Hammond, 1996c) is probably a better term here. That "object" may be a concept such as leadership, with the indicators being items on a leadership scale. Leadership may be linked with other concepts (e.g., morale) to create "superconcepts" such as organization climate. The relationship between concepts like leadership and morale would be indexed by the indicators of the two concepts. This representation fits gracefully into the quasi-rational or the perceptual end of the cognitive processes. Leadership, for example, is a concept understood in terms of particular words and deeds. The molecular analysis, of interest perhaps to the physiologist, would not be of value to the participant or to a would-be change agent. A Brunswikian, as a member of an organization, would achieve a representation of the organization that would involve seeing its various components as connected in some form that was both causal and probabilistic.

We have seen how this talk to the sophisticated scholars of Berkeley may be interpreted so as to provide speculation on how Brunswik used the idea that ontogeny recapitulates phylogeny to locate himself in the mainstream of psychological science and, almost alone of his fellow psychological theorists, foresaw (albeit dimly) the importance of systemic complexity in understanding the world. Now, we can see that after looking at the "achievement" of the participant observer in an organizational setting, the issues of representation, functional relationships, and probabilistic causal linkages loom large. Why did not Brunswik extend his thinking to social and organizational psychology? One answer, discussed above, is that the necessary mathematical models were not available to him, so that he did not have a way of representing the "world" in which he was interested. A second reason may have been that social and organizational psychology were not mainstream, not matters of interest to the gatekeepers of that psychology against which Brunswik measured himself. A third reason may have been that the cues or indicators that index reality in perception index a theoretical construct in organizations. These constructs take on substance only because the trace of their presence can be observed. We find, for example, the spoor of leadership in the areas of organization climate and performance.

At first glance, Brunswik's paper seems to teeter on the edge of inconsequence, hostage to a view of the development of science that is a historical curio. As we have seen, however, it contains ideas that have become the cornerstone of biology, and that allow psychology to be con-

nected to its roots in the everyday world. On one level, the paper shows a powerful and scholarly mind drawing out underlying resemblances between superficially different phenomena. On another level, we see a scientist demonstrating that, contrary to what he might fear that others believe, his work lay in a mainstream of the multichanneled river that is psychology. At the same time, we see how uncertainty about whether others would accept this argument, and a lack of scientific (i.e., mathematical) models for representing situations led this same powerful mind to be conservative in his claims, and to hold back from extending his theoretical framework into areas for which it seemed admirably fitted. Running through his address is a concern for evidence. There is a focus on facts. Evidence will always rein in conjecture, and so it did with Brunswik, the epitome of correspondence man (Hammond, 1996c).

We may finish, then, by concluding that Brunswik's obscure address tells us a little about the man himself, more about the interaction of the man with his way of going about science, and much about what new applications his work and ideas may be fitted for, and why these developments have not yet occurred. Despite his fears, his is no transient reputation; rather, his fame grows and endures.

NOTES

1. Kenneth R. Hammond made a number of invaluable comments on an earlier version of this paper.

2. In psychology the canon may be regarded as defined by introductory texts, since we may assume that the content of such texts consists of matters about which the discipline agrees. Of course, time and new theories and findings wreak changes in what is agreed on. Perhaps the disregard of Brunswik reflects the fact that, on one hand, the science of perception has moved on, and that, on the other hand, judgment ad decision making (the areas in which Brunswik has present-day influence) have never entered the canon. To judge on the basis of the number of pages given over to judgment and decision making in most introductory texts, human begins obey rather than decide, a consequence of being beasts in a monistic and material world rather than rational angels. Even when judgment and decision making are admitted to the canon (as, e.g., in the *Annual Review of Psychology*), Brunswik is ignored.

3. A. N. Whitehead (1932) aphorized the lot of the would-be theorist: "Systems, scientific and philosophic,

come and go. Each method of limited understanding is at length exhausted. In its prime each system is a triumphant success: in its decay it is an obstructive nuisance" (p. 203).

4. For example, http://www.brunswik.org/

5. The term *types* usually refers to animals or plants, although in this paper, Brunswik applied it to the development of science, writing, "The history of science is a part of phylogeny, representing as it does a particularly lofty aspect of the general cultural development" (p. 4).

6. In psychology the proposition that ontogeny recapitulates phylogeny was asserted most prominently by G. Stanley Hall, a man who could lay some claim to being the founder of organized psychology in the United States. Hall (1923) wrote, "Every child . . . recapitulates . . . every stage of development through which the human race has passed" (p. 315). Brunswik dismissed Hall, claiming that his work, based on faulty anthropology, had not stood the test of time. Half a century after Brunswik passed judgment on Hall, we can see that time is even-handed.

7. All page references, unless otherwise indicated, are to "Ontogenetic and Other Developmental Parallels to the History of Science."

8. Given that scientists who have notched achievements on their belt have usually had to swim against the tide, it is interesting that Brunswik, a man of some achievement himself, eventually tired of doing it alone. Most scientists, however, are able to gather around them a collection of apprentices, disciples, even sycophants, all of whom validate one another. Scientists may form their own societies and publish their own journals. A person may step into a deanship or a vice presidency and create another apologia for his or her life. These protective strategies seem to have been ignored by Brunswik. His case may be contrasted with that of B. F. Skinner, who also focused on molar behavior and encouraged the use of behavior technologies while the continuous criticism of his fellow scholars rained upon him.

9. Even Tolman, Brunswik's highly regarded if somewhat controversial American mentor, eventually lost faith in his own S-O-R formulation. California does not, it seems, breed the stolidity of the Midwest or the self-confidence of the East.

10. With the intellectual and cultural eclipse of central Europe leading to the decline of Romanticism and the death (or close thereto) of Gestalt psychology, intuition is now of little contemporary importance for judgment and decision making, or indeed any of the higher processes. This situation, however, may be changing as central Europe re-asserts itself.

11. This achievement is far from trivial. The construction of policy (a course of action designed to solve a problem of a community, organization, or polity, although more recently the term *policy* is being applied to individual courses of action for dealing with complex and/or continuing problems as in, e.g., a personal fitness policy) depends on, first, how we understand the world, and second, how we think (problem-solve and decide) on the foundation of that understanding. Psychologists have often been absent from the top table because they could not put perception and thought together with to-be-achieved criteria.

12. The term *correspondence* and *coherence* are explicated by Hammond (1996c). Very briefly, the term *correspondence* refers to the process by which a person achieves empirical accuracy in her or his grasp of the environment, and the term *coherence* refers to whether ideas and thought have logical consistency. In Hammond's (1996c) words, "The correspondence theory of truth focuses on the correspondence of ideas with facts, rather than the coherence of ideas with ideas" (p. 4). It is perhaps unfortunate for Brunswik that coherence possesses a profound aesthetic attraction. Ideas, even when they are plainly wrong, may have a compelling fascination. Facts are simply the workaday bricks and mortar of the scientific world. Brunswik, gifted with a plenitude of ideas, was yet a correspondence man with a respect for facts.

13. The Whig view of history, in one sentence, is that humankind has made steady progress over time, and that our civilization, the most advanced ever known, is the culmination of thousands of years of development.

14. It is interesting that Brunswik seems to have remained an intellectual liberal even though he was only eleven years of age when World War 1 began, a war that saw not only the end of the Austro-Hungarian Empire (Brunswik's home port) and the transfer of psychology's center of gravity from German-speaking Central Europe to English-speaking America, but also the end of utopian optimism. Indeed, Brunswik's own life instantiates in miniature those changes.

15. Tolman, of course, was a close collaborator of Brunswik's, and they found themselves in agreement on many of the important theoretical issues of the day.

16. These two words are taken from one of Brunswik's most memorable passages, in which he wrote, "The geocentric world view is more perceptual . . . and hence more egocentric or subjective then heliocentric. In fact, all the great 'Copernican revolutions' in the history of science are manifestations of what Freud called 'retreating narcissism.' Copernicus himself renounced the idea of dominance of man's domicile over the heavenly bodies; the second of these revolutions, by Darwin, dethroned man among the animals; the

third, by Kant, challenged the subject's cognitive mastery of reality; and still another, by Freud, exposed the conscious mind as not even being master within its own personality" (p. 20).

17. Surprisingly, he did not use the term *causal texture*, although it is discussed in Tolman and Brunswik's 1935 paper in the *Psychological Review*.

18. The term *policy* had a particular meaning for Brunswik. Here it is used in its standard sense of a course of action directed to guiding a system toward a goal.

19. The term *molar* connotes whole, integrated behavioral acts, in contrast to the term *molecular*, which refers to the muscular components of actions. Brunswik talked of "molarity," that is, "adequate complexity of scope" (p. 21).

20. Organizations provide the context within which much practical thinking occurs. Brunswik's conceptions relate gracefully to organizational behavior, as organizations are themselves may be represented as networks.

  REPRINT

Ontogenetic and Other Developmental Parallels to the History of Science
Egon Brunswik

It has been argued that in any natural development higher order products must pass through a necessary sequence of more primitive, preliminary stages.* The famed biogenetic law, conceiving of ontogenesis as a recapitulation of phylogenesis, is but one of a variety of possible applications of this general idea. Among other things, it has suffered from the danger of overspecification in that it became difficult to decide which particulars of phylogenesis were essential and which were incidental and thus dispensable. This also holds for the first major attempt to apply the biogenetic law to psychology, undertaken by the American psychologist G. Stanley Hall in his book on adolescence in 1904 (1). Hall asssumed that children pass through the stages of hunting, building, and so forth, as they mature, in alleged recapitulation of the history of mankind. This theory, based on faulty anthropology and stated in overly concrete categories without sufficient evidence, has not stood the test of time.

A more promising way to establish development parallelisms in psychology is by concentrating on certain more broadly conceived, fundamental modes of approach or organization, principles so basic and abstract as to be unaffected by situationally determined details of the adjustmental process. Aside from some psychologically noncommittal early formulations of Herbert Spencer and of Wundt centering about "homogeneity-heterogeneity" or "differentiation," most of the attempts along this line came predominantly from the European continent within the last thirty-odd years. Some of these, such as notably that of Heinz Werner (2), deal mainly with ontogeny, that is, *child development*, in relation to phylogeny, the latter in the form of comparative material from both *primitive cultures* and *animal experimentation*. From the standpoint of our topic, the history of science is a part of phylogeny, representing as it does a particularly lofty aspect of the general cultural development. The idea that children's theories may more or less spontaneously move along paths previously traveled by the great creators of scientific ideas has been championed especially by Piaget (3) and his collaborators at Geneva. We shall refer to some examples of his work below.

Perhaps even more daring than the search for

Reprinted from E. Brunswik (1959), Ontogenetic and other developmental parallels to the history of science. In H. M. Evans (Ed.), *Men and Moments in the History of Science* (pp. 3–21) (Seattle: University of Washington Press), by permission of University of Washington Press.

extraneous counterparts of ontogeny is the execution of the idea that the individual being contains a variety of developmental stages within himself. In modern psychology this *intraindividual genetic* approach has taken three major forms.

The first is incorporated in the conception of the adjustmental makeup of organisms as a *simultaneous hierarchy* of functions operating at different developmental levels. In the present context it may suffice to point to various efforts, in essence dating back to Helmholtz, of describing "perception" as a primitive mode of "thinking," more specifically of inductive reasoning. Some relation to the notions of the romantic natural philosophers of the early nineteenth century, notably Oken, concerning the simultaneous hierarchy of organs of different developmental status within the body of higher animals may here be discerned (4). In application to ontogeny it has been pointed out that the thinking of children is in many ways perceptionlike; as regards our present topic, we shall bring up cases in which early scientific theories show structural resemblance to certain specific patterns found in perception.

The second form of intraorganismic developmental comparison is given by the fact that the developmental level at which an organism operates seems to some extent to be determined by the nature of the demands of the stimulus situation; thus we have what may be called a task-induced hierarchy. For example, a simpler task may be handled by a more advanced function, while a more difficult or complex one of the same general kind may involve recourse, or "regression," to a lower developmental level. Among others, Werner (5) has advanced certain ideas along this line.

A third application of the comparative approach within the same individual is given by attempts to subsume certain relatively rapid process chains under the genetic point of view so that they appear as a *telescoping of the developmental process*. There are two subvarieties of this third case.

a. One concerns *practice-induced changes*. These are changes occurring in the course of what may broadly be labeled practice or familiarization, in contradistinction to learning proper. A practiced function or person is in certain ways comparable to a function or person at a higher developmental level. One of the most notable

attempts to establish exercise of a mental function as an effective substitute for general level of development, the latter involving both the natural level of intelligence and impairments through brain damage, has recently come from the American psychologist, Harry Harlow (6). The examples presented in this paper will be from other contexts, however.

b. The second subvariety of intraindividually telescoped development concerns what Sander (7) and others in the Leipzig school of developmental psychology have called "actualgenesis," as most drastically exemplified by the almost instantaneous growth of perceptual actuality as we open our eyes to a new scene. Sander brings forth evidence for his belief that every single cognitive act runs the gamut of an intrinsic genetic hierarchy, so that actualgenesis becomes a third partner to ontogenesis and phylogenesis within an expanded biogenetic scheme.

Let us turn to some concrete illustrations. Some of the examples cited will have ramifications with respect to more than one of the genetic parallelisms listed above.

Developmental Aspects of Criticism and the Constructive Interpretation of Error

We shall begin with experiments on the development of criticism in children undertaken as a University of Vienna doctoral dissertation by Anna B. Brind some twenty-five years ago, under the direction of this writer (8). There are several reasons for choosing this study as our first example. From the beginning its plan was geared to certain problems in the philosophy of science, specifically the ways in which new propositions are rejected or accepted. It has been abundantly observed by students or contemplative onlookers of the history of science that novelty tends at first to be met by stunned and rather indiscriminate rejection, followed by more thoughtful and specific criticism—a pattern that makes the history of science the drama it is. The very generality and atmospheric character of the attitudes involved make it possible to concentrate on formal modes of development rather than on its content, as we said at the beginning that we should. A further advantage of this study is a design which permits us to bring into the picture both stimulus-induced developmental levels and intraindividual tele-scoping, along with ontogenesis.

Brind's study constitutes an analysis of the de-velopment of the readiness to be critical of certain more or less blatantly erroneous sentences involv-ing factual untruths and logical incorrectness. Ten such sentences were randomly interspersed with an equal number of correct statements and presented to normal school children aged seven to fourteen, with forty subjects (boys and girls) at each year level.

For each of the sentences there was found an age level at which (1) a kind of naive credulity could be observed. Independent judgment seems to begin with (2) uncertainty or diffuse distress. Next comes a series of stages of criticism proper, characterized by growing discrimination between the correct and the incorrect sentences. The earli-est explicit type of criticism usually consists in (3) stereotyped rejection, or global, en bloc nega-tivism. Examples are "No," "Bad," "Can't be." This is followed by (4) specified rejection. By this is meant a circumscribed statement of the weak point in the statement. Taking as an example the sentence, "When it rains, it is dry," a case of specified rejection would be "Not dry." A still higher level is that of (5) positive correction, given for our example by such statements as, "It is wet."

The most advanced stages transcend criticism in the narrow sense of the word. We shall subsume them under the term (6) higher-order criticism. Here we find a series of parallel subcategories. Perhaps the most important is (a) constructive interpretation, in which an attitude of making the best of the material presented is taken. For our sample sentence, an example is, "Yes, it is dry if there is a roof overhead." Perhaps interpreta-tion is the result of a kind of social consideration of the person who stands behind the statement in question. In this case the attitude toward the author is a benevolent one, reflecting a trust in the good senses of one's fellow men together with an implicit understanding of the intrinsic limita-tions of communication and the ensuing need for the use of indirection and metaphor. Other subvarieties of higher-order criticism are given by various types of (b) negative reference to the au-thor of the sentence. An example is, "The man who has written this must be crazy."

The various forms of criticism proper and of higher-order criticism just listed are followed by a last stage in which the subjects merely express (7) amusement, disinterest, or even surfeit and

disgust in the task without taking the trouble of dealing with it in any specific way.

The sequence of the seven attitudes outlined in the preceding paragraphs was found to hold, first, when the total frequences of respective utter-ances of all subjects, grouped by age levels, were compared with one another. The lower the num-ber in our list of critical attitudes, the lower the age of the onset, the peak, and the decline of the relative frequencies. For our type of material, higher order criticism does not occur before the age of nine and fails to come into its own before age eleven. (Although it is true that such a cross-sectional approach is not ontogenetic in the literal sense of the word, this type of approach is widely accepted as a more practicable substitute for the truly ontogenetic, longitudinal approach, at least for a good many types of child-psychological prob-lems.)

The same sequence was found, second, when the responses of children of a similar age level to sentences of different degrees of difficulty were compared. This subsumes the material under what we have labeled above task-induced devel-opmental hierarchy. And third, the same sequence of stages was found when the responses given at the beginning of the experiment compared with those given by the same subjects at later stages of the same experiment. Protracted occupation of the same kind thus acted in the way of an artificial evolution, in the manner characterized above as practice-induced developmental tele-scoping.

In trying to relate Brind's results to the type of genetic series which we have come to know as the history of science and of ideas, we may for the moment ignore the fact that the crucial part of her material is false rather than true; as we all know, most of the really decisive restructurings in science were for long periods treated as false-hoods. We are also reminded of Schopenhauer's saying that each truth enjoys but a short life span of interested acknowledgment that lies between its being ridiculed as absurd and its being dis-carded as trivial. Our categories describing the sequence of critical attitudes are flexible as to content, yet fairly detailed in elaborating the vari-ous formal steps. We may therefore in this case confine our comparison to relatively indirect, generalized, or casual evidence.

The preliminary stage of naïve credulity may be seen as paralleled by the gullibility so fre-quently observed at the popular, prescientific level. Among eminent scientists observant of their own creative processes, Helmholtz—at a dinner in honor of his seventieth birthday—has referred to the thoughts "creeping quietly into my thinking without my suspecting their importance." The ensuing sequence of astonished bewilderment, emotional and total refusal, petty criticism, and the eventual turning to positive and "higher" forms of criticism is, within the field of psychology, best exemplified by the changing attitude toward psychoanalysis. After half a century of vacillation we have now reached the stage of interpreting psychoanalysis in a constructive manner and of trying to fit it into the pattern of standard experimentation (9).

The stage of constructive interpretation is that of real superiority. The partial truth implicit in so many of the "creative errors" in the history of science becomes clearly emphasized. Prominent among these is the opening up of a new problem area by means of a false solution (10). So far as the history of psychology is concerned (11) we may think of Mesmer's fantastic "animal magnetism" that turned into the sound doctrine of hypnotism, or of Gall's "phrenology" that gave rise to the serious treatment of brain localization of mental faculties, eventually helping to revise the classification of these faculties as well. In commenting on Brind's above-described results, Otto Selz, prominent member of the so-called Würzburg school of thought psychology, stressed the facilitation of problem solution by preceding mistakes in the history of science and of technology, along with the validity of the same principle for the dynamics of individual thinking processes (12).

The Gestalt psychologist, Köhler, has stressed the importance of "good error" in the problem-solving behavior of chimpanzees (13), thus furnishing a parallel from what Sander would call actualgenetic material at the phylogenetically lowered level of animal psychology. If a banana placed outside the cage could not be reached by using a single stick, some of the apes would spontaneously push out another stick by means of the first so that an optical bridge was formed connecting the hand with the banana. This was found to be a step preliminary to the crucial invention of mechanically joining two sticks of different diameter by inserting one into the other end by end, thus manufacturing a suitable tool for obtaining the fruit. The error of confusing the visual and the mechanical aspects of reality

committed by the apes has a counterpart in children when they confuse meteorology and astronomy, and in the history of science when the firmament is conceived of as a dome with the stars moving along its surface.

A sequence recently observed in the development of the views regarding the role of "metaphysics" and of other imperfect instruments of knowledge, such as subjective introspection or speculation as they concern psychology, is also to the point here. Classical writers of the school of logical positivism have stressed the untestable, "meaningless" character of metaphysical statements, taking the latter in their literal meaning. One of the most totally rejective formulations comes from Philipp Frank (14) when he speaks of the metaphysics of yesterday as the common sense of today and the nonsense of tomorrow. Such admonitions as "Positivism, not negativism!" perpetrated by one of the members of the next generation of the school, Herbert Feigl (15), are symptomatic of a trend toward more advanced forms of response that move in the direction of "making the best" of any and all of the products of human imagination. As this writer has pointed out elsewhere in greater detail (16), the so-called operational redefinitions of traditionally metaphysical or subjective concepts such as "purpose" (by Tolman), "hypothesis" (notably in animals; by Krech), "intentionality" (by this writer), and so forth, which since 1930 have been superseding John B. Watson's iconoclastic early behaviorism, must be seen as but another facet of the type of constructive interpretation which Brind has found to be an advanced form of criticism in her children. It stems from the conviction—appropriate to one engrossed in a discipline which still is in its adolescence—that not only science at large, but each science individually, and each unit of knowledge within it, must grow like an organism that passes through a variety of stages of increasing self-sufficiency and maturity; and that in this process the "genidentity" (to use a term of Kurt Lewin) of the problem line is maintained through the most bizarre and unrecognizable metamorphoses.

Theorizing in Children and in Early Science

Turning now from genetic sequences of such general attitudes as criticism to the more material content of science, the work of Piaget on the theorizing and the world view of children deserves particular attention. Since most of Piaget's books relating to the subject have been translated (17) we shall confine ourselves to a few examples. The validity of generalization of Piaget's findings regarding age levels or culture has been questioned as well as his adequacy of method; this writer feels, however, that so long as any children of any age anywhere produce the views found by Piaget with fair assurance of spontaneity in the sense of the absence of specific prior teachings, as seems to be the case, the major point has been maintained.

Most of Piaget's parallels related to the history of physics. They are based on the free-flowing speech of, and interviews with, children, mostly under the age of ten. Simple questions were asked, e.g., "How does it come that a boat floats on the water?" In some cases the children had to predict the outcome of simple experiments, e.g., whether a stone or a match would sink or not. The results show a remarkable specificity, as well as in many cases a remarkable deviation from the views which could reasonably have been imparted to the children by adults.

One of the central concepts in the terminology of Piaget is "conservation." The stable world of the adult as well as his physics is based upon the discovery of a number of invariants. Piaget maintains that these constants and laws enter the scope of the child slowly and under great difficulties. To begin with, up to the age of about eleven or twelve, children do not know of the principle of inertia. In order to explain the flight of a projectile, children below age ten will in most cases assume that the projector produces air which is constantly acting upon the projectile. For example, a ten-year-old child thought that without air the projectile would fall to the ground immediately, and that "the air went all the time and pushed it along." In fact, it is the very weight (mass) of the projectile which by resisting the push of air is seen as ultimately stopping the movement.

Piaget points out that this explanation of continued movement is strikingly similar to the famous explanation suggested by Aristotle, known as the theory of antiperistasis. According to this theory the air plays the part of a motor. Shaken by the projectile as it issues from the sling of the catapult, the air flows after it and drives it along. After the contact has been lost the original impulse is transferred to the medium traversed by the projectile in a way similar to magnetism. This faculty decreases at a distance because of the resistance in the actual mass of the projectile, its natural weight. Aristotle thus reveals himself as being a long way off the principle of inertia as we have known it since the days of Galileo and Descartes, and as it is gradually transmitted to our children through cultural channels. For Aristotle as well as for the child the world is filled with spontaneous movement and living forces including those of the air, that is, with immanent animism and artificialism. Motion cannot occur without a moving agent permanently acting upon the thing in motion. Weight by itself, on the other hand, is seen as but an obstacle to movement.

Another variety of this type of explanation found both in Aristotle and in children is the theory of the reflux of air behind the projectile. This theory runs in a vicious circle. It is assumed that first the air in front of the projectile is put under pressure by the projectile; escaping from that pressure the air next flows behind and eventually goes on to push the projectile forward. Similar is the explanation given by children of the movement of the clouds. They are supposed to advance owing to the air that they themselves produce and that moves behind them and pushes them along.

An example from psychology is given by the resemblance, again to rather minute detail, between children's theories of perception and those of Empedocles or Plato. According to the latter, vision is due to light given out by an object as it meets the flashes of light emanating from the pupil of the eye. Similarly, children about six years of age tend to confuse "seeing," which according to them occurs outside the eye, with "giving light." Street lamps are able to see. Unless they are shut, as they are at night, eyes give light like lamps. This material by Piaget ties in with an observation by G. Stanley Hall concerning a child asking his father: "Why don't our looks mix when they meet?"

Concerning the development of the concept of weight Piaget distinguishes three stages, at least two of which are pre-Archimedean. During the first stage it is implied that specific weight is the same for all bodies, so that weight and volume mean pretty much the same thing. A small piece of wood is considered necessarily heavier than a pebble of slightly lesser volume. In the second stage bulky objects no longer are conceived of as necessarily heavy. Yet the concept of specific weight is not yet correctly envisaged, different objects merely being regarded as made of more or less condensed or rarefied materials. One of the children, five and one-half, states that the pebble is full and heavy; wood is much heavier than the equal volume of water because it is packed whereas water is liquid. Weight is here seen as dependent on condensation and solidity. Traces of similar views can be found in Anaximenes and Empedocles. Eventually, but not before the age of nine or ten, a clearer conception of specific weight can be found at least in the case of such common substances as water, wood, and stone, overruling the earlier emphasis on compactness. Prior to this final stage, the weight of water is brought into the picture primarily as the cause of a current that is assumed to keep such objects as boats floating. In fact, according to very young children, boats float not because they are light but because they are heavy, thereby giving rise to strong counterforces and movements in the water that keep the boat floating. A kind of struggle between the water and the immersed object is envisaged, leading to the prediction that stones will float whereas matches will sink. In a slightly more advanced stage, boats are assumed to float because they are lighter than the total mass of water in the lake. Not before the final stage are they correctly perceived as floating in consequence of the fact that they are lighter than water at equal volumes.

Furthermore, children show difficulty in establishing for themselves the principle of conservation of weight. Objects are assumed to lose weight as they grow in bulk, for instance from a pellet to a bowl. The first thing grasped is absolute weight, and much later follows relative weight; the sequence from absolute to relative is one of the characteristic features of mental development in general. In a way similar to the pre-Socratics, it is assumed that air, fire, smoke, steam, and water have the power of transforming themselves into one another. This assumed possibility of transformation of anything into anything else may be largely responsible for the appeal held by the world of the fairy tale in the esteem of children.

In essence, any nonrecognition of conservation serves to make abstract issues unduly concrete and leads to confusion. This becomes especially clear in considering the problem of

conservation for such mathematical variables as number or volume. Max Wertheimer, the founder of the school of Gestalt psychology, has searched primitive cultures hardly touched by the dawn of science for evidence of the contamination of early concepts of number and has come up with an impressive array of instances of the use of different terms for the same number when the elements are arranged in different patterns or when different kinds of objects are involved (18). Piaget and his collaborators (19) have observed, among other things, that the scattering of a group of objects over a larger area than that of the original distribution tends to induce children to claim that now there are more, even if the scattering has been performed in plain view of the child. As to volume, the pouring of a liquid from one container into two smaller ones tends to give the impression of an increase, or else of a decrease, depending on whether there is cognitive assimilation to the increase in the number or to the decrease in the size of the new containers, as the more dominant feature of the change.

With all this, we have moved into the twilight region between concepts and percepts. It is of crucial significance that educated adults, while freeing themselves from illusory entanglements of number and volume so far as their thinking and scrutinized observation are concerned, can be shown still to fall for them in their more direct perceptions (20). The thinking of children, and that of prescientific primitives, thus turns out to be in important respects similar to that of intuitive perception, both adult and childlike. By intuitive perception we mean the fairly autonomous primitive instrument of cognition within ourselves as scientifically minded adults that functions with speed and spontaneity. To apply the terminology of Werner (21), "diffuse" cognition is superseded by "articulate" cognition; and this is the case in ontogenesis, in the phylogenesis of science, and in a simultaneous genetic hierarchy within the fully matured individual.

Egocentrism and Level of Abstraction in Concept Formation

To the scientifically trained mind the concepts under discussion in the preceding section, such as energy, weight, number, or volume, will appear as paradigms of objective, almost preordained modes of thought, and any deviation from them will likely appear as error or illusion. Yet there are other areas in the realm of concept formation where greater latitude seems to exist; their study brings out some of the more subtle points of what we may call competing "viewpoints" in the establishment and application of concepts.

A convenient and effective method of studying this problem is to present pairs of common words and to ask for a supraordinate concept. A study of this kind was conducted as a doctoral dissertation by A. Spielmann-Singer at the University of Vienna under the direction of Charlotte Bühler and of this writer (22). Special attention was paid to potential relevance for the emergence of the scientific point of view. Children from four to ten years of age (ten boys and ten girls for each age level) were presented with such word pairs as "streetcar and automobile," "spinach and lettuce," "cup and kettle," and so forth. The children were asked to find a word which would "fit both of them."

The results may be discussed under two major headings. One concerns the particular content of the guiding viewpoint of concept formation, with special emphasis on what Werner has described as "syncretism" and Piaget as "egocentrism," that is, the intrusion of subjective aspects into the objective classification. The other concerns specificity versus generality, or what is frequently labeled level of abstraction.

As to subjectivism, the youngest of our children showed a predilection for (1) classification in accordance with pleasantness versus unpleasantness; for example, "streetcar and automobile" was frequently answered by such phrases as, "They are fun." For our type of material, practically no answers of this type were found after the age of seven. Next was (2) concentration upon the practical usefulness of the objects in question, for example when "lettuce-spinach" was responded to by "to eat." There follows further detachment from the ego in the sense that (3) communality of sphere of life, of milieu, or of other perceptual grouping is being stressed; an example for our last-named pair is, "They grow in the garden." For our material, this type of response reaches its peak at the age of six. The most mature type of response concentrates upon (4) characteristics resting in the objects themselves. Here we approach most closely what is commonly called the objective or science-type point of view, or what in German is labeled *sachlich*. Examples are the description of "lettuce and spinach" as "green," or as "vegetables."

It goes without saying that in many instances the fourth, or objective attitude may coincide with the second, or utilitarian, as for instance in the case of "cup and kettle." Here we have to do with human artifacts made for particular purposes. Yet even in such cases it was possible to distinguish different degrees of egocentricity and to classify the answers accordingly.

For our material, objective, sciencelike responses are rare in the age brackets from four to six; they jump from 8 per cent at the age of six to 52 per cent at the age of seven, however—obviously in connection with entering school—and they reach 90 per cent at the age of ten.

Parallel hierarchies from subjectivistic to objectivistic types of classifications are abundant in the history of science. The popular prescientific classification of animals into "harmful" and "beneficial," or their classification in terms of common appearance or milieu (whales grouped with the fish) or in terms of other phenotypical characteristics come to mind at once. The geocentric world view is more perceptual—or "pictural," as Philipp Frank (23) would say—and hence more egocentric or subjective than the heliocentric. In fact, all the great "Copernican revolutions" in the history of science are manifestations of what Freud has called "retreating narcissism," (24) Copernicus himself renounced the idea of the dominance of man's domicile over the heavenly bodies; the second of these revolutions, by Darwin, dethroned man among the animals; the third, by Kant, challenged the subject's cognitive mastery of reality; and still another, by Freud, exposed the conscious mind as not even being master within its own personality.

Let us now turn to the second aspect of the development of concept formation, specificity versus generality, or level of abstraction. In Spielmann-Singer's data the concrete type of answer occupies a particularly basic position. Between 30 and 35 per cent of the children in the age groups from four to six gave answers that were erroneous by being too specific. An example is "made of iron" as a reply to "cup and kettle," leaving out all cups or kettles made of materials other than iron (or metal). This type of answer does, however, fade out almost completely after the age of seven so far as our material is concerned.

Overspecificity is superseded by another type of inappropriateness, overgeneralization, with a peak between 20 to 25 per cent at the age levels of seven and eight. An example of such an answer is "object." Since responses of this kind are apt to embrace both of the concepts presented, overgeneralization is not always an error in the strict sense of the word. But from the adult standpoint overgeneralization must be regarded as an easy escape with little value for the specific problem at hand. Overgeneralization is a transitory type of response. Within our material it plays very little role at first and shows a marked tendency to decline after age seven and eight.

From then on, there is increased emphasis on what the logician calls the *"genus proximum,"* that is, on concepts fully embracing the original items but avoiding as much as possible going beyond. For the pair "streetcar-automobile" such an answer is exemplified by "vehicle." At the age level of ten, 87 per cent of the answers fall in this category.

The sequence from the concrete to the very abstract and down again to the medium level of the *genus proximum*, which we have observed in the quasi-ontogenetic data just presented, can also be found in what we have introduced above as actual-genesis in the sense of Sander. Using the retrospective method as developed by the Würzburg school, Willwoll (25) studied this microdevelopment of individual problem solutions in educated adults. Pairs of words were presented and the experimental subjects were asked to find a supraordinate concept. The intermediate level of the *genus proximum* was found to be the latest and most difficult in most individual solutions except the more automatic ones. At the same time, finding this level is experienced as especially rewarding from the standpoint of the subject's self-imposed level of aspiration.

Both the ontogenetic and the actualgenetic findings just presented seem to be in conflict with the commonsense view of the development of scientific thought. According to this view the concrete level is the easiest to handle and the first to be acquired while each step up the ladder of abstraction involves added difficulty, so much so that the highest abstractions can be approached only by such princes of thought as the philosophers.

In reality, the vast generality of such universal "dichotomies" as "being versus becoming," or "mind versus matter," are probably relatively easy to come by. Indeed, they are an early product in the history of ideas, and there is evidence from child psychology that they are early in ontogenesis also. The over-all picture is somewhat complicated by the fact that such " metaphysical" concepts may have specific ties with the world of concrete objects or events by virtue of their perceptionlike or "pictural" (26) (see above) or "metaphorical" (27) character, and that these ties in a certain sense undo the all-embracingness of their meanings. But there can be little doubt that science proper tends to move at intermediate levels of abstraction. Much abstraction, but also much technological, operational, or methodological specification is required for the establishment of such concepts as correlation coefficient, or momentum. Only by virtue of such specification may we move from the metaphysical stage to the "positive" stage, as Comte has envisaged it, or from the "Aristotelian" to the "Galilean" modes of thought, as Lewin (28) has described them with an eye on the particular problems facing psychology in its historical development.

Perceptionlike Structures (Formalism) in Early Science

In the history of geography and of astronomy the theme of "perfect" form has exerted recurrent and lasting influence. Ancient geographers have shown their predilection for regularity of form by assuming that the shape of continents and islands was originally circular, triangular, or rectangular, existing irregularities being the result of deterioration in time (29). In assuming the circularity of the orbits of the planets, Copernicus was prompted by the same formalistic bias. Had Tycho Brahe not shared this formalism, he would not have refuted the Copernican system as a whole on the basis of certain inconsistencies with observation but would have revised it. Not before another generation had passed did Kepler struggle through to accept the ellipse in spite of the fact that it was less simple.

It will be noted that, in terms of our above discussion of stages of criticism, Tycho is an example of negativism, Kepler, of interpretation of data. The final stage of criticism, ridicule, in the present case of form, becomes mythology, best exemplified by Fechner's satire *Vergleichende An-*

atomie der Engel (1825). This presents the argument that since the sphere is the most perfect form, the angels, as the most perfect beings, must be spherical.

There is at least one area in which simplicity, circularity, and other features subsumable under "good form" are a reality, however. This area is the perception of form. An incomplete circle presented in short exposure tends to be experienced as a complete circle. Similarly, the negative afterimage of a square with one blunted corner will frequently appear either as a perfect square or else will show symmetrical corners blunted, and so forth. Generally speaking, under a variety of conditions of reduced stimulus impact, perceptual shapes will tend toward geometrically outstanding forms. Technically this is known as the "law of *Prägnanz.*" Most likely it is the result of dynamic self-organization within what such leaders in recent physiological Gestalt psychology as Köhler have termed "brain fields." (30)

We have already had occasion to characterize perception as a relatively primitive function in the simultaneous intraorganismic developmental hierarchy that makes up the adult human personality. By virtue of its formalism, early scientific thinking thus once more appears as a counterpart to a primitive subsystem of mature man.

The parallel can be expanded still further. Sander has subsumed short exposure and other reductions of the stimulus impact under his concept of actualgenesis (31), in the sense that under these conditions cognitive acts are cut off in the midst of their natural maturation process, even though in most cases this process may not require more than a few seconds, or perhaps only fractions of a second, for its completion. In the light of this challenging notion, good form is but an intermediate one of several stages perception is capable of reaching on its own. Early scientific thinking would then not only display features of a perception, as such, but also of perception handicapped in the fulfillment of its own developmental potential.

Conclusion: Developmental Parallels within the History of Science Itself

It takes but a simple reapplication of the various aspects of what we have labeled simultaneous intraorganismic genetic hierarchy to view science in any cross section of time as a conglomerate of efforts moving at different developmental levels, depending on the age of the various disciplines, the difficulty of the problem, the time elapsed since work on the problem has begun, and so forth.

Speculations of this kind have led this writer (32) to attempt for psychology what one of his reviewers, Gustav Bergmann, has felicitously labeled "structural history writing" in contrast with the "pragmatic" tracing of historical influences in terms of intellectual biography, which characterizes the customary actuarial historical narrative. Structural history writing presupposes the classification of problems and modes of approach in terms of genetic sequences. One of the ways in which this can be done is by a pattern analysis of the scope of the varying scientific edifices that have occupied the attention of psychologists.

In executing this plan it first appears that the scope of the traditional subjective—that is, speculative or introspectionistic—psychology has, within the last three centuries, expanded from considerations confined to the internal life (Descartes) to a sensationist-peripheralist emphasis (English empiricism and associationism) and eventually to a stage in which the external reference of the inner states becomes the major issue. (Both Brentano's act psychology and Lewin's topological-dynamic psychology are relatively clearcut examples of this third stage.)

Next it is discovered that, with a temporal lag that decreases from centuries to decades as we progress in time, there is a parallel development at a methodologically higher, more "objective" level, which goes through a similar sequence of basic pattern or scope. It begins with the physiological psychology encapsulated within the body, as the early and middle nineteenth century knew it, progresses to the classical behaviorism of Watson with its more pointed emphasis on the sensory and motor peripheries and their interrelationships (stimulus-response approach), and so far has culminated in the more complex, more "molar" forms of behaviorism and physiological psychology (e.g., Tolman, Lashley), in which the long-range, or distal, external correlates or referents of observed or hypothesized central or brain processes are the major issue.

From the genetic point of view both "objectivity" (scientific exactitude) and "molarity" (that is, adequate complexity of scope) are subsumable under the concept of difficult or late developmental level, so that an advancement in one is often found to go with a standstill or even a regression in the other, at least temporarily (33). The net effect is that each historical cross section simultaneously embraces a variety of developmental stages.

Structural analyses and comparisons of this kind are in the nature of things much more precarious than concrete fact finding or process tracing. Fortunately they can at least in part be supported by quantitative analyses of historical trends in psychology, which have of late become the vogue in a discipline very much aware of the necessity to introduce objective methods along its entire front. Most notable of these is a statistical trend documentation based on a content analysis of leading American psychological periodicals undertaken by Allport in collaboration with Bruner (34). It covers the crucial period in the growth of psychology from 1888 to 1938. Our claim of spiral recurrence of comparable historical sequences at increasingly higher levels of either difficulty or exactitude, which we have summarized in the preceding paragraphs, can be borne out by means of Allport and Bruner's charts dealing with the changing emphasis on certain fields or topics. There we find a number of U-shaped time distributions, which may be interpreted as parts of bimodal distributions; the latter in turn may be taken to point to a shifting in the "kind" of endeavor within the category in question. For example, the change from the purely internal or peripheralistic physiological psychology of the nineteenth century to the brain-and-achievement type of approach which we have reported as the favorite of today is reflected by a marked slump of interest in physiological problems at the beginning of this century.

In our opinion the fusion, just illustrated, between the structural, or broadly interpretational, approach to the history of science and an adequately categorized, rigorous but comprehensive method of objective trend documentation promises to render fruitful the application of genetic principles to the analysis of the history of science.

NOTE

This is a somewhat revised version of a paper read before the History of Science Dinner Club at Berkeley in 1939. While the essentials of the original presentation were left intact, it has been brought up to date in certain respects, primarily so far as the writer's own views relating to the subject are concerned.

REFERENCES

1. G. Stanley Hall, *Adolescence* (New York: D. Appleton and Co., 1904).
2. H. Werner, *Comparative Psychology of Mental Development* (rev. ed.; Chicago: Follett Publishing Co., 1948).
3. J. Piaget, *The Child's Conception of the World* (New York: Harcourt, Brace and Co., 1929), and J. Piaget, *The Child's Conception of Physical Causality* (New York: Harcourt, Brace and Co., 1930).
4. S. Bernfeld, "Zur Revision der Bioanalyse," *Imago*, XXIII (1937), 197–236.
5. Werner, *Comparative Psychology*.
6. Harry Harlow, "Thinking," *Theoretical Foundations of Psychology*, ed. H. Helson (New York: D. Van Nostrand Co., 1951), pp. 452–505.
7. F. Sander, "Structure, Totality of Experience, and Gestalt," *Psychologies of 1930*, ed. C. Murchison (Worcester, Mass.: Clark University Press, 1930), chap. x.
8. E. Brunswik, "Experimente über Kritik: Ein Beitrag zur Entwick-lungs-Psychologie des Denkens," *Bericht, XII Kongress für Psychologie*, ed. G. Kafka (Jena: Fischer, 1932).
9. Else Frenkel-Brunswik, "Psychoanalysis and the Unity of Science," *Proceedings of the American Academy of Arts and Sciences*, LXXX, No. 4 (1954).
10. J. Jastrow, ed., *The Story of Human Error* (New York: Appleton-Century, Inc., 1936).
11. G. Murphy, *Historical Introduction to Modern Psychology* (rev. ed.; New York: Harcourt, Brace and Co., 1949).
12. See Brunswik, "Experimente über Kritik."
13. W. Köhler, *Gestalt Psychology* (New York and London: H. Liveright, 1929).
14. P. Frank, "Foundations of Physics," *International Encyclopedia of Unified Science* (Chicago: University of Chicago Press), Vol. I, No. 7 (1946).
15. H. Feigl, "Logical Empiricism," *Readings in Philosophical Analysis*, ed. H. Feigl and W. Sellars (New York: Appleton-Century-Croft, Inc., 1949).
16. E. Brunswik, "The Conceptual Framework of Psychology," *International Encyclopedia of Unified Science* (Chicago: University of Chicago Press), Vol. I, No. 10 (1952).
17. Piaget, *Child's Conception of the World*; Piaget, *Child's Conception of Causality*.

18. M. Wertheimer, *Drei Abhandlungen zur Gestalt-theorie* (Erlangen: Philosophische Akademie, 1925).

19. J. Piaget and B. Inhelder, *Le développement des quantités chez l'enfant: Conservation et atomisme* (Neuchatel: Delachaux, 1941); J. Piaget and A. Szeminska, *Le genèse du nombre chez l'enfant* (Neuchatel: Delachaux, 1941).

20. E. Brunswik, *Wahrnehmung und Gegenstandswelt* (Leipzig and Vienna: Deuticke, 1934).

21. Werner, *Comparative Psychology*.

22. For a summary of some of the quantitative results see Charlotte Bühler, *Kindheit und Jugend* (3rd ed.; Leipzig: Hirzel, 1931).

23. P. Frank, *Modern Science and its Philosophy* (Cambridge, Mass.: Harvard University Press, 1949).

24. Brunswik, "Conceptual Framework of Psychology."

25. A. Willwoll, *Begriffsbildung: Eine psychologische Untersuchung* (Leipzig: Hirzel, 1926).

26. Frank, *Modern Science*.

27. S. C. Pepper, *World Hypotheses: A Study in Evidence* (Berkeley: University of California Press, 1948).

28. K. Lewin, "The Conflict Between Aristotelian and Galileian Modes of Thought in Contemporary Psychology," *Journal of General Psychology*, V (1931), 141–77; also in K. Lewin, *A Dynamic Theory of Personality* (New York: McGraw-Hill Book Co., 1935).

29. As Clyde Kluckhohn informs me (private communication), similar views are common among the Navajos.

30. Köhler, *Gestalt Psychology*.

31. Sander, "Structure, Totality of Experience, and Gestalt."

32. Brunswik, "Conceptual Framework of Psychology."

33. *Ibid.*, pp. 50 ff.

34. G. W. Allport, "The Psychologist's Frame of Reference," *Psychological Bulletin*, XXXVII (1940); 1–28; J. S. Bruner and G. W. Allport, "Fifty Years of Change in American Psychology," *ibid.*, pp. 757–76.

17

Historical and Thematic Relations of Psychology to Other Sciences [1956]

 COMMENT

The Emergence of Psychology as a Unique Science
Ray W. Cooksey

Brunswik's ideas regarding the convergence of history, theory, and method in psychology took concrete form and substance in the 1950s with the publication of his monograph *The Conceptual Framework of Psychology* in 1952. His monograph had a very rich texture and a density (some would say obscurity) to it that made its central ideas difficult to penetrate and understand (see the more detailed review and discussion of Brunswik's monograph, Chapter 12, this volume). After publication of the monograph, Brunswik appeared to focus his efforts on publicizing his ideas in a somewhat less concentrated and more digestible form. One such effort was a paper he presented to the Section of the History and Philosophy of Science at the Berkeley meeting of the American Association for the Advancement of Science in 1954. This paper was subsequently and posthumously published in *Scientific Monthly* in 1956 (Brunswik, 1956a).

Brunswik (1956a) sought to present, in a somewhat more transparent manner than was typical of him, a coherent discussion of the historical and thematic relationships he saw between psychology as a developing discipline of inquiry and other sciences. It was through this rigorous analysis that Brunswik highlighted the evolutionary path that psychology had taken from the earliest signs of its emergence as a science in the work of Fechner to its current (as of the 1950s) state as a science at the crossroads, divided as to theoretical focus and preferred methodological approach. Leary (1987) noted that Brunswik's historical analyses had their genesis over the decade leading up to the publication of his 1952 monograph and had formed the foundation of the history-of-psychology course that Brunswik taught. "Historical and Thematic Relations" condensed this analysis even further while opening it up for possible wider appreciation. Brunswik managed to keep the sweeping scope of his analysis intact in the 1956 paper while creating simpler visual representations and analytical discussions of what the analysis meant for psychology.

Brunswik stated his intentions in the 1956 paper clearly in his introduction and directly indicated the range of 'sciences' he wished to encompass in his analysis:

"In the light of a comparative science, psychology stands at the crossroads as perhaps none of the other disciplines does. I shall stress especially its relationships to the physical and biological sciences, including some of the relatively 'low-brow' cultural disciplines such as economics" (p. 286).

Brunswik's subsequent analysis developed four distinct yet interrelated themes. He traced, in Table 1 on page 152 of his paper (Table 17.1 here), the evolution of the focus of psychology from the early central emphasis established by physiology through the peripheral emphasis exemplified by the emerging nineteenth-century focus on reaction time as a dependent variable,

which anticipated the emergence of classical behaviorism, to the central-distal focus, which emphasized achievement in consideration of behavior from both stimulus and response perspectives.
An interesting methodological side effect of the
evolution of peripheralism, with its further evolution into the central-distal perspective, is the emphasis on correlation as the most appropriate
way of conceptualizing relations between behavioral events. Brunswik would place heavy emphasis on this conceptualization in other works where
he developed his lens model in the context of
probabilistic functionalism (e.g., Brunswik, 1952,
1955c).

Brunswik's second analytical theme in his 1956
paper focused on the struggle for unity between
psychology and its parent sciences with respect
to objectivity and theory construction, which created conflicting pressures with the quest for thematic diversity in the sciences (or, perhaps, disciplinary identity). His argument was illustrated in
Table 2 on page 154 of his paper (Table 17.2
here) using physics, sensory psychology, physiology, and personality psychology. On the surface,
his purpose appeared to be to illustrate how the
evolution of psychological concepts paralleled
those in other sciences. However, it seems equally
clear that he was sending a warning to the reader
about the dangers of going too far in such parallel
development:

"We must be on guard about excessive thematic
unity, especially if we are concerned with a
younger discipline [psychology] growing up in
the shadow of overwhelming parent sciences
[physics and physiology]. Formidable and even
grotesque examples of an excessive unity of a
highly uncritical kind can be brought forth from
ancient science. More or less arbitrary 'dichotomies' or other formalistic classification schemes
are combined to pervade an all-encompassing system" (p. 288).

The importance of Brunswik's message here cannot be overstated, and it underscores many of
the arguments he had made over the past three
decades. Psychology strove to be a "science" in
its own right but did so by modeling itself on its
parent disciplines. In doing so, it was hamstrung
in its quest for uniqueness of identity and method,
so that it was unable, as a discipline, to effectively
study the very phenomena it was interested in.
The echoes of this perspective were felt in Brunswik's arguments about the mindless adoption of
systematic experimental research design from the
agricultural sciences as the method to employ
when studying human behavior. Such direct
mimicry may have given psychologists access to
readily available tools for research and theorizing
but at the very dear cost of reducing the three-
dimensional, rich, and uneven texture of the jun-
gle of human existence to a two-dimensional,
uninteresting, and relatively barren desert.

In tracing the evolution of psychology as a
science, Brunswik (1956a) cited the thinking of
one of his contemporaries, Kurt Lewin:

Kurt Lewin . . . distinguished between Aristotelian
and Galileian modes of thought. . . . According to
Lewin, progress from the former to the latter
mode involves any or all of the following, partly
overlapping shifts: from dichotomy to gradations,
from qualitative appearance to quantitative reality, from subjective speculation to objectivism,
from classification to causation, from phenotype
to genotype, from static existence to dynamic
flow, from surface to depth, and from disjointed
description to the "nomothetic" search for laws.
(p. 290)

Brunswik's Table 3 (1956a, p. 156; Table 17.3
here) was intended to exemplify this evolution
by showing that the path from physics to astronomy to anatomy-physiology to biology to psychiatry to psychology, as evidenced by the work of
key focal individuals, provided clear signposts in
the shift from an Aristotelian mode of thinking
to a Galileian mode of thinking. This is a view
that Hammond (1978b, p. 14) was to mirror later
in his early presentations of cognitive continuum
theory, where Aristotelian thought was equated
with more intuitive modes of thought and Galileian thinking was equated with more analytical
modes of thinking. Brunswik further noted in his
historical analysis that the trends observed in the
evolution of psychology were beginning to be
seen in other social sciences as well: "We may
further remind ourselves of the fact that in the
social sciences—in many ways still younger than
psychology—elaborate dichotomous schemes are
still in vogue in some quarters right under our
eyes—for example in the work of Talcott Parsons" (p. 291). Brunswik was thus concerned that

the evolutionary path traced by psychology might be traced by other social sciences as well.

Although the message was somewhat complicated and distributed throughout Brunswik's paper, it seems that the fundamental statement Brunswik was making was that, having traveled down this historical evolutionary path, psychology had reached the critical stage where it needed to ask itself whether or not it had gone too far. For example, consider Brunswik's communication of his fundamental concern coupled with his thoughts regarding the nomothetic imperative associated with the shift toward Galileian thinking:

> At this point we must pause and take a look at the foundations of our discipline. There is nothing in the development of science that will inspire paralyzing awe and induce adolescent dependence as much as a headway in modes of conceptualization such as the natural sciences have been found to possess in relation to psychology. We must therefore be doubly on our guard against the intrusion of policies that are alien to our basic problems. In particular, we must ask ourselves whether the following of the nomothetic lead is an unmixed blessing for psychology. (p. 294)

Brunswik then laid out, in his Table 4 (p. 158; Table 17.4 here), what was probably his most interesting display of the historical tensions impacting on psychology. He said, in a prelude to his discussion of this display, that "psychology seems to drift toward a course halfway between factualism and nomotheticism—that is, toward probabilism" (p. 293). In Brunswik's interpretation, if one were to gather together the various, sometimes competing, strands of influence on modern psychology (functionalism and the environmental probabilism it implied, classical behaviorism, equifinality and thermodynamics from open systems theory, molar objectivism, correlational statistics juxtaposed with systematic ANOVA methods, input from other social disciplines such as biometrics, econometrics, engineering), one could project a path forward for a psychology that would look more like its own unique science and less like its natural science progenitors. This was the essence of Brunswik's message in his 1956 paper:

> Let us fall back on the thema of psychology as we have tried to develop it in analyzing the differences between physiology and physiological psy-

chology. We have conjectured that the emphasis on wide-spanning functional correlations at the expense of attention to the intervening technologic detail is one of the major characteristics that distinguishes psychology from its predecessors. . . . On further analysis, we note that the functional arcs that span toward, and gain their feedback from, the remote, "distal" environment—and these are the really important arcs—become entangled with the exigencies and risks inherent in the environment. So long as the organism does not develop, or fails in a given context to utilize completely, the powers of a full-fledged physicist observer and analyst; his environment remains for all practical purposes a semierratic medium; it is no more than partially controlled and no more than probabilistically predictable. The functional approach in psychology [Brunswik's "New Look" for psychology] must take cognizance of this basic limitation of the adjustive apparatus; it must link behavior and environment statistically in bivariate or multivariate correlation rather than with the predominant emphasis on strict laws which we have inherited from physics. (p. 294)

Brunswik concluded his paper with a review of his concept of representative design and the implications it carried for his perspective on where psychology should head as a science of probabilistic functionalism. He used this final development to hammer home his "warning against the uncritical transplantation of content-alien themas or instrumental scaffoldings, at least as long as we wish to prize and uphold our indigenous thematic identity above all else" (p. 295).

One could argue that, in his 1956 paper, Brunswik had at last found a comprehensible way to communicate at least some of his core ideas. His language, usually rich in texture and dense in content, had been pared back to some extent to allow the ideas to come forward without excessive interference from his typical linguistic complexity. Brunswik saw his ideas as the natural progression for psychology to follow if it was to move beyond the restrictive boundaries created for it by its own historical evolution:

> Representative design and the resultant probabilistic functionalism are nothing but the consistent projection of such a belief [that psychology was not a "fundamental discipline" in the sense of

the standard natural sciences] onto the plane of methodology and explicit theorizing. Since the statistical macroprobabilism of representative design would move psychology away from physics and other fundamental natural sciences with their nomothetic thema, considerable resistances must be expected along the way.

Our theoretical submissiveness to the physical sciences may be more readily overcome if we can show that the proposed reorientation would bring psychology closer to other, perhaps less glamorous but no less urgent or real, natural and social sciences [e.g., meteorology, economics, and communication theory] in which a macro-probabilism has long been recognized as a legitimate attitude. (pp. 295–296)

The above quote also shows that Brunswik knew he had set himself up for a very difficult uphill battle for acceptance of his ideas—a battle he did not win in his day, one where he severely underestimated the depth and completeness of

resistance that would be encountered. However, as Hammond (1996c) later showed, Brunswik's ideas have gained increasing acceptance over the decades since his death, and though the battle has not yet been won, several important skirmishes have at least been won within the focal discipline of the psychology of human judgment and decision making. The richness and interconnectedness of Brunswik's arguments and their implications for the influence of other "sciences" are reflected in current theoretical endeavors to embed the study of judgment and decision making into larger, more systemic frameworks where multivariate contextual determinants and influences remain entangled and problematic (see, for example, recent conceptual work by Brehmer, 1996; Cooksey, 1996a, 1996b, 2000; Hammond, 1996c; work reported in Part IIIA in the present volume; and, although typically not directly citing Brunswik's influence, the emergence of naturalistic decision-making perspectives and approaches in Zsambok & Klein, 1997).

 REPRINT

Historical and Thematic Relations of Psychology to Other Sciences
Egon Brunswik

Not quite a century has passed since experimental psychology began, in Gustav Theodor Fechner's treatise on the "psychophysics" of sensation in 1860, to emancipate itself as a science. The emancipation has taken place relative to the purely speculative approach of philosophy, on the one hand, and relative to the confinement to the human or animal body imposed within psychology's closest antecedent among the sciences, physiology, on the other. And not quite half of a century

Reprinted from *Scientific Monthly* (1956), 83, 151–161, copyright 1956, American Association for the Advancement of Science, reprinted with permission.

has elapsed since John B. Watson, in 1913, suggested that psychology abandon its original subjectivistic or introspectionistic concern with sensation and other data of consciousness and concentrate on the "behavior" of the organism as a physical body in a physical environment. Thus psychology was to be placed fully under the auspices of the methodologically most rigorous of its older sister disciplines, physics.

In the light of a comparative science, psychology stands at the crossroads as perhaps none of the other disciplines does. I shall stress especially its relationships to the physical and biological sciences, including some of the relatively "lowbrow" cultural disciplines such as economics.

From Physiology to Physiological Psychology

The emergence of what we may call the specific "thema" of psychology is best discussed by contrasting the physiological psychology of today with the physiology from which it has sprung. Some of the major physiological discoveries of the first half of the 19th century were more or less directly at the doorstep of psychology. Among these were the Bell-Magendie law, which asserts the structural and functional discreteness of the sensory and motor nerves, and the law of specific sense or nerve energies by Charles Bell, Johannes Müller, and Helmholtz, which recognizes the dependence of sensation on the receiving organism. Still another discovery, the establishment of the rate of nervous impulse by Müller and by Helmholtz, best represents the step-by-step tracing of internal processes which is so characteristic of physiology; this is symbolized by the straight line in diagram A of Table 17.1.

Compare this pattern with the counterpart of rate of nervous impulse in psychology proper, reaction time. The distinguishing characteristic of problems of this latter kind is the concentration on the over-all functional correlation of sensory input and motor output without primary concern for the details of the mediating process. This correlational peripheralism is described by the bridgelike arc in schema B of Table 17.1. In line with its gross, achievement-oriented character, the study of reaction time received its first impetus from difficulties with observational error in astronomy raised by Bessel in the 1820's; later it

became a favorite of Wilhelm Wundt, the founder of the first psychological laboratory at Leipzig in 1879, and of his American assistant, James McKeen Cattell, who applied it to his differential-psychological testing research at Columbia University.

The direct physical observability of both stimulus and response renders the study of reaction time a 19th century rudimentary anticipation of Watson's sensory-motor behaviorism and of Bekhterev's concurrent reflexology. More importantly, Fechner's psychophysics shared with the study of reaction time a relational rather than a process-centered emphasis. This was manifested in the famous Weber-Fechner law which expresses sensation as a direct mathematical function of the external stimulus. The fact that psychophysics is being considered almost unanimously the birth cry of psychology proper must be ascribed to this correlational feature.

Various conditioning and higher learning problems have recently been treated under the sensory-motor reflex schema by Skinner and others. Critics have bemoaned the fact that this approach, cutting short as it does from input to output, tends to bypass the brain; and the dean of historians of psychology, Edwin G. Boring, has criticized it as a "psychology of the empty organism" (1).

In the development of physiological psychology, the possibility of such an accusation is circumvented by the emergence of a third type of approach that at the same time does away with peripheralism in its various forms. It is described

TABLE 17.1 The emergence of physiological psychology from physiology

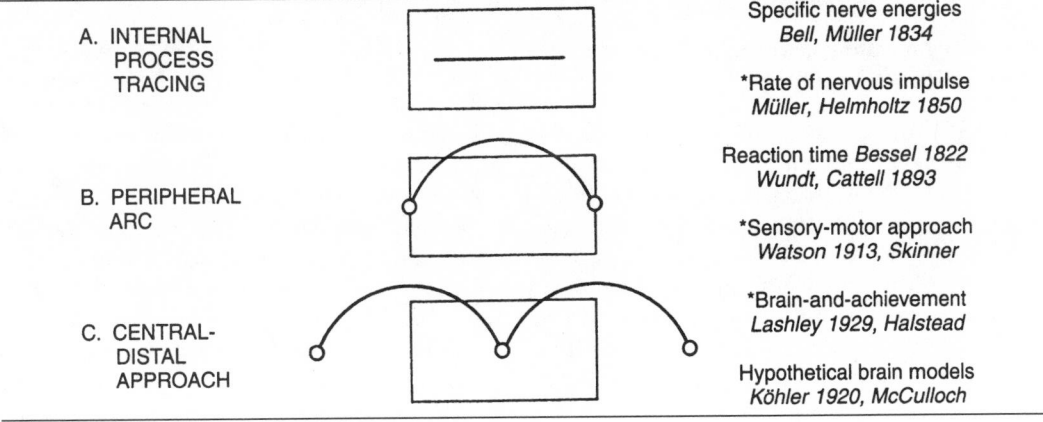

A. INTERNAL PROCESS TRACING		Specific nerve energies *Bell, Müller 1834* *Rate of nervous impulse *Müller, Helmholtz 1850*
B. PERIPHERAL ARC		Reaction time *Bessel 1822* *Wundt, Cattell 1893* *Sensory-motor approach *Watson 1913, Skinner*
C. CENTRAL-DISTAL APPROACH		*Brain-and-achievement *Lashley 1929, Halstead* Hypothetical brain models *Köhler 1920, McCulloch*

in Table 17.1 under diagram C. Occurrences in the brain—that is, "central" factors—are directly correlated with relatively remote, or "distal," results of behavior ("achievements"), such as the reaching of the end of mazes of varying intricacy by a rat (right arc; the arc to the left is shown to indicate that abstraction and related cognitive extrapolations into the causal ancestry of the stimulus impact are inseparably intertwined with all brain-and-achievement studies).

Foreshadowed by Gall's notorious "phrenology" in the early 19th century and by Flourens' pioneering of brain extirpation experiments soon thereafter, the central-distal approach reached its full scope in the brain-lesion study in rats by Lashley in 1929 (2). The same year brought Berger's report on brain waves and thus the beginning of electroencephalography with its wide use in modern psychiatry. More recently, Halstead has applied the statistical tool of factor analysis to the study of brain and intelligence at the human level (3). In contrast, the 1860's and 1870's witnessed the peripheralistically conceived brain-localization studies of Broca and of Fritsch and Hitzig in which the more narrowly sensory or motor aspects were stressed at the expense of organization and integration.

Of considerably shorter history than the empirical brain-and-achievement studies are the largely hypothetical studies of the brain which began with Köhler's theory of dynamic brain fields or "physical Gestalten" in 1920 (4). While the Gestalt-psychological approach is more purely central rather than genuinely central-distal, the distal, adjustmental aspects have come to share the limelight in the study of "teleological mechanisms" by McCulloch and other cyberneticists (5).

Psychology and the Ancient Speculative Unity of Science

One of the most prominent problems of a comparative science of science is that of the unity of the sciences (6). Most scientists agree that there must be unity with respect to the objectivity of both observation and the procedural aspects of theory construction. Physiological psychology and the school of behaviorism are primarily dedicated to the unification of psychology with the natural sciences along these lines. Equally important as the procedural unification is the thematic diversi-

fication of the sciences, however. I have therefore made it a point to begin these considerations with an example of such diversification of psychology from a neighboring discipline.

Close inspection shows (6) that considerable inhibitions stemming from vested intellectual interests must be overcome to achieve such differentiation among the sciences. We must be on guard against excessive thematic unity, especially if we are concerned with a younger discipline growing up in the shadow of overwhelming parent sciences.

Formidable and even grotesque examples of an excessive unity of a highly uncritical kind can be brought forth from ancient science. More or less arbitrary "dichotomies" or other formalistic classification schemes are combined to pervade an all-encompassing system. An example involving the psychology both of sensation and of personality along with physics and physiology is presented in Table 17.2. For the most part, the schema is based on the pre-Socratic cosmology of Empedocles and on the humoral doctrine of four temperaments of Hippocrates and Galen; the last two columns are relatively modern elaborations (7). The original dichotomies are developed into quadripartite systems either by doubling or by compounding so that a modicum of differentiation is achieved.

From the systematic point of view, two features must be especially emphasized in connection with Table 17.2. One is the arbitrariness of classification as revealed most drastically by the presence of alternative sets of columns for the same subject matter—for example a double dichotomy and a partly conflicting compound dichotomy for the sensory qualities. We may add that another of the pre-Socratics, Anaximander, chose air to be cold rather than dry.)

The other feature noteworthy in Table 17.2 is the apparent ease of transfer of four-ness from one area to another in the manner of an absolute one-to-one correspondence. Different areas of knowledge, capable of independent approach, are thus thrown together indiscriminately by means of vague analogy: this is comparable to what such child psychologists as Piaget or Heinz Werner have described as syncretic or diffuse modes of thought (8).

More specifically, Gestalt psychologists have criticized the ready assumption of a strict correspondence between physical stimuli and sensory

TABLE 17.2 Simple and compound dichotomies and a resultant pervasive system of corresponding quadripartite schemes in ancient physics and physiology and in personality psychology

Physics	Sensory psychology		Physiology	Personality psychology			
	Dichotomies of qualities (Alternatives:)					Temperaments and their behavioral aspects	Compound dichotomies (Alternatives:)
Cosmic elements	Double	Compound	Humors			Emotional response	Affective tone
(a)	(b)	(c)	(d)	(e)	(f)	(g)	(h)
Air	Dry	Warm-Moist	Blood	Sanguine	Hopeful	Weak-Quick	Pleasant-Excited
Earth	Cold	Cold-Dry	Black bile (Spleen)	Melancholic	Sad	Strong-Slow	Unpleasant-Calm
Fire	Warm	Warm-Dry	Yellow bile	Choleric	Irascible	Strong-Quick	Unpleasant-Excited
Water	Moist	Cold Moist	Phlegm (Mucus)	Phlegmatic	Apathetic	Weak-Slow	Pleasant-Calm

qualities as an undue "constancy hypothesis." It is in this surreptitious manner that physics and sensory psychology (Table 17.2, columns *a* to *c*) become symmetrical and thus in effect merge into one. It is even difficult to reconstruct which of the two areas of knowledge has the observational primacy over the other, although it is evident that there is a good deal of give and take.

In philosophy, it is easily seen that the implied operational indistinguishability of matter and mind (in this case, sensation) constitutes, or at least reinforces, naive realism; or else, by way of the horizontal dichotomy between columns, it helps to put dualism on an absolute basis. Once the constancy hypothesis of the coordination of the two realms has given rise to the accusation of "unnecessary duplication" (as in Occam's razor), this dualism in turn readily changes into either materialistic or idealistic monism. The regularity and symmetry which result from easy transfer and carry with them the flavor of Pythagorean number mystics may be criticized on the same grounds of subjectivism on which Schopenhauer criticized Kant's compulsive filling of all the plots in his 3×4 table of categories.

(In experimental psychology, the adoption of the constancy hypothesis in its radical form would lead to the obliteration of the stimulus-response problem of psychophysics which, as we have seen, lies at the roots of modern psychology; it would even lead to the at least theoretical impossibility of acknowledging any kind of illusion—as it has come close to doing in Locke's doctrine of primary qualities, such as size, shape or motion.)

Both the arbitrariness and the easy transfer that characterize early stages of science are further revealed in the fact that some systems are not dichotomous or fourfold but three-, five-, or sevenfold. In his capacity as a psychologist, Plato distinguished three major faculties (reason, emotion, and desire, the latter including the lowly sensation); he localized them in a corresponding hierarchy of physiological centers (brain, heart, and liver or "phren"—that is, diaphragm); and he further distinguished three corresponding sociopolitical personality types (philosopher, warrior, and worker. The ancient Chinese favored a fivefold scheme. In the doctrine of cosmic elements, the air of the Greeks is replaced by metal, and wood is added as a fifth element; the scheme is syncretically generalized to five tastes, five intestines, five sentiments, five poisons, five planets, five dynasties, and so forth (9). The relative merits of the various base numbers are not discussed here, although it may be granted that some of them are not without a realistic basis in certain limited areas (such as two-ness for sex, three-ness for man between input and output or the healthy medium between extremes, and so forth).

Relative Level of Maturity of Psychology

As has been noted in passing, the most distinctly psychological aspects of the doctrine of four temperaments have outlasted their counterparts in physics and physiology by centuries if not millenniums. Furthermore, this doctrine has flourished in much greater variety and thus is fraught with more ambiguity than its long-vanished correspondents in the natural sciences. Columns *g* and *h* of Table 17.2 show only two of the kinds of compound dichotomies usually suggested, both conceived in the Wundtian three-dimensional theory of emotion; Herbart used a combination of strong-weak and pleasant-unpleasant instead. There are at least 16 major thinkers who expended their efforts on the four temperaments in a feast of arbitrary classification. Among the persons concerned were Kant and such serious experimental psychologists of the past as Ribot, Külpe, Ebbinghaus, Höffding, and Meumann; on the contemporary scene we find the well-known German typologist, Ludwig Klages (7). This suggests that the relative youth of psychology is matched, at least in the personality area concerned, by a backwardness in its categorial structure, or "modes of thought."

In investigating the question of the relative maturity of psychology further, we note that dichotomizing and related forms of absolute classification, as well as their formalistic-syncretic transfer to other areas, are but two of several aspects of a broader prescientific syndrome. Auguste Comte put his finger on this syndrome in his distinction between what he called the metaphysical and the positive stages of science; with an eye on the special situation in psychology, Kurt Lewin, somewhat similarly, distinguished between Aristotelian and Galileian modes of thought (10). According to Lewin, progress from the former to the latter mode involves any or all of the following, partly overlapping shifts: from dichotomies to gradations, from qualitative appearance to quantitative reality, from subjective speculation to objectivism, from classification to causation, from phenotype to genotype, from static existence to dynamic flow, from surface to depth, and from disjointed description to the "nomothetic" search for laws.

We may try to assess the standing of psychology among the sciences by listing a few of the most crucial shifts in these respects (Table 17.3). Perhaps the earliest shift from phenotypical quality to genotypical quantity concerns physics. From Empedocles' qualitatively conceived fourfold scheme mentioned in a previous paragraph, the doctrine of elements moved on toward an essentially modern conception of physical reality in Democritus' atomic theory that stressed shape and size instead of sensation. This theory is far from free of subjective speculation or contamination by direct perceptual appearances (especially "synesthesia" from the tactile-kinesthetic sphere), to be sure, but the step from surface to underlying reality and from dichotomy to gradation is taken at least in intent. The step from perceptual appearances to an indirect, abstract construction of a much more dynamically conceived reality was next made in astronomy with the shift from the perceptually dominated geocentric to the nomothetically more economical Copernican system.

The biological sciences followed with the shift from static anatomy to dynamic physiology as epitomized by Harvey's discovery of the circulation of the blood, and with the shift from Linnaeus' phenotypical taxonomy to Darwin's genotypical evolutionary classification in botany and zoology. Transitions between dichotomizing and gradations also occurred—for example, when in the Middle Ages the four humors were ranked according to their "degree" of aliveness (11).

Confirming our suspicion, we note that corresponding steps in the psychological disciplines follow much later, mostly within the memory of ourselves or of our immediate elders. In psychiatry, there is a tradition of static description and cataloging which began in the early 17th century with Robert Burton's revealingly titled *Anatomy of Melancholy*, which continued with Pinel—the man who freed the insane from prison during the French revolution—and was still in evidence in Kraepelin until it was broken by Freud's "depth-psychological" revision of psychiatric classification, notably in the doctrine of neurosis. In psychology proper, there is the shift from Wundt's and Titchener's so-called "existential" inventory

TABLE 17.3 Shift in modes of classification and outlook from the subjective-qualitative-phenotypical-static ("Aristotelian") to the objective-quantitative-genotypical-dynamic ("Galileian") syndrome

Physics (Elements)	Astronomy	Anatomy-Physiology	Biology	Psychiatry	Psychology
Empedocles 5th B.C. ↓					
Democritus 4th B.C.	Ptolemy 2d A.D. ↓				
	Copernicus 1530	Vesalius 1543 ↓			
		Harvey 1628			
			Linnaeus 1738 ↓		
			Darwin 1859	Kraepelin 1883 ↓	
				Freud 1900	
					Titchener 1901 ↓
					Lewin 1935

and description of sensory experiences to Lewin's more dispositionally conceived notions of the internal psychological "field." Instead of Lewin, I might have mentioned some of his older Gestalt-phychological colleagues, notably Wertheimer and Köhler. Beginning in the 1910's, these workers set out to work on the intrinsic central dynamics of perception, and of thinking and problem solving; by virtue of their introspectionistic orientation, they are more comparable to Wundt and Titchener than to the more behaviorally oriented Lewin. Indeed, the simile has sometimes been used that while Titchener tried to dissect consciousness analytically like an anatomist, and his "sensations" thus are no better than a carcass of experience, the gestaltists with their "phenomenology" are more like physiologists in that they keep consciousness alive while studying it.

As in all structural interpretations of history, a table of examples can be no substitute for full documentation. Indeed, Hippocrates' humoral underpinning of the doctrine of temperaments may be set parallel to Democritus' geometric underpinning of the elements and offered as demonstration of the fact that at least part of psychology showed objectivistic intent as early as did physics. Yet humoral doctrine is physiology, not psychology; nor would the fact that much of ancient psychology was behavioristic from the outset change our impression that, in the handling of the

actual problems in the area, relatively primitive patterns of thought were the rule. I have already mentioned in discussing Table 17.2 that syncretic dichotomizing persists much longer and flourishes more abundantly in the psychological doctrine of the four temperaments than it does in the corresponding doctrines of the four physical elements or of the four physicological humors. We may further remind ourselves of the fact that in the social sciences—in many ways still younger than psychology—elaborate dichotomous schemes are still in vogue in some quarters right under our eyes—for example, in the work of Talcott Parsons.

Dependence of Psychology on the Natural Sciences

Next we turn to more direct cross-disciplinary comparisons that involve historical phase differences with respect to comparable categories and in which psychology appears at the receiving end. For chronologically arranged evidence, we may turn to Table 17.4. This table concentrates on the experimental and differential-psychological developments that constitute the core of modern psychology; developments in physiological and abnormal psychology which are incorporated in some of the preceding tables have been played

TABLE 17.4 Scientific background and cross-disciplinary relations of psychology with special emphasis on general systematic isomorphisms and on methodology

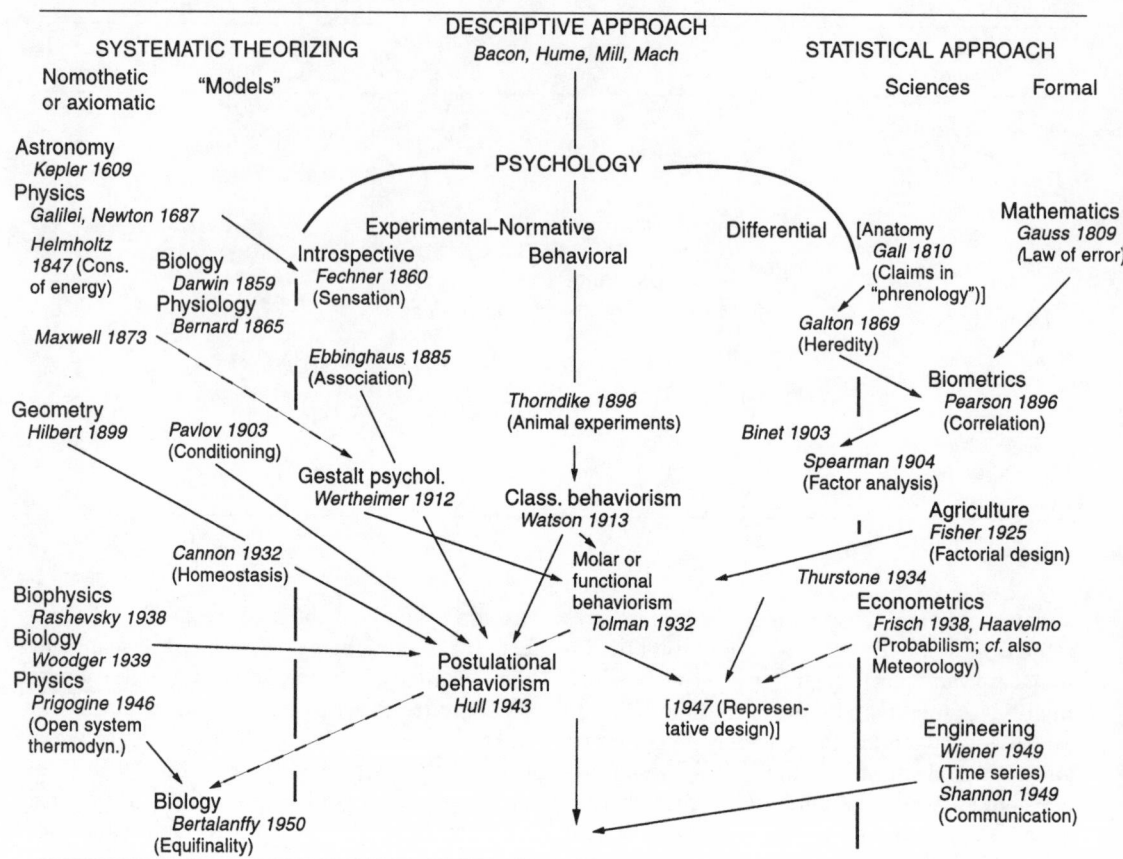

down or omitted. Special emphasis is given to conceptual outlook and methodology.

Our first consideration concerns the law-stating or nomothetic approach; it is traced at the left side of the table. While the actual establishment of natural law as it has been able to stand the test of time was brought about in astronomy and physics during the 17th century, psychology had to wait until Fechner (1860) for the beginnings of the experimental-nomothetic treatment of sensation, and until Ebbinghaus (1885) for that of memory by association. Solid arrows indicating these cross-disciplinary infusions generally point downward in a telltale manner in the respective parts of the table. Thus axiomatization, or more generally what Feigl called higher-order theory (12), was brought about in physics by Newton; much less impressive attempts in psychology—

further preceded and indeed prompted by Hilbert's axiomatization of geometry and by Woodger's efforts toward an axiomatization of biology (as his contribution to the *International Encyclopedia of Unified Science*)—had to wait until the work of Hull and his associates in the 1940's (13). A perusal of the writings of such nomothetically oriented psychologists as hull or Lewin reveals that the ostensible classic among physical laws, the law of falling bodies, is invoked as an exemplar with almost monotonous regularity.

The nomothetic ideal is paramount not only in the classical phase of experimental psychology in the 19th century and in the recent postulational behaviorism of Hull but also in Gestalt psychology and in the physiological theory of Gestalt referred to earlier in this article. Frequent reference to "dynamics" in a brain "field" suggests analogies to Maxwell's electromagnetic field theory. Warnings, pointing out that gravitation also acts in a field, have been sounded against pressing this analogy; a broken, rather than solid, arrow has therefore been used in Table 17.4. The fact remains, however, that the revolutionary element in Gestalt psychology is the breaking away from elementism and associationism and that the "machinelike" models to which these conceptions can be traced largely originated in classical mechanics. In addition, the coexistence of associationistic and of field-dynamic principles in modern psychological theory in certain ways resembles the duality of gravitation and electromagnetism of which modern physics has so long been tolerant.

The 20-odd years about the turn of the century were a particularly turbulent phase in the development of psychology—so much so that Karl Bühler has spoken of them as the constructive crisis of psychology (14). Gestalt psychology and classical behaviorism are but two especially clear-cut of at least four new psychological movements that sprang up in that period.

Another of these new movements is psychoanalysis. It shares with Gestalt psychology the insistence on the finding of regularities of a more complex scope. Freud, who had a distinguished active career in physiology prior to developing his dynamic theory of personality was, as was documented by Siegfried Bernfeld (15), strongly influenced by the physical thinking of his time. He was strongly influenced by Helmholtz' principle of conservation of energy in developing his basic models. As was further demonstrated by Else Frenkel-Brunswik at the joint symposium of the AAAS with the Institute for the Unity of Science in Boston in 1954 (16), Freud had a keen sense of the basic requirements of the philosophy of science, popular belief to the contrary notwithstanding.

In Watson's classical behaviorism, we note that its primary concern was the fulfillment of the physicalistic ideal of observational precision. In the American psychology of this period, the desire for fact-finding and the fear of the dangers of speculation temporarily took precedence over the nomothetic aim and led to a form of descriptive empiricism or factualism that had the earmarks of Bacon's "simple enumeration" or of the early antitheoretical positivism of Comte or Mach. In stressing fact more than law, the prime urgency of the "general" was challenged in favor of the "particular," and thus a first inroad was made on the nomothetic ideal of science insofar as it concerns psychology. As I will try to show in the next section, psychology seems to drift toward a course halfway between factualism and nomotheticism—that is, toward probabilism.

Two lines of development issue from classical behaviorism. One is the formalized, nomothetic behaviorism of Hull and his associates at Yale which I have already mentioned. The other and more radical departure is the "purposive" behaviorism of Edward C. Tolman at the University of California (17). It is best introduced by first referring to the fourth of the major crisis schools, frequently called American functionalism. Historically, this school precedes, parallels, and is about to outlive classical behaviorism. Under the influence of Darwin and other evolutionists, functionalism is characterized mainly by an emphasis on the readjustive value of behavior in coming to terms with the physical or social environment. An early representative was Thorndike with his problem-solving experiments with animals and his "trial-and-error" principle. In contrast to frequency of repetition, which played such a large part in the nonsense syllable experiments of Ebbinghaus and the "conditioning" experiments of the Russian physiologist, Pavlov, Thorndike stressed the importance of success and reward in learning ("law of effect").

Tolman's purposive behaviorism combines the constructive elements of classical behaviorism with those of functionalism and of Gestalt psychology in a program of animal and human experimentation and theory that is both "objective" and "molar." Its redefinition of purpose is operational, stressing the reaching of common end-stages from a set of differing initial or mediating stages. Thus it is not less or more "teleological" in the objectionable, vitalistic sense than Wiener's and McCulloch's cybernetics.

Convergence with a further type of influence from systematic theorizing in the physical sciences may develop if von Bertalanffy's attempted reduction of biological "equifinality," and thus of purposive behavior, to Prigogine's new open-system thermodynamics (18) should obtain the approval of physicists and biologists. It is one of the intrinsic limitations of high-complexity disciplines such as psychology that final judgment of reductive theory of this kind must remain outside his province. Since the verdict of history is not yet in, I have bracketed these developments in Table 17.4.

Claude Bernard's and Cannon's ideas on homeostasis have received increased attention in functional psychology, and Ashby has used them in his *Design for a Brain* (19). Ashby's book is part of a current vogue in brain models which has developed out of the earlier examples I have mentioned in connection with physiological psychology and which has recently received a further impetus from the interest in the engineering problems of complex calculating machines. With a more distinctly nomothetic slant, Rashevsky and his associates at the University of Chicago (20) have produced biophysical mathematical models that promise to be fruitful up to the level of social psychology and perhaps even in history.

Much of the work just mentioned, notably that on homeostasis and mathematical biophysics, proceeds under the assumption of a widespread isomorphy among outwardly diverse types of processes. Von Bertalanffy has therefore suggested the concerted development of a "general systems theory" (21). Such a theory could achieve a great deal toward the unification of the sciences under the auspices of the nomothetic-reductive approach that is so closely associated with the history of the natural sciences.

Diversification of Psychology as a Probabilistic Science

At this point we must pause and take a look at the foundations of our discipline. There is nothing in the development of science that will inspire paralyzing awe and induce adolescent dependence as much as will a headway in modes of conceptualization such as the natural sciences have been found to possess in relation to psychology. We must therefore be doubly on our guard against the intrusion of policies that are alien to our basic problems. In particular, we must ask ourselves whether the following of the nomothetic lead is an unmixed blessing for psychology.

Let us fall back on the thema of psychology as we have tried to develop it in analyzing the differences between physiology and physiological psychology. We have conjectured that the em-

phasis on wide-spanning functional correlations at the expense of attention to the intervening technologic detail is one of the major characteristics that distinguishes psychology from its predecessors (diagram C of Table 17.1). Tolman's molar behaviorism, and parallel developments in the study of perceptual "thing-constancy," can be shown to fall in essentially the same pattern, the fact notwithstanding that the focus in the central region remains hypothetical (6, 22).

On further analysis, we note that the functional arcs that span toward, and gain their feedback from, the remote, "distal" environment — and these are the really important arcs — become entangled with the exigencies and risks inherent in the environment. So long as the organism does not develop, or fails in a given context to utilize completely, the powers of a full-fledged physicist observer and analyst, his environment remains for all practical purposes a semierratic medium; it is no more than partially controlled and no more than probabilistically predictable. The functional approach in psychology must take cognizance of this basic limitation of the adjustive apparatus; it must link behavior and environment statistically in bivariate or multivariate correlation rather than with the predominant emphasis on strict law which we have inherited from physics.

It is perhaps more accurate to say that the nomothetic ideology was influenced by a somewhat naive and outdated high-school-type, thematic, cliché of physics which some of us have tacitly carried with us in the process of developing psychology into a science. As need not be reiterated here, physics itself has become statistical in the meantime. Yet we must not fall for easy analogy; we must make it clear that the statistical underpinning which experimental physics has received in statistical mechanics and quantum theory, being of a microscopic character, has little to do with the probabilism of functional psychology. Since the individual case or instance does not lose its identity in psychology, our form of probabilism is macroscopic rather than microscopic and thus of much greater consequence in the actual execution of our discipline.

The use of bivariate correlation statistics is most obviously inevitable in the study of individual differences. In reality, the two have developed in close contact with one another; I have therefore grouped them together on the right side of Table 4 rather than placing the statistical approach where it belongs—that is, halfway between the nomothetic and the purely fact-descriptive approach.

As long as correlation statistics was not available, problems of differential psychology were treated with an air of absoluteness that reminds one of the nomothetic approach. One of the most grotesque products of this would-be type of correlational study was the so-called "phrenology" of the anatomist, Gall, who tried to link mental faculties to the shape of the skull on the basis of the most casuistic evidence.

Psychology has from its beginnings been intertwined with statistics and its active development in a variety of ways. Classical psychophysics is closely linked to the study of unidimensional error distribution and thus to Laplace and Gauss, notably in such American psychophysicists as James McKeen Cattell. Bivariate correlation statistics was first introduced by Galton and Pearson and may even be considered to be a direct joint product of biometrics and psychometrics. The factor analysis of Spearman, of Thurstone, and of others is even more a distinctly differential-psychological development. Because of the partly mathematical character of most of these developments, I have placed them somewhere between differential psychology and formal statistics in Table 17.4. For the first time in this analysis, we witness a give-and-take between psychology and other disciplines (as brought out by the zig-zag course of arrows in the table); we may take this as an added omen of the inherently statistical character of psychology as a whole, briefly deduced in a preceding paragraph.

While statistical correlation and factoring, including the attendant representative sampling of individuals from a population, have traditionally been recognized as necessary in the area of individual differences as they occur in intelligence or personality testing, the possibility of studying the broader functional organism-environment relationships by these statistical methods has long been ignored. In certain essential respects, this even holds true for R. A. Fisher's factorial design and analysis of variance (23). The variables and their levels of strength are still arbitrarily selected rather than naturally samples; hence the results are subject to severe limitations of generalizability. By allowing multivariate analysis, however, Fisher's methods are definitely superior to the older univariate designs, especially in the study

of problems of higher complexity. It is therefore not astonishing that their first transfer from their original domain, agriculture, to psychology (24) fell within the framework of Tolman's molar-functional study of behavior; their use has since rapidly expanded over wide areas of experimental psychology.

To obviate the intrinsic shortcomings of the artificial, "systematic" designs of which factorial design is but an elaborate case, I have advocated that in psychological research not only individuals be representatively sampled from well-defined "populations" but also stimulus situations from well-defined natural-cultural "ecologies" (25); only by such "representative design" of experiments can the ecological generalizability of functional regularities of behavior and adaptation be ascertained. Representative sampling of situations from the ecology allows us to take cognizance of the occasional major failures that result from the fallibility of perceptual cues or behavioral means while at the same time fully recognizing the favorable cases also. Generalization of the achieved degree of success to the ecology as a whole becomes possible with the use of the routine technical criteria for sampling statistics hitherto confined to differential psychology. Since representative design has so far been used only in a limited set of contexts, it has been bracketed in Table 17.4.

As was pointed out by Hammond (26), certain parallels can be drawn between the situation created in psychology in representative design and the situation created in physics by relativity theory. In both cases, an earlier overgeneralization of classical results obtained within a limited type of universe is corrected. As has been pointed out by Hammond in a different context, factorial design is geared to the manufacturing type of problem situation that prevails in agriculture, while the organically developed natural-cultural range of generalization to which psychology must aspire demands other methods. As in the example from antiquity which was discussed in the second section, we are faced with a warning against the uncritical transplantation of content-alien themas or instrumental scaffoldings, at least as long as we wish to prize and uphold our indigenous thematic identity above all else.

Perhaps the first to see that psychology was not a "fundamental" discipline in the sense of the standard natural sciences was the Columbia psychologist, Woodworth (27). Representative design and the resultant probabilistic functionalism are nothing but the consistent projection of such a belief onto the plane of methodology and explicit theorizing. Since the statistical macroprobabilism of representative design would move psychology away from physics and other fundamental natural sciences with their nomothetic thema, considerable resistances must be expected along the way (28).

Our thematic submissiveness to the physical sciences may be more readily overcome if we can show that the proposed reorientation would bring psychology closer to other, perhaps less glamorous but no less urgent or real, natural and social sciences in which macroprobabilism has long been recognized as a legitimate attitude. Prominent among these admittedly and recognizably statistical disciplines are meteorology (29) and economics insofar as they use autocorrelation and intercorrelation, as theoretically stressed especially by Wiener (30), for probability prediction. Economics deserves special attention in view of the reinforcement which the statistical conception has received in the Norwegian school of econometrics, notably by Haavelmo (31). Within still another discipline, communication theory—as cast into mathematical form by Claude Shannon, with psychologically cogent commentary by Warren Weaver (32)—the study of message transmission through semierratic external media comes very close to the psychological problem of the anticipation of, and adjustment to, a distant world. Communication and psychological functioning also have in common the use of redundancy as a means of overcoming the low predictive probability of single signals of these instrumentalities (6, chapt. 2. and sect. 23). In probabilistic functionalism, this low predictive probability finds its counterpart in the limited "ecological validity" of cues or means, and the place of redundancy is taken by the intersubstitutability or "vicarious functioning."

Conclusion

The growing strength of behaviorism has long assured that the core of a procedural physicalism and thus of the essential operational aspects of the unity of science are rapidly becoming a matter of course in psychology. The time has come when unity of science is best served by stressing the thematic differentiation among the sciences within the over-all unity. In carrying this diversification to its logical conclusion, psychology emerges as a macrostatistical discipline, thus acquiring not only distinct thematic identity but also internal methodological unity. The acceptance of this probabilistic functionalism and of the attendant representative design of research may be facilitated, both inside and outside psychology, by a comparative methodology involving sciences of all shadings. The best way to emancipate psychology from the suggestive power of those nomothetic-reductionist natural sciences in the shadow of which it began its development is to demonstrate its structural affinity with disciplines already recognized as statistical on character.

REFERENCES

1. E. G. Boring, *History of Experimental Psychology* (Appleton-Century-Crofts, New York, ed. 2, 1950). This standard work should also be consulted for sources mentioned but not cited in full in this paper. For contributions to psychology outside of experimental psychology see G. Murphy, *Historical Introduction to Modern Psychology* (Harcourt-Brace, New York, rev. ed., 1949).
2. K. S. Lashley, *Brain Mechanisms and Intelligence* (Univ. of Chicago Press, Chicago, 1929).
3. W. C. Halstead, *Brain and Intelligence* (Univ. of Chicago Press, Chicago, 1947).
4. For a brief recent summary, see W. Köhler, *Sci. Monthly* **80**, 29 (1955).
5. "Teleological mechanisms," *Ann. N. Y. Acad. Sci.* **50**, No. 4 (1948).
6. E. Brunswik, *The Conceptual Framework of Psychology* (Univ. of Chicago Press, Chicago, 1952).
7. For further discussion and sources, see G. W. Allport, *Personality* (Holt, New York, 1937), pp. 63ff.
8. For a recent summary, see M. Scheerer, "Cognitive theory," in *Handbook of Social Psychology*, G. Lindzey. Ed. (Addison-Wesley, New York, 1954), vol. 1, pp. 91–142.
9. A. Forke, *The World Conception of the Chinese* (Probsthain, London, 1925).
10. K. Lewin, *Dynamic Theory of Personality* (McGraw-Hill, New York, 1935), pp. 1–42.
11. C. D. Leake, personal communication.
12. H. Feigl, "Some remarks on the meaning of scientific explanation," in *Readings in Philosophi-*

cal Analysis, H. Feigl and W. Sellars, Eds. (Appleton-Century-Crofts, New York, 1949), pp. 510–514.

13. C. L. Hull *et al.*, *Mathematico-Deductive Theory of Rote Learning* (Yale Univ. Press, New Haven, Conn., 1940); C. L. Hull, *Principles of Behavior* (Appleton-Century, New York, 1943).

14. K. Bühler, *Die Krise der Psychologie* (Fischer, Jena, ed. 2, 1929).

15. S. Bernfeld, *Psycholanalytic Quart.* **13**, 341 (1944).

16. E. Frenkel-Brunswik, *Sci. Monthly* **79**, 293 (1954). For a more extensive presentation, see the same author's "Psychoanalysis and the unity of science," published jointly with the Institute for the Unity of Science in the *Proc. Am. Acad. Arts and Sci.* **80**, No. 4 (1954).

17. E. C. Tolman, *Purposive Behavior in Animals and Men* (Century, New York, 1932).

18. L. von Bertalanffy, *Science* **111**, 23 (1950).

19. W. R. Ashby, *Design for a Brain* (Wiley, New York, 1952).

20. N. Rashevsky, *Mathematical Biophysics* (Univ. of Chicago Press, Chicago, rev. ed., 1948).

21. See the symposium on general systems theory, with von Bertalanffy, Hempel and others participating, in *Human Biology* **23**, 302 (1951).

22. E. C. Tolman and E. Brunswik, *Psychol. Rev.* **42**, 43 (1935).

23. R. A. Fisher, *Design of Experiments* (Oliver and Boyd, Edinburgh, Scotland, 1935).

24. R. S. Crutchfield and E. C. Tolman, *Psychol. Rev.* **47**, 38 (1940).

25. E. Burnswik, "Systematic and representative design of psychological experiments," *Univ. of California Syllabus Ser. No.* 304 (1947); also in *Berkeley Symposium on Mathematical Statistics and Probability*, J. Neyman, Ed. (Univ. of California Press, Berkeley, 1949), pp. 143–202.

26. K. R. Hammond, *Phil. Sci.* **18**, 208 (1951); *Psychol. Bull.* **51**, 150 (1954).

27. R. S. Woodworth, *Dynamic Psychology* (Columbia Univ. Press, New York, 1918).

28. A recent symposium in which I defended my views against such advocates of the nomothetic-reductionist point of view in psychology as L. Postman, E. R. Hilgard, D. Krech, and H. Feigl has been published in *Psychol. Rev.* (1955).

29. For an outline of statistical procedures in meteorology, see H. R. Byers, *General Meteorology* (McGraw-Hill, New York, 1944), pp. 486ff.

30. N. Weiner, *Extrapolation, Interpolation, and Smoothing of Stationary Time Series* (Wiley, New York, 1949).

31. T. Haavelmo, "Probability approach in econometrics," *Econometrica*, Suppl. (1944).

32. C. E. Shannon and W. Weaver, *Mathematical Theory of Communication* (Univ. of Illinois Press, Urbana, 1949).

18

Scope and Aspects of the Cognitive Problem [1957]

COMMENT
Last Words
Kenneth R. Hammond

One of the first conferences directly focused on cognition in the twentieth century was held at the University of Colorado in 1955. Brunswik, together with J. Bruner, Leon Festinger, Fritz Heider, Charles Osgood, and Amnon Rappoport, was invited to present a paper. It was to be his final effort and possibly spurred by his sense that his life was drawing to a close, possibly spurred by his high regard for his fellow participants, in this paper he made a strong effort to make the whole of his life's work intelligible to his peers. Whatever the cause, Brunswik was eloquent. Broad-ranging in his ideas, and deft in his historical and contemporary exposition of them, he was at his best. As a result, this chapter not only offers an excellent representation of Brunswik's final theoretical views but also illustrates their significance for the future.

Because he was ill and could not attend the conference, he asked me to read his paper to the audience. Whether he had premonitions or plans at this time about his not-far-off suicide is an unanswerable question. But there is no doubt that what we see in the first several paragraphs of this paper is an articulate statement of what he believed to be the task of psychology and his program of research for the achievement of the goals of that psychology. In his first sentence he put forward a definition of psychology as being "concerned with the interrelationships between organism and environment." This is a more-or-less trite as well as standard definition and, because it is so abstract, it is more-or-less ignored. But Brunswik took abstractions seriously and wouldn't let us ignore it, for in the second sentence he reminded us that "in this definition both organism and environment appear as equal partners" (p. 300), a fact that few psychologists have acknowledged and none have explicated. Explication of that fact had long constituted his life's work; it became his goal to urge psychologists to take that equality seriously, and that, he would argue, means developing a theory of the environment as well as a theory of the organism. Time and again, he would point out that whereas psychologists have developed countless theories about the organism, they have developed none about the environment, and, we might add, with the exception of Brunswik and Gibson, none have yet.

In his third sentence he stated that "both organism and environment will have to be seen as systems, each with properties of its own, yet hewn basically from the same block." We can understand the demand that each "will have to be seen as systems," but what could that strange metaphor "each with properties of its own, yet hewn from the same block" possibly mean? The following sentence tells us: "Each has surface and depth, or overt and covert regions." This in itself was an original thought, but in fact, it meant more. As he would later tell us (pp. 8–11), it also meant that vicarious mediation of information from the environment would be matched by vicarious functioning on the part of the organism.

These concepts, which begin to define the "properties" he would later elucidate in greater detail, have always troubled Brunswik's readers, although they are among his most important theoretical achievements. As a result, together with Thomas Stewart, Berndt Brehmer, and Derrick Steinman (Hammond et al., 1975), I would later introduce the "principle of parallel concepts" to signify that the same concepts apply to both organism and environment because the formal "properties" of each are the same and thus are "hewn from the same block." In more prosaic terms, environmental and organismic concepts parallel one another. (I am afraid, however, that my colleagues and I were no more successful in our prosaic efforts than Brunswik was in his more colorful metaphor; few psychologists have ever made use of this concept.) Finally, with a masterful sentence, he drew the logical conclusion, thus: "It follows that, much as psychology must be concerned with the texture of the organism or of its nervous processes and investigate them in depth, it must also be concerned with the texture of the environment (recall Tolman and Brunswik, 1935) as it extends in depth away from the common boundary" (p. 300). And that is what he tried to do—investigate the texture of both the environment and the organism—and he did so in such painstaking detail that few psychologists bothered to look at his work.

But they would have an excuse; it is hard to do what Brunswik asked of us (as Gibson noted; see Kirlik, Chapter 13, this volume). It is hard to theorize about the environment, and it is hard to translate such theory into an experimental design that will represent the ecology of interest and thus permit a generalization from laboratory to life. I am somewhat experienced in these problems. I tried to take seriously Brunswik's admonitions about distinguishing theoretically and empirically between surface and depth in a task, and I tried to vary the relationships between them, all the while being mindful of what representative design demanded of me (see Hammond, Hamm, Grassia, & Pearson, 1987; see also Hammond, Hamm, & Grassia, 1986). The fact that I attempted this only some thirty years after reading that masterful sentence is testimony to the fact that at least this psychologist found this task daunt-

ing (but doable in the age of the computer). Unfortunately, understanding my efforts was apparently daunting as well; the manuscript describing this effort was rejected by the *Psychological Review* (twice) in rather scornful terms. (It was subsequently published in an engineering journal, a discipline in which the problem of understanding the dynamics of the environment has always been paramount, rather than ignored, and reprinted in William Goldstein and Robin Hogarth's compendium of *Research on Judgment and Decision Making*, 1997).

When Brunswik emphasized the fact that both organism and environment have surface and depth, he began to offer a theory of tasks. Use of these concepts is a first and essential step, for it allows us to inquire about the nature of the region that separates surface and depth. (In the Hammond et al., 1975, article referred to above, this was called the "zone of ambiguity" in order to emphasize the need to articulate the parameters of this region.) Brunswik provided the details of his theory that applies to this region, for both organism and environment, an achievement no other psychologist, with the exception of J. J. Gibson, has even attempted, let alone matched. He did so, Gibson told us, for the reason that, "if anything still ails psychology in general, and the psychology of cognition specifically, it is the neglect of investigation of the environmental or ecological texture in favor of that of texture of organismic structures and processes" (p. 300). He then anticipated the "feminist revolution" of the 1960s and 1970s by noting, "This preoccupation of the psychologist with the organism at the expense of the environment is somewhat reminiscent of the position taken by those inflatedly masculine medieval theologians who granted a soul to men but denied it to women" and then reiterated his point that his goal "is to restore or establish the proper equality of standard in the treatment of organism and environment . . . in which equal justice is done to the inherent characteristics" of each.

Brunswik made good on his commitment by making the idea of "vicarious mediation" on the part of the environment and "vicarious functioning" on the part of the organism integral parts of his theory, thus "restor[ing] the proper equality of standard" he deemed so necessary to psychology. It is these features that also must be considered in the matter of representative design. Task circumstances must be examined for the manner in which each occurs. Later, just as Brunswik introduced probability in rat experiments on learning, others, notably B. Brehmer and Michael Doherty and his students would introduce vicarious mediation and vicarious functioning into human experiments on cognition in relation to what would be called multiple cue probability learning. Much would be learned from these experiments, and new concepts would be introduced (see James Holzworth, Chapter 21, this volume), but the entire enterprise would stem from the ideas made clear in this chapter by Brunswik.

In short, when Brunswik asks, "Let me now turn to the unfolding of the drama of cognition before the eyes of the curious onlooker," this chapter makes us realize that we are in the presence of someone who can be trusted to take us through the "unfolding" of this topic as no one else can, or has. New ideas are abundant, and although some have been explored, most of the ideas in this chapter still offer a rich menu of thought-provoking challenges to the psychologists of the twenty-first century.

 REPRINT

Scope and Aspects of the Cognitive Problem

Egon Brunswik

One of the broadest and most universally accepted definitions of psychology conceives of psychology as being concerned with the interrelationships between organism and environment. In this definition both organism and environment appear as equal partners. This is not to say that they must be equal in all aspects of structural detail. We know that this would mean carrying things too far. A better simile would be to compare the two partners with a married couple. Perhaps the organism could be seen as playing the role of the husband and the environment that of the wife, or the reverse may be argued as well.

At any rate, both organism and environment will have to be seen as systems, each with properties of its own, yet both hewn from basically the same block. Each has surface and depth, or overt and covert regions. As in any marriage, the inter-

relationship between the two systems has the essential characteristic of a "coming-to-terms." And this coming-to-terms is not merely a matter of the mutual boundary or surface areas. It concerns equally as much, or perhaps even more, the rapport between the central, covert layers of the two systems. It follows that, much as psychology must be concerned with the texture of the organism or of its nervous processes and must investigate them in depth, it also must be concerned with the texture of the environment as it extends in depth away from the common boundary.

It will have been noted that by environment we mean the measurable characteristics of the objective surroundings of the organism rather than the psychological environment or life space, in the sense in which Lewin has used this term. We may specify the sum total of these objective surroundings as the "ecology" of an individual or species.

It is the contention of this paper that if there is anything that still ails psychology in general, and the psychology of cognition specifically, it is the neglect of investigation of environmental or ecological texture in favor of that of the texture of organismic structures and processes. Both historically and systematically psychology has forgotten that it is a science of organism–environment relationships, and has become a science of the organism. No such drastic statement can be literally true, of course. Defenders of the traditional policies of psychology will point to the fact that almost anywhere in modern psychology the organism is seen as in contact and interaction with the environment, be this in the form of "input" or "output" or both. But my point is that the investigation is in the typical case not carried beyond these boundary points into the territory of the environment proper, while on the other hand it is richly engrossed in the organismic portions of the causal chains, those portions that connect input with output on the "inside." This preoccupation of the psychologist with the organism at the expense of the environment is somewhat reminiscent of the position taken by those inflatedly masculine medieval theologians who granted a soul to men but denied it to women; our point, then, is to restore or establish the proper equality of standards in the treatment of organism and environment—that is, the equality of subject and situation (or object) in which equal justice is done to the inherent characteristics of the organism and of the environment.

Cognitive Achievement, Strategy, Tactics

But let me be more specific. Let me concentrate on the problem of cognition, which we may define as the problem of the acquisition of knowledge. Within cognition, let me concentrate on the more general case, on the more intuitive type of cognition called perception. And let me assume that this special form of cognition may serve as a paradigm of the patterns prevailing elsewhere in behavior. Within perception, let me choose topics sufficiently complex so as to encompass cognitive patterns in all their potential ramifications. To make reasonably sure that this is the case, we should sample cognitive problems representatively much as, in the study of personality, we sample persons and then survey the full sample of problems as to their structural components. But perhaps we can substitute for this rather forbidding ideal a choice of problems of such a degree of spread and intricacy that it is very likely that none of the major aspects or phases of the cognitive problem will be left unrepresented.

The problems I propose to choose are those of three-dimensional perception of space and of the "things" in it, and of the physiognomic or social perception of personality traits from external appearance. Both of these groups of problems have been with us for a long time, and offer the possibility of studying historical climates as they may affect the approach to a certain problem. Both have been highly puzzling in a variety of ways, and have revealed a great many facets as the context of the problem was varied.

This richness, in turn, must be seen as the result of the fact that both groups of problems fulfill the requirement with which we have begun our considerations. Both of them do not halt at the boundary between organism and environment but penetrate into the very heart of the environment. If the respective cognitive achievements approach perfection, the type of object attained is a remote one, or, more precisely, one defined without reference to the particular retinal input elicited by it in a given situation. Using a pair of terms first suggested by Koffka (18) and by Heider (13), both thing-perception and social perception involve cognitive attainment of "distal" variables that are to a certain extent independently variable of the corresponding "proximal" or sensory input. The measured size of a physical body and the tested intelligence of a person are examples of distal variables, while the size of the retinal impact and the geometric relations in the face or photograph of the person whose intelligence is to be intuitively appraised are examples of relatively proximal variables.

The distinction between distal and proximal concerns the measured properties of the environment only, taking the chains of event to a point just prior to their impact on the organism. The first impact upon the organism, or the relatively outlying portions of the excitatory processes or mechanism, are usually called "peripheral." And the final stage of the cognitive process is "central." We need not be concerned here with the fact that the central event must in turn be encoded in verbalized judgment to become communicable and conveniently measurable.

The full scope of the cognitive problem, at least so far as external perception is concerned, would then seem to involve a theater stretching all the way from the distal to the central layers. Its prime aspect would seem to be the over-all correspondence between a certain distal and a certain central variable, so that the former could be considered successfully mapped into the latter. This first aspect we call cognitive "achievement" or "attainment," or also "functional validity" of the final response relative to the distal focus.

The second aspect of the cognitive problem concerns the gross characteristics or macrostructure of the pattern of proximal and peripheral mediation between the distal and central foci. This is the problem of the grand strategy of mediation. Of special importance in this context is the question of whether or not a single track of mediation is sufficient or whether a multiplicity of cues or mechanisms must be provided. It is here that the necessity of special inquiry into the texture of the environment per se becomes evident for the first time. Obviously, a single track of mediation can be sufficient only if the environment provides us with unequivocal proximal or peripheral indicators or cues. For example, if Aristotle had been right in his assumption that all those whose faces resemble that of a fox are sly, and if this should be true in reverse also, the single cue of foxlike appearance would be sufficient cognitively to attain slyness in others. But we suspect that such does not hold—as indeed such ideal relationships do not in the general case— and that therefore macromediation must use alternative pathways. In other words, it is subject to the same principle of "vicarious functioning," which since Hunter's presidential address in 1932 must be recognized as the basic definiens of all behavior.

A third aspect of the cognitive problem is given by the attempt to break down the cognitive process further into its component parts. It concerns the special technology of the machinery along each of the several possible tracks of mediation. It may therefore be labeled the problem of micromediation, or of mediational tactics. The special ways in which foxlike appearance, if any, may be established neurologically furnish an example of such a problem.

Ecological and Organismic Phase of the Cognitive Process

The threefold distinction among the achievement, the strategy, and the tactics of the cognitive process concerns the order of magnitude of the unit encompassed. Achievement and its strategy are molar problems; tactics is a molecular problem. There is a second way of subdividing the cognitive process, one that proceeds in terms of regional segmentation. Here the most obvious distinction is obtained by breaking up the overall achievement arc into an ecological and an organismic portion. The final distal–central correspondences may then be analyzed in terms of (a) distal–proximal correspondences, which are intraecological; (b) proximal–peripheral correspondences, which cross over the boundary from the environment into the organism; and (c) peripheral–central correspondences, which are intraorganismic. For most of the molar problems of cognition the distinction between the proximal and peripheral layers is of lesser importance, however, and only the first and third of our correspondence problems remain in prominence today.

We had already encountered the purely ecological portion of the cognitive process when we spoke of the possibility of its equivocality and of the ensuing necessity facing the organism of having to compensate for this equivocality by the use of additional or "vicarious" cues. The degree of distal–proximal correspondence involved here may be labeled "ecological validity." Just as the functional validity or correctness of judgment may be expressed by a correlation coefficient linking the central response variable with the distal variable, ecological validities may be expressed by correlations linking the proximal with the distal variable. Turning to our example from Aristotle, the over-all functional validity of judgments of slyness would be given by the degree of the statistical association of these judgments with tested slyness in the object. The ecological validity, on the other hand, would not involve the final judgment. It would merely be an expression of the degree of statistical association between tested slyness in the object and one of the potential mediators of this objective slyness to the perceiver: in our case, foxlike features. So long as we confine our attention to ecological validities we are therefore dealing with a sign–significate relationship in its capacity as a challenge to the cognitive powers of the perceiver, but we do not yet know whether or not the perceiver will be responsive to the cue. Since in the typical case these sign–significate relationships will be far from univocal and the ecological validity will therefore be far from perfect, some may even doubt whether the responding organism would be justified in using the proximal cue as a basis for judgment regarding the distal object.

Be this as it may, our next concern must be this second, intraorganismic portion of the cognitive process. We shall speak of this as the phase of the "utilization" of cues. Those who take the position that all of psychology must deal with the organism per se, rather than also spreading out into the environment, may wish to confine the term "cognitive process" to this second phase. We would prefer to do otherwise and consider utilization as something like the third act of a play, one that culminates and resolves an earlier setting or impasse and that cannot be understood without such external build-up. The third act is the crux of a play. There are good third acts and there are poor or weak ones, depending on how the potential of the build-up is realized. Similarly, in cognition, the utilization of the sensory input relative to the distal object may be appropriate or not. We may call it appropriate in a generalized sense if the strength of utilization of a cue is in line with the degree of its ecological validity; but we must remember that individual cognitive failure is compatible with such general appropriateness in all instances running counter to the prevalent trend of ecological validity.

Prescientific Approach to Cognition: Cognitive Absolutism

Let me now turn to the unfolding of the drama of cognition before the eyes of the curious onlooker. Let me distinguish two types of such onlookers. One is exemplified by the philosophers, including those casual scientists in whose minds incidental observation, practical problems, and abstract speculation are found in curious mixture. The other is the scientist proper. The latter type of onlooker supersedes the former in the course of history, although there is a great deal of overlapping.

Let us see how the two types of approach have gone about handling the cognitive problem. First, the philosophers have tended to proceed primarily at the most global level. In our own somewhat disenchanting terminology this means concentration on the achievement problem at the expense

of those of the strategy and tactics of mediation. Kant's formulation as to whether the "thing in itself" is knowable is perhaps the penultimate in a long chain of different phrasings of the problem of achievement as they spring from the original blandness of naïve realism.

A second feature of the philosophical approach to cognition is its tendency toward absolute, all-or-none solutions of the achievement problem. In naïve realism, at least in its most extreme form, perfect functional validity is taken for granted in such a manner that stimulus and response, or reality and appearance, become in effect one and the same. But soon the pendulum swings to the opposite extreme, skepticism. Once the possibility of error is discovered, there seem to be at first no bounds to the generalization of error. Skepticism thus has been said to proceed by the assumption "once a liar, always a liar." But it was a great skeptic, Democritus, who, by the good services of his observations on perceptual error, came to assign independent status to the stimulus, and indeed to define it in essentially quantitative, mensurational terms. Because he opened the door to the operational approach to the problem of cognition, we may agree with those who rank Democritus on a par with the two acknowledged great men of ancient philosophy, Plato and Aristotle. It is only by an operational approach that we may discover that cognition may be sometimes right and sometimes wrong, and that therefore our treatment of the cognitive problem must be probabilistic. As we will see, cognitive absolutism is still rampant in modern perception psychology, and it appears in a variety of rather treacherous disguises.

The fact that philosophers tended to concentrate on the achievement aspect by no means blinded them to the demands of the mediation problem. But in entering this area they did so predominantly in their secondary capacity as amateur scientists, and sometimes the mechanics of practical aspects became altogether dominant. Physiognomic perception has always been a ball tossed among philosophy, medicine, and the country fair. And the first to list the depth cues by which the painter could restore the three-dimensionality of his original to his picture was a great artist and engineer, Leonardo da Vinci. Philosophers took over promptly from there, with Descartes and Berkeley in the forefront of those who helped to round out our knowledge of the strategy of three-dimensional perception.

Classification of Cues in Terms of Peripheral Tactics

This was about the state of affairs when psychology began to emerge in its own right about a century ago, and thus the problem of cognition became capable of scientific treatment. The overall skeleton of the problem was there, even though the traditional metaphysical formulations all but hid the fact that the achievement problem was scientifically meaningful; there was some scattered attention to mediational strategy, but practically nothing was filled in regarding mediational tactics.

Two major alternatives seem open at this point: either science could retrace the process of analysis from top to bottom or it could take a reverse course and begin with tactics. The latter is what actually happened. At first glance this proposition seems to be begging the question. How could one study tactics if one did not have a clear picture of the context of these tactics? But we must remember that in a vague and at the same time somewhat absolute way the problem of cognition had been posed with some measure of success in philosophy, and that this anticipatory treatment was sufficient to furnish some kind of informal matrix for the problems of tactics to hold on to.

Tactics is, as we have seen, a form of elementism, the one of the first things we all have learned in history is that nineteenth-century psychology was elementistic. The point we wish to stress in the present context is that the elementism of the "punctiform sensations reunited by the bond of association," which usually serves as the prime paradigm for elementism, is but one of many manifestations within a much richer syndrome. The type of elementism which we should like to expose by the rather crude summary statement that, in psychological science, the study of cognition tends to begin with the study of cognitive tactics has little to do with the introspective sensationism of the period. Rather, it lays stress on the objective processes involved in cognition.

Problems of tactics are characterized by (a) concentration on a single track of mediation, (b) encapsulation within the organismic portion of this cognitive track, (c) occupation with tracing this track step by step, and thus (d) concentration on the peripheral physiological phase, that phase which constitutes the beginning of the intraorganismic leg of the cognitive process.

An example is furnished by the traditional modes of classification of the so-called perceptual depth criteria. As we have hinted above, the difficulties of appraising depth on the basis of two-dimensional retinal projection had been sufficiently realized during the philosophical era, and it had been acknowledged that utilization of a variety of such cues was an essential strategic requirement. Lists of such cues were thus inherited from an earlier phase of history, but their classification had yet to be undertaken. Three major traditional classificatory schemes may be distinguished. They all reveal concentration of attention on the tactics of the organism.

The first of the traditional tactical classifications is that into primary versus secondary cues. There are only three primary cues: binocular disparity, binocular convergence, and accommodation. Closer inspection shows that in each case there is a gross peripheral organ or mechanism with which the functioning of the cue may be identified. In the case of binocular disparity this is the presence of a neurologically integrated double eye with the optic chiasma and the respective centers. In the case of convergence there are the extrinsic muscles controlling the rotation of the eyeball. And in the case of accommodation there is the ciliary muscle controlling the curvature of the lens. None of the other depth criteria can boast such obvious peripheral machinery. Thus we find them relegated to a "secondary" role, like paupers without a house or a car of their own. Their utilization potential is also seen as marred; only the primary cues are said to be capable of furnishing genuine experiences of depth, the secondary cues leading at best to pale surrogates without genuine plasticity.

The presence of a striking peripheral physiological mechanism turns out to be a status symbol of even greater consequences. It is the existence of primary cues that lends some of the major support to the doctrine of nativism regarding space, much as if such more centrally determined principles as the autochthonous dynamics of the brain field which the Gestaltists have later brought into the picture were incapable of ever reaching the noble status of innateness simply because there was no special peripheral involvement. Secondary depth cues were thus automatically considered "empirical" cues based on associative learning. A special philosophical lure is attached to this controversy by the fact that nativism is a distant—or perhaps not so distant—relative of rationalism, and that in turn rationalism remained the dominant philosophy on the European Continent. The paradoxical situation thus arose that rationalism was implicitly served by what could be called peripheral "physiologism," bespeaking the elevation in scientific prestige accorded at least temporarily to the hitherto belittled surface region of the organism.

The second tactical classification of the depth criteria may be passed over briefly. It is given by the distinction between monocular and binocular cues. Only accommodation switches position under this new scheme. But again the major category of order is the involvement versus the irrelevance of a peripheral receptor organ.

The third tactical classification is in terms of the sensory system involved. Here the visual cues are juxtaposed to the nonvisual, notably to the "tactile-kinesthetic" cues. Only convergence and accommodation are in the latter category, while binocular disparity, the first of the original primary cues, is now grouped with the secondary criteria. Classification of psychological events in terms of the sensory system to which they belong must be considered, even though still prevalent in many texts, another relic of nineteenth-century peripheralism.

Beginnings of Ecological Analysis

Let us now turn to the treatment of cues in terms of the environmental or ecological portion of the mediating process. The emphasis on this external portion is present in much of traditional speculative physiognomics. Coming back to our example from Aristotle, we note that the statement is concerned primarily with the alleged fact that foxlike features are in reality associated with foxlike character, and only secondarily with the problem of whether or not this sign is being picked up or "utilized" by the perceiver; it is not at all concerned with the details of how such utilization may work in the way of tactical technicality, that

is, what the nervous pathways organizing the impact may be like. The same holds for Gall's phrenology or the more recent constitutional typologies.

What is new in these latter attempts may be classified under two main headings. One concerns the machinery by which the association between distal variable and cue comes about; if you will permit my subordinating this machinery under the over-all purposive unity of the cognitive act, we may call this the ecological tactics of the cue. The second concerns the degree of association between distal variable and cue. As we have observed earlier, historical attempts show a predilection for making absolute the object-cue relationship, as if we were dealing with a kind of language emitted by the object in accordance with the strict rules observed by a rational being when engaged in speaking. Newer attempts realize that the voice of nature is not quite like the voice of reason; they recognize that nature may scatter its effects more irregularly. Definite limitations in what we have called the ecological validity of a cue are thus being more readily admitted.

Concern with ecological tactics and concern with ecological validity are of course intimately interwoven. If we know the machinery of a cue, we may at the same time realize that other machineries may produce the same cue without being backed by the same distal event; by the same token, we may learn how to "fake" the cue, that is, how to create a misleading instance artificially. In other words, we will realize that in the general case we will have to treat cognition as based on equivocal rather than univocal sign–significate relationships or, as Thurstone once said about perception, as based on insufficient evidence.

Ecological validity is a statistical concept based on the principles of contingency or correlation and requiring the coolheaded gathering of a representative array of information. In the general case it involves the integration of both positive and negative, confirming and disconfirming (misleading) instances of concomitance of the distal variable with the cue variable. Small wonder, then, that in the discovery of the limitations of ecological validity the more casuistic study of "exceptions" to the rule comes first; among them, those exceptions that can be produced artificially have exerted particular attraction, perhaps as a result of the same dialectics that marks the switch from the absolutism of naïve realism to the utter negativism of the skeptics.

Turning to the depth cues again, we find that among the various classifications proposed in listing them there is one which is unashamedly based on the possibility of ecological "faking." This is the designation of certain cues as "painter's cues," that is, those configurations which the painter may use to create the impression of depth without depth being actually present. It will be remembered that the description of these cues was one of Leonardo's pet subjects, far antedating the various types of description in terms of organismic tactics which we have listed above. In terms of these later classification schemes the painter's cues encompass all cues except the binocular cues and those involving motion.

An early example of the fact that cues conceived primarily in peripheral tactical terms during the nineteenth century were originally looked upon with an eye more on the ecology is given by the cue of accommodation. In terms of classical nineteenth-century analysis this is a primary, monocular, kinesthetic cue. But in Berkeley's *New Theory of Vision* of 1709 the cue appears under the label of "blurredness," referring to the lack of sharpness of objects out of focus as contrasted with the sharpness of the objects in proper focus. The emphasis is on the proximal retinal image and its ecological history rather than on the peripheral machinery within the organism. Since the blurredness of the object out of focus is as much a confirming instance of the cue as is the sharpness of the object in proper focus, the present example does not involve limitations in the ecological validity of the cue, however.

Cues as Proximal Variables

In the same vein we may insert another remark merely reflecting on the neglect of ecological consideration in classical experimental psychology. Ideally, the most appropriate cutting-in level in the definition of a distance cue appears to be the proximal level. Blurredness versus sharpness of the retinal image, if offered without further commentary, is an example of a purely proximal definition of a cue variable. But we notice that in many of the current textbook designations of depth cues—the word "designation" is used here in contradistinc-

tion to "classification" (which is usually peripheral)—proximal and ecological aspects are intertwined in a rather unhappy confusion.

For example, we hear of a cue variously labeled as "interception," "interposition," "covering," or "overlapping." All these terms refer to the ecological history of the retinal image, indicating that a nearer object blocks out part of a farther object. Without exception, the examples offered for operation of the cue involve objects of some intrinsic regularity, such as circular discs, rectangles, boxes, and so on. It soon becomes evident that the retinal situation involves the disruption of what Wertheimer has called the "good continuation" of the contours of these overlapped objects. The proximal nature of the cue would thus most aptly be described as "poor continuation (coupled with good continuation and completeness of an intersecting object)." The recent experiments by Ratoosh (24) and by Chapanis and McCleary (5) on the utilization of this cue confirm this interpretation in terms of Gestalt factors. Describing the cue by such ecological terms as "overlapping" or "interception" involves the same absolute view of the cue that underlies Aristotle's case of foxlike appearance; it tacitly implies that the characteristic combination of poor with good continuation to which we have just referred is *always* the result of a three-dimensional arrangement, with the object that shows good continuation in front and the object that shows poor continuation in the back. In reality, the so-called interception cue is a painter's cue and thus one that can be reproduced on a flat surface; in addition, an objectively moon-shaped object could well be combined with an object in the shape of a frying-pan in such a way that the former is in reality in front of the latter and neither is in reality characterized by good continuation, thus furnishing a misleading instance of the cue.

Perhaps more than anyone else, it was Gibson (11) who helped to free the definition of the perceptual depth cues from its unrecognized entanglement with ecology. His definitions, notably those in terms of "retinal gradients," are clearly focused on the proximal geometry per se. Gibson's own "expanse" cue, describing the rapid increase in the size of the retinal image of a landing airplane, might well have become known by some such name as the "approach" cue if the sloppy traditional labeling practices had been followed, thus nipping in the bud the analysis of the interrelationships between cue and ecology.

Classification of Cues in Terms of Ecological Validity: Representative Design

But the separation of issues effected by Gibson, while an important step in the right direction, constitutes but one of the preconditions for the execution of textural ecology and its rescue from absolutism. When I began some fifteen years ago to realize the urgency for the analysis of depth cues of this latter task, along with its formidable proportions, nothing but some physiognomic studies existed to point the way. These latter shared with the casuistic treatment of misleading instances of depth cues of which we have spoken above a rather markedly negativistic attitude. These studies involved correlational statistics, to be sure, and were on rather solid ground; but in claiming low or zero correlations between physical and mental characteristics such leading authors in the field as Donald G. Paterson (23) or Cleeton and Knight (6) unmistakably revealed their gusto and delight in exploding the myths of physiognomics. Again, the pendulum swings from naïve realism to utter skepticism. While this may to a certain extent be justified in physiognomics, it certainly does not hold true for depth perception. Here we know almost offhand that many of the depth cues will be fairly dependable, but we would like to know just exactly how dependable they are.

Perhaps the greatest boon to be gained from correlational physiognomics was the realization of the fact that any investigation in textural ecology inherently requires sampling from a population or universe. In the case of the objects of physiognomic perception this requirement was as good as automatic, because the actual or potential social objects involved were themselves persons and thus fell within the traditional domain of application of the sampling practices. But this precedent did not hold for the universe of situations involving depth perception. It thus had to be newly postulated that ecological objects or situations, even if not persons, should be representatively sampled: only by such "representative design" would we be enabled to estimate the over-all ecological validities inherent in the texture of a certain ecological universe or subuniverse. To approximate roughly such representativeness, pictures from *Life* magazine were at first selected. Instances involving a rather broad variety of depth cues were analyzed, and the corresponding real depths were intellectually reconstructed as well as possible from the context of the picture. It turned out that on the basis of this preliminary evidence so-called interception was perhaps the ecologically most valid of all depth cues; that is to say, of all the characteristic intertwinings of poor with good continuation of which we have spoken above as characterizing the cue proximally (and in a picture), practically all instances were traceable to objective depth arrangements with the poor-continuation object in the back rather than in front. Binocular disparity, in the eyes of nineteenth-century psychology the monarch of the distance cues, seemed a poor second by comparison; its ecological validity is marred by the fact that in all photographic reproduction of three-dimensional reality the cue suggests two-dimensionality. (In our special case, the presence of pictures within the pictures was considered for this part of the analysis, whereas the magazine pictures themselves were treated as if given in three dimensions.) For the obviously less valid depth cues, known as vertical position, space-filling (number of distinguishable steps between objects), and color, Seidner (26) has done a series of more thorough investigations and has come out with significant ecological validities ranging up to .4.

One of the great merits of the school of Gestalt psychology is the fact that it has called our attention to the presence of so-called tacit presuppositions in our science. We all are familiar with the famed "constancy hypothesis," an unverbalized presupposition inherent in classical nineteenth-century psychology, according to which sensations are univocally related to the elements of peripheral excitation. The original constancy hypothesis thus is a peripheral-central assumption. We may suspect, however, that other regions too may be interconnected by surreptitious constancy hypotheses. For example, the point may be made that ignoring the problem of ecological validity bespeaks the presence of a distal-proximal constancy hypothesis so far as the depth cues are concerned. This suspicion is confirmed by the fact that a physical law is frequently invoked as underlying the operation of a cue: for example, the law of triangulation or the various laws of physical optics. Such reference to law implies a tendency to forget that general laws become univocal predictors only if further specifications concerning the particulars of the mediating strata—such as the presence or absence of lenses or screens—is made. True enough that the "faking" of cues in consequence of contingencies or artificialities along this line is recognized as a possibility, and in fact is generously employed as a device of experimental analysis. Yet in the classification of cues we search in vain for an indication of a hierarchical conception as to their signification potential. Ecological classification is not entirely absent in classical experimental space psychology, to be sure. But we find it confined to relatively secondary considerations, such as the distinction between cues operating best at small versus large distances (say, binocular disparity as against so-called aerial perspective) or between cues giving a metric indication of depth as opposed to those merely indicating order (say, binocular disparity as opposed to interception). As to dependability in the sense of relative frequency of positive versus misleading instances, cues tend to be tacitly treated as if on a par in absolute perfection. Their status in the eyes of classical psychology thus resembles somewhat that of an unquestioned social stereotype as formed by the man on the street: unthinkingly made absolute yet often misleading.

Cue Utilization and Its Vicariousness

One of the effects of this oversimplified picture of the ecology was a crippling of the scope of the problems of organismic strategy. These problems should be handled in close contact with those of ecological validity. Proper cognitive adjustment demands (a) that vicarious utilization of many cues be present when validities are imperfect, and (b) that hierarchy of utilization (relative strength in rivalry) follow hierarchy of validity. Neither vicariousness nor rivalry can thus be properly understood without the fact of limited ecological validity.

This is the more to be noted, as we know, from other fields and from the over-all theory of psychology that vicarious functioning is one of the most fundamental principles, if not *the* most fundamental principle, of behavior. When Hunter (16) introduced the term, this was done in search of a definition of the subject matter of psychology, and in the status of the defining criterion. In effect, vicarious functioning plays the major role in the definitions by McDougall (22) and by Tolman (28) of the purposiveness of behavior. Hull (15) has incorporated it in his theory of the habit-family-hierarchy, a theory that was never surpassed as to level of complexity in his subsequent work. Psychoanalytic mechanisms are an expression of vicarious functioning; in her work on the interrelationships between motivation and overt behavior, Else Frenkel-Brunswik (8) has given quantitative expression to the possibility of "alternative manifestations" of common underlying drives, thus projecting onto an operational plane the psychoanalytic distinction between the latent and the manifest, and the vicariousness in their interrelationship.

Vicarious functioning encompasses both the divergent and the convergent part of the lenslike patterns that characterize all achievement. In the field of cognition, it is the divergent part—ecological validity—which is ecological and the convergent part—utilization—which is organismic. While isolative or absolute experiments on the utilization of depth cues have a long history, experiments in the relative utilization or rivalry of depth cues came into their own but thirty years ago; none of them have so far pitted cues against each other under the principles of representative design. But at least some good evidence has been assembled on the fact that binocular disparity can be overpowered by interception or by combinations of other cues, quite as it should be in view of its limited validity, at least in a cultural ecology.

Parallel problems arise in the field of physiognomics and social perception. Vicariousness is predicated upon limited ecological validity and in turn raises the problem of rivalry in utilization. A wide area of the pathology of cue-utilization is thus opened up, development of which may profit from the academic theory of depth perception as it may from its more indigenous roots in personality psychology. That the proper recognition of the vicarious functioning of cues may be one of the chief incentives for the introduction of representative design into the diagnostic process has been pointed out by Hammond (12). Hammond and his collaborators at Colorado also are among the pioneers in the study of the pathology of mediation in the diagnostician. A monograph by Smedslund (27) in Oslo on the probability learning of multiple cues illuminates the selective or distortive use of artificial cue systems in neurotics or in those who, in the terminology of Frenkel-Brunswik (9), show extreme "intolerance of ambiguity."

Ratiomorphic Explication of the Cognitive Process: Gestalt Principles and Probability Learning

On the other hand, it must also be granted that an element of maladaptiveness and thus, in a sense, of pathology, is intrinsic to any utilization of cues that are not perfectly dependable. As in any stereotype or as in wagering, there must always be what Reichenbach has called a "posit," that is, an implicit perceptual hypothesis; yet this hypothesis will be wrong in all the misleading instances of the cue. It may be helpful to try to explicate these underlying hypotheses in a rational manner or, in brief, to develop what may be called a "ratiomorphic" (3) theory of perceptual utilization. In essence this would constitute an expansion of Helmholtz's doctrine of unconscious inference (14). In the days of Gestalt psychology it would have taken some defensive argument before one could have revived such skeletons in the closet. In our day of "hypotheses in rats" (21), of information theory, of calculating machines, of the open recognition of "teleological mechanisms" (1), and of the explicit comparison of nervous activity with two-valued logic, such defensiveness seems no longer necessary.

All ratiomorphic explication must take recourse to some form of regularity or law. As we have anticipated, physical law seems readily available to serve as a template for the explication of the primary depth cues; along with ready physiological identifiability this is perhaps partly why these cues were singled out from the others.

More intriguing and more rewarding from the point of view of our understanding of perception is the ratiomorphic explication of the so-called secondary cues. This may be undertaken by pinning down those ecological conditions under which the cue would be ideally correct. For example, the cue of interception would be ecologically fully valid if all object contours were in reality characterized by good continuation. Its implicit

hypothesis is therefore, briefly, that all objects are of regular shape; perception behaves *as if* good continuation were a universal natural law. Similarly, linear perspective and Gibson's density- or texture-gradients work on the assumption that all objects appearing to be otherwise equal, such as telephone poles, trees, railroad ties, brush, or pebbles on a beach, are in reality equal in size as well. Or the cue of vertical position is predicated on the assumption that we are looking at objects below the horizon which are of equal objective elevation. And, finally, the light-and-shade cue operates, at least predominantly, as if it were a law that light comes from above rather than from below.

Some of the explicated hypotheses would seem to be readily subsumable under the well known principles of Gestalt organization, usually encompassed by the law of pregnance. But obviously such factors as light-and-shade distribution or some of the assumptions underlying the vertical position cue demand a more empirical interpretation. In collaboration with Kamiya (4) it could be established that at least one of the allegedly autochthonous Gestalt factors, "nearness" in the visual field, possesses at least a modicum of ecological validity with respect to distal object manipulability. It thus seems that an interpretation fitting all cues or organization principles could best be derived by assuming that their underlying hypotheses are the outcome of some generalizing type of probability learning rather than of principles intrinsic to Gestalt dynamics.

Ratiomorphic explication is but one of several aspects of the utilization problem, that is, of the intraorganismic leg of the cognitive process. While the sheer fact of utilization may seem to yield to "explanation" in terms of mediational technology, ratiomorphic explication deals, as we have just argued, with the underlying rationale of cognition in a way that cannot be divorced from the ecological leg of the process. It is only by comparing the reconstructed perceptual hypotheses with the ecological validities that their character mentioned above as crude overgeneralizations or stereotypes is revealed. It is obvious at once that they not only fail to represent universal law; they do not even represent ecological or local law so long as the term "law" is used in the usual, strict sense.

The picture of the cognitive absolutism of the perceptual system which we have just drawn holds only so long as we assume an unmitigated exploitation of the cue on the part of the responding system. But such radical response is in reality not the case. The facts of rivalry and compromise to which we have referred above suggest that cues will yield to conflicting evidence, perhaps even in an ecologically rather well adjusted "hierarchy" of relative utilization strength. In the light of this, all the above perceptual hypotheses should be reformulated as involving not absolute law but relative frequency.

Distribution Hypotheses and Correlation Hypotheses in Perception

At this point we are reminded of certain previous uses of the term "perceptual hypothesis," notably in the framework of the so-called hypothesis-information theory of perception proposed by Bruner (2) and by Postman (25). Some of their experiments on the subject center about the theme that certain stimuli or configurations occur more frequently than others and therefore are more readily perceived. Possibly Gibson's (10) observation about the progressively decreasing apparent curvature of curved lines under prolonged observation, or some of Köhler and Wallach's (20) figural displacements could be similarly explicated as a refusal on the part of perception to accept infrequent facts or relationships, although I doubt that the authors would agree with such ratiomorphic reformulation. Ivo Kohler's (19) observation that for persons wearing special systems of lenses, familiar letters tend to remain in their normal orientation, even if left-right reversal is effective in the rest of the field, belongs in the same category.

The facts listed in the preceding paragraph have in common that they involve what may be called "distribution hypotheses," that is, expectations regarding frequencies along a single dimension (or a set of isolated dimensions), as revealed by perceptual belief in the recurrence of the probable in accordance with past distribution and by mounting perceptual disbelief in the fact of a serious threat toward an upsetting of this distribution. In this latter respect there is a resemblance to Jarvik's (17) "negative recency effect," a case similar to the so-called "gambler's fallacy." Here too there is increasing skepticism concerning the future occurrence of what is generally rare, even

though—or even because—it has been prevalent in the immediately preceding series of events.

The case of depth cues, on the other hand, involves "correlation hypotheses." Although the hypotheses underlying cue utilization are in the nature of distribution hypotheses in the above unidimensional sense (say, concerning the prevalence of good continuation in our nature-culture), they are not really put to test in the experimental situation, as is the case for the experiments just cited. Rather, they are developed, in a series of experiential or quasilogical steps, in to some bidimensional sign–significate hypotheses (in our example, concerning the indicative power of poor as against good continuation with respect to depth); and the testing of these hypotheses, if it is to take place at all, lies in the more distant future. The old semantic criterion for sign function, "something stands for something else," is fulfilled only in the case of a correlation hypothesis; the cue itself is not challenged from the frequency point of view, but what is involved is merely the frequency of its association with the significate. Only correlation hypotheses are able really to venture out into the distal environment and thus to become related to the problems of textural ecology as we have defined them; distribution hypotheses and the study of their effects must in the nature of things remain essentially proximal in character.

The Crippling of the Cognitive Problem by Tied-Variable Designs: Encapsulation within the Skin

Above we have spoken of the pathology of the perceiver. There also is a pathology of the science that deals with the perceiver. Pathology is not meant in any grossly dramatic sense here; we merely wish to point out that there may be in the design of cognitive research certain unrealistic and perhaps formalistic predilections that narrow our scope of the problem. At least some of them are traceable to the all-or-none absolutism regarding ecological validity of which we have spoken above.

Systematic psychological experiments involving depth perception may be grouped into two major categories, those thriving on a confirming instance of the cue under neglect of the misleading case, and those thriving on the misleading case at the neglect of the confirming case. In the most recent experimental work on perception the former, apparently more positive policy is represented by some, although by no means all, of the work of Gibson, while the latter is predominant in the work of Ames and the Princeton group. Sometimes the declared aim is to study the utilization of cues, notably in the misleading-case type of distortive experiment that provokes gross illusion. Sometimes the declared aim is to study the problem of achievement, that is that most encompassing type of cognitive problem that takes us back to the beginning of our considerations. Perceptual size constancy is such a problem. Gibson has reported on experiments in which size constancy was practically perfect (11, Chap. 9). But closer inspection of his experimental design reveals that he had chosen his experimental conditions so as to represent an idealized rather than the real ecology. By performing his experiment in an open field with even texture and density he artificially made absolute, in the temporary subecology of his experiment, the "law" presumed by the perceptual hypothesis underlying the utilization of the cue. In the terminology of representative design he thus artificially tied — that is, confounded to a perfect degree — the distal and the proximal variables. Size constancy is automatic in this case, or it is an artifact of the design, provided that the cue is being utilized by the organism. That is to say, the experiment has no distal relevance; it does not really venture out into the ecology. All it does is to test the utilization of the cue, which is a purely intraorganismic problem. Idealization of the ecology thus leads to encapsulation of research within the skin.

The Princetonians, on the other hand, have a distinguished line of ancestry to the so-called "transdermal transactionism" of John Dewey and Arthur F. Bentley (7), which would seem to commit them to a search for genuinely distal research policies. But just as Gibson's rose-colored experiments, as we have seen, do not really pierce the skin, the Princetonians' bleakly distortive experiments do not pierce the skin either. In terms of representative design, theirs is a policy in which cue variable and distal variable are tied inversely, creating *ad hoc* a perfect negative ecological validity. These experiments, too, merely probe into cue utilization, that is, into strategy and mechanism, stressing the negative side of achievement but failing to reflect it proportionally.

If tested under representative situational conditions, size constancy is high but not absolute as measured in correlational terms; in other words, relatively high accuracy is the rule but there are large exceptions. So long as the cognitive problem is kept in mind in its full scope, such a probabilistic approach in terms of a mapping of functional validities is the only adequate approach to the problem of accuracy of achievement.

In another paper, Dr. Osgood provides a cogent analysis of the riddles of the "little black box," as we like to fancy the intraorganismic world in general and the nervous system in particular to be. What we have attempted to show here is that there also are riddles of what most of us have tended to treat as a "big white box," or, still better, a "big open box"; that is, our surroundings. Since physics has taught us the most universal laws of the external world, and geography provides the particulars, no exigencies seem to be left. But as it is the intermediate level of generality which provides the little black box with problems all its own, the ecology too is full of particular semiregularities all its own to which we have become somewhat blinded by the shining streaks of light of the purely nomothetic approach. As we have seen especially in the ratiomorphic explication of some of the secondary depth criteria, the cognitive system struggles hard to get hold of just these intermediate generalities. As we may gather from the psychology of learning, *ad hoc* regularities of limited spatial or temporal scope, or even of but partial validity, are the bread of the adjusting organism; the general laws of physics are more like the butter which none but the most highly developed strata of the cognitive system can afford.

Or to say this still differently: in the psychological applications of communication theory it is usually the organism that appears as the source of noise; in reality, however, the limited ecological validities of proximal cues relative to distal object variables furnish a perfect environmental counterpart to this internal noise. The translation of depth into depth cues is a case of probabilistic encoding even though this encoding takes place by virtue of the causal chains of nature-culture rather than by virtue of human fiat. Osgood's scheme begins with the decoding on the part of the organism of the messages from the environment, that is, with what we call utilization. Should it not then be recognized that equal attention must be given to the predicaments of the encoding process, a process which of necessity must precede any decoding? Only in this manner can the textural analogies between the macrocosm of the environment and the microcosm of the organism be developed and utilized to the best advantage of psychology.

To sum up: while philosophy and other antecedents of psychology have set the broad framework of the cognitive problem, starting from the most encompassing aspect of achievement and remaining aware of environmental texture when working down to organismic strategy, psychology proper took the reverse course, beginning with the microproblems of cognitive tactics and tending to encapsulate within the organism. We have tried to show that only by detailed analysis of ecological textures can the cognitive problem be restored from mere utilization problems to its full scope of achievement problems and thus again become the key to the core question of psychology, that of the adjustment of the organism to a complex environment.

REFERENCES

1. *Annals of the New York Academy of Science*. Vol. 50, No. 4 (1948).
2. Blake, R. R., and G. V. Ramsey (eds.) *Perception—An Approach to Personality*. New York: Ronald (1951).
3. Brunswik, E. Ratiomorphic models of perception and thinking. *Proc. 14th Internat. Congress Psychol.*, ed. M. Mailloux. Montreal (1954).
4. Brunswik, E., and J. Kamiya. Ecological cue-validity of "proximity" and of other Gestalt factors. *Amer. J. Psychol.*, 66:20–32 (1953).
5. Chapanis, A., and R. A. McCleary. Interposition as a cue for the perception of relative distance. *J. gen. Psychol.*, 48:113–132 (1953).
6. Cleeton, G. U., and F. B. Knight. Validity of character judgments based on external criteria. *J. appl. Psychol.*, 8:215–231 (1924).
7. Dewey, J., and A. F. Bentley. *Knowing and the Known*. Boston: Beacon Press (1949).
8. Frenkel-Brunswik, E. Motivation and behavior. *Genet. Psychol. Monogr.*, 26:121–265 (1942).
9. Frenkel-Brunswik, E. Intolerance of ambiguity as an emotional and perceptual personality variable. *J. Pers.*, 18:108–143 (1949).
10. Gibson, J. J. Adaptation, after-effect, & contrast in the perception of curved lines. *J. Exper. Psychol.*, 16:1–31 (1933).
11. Gibson, J. J. *The Perception of the Visual World*. Boston: Houghton Mifflin (1950).
12. Hammond, K. R. Probabilistic functioning and the clinical method. *Psychol. Rev.*, 62:255–262 (1955).
13. Heider, F. Environmental determinants in psychological theories. *Psychol. Rev.*, 46:383–410 (1939).
14. Helmholtz, H. *Handbuch der physiologischen Optik*, Vol. 3, 1866; trans. from 3d ed. by J. P. C. Southall. Rochester: Opt. Soc. of Amer. (1925).
15. Hull, C. L. The concept of the habit-family-hierarchy and maze learning. *Psychol. Rev.*, 41:33–54 and 134–154 (1934).
16. Hunter, W. S. *Human Behavior*. Chicago: Univ. of Chicago Press (1928).
17. Jarvik, M. E. Probability learning and a negative recency effect in the serial anticipation of alternative symbols. *J. exp. Psychol.*, 41:291–297 (1951).
18. Koffka, K. *Principles of Gestalt Psychology*. New York: Harcourt Brace (1935).
19. Kohler, I. *Über Aufbau und Wandlungen der Wahrnehmungswelt*. Vienna: Rohrer (1951).
20. Köhler, W., and H. Wallach. Figural aftereffects: an investigation of visual processes. *Proc. Amer. Phil. Soc.*, 88:269–357 (1944).
21. Krechevsky, I. Hypotheses in rats. *Psychol. Rev.*, 39:516–532 (1932).
22. McDougall, W. *Introduction to Social Psychology*. London: Methuen (1908).
23. Paterson, D. G. *Physique and Intellect*. New York: Appleton-Century (1930).
24. Ratoosh, P. On interposition as a cue for the perception of distance. *Proc. Nat. Acad., Sci.*, Wash., 35:257–259 (1949).
25. Rohrer, J. H., and M. Sherif. (eds.) *Social Psychology at the Crossroads*. New York: Harper (1951).
26. Seidner, S. E. Ecological validity of visual depth criteria. Univ. of California doctoral dissertation (in progress).
27. Smedslund, J. *Multiple-probability Learning*. Oslo: Akademisk Forlag (1955).
28. Tolman, E. C. *Purposive Behavior in Animals and Men*. New York: Century (1932).

PART III

APPLICATIONS

A.

Theoretical and Methodological
Contributions to Psychology

19

The Contribution of Representative Design to Calibration Research

Michael E. Doherty, Gregory L. Brake, and Gernot D. Kleiter

Most followers of Brunswik would, we think, identify representative design (Brunswik, 1944, 1956b) as one of the most critical of Brunswik's methodological contributions. The idea of representative design epitomizes Brunswik's system; it includes the need to pay as much attention to the environment as to the subject, the need to sample environments as well as subjects, the need to represent environments in all of their entangled dimensions in depth, and the need to adopt an idiographic-statistical approach to the study of behavior. Most followers of Brunswik would also, we think, identify vicarious functioning as the single most critical of Brunswik's theoretical concepts. They are not unrelated; a fully representative design allows the experimental subject to function vicariously and thus to attain a high level of achievement. The present paper illustrates the potential contribution of Brunswik's ideas to a topic that has been hitherto "beyond the pale." That application is to research on the calibration of subjective probabilities, a research area that has hitherto generally been considered to be in the domain of the heuristics and biases.

The goal of this paper is to demonstrate the implications of representative design for studying the calibration of subjective probability judgments, that is, the degree to which people's judgments of the probabilities of a set of events match the actual event outcomes. The experiments that we will briefly describe have employed not only random sampling of situations, but also the statistical description of the environment and of the subjects in the same statistical concepts. Successful adaptation necessitates that people utilize informational cues according to extent that they are ecologically valid (Brunswik, 1944; Cooksey, 1996b); hence, both cue utilization and ecological validity should be measured, ideally in the same terms. In previous calibration research, it has been possible to assess neither cue utilization nor ecological validity, because the tasks used involved either recall from memory or inferences based on information in memory and commonly involved asking subjects to answer almanac questions.

Calibration research is, in a fundamental way, akin to research based on Brunswik's lens model. In both lines of research, the focus is on empirical accuracy, or correspondence between judgments and environmental outcomes, rather than on the coherence of judgments with some formal model (Cooksey, 1996b; Hammond, 1996b). Hammond (1996d) suggested that the distinction between coherence and correspondence is at least partially responsible for the division between the social-judgment-theoretic and the heuristics and biases programs of research. In spite of the fact that calibration research has long been classified with the heuristics and biases program, recent ecological theories of overconfidence (e.g., Gigerenzer, Hoffrage, & Kleinbölting, 1991; Juslin, Olsson, & Björkman, 1997; Soll, 1996) have been greatly influenced by Brunswik's theoretical ideas. These investigators have made significant methodological contributions to the calibration literature, especially with respect to Brunswik's call for proper sampling of the environment (see especially Juslin, 1994). The research described below continues in that tradition but more fully adopts the methodology of representative design, in the sense that we confronted our subjects with multiple, entangled cues that allowed the exercise of vicarious functioning.

The research we discuss in this paper was conceptualized theoretically and methodologically within both the calibration and the representative-design, or lens-model, frameworks. Subjects made probability judgments about events with known outcomes, with the events described in terms of a rich set of cues, using the double-system case of the lens model (Cooksey, 1996b).

Description of the Task Environment

In a series of studies, described fully in Brake (1998), some subjects made probability judgments about the desirability of roommates, others about the outcomes of baseball games. Given the brevity of this paper, we focus on the latter. The research environment was selected because there is an extensive historical database consisting of both qualitative and quantitative information, and because there is an ample supply of expert subjects who would find such a task interesting. The environment comprised 150 games randomly sampled from the 1992 major league baseball season, specifically partial game summaries taken verbatim from the sports pages of the newspaper *USA Today*. Each summary was coded for analysis in terms of five cue variables, and the separately presented final season records of the teams provided a sixth variable. Table 19.1 details the statistical structure of the task environment, although in some conditions some variables were dropped out in manipulations of task difficulty. The hit rate of a multiple logistic regression model of the environment for the full cue set (i.e., the percentage of the games correctly predicted by the model) was 87 percent; ordinary least squares (OLS) multiple regression analysis produced an R_e of .73.

In a series of studies, highly knowledgeable subjects predicted the outcomes of the 150 games based on the partial game summaries, doing so on either half-scale or full-scale probability scales. In all studies, a third of the game summaries presented three innings of information, a third five, and a third seven. In different studies, subjects performed the tasks on booklets or on computers. There were forty subjects in three studies with full cue sets, and we will present them together.

Calibration and Lens Model Assessments of Subjects' Performance on the Task

Subjects showed exceptional ability to predict the outcomes of the games, with a mean percentage of correct predictions of 83 percent, in contrast with the multiple logistic regression performance of 87 percent. The results showed marked underconfidence with both single-event probabilities and frequency judgments. The finding of underconfidence in this task is consistent with a well-established result in the calibration literature, the hard-easy effect (Lichtenstein & Fischhoff, 1977; Suantak, Bolger, & Ferrell, 1996). The subjects did well, but not perfectly. The subjects' Brier scores, the measure of correspondence in the calibration literature (being the mean squared deviation between the subjective probabilities and the 0,1 codings of the outcome variable), were about .15, which reflects fairly good but far from perfect correspondence between judgments and outcomes. The related lens model measure of correspondence, r_a, similarly reflected good but imper-

TABLE 19.1 The statistical structure of the baseball task environment, including cue intercorrelations and descriptive statistics for each of the cues. Beta weights are taken from the OLS multiple regression model of the environment

	Wins	Pitchers	Closers	Inn	Runs	HFA	$I \times R$	Outcome
Mean	0.79	−0.09	0.03	5.00	0.11	0.53	1.02	0.51
SD	14.19	1.69	0.65	1.64	3.14	0.5	17.71	0.50
Wins								
Pitchers	−.11							
Closers	.14	.11						
Innings	.01	.04	−.03					
Runs	.20	−.30	.19	.09				
HFA	.11	−.11	.03	−.08	.26			
Inn × Runs	.20	−.28	.21	.07	.96	.25		
Outcome	.40	−.20	.38	.10	.62	.12	.59	
β	.27	−.05	.26	.05	.61	−.05	.11	

fect correspondence, with mean values of r_a across the three studies being about .70.

The Contribution of the Brunswikian Approach

Given that we have a full double-system lens-model representative design, the subjects' performance can be illuminated in a way that is not normally possible in calibration research. The above report of the wide arching measure, r_a, immediately suggests that we can bring the lens model equation (see Stewart, Chapter 27, this volume) to bear. We can see the extent to which the subjects' models corresponded to the model of the environment; mean G values were about .95. We can determine whether the subjects were able to match variation in the environment not described in the linear model; mean C values were about .30. More interestingly, the correspondence between ecological validities and cue utilization coefficients could be examined, and the calibration and lens model indices could be correlated with each other and with aspects of the environment. Certain of the calibration indices and lens model measures assess similar features of performance; hence, they must, of statistical necessity, be highly correlated; the correlation between r_a and the Brier score, across twenty-nine subjects, was −.90 (low Brier scores reflect high achievement). But some interesting and unexpected relationships were uncovered. Perhaps the most interesting and surprising of them was the correlation between the number of cues that subjects used (that is, that had statistically significant cue utilization coefficients) and the achievement indices of the subject; for two studies with a total of twenty-nine subjects, the correlation between r_a and the number of cues used by subjects was .54, and the correlation between the Brier score and the number of cues used was −.59. That is, the subjects who used more information were more accurate. That may sound obvious, but it is far from necessarily so!

A major advantage of using a representative design is that it permits measurement of task difficulty independent of the percentage of correct responses. The hard-easy effect posits that subjects tend to be underconfident with easy items and overconfident with hard items, with the cross-

over empirically being in the neighborhood of 70 percent correct. But there is an unsatisfactory element of circularity in defining task difficulty strictly in terms of the subjects' performance (Juslin, 1993; Wallsten, 1996). Task difficulty was assessed objectively in the study just described. According to the multiple logistic regression, the task difficulty level could be described as being approximately 87 percent. According to the OLS regression, the approximate estimate is given by R_e, which was .73. We say approximate because not all of the information in the game summaries was amenable to coding (e.g., player names); hence, the task may be slightly more predictable to an expert.

The representative design and the attendant availability of such statistical measures as just described allow not only the *assessment* of difficulty, but its *manipulation*. Given that our task was highly predictable (that is, easy) and our subjects were underconfident, the next step was to increase task difficulty by reducing the information available to the subjects.

Manipulation of Difficulty of the Task Environment

Four levels of task difficulty were created simply by providing subjects with differing levels of information. Two methods were used to accomplish the reduction of task difficulty. The first was to reduce the number of cues available to the subjects. The second was to make cue information available to the subjects about only one of the two teams, a manipulation intended to test a hypothesis concerning the effect of multiple hypothesis testing (Doherty et al., 1996).

Multiple logistic and OLS regression analyses were performed on the four resulting task environments. The percentages correct from the multiple logistic regression analyses were 83 percent, 71 percent, 69 percent, and 64 percent. Thus, the percentages correct ranged from quite high to rather low, bearing in mind that chance is 50 percent for such predictions. The corresponding R_e values were .68, .52, .40, and .28. If the hard-easy effect is explained by variation in task difficulty, then the underconfidence found with the full cue set should have given way to good calibration and then overconfidence as task predictability diminished. It did. Task difficulty does not appear to be the whole story, though, as the relationship between difficulty and confidence was not perfect.

Cue Weighting

Overall, participants in these studies tended to underweight valid cues. They may have been unaware of the fact that even small run differences are fairly good predictors of game outcome (Slegers, Brake, & Doherty, 2000). This underweighting of cues may have been responsible for the underconfidence obtained. This is consistent with a model proposed by Griffin and Tversky (1992), which suggests that people tend to be insufficiently sensitive to the predictive validity (or, in lens model terminology, ecological validity) of evidence when judging probability. Additional examination of the relationships among cue utilization, ecological validity, and confidence may lead to the development and evaluation of plausible process models that can account for overconfidence and the hard-easy effect found so consistently in the calibration literature. Furthermore, the relationship among cue utilization and ecological validity may have implications for debiasing. Training as a means of improving calibration has met with very limited success, though several researchers have proposed methods for improving the calibration of subjective probabilities, among them, providing outcome feedback to judges. It appears to us that cognitive feedback (Balzer, Doherty, & O'Connor, 1989; Doherty & Balzer, 1988) has a much better chance of being useful in improving the calibration of subjective probability judgments. As the just cited reviews show, task information has powerful influences on behavior. One possible intervention using cognitive feedback would be to give subjects, in addition to ecological validities, information about the relevant statistical features of the ecology for which their calibration is being assessed, such as the central tendency and variability of the probabilities predicted by the ecological equation.

Conclusion

As any good Brunswikian would say, the task matters! The analysis of cognitive processes cannot be investigated in a fully meaningful way without a corresponding, or rather a propaedeutic, task analysis.

ACKNOWLEDGMENT

This manuscript was prepared with the support of National Science Foundation grant SBR-9422253 to Bowling Green State University, Michael E. Doherty and Clifford R. Mynatt, principal investigators.

20

Assessing Self-Insight via Policy Capturing and Cognitive Feedback

Michael E. Doherty and Barbara A. Reilly

The investigation of the extent to which people have insight has a long history. One could start the modern history with the controversial theories of Freud, who postulated that there were inaccessible areas of mind, the so-called unconscious, as well as accessible areas, the so-called conscious. Or one could start with the Gestalt psychologists, who meant by insight a sudden restructuring of the perceptual situation, "a patterning of the perceptual field in such a way that the significant relations are apparent; . . . the formation of a *Gestalt* in which the relevant factors fall into place with respect to the whole" (Heidbreder, 1933, p. 355). There must be myriad other meanings between the two poles just mentioned, with Freud focusing on the development of insight into aspects of oneself, and the Gestalt psychologists focusing on the development of insight into aspects of the environment.

While Brunswik did not deal extensively in his research with the study of insight (but see Brunswik & Herma, 1951, pp. 288 ff.), he was acutely aware of both meanings just noted, the first through the distinguished psychoanalytic career of his wife, Else Frenkel-Brunswik, and the second through his intimate knowledge of Gestalt psychology. Brunswik's ideas have had a significant influence on major developments that have furthered our understanding of insight. Fittingly, the dimension of insight to which Brunswikian research has been relevant is the extent to which a person has insight into the extent to his or her understanding of a task environment!

The specific background of our story begins not with Freud or the Gestalt psychologists, but with Brunswikian research on policy capturing, with cognitive feedback, and with Hammond's (1996c) treatment of intuition and analysis in his cognitive continuum theory. Cook and Stewart (1975) summarized the then scant work on the agreement between the statistical weights of a policy equation and the subjective weights that were provided by subjects who had been asked to describe their judgment policies in policy-capturing tasks, and they assessed seven methods of obtaining subjective descriptions. The role of cognitive feedback is central to the story to be told, because it was in the cognitive feedback stage of some of our policy-capturing research that evidence of a significant degree of insight emerged. Cognitive continuum theory is relevant in that Hammond posits that the ability to report one's judgment process is one of the criterial attributes discriminating analytical from intuitive cognition.

The Received View of Insight in the 1970s and 1980s

An influential review by Slovic and Lichtenstein (1971) set a pessimistic tone for the 1970s and 1980s, with respect to insight. Nisbett and Wilson (1977), in their "Telling More than We Can Know: Verbal Reports on Mental Processes," cited Slovic and Lichtenstein's conclusion that people were unable to report accurately the weights that they used in making a series of multiattribute judgments. Nisbett and Wilson presented a very dour view of human insight across situations. After saying that the presence of "at least some correspondence between subjective and objective weights" was the only evidence they had been able to uncover that "people can be at all accurate in reporting about the effects of stimuli on their responses" (p. 254), Nisbett and Wilson went on to dismiss that correspondence as "nothing more than the ability to describe the formal rules of evaluation." They opened their paper with a strong negative conclusion: "Evidence is reviewed which suggests that there may be little or no direct introspective access to higher order cognitive processes" (p. 231). To how many students in judgment and decision-making classes in the 1970s and 1980s did the first author of this paper soberly pronounce this conclusion? How many graduate students did policy-capturing studies, and found the expected mediocre match between subjective weights and any of a number of indices of cue usage? A more complete review of the relevant literature is given in Reilly and Doherty (1992).

A Small Bit of Evidence Contrary to the Received View

In the 1980s, a doctoral student of a colleague in industrial-organizational psychology was running a policy-capturing dissertation, the subjects for which were experienced fire captains in another state. As part of the incentive for serving in the study, the student returned to the fire captains and explained their policies to them; he gave them cognitive feedback. They said that he was giving them the wrong feedback, that the weights he was showing them could not be theirs, as they did not reflect how they had made their judgments. The student explained that the weights were in fact correct, that it had been demonstrated that people did not know their own policies. The fire captains were adamant. *The fire captains were right!* The feedback forms had been miscoded. That was unsettling, but it might easily be attributed to an exception or a fluke or just tucked away in memory as an anomaly, à la Kuhn (1962), festering there until more anomalies came along to upset the paradigm.

Powerful Evidence Contrary to the Received View

In 1987, the second author was completing her master's thesis research, a policy-capturing study in which forty senior accounting majors had made desirability ratings of 160 hypothetical accounting jobs, each job defined by nineteen cues. She decided at the last minute to see whether the subjects might recognize their own policies, as an operation that would be an entirely novel way of assessing insight. Most of her subjects had already had their feedback mailed to them, but

eleven returned for individual feedback. She first showed each one a matrix of forty subjects by nineteen usefulness indices (Darlington, 1968) and then asked each subject to identify himself or herself and then make a second choice. Of the eleven, seven selected themselves on their first choice, two others on their second! For the first choices, seven out of eleven, given the probability of success of .025 (1/40), yielded a p value under the null hypothesis of 1.84×10^{-9}. Our (Reilly & Doherty, 1989) conclusion was that people had far better insight than had previously been believed, but that people could not express the insight that they did have by the typical methods of producing subjective weights.

That study was quickly followed up by Reilly and Doherty (1992), in which a different substantive task was used. In this investigation, subjects rated how much they would like hypothetical roommates. In a desire to be able to generalize over formal as well as substantive task characteristics, the number of cues and cue intercorrelation were also manipulated. Some subjects saw four cues, others twelve. Some subjects were faced with orthogonal cues; others served in a representative design. Subjects in all four conditions were able to recognize their own policies at well beyond traditional levels of significance. An interesting finding in this investigation was that the subjects in the two representative designs behaved quite differently from those in the orthogonal designs. Even though the cue means and variances were the same, the representative subjects rated the profiles significantly higher than did the orthogonal subjects, and the intercorrelations among the subjects in the representative designs were far higher than those in the orthogonal designs.

Reilly (1996) extended this research to the assessment of insight into others, as well as obtaining further data on into one's own judgment policy. Her subjects were fifty pairs of roommates who had lived together for at least six months in dormitories. Each subject rated 100 hypothetical roommates, as above, and later were asked to select their own judgment policy from a matrix of twenty (policies) by twelve (usefulness indices). Fully sixty-two of 100 subjects successfully recognized their own policies, a probability under the null hypothesis of 1.80×10^{-54}, and 33 successfully recognized their roommate's policies, ($p = 1.22 \times 110^{-18}$). Subjects who correctly identified themselves recognized their own policies were also significantly better at describing them; that is, the mean correlation between their subjective weights and usefulness indices were higher for the recognizers (mean $r = .63$) than for the non-recognizers (mean $r = .32$). Interestingly, those subjects displaying self and other insight rated their relationships with their roommates as significantly less marked by conflict.

Subsequent to the earlier studies, similar results concerning insight into one's own judgment policies were found with physicians by both Wigton (personal communication) and Harries, Evans, and Dennis (1997).

The Role of Environmental Variation in Self-Knowledge

We are not arguing here that people have good insight in all possible circumstances; that would fly in the face of too much experimental evidence. We are arguing, and have shown definitively, that people do have insight into their judgment policies when those policies describe repeated multiattribute judgments. The question is why? We could do worse than to return to our roots in Brunswik for some possible ideas here.

In developing his system, intended had he lived out a complete research career, to be a general system of psychology, Brunswik relied heavily on the psychology of perception. What is more fundamental to the perceptual act than change, than variation in the ecology? If the environment presents constant stimulation, we adapt to it; that is, we do not attend to it.

Consider a comparison between policy capturing and the typical psychological rule-of-one-variable design, especially a between-subjects design. In the former, a subject makes a large number of multiattribute judgments in which the very essence of the paradigm involves variation of all of the attributes on every trial. In the latter, a subject is exposed essentially to a single observation of an experimental environment in which he or she sees but one level of the independent variable. There may be an "independent variable" in the study, but there is *no* variation in the environment, *so far as the subject is concerned*. In an even more extreme circumstance, Nisbett and Wilson (1977) reported one group study in which

they deliberately held the relevant aspect of the environment completely constant, completely without variation. They had subjects choose which of four pairs of nylon stocking was the best quality of the four. The rightmost of the four pairs was chosen as having the highest quality, even though all four pairs were identical. Not a single subject volunteered that the position of the stockings had anything to do with his or her preference. It would take a comprehensive review to ascertain how many of the investigations supporting the proposition that we have poor insight might be characterized as asking the subject to respond to a constant, which we hasten to add is less a criticism of the interpretation of such studies as showing a lack of insight than it is a limitation on their generalizability.

We can only speculate about the process or processes by which perceived variation is translated into self-insight. We remind the reader that the insight about which we are speaking is insight into the extent to which the subject has understanding of a task environment. And the interaction with that task environment is iterative: The subject is producing varying responses as the cues vary, so the variation is more than just salient; it is, as implied above, the very essence of the policy-capturing paradigm. When things in the environment vary, we pay attention, and we know what we pay attention to, in judgment as in perception.

Implications Beyond Insight

As argued in Reilly and Doherty (1992), the fact of insight supports the proposition that a regression model, whether or not weighting and averaging veridically reflects the judgmental processes, "is much more than a mere prediction device, much more than an equation relating the output to the input.... A regression model is an imperfect, paramorphic model, as are all models, scientific and otherwise" (Reilly & Doherty, 1992, pp. 306 ff.; see also Doherty & Brehmer, 1997; Hoffman, 1960).

Finally, we note that it should not be too surprising that we get superior insight when we use the recognition measure rather than have the subject produce weights. We return to the perceptual analogy: I can recognize myself in a mirror or a picture far better than I can describe myself!

21

Judgment Analysis

R. James Holzworth

Judgment analysis is a term that did not exist in psychology until after World War II. It is closely related to *decision analysis*, of course, and the two have been confused. In 1971, for example, Slovic and Lichtenstein refused to distinguish between the terms *judgment* and *decision* and stated forthrightly that they would "use these terms interchangeably." Later, in a 1977 review, they did not address the distinction at all. But by 1980, Hammond, McClelland, and Mumpower (1980) had become concerned about the ambiguity in the usage of these terms and did address the matter directly. They observed that "the title of R. N. Shepard's talk at the AAAS meetings in 1962 ("Use of judgments in making optimal decisions") provides a further illustration of the uncertain status of the distinction between these two terms: Could that title have just as well read: 'Use of decisions in making optimal judgments'?" (p. 56). Hammond et al. went on to say that they would make a distinction between judgment and decision "because we believe that . . . the development of a cumulative scientific discipline will best be served by indicating that the work of the researchers may very well be complementary. Specifically, . . . we believe that *instituting* that distinction . . . will be useful in identifying the complementary nature of the intended functions of the theories" (p. 57). That conclusion seems to have been justified by later developments.

By 1980, it had become clear that decision analysis had pursued the question of the *rationality* of the decision process, while judgment analysis had pursued the question of the empirical *accuracy* of human judgments under various conditions. By 1996, Hammond would find this conclusion sufficiently firm to assign decision analysis to the *coherence* metatheory of truth, and judgment analysis to the *correspondence* metatheory of truth. If that assignment stands up to criticism, there seems little likelihood that the situation will return to that of 1971.

Interest in clinical judgment had spurred Paul Meehl to write his landmark book *Clinical vs. Statistical Prediction* in 1954. But judgment analysis as a field of endeavor got its start as a systematic approach to cognition with Hammond's article titled "Probabilistic Functionalism and the Clinical Method" (published in the *Psychological Review* in 1955). For whereas Meehl's book showed the superiority of statistical prediction over clinical prediction and thus cast doubt on the value of the latter, Hammond's article took a theoretical approach to the analysis of judgment. Brunswik's lens model was used to analyze, or externalize, the judgment processes of clinical psychologists, thus demonstrating that the lens model could be generalized from visual perception to clinical judgment. *Judgment analysis*, as the term is used now, was born at that point. (See Hammond, 1996c, for a historical review of the clinical vs. statistical prediction dispute.)

Fundamental Concepts

As the reader of this volume will be well aware, the fundamental Brunswikian concepts involved in analyzing judgment under uncertainty are those included in the lens model; thus, uncertainty in the external system, uncertainty in the subject's cognitive system, the ecological validity of multiple fallible indicators and their use, and the interdependence or redundancy among the indicators, as well as the reliability of the indicators, together with the function forms of the indicators and their usage, as well as the form of the organizing principle, are ascertained empirically. Cooksey presented all of the details of the appropriate procedures in his "Judgment Analysis" (1996b). In a nutshell, judgment analysis (JA) reflects the idea that within the correspondence metatheory, judgments are based on multiple fallible indicators; as for example, when someone makes a judgment about the weather, it is based on the presence of clouds, wind, and the presence or absence of rain. (See Albright and Malloy, Chapter 22, and Doherty and Reilly, Chapter 20, this volume, for examples.)

Conducting Analyses of Human Judgment

JA is used in many applications for a number of reasons, including assessing judgment accuracy and achievement, modeling judgment policies ("policy capturing"), training for improved judgment, comparing judgment policies, judgmental bootstrapping, monitoring judgments, clinical trials and assessment, and providing decision support. Excellent resources for those interested in conducting JA are Cooksey (1996b), Doherty (1996), and Stewart (1988).

Cooksey (1996b) listed eight stages of JA: (1) Conceptualize the judgment problem; (2) understand the ecology; (3) identify relevant cues and dimension of judgment; (4) sample cue profiles; (5) sample judges; (6) obtain judgments; (7) capture policies; and (8) compare policies. The first five stages are a great challenge to those committed to the spirit of representative sampling (Brunswik, 1943). Very often the judgment problem is conceptualized with the assistance of subject matter experts, some of whom participate as judges in the research project. Understanding the ecology, identifying relevant cues and dimension of judgment, sampling and/or creating cue profiles, and finding willing participants to make judgments are all tasks that must be done carefully for a successful JA effort. At Stage 6, explicit judgments are made concerning the carefully prepared cue profiles. Sometimes, judges are asked to describe their policies in some ways (cue weights, function forms, and aggregation rules) during or at the completion of Stage 6, but there is evidence that people often lack insight into their own judgment policies (Brehmer & Brehmer, 1988). Lack of insight is demonstrated by low correspondence between spoken estimates of cue importance weights and statistically derived importance weights. Judges are often surprised when presented the relatively large number of cue profiles needed to produce stable results. Stage 7 of JA involves use of one or more statistical techniques to derive algebraic models of judgment from the data gathered in Stage 6. The most commonly used technique is multiple regression when both judgments and cues are continuous variables (see

Cooksey, 1996b). Stage 7 concerns detailed data analyses for each individual judge. At Stage 8, results from individual judges are compared in a variety of ways, depending upon the purpose of the research project.

Landmark Judgment Studies

A number of studies have contributed significantly to the evolution of JA methodology. These studies may be considered landmarks. The first was conducted by Hammond (1955), who applied Brunswik's ideas concerning vicarious functioning and representative design to clinical psychology. Concurrent development of the multiple cue probability learning (MCPL) paradigm and lens model equation (Hammond, Hursch, & Todd, 1964; Hursch, Hammond, & Hursch, 1964; Tucker, 1964) promoted and facilitated research on human judgment in general. Hammond, Wilkins, and Todd (1966) widened the focus of JA research to include issues of interpersonal perception and interpersonal learning (IPL). Researchers began comparing cognitive systems of two or more persons; agreement, as well as achievement, became an important judgment performance measure. In 1972, Hammond and Summers introduced the concept of *cognitive control*, referring to the extent to which a person is able to use a particular judgment policy consistently. Addressing a significant social issue, Balke, Hammond, and Meyer (1973) applied concepts of self-understanding and cognitive control to labor-management relations. Interactive computer graphics were developed to help union and management negotiators gain insight into their own and each others' policies. By the early 1970s, a great deal of attention was being given to vicarious functioning and the mediational correlations of proximal cues with human judgments. Then came a publication that shook the confidence of judgment researchers, if not their philosophies. Dawes and Corrigan (1974; Dawes, 1979) argued that proper, even improper, linear models of human judgment processes are superior to unaided human intuition when predicting a numerical criterion from numerical cues. These researchers refocused attention on distal correlations and made mediational correlations secondary again. Differential weighting of cues is less critical than knowing what cues are important and how to combine them. In 1976, Hammond and Adelman reported use of JA to help resolve a serious dispute concerning selection of handgun ammunition for the Denver Police Department. The success of their contribution not only demonstrated the importance of measuring individual differences in human social values but also opened new possibilities for JA (also see Hammond, Harvey, & Hastie, 1992).

What We Know about Human Judgment

We now know a great deal about human judgment from using JA (see Brehmer & Brehmer, 1988). The judgment process is adequately described by a linear model incorporating fewer cues than most people believe are necessary. Judges are somewhat inconsistent in cue usage. There are sometimes wide individual differences in cue usage. Judges may have little insight into their own judgment policies. They can make better use of cognitive feedback than outcome feedback. They can recognize, if not describe, their judgment policies.

Linear Models of Judgment

Perhaps *the* major issue of debate concerning the JA approach is whether judgment polices are accurately represented by linear, algebraic statistical models. Hoffman (1960) characterized linear models as "paramorphic representations" of judgment processes, which has since become a pejorative term because it implies that equations resulting from JA are not "really" models of judgment. Doherty and Brehmer (1997) put this issue to rest, claiming linear equations are legitimate models within the scientific community:

> Human judgment entails a set of imperfectly reliable processes by which the person identifies relevant variables, gives weights to these variables according to their perceived importance, and combines them into a judgment. The combination rule may well depend on the task . . . , but in a great many task environments the combination rule appears to be well-described by a linear model. If there is to be a challenge to the use of linear models in the scientific study of human judgment, the challenge should be directed at this *conception* of the judgment process, rather

than at the use of regression analysis or the analysis of variance. The conception of human judgment emerging from regression studies of human judgment can be refuted only by evidence that shows that judgment is something other than a matter of combining pieces of information that are weighted according to their importance. So far, such evidence has failed to materialize. (pp. 546–547)

Hammond (1996c) points to evidence suggesting that the linear model (i.e., adding or averaging multiple cues) is a genetic endowment of *Homo sapiens*.

Judges Are Inconsistent in Cue Utilization

Judgment response variance is never completely accounted for by all cues used in JA, as evidenced by squared multiple correlations between judgments and cues less than the maximum value of 1.00. Either the analyst has not accounted for all systematic variance (e.g., configural cue utilization), or a judge has been utilizing cues in an inconsistent manner (the "imperfectly reliable processes" referred to in the above quote by Doherty and Brehmer). Hammond and Summers (1972) made inconsistent judgment a topic of great interest and stimulated much research on cognitive control and cognitive conflict. Poor performance in cognitive tasks, and conflicting judgments between individuals, is often due to incomplete cognitive control rather than incomplete knowledge of a task or conflicting personal motives. Investigation of vicarious functioning is critical to increased understanding of the consequences of limited or impaired cognitive control.

Judges May Have Little Insight into Their Own Judgment Policies

Here is a controversial conclusion reached in many judgment studies, but it may be premature (see Doherty and Reilly, Chapter 20, this volume). Insight is usually operationally defined as the degree of correspondence between spoken estimates of cue importance and statistically derived importance weights. Reilly and Doherty (1989, 1992) demonstrated that people have more insight into their own judgment policies than one would conclude from using the standard correspondence measure. Holzworth (1996) has shown that people's intuitions about their judgment policies may be incorporated into their statistical models, producing more valid models of judgment.

A New Development

The traditional focus of judgment analysis is for the judgment analyst to discover the subject's judgment policy through careful study and then, if required, to think through the implications of various policies that people might hold: What would be the likely outcomes of the behavioral implementation of this policy or that one? Recently, however, the reverse course has been taken. That is, after observing certain behavior, inferences are made by interested parties about the judgment policies that produced them, or are thought to have produced them. This has been most visible in connection with practices of the police in detaining and searching members of minority groups, a practice that has come to be known as *profiling*. That is, the public, or interested sections thereof, attributes a certain "profile" (of specific indicators and their weights) to the police and charges that the police unfairly act on it. The critics of the police contend that the profile, or the judgment policy of police officers, contains, most prominently, race and race-related indicators to infer the likelihood of criminal activity. As a result, it is claimed, blacks and other minorities are unfairly singled out for questioning, and this has been a prominent topic for news articles and editorials, most of which claim injustice and demand investigation and change.

Students of JA will recognize that only part of the information necessary for settling this important matter has been presented. They will want to know (1) do police officers in fact hold such judgment policies (behavioral data make the charge plausible) and (2) what are the ecological validities of the indicators, as well as (3) information regarding other parameters of the judgment policies of the police officers. They will recognize that this is an important problem that should not be debated without the information that an application of JA can and should provide. Whether this step will be taken in the heated environment in which such problems are currently argued is certainly doubtful, but students of JA should continue to develop their competence in preparation for the day on which it will be demanded.

JA Crucial to Cognitive Psychology

Brunswik's principles of achievement and vicarious functioning, and of representative design and sampling issues, all basic to JA, will always be crucial to cognitive psychology. After proclaiming vicarious functioning perhaps *the* most fundamental principle of behavior, Brunswik (1957) added: "Vicarious functioning encompasses both the divergent and the convergent part of the lenslike patterns that characterize all achievement. In the field of cognition, it is the divergent part—ecological validity—which is ecological and the convergent part—utilization—which is organismic." (p. 22)

Recently, Stewart, Roebber, and Bosart (1997) reminded us that an understanding of the task environment is essential for understanding the accuracy of judgment. They painted a positive picture of human judgment, concluding that "in many fields of expert judgment, performance is near the limit imposed by environmental uncertainty" (p. 217). JA will continue to be a useful tool, perhaps in conjunction with other methods (e.g., verbal protocol analysis; Ericsson & Simon, 1993) in attempts to understand human judgment and thought processes, because it is based on a philosophy that encourages in-depth investigation of environmental and tasks systems as well as cognitive systems.

22

Brunswik's Theoretical and Methodological Contributions to Research in Interpersonal Perception

Linda Albright and Thomas E. Malloy

Brunswik believed that the processes of social and nonsocial perception were similar (Brunswik, 1934b) and that representative design was the optimal method for the study of both types of perception. He also contended that research in social perception, in particular, "brings home in a most natural way the necessity of representative design of experiments as the methodological counterpart of probabilistic functionalism" (1950, p. 61). That is, because the stimuli in social perception research are people, whose characteristics can not be separated and manipulated orthogonally, representative covariation is the only methodological option. To illustrate this point, Brunswik (1956b) stated:

> To make the analogy with classical psychophysical experiments complete, other personality features or external characteristics, such as will power, or the height of the forehead, would either have to be made to vary—e.g., by artificial selection of the social objects—in perfect correlation with IQ . . . or else have to be held constant at a precise value. It is evident that such an experiment, if actually set up, would defeat its very purpose on account of the unnaturalness of the personality patterns . . . as compared with those in actual social reality. (p. 27)

Later experiments in social perception used systematic covariation, but what Brunswik did not foresee was that such a procedure would be accomplished by representing social objects through verbal descriptions. Whether these studies generalize to those that present actual targets and in which there is a natural covariation of cues remains an empirical question, however.

In this article we show how Brunswik's seminal conceptual and methodological principles have been implemented in current research in interpersonal perception. We begin by describing some of Brunswik's own research, in which he examined the validity of judgments of personality traits on the basis of photographs. Then, we consider some statistical issues that arise in the idiographic approach to analysis. Finally, we show how Brunswik's principles have been applied and, to some extent, extended in current research in interpersonal perception.

Brunswik's Approach to Research in Social Perception

Implementing the principles of probabilistic functionalism and representative design in research on social perception translates essentially into measuring the responses of multiple judges to multiple targets, or "social objects" in Brunswik's terms. In addition, measures of the mediating external cues and of the distal stimulus must be obtained. From a lens model perspective, Brunswik considered the study of social perception as representing the broadest reach of the arch connecting the variables of experimental research in perception, because the initial focus consists of covert-distal stimuli (e.g., personality characteristics, attitudes, and motives). In the study of social perception as well as nonsocial perception, Brunswik deplored the double standard for the sampling of subjects and the sampling of stimulus objects. In the context of citing particular examples of this double standard in social perception research, Brunswik (1956b) concluded that, "in the typical case, they have a pitifully small ecological N to go with a populational n of adequate size" (p. 40).

In Brunswik's (1945) study of social perception, all members of a subunit of the Army Specialized Training Program at the University of California (N = 46) were judged on the basis of a photograph by twenty-five students at the University of California who were unacquainted with the targets. Judges rated the targets on intelligence, energy, likability, and good looks. These judgments were compared to judgments of the same characteristics made by close acquaintances. Brunswik believed that judgments made by close acquaintances were closest to the "unattainable ideal of an objective appraisal of their personalities" (Brunswik, 1956b, p. 28). Measures of functional validity (correlations between the averaged ratings of the strangers and averaged ratings of the close acquaintances) were low on judgments of intelligence, moderate on judgments of energy and likability, and high on judgments on good looks. Analyses of ecological intertrait relationships showed strong connections among measures of energy, likability, and good looks. However, strong "halo effects" (correlations between the judgments of different traits that were made by strangers) occurred among all four traits. The low level of achievement for the trait intelligence appeared to be due to weak ecological trait-cue relationships between distal measures of intelligence and mediating external cues.

The findings presented above reflect only a few of the phenomena that can be addressed through the use of representative design; indeed, Brunswik (1956b) outlined the following eight usages of the correlation coefficient, which are displayed in Table 22.1. Translated into the context of social perception, *test reliability* refers to the degree to which individual differences in achievement (judgmental accuracy) are reliable and can be estimated by correlating judges' achievement scores on one index of the trait with their achievement scores on another index of the same trait. *Test validity* refers to the degree to which individual differences in achievement (judgmental accuracy) are valid and can be estimated by correlating judges' achievement scores with an external criterion. *Agreement among judges* refers to the extent to which different judges agree in their judgments of the targets on a given trait and can be measured by correlating the judgments of all possible pairs of judges and

TABLE 22.1 Brunswik's Eight Usages of the Correlation Coefficient

Phenomenon	Symbol[a]
Differential psychology	
Test reliability	r_{11}
Test validity	r_{12}
Functional psychology	
Agreement among judges	$r_{R_iR_j}$
Self-consistency of judge	$r_{RR'}$
Halo effect	$r_{R_aR_b}$
Achievement	r_{SR}
Psychological ecology	
Ecological reliability	$r_{SS'}$
Ecological validity	$r_{S_1S_2}$

Note. Adapted from Brunswik (1956b, Table 2). 1 and 2 refer to achievement scores on particular traits. Ri and Rj refer to judgments of a given trait made by different judges. R and R' refer to two judgments of the same trait made by the same judge. Ra and Rb refer to judgments of different traits made by the same judge. S and S' refer to measures of the same trait at different times. S1 and S2 refer to distal and proximal measures of the same trait.

[a]Notation used by Brunswik (1956b).

then averaging these correlations. *Self-consistency of judge* refers to the extent to which the judge's responses are reliable measures and can be estimated by correlating for each judge their judgments of two indicators of the same trait and then averaging across judges for an overall estimate of self-consistency. *Halo effects* refer to the extent to which the judge maintains a particular level of positivity when judging different traits and can be estimated by correlating a judge's ratings of different traits and averaging across judges. *Functional validity* refers to the extent to which judgments are valid reflections of social reality and can be estimated by correlating judgments with an external, objective measure of the trait. *Ecological reliability* refers to the extent to which the trait remains constant or stable over time and can be estimated by correlating the same measure of the trait at two different times. Finally, *ecological validity* refers to the extent to which proximal cues are valid reflections of the distal trait and can be estimated by correlating the measure of the proximal cue with the measures of the trait.

Brunswik advocated an idiographic approach to the statistical analysis of the data, as described for each of the phenomena above (except ecological reliability and validity, which refer to the environment). Because the stimuli are persons in social perception research, the idiographic approach to estimating functional validity can produce artifactual results.

Statistical Issues in the Idiographic Approach to Estimation of Functional Validity

When the data consist of multiple judges who rate multiple targets on multiple traits, there are two general approaches to the estimation of functional validity. One can average the multiple judges' ratings on a given trait for each target and then correlate the averaged judgments with objective measures of the trait. In this case, the unit of analysis is target and the correlation is an estimate of overall functional validity for the sample. Brunswik referred to these averaged ratings (across judges) as "the composite judge." Although this was the analytic method used in the analysis of his 1945 study, he believed that this approach "obliterated inter-subject differences," so that the "entire investigation may as well have been done with one subject only" (Brunswik, 1956b, p. 31). The alternative approach is to correlate for each judge his or her ratings of the targets on a given trait with objective measures of each target's standing on the trait. In this case, target is the unit of analysis, and the correlation is a measure of achievement for each judge. The various judges' performances can be aggregated in a variety of ways, such as averaging across judges or by way of cluster analysis. Alternatively, they may be correlated with some other variable, as in test validity.

Research on the accuracy of judgments of personality and other characteristics conducted in the 1940s and 1950s used an idiographic approach. The major purpose behind this research was to address applied problems, such as what characteristics were associated with being a good judge of personality. The analytic approach most commonly used in the research of this period was to compute for each judge the overall discrepancy (arithmetic difference) between targets' self-ratings on different traits and judges' ratings of the targets on the same traits. The lower the discrepancy, the more accurate the judge. The discrepancy scores were then correlated with other individual difference measures to determine what characteristics were associated with being a good judge of personality.

In a landmark article published in 1955, Lee J. Cronbach showed that these global measures of accuracy could reflect any of four types of accuracy, which he called "elevation," "differential elevation," "stereotype accuracy," and "differential accuracy." *Elevation* refers to the ability to judge how favorably people judge themselves in general (across targets and traits) and is produced by a correspondence between the parts of the scale used by the judge and by the targets. *Differential elevation* reflects the ability to judge how favorably different targets judge themselves (across traits) and is produced by a correspondence between the part of the scale used typically by each target and the part used by each judge in his or her ratings of each target. *Stereotype accuracy* refers to the ability to know how favorably people in general judge themselves on particular traits and is produced by a correspondence between parts of the scale used for each trait by the targets and by the judge. Finally, *differential accuracy* refers to the ability to judge how different targets judge themselves on different traits and is produced by a correspond between each target's rating of each trait and the judge's rating of each target on each trait. Differential accuracy is the most precise measure of the ability to judge personality.

Cronbach's analysis implied that accuracy scores needed to be partitioned into their component sources to be interpretable. Because this approach added to the computational burden in the precomputer era, research on accuracy in social perception ended temporarily (Kenny & Albright, 1987). Although Brunswik's correlational approach to estimating accuracy avoids some of the Cronbachian artifacts, the point remains that a person's judgment of a characteristic of another person consists of multiple sources of variance. Current research on the accuracy of social perception reflects this basis tenet.

Application of Brunswikian Principles in Current Research on Interpersonal Perception

Because different approaches to the study of social perception have emerged and maintained, the term *interpersonal perception* is now used to refer to research in which the targets of judgment are real, as opposed to hypothetical, people. All research on interpersonal perception is Brunswikian, because the use of real people as targets of judgment invokes the principle of representative covariation. Because Brunswik was the first to conduct a theoretically based and comprehensive (i.e., he examined numerous phenomena in addition to accuracy) study of social perception, he was the originator of the interpersonal approach to social perception research. We describe below two current lines of research that employ Brunswikian principles (see Funder's and Gillis' chapters, this volume, for other current research).

Using a lens model framework, Robert Gifford and his colleagues have investigated the mediational role of nonverbal behavior in judgments of personality in a series of studies (Gifford, Ng, & Wilkinson, 1985; Gifford, 1991, 1994). For example, Gifford (1994) demonstrated links between personality characteristics and various types of nonverbal behavior (i.e., ecological validity), links between judgments of personality characteristics and nonverbal behavior (cue utilization), and links between judgments of personality and self-ratings of personality (functional validity). Specifically, Gifford (1994) found strong correlations between judgments of introversion and extroversion and smiling, gesturing, nodding, and eye contact, and he found moderate to strong correlations between judgments of introversion and extroversion and self-ratings of these traits. Given that judges were unacquainted with the targets and that verbal and behavioral information was not available to judges, this research provides strong evidence that these nonverbal behaviors are valid cues for the judgment of introversion and extroversion.

Brunswik's contributions to the study of interpersonal perception can also be seen in David Kenny's social relations model (SRM). Whereas Gifford's research incorporates the principles of probabilistic functionalism, the SRM incorporates and extends the principles of representative design. Briefly stated (see Kenny, 1994 for more elaboration), the SRM assumes that a perceiver's judgment of a target consists of four components, called the perceiver effect (the way a perceiver tends to judge others in general), the target effect (the way a target tends to be judged by others in general), the relationship effect (the way a perceiver uniquely judges targets), and error. These components are estimated by having a random sample of judges rate a random sample of targets. Random sampling of targets employs the

principle of representative variation (in that traits are assumed to vary representatively) and the principle of representative covariation (in that the covariation of traits is allowed to remain in its "multivariate pattern of potential observation"; Brunswik, 1956b, p. 10). However, the SRM incorporates the principle of representative covariation in a unique way. If the judges and targets rate each other, the SRM allows and estimates the correlation between one's perceiver and target effects and the correlation between two individuals' relationship effects. The perceiver-target correlation estimates the extent to which people tend to judge others the way they are judged by others. The relationship correlation estimates dyadic reciprocity; the extent to which one individual's unique judgment of another relates to the other's unique judgment of the individual.

In a study of well-acquainted individuals, Malloy and Albright (1990) estimated these two correlations but considered the relationship between the two relevant components of different variables. That is, members of small groups judged each other on several personality traits and also predicted how each person would judge them. Correlations between their perceiver effects on the predictions (the way people thought they were judged generally) and their target effects on the trait judgments (how they were judged generally) were strong. People predicted accurately how they were judged by others in general, a phenomenon called *generalized meta-accuracy*. Correlations between their relationship effects on the predictions (the way people thought they were judged uniquely by specific others) and their relationship effects on the trait judgments (the way they were uniquely judged) were low. People did not accurately predict how they were uniquely judged by specific others, a phenomenon called *dyadic meta-accuracy*.

Conclusion

Brunswik provided the field of social perception with a conceptual model and a theoretically based methodology that is naturally suited for the study of interpersonal judgment. With the development of generalizability theory (Cronbach, Gleser, Nanda, & Rajaratnam, 1972) and the further refinement and extension to broader levels of analysis (the separation individual and dyadic interpersonal phenomena), the potential exists for a modern realization of the rich conceptual and methodological vision of Egon Brunswik. Further, technological development in computer image analysis has made it possible to obtain objective and precise measures of stimuli, such as facial expression and the emotional states

that underly them (Bartlett, Hager, Ekman, & Sejnowski, 1999). With the availability of such measurement, research in social perception represents the broadest reach of the arch connecting the variables of research in perception not only in a conceptual sense, but in an empirical one as well.

23

Hierarchical Linear Models for the Nomothetic Aggregation of Idiographic Descriptions of Judgment

Stephen G. Schilling and James H. Hogge

In this chapter, we explain how hierarchical linear models (Bryk & Raudenbush, 1992) can serve as an analytic framework that considers a set of judges simultaneously, both idiographically (incorporating reliable individual differences between judges' policies) and nomothetically (examining evidence of generality across individuals). Beginning with a summary of the distinction between the idiographic and nomothetic orientations and Brunswik's view of the tension between the two approaches, we note previous strategies that have been employed to aggregate idiographic judgment data. Next, we provide a brief overview of hierarchical linear models and show how they can be used to analyze a set of judgments based on multiple cues. Finally, we summarize the specific advantages of hierarchical linear models for the Brunswikian judgment analyst.

Individuality and Generalization in Judgment Analysis

The distinction between idiographic and nomothetic approaches to the study of human behavior entered the lexicon of psychology through the

pen of Gordon Allport (1937), who borrowed the terms from the German philosopher Wilhelm Windelband, (1894, 1904, 1998). Windelband used *idiographic* (literally, "describing individuality") and *nomothetic* (literally, "laying down laws") to characterize entire disciplines. According to Windelband, idiographic disciplines, such as history, seek to understand a particular event, while nomothetic disciplines, such as the natural sciences, seek only general laws. Allport (1937, p. 22) suggested that although psychology was striving to become "a completely nomothetic discipline," "a psychology of personality would essentially be idiographic" because, for Allport, the study of personality was the study of individuality. Having introduced these two new terms, however, Allport offered additional advice:

> The dichotomy, however, is too sharp: it requires a psychology divided against itself. . . . It is more helpful to regard the two methods as overlapping and contributing to one another. In the field of medicine, diagnosis and therapy are idiographic procedures, but both rest intimately upon a knowledge of the common factors in disease,

determined by the nomothetic sciences of bacteriology and biochemistry. Likewise, biography is clearly idiographic, and yet in the best biographies one finds an artful blend of generalization with individual portraiture. A complete study of the individual will embrace both approaches. (p. 22)

Although Allport's contemporaries quickly adopted these new terms (albeit with some confusion, at least partially inherited from Allport himself; see Lamiell, 1998), they apparently overlooked his cautionary note. Instead, the distinction between the two terms led to polarization of the field and continuing controversy (see, for example, Allport, 1962; Beck, 1953; Eysenck, 1954; Falk, 1956; Holt, 1962; Lamiell, 1997). Regrettably, many researchers tended to regard the two approaches as mutually exclusive, to adopt either an idiographic or a nomothetic approach, and to turn a blind eye to the utility of the other perspective.

Brunswik's Idiographic-Statistical Approach

Brunswik (1955a, p. 237) complained that "the nomothetic-reductionist-systematic type of approach has in the past been overstressed at the expense of the probabilistic-functional-representative approach," and asserted that "we must balance psychology in the molar and molecular realm." In other words, he advocated multiple levels of analysis: "Each level of parsimony and of generalization, from the most disjointedly enumerative description to the most universal of laws, entails a challenge of its own. As there must be a balance of occupations in a society so that all the potential demands are filled, so in science at large there must be an equitable distribution among the variety of potential themata. Insistence on reduction as a universal goal of science can only result in blighted spots on the landmap of scientific enterprise" (pp. 236–237). Brunswik certainly was aware of the idiographic-nomothetic controversy, and like many other writers, he found it useful to reconceptualize the issue. In particular, he linked statistics to the idiographic approach.

In an introduction to Brunswikian theory and

methods written twenty-five years later, Hammond (1980, p. 3) noted that

> Brunswik uses the term *idiographic-statistical* to indicate that each person's behavior should meet a statistical test of regularity or dependability before the behavioral data can be defined as a function of situational variables. *Idiographic-statistical* therefore means that significance tests should be applied to each subject's behavior. Of course, this step can hardly be taken unless there are a sufficient number of situations or trials for statistical tests to be made, and therefore the idiographic-statistical approach is directly tied to the representative design of experiments.

More recently, methodological recommendations by Stewart (1988) and Cooksey (1996b) have also included the caution that the aggregation of individual data and generalizations about the population of individuals should be deferred until the data are understood for each individual. In other words, the idiographic-statistical level of analysis should be followed by the nomothetic level of analysis.

Previous Approaches to the Aggregation of Idiographic Descriptions of Judgment

Unfortunately, Brunswik provided little analytic guidance beyond the very general outline mentioned above, so investigators have been left to develop and explore various approaches to aggregating judgment data. For comparisons of predefined groups of judges, specific techniques have included univariate or multivariate ANOVA applied to summary information for each judge. Examples include R^2 or G (e.g., Adelman, 1977; Hogge & Murrell, 1991) and either individual lens model cue weights or correlations (Dean, Hammond, & Summers, 1972; Ruble & Crosier, 1990; Stewart, Moninger, Heidemann, & Reagan-Cirincione, 1992). When no predefined groups of judges exist, investigators have applied cluster analytic techniques to the same information (e.g., Adelman, Stewart, & Hammond, 1975; Rohrbaugh, 1977; Young, 1982; Hamm, 1983; Cooksey, Freebody, & Bennett, 1990; Graves & Karren, 1992). All of these techniques lack a framework that unifies the idiographic and nomothetic levels of analysis. Fortunately, such an analytic framework is provided by hierarchical linear models (HLM).

Unification of the Idiographic and Nomothetic Levels in the Analysis of Judgment

The HLM framework provides a coherent means of nomothetic (group-level) aggregation and significance testing, simultaneously incorporating estimation of idiographic (individual-level) judgment models. Within the HLM methodology, this is accomplished by means of a comprehensive model that incorporates models corresponding to these two levels of analysis.

Our HLM approach to the analysis of judgments based on multiple cues parallels Meehl's (1954, p. 64) formulation that reconciles individuality (identified with the idiographic perspective) and generalization across individuals (the nomothetic perspective). According to Meehl, a law is simultaneously nomothetic in its form, idiographic in its parameters, and strongly idiographic in its "end terms" (the response properties of the organism). For example, the social judgment theory generalization that a linear model is sufficient to describe the relationship of judgments to a particular set of cues is nomothetic in its form in the sense that it has been found to be true for *groups* of judges considering the particular set of cues. At the same time, however, the weights (parameters) of the linear model differ (idiographically) from judge to judge; furthermore, a particular (and unusual) judge may exhibit nonlinearity or respond to the set of cues in some other idiosyncratic way.

The Idiographic Level of Analysis in HLM

A hierarchical analysis of judgments based upon multiple cues begins with the specification of a general model for each judge's ratings (see Equation 1 of Appendix A). The judge's weights for each cue are simply the linear terms associated with each cue in the multiple regression model; the model allows for the possibility of nonlinear cue-rating relationships by including both quadratic and linear terms. In HLM terminology, this is a *Level 1 model*; in Brunswik's terminology,

this is the *idiographic-statistical model*. Because this general model is applied separately to each judge's ratings as suggested by Meehl (1954), the parameters (i.e., the regression weights) of the nomothetic law expressed by the general model may vary idiographically for each judge. The idiographic nature of the HLM formulation permits the investigator to determine if the judges differed with respect to the weights they gave particular cues by examining variability across judges of the linear or quadratic terms for those cues.

The Nomothetic Level of Analysis in HLM

The HLM model specification is completed with a *Level 2 model* (see Equation 2 of Appendix A) that expresses each regression weight for each judge as a function of the unique component of the regression weight for that judge and the average level of the corresponding linear or quadratic term over all judges. The components of the idiographic-statistical models that are the same across judges are modeled by the average level of the particular linear or quadratic term. The Level 2 model thereby accomplishes the aggregation of idiographic descriptions of individual judges and thus corresponds to the first part the nomothetic level of analysis. Significance tests (z-mean effects in this portion of the analysis) tell the investigator which linear or quadratic terms of cues were utilized by the group of judges. If the z value for a given average effect is statistically significant, then the investigator can conclude that utilization of the corresponding term differs from zero in the population from which the judges were drawn. In HLM terminology, the average levels for a particular model are called *fixed effects*.

The second aspect of the nomothetic level of analysis, typically ignored in traditional experimental design/ANOVA approaches to psychological inquiry, is measuring variability across judges. This is assessed by examining the variance component associated with a particular linear or quadratic term. If the variance component associated with a particular term is zero or close to zero, then judges did not differ in the weight they gave that term. If the variance component is large, then there was considerable variability among the judges in the weight they gave that term. In HLM terminology, the unique components for a particular model are called *random effects*.

Testing the Fit of the Comprehensive Hierarchical Linear Model

Together, the Level 1 model and the Level 2 model constitute a comprehensive hierarchical linear model whose parameters can be estimated via a combination of maximum likelihood and empirical Bayesian techniques, as explained in Appendix A. Because the general Level 1 model includes all of the cues and allows for the possibility of nonlinear cue-rating relationships, it may be more complex than required for a particular set of data. Accordingly, a sequential model-fitting process is used to determine the extent to which the Level 1 model can be simplified.

Indices of model fit

As explained in Appendix A, three indices of model fit should be examined: the maximized log-likelihood (MLL), the Akaike information criterion criterion (AIC), and the Bayesian information criterion (BIC). Because the three indices generally track one another closely, the MLL is treated as the primary criterion on which to base significance tests.

Testing differences between models

In general, a simplified version of a model (i.e., a special case of the model in which one or more linear or quadratic terms have been deleted) is acceptable if it results in a nonsignificant decrease in the MLL. The significance of the decrease in the MLL can be tested with the likelihood ratio chi-square difference between the two models. The formula for this chi-square appears in Appendix A.

The Model-Fitting Process

With software like SAS (SAS Institute Inc., 1990) or the S-Plus lme module (MathSoft Inc., 1998), a final hierarchical linear model is identified with the following model-fitting process:

1. A model with all linear and quadratic fixed effects and all linear and quadratic random effects is fitted, and the variance estimates associated with each random effect are examined to determine which random effects can be omit-

ted from the model. In other words, linear or quadratic terms that the judges did not use are omitted.

2. The cues (linear or quadratic terms) associated with the smallest variance estimates are successively omitted from the model, with indices of model fit being examined and the chi-square test applied to see if omitting these terms results in significantly poorer model fit.

3. When all unnecessary terms have been omitted, small fixed effects can be omitted and model fit examined as in the previous step.

4. When no further terms can be removed without a significantly poorer fit, a final hierarchical linear model has been identified.

Hierarchical Analysis of an Example of Judgments Based on Multiple Cues

Hogge and Murrell (1994) investigated the assessment of the professional competence of British nursing students by hospital nurses responsible for the supervision and evaluation of their practice. Twenty nurses were given a summary of seven performance criteria (Figure 23.1) taken from the nursing school's student handbook. These criteria were used as the basis of the evaluation of the competence of general nursing students in the last six months of their training.

Next, the nurses rated the overall competence of each of twenty-five randomly generated hypothetical nursing students whose performance with respect to the seven criteria had been summarized on profile sheets (Figure 23.2). The same 5-point scale (with 3 = passing) was used for both the criteria and the rating of overall competence.

An Initial Analysis: Fitting Individual Regression Functions

In order to facilitate an understanding of what is accomplished by applying the hierarchical linear model approach, we began by fitting individual regression functions for each judge. Then we computed summary statistics based on the fitted parameters of the individual regressions. The results of this analysis are presented in Table 23.1. The first part of the table presents the variances and standard deviations of the fitted parameters across judges; the second part presents means of the fitted parameters across judges.

ACCOUNTABILITY	Individual accountability and an understanding of the concepts of professional accountability.
	Development of "self" as a resourceful, creative, innovative and questioning person.
	Protection of the personal and confidential rights of patients and clients.
	Awareness of the roles of individual members of the multidisciplinary health care team.
	Functions efficiently in a team and assists in a multidisciplinary approach where appropriate.
	Safe to undertake administration of medications with a witness under supervision.
KNOWLEDGE BASE	Appreciation of research and relevant literature.
	Awareness of social and political factors that adversely affect the physical, mental and social well-being of patients or clients.
	Recognition of common causal factors that contribute to and those that adversely affect the physical, mental and social well-being of patients or clients.
	Identification of the social and health implications of physical and mental handicap or disease, and pregnancy / childbearing for the individual, his or her friends, family and community.
	Knowledge of the normal development of the foetus, the infant, the child, the adolescent and the young, middle-aged and elderly adult.
	Knowledge and understanding to meet the requirements of legislation relevant to nursing.
	A safe level of knowledge and understanding of medications.
	Knowledge necessary to meet the health and nursing needs of individuals.
ASSESSMENT	Ability to make an objective and subjective assessment of physical, psychological, social and spiritual needs with patients/clients and from other sources. Identification of health-related learning needs of patients, clients, families or friends and participation in health promotion. Recognition of potential risks and ensuring of safety. Gathering and evaluating information about resources, social networks and support systems.
PLANNING	Devising a plan of care reflecting an appreciation and evaluation of the principles of a problem-solving approach through selection, assessment and interpretation of data. Writing individual case plans involving the client or patient or other according to his/her ability and taking into account available resources.
IMPLEMENTATION	Development of helpful, caring relationships with patients, clients and their families and friends. Use of leadership/followership skills to meet goals and enhance quality of nursing care. Skills necessary to meet the health requirements of individuals and of groups. Enabling patients or clients to progress from varying degrees of dependence to maximum independence, or to a peaceful death.
EVALUATION	Ability to evaluation progress towards agreed objectives. Ability to modify the health care plan where necessary. Ability to reflect on the process and outcomes of care given. Skills needed to guide and supervise nursing care; to participate in evaluation of nursing practice through quality assurance programs and to facilitate changes in health care provision; to promote cost containment through appropriate use of human and material resources; to promote a safe environment for patients and health care providers; to recognise own learning needs and see opportunities to meet them; and to act as a Health Educator and to refer individuals and their families appropriately.
SPECIFIC NURSING INTERVENTIONS AND SKILLS	Maintaining a safe environment and assessment. Emergency care, high dependency care and medical treatment. Management of eating, drinking and eliminating. Work with breathing and cardiac functions. Maintaining fluid and electrolyte balance and the administrations of medications. Personal cleansing, temperature regulation and the significant observations of the skin. Mobilizing and orthopaedic nursing care. Special senses and ENT nursing. Prevention of infection.

FIGURE 23.1 Performance criteria for general nursing students.

NURSING STUDENT NUMBER 3

Accountability	4	Credit
Knowledge	3	Pass
Assessment	3	Passs
Planning	2	Borderline
Implementation	3	Pass
Evaluation	5	Distinction
Nursing Skills	4	Credit
Overall Competence	5	Distinction
(Please circle	4	Credit
your rating)	3	Pass
	2	Borderline
	1	Refer

FIGURE 23.2 Sample judgment task profile.

From an examination of the first part of Table 23.1 it is clear that the fitted regression parameters for the intercept and the Cue 2 effect exhibit variability across judges; however, it is difficult to determine if there is variability among the other parameters. The second part of the table suggests that, on average, the linear effects for Cues 2 (knowledge) and 4 (planning) and the quadratic effect for Cues 2 and 3 (assessment) are not needed. A researcher performing traditional nomothethic aggregation based only on the data in the second part of Table 41.1 might determine that Cue 2 is unimportant. But this is belied by our earlier finding that the judges exhibit considerable variation in the importance they attach to Cue 2. What is needed is a means for integrating both results in a nomothetic model. In what follows, we will see that the HLM framework provides a means for integrating both approaches.

Fitting the Hierarchical Linear Model

Table 23.2 contains a summary of the model-fitting process for these data (Appendix B contains the S-Plus commands used to conduct the analysis of the data; in addition, the corresponding SAS commands are included). Following the model-fitting process described above, we begin with the most elaborate model (Model 1, with all linear and quadratic fixed and random effects). In the next stage of the model-fitting process, the only random effects are linear Cue 2 (knowledge) and 7 (nursing skills) effects and the intercept effect (random intercepts are included in virtually all HLM models). This change produced no appreciable increase in the MLL and noticeable improvement in both the AIC and BIC indices. Omitting the random effect for Cue 7 produced a decrease of approximately 4.3 in the MLL and a chi-square of 8.6 on 3 degrees of freedom (significant at the .05 level), with no improvement in the AIC and only a slight improvement in the BIC; hence, the random effect for Cue 7 was retained. Finally, in Step 3, omitting the fixed quadratic effects for Cues 2, 3 and the fixed linear effect for Cue 7 actually increased the MLL, with appreciable decreases in the other fit indices. Parameter estimates for this final model appear in Table 23.3.

Interpretation of Results

Earlier, we identified two separate aspects of the nomothetic level of analysis: variability of cue weights between judges and average cue weights across judges. To emphasize the relationships between HLM models and each of these aspects, we deal with them separately.

Cues that were eliminated in Step 2 of the model-fitting process have been omitted from Panel A of Table 23.3 because their variance components were not significantly different from zero.

TABLE 23.1 Summary Statistics for Individual Regressions

A. Parameter variances and standard deviations	Variance	Std. Dev.
Intercept	0.264	0.514
Cue 1 (knowledge)	0.014	0.119
Cue 2 (knowledge)	0.050	0.224
Cue 3 (knowledge)	0.010	0.100
Cue 4 (knowledge)	0.009	0.095
Cue 5 (knowledge)	0.005	0.072
Cue 6 (knowledge)	0.004	0.060
Cue 7 (nursing skills)	0.006	0.078
Cue 1 squared	0.002	0.040
Cue 2 squared	0.005	0.073
Cue 3 squared	0.007	0.081
Cue 4 squared	0.007	0.086
Cue 5 squared	0.003	0.053
Cue 6 squared	0.002	0.046
Cue 7 squared	0.003	0.052

B. Mean parameter values Parameter	Mean	Std. Error	z Value
Intercept	2.889	0.115	25.12
Cue 1 (accountability)	0.101	0.027	3.80
Cue 2 (knowledge)	−0.086	0.050	−1.71
Cue 3 (assessment)	0.259	0.022	11.55
Cue 4 (planning)	0.011	0.021	0.51
Cue 5 (implementation)	0.112	0.016	6.97
Cue 6 (evaluation)	0.102	0.013	7.58
Cue 7 (nursing skills)	0.205	0.017	11.81
Cue 1 squared	−0.095	0.009	−10.52
Cue 2 squared	0.023	0.016	1.38
Cue 3 squared	−0.028	0.018	−1.54
Cue 4 squared	−0.142	0.019	−7.35
Cue 5 squared	−0.151	0.012	−12.83
Cue 6 squared	0.038	0.010	3.66
Cue 7 squared	−0.076	0.012	−6.45

TABLE 23.2 Hierarchical Linear Model Comparisons

Model	MLL[a]	AIC[b]	BIC[c]
1. All random and fixed effects	−917.5	1938.9	2194.1
2. Cues 2 and 7 random—all fixed effects	−925.2	1894.4	2002.3
3. Cue 2 random—all fixed effects	−929.5	1896.9	1990.1
4. Cues 2 and 7 random—all linear effects; quadratic effects for Cues 1, 4, 5, 6, 7	−921.1	1882.2	1980.3

[a]Maximized log-likelihood.

[b]Akaike information criterion.

[c]Bayesian information criterion.

TABLE 23.3 Parameter Estimates for Model 4

A. Random effects	Variance	Std. Dev.
Intercept	0.147	0.383
Cue 2 (knowledge)	0.020	0.141
Cue 7 (nursing skills)	0.003	0.055
Residual	0.318	0.564

B. Correlations among random effects	Intercept	Cue 2
Cue 2 (knowledge)	0.994	
Cue 7 (nursing skills)	0.412	0.509

C. Fixed effects Parameter	Estimate	Std. Error	z Value
Intercept	2.839	0.113	25.14
Cue 1 (accountability)	0.102	0.018	5.61
Cue 2 (knowledge)	−0.068	0.039	−1.74
Cue 3 (assessment)	0.240	0.016	14.60
Cue 4 (planning)	0.023	0.019	1.20
Cue 5 (implementation)	0.104	0.015	6.83
Cue 6 (evaluation)	0.095	0.018	5.34
Cue 7 (nursing skills)	0.189	0.017	10.84
Cue 1 squared	−0.093	0.013	−7.13
Cue 4 squared	−0.144	0.017	−8.49
Cue 5 squared	−0.132	0.015	−8.62
Cue 6 squared	0.039	0.013	3.02
Cue 7 squared	−0.085	0.012	−6.84

The results in Panel A show that there was significant variability among the nurses in the linear weights they assigned to both Cues 2 (knowledge) and Cue 7 (nursing skills). Also, the significant variance component for the intercept indicates that there was mean variability among the nurses (i.e., they tended to use different portions of the 5-point rating scale).

The significance tests for the fixed effects (Panel C of Table 23.3) tell the investigator which cues were utilized on average across the group of judges. Cues with significant random effects are retained in the final model despite nonsignificant z values because, although the average sample weight was not significantly different from zero, some judges assigned the cue nonzero (but offsetting) weights. Also, by convention, the final model contains the linear term of any cue found to have a significant quadratic effect.

Using a critical z value of ±1.96 (.05 significance level), the results in Panel C indicate that, on the basis of this sample of twenty judges, the most appropriate judgment model for a judge

randomly selected from the corresponding population would include the intercept, linear terms for all of the cues, and quadratic terms for Cues 1 (accountability), 4 (planning), 5 (implementation), 6 (evaluation), and 7 (nursing skills).

A Technical Issue in Implementing an HLM Analysis

A potential area of concern for the final model is the high correlation between the random effects for the intercept and Cue 2 (see Panel B of Table 23.3). High correlations between random effects can sometimes cause unstable estimates akin to the effects of multicollinearity in multiple regression. One common remedy is to recenter the independent variables closer to a point of intersection of the response planes estimated for individual judges. In the case of the present data, this would mean centering each independent variable about 1. The rationale is that one might expect that all judges would tend to give low ratings for such a case. In fact, applying this new centering reduces the correlation from 0.994 to −0.755. Comparison of the results for these parameterizations shows that both centerings produce very similar correlation matrices.

Advantages of the Hierarchical Analysis of Judgments

When undertaken after the ratings of judges have been analyzed and understood at the individual level, the analytic framework of HLM offers several advantages for the Brunswikian judgment analyst:

1. Judges are simultaneously modeled at the idiographic and nomothetic levels; thus, the idiographic descriptions of judges are represented in a comprehensive model that also portrays judgment-cue relationships at a group level. In essence, the HLM framework can be seen as paralleling Meehl's (1954) characterization of behavioral laws as nomothetic in their form for a given group, but idiographic in their parameters for a particular individual.
2. The comprehensive HLM models described above permit the detection of both linear and quadratic relationships between the cues and judges' ratings; moreover, the technique we have described clearly indicates whether quadratic relationships detected in idiographic descriptions of individual judges should be included in an overall, nomothetic description of the aggregated data.
3. The method we have described leads the investigator to a parsimonious nomothetic model of the aggregated judgment data. Model fitting is guided by indices of model fit and a significance test that is used to determine which linear and quadratic terms can be omitted during the model-fitting process.
4. Additional significance tests permit the detection of
   a. differences among the judges with respect to the weights they assign individual cues (idiographic level of analysis) and
   b. appreciable cue utilization in the population from which the sample of judges was drawn (nomothetic level of analysis).

In short, the HLM methodology provides a coherent means of model aggregation and testing that effectively unifies the idiographic and nomothetic levels of analysis. As recommended by Cooksey (1996b), Hammond (1980), Stewart (1988), and others, analyses within the HLM framework follow the application of significance tests to descriptions of the behavior of individual subjects; thus, this method supplements, not supplants, Brunswik's idiographic-statistical approach. In addition, as described by Hogge and Schilling (1998), the HLM framework can easily be extended to the examination of group differences, thus achieving further methodological unification without compromising Brunswik's fundamental analytic perspective.

Appendix A: Specification of Hierarchical Linear Models

Our application of hierarchical linear models (HLM) to judgment data requires the specification of models at two levels corresponding, respectively, to the idiographic and nomothetic levels of analysis.

General Model for Individual Judges

A hierarchical analysis of judgment based upon multiple cues begins with the specification of a general model that allows for the possibility of nonlinear cue-rating relationships by including both linear and quadratic terms:

$$Y_{ij} = \beta_{0j} + \beta_{1j}\dot{X}_{1i} + \cdots + \beta_{qj}\dot{X}_{qi}$$
$$+ \beta_{q+1j}\dot{X}_{1i}^2 + \cdots + \beta_{pj}\dot{X}_{qi}^2 + \varepsilon_{ij}$$
$$\varepsilon_{ij} \sim N(0,\sigma^2), \tag{1}$$

where Y_{ij} is Judge j's rating of Person i, $\dot{X}_{mi}$ is a mean-centered[1] value for Cue m on Person i, β_{kj} is a judge-specific regression coefficient, ε_{ij} is random error, and σ^2 is the variance of the random error. In HLM terminology, this is a *Level 1 model*; it corresponds to the ideographic level of analysis.

Model for Aggregation of Ideographic Descriptions of Judges

The HLM model specification is completed with a nomothetic *Level 2 model* for the regression coefficients of the level 1 model:

$$\beta_{kj} = \gamma_k + u_{kj}, \mathbf{u}_j \sim N(\mathbf{0}, \mathbf{T}). \tag{2}$$

Here γ_k is the mean effect of the cue over all judges, u_{kj} is the unique component of β_{kj} for Judge j, and $\mathbf{T}$ is the variance/covariance matrix associated with the vector of random effects $\mathbf{u}_j$. In HLM, the γ_k's and $\mathbf{T}$'s, and σ^2 are the structural parameters of the model and are estimated via maximum likelihood (for details, see Bryk & Raudenbush, 1992), while the β_{kj}'s are estimated via empirical Bayesian techniques.

Estimates of the individual regression components, $\tilde{\beta}_{kj}$, combine information from the least squares estimates $\hat{\beta}_{kj}$ used in SJT and the mean estimates $\hat{\gamma}_k$ by forming an optimal weighted combination of the two. Let $\hat{\mathbf{T}}$ be the estimated variance/covariance matrix, and let $\mathbf{V}_j = \hat{\sigma}^2 \mathbf{X}'_j \mathbf{X}_j$ be the variance/covariance matrix of the least squares regression coefficients. Then, an optimal Bayesian weighting procedure yields the following estimates of $\tilde{\beta}_{kj}$:

$$\tilde{\boldsymbol{\beta}}_j = (V_j^{-1} + \hat{\mathbf{T}}^{-1})^{-1}(V_j^{-1}\,\hat{\boldsymbol{\beta}}_j + \hat{\mathbf{T}}^{-1}\hat{\boldsymbol{\Gamma}}), \qquad (3)$$

where $\tilde{\boldsymbol{\beta}}_j$, $\hat{\boldsymbol{\beta}}_j$, and $\hat{\boldsymbol{\Gamma}}$ are vectors containing the Bayesian, least squares, and mean estimates $\hat{\beta}_{kj}$, $\tilde{\beta}_{kj}$, and $\hat{\gamma}_k$, respectively (for details, see Bryk & Raudenbush, 1992).

Indices of Model Fit

We recommend examining three indices of model fit: the maximized log-likelihood (MLL), the Akaike information criterion (AIC), and the Bayesian information criterion (BIC).

In general, a linear subset of a model (i.e., a special case of the model in which one or more of its parameters have been set to zero) is acceptable if the corresponding decrease in the MLL is not statistically significant. The significance of the decrease in the MLL can be tested with the likelihood ratio chi-square difference between the two models. If model M_2 is a linear subset of model M_1, p_1 and p_2 are the numbers of parameters in the two models, and $\hat{\theta}_1$ and $\hat{\theta}_2$ are the corresponding vectors of parameter estimates, then

$$G^2(M_2\,|\,M_1) = -2(l(\hat{\theta}_2\,|\,y) - l(\hat{\theta}_1\,|\,y)) \qquad (4)$$

is the likelihood ratio chi-square difference between the two models and is chi-square distributed with $p_1 - p_2$ degrees of freedom. This significance test is used to determine which effects can

be omitted during the model fitting process described in the body of this chapter.

The AIC and BIC are the likelihood-based equivalents of adjusted R^2 indices in multiple regression, but with *smaller* values indicating better fit. The main practical difference between the AIC and BIC is that the BIC tends to penalize more heavily for greater numbers of parameters (Aitken, 1980) and is thus the more conservative of the two indices.

Appendix B: SAS and S-Plus Commands

SAS Commands for Saturated Model

```
data nurse;
input judge nurse cue1 cue2 cue3 cue4 cue5 cue6 cue7
cue1sq cue2sq cue3sq cue4sq cue5sq cue6sq cue7sq
rating;
cards;
    *
    *
    *
;
proc mixed;

model rating = cue1 cue2 cue3 cue4 cue5 cue6 cue7
/* The Fixed Part of the Model */
cue1sq cue2sq cue3sq cue4sq cue5sq cue6sq cue7sq/
sol;

random cue1 cue2 cue3 cue4 cue5 cue6 cue7/* The
Random Part of the
Model */
cue1sq cue2sq cue3sq cue4sq cue5sq cue6sq cue7sq/
sub = judge type = un;

run;
```

S-Plus Commands for Saturated Model

```
nurse1.fit <- lme(fixed = rating ~ cue1 cue2 cue3
cue4 cue5 cue6 cue7
+ cue1sq cue2sq cue3sq cue4sq cue5sq cue6sq
cue7sq,
+ random = ~ cue1 cue2 cue3 cue4 cue5 cue6 cue7
+ cue1sq cue2sq cue3sq cue4sq cue5sq cue6sq
cue7sq, cluster = ~ judge,
+ data = nurse)
```

NOTE

1. $\dot{X}_{mij} = (X_{mij} - \bar{X}_{m\cdot j})$

24

Vicarious Functioning Reconsidered: A Fast and Frugal Lens Model

Gerd Gigerenzer and Elke M. Kurz

When Egon Brunswik left Vienna for Berkeley in 1937, he began to abandon his favorite tool—a measurement tool known as the *Brunswik ratio*. The ratio measured the degree of perceptual constancy. In its place, Brunswik (1940b) adopted new tools from the Anglo-American statistical tradition—correlation and regression. Then, he measured the degree to which perception attains the distal stimulus by a correlation coefficient called *functional validity*.

New tools often inspire new theories, a source of new ideas known as the *tools-to-theories heuristic* (Gigerenzer, 1991). Brunswik used this heuristic, and so have many others. After he had switched to correlations as his new tool, his concept of the mind changed, too. He began to regard the mind as an "intuitive statistician," and he suggested that the intuitive statistician would use the same new tools: correlation and regression. In particular, *vicarious functioning*, which Brunswik considered the most fundamental principle of a science of perception and behavior, began to be modeled by multiple regression (as first fleshed out by Hammond, Hursch, & Todd, 1964; see also Tucker, 1964; Stewart, 1976).

Vicarious functioning carried a rich meaning for Brunswik. He agreed with W. S. Hunter that the "flexibility and exchangeability of pathways relative to an end," that is, vicarious functioning, was the defining and unifying criterion of psychology (Brunswik, 1952). Brunswik's classical examples were the substitution mechanisms in psychoanalytic theory, the habit family hierarchy in Hull's behaviorism, and hierarchies of perceptual cues. The psychoanalytic work of his wife, Else Frenkel-Brunswik (e.g., 1942), stressed the fact that one cause can manifest itself in various symptoms—rationalization, hysteric conversation, regression, cathexis, and narcissism, among others. If one symptom is blocked or not available,

it can be substituted by another. Similarly, in Hull's habit family hierarchy, if a habit is not successful in a situation, it will be replaced with the next one in the hierarchy. In Brunswik's perceptual research, vicarious functioning had a very specific meaning: It signified the divergent as well as the convergent part of his lens model, the first being ecological validity and the second utilization. Both of these complementary aspects of vicarious functioning were modeled by correlation statistics.

In this chapter, we propose a radically different way to model vicarious functioning: the framework of *fast and frugal heuristics* (Gigerenzer, Todd, & the ABC Research Group, 1999). Simple heuristics are psychologically plausible alternatives to multiple regression, and we argue that they are consistent with Brunswik's own ideas. The adaptive value of vicarious functioning is not only in making accurate judgments, but also in being able to make judgments quickly and with limited knowledge. We illustrate a fast and frugal lens model (there are several, depending on the task and the heuristic) and report a counterintuitive result: In making inferences about real-world criteria (the "distal" stimuli), the fast and frugal lens not only was as accurate but also was even more accurate than the computationally complex multiple regression model.

Vicarious Functioning Reconsidered

The idea of vicarious functioning is an extension of Brunswik's earlier notion of cue learning, which in turn is based on Helmholtz's controversial concept of unconscious inferences and Bühler's duplicity principle (details in Doherty & Kurz, 1996; Gigerenzer & Murray, 1987, pp. 61–81). Vicarious functioning describes adaptive cognitive processes that can handle two constraints: the presence of *uncertainty* and the need for *substitution*. A cue (e.g., the retinal image of an object) is only an *uncertain* indicator of a distal stimulus (e.g., the distance to the object), and a cue may not always be present; thus, an adaptive system has to rely on multiple cues that can be *substituted* for each other.

Is multiple regression an appropriate model of vicarious functioning in all situations? What cognitive processes does it imply, and which does it neglect? We begin by pointing out two cognitive processes implied by the multiple regression model and the evidence that one of these two seems to be dispensable in many situations. Then we will draw attention to two processes inherent in vicarious functioning that multiple regression does not model.

Weighting and Summing?

Two fundamental processes in multiple regression are the weighting of cues and the summing of the cue values (Kurz & Martignon, 1998). Weighting and summing have been used to define rational judgment at least since the Enlightenment—the concepts of expected value and utility, Benjamin Franklin's moral algebra, and *Homo economicus* all rely on these two principles. Why should vicarious functioning not work this way, too?

The first blow was delivered to weighting. In the 1970s and 1980s, Robyn Dawes (e.g., 1979) and his colleagues studied predictive accuracy, that is, situations in which the regression weights were computed from one sample and used to make predictions for a new sample. They showed that simple unit weights, such as +1 and −1, typically led to the same predictive accuracy as the "optimal" weights in multiple regression. Weighting does not seem to matter, as long one gets the sign right. Of course, multiple regression would be more accurate than Dawes's unit weight rule in *fitting* given data (as opposed to *predicting* new data), as models generally do when they have more free parameters. But the purpose of vicarious functioning is to predict what is not yet known rather than to fit what is already known. Thus, the question is: If summing without weighting is as accurate as multiple regression, and much simpler to perform, why should mechanisms of vicarious functioning have evolved that try to estimate regression weights?

The second blow was delivered to summing. During the 1990s, the counterintuitive evidence accumulated that fast and frugal heuristics that do not sum cue values but rely only on the first cue that differentiates between two alternatives can be more accurate than multiple regression (Gigerenzer, Czerlinski, & Martignon, 1999; Gigerenzer & Goldstein, 1996). For instance, the *Take The Best* heuristic (see below) uses a simple form of weighting (namely, ordering cues), but it does not sum the cues. Thus, the question is: If weighting without summing can be as accurate as multiple regression, why should mechanisms of vicarious functioning have evolved that try to sum cue values?

It seems that either weighting or summing is dispensable, but not both. But this is not yet the whole story: Weighting and summing model only a part of vicarious functioning. Two cognitive processes in vicarious functioning are not captured by weighted or unweighted linear models.

Searching and Stopping!

Multiple regression models one of three processes involved in vicarious functioning, the *decision rule* ("judgment policy"), by assuming the use of weighting and summing. It does not model two processes that precede a decision, *rules for search*, which give direction to the search for cues, and *rules for stopping*, which stop this search at some point. Modeling search and stopping is paramount for situations involving limited time, limited knowledge, and other constraints. For instance, when deciding about whom to hire, whom to marry, or which stock to buy, one needs to search for cues—in internal memory or in the external world—and this search cannot go on endlessly. Limited search and stopping rules are the essence of bounded rationality (Simon, 1955), as opposed to the fiction of unbounded rationality. The study of search and stopping rules, however, is bypassed in many experimental designs in which all cues are laid out conveniently in front of a participant, who is not supposed to search for further cues. Convenient packaging, however, does not capture the spirit of representative design, nor that of vicarious functioning. The focus on multiple regression in Brunswikian research has thrown search and stopping out of focus.

In the following, we propose an alternative

conception of vicarious functioning that uses weighting but not summing and that models search and stopping. It is a step toward a class of psychologically plausible models of vicarious functioning in human judgment.

A Fast and Frugal Lens Model

The term *fast and frugal* signifies cognitive processes that allow one to make judgments that are reached under limited time and with limited knowledge and that do not try to optimize. *Optimizing* may involve computing the optimal linear weights or the Bayesian conditional probabilities, and *optimizing* has been the classical definition of rationality. Brunswik, however, did not think that the cognitive system is rational, only ratiomorphic or quasi-rational. But he was not clear about the mechanism of these quasi-rational processes. Heuristics that are fast (that is, involve little computation) and frugal (that is, search for only few cues) can define the quasi rationality of Brunswik's lens model.

How would a fast and frugal lens function? It embodies heuristics, principles for search, stopping, and decision. We explain its functioning for two-alternative choice tasks, such as to infer which of two U.S. cities has a higher homelessness rate, or which of two soccer teams will win a game. The specific heuristic we use is the Take The Best heuristic, which is derived from probabilistic mental models theory (Gigerenzer, Hoffrage, & Kleinbölting, 1991). This heuristic is just one illustration; there are other heuristics of similar design and for other tasks, such as for estimation and classification (see Gigerenzer, Todd & the ABC Research Group, 1999). For simplicity, we assume that all cue values are binary (positive or negative, with positive indicating higher criterion values) and ignore the recognition heuristic, the initial step of Take The Best (see Gigerenzer & Goldstein, 1996):

Step 1. *Search rule*: Choose the cue with the highest validity that has not yet been tried for this task. Look up the cue values of the two objects.

Step 2. *Stopping rule*: If one object has a positive cue value and the other does not (i.e., either negative or unknown value) then stop search and go on to Step 3. Otherwise go back to Step 1 and

search for another cue. If no further cue is found, then guess.

Step 3. *Decision rule*: Predict that the object with the positive cue value has the higher value on the criterion. (See Figure 24.1.)

This fast and frugal lens uses *one-reason decision making*; that is, the decision is based on only one cue. Take The Best orders cues according to their validities v_i:

$$v_i = \frac{R_i}{R_i + W_i},$$

where R_i is the number of right (correct) inferences, and W_i is the number of wrong inferences based on Cue i alone (among all cases where one object has a positive value and the other does not). Ordering cues according to v_i is fast, but not "optimal." For instance, this order does not try to account for conditional validities of cues, that is, dependencies between cues.

How Accurate Is a Fast and Frugal Lens?

How does the fast and frugal lens compare to the multiple regression lens? We tested four models of vicarious functioning, including Take The Best and multiple regression, in twenty real-world environments. The two other models were Dawes's rule, a linear model that uses unit weights (+1 or −1), as mentioned above, and the Minimalist heuristic, which is like Take The Best except that it is even simpler because it looks up cues in a random order (thus, the only difference is in Step 1). The criteria to be predicted in the twenty environments included economic variables such as selling prices of houses and professors' salaries; psychological variables such as predicting the perceived attractiveness of famous men and women; demographic variables such as mortality rates in U.S. cities and population sizes of German cities; environmental variables such as amount of rainfall, ozone, and oxidants; health variables such as obesity at age eighteen, and sociological variables such as dropout rates in Chicago public high schools. The task was always to predict which of two objects scored higher on a criterion. The data sets ranged from seventeen objects to 395 objects, and from three cues (the minimum to distinguish among the strategies) to nineteen cues (for details see Czerlinski, Gigerenzer, & Goldstein, 1999).

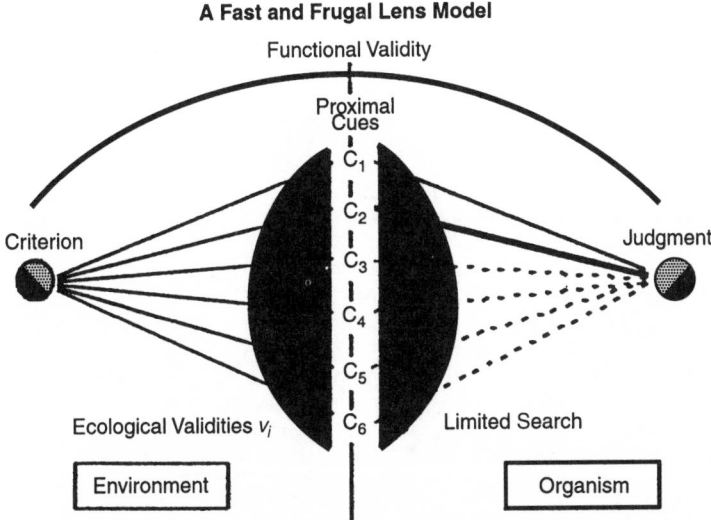

FIGURE 24.1 Illustration of a fast and frugal lens model. The task is to infer which of two objects has a higher value on a criterion. Cues are binary and looked up in the order of their estimated validity. The first cue, C_1, does not discriminate (light line), but the second cue does (dark line). Search is stopped, and the values of C_2 determine the inference. Information concerning other cues is not searched (broken lines).

For each of the twenty tasks, each of the four strategies estimated its parameters (the sign, the order, or the beta weights of the cues) using one half of the objects, and then used these parameters to make predictions about the other half of the objects. This procedure is known as *cross-validation*.

What price does one-reason decision making have to pay for being fast and frugal? Table 24.1 shows how frugal the two heuristics actually were: on average, they searched for fewer than a third of the cues (similar to the illustration in Figure 24.1), whereas the two linear strategies always looked up all cue values (which averaged 7.7 across the twenty environments). How much more accurate were the two linear models than the heuristics? Table 24.1 shows a counterintuitive result: The fast and frugal lens model (using Take The Best) achieved the greatest predictive accuracy, with an average of 71 percent, compared to multiple regression and Dawes's rule with 68 percent and 69 percent, respectively.

This result seems paradoxical because multiple regression processed all the information that Take The Best had, and more. There are two factors that explain this result: the *robustness* and

the *ecological rationality* of the fast and frugal lens. The fast and frugal lens is relatively robust, whereas multiple regression overfits. This can be seen from the "fitting" column in Table 24.1. In this condition, Czerlinski, Gigerenzer, and Goldstein (1999) gave all four strategies the complete information about all objects (i.e., no cross-validation), and they fit the data as well as they could. In this case, multiple regression achieved the highest accuracy. The difference between the fitting and the predictive accuracy columns reveals that multiple regression overfitted more than any of the other three strategies.

Dawes's rule lives up to its reputation as a robust strategy, and, consistent with earlier demonstrations, its predictive accuracy matched that of multiple regression. The most frugal strategy, the Minimalist, had to pay some price for simplicity, but not a high one: Its performance was not too far behind that of the two linear strategies in predictive accuracy.

Ecological Rationality

We mentioned overfitting as one reason that the fast and frugal lens performed better than the

TABLE 24.1 Performance of a Fast and Frugal Lens Using a Heuristic (Minimalist or Take the Best) Compared to Two Linear Strategies (Dawes's Rule, Multiple Regression) across Twenty Data Sets

Strategy	Frugality	Accuracy (% correct)	
		Fitting	Predictive Accuracy
Minimalist	2.2	69	65
Take The Best	2.4	75	71
Dawes's rule	7.7	73	69
Multiple regression	7.7	77	68

Note: The average number of cues was 7.7. Performance was measured in terms of frugality (average number of cues looked up) and accuracy (percentage correct). Accuracy was measured both for fitting given data (test set = training set), and for predicting new data, that is, predictive accuracy (test set ≠ training set). The average number of cues looked up was about the same for fitting and generalization (see Czerlinski, Gigerenzer, and Goldstein, 1999).

multiple regression lens. But there is another reason that explains why and when fast and frugal heuristics perform well, even in a purely fitting task (recall that Take The Best was very close to multiple regression even in fitting; see Table 24.1). This second reason is a match between the structure of the (known) information in the environment and that of the heuristic. Brunswik had seen the importance of analyzing the structure of environments in order to understand the mechanisms of the mind, but there is room for improvement in his first attempt to capture the structure in terms of correlation coefficients.

What we call *ecological rationality* is an elaboration of the Brunswikian program of studying the texture of environments. Heuristics are not rational in the classical sense of coherence—the Minimalist, for instance, can produce intransitive judgments. They derive their rationality through a match with the structure of the environment, not with the laws of logic or probability. Martignon and Hoffrage (1999) introduced two characteristics of environments that explain when and why a fast and frugal lens that operates with Take The Best is accurate: *noncompensatory* and *scarce* information.

Noncompensatory Information

The fast and frugal lens is noncompensatory: The decision based on the first cue that discriminates (in the example: C_2) cannot be reversed by the other cues (C_3, C_4, . . .), nor by a combination

of them. A noncompensatory set of cues is a set in which each weight is larger than the sum of all other weights to come, such as 1/2, 1/4, 1/8, ... To the extent that cues are noncompensatory, Take The Best will be as accurate as the best linear model. The following theorem states an important property of noncompensatory models and is easily proved (Hoffrage & Martignon, in press).

> *Theorem:* Take The Best is equivalent—in accuracy, not in process—to a weighted linear model whose weights form a noncompensatory set.

If multiple regression happens to have a noncompensatory set of weights (in which the order of this set corresponds to the order of cue validities), then its accuracy is equivalent to that of Take The Best. For instance, among the twenty environments, Martignon and Hoffrage (1999) found four in which this was the case. The important difference between the fast and frugal heuristics and multiple regression or optimization methods is that a fast and frugal lens does not try to compute optimal weights. These heuristics just "bet" that the environment has a structure they can exploit.

Scarce Information

In order to illustrate the concept of scarce information, let us recall an important fact from information theory: A class of N objects contains $logN$ bits of information. This means that if we were to encode each object in the class by means of binary cue profiles of the same length, this length should be at least $logN$ if each object is to have a unique profile. For instance, eight objects can be perfectly predicted by three ($log8 = 3$) binary cues. If there were only two cues, perfect predictability simply could not be achieved.

> *Definition*: A set of M cues provides *scarce* information for a reference class of N objects if $M < logN$.

Based on this definition, the following theorem relates the performance of Take The Best to that of Dawes's rule.

> *Theorem*: In the case of scarce information and small numbers of objects (up to 2^{10}), Take The Best is on average more accurate than Dawes's rule.

The proof is in Hoffrage and Martignon (in press). The phrase "on average" means across all possible environments, that is, all combinations of binary entries for NM matrices. The intuition underlying the theorem is the following: In scarce environments, Dawes's rule can take little advantage of its strongest property, namely, compensation. If, in a scarce environment, cues are redundant—that is, if a subset of these cues does not add new information—things will be even worse for Dawes's rule. Take The Best suffers less from redundancy because decisions are made at a very early stage.

The Adaptive Toolbox

We illustrated the mechanism of a fast and frugal lens for a two-alternative choice task. Other types of tasks, such as estimation (Hertwig, Hoffrage, & Martignon, 1999) and classification (Berretty, Todd, & Martignon, 1999), can be performed by heuristics based on similar building blocks that define search, stopping, and decision. This collection of heuristics and their building blocks is what we call the *adaptive toolbox*—specialized mechanisms of cognition and learning that have evolved in the human mind (Gigerenzer, Todd, & the ABC Research Group, 1999). The adaptive toolbox refers to vicarious functioning on the level of heuristics, rather than to cues. An adaptive mind should be able to substitute heuristics just as it does cues.

The specific fast and frugal lens we proposed here embodies limited search and stopping, which the multiple regression model does not incorporate. The fast and frugal lens relies on a simple form of weighting (ordering by validities v_l) but does not use summing or other forms of integrating cue values. Its strength is in its robustness, ecological rationality, and psychological plausibility (Rieskamp & Hoffrage, 1999).

The fast and frugal lens combines Brunswik's ideas of vicarious functioning with the notion of bounded rationality (Simon, 1955). The emphasis on cue substitution as opposed to cue integration is consistent with some of Brunswik's favorite examples: the alternative manifestation and substitution of symptoms in Frenkel-Brunswik's (1942) psychoanalytic work and the substitution of behavior in Hull's hierarchical habit family. And cue substitution is certainly also consistent with an emphasis on the mere rank order of cues (Brunswik, 1947): "In a well-adjusted organism or species, however, the rank order of utilization in what may be called the 'or-assembly' of cues, or the 'cue family hierarchy,' should be the same as the order of their ecological validity"(p. 48). Multiple regression is not the last word on vicarious functioning. We propose taking Brunswik's notion of the quasi-rational nature of vicarious functioning seriously and model it with adaptive heuristics.

25

Multiple Cue Probability Learning

R. James Holzworth

Brunswik's principal research interest began with visual perception, specifically the perceptual constancies. But his theorizing was at such a high level of generality, even while he was in Vienna, that his concepts of uncertainty, ecological validity, and vicarious functioning could easily be seen to apply to other circumstances, once one was willing to look. Although Brunswik had introduced the concept of probability to the topic of learning in his 1939 rat learning experiment, his success was utterly ignored by the learning establishment (see Doherty, this volume). The demonstration of the potential for the generalization of the lens model to learning had to wait until 1954, when Smedslund (1955) in Norway carried it out in his doctoral thesis. It was he who first saw the manner in which all these concepts could be generalized to learning, roughly at the same time that Hammond (1955) made the same extension beyond visual perception to the context of clinical judgment.

In one of his last articles to be published, Brunswik (1957) emphasized that his goal was to "restore or establish the proper equality of standards in the treatment of organism and environment [in] which equal justice is done to the inherent characteristics of the organism and of the environment" (p. 6). One glance at the lens model makes it clear that "equal justice" is exactly what the lens model can provide. The diagram of the model makes clear that equal attention is given to both organism and environment. And this "equal justice" model is what was carried out in the field of learning for the first time with the introduction of the multiple cue probability learning (MCPL) paradigm by Jan Smedslund, and the use of the lens model by Hammond in relation to clinical judgment.

The learning theorists of the 1930s and later, however, were uninterested in giving equal attention to both organism and environment; rather, they "stuffed" the organism, one might say, with numerous hypothetical constructs that were in-

tended to explain its behavior. Their purpose in creating the T-maze paradigm was only to test the hypothesis of interest; there was no regard for, or interest in, how environments might actually be constructed. As a result, no thought whatever was given to how the results of an experiment might be generalized to any environment. Although Estes (1950, 1964) adapted his stimulus-sampling theory to *non*contingent human probability learning experiments and prescribed how probabilities of various predictive responses by the learner changed as a function of events (reinforcement), no attention was paid to contextual characteristics of learning environments. Instead, the focus was on whether organisms attempt to maximize or match S-R reinforcement contingencies. Efforts to answer this question led Herrnstein (1979, 1990), while disregarding the work of Mats Björkman (1967, 1969), to conclude that "melioration" is the common tendency—a rise or fall in the reinforcement of a response causes the rate of occurrence of the response to change in the same direction.

The MCPL paradigm did, however, provide equal justice to the organism and the environment by describing the degree of uncertainty in the task environment, the ecological validities of the cues, and the intercorrelations (redundancy) among the cues, thus making explicit—and controllable—a degree of complexity never imagined by the stimulus-response (S-R) learning psychologists. And the MCPL paradigm offered justice to the organism by describing the subject's performance in terms of the uncertainty in the response system, differential cue utilization, and achievement, or learning. Thus, by providing equal justice, it made a complete break with the learning theory of the day, which was soon to die a quiet death, apparently because of the barren nature of its implications beyond the T maze.

This was especially true once the Lens Model Equation (LME) was developed by Tucker in 1964 (see Stewart, chapter 27 of this volume).

One of the new concepts introduced by this equation, which is based on multiple regression (MR) statistics, was the "limit of achievement." This concept indicated that once the systematic variance in the task has been accounted for by the linear model, the limit of achievement has been identified; better performance cannot be achieved. Thus, the LME offers a measure of that degree of learning, or achievement, that cannot be surpassed, and that limit will ordinarily be a direct function of the degree of irreducible uncertainty in the task. I mention this concept because it would have been hardly imaginable to the S-R learning theorist, for these theorists had always assumed that perfection was always possible in learning, and in the tasks the S-R psychologist was persistently employing, over and over again, perfection always was possible because the task was a fully determined one. However, in the MCPL paradigm, the amount of irreducible uncertainty in the task was set by the experimenter— who set the amount of randomness in the task— and, therefore, the question of whether the subject reached the "limit of achievement" could be empirically examined. And it was this approach that made visible a new and important distinction, namely, the distinction between the *formal and substantive properties* of the task (see Hammond, 1966a, for the introduction of these terms). The MCPL tasks were always described in terms of their formal properties because the degree of uncertainty in the task was specified, as were the ecological validities and the intercor-

relations among the cues. The term *substantive properties* refers to properties of materials used to build the task (e.g., text used to define cues, diagrams used to express cue values). Tasks could be varied and compared with respect to their formal properties, as well as their substantive ones, as a matter of course (see, e.g., Adelman, 1981).

Roughly coterminus with the death of S-R learning theory, MCPL became a prolific field of endeavor. It did not, of course, attract established learning researchers already committed to the S-R model, who must have found it mystifying and rarely cited it (see Doherty, this volume). It did, however, attract young psychologists, who found that it provided an exciting research paradigm that offered a variety of new topics to explore (see Brehmer & Joyce, 1988; Cooksey, 1996b, for reviews). Figure 25.1 presents the history of MCPL studies and shows that they reached a peak in the early 1970s and diminished in frequency regularly until the present. Reasons for the decline in publication rate have been offered by Estes (1976). Referring to MCPL as well as other probability learning paradigms, Estes wrote:

> Probability learning has been somewhat eclipsed in the literature of cognitive psychology by an increasing preoccupation with psycholinguistics and the semantic aspects of memory. Nonetheless, it should be recognized that we are scarcely in a position to close the chapter of research on this aspect of human learning. First, the reasons,

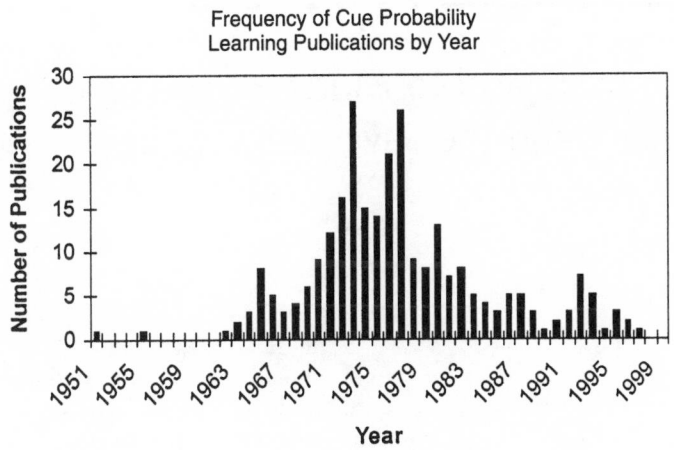

FIGURE 25.1 Publications of cue probability learning research.

both theoretical and practical, that were responsible for the interest in probability learning during the 1950s have by no means evaporated. Rather, it continues to be apparent that probability learning constitutes a major interface between cognitive psychology and the practical world. (p. 37)

Some of the "practical" concerns to which Estes was referring include economics, clinical judgment, and medical diagnosis (see also Klayman, 1988).

What Does the Future Hold for MCPL Studies?

Many MCPL studies have implications for training (e.g., clinical judgment, medical training), and a greater emphasis on training issues may lead researchers to focus on new problem areas. For example, within industrial psychology, a training perspective raises issues such as factors affecting learning and performance on the job (e.g., divided attention, fatigue, noise, stress) and methods of providing cognitive feedback so that workers may perform better (e.g., job design, electronic monitoring). In the spirit of probabilistic functionalism, Alexander Kirlik and associates (Kirlik & Bisantz, 1999; Kirlik, Fisk, Walker, & Rothrock, 1999) have been investigating design and training problems in dynamic, high-technol-

ogy, and high-consequence environments for the U.S. Navy. Recent research on goal setting also expands the picture of MCPL (DeShon & Alexander, 1996; see also Adelman, this volume, and Kirlik, this volume; see especially Chasseigne and Mullet, this volume, and Chasseigne, Mullet, and Stewart (1997) for an example of the use of the MCPL paradigm in studies of the elderly).

Conclusion

The MCPL research paradigm served its usefulness by providing a means for demonstrating that Brunswik's probabilistic theory about cognition and his explication of it in terms of the lens model could be directly translated into fruitful research. Moreover, it demonstrated that the LME and its associated concepts could provide new substantive information about probabilistic learning under generalizable conditions, and it made it evident what generalization would entail. It is no longer necessary to show that such experiments can be done with profit; it is clear that the MCPL paradigm has a useful place in particular fields of application as well as in relation to theoretical issues (for an example, see Hammond, Hamm, Grassia, & Pearson, 1987; see also Hammond, Hamm, & Grassia, 1986).

26

From Ecological to Moral Psychology: Morality and the Psychology of Egon Brunswik

Bo Earle

Introduction

Moral judgment and behavior are uniquely resistant to psychological analysis because morality generally is defined in terms that do not admit of psychological predication. Principal among

these is the idea of *freedom*. An agent can act morally only on the condition that it is also free to do otherwise. Correspondingly, to evaluate actions for their moral content is necessarily to construe them as expressions of a self-determining, autonomous will. Such autonomy is not only essential to the idea of morality, but is also integral to the self-understanding in the Western world in the modern era. For this self-understanding is founded on a conception of a kind of dignity and value intrinsic to every individual, predicated solely on the capacity for free self-determination. In the fully emancipated state envisioned by the philosophers of the Enlightenment, the modern, autonomous subject need appeal no further than to the court of its own rationality for justification of its knowledge of and conduct in the world around it.[1] Thus, regardless of whatever the psychological dimension of moral behavior may in fact be, moral psychology faces the purely conceptual dilemma that to account for moral behavior psychologically is to undermine the exalted autonomy by virtue of which such behavior is counted as "moral" to begin with. In order to elucidate the psychological component of moral behavior, therefore, moral psychology must be concerned first and foremost that it does not effectively deny the properly moral component of such behavior.

Contemporary attempts to temper, if not resolve, this dilemma and its practical implications commonly construe the psychological processes underlying moral judgment as mitigating rather than repudiating the Enlightenment conception of morality. Cass Sunstein's (1997) psychological argument for debiasing legal procedures offers a prime example of this tactic. When considered in juxtaposition to Brunswikian psychology, however, it is clear that this approach fails to resolve the opposition of psychology and morality and, on the contrary, remains beholden to a formal and abstract conception of rational validity. By contrast, Brunswikian psychology, by measuring cognitive achievement according to ecological functionality rather than abstract criteria of rational validity, provides a more promising basis for resolving this dilemma. In the following, the respective theoretical premises of Sunstein and Brunswik are contrasted in order to suggest that Brunswikian theory constitutes a distinct and highly promising new approach to the psychology of moral judgment.

Cognitive Competence as Ecological Functionality

Brunswik's work throughout his career was premised on an idea that at first blush will hardly appear unfamiliar to contemporary theoretical psychologists: that the context of a particular decision-making situation bears a strong correlation to the process by which the decision is made and consequently also the decision itself. Brunswik's innovation, however, was to define context not as something to which objective, rational analysis and synthetic reason are ultimately opposed, but as their *genuine origin and formative foundation*. Thus, rather than measuring the error- and bias-inducing effects of context against the absolute standard of reason abstracted from all context (the approach exemplified by Sunstein, as we will see), Brunswik measured cognitive achievement according to the efficacy it demonstrates in respect to the demands of particular environmental contexts.

Measuring Cognitive Competence in Uncertain Ecologies

In Brunswik's view, our pride in the occasional capacity of cognition to abstract itself from its primary, ecological function lulls us into treating objective analysis as the model of correct thinking per se. In fact, such analysis constitutes a very specialized function of cognition, and it is a mistake to think that it could replace or provide any kind evaluative standard for the primary, ecological modes thinking. For, Brunswik (1952) contended, these latter

> must appear as the more truly behavior-like function when compared with deductive reasoning with its machine-like, precariously one-tracked tight-rope modes of procedure. The constantly looming catastrophes of the intellect would be found more often developing into catastrophes of action were it not for the mellowing effect of the darker, more feeling-like and thus more dramatically convincing primordial (that is, perceptual) layers of cognitive adjustment. (p. 90)

To be situated in a particular environment is to be at least partially blinded to the laws governing it; for, although one might understand such laws very well in the abstract, being environmentally situated necessarily implies being subject to an influx of phenomena beyond one's capacity to thoroughly enumerate in objective terms. To offer such enumeration is by definition to remove oneself from the environment: to isolate it from oneself as the object of explication, rather than the proper medium of behavior. "The universal lawfulness of the world is of limited comfort to the perceiver or behaver not in a position to apply these laws" (Brunswik, 1955c, p. 209); "his environment remains for all practical purposes a semierratic medium; it is no more than partially controlled and no more than probabilistically predictable" (Brunswik, 1956a, p. 158).

If the medium of perceptual and behavioral achievement is "semierratic" and only "partially controlled," then such achievement cannot be accounted for mechanistically in terms of univocal causal relations, regardless of how well such accounts might apply to artificially isolated, entirely controlled, physical events. "Concise mechanical description, in accordance with the conceptual system of physics," Brunswik (1992) wrote, leads to a characterization of behavior in terms of "periodic, stationary chains of events, in the course of which particular conditions and activities consistently reappear with relatively little modification"; but "what is remarkable," Brunswik contended, "is that the causal chains by which these recurrent forms are combined themselves exhibit far less uniformity than the products to which they consistently give rise" (p. 215).[2]

This point is central to Brunswik's theoretical innovation. My conviction that the contents of my environment are as they appear results not from any analytical inference on my part that such contents are necessary correlates of data given to my retina, but from criteria or cues internal to my perception itself: According to Brunswik, my certainty is given immediately by the faculty of the *Anschauung*, the intuition/perception (or, literally, the "seeing into") by virtue of which the contents of my environment appear to me as such contents. The ability to maintain a stable, coherent view of the world and its contents, and to behave in a consequent manner in relation to them, cannot be accounted for mechanistically, for every environmentally situated perspective negotiates its environment via criteria that are meaningless in abstraction from the particular activities and purposes in which that negotiation consists. But disengaged, objective analysis entails just such abstraction.

The Depth and Texture of Social Perception

Thus, in contrast to the behaviorists, although Brunswik was indeed committed to construing perception in relation to empirical conditions, he denied that this necessarily implies construing it in causal relation to them. Rather, Brunswik depicted the behavioral ecology in which perception is carried out in terms of "depth" and "texture." Depth denotes the intentional character of ecological behavior; its orientation toward objects is not directly represented in the immediate data of the senses. Texture describes the relative probability that a particular environmental cue actually indicates the object "intended" by the organism. At the same time, however, depth applies also to the subject; for although Brunswik (1943, p. 258) likened the "wager" underlying behavior to an assessment of relative probabilities, it is almost entirely the work of the intuition, for even the most routine environmental negotiation demands such wagers with a frequency that is beyond the capacity of conscious deliberation. On the basis of the interrelation of these two realms of "depth," Brunswik postulated an ecological holism. "Both organism and environment will have to be seen as systems," Brunswik (1957) wrote, "Each with properties of its own, yet both hewn from basically the same block. Each has surface and depth, or overt and covert regions. . . . The interrelationship between the two systems has the essential characteristic of a 'coming-to-terms.' And this coming-to-terms is not merely a matter of the mutual boundary or surface areas. It concerns equally as much, or perhaps even more, the rapport between the central, covert layers of the two systems" (p. 5).

Brunswik construed this "coming-to-terms" as a relation of the subjective *Anschauung* to objective "depth criteria" (*Tiefenkriterien*) (Brunswik, 1934b, pp. 49, 109).[3] The representative example of "criterial perception" is the recognition of the mental states of others. Brunswik (1950) maintained that in a social ecology, the "most relevant layer" of perception is that constituted by socially malleable objects (p. 57). As early as the early 1930s, Brunswik designed experiments to examine perception of not only basic moods and emotions but also more explicitly socially determined properties, such as "character," "likeability," "intelligence," and "energy" (Brunswik, 1934b, pp. 210–222; cf. Brunswik, 1956b). These experiments measured the correlation of the perception of such properties with schematic depictions of facial features, such as length of nose, height of forehead, and distance between the eyes, which patently bear no causal or "symptomatic" relation to them. These experiments make clear the absolute incommensurability of behavioristic causality with Brunswik's concept of *Tiefenkriterien*, for the latter are explicitly premised on the proposition that the perception of "deep" properties demands no analytic inference of causal relationships.

Brunswik explained the perceptual stability or "constancy" of such properties by distinguishing, like Husserl, between the "content" and the "object" of perception. Perception does consist of "real things," but these are not represented in the discrete identities of objects themselves, but in the objective properties (color, shape, weight, etc.) of which they are composed. Such properties constitute the "real content" of perception: Objects are thus not *identified* as discrete entities unto themselves so much as they are *classified* according to their constituent properties. As Kevin Mulligan (1997) noted, however, what clearly distinguishes Brunswik's conception of perceptual classification from that of Husserl is the contention that such classification would be impossible were it not for the stability that classificatory categories can maintain by virtue of their integral role in the general ecological system. Hence, Brunswik's contention that such categories cannot be identified with the discreet object perceived: They are incapable of analytical precision because they do not admit of univocal application. Rather, they are, Brunswik (1935a) wrote, always at least partially *"submerged in their functional, mediatory role"* (p. 85);[4] they are inextricable from their functional role within the total ecological system and thus are incapable of neutral, analytical description of that system from a perspective exterior to it.

The significance of this point to moral psychology is corroborated by George Lakoff's (1987) study of categories and classification, which Brunswik's theory clearly anticipated. Just as Brunswik argued that the "most relevant layer" of perception consists in properties defined according to their ecological function, Lakoff showed that concepts of greater functional pertinence—what he called "basic level concepts"—have an epistemic priority over more abstract, generalized concepts, *although the latter are capable of far greater analytical rigor*. Thus, for instance, in the conceptual hierarchy *woodwind/saxophone/alto saxophone*, or *vehicle/car/VW*, it is the middle "basic" concept that is both easiest for people to learn and used most frequently, although it is rarely if ever the most accurate or unambiguous. "Basic" concepts, Lakoff contended, are by far the most frequently used, across all discursive contexts and languages. The significance for morality could not be greater, for clearly, in a moral context, the basic concepts will *not* be the abstractions that currently tend to dominate moral discourse (e.g., "freedom," "justice," right," and "wrong") but rather terms of more concrete and immediate functional pertinence, such as "courageous," "honest," "generous," and "cruel." For instance in the hierarchy *wrong/cruel/cruel to animals*, it is not the abstract idea of what it means to "do wrong" but the basic concept of "cruelty" that is morally most relevant; for relative to such abstraction, "cruelty" will have a more significant and certainly far more tangible functional role in the ecology in which it is applied.

The Criteria of Moral Judgments

Just as perception generally could not be achieved in the absence of ecological cues (e.g., of depth), social perception—particular, moral judgment—is essentially dependent on determinate cues, or criteria of morality. A Brunswikian moral psychology would allow us to recognize the actual, functionally concrete cues informing judgments that invoke abstractions like "freedom" and "human rights" as their ostensible criteria. Such abstractions are, Michael Ignatieff (1997) wrote, "fiction[s] in the sense that [they] require a self-conscious screening-out of certain empirical realities in the name of moral convention. . . . We are asked to deny plain facts and look beneath them to some elementary essence we all supposedly have in common" (p. 64). The impossibility of adequately accounting for moral behavior and substantiating moral judgment on the basis of such fictions alone is born out by any of a number of contemporary public debates. The putatively self-evident univocality of what participants in Clinton's impeachment referred to monumentally as "the Law" was patently belied by the confusion and partisanship that those same participants manifested in the impeachment proceedings. Indeed, this discrepancy attests pointedly to the fact that, to whatever extent ours is, in fact, "a government of laws, not men," it is so not by virtue of any conformity of our leaders' judgment and behavior to canonical legal principles but, on the contrary, precisely by the *circumscription* of their judgment and behavior by the procedural requirements of the Constitution. The essential distinction between actual moral judgments and the democratic procedures by means of which functional compromises are achieved among conflicting judgments is, as de Tocqueville famously pointed out, too frequently obscured by American reverence for the Constitution and the abstract liberties and rights it champions. A perfect example of the distinction between an actual moral judgment, grounded in concrete ecological cues, and a merely procedural sophism masquerading as a moral judgment is given in the abortion debate. The prolife position postulates a genuinely moral criterion: that humanity is manifest in the human form. Since a fetus exhibits a recognizably human form and thus meets the criterion for humanity, abortion is tantamount to murder. The prochoice position lamentably advances no alternative criterion; as a result, no amount of pontification concerning the entirely abstract idea—what Ignatieff would call "fiction"—of a supposed "right" to bodily self-determination addresses the salient question, namely, by what criteria do we recognize human life if not the human form? Could there be such criteria manifest in the actual choice-making behavior of real women? Could, for instance, the decision not to become a mother in certain circumstances be defended on the basis of our positive conceptions of the proper role of *motherhood* itself? There is certainly a plausible, albeit difficult, case to be made that such positive conceptions of the prerogatives of motherhood represent a more compelling manifestation of moral value in than the inert human form. Making such a case however would require the pro-choice side to forego the comfort of the analytical rigor of the rights-based approach to morality; not merely to defend certain women's reproductive behavior on the weak but analytically unimpeachable basis of rights, but to positively endorse it on the basis of a strong but analytically unsanctioned assertion that it exhibits something of what makes human life valuable; i.e., a criterion of morality.

Referring to the democratic process, or to abstract "fictions" like universal rights, to justify moral positions in fact only undermines such positions by denying them any genuinely compel-ling moral end or purpose. Michael Sandel (1996) made this point with regard to Supreme Court rulings expressing toleration for homosexual practices on the basis of the right to privacy. These rulings

> tolerate homosexuality at the price of demeaning it; [they] put homosexuality on a par with obscenity—a base thing that should nonetheless be tolerated so long as it takes place in private. . . . The problem with the neutral case for toleration is the opposite side of its appeal; it leaves wholly unchallenged the adverse views of homosexuality itself. But unless those views can be plausibly addressed, even a court ruling in their favor is unlikely to win for homosexuals more than a thin and fragile toleration. A fuller respect would require, if not admiration, at least some appreciation of the lives homosexuals live. But such appreciation is unlikely to be cultivated by a legal and political discourse conducted in terms of autonomy rights alone. (p. 107)

Cognitive Competence as Rational Validity

The penchant of philosophers to explain moral behavior by reference to the most general, abstract concepts rather than to the functionally most pertinent, basic concepts is identical in intent to the penchant of psychologists to explain behavior generally by reference to the artificial conditions of controlled environments. In both cases, it is the analytical rigor provided by universalizable conceptual frameworks that is pursued, although, as Brunswik showed, in neither case does such "universal lawfulness" bear significantly on the actual situation and achievement of the "perceiver or behaver not in a position to apply those laws." (Brunswik, 1955, p. 209) It is precisely the immateriality of "universal lawfulness" to context-specific moral behavior that undermines Sunstein's (1997) "Behavioral Analysis of Law." Sunstein argues that developments in the study of judgment and decision making "call for qualification of rational choice models," on the grounds that "cognitive errors and motivational distortions . . . press behavior far from the anticipated directions" (p. 1175). The primary qualification considered by Sunstein with respect to the law concerns the way in which "preferences and values are sometimes constructed rather than elicited by social situations" (p. 1176); "Thus law can construct . . . preferences both internally, by affecting what goes on in court, and externally, by affecting what happens in ordinary transactions—market and nonmarket" (p. 1177).

Although Sunstein is informative in respect to the ways in which procedure and context construct preferences and values, such procedural considerations only beg the question of the actual desirability of the various particular preferences and values themselves. As a result, Sunstein equivocated on whether the kind of behavioral data his study cites can contribute to assessing the actual moral authority of legal judgments: "None of these points makes a firm case for legal paternalism, particularly since bureaucrats may be subject to the same cognitive and motivational distortions as everyone else" (p. 1178). Sunstein's concern was exclusively for legal procedure, rather than for the ends and purposes the law exists to serve. Sunstein did hold out hope that through procedural "corrections" our innate, less than perfectly rational decision-making processes might be sufficiently "debiased" be provided with an internally coherent, formal rationality. But such debiasing procedures secure rationality for the *form* of decision-making processes only by effacing the question of the adequacy of their content, and it is precisely this latter question that the ineluctable moral element in legal judgments poses most trenchantly.

Pretending that the rationality of legal judgments can be measured exclusively in respect to their formal coherence, Sunstein relativized the actual moral ends or criteria governing legal judgments. But it is precisely the moral nature of such criteria that distinguishes legal judgments from purely technical, cost-benefit assessments. While such relativization may prove most efficacious in a technical context where exclusively utilitarian criteria are at stake, *moral and legal judgments are defined by their irreducibility to criteria of utility alone.* Thus, despite his critique of rational choice theory, Sunstein's approach maintains the fundamental opposition of psychology and morality because the debiasing procedures he recommended do not resolve that opposition but only artificially and provisionally suspend it, relativizing the criteria of legal judgments as if criteria of morality could be assimilated entirely to criteria of utility.

Now, the question of the extent to which utility should figure in moral judgments is certainly le-

gitimate. The crucial point to recognize, however, is that regardless of one's position on this question—even if one were to claim that moral questions should always be decided by maximizing utility—*no* position on this question could possibly be defended according to utilitarian criteria alone. Rather, even an uncompromising utilitarian must make a decidedly *moral* argument to the effect that utility is the best measure of morality; and no such argument could possibly be convincing that did not first offer a distinctive *criterion of morality* that utility could then be shown to satisfy.

Sunstein's entirely procedural conception of rationality accomplishes precisely the inverse: It assimilates moral criteria to criteria of utility. Although Sunstein attended to contextual influences that rational choice theory ignores, he did so only to artificially counterbalance them with debiasing procedures intended to put the decision maker back in conformity with formal, analytical models of rationality. Sunstein refused to recognize the rationality of any cognition that fails to conform to such models, and he consequently could not conceive of legal and moral rationality otherwise than in opposition to the putative constraints imposed by context and psychology generally. Procedural correction of the psychological biases imposed by context, bringing judgment in conformity to rational models, does not resolve the opposition of psychology and morality but only suspends it in the *particular* context of artificial procedures that assimilate morality to utility.

Sunstein's attempt to resolve the opposition of morality and psychology, although unsuccessful, is instructive because it demonstrates that such a resolution requires admitting into the purview of "rationality" forms of cognition that fail to exhibit strict analytical coherence; for it is only by recognizing the way in which moral judgments respond to criteria incommensurable with analytical utility assessments that a psychology of moral behavior might proceed without denying the moral nature of its object.

As the preceding discussions have hopefully indicated, it is the great promise of Brunswikian psychology in respect to morality to accomplish precisely this, that is, to elucidate the actual criteria of moral judgments according to their local, ecological function. In lieu of endless analytic disputation of the abstract and ultimately indeterminate concepts with which morality is traditionally concerned ("rational validity," "freedom," "autonomy," etc.), a Brunswikian moral psychology promises to provide a *functionally determinate* definition of *basic* moral concepts such as "cruelty," "generosity," "virtue," and "vice," in respect to the concrete, functional cues according to which such concepts are in fact recognized in actual social ecologies. Thus, basic moral concepts would be defined in a manner essentially analogous to Brunswik's own definition of socially malleable personality traits such as "likeability" and "character" according to the functional cues by which such traits are perceived. In respect to the debates over abortion and homosexuality, the liberal camp in particular would stand to gain immensely from learning what many conservatives know very well: that moral judgments, as opposed to technical and utilitarian judgments, persuade less by virtue of analytical coherence than by virtue of harnessing concrete, ecologically determinate criteria of morality.

"Ratiomorphism" as a Holistic Theory of Cognitive Achievement

Brunswikian theory presents thought and behavior as fundamentally inextricable. Both are construed according to a model of what Brunswik termed "ratiomorphism." "Only by at least implicit recognition of this underlying communality," Brunswik (1966b) wrote, "are we enabled to proceed to differentiation between relatively autonomous cognitive subsystems at the more molar level of strategy and of achievement. In this light perception and the different varieties of thinking begin to reveal themselves as but different forms of imperfect reasoning. . . . All intuition and all irrationality thus appear but as aspects of rationality" (p. 490). Brunswik's conception of thinking, intuition, and perception as only various "ratiomorphisms" fundamentally refutes the general premise that coherence of experience is possible only by virtue of the conformity of cognition with formal models of analytical rationality. For Brunswik, it was the faculty of the *Anschauung*, comprising intuition and perception alike, that provided the formative basis of cognition, and what preserved the intuition from contingency and inscrutability was not any fortuitous congruence with abstract concepts, but the structural stability it was provided by virtue of its eco-

logical function. In Brunswik's account, it is ecological functionality that makes possible all ratiomorphic achievement, from basic perception to "all the different varieties of thinking," including moral judgment. Ecological functionality provides not only for the efficacy of such perceptual and behavioral achievement in particular cases; just as important, it provides a systemic, structural basis for confidence in the stability and dependability of such achievement, and thus also for confidence in the probability that its efficacy will also persist into the future. It is precisely such confidence that neither Sunstein's debiasing procedures, designed to make moral behavior conform to universal rational norms, nor liberal moral arguments invoking abstract concepts of "universal rights" and "free choice" can provide.

Conclusion

It is Brunswik's conception of knowledge and of ratiomorphism generally as competence implicit to ecological interchange that marks his fundamental break with the traditional conception of cognitive competence, and that likewise marks the promise of Brunswikian psychology in application to ethics. Construed in terms of functional validity, knowledge is inextricable from the particular practices and ecologies to which it is applied. It essentially inheres in such practices and cannot be abstracted from them. The conception of the subject as inextricable from its practices, and of knowledge as familiarity with and competence in negotiating particular ecologies, is fundamentally incommensurable with the prevailing view of moral psychology today, of which Sunstein (1997) is exemplary. Sunstein ostensibly dispenses with models of rational decision-making processes only to covertly reaffirm them as the standard against which the biasing effects of context are measured. By contrast, a Brunswikian moral psychology would represent a genuinely new account of moral behavior, which resolves the opposition of psychology and morality by construing the latter not in opposition to the psychological effects of social and environmental contexts but as coextensive with them; as, in other words, but one of the variety of ratiomorphic strategies by which subject and environment "come to terms." A Brunswikian moral psychology would thus promise to redirect the currently prevalent but ultimately futile and even counterproductive concern for the strictly analytical coherence and justifiability of knowledge and ethical life toward the infinitely more salutary and pertinent issue of the stability and integrity of the particular social practices that make possible not only properly moral judgment and behavior but also knowledge and perception generally.

NOTES

This chapter is a slightly edited version of Earle, B. (2000), From ecological to moral psychology: Morality and the psychology of Egon Brunswik. Journal of Theoretical and Philosophical Psychology, Vol. 20, pp. 196–207. Reprinted here by permission.

1. Cf. Isaiah Berlin (1969, p. 126): "Benjamin Constant, . . . Jefferson, Burke, Paine, Mill, compiled different catalogues of individual liberties, but the argument for keeping authority at bay is always substantially the same. We must preserve a minimum area of personal freedom if we are not to 'degrade or deny our nature.'" Also cf. Alasdaire MacIntyre (1981, p. 42): "[The] concept of authority as excluding reason, is . . . a peculiarly . . . modern concept, fashioned in a culture to which the notion of authority is alien and repugnant, so that appeals to authority appear irrational."

2. My translation. The perceived necessity of providing a thoroughgoing, mechanistic account of human behavior is convincingly repudiated by Charles Taylor (1985) as a misguided preoccupation of contemporary psychology.

3. Elsewhere Brunswik wrote in Husserl's idiom of *Tiefenmotive* (Brunswik, 1935a, p. 83).

4. "gehen in ihrer funktionalen Vermittlerrolle unter."

27

The Lens Model Equation

Thomas R. Stewart

The lens model equation (LME) is a quantitative expression of Brunswik's lens model and probabilistic functionalism. Since its introduction in 1964, the LME has led to advances in the study of expert judgment, multiple cue probability learning, interpersonal learning, and conflict. In this brief chapter, I will summarize the history of the lens model equation, describe its relation to Brunswikian theory, and discuss future directions for LME research.

History of the Lens Model Equation

The seeds of the eventual development of the lens model equation can be found in Hammond's 1955 paper entitled "Probabilistic Functionalism and the Clinical Method." Hammond argued the importance of the partition between organism and the environment and shows, with two examples, how both the subject and the object side of the lens model can be analyzed by the same method—multiple regression analysis. This symmetry of method is at the heart of the LME. What is missing, however, is an analysis of the *relation* between the two sides of the lens.

Hursch, Hammond, and Hursch (1964) corrected this omission by deriving the original lens model equation. They used it to explore the effects of statistical properties of both the environment and the response process on the results of multiple cue probability studies. Ironically, the LME was not the central focus of their paper. In fact, there are so many equations in the paper that one can identify the LME only with difficulty and the advantage of hindsight. Hammond, Hursch, and Todd (1964) made a slight notational modification and featured the LME prominently on the second page of their paper (although neither paper uses the term *lens model equation*, which became popular only later). The Hammond, Hursch, and Todd (1964) version of the LME is:

$$r_a = \frac{R_e^2 + R_s^2 - \Sigma d}{2} + C\sqrt{(1 - R_e^2)(1 - R_s^2)},$$

where $\Sigma d = \Sigma(r_{e_i} - r_{s_i})(\beta_{e_i} - \beta_{s_i})$.

r_a is the correlation between the subject's judgment (Y_s) and the distal variable (Y_e).

R_e is the multiple correlation for the environment, or object, side of the lens model, that is, the multiple correlation between the distal variable and the cues.

R_s is the multiple correlation for the subject side of the lens model, that is, the multiple correlation between the subject's judgment and the cues.

r_{e_i} is the correlation between Cue i and the distal variable.

r_{s_i} is the correlation between Cue i and the subject's judgment.

β_{e_i} is the standardized regression weight (beta) for Cue i from the regression of the distal variable on the cues.

β_{s_i} is the standardized regression weight (beta) for Cue i from the regression of the subject's judgment on the cues.

C is the correlation between the residuals from the two regression equations.

This equation describes achievement (r_a) as the sum of two terms. The first term captures the component of achievement that is attributable to the cue validities and cue utilizations. The second term captures the component of achievement that cannot be accounted for by the regression models of the environment and the judge. But there is more. The first term also provides measures of the predictability of the environment (R_e), the consistency of the judge (R_s), and the match between the cue validities and cue utilizations (Σd—a parameter that Brunswik would have considered of great importance). Thus, for the first

time, it was possible to analyze cognitive performance into the part that was due to the environment, the part that was due to the judge, and the relation between them.

Ledyard Tucker was asked to review the 1964 LME papers for *Psychological Review*. In his review, he suggested an alternative formulation for the lens model equation that was eventually published (Tucker, 1964) and became the standard form of the LME. Tucker rewrote the first term to produce the following equation:

$$r_a = GR_eR_s + C\sqrt{1 - R_e^2}\sqrt{1 - R_s^2}$$

Tucker's new parameter, G, is the correlation between the predicted scores from the two regression models. G is an alternative to Σd. As Tucker pointed out, this version of the equation has an elegant parallelism: Both terms on the right side involve a correlation between components of the distal variable and components of the judgment.

Tucker's formulation has been nearly universally adopted (although Σd has been used as recently as 1992; see Gangestad et al., 1992). In his comprehensive text on judgment analysis, Cooksey (1996b) did not even bother to mention Σd. However, since the relative advantages or disadvantages of the two forms of the LME have not been described in the literature, there might be circumstances when Σd would be preferred to G, as Tucker himself suggested (1964, p. 529). However, analysis of the properties of G and Σd indicates that G is always preferred.[1]

There have been several expansions of the LME since the original 1964 papers. Castellan (1972) generalized the LME to multiple criteria. Stenson (1974) showed how G could be estimated from the environmental and subject reliabilities if the cues were unknown, demonstrating the relation between G and correction for attenuation of a validity coefficient in test theory. Stewart (1976) developed a hierarchical formulation that made it possible to isolate the contributions of different sets of variables. Cooksey and Freebody (1985) developed a fully generalized lens model equation that encompassed both the Castellan multivariate and the Stewart hierarchical formulations. Stewart (1990) combined the LME with a decomposition of the Brier skill score, incorporating regression and base-rate bias into the formulation. Based on an expanded version of the lens model, Stewart and Lusk (1994) decomposed R_e into environmental predictability and fidelity of the information system and R_s into reliability of information acquisition and reliability of information processing. The more general forms of the LME have rarely been applied.

Since its original development and use in studies of judgment and multiple cue probability learning, the LME has been adapted for use in studies of interpersonal learning (Hammond, Wilkins, & Todd, 1966) and to studies of conflict (Hammond, 1965). More recently, it has been used in a remarkable variety of judgment studies. For example, Gifford (1994) used the LME to study encoding and decoding of interpersonal dispositions from nonverbal cues. Lee and Yates (1992) studied how judgments change as the number of cues increases. Fiedler and Walka (1993) studied judgments of the veracity of reports on minor delinquency. Hepworth (1991) suggested the use of the lens model as a framework for the assessment of student nurses. Tape, Kripal, and Wigton (1992) studied methods of learning in a medical context. Cooper and Werner (1990) used it to study predictions of violence. Gangestad et al. (1992) used the LME in a study of person perception. Stewart et al. (1989) and Stewart, Roebber, and Bosart (1997) used the LME to analyze the skill of weather forecasters. Balzer, Doherty, and O'Connor (1989) reviewed a number of studies that had used the LME to analyze the effects of cognitive feedback. Sniezek (1986) used it in a study of probability learning tasks. Wigton et al. (1990) investigated the effects of cognitive feedback on diagnostic judgments of pharyngitis for physicians and medical students. Ashton (1992) used it to study judgmental achievement of auditors. O'Boyle et al. (1992) employed the LME in a study of quality-of-life measures for patients. Sengupta and Te'eni (1993) studied group decision support systems. Clearly, the LME is a powerful and versatile tool for judgment research.

The LME, the Lens Model, and Brunswik's Probabilistic Functionalism

Mathematically, the LME is simply a formula for analyzing the correlation between any two variables with respect to another set of variables.

It is a variant of partial correlation methods that break correlations down into components that are and are not related to other variables. It is also a form of the classic formula relating the correlation between two tests to their reliabilities and the correlation between the true scores (Brehmer, 1988). The importance of the LME derives not simply from its mathematical properties, but from the close correspondence between those properties and Brunswik's lens model.

Following are five requirements for a quantitative analysis that is consistent with Brunswikian theory:

1. Symmetry and parallelism: Both the environment and the organism must be represented and analyzed in parallel terms (see especially, Brunswik, 1957, this volume).
2. Probabilism: The method must account for probabilistic relations among variables in both the environment and organismic systems.
3. Vicarious functioning: Since vicarious functioning is central to behavior, the method must account for it.
4. Representative design: The method must permit representative design of experiments. In particular, it must be possible to analyze studies that allow vicarious functioning.
5. Functionalism: Since behavior is goal-directed, the organism's goal must be included in the analysis.

The following is a discussion of how the LME meets each of these requirements.

Symmetry

The LME provides a beautiful representation of the symmetry of the lens model. Parallel regressions are applied to environment and organism, and the LME includes parallel terms for the environment and the organism, as well as terms that describe the relation between them.

Probabilism

Because the LME is based on correlational statistics and regression analysis, the uncertainty inherent in both the environment and the organism is directly represented. The multiple correlations (R_e and R_s) measure linear determinancy, that is, the strength of the relation between a linear function of the cues and the distal variable or the judgment, respectively. To the extent that these multiple correlations are less than 1.0, these cue-variable relations are probabilistic (assuming that the form of the regression model is correct).

Probabilistic relations between each cue and the distal variable (ecological validities) or the judgment (cue utilizations) are incorporated into R_e, R_s, and G.

Vicarious Functioning

Vicarious functioning requires correlated cues. Because the LME is based on regression analysis, it can be applied to designs that include such correlations. However, the LME does not provide a direct measure of vicarious functioning. That is, the LME itself cannot tell us whether a judge is taking advantage of the opportunity for vicarious functioning, nor does it measure the contribution of vicarious functioning to achievement. However, a measure of the potential for vicarious functioning can be developed as follows.

G is influenced by the correlations among the cues and therefore reflects the potential for vicarious functioning. For some tasks, subjects can achieve high G by using patterns of cue utilization that differ markedly from their ecological validities and from the cue utilizations of other subjects who also have high G. But G is a nonspecific measure. It is influenced not only by vicarious functioning, but by other factors as well.

The following matrix formula for G can be used to explore vicarious functioning.

$$G = \frac{\beta_e' R \beta_s}{\sqrt{\beta_e' R \beta_e} \sqrt{\beta_s' R \beta_s}}.$$

β_e is a vector of standardized regression weights for the environment.
β_s is a vector of standardized regression weights for the judge.
R is the matrix of cue intercorrelations.

Note that β_e and β_s are determined by R and by the cue validities and cue utilizations, respectively.

β_e and R combine multiplicatively to determine the opportunity for the judge to use vicarious functioning. Operationally, vicarious func-

tioning means that the judge can employ a wide range of weights (β_s) and still achieve a high value of G. The conditions under which this may occur can be derived from the above formula. Specifically, when $\beta_e' R$ produces a vector of numbers that are closely spaced (i.e., have low variability), then the potential for vicarious functioning is high. For tasks having the same number of cues, examination $\beta_e' R$ could be the basis for an index comparing the degree to which different tasks provide opportunities for vicarious functioning. This exploration of G leads to an important insight: Opportunities for vicarious functioning depend not only on the intercorrelations among the cues, but on a combination of those correlations and the ecological validities of the cues. As far as we know, Brunswik was not aware of the importance of *both* cue intercorrelations and ecological validities in vicarious functioning.

Representative Design

As stated above, the LME can be used to analyze data that are gathered under representative conditions. Furthermore, generalizations based on the use of the LME *require* representative design. Of course, the LME can also be applied to data that were *not* gathered using a representative design. But without an appropriate design, results obtained using LME, or any other analytical method, are meaningless.

There has been misunderstanding among psychologists regarding the meaning of representative design. In judgment research, representative design is often equated with the use of correlated cues. Representative design is often taken to mean that cases must be drawn randomly from some natural environment, and that the natural setting for judgment must be reproduced in the experiment.

In fact, representative design does not require correlated cues, random sampling from a natural environment, or reproduction of the setting where judgments are made. The essential characteristic of representative design is that the experimenter carefully specify what generalizations are to be made from the experiment and then set up the experiment to support those generalizations. This requires a careful examination of the environment and the process being studied. The resulting design may or may not include correlated cues and may or may not require faithful reproduction of the context for judgment.

The confusion about representative design and correlated cues resulted from Brunswik's emphasis on vicarious functioning and his argument that traditional orthogonal research designs eliminated the possibility of such functioning. With regard to vicarious functioning, therefore, representative design means correlated cues. In studies where vicarious functioning is not central, representative design does not necessarily require correlated cues.

Functionalism

The LME is an inherently functional representation of behavior because it analyzes achievement (r_a). This correlation measures the extent to which the judge achieves the goal of making accurate judgments about the distal variable. The LME decomposes that correlation, thus clarifying the components of achievement.

In summary, the LME is consistent with Brunswikian theory and truly deserves to be called the *lens model equation*.

The Future of the LME: Continued Application and Methodological Studies

A search of the Social Science Citation Index from 1969 to 1998 identified more than 140 papers that cited at least one of the original 1964 papers. Although the rate of citation fell from about six or seven papers per year in the 1970s to two or three papers per year in the 1990s, it is remarkable that these thirty-five-year-old papers are still being regularly cited. This is clear evidence of the continuing value of the LME for analyzing judgment. Still, one might ask why it is not being used more frequently.

There are several possible reasons. One is lack of awareness. There are papers that could make good use of the LME but don't. Another reason is the difficulty in calculating LME parameters. Only one software package (POLICY PC) computes lens model parameters. It is possible to compute them with statistical packages such as SPSS or SAS, but several steps are required. In addition, most psychologists have not been taught LME analysis. They have to learn it on their own. Another reason is that, in many studies, the required data about the environment (criterion data) are lacking. Without criterion data, the LME cannot be used to analyze achievement. It can still be used to analyze agreement between judges, but many investigators do not appear to realize that can be done, or to appreciate its value.

Future efforts should be made to correct the underutilization of LME analysis by increasing awareness among psychologists and making computational procedures more available.

At the same time, more detailed study of the behavior of LME parameters (G, C R_s, R_e) is needed. While there have been several studies of the parameters of the LME (see Cooksey, 1996b, pp. 212 ff., for a review), little is known about their statistical properties. The current capability to conduct extensive simulations on personal computers should be exploited to conduct the research on critical statistical issues in the interpretation of LME results (such as the distributions of G and C). Castellan's (1992) study of the properties of G under a variety of assumptions is a good example of the kind of research that is needed.

In conclusion, the LME is a proven tool for Brunswikian research that could be applied more frequently and should be the focus of detailed methodological study in order to advance our understanding of judgment under uncertainty.

NOTE

I thank Elise Axelrad Weaver for helpful comments on an earlier version of this chapter.

1. The relation between G and Σd is expressed in the following equation:

$$\Sigma d = R_e^2 + R_s^2 - 2GR_eR_s.$$

This means that, for fixed R_e and R_s, Σd is just a linear function of G. It also shows that Σd is not independent of the multiple correlations for environment or judge. This lack of independence has unfortunate implications. The best value of Σd would seem to be 0, indicating a perfect match between environment and judge, but this value can be achieved only when $R_e^2 + R_s^2 = 2GR_eR_s$. This equation is satisfied when $G = 1.0$ and $R_e = R_s$, but there are many other possible solutions as well. As a result, $\Sigma d = 0.0$ does not produce the best possible achievement. For a given R_e, maximum achievement is reached when $R_s = 1.0$

and $\Sigma d = (1 - R_e)^2$. In other words, in order to maximize performance, Σd must be greater than 0 (unless $R_e = 1.0$). This is a strange and counterintuitive result, which certainly would have surprised Brunswik. From Tucker's version of the LME, it is clear that achievement is maximized when both R_s are G are 1.0, a simple and intuitive result. To summarize, Σd confounds the effects of cue utilization and R_s, while G clearly separates them. G is always preferred to Σd. The standard practice of using Tucker's version of the LME is correct.

B.

Overviews of Applications to
Substantive Problems

28

The Realistic Accuracy Model and Brunswik's Approach to Social Judgment

David C. Funder

A rereading of Egon Brunswik's collected articles and his classic 1956 book makes it clear that Brunswik was, among many other roles, a preacher. He had several messages that he was powerfully motivated to get across to an audience that seemed slow to grasp the point, and he argued them again and again. One of the most important of these messages was that psychology needed to study more than just processes within the person, or "organism." Every person lives within and interacts with an environment. Any study of the person that failed to integrate an analysis of the environment, and the person's interaction with it, would fall far short of what psychology needs. In Brunswik's (1957) words:

It is the contention of this paper ["Scope and Aspects of the Cognitive Problem"] that if there is anything that still ails psychology in general, and the psychology of cognition especially, it is the neglect of investigation of environmental or ecological texture in favor of that of the texture of organismic structures and processes. Both historically and systematically psychology has forgotten that it is a science of organism-environment relationships, and has become a science of the organism. (p. 6).[1]

While it would be pleasant to report that psychology remedied this state of affairs over the next forty years, it would not be correct. Psychology's examination of perception and judgment still concentrates almost exclusively on processes that occur within the skull of the perceiver or judge and almost completely ignores the environment that people must perceive and judge and within which they must function.

Brunswik and Social Perception

While most of Brunswik's work dealt with perception of the physical environment, and particularly the problem of size constancy, near the end of his career he began to turn his attention increasingly onto social perception. His initial work in this area dealt with the perception of "physiognomic" cues such as facial features and body size. However, it is perhaps telling that the final section of his 1956 book (Part eighteen) turned to issues of clinical psychology and the special issues that arise when the stimulus to perception and judgment is a person. If it is important to remember the environment when studying physical perception, Brunswik observed, this principle is even more important when the topic is social perception and the important environmental stimuli are themselves persons: "The most dramatic case we could make for representative design was that of the perception of social objects. In this case both subjects and objects are persons; if the former are to be sampled representatively this could hardly be denied to the latter. Yet . . . the traditional ways of handling stimuli systematically rather than representatively are so ingrained that this simple logic has prevailed only in exceptional instances" (1956b, p. 131).

In other words, social perception is an even better venue for application of representative design, the lens model, and probablistic functionalism than is physical perception. In physical perception, the relationships between reality, cues, and perception are often nearly 1 : 1 : 1. In social perception, the uncertainty at each step—a core concern of the lens model—is much more obvious. Brunswik (1950) commented that the study of social perception "may help in stressing the probabalistic, rather than strictly 'nomothetic,' character of studies dealing with complex textures of interwoven factors in the physical or social environment" (p. 61).

Brunswik would not have been encouraged if he had foreseen that well into the 1980s, the study of social perception would still be focused almost exclusively on the examination of processes that occur solely within the perceptual and cognitive systems of the social perceiver. To this day, the stimulus inputs provided to subjects in the typical study of social perception are artificial, arbitrary, and systematically orthogonalized. All three of these aspects of contemporary research are serious mistakes from a Brunswikian perspective, and their persistence throughout the literature has produced a large corpus of research on person perception that makes almost no reference to the persons perceived.

A contemporary of Brunswik who was an important figure in personality and social psychology saw what was happening from the very beginning and expressed his worries quite clearly. Gordon Allport wrote:

> Recently I attended a conference of psychologists working on the problem of the "perception of persons" (see Tagiuri & Petrullo, 1958). At this conference one heard much about perception but little about persons, the object of perception. The reason, I think, is that the participants . . . much preferred to . . . evade the question of what the person is really like (1958, p. 243)

> In many investigations of "person perception," to try to discover the traits residing within a personality is regarded as either naïve or impossible. Studies, therefore, concentrate only on the *process* of perceiving or judging, and reject the problem of validating the perception and judgment. (1966, p. 2; emphasis in the original)

The conference that Allport attended, and that so disturbed him, turned out to be a harbinger of the dominant perspective for the next three decades, if not longer. Social psychologists conducted a vast number of studies that concentrated exclusively on the process of judgment and thereby learned a good deal about how people combine various bits of verbal information about people (e.g., Asch, 1946; Hastie, et al., 1980). However, as Allport feared, this research yielded little knowledge about how well or even whether there was any match between the judgment and reality.

By the 1980s, therefore, a reinjection of Brunswikian theory into social psychology was desperately needed. The particular aspect of Brunswik's writings that was most directly germane to person perception was his insistence that the environment must be studied in parallel with subjects' perceptions of it. Brunswik was explicit about what he meant by *environment* in this context. He meant the actual, "*distal* variables that are to a certain extent independently variable of the corresponding *proximal* or sensory input" (1957, p. 7; emphasis in the original). Examples of distal variables range from the measured size of a physical body and measured intelligence to personality traits.

As examples of distal stimuli, personality traits are particularly appropriate for Brunswikian analysis. While no one has ever seen a trait of personality directly, traits give off numerous potential cues, many of which are misleading and some of which are actually informative under some circumstances. The social perceiver has no choice but to assemble as many cues as possible over the time of acquaintance and then somehow integrate them into a judgment that might be right, but because of the loose association between cues and reality stands an appreciable chance of being wrong. This is the quintessential Brunswikian situation.

The Two Great Ecologists

This uncertain situation is what makes Brunswik's approach more suitable to the study of social perception than is that of another ecologically oriented theorist who has his own latter-day revivalists in the field of social perception, J. J. Gibson (see Zebrowitz & Collins, 1997). Gibson (e.g., 1979) shared with Brunswik a view that one needed to understand how nature is revealed through stimuli, in order to understand perception and judgment. But Gibson saw the connection between stimuli and perception as "direct"—as unmediated by cognitive processes. Exactly what Gibson meant by "direct perception" was never clear to most readers. Perhaps he did not really mean this phrase literally at all and was just trying to counter the overcognitivization of psychology by drawing attention to the environment, much as Skinner (e.g., 1938/1966) tried to do by denying altogether the existence of mental life. Be that as it may, Gibson's approach does seem inconsistent with one of the essential tenets of Brunswik's approach, that all perception is inherently probablistic.

This recognition of probablism, which is helpful for understanding the perception of the physical world, is essential for understanding social perception. For example, a twitching foot might usually indicate that a person is nervous and might so be what Brunswik would call an "ecologically valid" cue that is likely to indicate the presence of anxiety. But it might also be uninformative or misleading, because sometimes some people twitch their feet when they are not nervous, and sometimes they twitch their feet when they are happy and excited.

To the extent that the concern is with perceptions and judgments of phenomena that can at best only partially and probably be known, Brunswik's probablistic functionalism is exactly what is required. The same explicit acknowledgment of probabilism that makes it appropriate for weather forecasting (Lusk & Hammond, 1991) also makes it a good match to the problem of social perception. Gibson's approach is better suited to object perception in the here-and-now. This situation does not greatly resemble the task of figuring out the nature of someone's personality, a task where so much is *not* here, now.

Brunswik and the Criterion Problem for Social Perception

Even though it still does not often cite him by name, modern research on accuracy in social judgment has become increasingly Brunswikian in recent years. When various investigators, including me, first began to revive this topic in about 1980, the approach was only loosely Brunswikian in the sense that we correlated subjects' judgments of personality traits with independently derived indicators of what the traits in these subjects might actually be (e.g., Funder, 1980; Funder & Colvin, 1991[2]). This approach, as obvious as it might seem, was drastically at odds with the then-dominant approach described above, in which perceiver-subjects were provided with artificial and experimentally controlled "social" stimuli. The dominant approach aimed at modeling (and sometimes finding fault with) the processes of cognition going on in the perceivers' heads. The alternative approach aimed at mapping the relations between perception and judgment, on the one hand, and social reality, on the other.

This latter goal led accuracy researchers into an important difficulty, one that was sufficient to discourage some social psychologists from addressing the topic at all (Jones, 1985): the criterion problem. When studying physical perception, the investigator can use measuring tapes and scales to determine the nature of reality and then compare subjects' perceptions to those concrete indicators. Even the study of weather forecasting ends up with an actual, easily observed weather event. When the topic is social perception, the situation is much stickier. If a subject judges a target person to be friendly, on what basis can a psychologist (or anyone else) assess this judgment as right or wrong?

The answer to this question is to be found in Brunswik's principle of probablilistic functionalism. Brunswik emphasized how the probablistic association between cues and reality implies that one needs to acquire and use as many cues as possible, so that they can be combined and correct and substitute for each other "vicariously." This principle is nowhere more applicable than in the case of social perception. There exists no one certain criterion one can use to appraise the accuracy of social judgment. Instead, there exist only many different criteria, each of which is extremely *un*certain.

Broadly speaking, three classes of criteria have been used to assess the accuracy of interpersonal judgment (Funder & West, 1993). The first is self-other agreement: Does the judge's view of a person correspond with the person's view of himself or herself? This is a reasonable criterion and is by far the most widely used. But it is obviously fallible. People often distort their self-views, conceal their self-views, or simply are self-ignorant.

A second criterion is other-other agreement (also called *consensus*; Kenny, 1994). Do two (or more) judges agree with each other about what the person is like (see Brunswik, 1956b, pp. 35–36)? Consensus is a reasonable criterion, and its use is supported by findings that the same variables that ought to increase accuracy (e.g., greater acquaintanceship, trait visibility) in fact do tend to increase consensus (Funder & Colvin, 1988). But it, too, is fallible, because a community of observers can in principle all agree yet all be wrong.

The third criterion is behavioral prediction. Can a judge's rating of a personality trait be used to correctly predict what the person who is rated will do in the future? This is the most difficult criterion to employ, for two reasons. First, direct observations of personality-relevant behavior are difficult to come by and to reliably code into meaningful but numerically analyzable form (Funder, Furr, & Colvin, 1998). Second, it is difficult to ascertain exactly which behaviors should be predictable from which personality ratings. For example, if ratings of friendliness correctly predict subjects' propensities to smile, perhaps this indicates the ratings are valid. But what if they do not? Surely there are other indicators of friendliness, and we may have chosen the wrong one, rather than the ratings being wrong.

This is why, in a move Brunswik would surely endorse, accuracy researchers have learned they must constantly gather as many criteria for accuracy as possible rather than rely on any one (e.g., Funder, 1987). For accuracy researchers, probablistic functionalism is as important to the choice of a criterion as it is to understanding subjects' judgments. This, I propose, makes Brunswik exactly twice as relevant to the study of person perception as to the study of physical perception.

The Realistic Accuracy Model

My own laboratory and several others spent about ten years studying the variables that affect the accuracy of personality judgment, as appraised by the criteria noted above. These variables can be sorted into four broad categories (Funder, 1993). The first is judgmental ability, the tendency of some judges to be more accurate than others. (This has proven to be the most difficult moderator of accuracy to study, for a variety of reasons.) The second is "judgability," the tendency of some targets to be easier to judge than others (e.g., Colvin, 1993a, 1993b). The third moderator of accuracy is the nature of the trait being judged. For reasons of visibility and social desirability, among others, some traits are easier to judge than others (Funder & Dobroth, 1987; John & Robins, 1993). The fourth is information, a variable that has two facets. The first is quantity; more information (e.g., as gathered through longer acquaintanceship) produces more accuracy than less information, everything else being equal (e.g., Funder & Colvin, 1988; Blackman & Funder, 1998). The second facet is quality, the idea that some kinds of information are more

informative in general and for particular traits than other information (e.g., Andersen, 1984).

While this four-variable scheme is a useful way to organize empirical findings concerning the accuracy of personality judgment, more is needed. To enhance understanding and to propose new moderators, a theoretical model is needed that describes the process by which accurate personality judgment can be attained. To this end, I have proposed the realistic accuracy model (or RAM; Funder, 1995). The purpose of the model is to answer the following straightforward question: Assuming accurate personality judgment ever happens, how is such accuracy possible?

According to RAM, four things must happen in sequence. First, the target of judgment must emit some sort of information that is *relevant* to the judgment being made. Typically, this is a personality-relevant behavior but might be an aspect of physical appearance. Second, this information must be *available* to a social perceiver. For example, the perceiver must be present, and not absent, when the relevant behavior is performed. Third, this information must then be *detected*, or register somehow on the perceiver's nervous system. For example, the judge must not be so distracted that he or she fails to notice what is right in front of him or her. Fourth and finally, the information must be correctly *utilized* or interpreted before a correct judgment can be rendered. The model is represented schematically in Figure 28.1.

This model yields several implications (Funder, 1995, 1999). One of the most important is that accurate judgment is difficult. Only if all four of the steps outlined—relevance, availability, detection, and utilization—are successfully traversed will accurate personality judgment be attained. And any imperfection at any step will be multiplied with the imperfections of the other steps to contribute to inaccuracy. One theme that emerges from Brunswik's writings is the way he seemed to continually marvel at how well perceptual and judgmental processes generally succeed under such uncertain and constantly changing circumstances. The realistic accuracy model leads to the same appreciation.

Of course, perhaps it should, because RAM is obviously derived from the lens model. The first two stages, relevance and availability, are part of the "environment" side of the lens. The latter two stages, detection and utilization, are part of

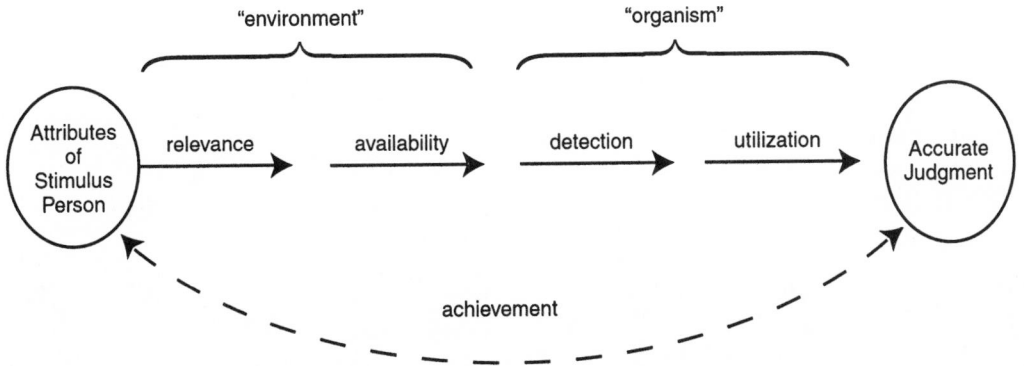

FIGURE 28.1 The realistic accuracy model.

the "organism" side (see e.g., Brunswik, 1940b, p. 72[3]). It shares also the "direction of causal sequence" that Brunswik espoused, flowing from left to right. RAM's separation of Brunswik's two (environment and organism) stages into four stages is a refinement that helps adapt the model to the special case of social perception. But at its heart the realistic accuracy model is a Brunswikian lens.

NOTES

The research described in this chapter was supported by National Institute of Mental Health Grant R01-MH42427.

1. A moment later, Brunswik tried to soften this complaint by adding, "No such drastic statement can be literally true, of course." A moment after that, he hardened again by comparing the cognitive psychologists with "inflatedly masculine medieval theologians" (p. 6). His feelings on this issue were strong.

2. I cite only my own work here, but several other investigators were involved in the revival of accuracy research, including Peter Borkenau, William Ickes, David Kenny, William Swann, Leslie Zebrowitz, and others. For a review see Funder (1999).

3. I choose this reference because, of the several published renderings of the lens, this early example is the one that RAM most closely resembles.

29

Application of the Lens Model to the Evaluation of Professional Performance

James H. Hogge

The evaluation of professional performance, whether formal or informal, quantitative or qualitative, requires the formation of global judgments of overall performance based upon several indicators (i.e., aspects of performance). For example, reviews of the performance of university faculty by administrators responsible for determining an-

nual salary increases traditionally are based on information about scholarly productivity, quality of teaching, and service in other ways both inside and outside the university. In addition, similar criteria are typically considered by university promotion and tenure committees. Although both evaluators and evaluees recognize that the evaluation of professional performance is a value-laden process, explication of those values is usually haphazard at best and inadequate for effective communication among participants. What is needed is an analytic framework within which the evaluation process can be represented and the role and nature of values can be clarified.

This chapter explains how Brunswik's (1952) lens model may be used to study and improve the quantitative evaluation of professional performance. The following pages deal with conceptualization of the evaluation process in terms of the lens model; the relationship of the lens model to representative design; the operationalization of values underlying the evaluation process; examination of evaluative consensus by means of the lens model equation, comparisons of predefined groups of evaluators, and identification of subgroups of evaluators with similar judgment policies; and a summary of the advantages of using the lens model to study the evaluation of professional competence.

Viewing Professional Performance through Brunswik's Lens

Although Brunswik's primary area of inquiry could be described as perception, he thought about his work in terms of the entire discipline of psychology. In "Psychology as a Science of Objective Relations" (1937), for example, he summarized his view as follows:

> The primary subject-matter of psychology is defined by a formal criterion as the objective pattern of couplings which an organism, in its causal intercourse with the environment, was able to focalize in a fairly "constant" way upon more or less remote (life-sustaining) types of "objects," despite the disturbing variability (multiplicity and ambiguity) of the single mediating stimulus-cues and means. Psychology is, therefore, a science of the relational achievements at the command of the organism, of well-established far-reaching (cognitive or effective) success—quantifiable in terms of its "objects attained"—, rather than of mediation processes, as such. (p. 260)

To facilitate discussion of these fundamental notions, Brunswik chose a lens analogy.

The Original Lens Model

Figure 29.1 is Brunswik's original lens model (Brunswik, 1952, p. 20). It portrays the process leading to an organism's perception (terminal focal variable)—mediated by a set of proximal variables—of a distal environmental variable (initial focal variable). The lines between the cues and the initial focal variable represent the ecological (environmental) validities of the cues, while the lines between the cues and the terminal focal variable portray the utilization of the cues by the organism. Brunswik (1952) noted that "the total pattern involved, when viewed as a composite picture of numerous cases of individual mediation from initial to terminal focus, bears resemblance to a bundle of rays scattering from a light-source and brought back to convergence in a distant second point by a convex lens" (p. 20).

As Brunswik (1952) described the process in probabilistic terms:

> Any organism has to cope with an environment full of uncertainties. Forced to react quickly or within reasonable limits of time, it must respond before direct contact with the relevant remote conditions in the environment, such as foodstuffs or traps, friends or enemies, can be established. The probability character of intra-environmental relationships, their limited "ecological validity," becomes of concern in two regional contexts: on the reception or stimulus side as the equivocality of relationships between physical or social objects and proximal sensory stimuli or cues, and on the effection or reaction side as the equivocality of relationships between proximal outgoing behavioral responses, or means, and their more remote distal results and effects. In one or the other of these ways behavioral responses are, to apply a saying by Thurstone, of necessity based upon "insufficient evidence." (p. 22)

As suggested by Hammond (1980), "The complicated (but precise) language used by Brunswik . . . may have been necessary for methodological arguments, but such language is clearly not likely to move run of the mill scientists to change their research practices, even if some of them happened to read it" (p. 7). If Brunswik's ideas and his lens model were to have broader influence, they needed to be presented in a form with

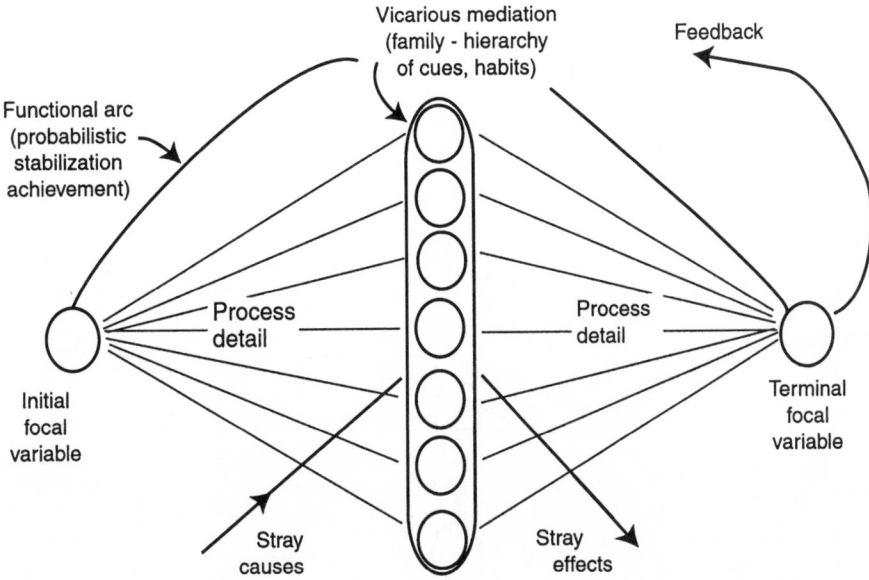

FIGURE 29.1 Brunswik's original lens model. From Brunswik, 1952, p. 20.

broader appeal. Cooksey (1996b) and Hammond (1996c) described how this was accomplished via social judgment theory.

The Lens Model in Social Judgment Theory

Hursch, Hammond, and Hursch (1964) adapted the lens model for the study of human judgment and presented it in a restricted form (Figure 29.2, from Hammond, Stewart, Brehmer, & Steinmann, 1975, p. 274) that became associated with social judgment theory (SJT). In this version of the lens model, the terminal focal variable is human judgment, and the initial terminal variable is termed the *criterion*, a distal (not directly knowable) environmental variable estimated by the judgments. Because actual criterion values are available, the accuracy of the judgments (*achievement*) can be summarized by the correlation between the judgments and the actual values of the distal variable. If a subject is asked to make judgments about an unknown or unmeasured criterion, the SJT lens model becomes the single-system design portrayed in Figure 29.3 (adapted from Cooksey, 1996b, p. 56). In this case, multiple regression may be used to model the subject's judgments as a function of the cues, but the concept (and assessment) of the objective accuracy of the judgments does not apply because an objective criterion is not available.

An *n*-System Lens Model of the Evaluation of Professional Performance

Because of the general lack of objective criteria for the assessment of professional competence, it is conventional to turn to multiple (*n*) evaluators. An expanded version of the SJT lens model (Figure 29.4, adapted from Cooksey, 1996b, p. 78) portrays several evaluators' estimates of "true" professional performance as probabilistically related to a set of cues that consist of several aspects of professional performance on which an evaluation of overall professional performance is to be based. Like the true score in classical test theory (Nunnally, 1978), true professional performance is not subject to objective verification. Instead, the emphasis is on the examination of agreement among the evaluators and comparison of their judgment systems as modeled by multiple regression. A particular evaluator is assumed to utilize the cues in accordance with his or her beliefs about their (imperfect) ecological validities. In other words, the evaluator's beliefs about the rela-

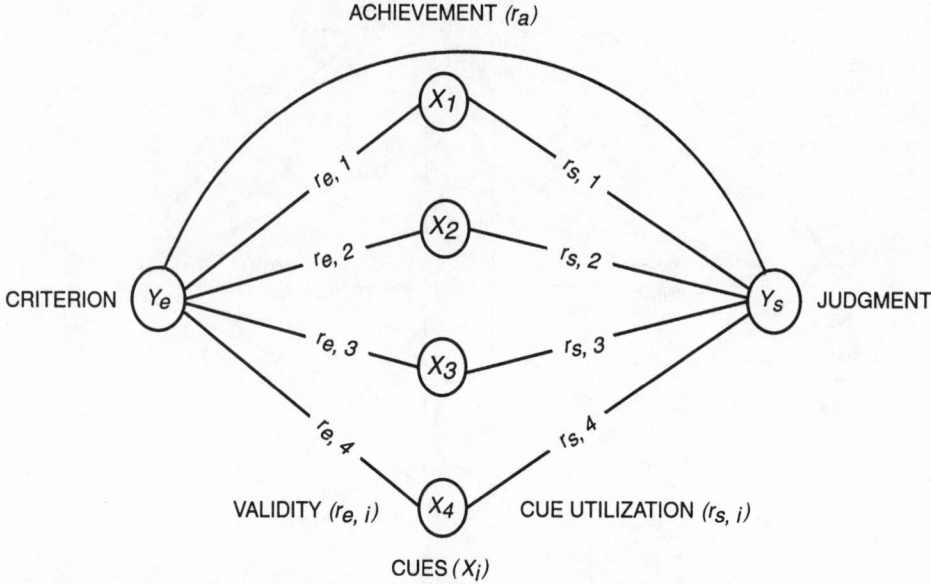

FIGURE 29.2 The lens model adapted for social judgment theory. From Hammond et al., 1975, p. 274.

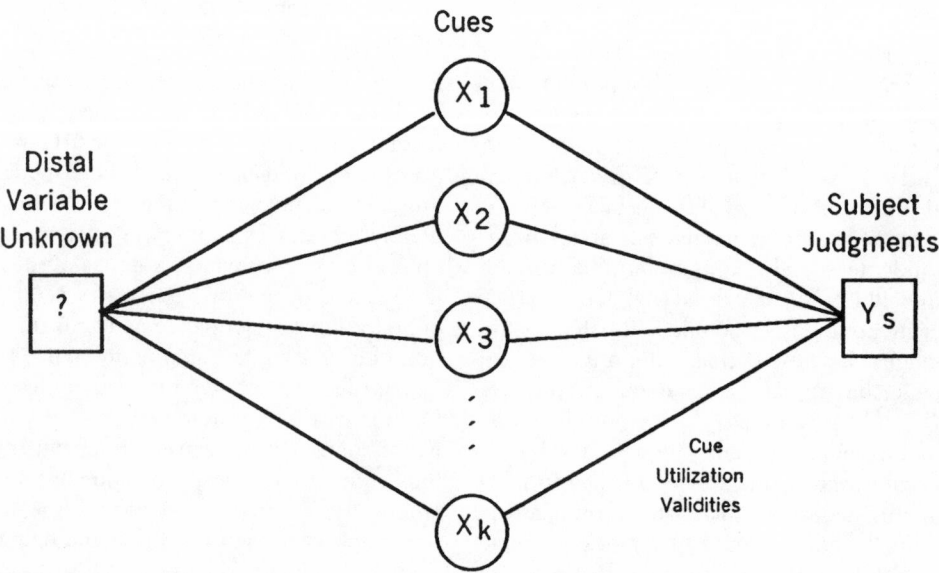

FIGURE 29.3 Single-system lens model (distal variable unknown or unmeasured). Adapted from Cooksey, 1996b, p. 56.

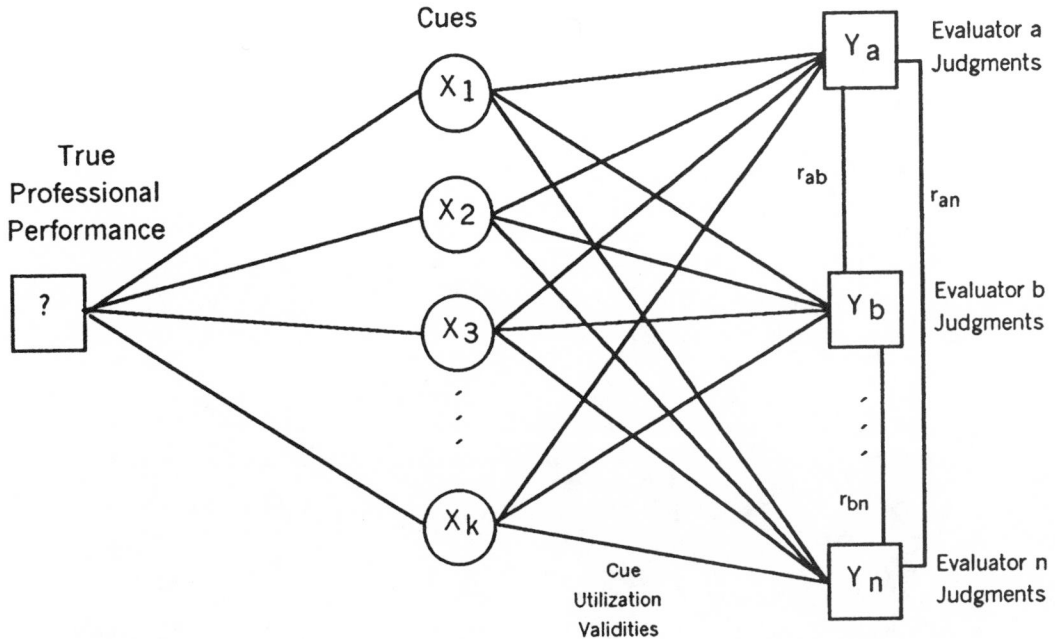

FIGURE 29.4 The *n*-system lens model for study of agreement among evaluators. Adapted from Cooksey, 1996b, p. 78.

tionships between the cues and an "impalpable criterion" (Hammond, 1980, p. 8) reflect the evaluator's values (Hammond & Adelman, 1976; Adelman, 1988): Differential weighting (utilization) of the cues by the evaluator is likely as his or her values come into play.

The Lens Model and Representative Design

In contrast to orthodox systematic design, which emphasizes subject sampling and seeks to disentangle variables in the environment, and then to test the effect of one variable at a time, Brunswik's (1952, 1955c, 1956b) representative design emphasizes environmental sampling and leaves variables entangled as they naturally occur. In the present context, evaluators correspond to subjects, and environmental sampling is accomplished by sampling sets of values of the cues on which judgments of professional performance are based.

Because it usually is impractical to require each evaluator to judge a set of concrete examples of professional performance (e.g., videotaped examples of professional performance), studies of the evaluation of professional performance are often based on profiles of cue values presented on sheets of paper. For example, Hogge and Murrell (1991) asked classroom teachers and university teacher educators to judge the overall competence of fifty hypothetical student teachers whose levels of competence with respect to six aspects of teaching competence (the cues) were summarized in profiles on sheets of paper (see Figure 29.5). Such artificial profiles involve cues that would, in a naturalistic situation (e.g., an actual classroom performance), have to be inferred from various kinds of specific behavior. Because the cues are abstractions of the behavior of hypothetical, rather than real, cases, the judgment task produces data that, at best, permit description of the value systems of the evaluators. Hypothetical profiles have been used in a wide variety of other applications of the lens model, including, for example, assessment of the relative desirability of police handgun ammunition based on stopping effectiveness, severity of injury, and threat to bystanders (Hammond & Adelman, 1976); judgments of the degree to which various airport development scenarios would be in the public interest (Parkin, 1993); ratings of the acceptability

STUDENT TEACHER NUMBER 1

Teacher/Pupil Relationships	5	Distinction
Preparation and Management	5	Distinction
Curriculum Content	2	Borderline
Classroom Interaction	3	Pass
Assessment and Records	4	Credit
Self-Evaluation	3	Pass
Overall Competence	5	Distinction
(Please circle your rating)	4	Credit
	3	Pass
	2	Borderline
	1	Fail

FIGURE 29.5 Sample judgment task profile.

of sample contracts representing differing combinations of values with respect to duration of contract, wage increases, number and use of machine operators, and number of strikers to be recalled (Balke, Hammond, & Meyer, 1973); and judgments about the stability of hypothetical marriages characterized in terms of degree of communication, degree of sexual compatibility, degree of mutual respect, adequacy of finances, degree of common interests, and similarity of family and social background (Dhir & Markman, 1984).

Operationalization of Values

An evaluator's judgment system (and, hence, value system) may be modeled with multiple linear regression,[1] yielding the following equation for k cues:

$$\text{Estimated professional performance} = W_1X_1 + W_2X_2 + \ldots + W_kX_k$$

In this equation, estimated professional performance is the estimate of the distal variable (the impalpable criterion), X_i is a particular cue (aspect of professional performance), and W_i is the corresponding relative weight (as defined by Cooksey, 1996b, p. 170, rather than the formulation originally proposed by Hoffmann, 1960). In accordance with Hammond and Adelman (1976) and Adelman (1988), the W_i can be taken as operationalizations of the evaluator's *imple-*

mented values (Hogge & Murrell, 1991) with respect to the evaluative task. Unfortunately, judges dealing with a variety of cues typically report patterns of cue utilization that differ from those exhibited in their ratings of real or hypothetical cases (Hammond et al., 1975; Brehmer & Brehmer, 1988). In other words, their *expressed values* (statements about the relative importance of cues) tend to differ from their *implemented values* (the relative weights computed from a regression model of their judgments).

Because this discrepancy between expressed and implemented values can yield evaluations that are inconsistent with one's statements about the relative importance of aspects of professional performance, it tends to disrupt communication between evaluator and evaluee. If, for example, senior members of the faculty of a particular department state that excellence in teaching and prominence in scholarship are of equal importance in assessing the tenurability of faculty members but, in fact, place greater weight on scholarship than on teaching, junior faculty members could disastrously misdirect their professional energies in the years leading up to their tenure reviews. A particularly striking example of discrepancies between expressed and implemented values was reported by Balke et al. (1973). Based on a reenactment of labor-management negotiations, including evaluations of hypothetical settlement contracts by all participants, Balke et al. found that even after months of discussions, union and management negotiators poorly understood their counterparts' implemented values. More important, both groups of negotiators exhibited poor *self*-insight. These results may explain why such negotiations are often very difficult and tend to break down amid accusations of bad faith.

Discussions of insight into the judgment process can be found in Brehmer and Brehmer (1988); Cooksey (1996b); Doherty and Balzer (1988); Hammond (1996c); Harries, Evans, and Dennis (1997); Reilly (1996); Reilly and Doherty (1989, 1992); and Doherty and Reilly (Chapter 20, this volume).

Examining Evaluative Consensus

Within the framework of the lens model, examination of the evaluative consensus begins with the idiographic modeling of the judgment systems (implemented values) of individual evaluators with multiple linear regression. After evaluators are understood at the individual level, information from the regression analyses can be used in further exploration of interevaluator agreement (by means of the lens model equation), nomothetic (group-level) comparisons of evaluators, and the identification of evaluators with similar judgment policies (implemented values). In addition, as described by Schilling and Hogge (Chapter 23, this volume), hierarchical linear models (Bryk & Raudenbush, 1992) can be used as an analytic framework that considers all evaluators simultaneously, both individually and collectively.

The Lens Model Equation

The agreement, r_{ij}, between two evaluators can be decomposed by the lens model equation (LME) that was developed by Hursch et al. (1964) and modified by Tucker (1964):

$$r_{ij} = R_i R_j G + C\sqrt{(1 - R_i^2)(1 - R_j^2)}. \qquad (1)$$

R_i and R_j are the multiple correlations for the prediction of the judgments of Evaluators i and j based on the same cues for the same cases. R_i and R_j are indices of *cognitive control* (Hammond et al., 1975). G is the correlation between the predictions produced by the multiple regression models of the two evaluators and can be interpre-

ted as the agreement that would be obtained if both evaluators achieved perfect cognitive control (i.e., if $R_i = R_j = 1.0$). C is the correlation between the residuals (discrepancies between actual and predicted ratings) of the two models.

$R_i R_j G$ is the linear component of r_{ij} and is the amount of agreement that can be explained by linear models with the cues as predictors. $C\sqrt{(1 - R_i^2)(1 - R_j^2)}$, the second term in equation (1), has been called the configural component (Cooksey, 1996b) and represents unmodeled aspects of agreement between the two evaluators. According to Cooksey:

> The value of the C coefficient may reflect: (1) common reliance on cues not included in either model (this should not be considered as "configural" cue usage); (2) nonlinearity of cue function forms common to both [evaluators] (this aspect is considered by many to be connoted by the term "configurality"); (3) cue interactions in common to both [evaluators] (this is the traditional connotation of the term "configurality"); and/or (4) chance agreement between random model errors from both [evaluators] (this also cannot be considered to be "configural" processing and is more likely to occur in small judgment profile samples). (p. 211)

Because SJT studies have found that "linear additive organizational principles are often adequate to explain judgment processes" (Hammond et al., 1975, p. 305), the configural component is often ignored (i.e., C is assumed to be essentially zero), thus reducing equation (1) to

$$r_{ij} = R_i R_j G. \qquad (2)$$

This simplified form of the LME thus suggests that agreement between two evaluators is simply a function of their cognitive control and the agreement between their value systems (patterns of cue utilization).

Application of Lens Model Equation

Inspection of R_i, R_j, and G for a particular pair of evaluators can suggest the most promising strategies for improving interevaluator agreement (i.e., increasing r_{ij}). A comparatively high value of G combined with low values of R_i and R_j indicates that agreement would be improved if the evaluators applied their judgment policies more consistently; thus, an emphasis should be placed on training the evaluators to improve their cognitive control. If, however, G is low, then the two evaluators should receive training to increase the similarity of their judgment policies.

Table 29.1 contains LME statistics for two pairs of nurses who judged the overall professional performance of hypothetical nursing students (Hogge & Murrell, 1994). In both pairs, the relatively low cognitive control of Nurse 19 (R_{19} = .63) attenuates the observed agreement (r_{ij}) between each pair of nurses. The G value of .91 for Nurses 4 and 19 indicates that the observed agreement (r_{ij} = .69) between them could be improved if Nurse 19 achieved higher cognitive control; however, the G value of only .40 for Nurses 12 and 19 reveals a fundamental policy difference that should be addressed with appropriate training. Of course, as noted above, use of the LME in this fashion involves the assumption that the configural component of the equation is of negligible size.

Improvement of cognitive control (R) and/or correspondence between evaluators' implemented values (G) can be accomplished with cognitive feedback, which is explained by Cooksey (1996b).

Comparisons of Groups of Evaluators

Univariate or multivariate analysis of variance (ANOVA) techniques may be used to compare predefined subgroups (e.g., professional specializations) of evaluators with respect to such dependent variables as R^2 or G. For example, Hogge and Murrell (1991) compared the squared multiple correlations of classroom teachers and teacher educators who had evaluated the performance of hypothetical student teachers. If correlations are to be used as the dependent variable in an ANOVA, they should first be transformed to Fisher's (1921) z_r as was done by Browne and Gillis (1982)

in comparing the cue utilization correlations of undergraduate and graduate students and faculty members who had judged the effectiveness of hypothetical art teachers. (For additional details about the Fisher transformation, see Cooksey, 1996b, p. 245, or any comprehensive statistics text. Cooksey also provides an extensive discussion of nomothetic comparisons using ANOVA techniques.)

The Identification of Evaluators with Similar Judgment Policies

If no subgroups of evaluators have been defined prior to the collection of data, then techniques that cluster the evaluators on the basis of cue weight profile similarity may be used to produce statistically defensible groupings, or typologies, of evaluators. Appropriate methods include the JAN technique (Christal & Bottenberg, 1968) and the ISODATA algorithm (Ball & Hall, 1967; Cooksey, 1982). For an introduction to clustering techniques used by SJT researchers, see Cooksey (1996b).

Advantages of This Approach

The use of the lens model and SJT to study the evaluation of professional performance offers advantages difficult to duplicate with other paradigms:

1. Through idiographic modeling with multiple linear regression, the value systems of evaluators are made explicit in a way that facilitates their examination. Thus, as noted above, both evaluators and evaluees can progress from general recognition that evaluation is a value-laden process to a more precise understanding of how values are actually influencing judgments about the quality of professional performance.

2. The clarification of both expressed and implemented values can improve communication among evaluators and evaluees. This clarification is particularly important in situations where the evaluator also serves as supervisor (e.g., a classroom teacher supervising practice teaching) because it can help both persons recognize which aspects of professional performance are most predictive of overall evalua-

TABLE 29.1 Lens Model Equation Statistics for Two Pairs of Nurse-Evaluators

Nurse Pair	r_{ij}	R_i	R_j	G
4,19	.69	.79	.63	.91
12,19	.22	.91	.63	.40

tive judgments. Supervision can then have a more productive focus.

3. Interevaluator agreement is decomposed by the lens model equation into components that can guide training of evaluators to improve the consensus among them and, hence, the reliability of the assessment of professional performance. Specifically, this decomposition makes it possible to determine whether inadequate agreement is due to low cognitive control (a small value of R) of either or both of the evaluators, to differences in the implemented values of the evaluators (a small value of G), or to a combination of these problems. Low cognitive control can be improved through practice (including cognitive feedback) in applying one's implemented values, while differences in implemented values can be addressed by means of discussion and practice (also supported by cognitive feedback) in judging the same cases.

4. Statistics obtained in the modeling process (e.g., R^2) and from the decomposition of interevaluator agreement (e.g., G) can be used as the basis of comparisons of groups of evaluators. For example, these indices could be used as dependent variables in an investigation of differences between university teacher education faculty members who teach instructional methods courses and classroom teachers who supervise the practice teaching of students who have completed the methods courses.

5. Further examination of the evaluative consensus through cluster analytic methods can lead to the description of evaluative typologies consisting of evaluators with similar value systems. This approach is particularly appropriate when no a priori groups of the evaluators exist. Evaluators within the same typology can then be studied to determine what other characteristics differentiate them from evaluators in differing typologies.

Future applications of the SJT paradigm to the evaluation of professional performance should investigate in more detail the consequences of various levels of discrepancy between expressed and implemented values and the effectiveness of training to improve awareness of one's implemented values. Some (e.g., Fischhoff, 1991; Fischhoff, Slovic, & Lichtenstein, 1980) would suggest that it is primarily expressed values that are labile and therefore most likely to change, while others (e.g., Brehmer & Brehmer, 1988; Hammond & Grassia, 1985) would also expect changes in implemented values. But regardless of how they come about, effective communication about values and increased consistency of word and deed in the assessment of professional performance are worthwhile goals to pursue.

NOTE

1. Alternative approaches to modeling inferences based on probability cues are, of course, possible. See, for example, the discussion of process models in Carroll and Johnson (1990) and the "take the best algorithm" (Gigerenzer, Chapter 24 this volume; Gigerenzer & Goldstein, 1996). Further evaluation of the take-the-best algorithm was conducted by Harries and Dhami (1998).

30

Brunswik and Medical Science

Robert S. Wigton

Errors in judgment must occur in the practice of an art which consists largely in balancing probabilities. (Sir William Osler, 1897)   (cited in Bean, 1961)

The more I learn about medicine, the more I am impressed with its probabilistic nature. All diagnoses are uncertain no matter how classic the presenting signs and symptoms. All prognoses are uncertain no matter how effective the treatments. Exposure to agents that "cause" illness may or may not lead to clinical disease, and the manifestations of disease may differ from patient to patient. Although Brunswik's work is unknown to nearly all physicians, there are striking parallels between what medicine has learned and his views of the causal texture of the environment. The dominant feature of nearly all medical decision making is a healthy dose of irreducible uncertainty, inevitable error, and an abundance of fallible indicators. As an example of the irreducible uncertainty in medicine, consider urinary tract infection, a common and well-studied illness. Medical texts list fifteen to twenty-five clinical findings, tests, and predisposing factors that are common features of urinary tract infection. The test most physicians depend on, the presence of white blood cells on microscopic examination of the urine, explains less than 20 percent of the variance in the diagnosis. The best clinical prediction rule incorporating all symptoms, findings, and tests leaves 70 percent or more of the variance unexplained. This diagnostic problem also shows how vicarious functioning can be important in actual practice. Patients with urinary tract infection may complain of various symptoms, including painful urination, frequency of urination, small volume of urine, and lower abdominal pain. These symptoms are highly intercorrelated, and physicians must learn not to conclude that more of these symptoms does not mean the diagnosis is more certain.

For another example, consider the diagnosis of streptococcal pharyngitis. It is difficult to distinguish which sore throats are caused by streptococcal infection (and need penicillin) and which are caused by viral infections based on clinical findings (multiple fallible indicators). The optimal linear model (which has been shown to outperform clinicians in predicting the culture results) has a variance explained of no more than 30 percent (Wigton, Connor, & Centor 1986). Vicarious functioning, again, is clinically important, since it is easy to think that the many signs of infection of the throat (swollen tonsils, red throat, exudate, pain on swallowing) add additional information when, in fact, they do not.

The fallibility of diagnosis, therapy, and prognosis is referred to as the "art" of medicine, as contrasted to the "science." As early as the 1880s, Sir William Osler, the father of modern internal medicine, recognized the art of medicine to be its probabilistic nature (Bean, 1961). Many years would pass, however, before formal systems would appear to deal with it. In the 1960s, Lee Lusted and others brought the tools of Bayesian analysis and signal detection theory to medical diagnosis (Ledley & Lusted, 1959). At the same time, Alvan Feinstein (1967) recognized the probabilistic nature of clinical signs and symptoms and urged more precise, reproducible recording of data and development of mathematical tools to help deal with the low correlation between clinical findings and diagnosis. He, like Brunswik years before, recognized the failure of general rules (nomothetic approach) in situations where the combination of disease process and the individual patient characteristics may produce a unique (idiographic) manifestation of illness (Feinstein, 1967).

Brunswik's concept of the lens model of the ecology foreshadowed the extensive development of clinical prediction rules in medicine. Using multivariable regression, researchers have studied many hundreds of clinical outcomes to derive prediction rules to increase the accuracy of diagnosis or prediction. Brunswikians recognize this as defining the left, or ecological, side of the lens model. The earliest interest came from attempts to define risk factors for developing heart disease, and interest later spread to clinical diagnosis, management, and prognosis. From this and similar work, we all know at least some of the risk factors for heart disease (cholesterol, smoking, diabetes, hypertension, obesity), but only a few of the clinical prediction rules have found their way into day-to-day clinical medicine. Examples of successful rules are a rule for predicting fracture in ankle injury (Stiell et al., 1994) and a rule for predicting whether a patient with chest pain has had a heart attack (Goldman et al., 1988).

Besides the lens model, other elements of Brunswik's work, while largely unknown to medical researchers, also foreshadowed the direction of experimental work in medicine decades later. Brunswik's insistence on representative design has strong parallels in medical experimental design. Brunswik's emphasis on the importance of correlational relationships in environmental phenomena parallels some of the dominant movements in clinical research today: evidence based medicine and outcomes research. He stressed measurement of actual relationships in the environment rather than the laboratory. Because of its strong base in laboratory science (e.g., physiology, biochemistry, microbiology), much of clinical practice derived from extrapolations from laboratory study and emphasized the coherence of clinical practices with laboratory-based theory. This coherence approach served well, but recent advances in methods for measuring outcomes of care have shown where theory was misleading. Investigators recommended, for example, that physicians select the best drug for treating hypertension by measuring the serum renin. This tailored the drug to take advantage of the renin-angiotensin system, important in the body's control of blood pressure. A recent study found, however, that serum renin is a very weak predictor of efficacy and that clinicians are better off using a simple rule based on age and race (Preston et al., 1998). The increased attention to outcome measurement has brought about a new emphasis on evidence-based medicine. Evidence-based medicine urges us to prefer the therapy or strategy with the largest clinical effect that is supported by observations that we feel are valid based on critical appraisal. As in meta-analysis, evidence is accorded more weight depending on the methodological rigor of the study. These developments in medicine have paralleled the natural evolution of Brunswik theorists to emphasize correspondence versus coherence theories of truth.

Finally, there is a rich tradition of Brunswikian research in medical judgment. Because it is easy to find medical judgment tasks with multiple fallible indicators, they have been excellent subjects of lens model research. (For reviews, see Wigton, 1988, 1996.) As in other areas, medical applications of the lens model have found that clinicians' strategies vary widely, that a linear model of the diagnostician/judge can accurately predict future judgments, that self-described and lens-model-derived strategies differ, that judges use unexpected cues, and that achievement improves with feedback. One approach to helping physicians operate in a probabilistic environment is to improve the accuracy of their estimates of the probability of the outcome. Work with clinicians in actual clinical practice, however, suggests that improving the accuracy of their probability estimates does not necessarily produce the expected change in therapeutic decisions (Poses, Cebul, & Wigton, 1995). Several investigators have shown that without training, physicians' probability estimates are not particularly accurate (Knaus et al., 1995). In the context of the lens model, feedback of probability information can improve both diagnostic accuracy and calibration (Wigton et al., 1990; Tape et al., 1991). The practical side of these applications can be seen in the recent demonstrations that innovative uses of prediction rules can improve care. For example, Selker and colleagues (1998) programmed ECG machines to print the probability of acute heart disease as calculated from a clinical prediction rule. Physicians were able to use this information along with the conventional ECG results and clinical findings to make more accurate diagnoses and better management decisions. In view of the time it has taken for medical research to catch up with some of the discoveries Brunswik foreshadowed years ago, I anticipate seeing continued applications of his work in medicine for years to come.

31

The Perception and Judgment of Rapport

John S. Gillis and Frank Bernieri

rapport *n.* 1. relationship or communication, esp. when useful and harmonious. (*The Concise Oxford Dictionary*, 1995)

A central premise of social judgment theory is that the perceptual processes that allow us to respond to, and interact with, our social environment are not qualitatively different from those we employ for our physical environment. Judging the level of sexual receptivity in a potential mate, or the level of hostile or competitive intent in a coworker, is based on the same cognitive process as judging the correct distance between two stones that we plan to hop on in order to cross a fast-flowing stream. Humans must perceive, identify, and react to emotions, personality traits, social structure (e.g., status, kinship), and social relations (e.g., love, rapport, and competitiveness versus cooperativeness) that constitute their social environment just as they must perceive and react to the physical objects making up their natural environment. Failure to do so effectively, in fact, is associated with psychopathology and maladjustment. This chapter describes a program of research the general objective of which is to describe how people judge elements of their social ecology. We focus on a single social construct, that of *rapport*, to simplify our discussion, but we maintain that our approach is generalizable to the myriad other psychological constructs we deal with regularly.

Our program of research on the perception of rapport is guided by Brunswik's suggestions in both general and specific ways. We believe that we are indeed studying perceptual responses with all of the "necessary imperfections" imposed on them by the "comparative chaos," the irreducible "ambiguity in the causal texture of the environment" (Brunswik, 1943, pp. 257–258). The work began, as Brunswik directed, with studies of the ecology, the interpersonal environment of two-person interactions that judges would later attempt to assess. We were concerned with the manner in which, and the extent to which, interpersonal rapport, the positivity of a relationship, was reflected in observable features of the behavioral stream generated by two individuals engaged in a social interaction.

Here, rapport was the distal variable, one side of the ecological causal chain that produces observable features among or between interacting individuals that are accessible to a perceiver. As Brunswik (1943) anticipated, we have found in our studies of the rapport ecology ambiguities in the chain from "cause to effect" and "effect to cause." That is, there was no single feature, behavior, or circumstance that invariably gave evidence of the state of the distal variable ("rapport" as reported by the interactants themselves). And various stimulus features were associated with more than one distal variable. Brunswik had thus given us a sequential guide to how to proceed with our work: to begin by studying the ecology. Our ecological data are actual dyadic social interactions produced by ordinary people interacting with virtually no constraints and recorded on videotape. Thus, we are satisfying, with both the size and the character of our ecology, Brunswik's (1943) call for "representative samples" (p. 264). The variables our subjects deal with perceptually appear as they do in the everyday world of those individuals. The approach we describe thus observes the covariance of an individual's perception across a representative set of social events, or interactions.

In what follows we describe (1) how we incorporated Brunswik's ideas into a study of interpersonal perception, (2) how our studies are conducted, and (3) what we have found.

The Lens Model and Interpersonal Perception

Brunswik's (1956b, 1966) description of the functioning and interrelationship of the ecology and the perceiving organism is represented most succinctly in his lens model. Summarizing the vital aspects of both systems, Brunswik (1956b) noted that "the general pattern of the mediational strategy of the organism is predicated upon the limited ecological validity or trustworthiness of cues . . . this forces a probabilistic strategy upon the organism. To improve its bet it must accumulate and combine cues. . . . Hence the lens-like model . . . which may be taken to represent the basic unit of psychological functioning" (p. 20). The lens model thus presents a schema in which the basic unit of perceiver and target can be studied with its probabilistic contingencies.

The Perception of Rapport within the Lens Model

Our focus has been on two principal questions: How is rapport encoded in face-to-face interactions? How do social observers decode it? The criterion measure of this distal variable, from which observer-target agreement was determined, is derived from the self-reports of the interactants themselves. We defined rapport, after Tickle-Degnen and Rosenthal (1990), as a composite of three distinct qualities—coordination, mutual attentiveness, and positivity—each of which is presumably encoded in the behavioral stream. Cues, or indicators, consisted of all nonverbal aspects of the videotaped interactions which could be coded. We sought to determine (1) which observable cues, if any, had ecological validity as indicators of rapport; (2) whether observers of rapport were influenced by changes in these cues; and finally, (3) whether behavioral manifestations of rapport and the cues used by observers to assess it varied across different interaction contexts.

When applied to the perception of rapport, a lens model analysis yields quantitative indices not only of observer-target agreement in rapport assessment (r_a) but of the role played by sources of information (cues) in the way the attribute is revealed by the target person (r_e), or in our work by the dyad interactants, and the way such cues are evaluated by observers or perceiver (r_s) (see Figure 31.1). Such indices provide information about the bases for accurate judgments or the lack thereof.

Procedures

We work with a video archive of 120 male and female college students who were videotaped in both cooperative interactions and mildly adversarial debates. Interactions were self-terminated and lasted from five to thirty minutes. From this set of interactions, fifty have been selected and a brief (fifty-second) excerpt taken from each. These fifty excerpts constituted the situations for the observers.

A meta-analysis by Ambady and Rosenthal (1992) revealed that the information contained within very brief samples (thirty seconds or less) of the behavioral stream can be powerfully predictive of various behavioral outcomes. Surprisingly, increasing the length of behavior analyzed from thirty seconds to five minutes had no impact on predictive validity (see also Ambady & Rosenthal, 1993). For at least some subset of important behavioral and social outcomes, a thin slice of an entire interaction contains as much predictive validity as a much larger slice. This innovation of using relatively "thin slices" of the complete behavioral stream was critical in that it enabled us to present a bona fide set of instances of the appearances of rapport to an individual subject in order to assess how his or her judgments might covary with various indicators, as well as his or her overall accuracy.

From the tape containing the fifty video clips, a comprehensive set of potential behavioral cues to rapport (e.g., the number of times interactants smiled, the distance they chose to sit from their partners, the number of nervous behaviors they demonstrated, and their rated levels of expressiveness and animation) was selected. Several dozen such cues were nominated for coding on the basis of their theoretical relevance to rapport, but in the end, virtually every dimension of the tapes that could be quantified and that varied across interactions was coded. Eventually, more than seventy distinct features were coded reliably. Because of the high intercorrelations among cues (duration and frequency of smiles, for example), this list was reduced to a final set of seventeen cues (see Bernieri, Gillis, Davis, & Grahe, 1996, for the behaviors in this set). Nor were these final cues entirely independent of each other. Nonorthogonality, of course, is necessary for vicarious mediation because several cues would be transmitting the same information. Variations in the levels of these seventeen cues were correlated across the fifty video excerpts with the interactants' reports of rapport. Their steps constituted our analysis of the environment.

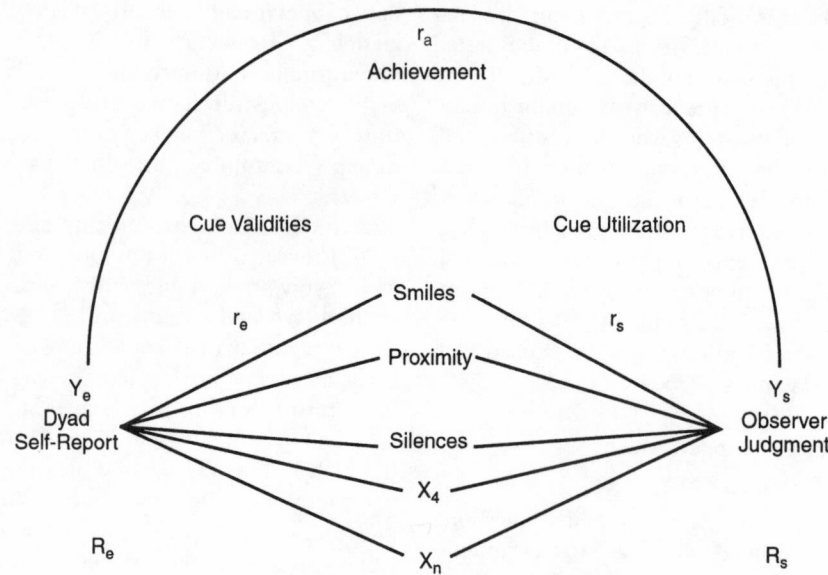

FIGURE 31.1 Brunswik's lens model adapted for the study of rapport and its judgment.

Observers or judges—those on the organismic side of the lens model—have generally been American university students, and the findings cited here have been obtained from such subjects. We have, however, also presented the tapes to samples from Australia, Greece, Mexico, Indonesia, Pakistan, Belgium, India, Lebanon, and Colombia with little difference in results on the decoding side. The judge's task is to observe the fifty interaction segments, the fifty dyads, and to estimate for each dyad the level of rapport being experienced by the interactants. The judges' accuracy, indicated as achievement (r_a) in the lens model, is determined by correlating their rapport assessments with those reported by the interactants over the fifty trials. Finally, their use of the behavioral indicators of rapport is determined by correlating their judgments, again, over the fifty viewed interactions, with the coded values of the cues for those same interactions. This lens model analysis is patterned after that outlined in Beal, Gillis, and Stewart (1978) and follows the general scheme suggested by Brunswik (1956b).

Findings

Ecology

The conception, design, and analyses of our studies follow directly from Brunswik's suggestions,

yet the most remarkable aspect of our work is the manner in which he anticipated many of our findings; his broad view of the organism-environment interaction was borne out in the specifics of our data. The ecology with which observers had to deal, despite all the ambiguities in its causal texture, did indeed carry sufficient information to allow accurate assessments of the distal variable, subtle and complex though it was. Interactants' self- reports of rapport, our criterion, could be predicted from features coded within the nonverbal behavioral stream. Over half of the criterion variance was accounted for by a subset of five coded behaviors: (1) frequency and duration of silences, (2) amount of female gesturing, (3) the physical distance maintained between interactants, (4) the number of postural shifts, and (5) the racial mix of the dyad. The fact that cues coded from a mere fifty-second slice of a much longer ongoing interaction were strongly predictive of the ultimate interaction outcome suggests that rapport is encoded chronically and redundantly throughout an interaction sequence, as opposed to sporadically and idiosyncratically through specific behavioral events or discrete actions. Thus, our Brunswikian analysis of rapport made salient its critical behavioral features.

Although rapport was strongly determined by the prevailing ecology, there were indeed ambiguities from "cause to effect" and "effect to cause." In the former case, no single behavior cue emerged as a perfectly valid indicator of rapport. There were, rather, a number of cues having partial linkages to that criterion. And such cues can be arranged hierarchically according to the extent of their linkage (a "cue family"; Brunswik, 1937), the aforementioned subset of five being at the top of this hierarchy. The fact that the five-cue model loses little predictive power compared to the entire array of seventeen coded cues is, of course, accounted for by the redundancy in information conveyed by the proximal cues (Brunswik, 1943). And all of this derives from our attention to an analysis of the environment, one of the "comparatively neglected tasks" to which Brunswik directed us.

Effect-to-cause ambiguities—the same proximal cues being consequences of various distal states—are not highlighted in our work, as we have typically focused on the single variable of rapport. However, the nonverbal behavior literature (Knapp & Hall, 1997) is replete with documented cases where behaviors such as smiling and gaze are diagnostic of extremely different psychological states (e.g., happiness, nervousness) and motivations (e.g., attraction, ingratiation, deception). In our own lab, we have found evidence that some cues are, depending on context, valid indicators of individual's emotional states in addition to predicting the state of the dyadic relationship (Bernieri, Gillis, & Curtis, 1998).

Achievement

Observer judgments of rapport based on a brief sample of the behavioral stream were correlated significantly with rapport reported by the interactants. Although accurate beyond chance levels, observers performed well below the theoretical maximum indicated by the strength of the cues-to-criterion statistical relationship. Judges were inaccurate mostly because they gave undue weight to animation cues, such as smiling and gestures, that had little validity. This conclusion emerges from our comparisons of the hierarchies of object-cue probabilities in the environment and the hierarchies of utility on the organismic side of the lens (Bernieri, Gillis, Davis, & Grahe, 1996).

This mistaken focus on animation-intensity-related cues supports Brunswik's notion that there may be "intuitive responsiveness" in social perception tasks to "environmental correlations as low as .15" (roughly the validities of gestures and smiling across our tasks; Brunswik, 1943, p. 260). One intriguing explanation is that judgment policies for social constructs may be more or less rigid and overgeneralized to different contexts that might change the nature of the social ecology. Thus, a policy that is developed and works reasonably well within one frequently experienced context may be applied rigidly and less successfully in a different context. It is possible that our observers may perform more accurately within the ecologies they normally experience than in the ecology we set up in the lab. This notion was supported by our observations that when we altered the rapport context from a friendly adversarial situation, where friends might be debating the merits of a recent Hollywood movie, to a more cooperative situation, where they were planning a fantasy "free trip around the world" vacation, the ecology changed so that animation intensity cues that had not worked earlier were more valid, making the observer's use of these cues more useful in this different context. Thus, we conclude that social perception policies, once established, may be robust and resistant to change in novel social environments. If our conclusion is true, knowing this state of affairs would be of great theoretical importance to professional and clinical psychologists when planning interventions designed to improve social adjustment.

Brunswik did not address the impact or demand character that certain dramatic cues could exert on the perceiving organism, although, with his interest in physiognomic relationships (Brunswik & Reiter, 1937), he may not have been surprised that such cues as smiling and facial expressiveness carried such weight. In one study, we tested the tenacity of initial policies by explicitly instructing observers which cues to ignore and which to utilize within our stimulus array (Gillis, Bernieri, & Wooten, 1995). The instructions should have improved their performance. Although judges understood our instructions and stated that they had complied with them, we found little evidence that they, in fact, had. When told to ignore smiling and animation intensity (i.e., general expressivity), their judgments of rapport correlated with these cues as strongly as did the judgments of those observers who had not been given these instructions. With regard to the kinds of social perception we are studying, Brunswik's (1937) description of intuitive perception as "relatively . . . stereotyped, superficial, confused, unanalytical, and sometimes narrow in its admission of and its way of evaluating cues" (p. 257) seems accurate.

Judgment policies

At least among untrained observers, there appear to be consensual implicit theories concerning the manner in which the positivity or negativity of social interactions is manifest. Subjects rely on these same cues, whether they are assessing rapport in an adversarial or a cooperative interaction context and whether they are judging the affective state of a dyad or a single individual (Bernieri, Gillis, & Curtis, 1998).

Judgment policies among individuals are not, of course, in perfect agreement; they do vary somewhat, as does judgment accuracy. What is interesting, however, is that we have been unable to uncover stable individual differences that predict this variation. For example, accurate judges did not differ from inaccurate judges on any personality, motivation, or intelligence measure that was clearly related to the task (Bernieri & Gillis, 1995b). Therefore, we have yet to uncover exactly what consequence differing social judgment policies might have on individuals.

Interestingly, whereas individual-to-individual variations have been noted, the median or typical judgment policy for a sample of observers within varying cultures seems remarkably stable. Sample representative implicit theories of social perception appear to cut across cultures, as we have found very similar cue utilization biases in samples from Greece, India, Belgium, Lebanon, and Indonesia (Grahe et al., 1999). Although Brunswik was not, to our knowledge, concerned with cross-cultural studies, his tendency to minimize the importance of cross-cultural differences seems to be vindicated here. (Details of procedure and description of our scales can be found in Gillis, Bernieri, & Wooten, 1995; Bernieri, Gillis, Davis, & Grahe, 1996).

Thus, we have found Brunswik's approach to be well suited to examining the social perception of rapport. Although not without limitations, the lens model analysis requires researchers to acknowledge that a social ecology does, in fact, exist and that perceivers are responding to it. Brunswik anticipated much of what we found and provided the schema by which our work continues to be organized. We continue to study real targets, observed in representative contexts, and to use an accuracy criterion drawn from the social environment. Much of what we have learned, and will learn, would not become apparent had we not come to our task with Brunswik's guidelines.

32

The Relationship between Strategy and Achievement as the Basic Unit of Group Functioning

John Rohrbaugh

As Brunswik (1956b) noted that the lens model "summarizes the relationship between achievement and strategy and may be taken to exemplify the basic unit of psychological functioning" (p. 141), so, too, is the lens model currently being used to represent the information processing that occurs within a group (Hinze, Tindale, & Vollrath, 1997). Much to his credit, Brunswik (1956b, p. 141) never suggested that the lens would be "a fully rational model of achievement" but, instead, "a mere 'ratio-morphic'" or reasoning-like framework for inquiry. Such a model is well suited to group study, since ratiomorphism should "not be confused with rationalism or with intellectualism; . . . it even helps us to nail down more concretely the rather important secondary differences between 'perception' and 'thinking'" (Brunswik, 1956b, p. 141).

There is no doubt that the Brunswikian psychology of perception (in particular) and cognition (in general) has been playing an increasingly important role in contemporary studies of group functioning. Since 1975, when Rohrbaugh undertook the first formal laboratory research in social psychology to extend the study of cognitive conflict tasks beyond the dyad to involve three to six participants in a single group process (see Rohrbaugh, 1988), the use of Brunswikian concepts and methods has become a prominent feature of group research. This assertion can be well documented by considering recent work in *group strategy* and *group achievement* as described below. First, however, primary consideration must be given to *group task*, without which neither strategy nor achievement can be understood.

Group Task

Psychological research on group strategy and group achievement languished for years because of its "encapsulation" (Brunswik, 1952, pp. 77–84). That is, it remained a psychology concerned only with the central and peripheral aspects of groups without attention to more distal features of their task environment. Ivan Steiner (1972), in reviewing a half century of group research, was one of the first investigators both to argue for a conceptual framework that would describe group work and to demonstrate that such differentiation in the nature of the task environment explained much of the observed variability in group performance. Although groups had been presented with a wide variety of specific judgment-making tasks (i.e., in Steiner's typology, unitary, optimizing, and discretionary) over the decades of investigation, the opportunity to observe their inferences about multiple situations through representative design in single experiments was a substantial advance in research method. Joseph McGrath's (1984) *Groups: Interaction and Performance* de-

voted a full chapter to the cognitive conflict tasks that Brunswikian researchers had introduced as an innovative approach to group study.

Rohrbaugh (1979) argued that the cognitive conflict tasks presented to groups should be positioned on a continuum of "intentional depth" (Brunswik, 1934b, pp. 222–225), depending (at least in part) upon the number of relevant cues in the task environment and the degree of equivalence between the ecological validity and utilization of each. The ease of making appropriate inferences about tasks with little intentional depth allows them to be undertaken successfully by groups with slight or no interaction; in fact, merely averaging individual estimates without discussion is an adequate response. However, it is the study of groups at work on problems of considerable intentional depth that merits attention, since these tasks clearly differentiate the functional advantages of specific group strategies. According to Brunswik (1943), "Ambiguity of cues and means relative to the vitally relevant objects and results must find its counterpart in an ambiguity and flexibility of the proximal-peripheral mediatory processes in the organism" (pp. 257–258) and, one can now add, in the group. Such vicarious functioning should be the central focus of group research.

Group Strategy

In tasks that carry the threat of considerable intentional depth (as many tasks do), groups must assume "an uncertainty-geared probabilistic strategy . . . to improve the cognitive 'wager'" (Brunswik, 1956b, p. 140). Mechanistic, rule-based group procedures to establish strategy such as averaging, voting, and Delphi-like approaches have been disappointing all too frequently (Reagan-Cirincione & Rohrbaugh, 1992a). Similarly, groups that rely on a single member to establish group strategy through the identification of their "best expert" are not well served either (Henry, 1995). In contrast, Sengupta and Te'eni (1993) have demonstrated that groups perform well on a multicue task when their members share information and compare individual strategies to work toward consensual judgments, so-called estimate-feedback-talk processes (Reagan-Cirincione & Rohrbaugh, 1992a; Reagan-Cirincione, 1994).

A multilevel theory of group decision making (Hedlund, Ilgen, & Hollenbeck, 1998; Hollenbeck et al., 1998) has been proposed that rests largely on Brunswik's lens model to guide the identification of key conditions at each level of analysis: team level, dyadic level, decision level, and individual level. Team informity, for example, is a measure of the degree to which members have all the cue information necessary to perform their roles; dyadic sensitivity reflects the success of the group leader in correctly weighting each member's recommendation; staff validity is the correlation between each member's judgment and the actual distal state. Although multilevel theory is restricted to situations in which a group leader, informed by member input, makes the final decision for the group, this line of research is advancing substantially the explanation of group strategy-achievement relations.

Group Achievement

Unlike the typical research design that poses a single question or problem for group evaluation (i.e., "one-shot" judgment studies in which the only measure of accuracy is the sole criterion-response discrepancy), representative design evoking multiple group judgments concerning a variety of multicue task situations (Gigone & Hastie, 1993, 1996) permits the attribution of imperfect achievement (functional validity) to such differing error sources as inappropriate cue utilization and environmental ambiguity. Brunswik (1943), for example, noted "the necessary imperfection, inflicted upon achievements . . . by the ambiguity in the causal texture of the environment. . . . Because of this environmental ambiguity, no matter how smoothly the organismic instruments and mechanisms may function, relationships cannot be foolproof" (pp. 258–259).

Even the earliest group studies in the Brunswikian tradition (Rohrbaugh, 1979, 1981; Harmon & Rohrbaugh, 1990) measured group achievement by correlating a well-selected series of actual distal conditions from a somewhat ambiguous environment with corresponding, cue-based predictions from group judgment policies. Gigone and Hastie (1997), in their lens model representation of the group judgment process, argued for the central importance of this correlational "match of the group's judgment policy and the environment"

and noted how group discussion might improve achievement should members "decide that a particular [ecologically valid] cue is important and therefore weight that cue more heavily than did any group member" (p. 165).

Improving Group Functioning

Cooksey (1996b, pp. 265–270) provided a thorough overview of the recent efforts to improve group performance by strengthening the relationship between strategy and achievement. Using a specific iterative form of an "estimate-feedback-talk" process with two tasks of considerable intentional depth, Patricia Reagan-Cirincione (1994) demonstrated, for example, that a group intervention focused very directly on modifying cue utilizations in accord with ecological validities could lead to great group achievement. In fact, her eight-stage process involving both direct facilitation and computer support led, in over 80 percent of the experimental meetings, to greater group achievement than by *any* of the group's members individually. Such a dramatic adaptive advantage may be attributable to the joint emphasis of the group intervention on improvements in both cognitive and behavioral aspects of group functioning.

Although no parallel experiments in field settings have been conducted as yet, a large number of decision conferences have been conducted that incorporate both direct facilitation and computer support to enhance cognitive processing and social interaction occurring within the meetings (McCartt & Rohrbaugh, 1995; Rohrbaugh, 1992). During a typical two-day decision conference, a group is assisted by a facilitator who works directly with the participants to help structure and focus the discussion, as well as encourage creative thought. Also present at the meeting is a judgment analyst to provide the computer support necessary to construct cases for on-the-spot judgment elicitation and to display immediately the characteristics of alternative judgment policies. Over the past fifteen years, field research has focused on the application of decision conferencing to cognitive conflict tasks has been encouraging (see, for example, Rohrbaugh, 1984; Milter & Rohrbaugh, 1988).

Groups of experts and management teams are concerned constantly with obtaining the most accurate assessments and forecasts possible, and they must be prepared continuously to update and enhance their judgment-making routines. Theoretically, the choice of an appropriate process to aggregate individual judgments into a collective strategy must take into account the level of bias evoked by the task. Any reasonable process of aggregation (including simple averaging techniques) is more than sufficient if the errors of judgment are randomly distributed, but mathematical aggregation schemes starkly fail when prospective group members share some systematic bias (Reagan-Cirincione & Rohrbaugh, 1992b; see also Gigone & Hastie, 1997). Since it is impossible to know how much bias is evoked by actual cognitive conflict tasks, particularly forecasting tasks with considerable intentional depth, it is prudent to assume that every important cognitive conflict task may evoke a great deal of bias.

From Past to Future Research

Perhaps the greatest irony in the field of group research, initiated nearly a century ago with such studies as Munsterberg's (1914) investigation of group judgments about the relative numbers of dots inscribed on cards and Knight's (1921) investigation of group judgments about room temperatures, is the recently reemerging conceptualization of groups as information processors. "Researchers *have begun to consider* (emphasis ours) that, much like individuals, groups process relevant and available information to perform intellectual tasks. . . . At the group level, information processing involves the degree to which information, ideas, or cognitive processes are shared, and are being shared, among the group members and how this sharing of information affects both individual- and group-level outcomes" (Hinze, Tindale, & Vollrath, 1997, p. 43).

In principle, most "decision-making" tasks (McGrath, 1984, pp. 62–64) might be studied with respect to the cognitive conflict inherent in the process of group functioning. Certainly, members of juries, for example, not only have different preferences but also may have systematically different cue utilizations, as well. Virtually any choice presented to a "decision-making" group requires at least implicit trade-offs to be made by participants with respect to the strengths and weaknesses, the costs and benefits, the pros and cons, of alternative courses of action. The most that can be done is "to compromise between cues" so that the "posit approaches the 'best bet' on the basis of all the probabilities, or past relative frequencies, of relevant interrelationships lumped together" (Brunswik, 1943, p. 258).

The improvement of these cognitive "wagers" deserves even more attention in the small-group literature. Conspicuously absent in the literature, for example, is research directly comparing the performance of groups when problems have been framed alternatively as "decision-making" tasks (where only the final choice is the object of study) or as cognitive conflict tasks (where the process of judgment receives primary attention). Such a line of inquiry would make far more clear the relationship of task definition to the development of group strategy and increased achievement. It would be the next important legacy of Egon Brunswik to the study of group functioning.

33

Brunswikian Research on Social Perception, Interpersonal Learning and Conflict, and Negotiation

Jeryl L. Mumpower

Brunswik emphasized the critical importance of the relationship between environment and organism in social as well as physical domains. Brunswik's insistence on the central role of the interaction between organism and environment for a functional psychology has now inspired more than four decades of productive research on social and interpersonal processes. Some of this research follows directly along lines that Brunswik himself initiated. In other instances, Brunswikian ideas have been extended in fruitful ways that his own work never explicitly anticipated.

This chapter focuses on Brunswikian research in the fields of social perception, interpersonal learning, interpersonal conflict, and negotiation. Each topic is discussed in turn.

Social Perception

As depicted in the lens model in Figure 33.1, persons are themselves the focal objects in *social perception*. The problem for the judge is to make inferences about distal variables—personality traits, personal qualities, and the like—on the basis of proximal cues that are directly observable but only probabilistically related to the other person's more fundamental characteristics, which are of ultimate interest to the judge. The judge's achievement is assessed in terms of the degree to which those inferences correspond to the other person's actual characteristics.

As part of his own research on social perception, Brunswik investigated persons' use of external physical characteristics (such as height and weight) as proximal cues to distal variables such as intelligence (1939b, 1943, 1945). Using both photographs and schematized line drawings, he found that persons were generally appropriately responsive, even though the ecological validity of these cues was quite modest, on the order of about .15.

Brunswik's approach to the study of social perception was not appreciated or emulated by social psychological researchers during the intervening decades. Not only did mainstream research on social perception pay little attention to concepts of environmental depth and texture (i.e., the relation between proximal cues and distal variables), but researchers in the field also neglected Brunswik's admonitions (1950, 1955c) about the importance of representative sampling of persons in the roles of objects. In reviewing contemporaneous research, Brunswik (1955c) noted that social perception research typically neglected to include a sizable number of social objects alongside the customary large number of subjects, "with fallacies of generalization ensuing" (p. 213). Little changed in ensuing years, as mainstream researchers continued to rely on tiny numbers of social objects to be judged (Hammond, 1996c, p. 138). Moreover, mainstream research on social perception somehow managed to avoid almost entirely what Brunswik viewed as the central issue for such research—the accuracy of such perceptions (see Hammond, 1996c, pp. 138–143).

Happily, this trend has been reversed in recent years by several researchers working within the Brunswikian tradition, who have focused precisely on the topic of the accuracy of social perceptions, concerning both personality and interpersonal interactions. Two streams of research are notable in this regard. Research by Funder and his colleagues (Funder 1987, 1995, 1996;

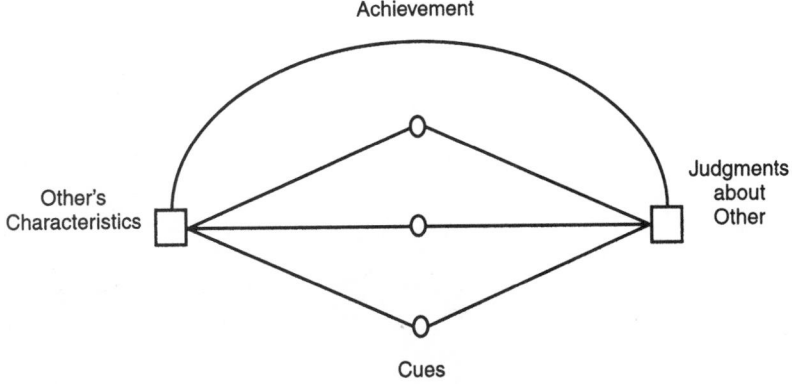

FIGURE 33.1 Social perception.

Funder & Sneed, 1993; Funder & West, 1993) has focused on the various factors that make judgments about the personality of other persons more and less likely to be accurate. Funder's work has investigated four categories of factors that may influence judgmental accuracy: "good judge" factors (which make some people better judges of personality than others); "good target" factors (which make some people easier to judge than others); "good trait" factors (which make some personality traits easier to judge accurately than others); and "good information" (the possibility that more or just better information leads to enhanced accuracy in personality judgment.)

Similarly, Bernieri and Gillis and their colleagues (Bernieri, Gillis, Davis, & Grahe,1996; Bernieri & Gillis, 1995a, 1995b; Bernieri, Zuckerman, Koestner, & Rosenthal,1994; Gillis, Bernieri, & Wooten, 1995) have taken a Brunswikian approach to the study of social perception. For instance, one line of their research has focused on identifying cues that judges use to make judgments about the degree of rapport between two interacting persons who are observed for a brief period of time, and about the degree of accuracy of such judgments.

Interpersonal Learning and Interpersonal Conflict

While the reemergence of Brunswikian approaches to the study of social perception is heartening, the greater influence of Brunswikian thought in this area has been on the study of

interpersonal learning and interpersonal conflict. Brunswikian-inspired approaches to both these topics emerged about ten years after his death, at about the same time, and have influenced research in the field ever since. The interpersonal learning (IPL) paradigm was introduced by Hammond, Wilkins, and Todd (1966; also, see Earle, 1973). The interpersonal conflict (IPC) paradigm was introduced by Hammond (1965, 1973). The basic elements of the IPL and IPC approaches are depicted in a lens model representation in Figure 33.2.

Both paradigms extend Brunswik's fundamental double-system lens model to a triple-system case in which there are two independent judges. (For a good overview of the triple-system case, see Cooksey, 1996b.) The judges face a common task, which can be described in terms of an environmental criterion (distal state) with which multiple proximal cues are associated. Judges infer the true value of the criterion on the basis of available proximal cues, each of which has an imperfect degree of ecological validity. Using the techniques of social judgment theory, judgment policy models (see Stewart, 1988) can be constructed to describe—in terms of weights, function forms, organizing principle, and consistency—the manner in which each judge combines information from the proximal cues to make an inference about the distal state. For each judge, achievement, or the predictive accuracy of the judgments with respect to the criterion, can be independently assessed.

The difference between the IPL and IPC para-

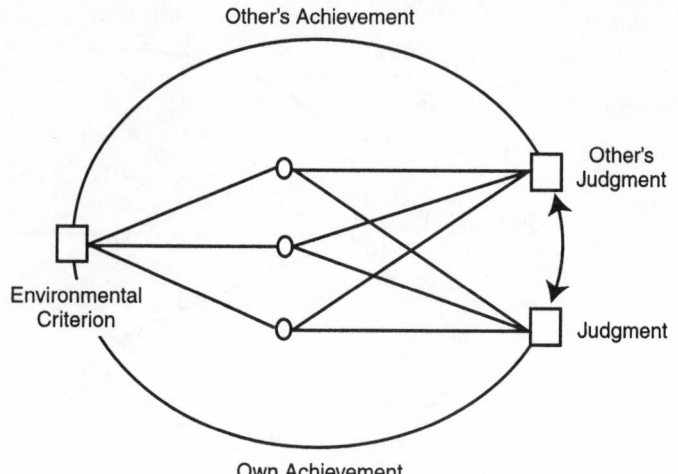

FIGURE 33.2 Interpersonal
learning and interpersonal conflict.

digms lies in the specific elements of the triple-system model on which attention is focused. In the IPL paradigm, the focus may be on either learning about or learning from the other person. *IPL about the other* is concerned with person insight, that is, the judge's understanding of and ability to predict how the other will behave (i.e., make judgments) in the task environment. The ability to predict accurately the other person's judgments requires an understanding of the weights, function forms, and organizing principle the other person uses to combine information from the proximal cues into a judgment. The degree of accuracy is also affected by the degree of consistency with which the other person makes judgments and the degree of consistency with which the judge makes predictions.

Research on *IPL from the other* focuses on understanding how a judge acquires knowledge about appropriate cue utilization (i.e., appropriate weights, function forms, and organizing principle) from observing the judgments that another person makes. Clearly, to learn from another person, one needs to learn about the other, so the two forms of IPL are closely coupled. IPL-about is always required for IPL-from: It is impossible to learn about a task from another person if one does not learn how the other person interacts with the task. The reverse does not necessarily hold true, of course. One can learn to predict accurately how another person will behave in a

given task environment without learning anything about how one should behave.

The two forms of IPL differ in another important respect. In IPL-from, it is essential that there be an explicit environmental criterion that is knowable, at least in theory. IPL-about, however, does not require that an environmental criterion be available or of interest. For IPL-about, research can focus simply on persons' abilities to predict one another's judgments, even in contexts in which the idea of predictive accuracy is irrelevant (e.g., Balke, Hammond, & Meyer, 1973; Miller, 1973).

Research in the IPC paradigm is motivated by the observation that not all conflict and disagreement stem from differences in motivation or in ends. Cognitive conflict may also arise—what Hammond (1973) described as differences over what people "believe to be the efficient, just, and moral ways to solve their problems" (p. 189). Hammond and Grassia (1985) made a similar point: "People dispute many things besides differential gains, or who gets what. They also disagree about (a) the facts (what is, what was), (b) the future (what will be), (c) values (what ought to be), and (d) action (what to do)" (p. 233).

In terms of the lens model representation in Figure 33.2, there are at least four potential sources of cognitive conflict. Judges may disagree about the relative importance of the available proximal cues (i.e., their relative weights); they may disagree about the relationship between values of cues and values of the criterion (i.e., the proper function forms for cues); they may disagree about the appropriate rule for combining information from cues into a judgment (i.e., the organizing principle); they may disagree because one or both judges are not able to make judgments consistently. Although the theoretical framework, befitting its Brunswikian heritage, was originally developed for situations in which an environmental criterion is present, interpersonal conflict may arise also in situations in which there is no environmental criterion.

Over three decades of research within the IPL and IPC paradigms has resulted in an impressive body of accumulated knowledge that contains a number of important, often nonintuitive conclusions about interpersonal learning and conflict. To cite just a few examples: Judges often fail to understand each other's judgment policies and sometimes lack good insight into their own judgment policies. Judges are unlikely to recognize shortcomings in terms of their lack of understanding of others' or their own judgment policies. Conflict may be exacerbated by encouraging persons to talk with one another, even if they try to communicate honestly and accurately. Successfully persuading another person to change his or her own mind and move closer to one's own position may sometimes escalate rather than decrease conflict, because of the difficulty in executing new judgment policies consistently. Disagreement tends to be greater when the unpredictability of the task is greater, because participants exercise less good levels of cognitive control in less predictable environments. Complex tasks involving larger numbers of cues and nonlinear function forms are more difficult to execute consistently, so that there are greater apparent levels of disagreement ("false disagreement") because differences in judgments are exaggerated by inconsistency. The causal texture of the task, in the form of intercorrelations among proximal cues, may mask policy differences ("false agreement"), if highly intercorrelated cues lead to similar judgments despite underlying differences in judgment policies. Judges who rely on linear cues will adhere to use of that cue longer than will judges who rely on nonlinear cues when they encounter new circumstances in which they should learn from each other to revise their judgment policies.

Further discussions of these and additional results can be found in several useful discussions and reviews of IPL and IPC research (Brehmer, 1976; Cooksey, 1996b; Hammond & Grassia, 1985; Mumpower, 1988; Rohrbaugh, 1988.)

Clearly, the fundamental notions of Brunswik's lens model may be extended not just to the triple-system case but also to n-system cases, in which multiple judges interact with one another. Rohrbaugh was one of the first researchers to extend Brunswikian ideas from dyads to small-group contexts—a research tradition that he and his colleagues have now carried out for more than twenty years (Rohrbaugh, 1977, 1988, 1997).

Negotiation

Most recently, a Brunswikian-influenced approach to the study of negotiation has emerged, led by the work of Mumpower, Rohrbaugh, their colleagues, and others (Darling, Mumpower, Rohrbaugh, & Vari, 1999; Milter, Darling, & Mumpower, 1996; Mumpower, 1991, 1998; Mumpower & Rohrbaugh, 1996). The main thrust of this research has been inspired by a quintessentially Brunswikian notion: that it is impossible to understand the behavior of negotiators, or to develop comprehensive theories of negotiation behavior, without analysis of negotiation task environments. In contrast, mainstream negotiation research has paid almost no attention to the structure of the negotiation tasks, failing to recognize the critical importance of task structure for understanding the process, dynamics, and outcome of negotiations. This is true even for that growing and now substantial portion of the negotiation research field that takes a behavioral decision theory perspective (for a happy exception to this generalization, see Raiffa, 1982).

The Brunswikian approach to negotiation is illustrated in Figure 33.3. In many negotiation tasks, there is no environmental criterion, or it is irrelevant, as indicated by the absence of depth on the environmental side of the lens model in Figure 33.3. For example, negotiators in a labor-management dispute (see Mumpower, Schuman, & Zumbolo, 1988, for an example of just such a dispute, analyzed from a Brunswikian perspective) may evaluate the desirability of potential

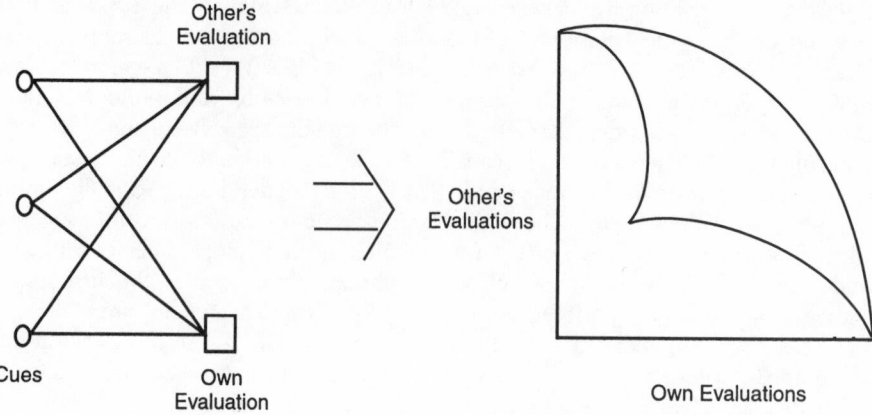

FIGURE 33:3 Negotiation.

contracts consisting of packages of proposed settlement levels for the various disputed issues (e.g., wage levels, health benefits, length of contract, and so forth). The issues in dispute, therefore, constitute the cues on the basis of which negotiators make judgments about the desirability of potential contracts.

As depicted on the right side of Figure 33.3, the joint distribution of negotiators' evaluations across all potential contracts (estimated by developing and applying judgment policy models) defines the *feasible settlement space*. The northeasterly edge of that feasible settlement space constitutes the *efficient frontier*, or the set of contracts for which no other agreement is possible that would improve one negotiator's evaluations of desirability without diminishing the other's. Psychologically speaking, the feasible settlement space and efficient frontier reveal the opportunities the problem affords, as well as the constraints the negotiation task structure imposes on the negotiators.

Brunswik argued in his 1956 book that careful analysis of the environment was essential and critical—he used the term *propadeutic*—for a functional psychology. Just as Brunswik would have thought, research has repeatedly demonstrated that the structure of negotiation tasks influences both the process and the outcome of negotiation processes in ways that could never be predicted or understood without prior analysis of the negotiation task environment structure.

Mumpower and Rohrbaugh (1996) summarized the importance of the Brunswikian perspective for the study of negotiation:

The distinctive feature of negotiation, unlike other task structures, is that the relevant environmental characteristics are not a set of exogenous variables that exist independently of the negotiators themselves. Negotiation problem structure is a synergistic function of the sets of preference and value trade-offs that the negotiators bring to the table. To wit, the negotiators jointly define the task structure. If either negotiators' set of preferences and values changes, then, the negotiation problem structure will also change, but neither negotiator is able independently to shape the negotiation problem structure into a form of his or her own liking.

Negotiators are mutually interdependent; their interaction defines the structure of the problem with which they must grapple. Moreover, because negotiators never have access to complete information about the other's preferences, and, arguably, may not have complete access to their own, they are unlikely to understand precisely the character of the problem structure that they jointly face.

Our arguments about the critical importance

of the problem structure concept for modeling and supporting negotiations have their basis in the ideas of Egon Brunswik (1952, 1956b). Brunswik argued that no coherent theory or model of human behavior could be developed that did not also include a theory or model of the environmental system (the task) with which the person interacted. In short, he argued that people's behaviors could not be understood independently of the environmental task. We believe the same holds true for negotiation. (pp. 406–407)

Conclusion

Mumpower and Rohrbaugh's preceding comments concerning the critical importance of task environment for negotiation research holds no less true in the areas of social perception, interpersonal learning, and interpersonal conflict. Brunswik taught that a psychology that ignores the task environment is doomed to be partial, incomplete, imperfect, and, consequently, frustratingly inadequate in its descriptive and predictive capacity.

34

Understanding the Effects of Psychiatric Drugs on Social Judgment

John Gillis

EDITORS' NOTE: Although this article was originally published in 1980, we reprint it here with minor editorial revisions because it demonstrates the broad scope and practical application of Brunswikian theory and method.[1] The research reaches far beyond the conventional experimental-control method that is focused on determining the effect of a variable to analyze important psychological functions in terms of the idiographic-statistical method that focuses on individual behavior. Even the topics being studied—interpersonal learning and interpersonal conflict among psychotic individuals—had never before been investigated, nor have they since, in spite of the fact that Gillis showed how valuable the lens model and its expansion are for this purpose. One might say that just as the experimental psychologists ignored the significance of Brunswik's ideas for their field, so the clinical psychologists have ignored his ideas—the practicality and productivity of which are here demonstrated by Gillis—for their field.

This chapter concerns the application of Brunswik's theory and method to the evaluation of the effects of psychoactive drugs on cognition, particularly social judgment. Although psychiatric drug effects were not among the research issues to which Brunswik gave attention (indeed, he might have been surprised had the relevance of his ideas to this problem been suggested to him), his ideas structured this entire research enterprise, and much of what was learned about these drugs could not have been easily discovered without them.

The work described here was guided by the same two fundamental principles (representative design and the idiographic-statistical approach) that guided the work of the other contributors to this volume. Brunswik's concern for the importance of the relevant features of the environment was reflected in the nature of the tasks in which drug influences were assessed. That is, tasks were designed to be representative of the patient's ecology with regard to their formal and substantive characteristics. Furthermore, patients were required to exercise their judgment under different conditions, along with and in the presence of others, where interpersonal learning and conflict could appear.

Brunswik's emphasis on the idiographic-statistical approach led to a focus on each individual's ability to cope with uncertain task environments. This approach is in contrast to the nomothetic designs typical of drug research, in which drugs are given to large numbers of individuals in order to determine how the drugs affect a single response.

The Problem

Despite the demonstrated capacity of antipsychotic drugs to alleviate symptoms, remarkably little information exists as to their effects on such important psychological functions as motivation, perception, and judgment, although each of these functions is obviously critical to a patient's (or anyone else's) adjustment. (Learning is one psychological process on which antipsychotic drug effects have been assessed: For example, the evidence regarding the drug chlorpromazine (Hartlage, 1965) suggests that it impairs learning across a variety of tasks in both humans and animals.) As a result, although antipsychotic drugs are firmly established as treatment agents, significant gaps exist in our knowledge of their effects on fundamental psychological processes. Studies of the cognitive and judgmental effects of these agents are needed.

The Nature of Maladjustment

Current gaps in knowledge about the nature of maladjustment are particularly serious because they exist in areas central to the definition and detection of abnormal behavior. Persons are, in many cases, considered disordered precisely because they lack motivation, evidence poor judgment, and have difficulties in learning appropriate responses, social and otherwise. If drug effects on the psychiatric patient are to be fully assessed, information about the influence of drugs on these functions must be obtained.

The Lack of Differential Clinical Effects among Psychiatric Drugs

Although the symptomatic effectiveness of chemotherapy is no longer in question, there are often few reasons for choosing one psychiatric drug rather than another in treating a specific disorder; that is, there are few demonstrated differences among drugs in clinical efficacy. As Baldessarini (1978) noted, "Available controlled clinical trials . . . do not permit a rational selection of a class of agents, much less a particular drug, for a specific type of psychotic patient" (p. 393). But if the various agents within a class cannot be distinguished as to symptomatic effectiveness, then potential differences in psychological effects assume considerable importance. Thus, for example, if several phenothiazines yield equal levels of symptom diminution, evidence that they have different consequences for judgment and learning would provide a sound basis for choosing among them. If such differences do exits and can be reliably identified, the clinician would then be able to prescribe agents that both alleviate symptoms and facilitate cognitive functioning—or at least, minimize its impairment. Because each prescriptive choice involves a clinical cost for a clinical gain, the full spectrum of drug consequences—both psychological and physiological—must be mapped before the extent of such benefits and liabilities can be known. Adding cognitive assessments to the known consequences of drugs will expand the profile of drug effects so that more informed clinical decisions can be made.

The Nature of Concomitant Psychological Therapy

Regardless of the view one takes of psychological therapies—whether they be individual or group psychotherapy or milieu programs—it is clear that they all involve learning. If a patient's situation is to improve, he or she must somehow learn to behave differently, respond emotionally in a more adaptive fashion, and view himself or herself and others in a new way. The extent to which learning is facilitated by psychoactive agents, psychological therapies will be useful adjuncts to chemotherapy. If learning is impaired by the drugs, however, the effects of psychological treatment can be expected to be diminished. Studies of the effects of drugs on cognition should, therefore, help clarify the interactions between chemical and psychological treatments.

Multiple-Cue Probability Learning (MCPL) Tasks

Typical drug studies (Gillis, 1975, 1978; Gillis & Parkison, 1977) have included three-cue tasks. Cues in these tasks have generally been represented by bar graphs, with cue values indicated by the height of the bars. Both linear and nonlinear cue-criterion relationships have been investigated. Both outcome feedback (subjects receive the correct criterion value after each trial) and the ecologically more representative cognitive feedback (Hammond, 1971; Hammond, Stewart, Brehmer, & Steinmann, 1975) have been given.

In order to improve his or her performance in an MCPL task, a subject must learn (1) the correct weights of the cues involved, (2) the functional relationships between cues and the criterion, and (3) the appropriate way of organizing information with a high degree of consistency. The investigator may observe not only the rate at which the subject's judgment improves but also the manner in which this is accomplished. In addition, the investigator may observe whether learning is limited by (1) a failure to acquire the correct knowledge of the judgment task or (2) a failure to apply effectively the knowledge acquired (Hammond & Summers, 1972).

The distinction between task knowledge and its consistent application, referred to as *cognitive control*, has been a useful one for drug research. The distinction arises from Tucker's (1964) modification of the lens model equation. Following Tucker's suggestion, MCPL performance is analyzed according to the following proposition:

$$R_a = GR_eR_s$$

Where r_a = achievement, or judgmental accuracy;

G = knowledge, an index of the extent to which the subject has correctly detected the properties of the task. Statistically, G represents the correlation between a subject's judgments and criterion values after each has been corrected for inconsistency;

R_e = the consistency of the judgmental task system, that is, the multiple correlation between the values of the available cues and the values of the criterion; and

R_s = the control or consistency of the subject's judgmental system, that is, the multiple correlation between the several cue values and a subject's judgments over trials.

(Nonlinearity is dealt with by appropriate transformations.)

Since R_e is constant for all subjects in a given study (that is, all subjects deal with the same MCPL tasks), performance can be analyzed and drug influences compared on the knowledge (G) and control (R_s) components (see Stewart, this volume).

Narrow- Versus Wide-Focus MCPL Tasks

It is possible to vary several parameters of the MCPL tasks, for example, the content, number of cues, functional relations between cues and criterion, and predictability of the task criterion. There has been some work with regard to each of these parameters in drug research. Especially useful have been those tasks labeled *narrow-* and *wide-focus*. While relatively simple in structure, these measures have yielded consistently interesting differences in several studies.

Narrow- and wide-focus tasks represent the most direct link of the research program to Brunswik. They were originally designed (Gillis, 1969) to study what Brunswik referred to as perception, or intuition, and thinking, respectively; task properties were developed to induce these contrasting modes of cognition. Brunswik suggested that certain important differences—in process and result—characterized the two modes. He described intuition as "uncertainty-geared" and depending on "relatively superficial and stereotyped cues of limited ecological validity, preferably a multitude of them" (1956b, p. 89). Intuition is thus multitrack, with its dependence on several intersubstitutable cues, the relatively large number of cues acting as a check against grossly erroneous judgments. Analytical thinking, on the other hand, is said to be certainty-geared and to function according to some set of precise and subjectively acknowledged rules. While intuition depends on several cues, analytical thinking is single-track and based on few. (For a recent discussion, see Cooksey, 1996b; Hammond, 1996c.)

This single- versus multitrack property was the basis for constructing MCPL tasks for drug studies. Because it was not possible with these tasks to induce all important aspects of the two modes of cognitions, the terms *narrow-* and *wide-focus* have been substituted for *analytical* and *intuitive*.

Each of these forms of MCPL tasks, as applied to drug research, includes three cues, each of which is related in a probabilistic (most often, linear) way to the criterion. In the narrow-focus task, only one cue has any significant predictive validity; the remaining cues having near-zero correlations with the criterion. In the wide-focus task, each of the three cues has a significant and roughly equal predictive validity.

MCPL Results: Differential Drug Influences on Learning[2]

MCPL tasks have been used in almost a dozen psychopharmacological studies. A brief survey of the results of these investigations indicates that various antipsychotic agents do indeed exert differential influences on performance in these tasks. The initial attempt to use MCPL tasks in drug research (Gillis, 1975) revealed that subjects receiving the high-potency agent thiothixene performed better than those receiving chlorpromazine. These differences were particularly pronounced on a narrow-focus task and were apparent on each of the performance indices—achievement, knowledge, and control—described earlier. Further studies continued to testify to the sensitivity of MCPL tasks to psychotherapeutic drugs. The present author (1977) noted differences, for example, among three widely used antipsychotic compounds and found (Gillis & Parkison, 1977) that patients receiving a slow-acting injectable agent performed significantly better than those on any of a variety of oral antipsychotic preparations.

It is uncertain whether the findings of differential drug influences yielded by MCPL tasks could have been obtained with conventional methods. To this author's knowledge, no literature directly comparing the effects of various phenothiazines or injectable and oral agents on such functions exists. What is clear is that MCPL tasks have detected differential drug effects among agents that do not differ in apparent clinical efficacy (Gillis & Moss, 1975; Gillis & Parkison, 1979). Because there often exists little reason for a clinician to select one drug rather than another (particularly when both are from the same class of medications, such as antipsychotics or antidepressives), evidence that certain agents affect learning differently (even while continuing to alleviate symptoms) provides a new basis for choice among therapeutic agents.

Not only do MCPL findings point up differential drug influences, but in some instances, they also point to the reasons for these differences. Subjects receiving the drug thoridazine, for example, performed more poorly than those on haloperidol because they failed to use cognitive feedback as effectively (Gillis, 1977). Placebo subjects performed better than those receiving either of two active antipsychotics not only because they were more aware of the task characteristics but also because they could implement this knowledge more consistently (Gillis, 1975)—that is, they exerted better cognitive control.

Interpersonal Conflict (IPC) Tasks

Its obvious importance notwithstanding, cognitive conflict between persons has received too little attention from psychologists (see Hammond, this volume). One important research task is studying such conflict to determine the methods by which persons go about resolving their differences, the limits of such attempts at a solution, and the conditions likely to facilitate or impede resolution.

As Brehmer (1976) suggested, the paucity of attention given to interpersonal cognitive conflict may stem from the absence of a theoretical framework for such conflicts. Social judgment theory has now provided such a framework, based on Brunswik's theoretical and methodological views. Specifically, the IPC paradigm provides for

1. Irreducible uncertainty in the tasks about which subjects are in disagreement.
2. Idiographic-statistical design (that is, a design in which the performance of each subject is analyzed over trials).
3. Adequate sampling of environmental form and content.
4. Task and cognitive systems conceptualized in the same terms.
5. The descriptions of both systems in statistical terms.
6. The appropriate statistical method, describing both the uncertainty and the regularities of such systems by correlation.

The IPC or cognitive conflict paradigm has two stages—a training stage, in which subjects learn to use information in different ways, and an interactive or conflict stage, in which subjects with different training are brought together to work jointly on judgment problems.

Training

In my studies of the effects of three antipsychotic drugs on conflict resolution between psychotic patients, I have used stimulus materials for the training stage that consist of sixty cards, each representing three characteristics of a different teacher. The patient's task is to learn to judge the quality of each of these teachers. Two 10-point scales (vertical bar graphs as used in MCPL tasks) are depicted on each card—one giving information regarding the intelligence of the teacher and another designating the level of discipline he or she maintains in the classroom. Both scales provide ten levels at which intelligence or discipline can be indicated, the level of each variable being represented by a darkened column on the scales. The criterion the patients are attempting to predict, *quality of teacher*, ranges from 1 to 20, higher scores being associated with better teachers.

Patients are studied in pairs; they are given different sets of training tasks. For one patient in a pair, virtually all of the variance in the criterion is attributable to the intelligence variable, the correlation between *discipline* and *quality of teacher* being essentially zero; for the other patient, this cue-criterion relationship is reversed. The training tasks are further differentiated in that the cue-criterion relationship is linear in one of these (intelligence and quality), while the discipline cue is related to teacher quality in a curvilinear fashion. Congruent with Brunswik's notions about environmental uncertainty, there are no perfect solutions for the tasks. Predictability is high, however, the multiple correlation between cues and criterion being set at .96. Subjects are randomly assigned to one of the two training conditions. After different cue-dependency training, conflicts in judgment occur between subjects as a result of different cognitive systems (or judgment policies).

Although interpersonal cognitive conflict has most often been accomplished by setting up the conflict situation just described, it is also possible to omit this stage entirely if subjects with naturally opposed (and consistent) judgment policies can be identified. The former procedure had been found to be simpler with psychiatric patients (Gillis & Moss, 1975).

Interactive (Conflict) Stage

Two patients were trained to use different cues (either *intelligence* or *discipline*) to make joint decisions in a second, interactive stage consisting of twenty trials. Patients are told that although they will be making essentially the same kinds of decisions as they did before, they will, on those new trials, be required to reach a jointly acceptable prediction as well as making individual deci-

sions. They are not informed that they have been trained differently.

In the interactive stage, the task system is changed; the cues are now arranged to be equally valid. Maximally accurate joint decisions therefore require that each subject give up some dependency on the cue on which he or she has been trained to depend and acquire dependency on the cue on which the other has been trained. Thus, a compromise is required in order to achieve judgmental accuracy.

A variety of quantitative indices can be derived from the cognitive conflict research paradigm (see, for example, Hammond, 1965). In the present case, the major parameters examined include those described earlier for MCPL tasks: *achievement* (R_a), *knowledge* (G), and *control* (R), all of which can be assessed for both training and conflict trials. In addition, the investigator can assess (1) the extent of agreement between the two interacting subjects, (2) the extent to which subjects change their strategies over time, and (3) the degree to which they are willing to compromise. All of these indices have been examined in one or more studies as measures of psychoactive drug effects.

IPC Results: Drug Effects on Conflict Resolution

In the two studies in which the IPC paradigm was employed, it was demonstrated to be appropriate for use with psychiatric samples, and its parameters were shown to be sensitive to the introduction of antipsychotic drugs. The teacher task was used to study the effects of two antipsychotic (chlorpromazine and thiothixene) and a placebo on conflict resolution in acutely disturbed schizophrenics (Gillis, 1975). Subjects receiving chlorpromazine were found to be significantly less effective at resolving conflict than those in the other treatment conditions. They resolved their differences more slowly and less effectively than those on placebo or thiothixene. These differences were due to the inability of chlorpromazine subjects to use information in a consistent, controlled fashion. Because these patients were inconsistent (lacked cognitive control) in their judgments, they actually became increasingly dissimilar as experimental trials progressed, and conflict therefore increased. An important effect of the drug was thus revealed: Chlorpromazine impairs the ability of schizophrenic patients to resolve differences with others; and lack of cognitive control was identified as the source of the effect. (See Brehmer, 1976, for a description of the generality of this finding in normal adults.)

A second study (Gillis, 1979a) of three antipsychotic agents (not including chlorpromazine) yielded no significant IPL differences between them. Patients receiving a high-potency agent (haloperidol), however, performed slightly better than those receiving thioridazine on all of the IPC measures.

The cognitive conflict model research paradigm thus gives promise of discovering important differences among antipsychotic drugs; there are no other approaches being currently used in psychopharmacological research that would allow detection of the important effects discussed here.

Interpersonal Learning

Hammond (1975) noted that, in addition to the problem of managing conflict, two significant questions concerning interpersonal transactions remain: What does one person learn from the other person as a result of the judgmental system of the other? Both processes are key functions in social life, and failure in either is apt to be significant.

As with failure in conflict management and social judgment in general, difficulties with interpersonal learning commonly appear among psychiatric patients. Further, as noted earlier, all forms of psychological therapy, regardless of theoretical foundations, involves learning, and virtually all therapeutic learning is accomplished within an interpersonal context. If a drug facilitates learning in this circumstance, it should enhance the total treatment process. But if it impairs the ability to learn from another person, this fact should be known to clinicians prescribing the medication. The IPL paradigm provides a method by which precise, quantitative measures can assess the nature and magnitude of interpersonal learning effects induced by psychiatric drugs. It thus provides objective indices of some of the

important costs that accompany the administration of a given agent to patients.

Like the conflict research paradigm, the IPL paradigm incorporates the two principles that Brunswik deemed essential: representative design and the idiographic-statistical approach.

Learning about Another Person

The IPL research paradigm permits evaluations of what one learns from and about another person (Hammond, 1975; Hammond, Wilkins, & Todd, 1966). The latter has been the focus of most drug research.

Learning about another person is ordinarily epiphenomenal; people are seldom directed to learn about one another. Learning about the other is generally, although by no means always, incidental to the circumstances in which differing judgments are produced. When judgments differ, however, people become more or less sensitive to the nature of one another's policies. Clearly, the quality of the interchange between people is enhanced if each can correctly discern the characteristics of the other's policy. If two persons can, in fact, learn about one another's judgmental policy, each will guide his or her behavior appropriately in relation to the other. Failure to understand the other, which will result in the inability to predict his or her judgments, will, however, lead to a variety of differences in social interactions. Whether a drug facilitates or impairs one's ability to understand and predict another's behavior, then, will have an important effect on social interaction.

The IPC paradigm permits the analysis of the extent to which one person has learned about the other. Once those predictions are made, the investigator may study the details of each subject's inaccuracies, should they occur. That is, the investigator may ascertain whether Subject A has failed to predict Subject B's judgments because A does not know (1) the manner in which B weighs the various cues, (2) which function forms B applies to them, or (3) how B organizes the information, (4) because A fails to apply his or her knowledge of B with consistency, or (5) because B is so inconsistent that accurate prediction of his or her judgments would be difficult for anyone. In short, detailed examination of the effects of a drug on cognitive adaptive functions are possible within the IPL research paradigm.

Procedures and Measures in IPL

Following the conflict phase of the IPC paradigm, subjects are asked to participate in a second series of trials. In this stage they are asked to look at the data on each cue card, make a judgment of the value of the criterion, and, in addition, predict what judgment their partner will make in response to the same data. The latter is not an unreasonable request, inasmuch as the two persons have been comparing judgments with regard to these same cues for at least twenty trials and have been discussing their judgments for roughly an hour or more.

This simple procedure produces considerable information bearing directly on the question of how much each person has learned about the other. A comparison of A's predictions for B with the actual judgments B makes provides a measure of predictive accuracy. In addition, it is possible to compare the predictions A makes for B with A's own judgments about the cue cards. This comparison provides a measure of assumed similarity, for if A predicts that B would make the same judgment that he or she makes, then A implicitly assumes that B is highly similar to him or her. Also, comparing A's judgments with B's judgments provides a measure of actual similarity. The effects of various antipsychotic drugs on all three measures have been studied on several occasions.

IPL Results: Effects of Drugs on Interpersonal Learning

IPL tasks have proved to be quite appropriate for work with psychotic patients. The major findings are:

1. Patients receiving placebos learn more effectively about others than those receiving chlorpromazine (Gillis, 1975).
2. Antipsychotic agents exert differential influences on IPL; the widely used drug thioridazine, for example, impairs IPL less than mesoridazone (Gillis & Davis, 1977). Patients receiving the high-potency agent haloperidol seem to learn more effectively than those re-

ceiving phenothiazines either alone or in combination with other drugs (Gillis & Moss, 1978). In general, the more the sedating and the greater the anticholinergic effect of an antipsychotic, the more severely it interferes with the ability to learn about how other people arrive at their judgments under conditions of uncertainty.
3. When antipsychotic drugs are combined with antidepressant drugs (as is frequently done in current chemotherapeutic practice), the results are much the same as when antipsychotic drugs are used alone.
4. Although phenothiazines generally impair IPL, patients who receive the phenothiazine fluphenazine decanoate in a slow-acting, injectable form are not impaired, although the injectable drug is effective in alleviating psychotic symptoms (Gillis & Parkison, 1979).

In short, the research on IPL points to at least one psychotherapeutic drug that alleviates symptoms without impairing the ability to learn about others. If this result is substantiated in further research, its implications will obviously be considerable.

This brief account of results illustrates the productivity of the IPL research paradigm. As in the MCPL and IPC tasks, not only can the relative influences of various drugs on cognitive functioning be detected, but the nature of these differences can also be identified. The generally proficient IPL performance of fluphenazine patients, for example, can be traced to their being significantly more consistent—that is, having more cognitive control—than those receiving chlorpromazine (Gillis & Parkison, 1979). Similarly, in their application of task knowledge, thioridazine patients were significantly more consistent (had higher R_{2s} in the LME) than mesoridazone subjects; and the groups did not differ with regard to the accuracy of their task knowledge (Gillis & Davis, 1977)—that is, G in the lens model equation.

Conclusion

In drug research, the study of the process of judgment is clearly valuable because functional deficits in judgment create interpersonal difficulties that result in hospitalization. It might be expected, then, that therapeutic drugs would be required to improve a patient's behavior in this regard and thus facilitate effectiveness in a social context. But if that is too large an expectation at this point, at the very least clinicians, before writing prescriptions, should know about the effects of specific drugs on judgment and on such important matters as the resolution of cognitive conflict and interpersonal learning. It is now clear that such critically important information can be discovered through the application of Brunswik's revolutionary theoretical and methodological

principles. The history of research in this area indicates that such information is not apt to be discovered by other methods.

NOTES

1. This chapter originally appeared in *New Directions for Methodology of Social and Behavioral Science,* 3 (1980), pp. 25–36. Reprinted by permission of Jossey Bass, Inc., Publishers.

2. This section focuses on the utility of the methods; a summary of substantive findings on drug differences can be found in Gillis (1979b) and Hammond and Joyce (1975).

35

Human Factors

Alex Kirlik

Human factors research is largely concerned with the analysis and design of human-machine systems (HMS) and human-computer interaction (HCI). Thus, the objects of human factors study can be seen to be irreducibly ecological: *systems* comprised of both people and their technological environments, and *interactions* among these system components. Additionally, the practical purposes (e.g., transportation, production, management, defense) for which HMS and HCI systems are designed naturally promote a *functional* attitude toward modeling and performance evaluation. These observations on the ecological nature of human factors are not new. In his 1957 article "Psychology and the Design of Machines" Franklin Taylor observed that human factors research "argues against maintaining separate sciences and construct languages: one for the environment and the other for that which is environed" (p. 258). This same year saw publication of Brunswik's admonition to psychologists that "both organism and environment will have to be seen as systems, each with properties of its own, yet both hewn from the same block" (Brunswik, 1957, p. 5), and more

important, a set of concrete proposals for carrying out an ecological, functionalist enterprise (Brunswik, 1956b).

Against this backdrop it may seem somewhat surprising that Brunswikian ideas had hardly any impact on human factors research and practice of the 1960s, 1970s, and 1980s. Neither of the classic (and still widely used) texts in human factors (Kantowitz & Sorkin, 1983) or engineering psychology (Wickens, 1992) makes any reference to Brunswik. But times are changing. More recent years have seen the publication of task analysis techniques (Kirlik, 1995), design frameworks (Flach & Dominguez, 1995), and methodological analyses (Vicente, 1997; Kirlik, in press) that explicitly and self-consciously apply Brunswikian ideas to modern human factors theory and method. David Woods (1995), a pioneer in cognitive human factors (or "cognitive engineering") and current president of the Human Factors and Ergonomics Society, has proposed a "context-bound" methodology as an alternative to human factors' historical focus on systematically designed laboratory experimentation using abstract, spartan tasks: "The context-bound approach . . . is characterized by studies of specific meaningful tasks as carried out by actual practitioners; models of errors and expertise in context are a critical focus; results are organized by cognitive characteristics of the interaction between people and technology. . . . The research methods are based on field study techniques and detailed protocol analysis of the process of solving a problem" (p. 180).

Something about the human factors enterprise has changed in recent years so that many are now rediscovering the merit in Brunswik's (1955c) plea that we must "resist the temptation of the systematic experimentalist to interfere, and must introduce a laissez-faire policy for the ecology" (p. 198).

In the remaining sections of this chapter, I will discuss how Brunswikian ideas, particularly functionalist theory and representative design, offer a precise and insightful way of framing methodological issues in a problem-driven design domain such as human factors. In particular, I will try to show that the historical transition from systematic laboratory experimentation to more representatively designed investigations is merely the natural, adaptive response of a problem-driven field to its changing problem base, rather than a move toward ecological enlightenment as some modern writers would have us think. Human factors as a whole will certainly not benefit by replacing one brand of methodological dogmatism with another, and discussions along such lines typically generate more heat than light (e.g., Dowell & Long, 1998, and its associated peer commentary). Second, and perhaps more relevant to Brunswikian psychology, I will point out how the history of human factors methodological successes and failures sheds light on, and lends confirmation to, functionalist theory and representative design.

Appropriate versus Premature Generalization in Human Factors Research

Much of the human factors research before the 1980s focused on the problems of coupling human operators and the surface or proximal features of their task environments (see the previously cited texts). This type of research led to the characterization of human factors as primarily concerned with "knobs and dials." The ability of an operator to manipulate a control and read a display is important—and remains so today. But due to the low levels of technological sophistication and automation in early human-machine systems, the proximal information and actions available at an interface were very tightly coupled to their remote (distal) referents and effects. As a result, there was little in the way of a task demand placed upon the system operator involving the "cognitive attainment of 'distal' variables that are to a certain extent independently variable of the corresponding 'proximal' or sensory input" (Brunswik, 1957, p. 7). The pressing human factors problems in designing an automobile interface, for example, concern reachability, visibility, and so on of displays and controls: If an analyst determines that a design requires the driver to reason beyond these proximal variables to covert distal variables, the most efficient solution to the problem will be to redesign the technology so the operator no longer has to do so. But Brunswik would have objected on principle to such "knobs and dials" research, as "having no distal relevance; it does not really venture out into the ecology" (1957, p. 28). That may be so, but a problem-driven field such as human factors will appropriately venture only so far as it must to deal with its problems. One likely reason that traditional human factors texts do not recommend functionalist theory is that performance in many low-technology contexts depends most heavily on efficient proximal interaction, because he technology itself takes care of the proximal-distal relationships.

A second (legitimate) reason why the Brunswikian approach has been slow to take hold in human factors concerns the nature of the generalizations necessary to appropriately inform design. The central theme of Brunswik's concept of representative design is the use of statistical sampling of environmental conditions in addition to sampling of human subjects, to allow for generalizations both to target human populations and to target environmental conditions. As noted by Hammond (1986), the experimental designs and inferential methods developed by agricultural statisticians and subsequently adopted by experimental psychologists were ill suited to the task of generalization over conditions: "Those agricultural statisticians had no interest in generalization over conditions but only over subjects, i.e., plants and animals. Their interest in treatments was specific; e.g., does *this* chemical have an effect or doesn't it? If it does, then the farmer will create a new world for the plant and animal in which the new chemical will appear. Generalization by argumentation is unnecessary; the results apply because the farmer *makes* them apply. (Hammond, 1986, p. 431; emphasis in original).

The sophisticated techniques of representative design ensure generalization over conditions, but these techniques are methodological overkill when, like a farmer, a researcher can simply *make* results apply by reproducing the exact conditions tested in experimentation. And a good deal of human factors research, regardless of the technological sophistication of the application domain, is a lot like farming in this regard. If Display A is superior to Display B for the task of landing a particular aircraft, we will insert Display A into the cockpit environment, with transfer of experimental results carried along by the display itself, so to speak. Generalization will be limited only by the potential interaction of display design features with experimentally unrepresented features of the target operational context. Many, but not all, human-machine task environments are nearly decomposable in this regard, and in such cases, procedures for sampling environmental conditions are not needed.

To summarize, the full resources of functionalist theory may not be required to deal with human factors problems focusing solely on human interaction with (proximal) displays and controls, and representative design may not be required for problems in which design-related experimental results can be physically, rather than statistically, generalized. But clearly many human factors design problems do not meet these conditions. And if Brunswik was correct about the conditions under which traditional, systematic experimental designs would both succeed and fail to provide appropriate generalization, we should expect to find a signature of such successes and failures in the empirical human factors record. Consider Carroll's (1991) interpretation of the empirical record:

The scientific method impels dichotomous contrasts, and this works well only if the required

controls are possible and appropriate. In HCI these requirements are generally not met. The chaotic and uncontrolled nature of complex activity like programming forced the use of extreme contrasts (structured versus random programs, organized versus random menus) in order to attain statistically significant results. . . . The paradigm of direct empirical contrasts persists in HCI but its use is more limited: Alternatives are contrasted to determine which of *those two* alternatives are better, not to apply or to extract general principles. (pp. 4–5; emphasis in original).

The history of systematic experimental HCI research is what Brunswik taught us to expect. The path ahead, of course, lies in seeing (like Brunswik) that while traditional psychology methodology may "impel" experimentation using "dichotomous contrasts," such designs are hardly required by "the" scientific method.

Functional Theory and Representative Design in Human Factors

If my Brunswikian classification of human factors design problems is on the right track, the reasons that human factors researchers are now beginning to embrace Brunswikian theory and method should be found in examining how the discipline's problem base is changing. The classification suggests that functionalist theory and representative design will be required resources for human factors research when:

1. Issues associated with appropriately coupling the human operator with proximal interface design features are of less consequence than issues arising out of how the operator uses proximal variables in the "cognitive attainment" of distal variables (i.e., when the functional role of the interface is to *mediate* interaction with a target context, rather than to serve as the target of interaction).
2. Generalization is required beyond explicitly sampled conditions (i.e., predictive techniques are required).

Concerning the first point, consider the critique of traditional HCI research offered by Jens Rasmussen (1990), a founder of cognitive engineering and proponent of ecologically oriented research methods:

> Basically, HCI, as a discipline, deals with the interaction of users with computers in terms of general aspects of communication languages, irrespective of the context of the work in which the systems are used. Clearly this approach is important for the development and optimization of separate tools . . . just like a ball point pen or typewriter can be optimized ergonomically without considering what the topic of the writing is. . . . Consequently, such studies are well suited for laboratory experiments by behavioristic methods, isolated from the complexity of the actual work domain (not without reason, the word processor has been called the Skinner box of HCI). (p. 326).

In Brunswikian terms, Rasmussen was clearly speaking of the inherent limitations of research methods that focus solely on interaction with the proximal environment, excluding study of how the proximal environment serves as a mediator to a distal context that is the actual, meaningful target of human interaction. Rasmussen went on to additionally motivate the need for ecologically oriented research methods in high-technology, high-risk systems: "For such systems, the potential consequences of human errors and mistakes may be very large, and a low probability of such events may be required. Therefore, design cannot be based on direct empirical evidence from actual accidents but has to be judged by predictive models of the human-system interaction" (p. 327).

Rasmussen's observation goes directly to our second previous point, that representative design will be required when generalization beyond known conditions is required. I do not believe it is a coincidence that a leader in the cognitive engineering field motivates the need for a more representative research approach by appeal to two features of the problem base that also provide the raison d'être for functionalist theory and representative design.

Conclusion

This overview of human factors research suggests that Brunswik may have been ahead of his time in more ways than one. The many subtle distinctions in his theoretical system are difficult to grasp, and the "concrete" examples he used to illustrate them (e.g., probabilistic proximal-distal relationships in depth perception) are unfamiliar to everyday awareness. Additionally, the many stringent requirements of his methodological approach must have seemed like overkill to those successfully performing and publishing experimental work with only a fraction of the effort. Today, we are much more likely to have concrete experience with probabilistic proximal-distal variables, in our interactions with technological interfaces that are often both inadequately informative and difficult to manipulate to achieve our ultimate, distal goals. Human factors researchers investigating these problems are becoming acutely aware of the need to represent these often complex environmental structures in their experimental designs, and even of the need to obtain expert knowledge of the task environments under study in order to understand the behavior of system operators. Perhaps we are reaching the point were we have finally created an empirical world of such complexity as to finally make obvious the need for the full resources of Brunswikian theory and methods.

36

Representative Design: Cognitive Science from a Brunswikian Perspective

Peter Juslin

In the end the greatness of a scientist is measured foremost not in terms of well-designed experiments or the elegant fitting of models, but in the deliverance of a profoundly important message. Egon Brunswik had such a message. Several of the issues he raised in his 1955 *Psychological Review* article appear noncontroversial in present-day cognitive science (although seldom, it seems, because of the direct impact of Brunswik's writings). For example, models with probabilistic notions, which stress the purposive, "distal-over-proximal" nature of cognitive processing, are commonplace in cognitive science. Nonetheless, it seems fair to conclude that the most important part of the story told by Brunswik remains largely unappreciated by mainstream psychology: that the proper object of study for a scientific psychology is the *organism-environment system* as a whole, where the behavior of the organism is molded by the forces of adaptation and intertwined with the properties of the environment.

It might seem odd to take lessons in cognitive science from a man who at times dismissed cognitive processes as "processing details." Arguably, however, the ecological and functional aspects of Brunswik's probabilistic functionalism are only further highlighted with the event of cognitive science. Classical experimental psychology often results in the accumulation of intriguing but disparate phenomena. Thus, cognitive psychology is often criticized on the grounds of undue fragmentation; we tend to end up with a new theory for every experimental paradigm that we address.

One aim of cognitive science is to create computational models of the cognitive processes that mediate between the *Proximal Input* and the organism *Response*. In general, the models are defined by some *cognitive activity or goal* (for example, depth perception), rather than by reference to specific experimental paradigms. While the empirical approach presented by experimental psychology can afford to neglect a careful analysis of the environment, a cognitive algorithm intended to produce intelligent behavior in a wide and real-life-like context cannot. No cognitive algorithm exists without the "behavioral support" of some task environment, and any useful candidate will efficiently exploit the properties of the environment. Hence, a natural environment need be not only a nuisance in its bewildering complexity but also a *natural resource* that affords efficient exploitation.

In this commentary, I briefly present an example of the application of how representative design can be usefully related to present-day cognitive science by reference to recent research on the overconfidence phenomenon.

An Example: The Overconfidence Phenomenon

A common finding in research on *realism of confidence* has been that people overestimate the validity of their general knowledge, the so-called overconfidence phenomenon. According to the most common experimental paradigm, the participants are presented with a large set of two-alternative general-knowledge items like "Which country has the larger population: (a) Finland, or (b) Zambia?" For each item, a participant is to decide on one of the two answers, and to assess confidence in this decision as a probability between .5 and 1. In most studies, the mean confidence has been higher than the proportion of correct answers. For twenty years or so, this result has primarily been interpreted in terms of a *cognitive overconfidence bias*.

This interpretation was challenged in the early 1990s by the introduction of Brunswikian ideas, a movement spearheaded by Gigerenzer with colleagues, and by the theory of *probabilistic mental models* (PMMs; Gigerenzer, Hoffrage, & Klein-bölting, 1991). At the time, similar studies were performed in our laboratory in Uppsala (later reported in Björkman, 1994; Juslin, 1993, 1994). In a theoretical review of the area from 1994 (McClelland & Bolger, 1994), these researches were collectively referred to as the *ecological models*.

The ecological models assume that people often rely on *probabilistic cues* to infer the correct answers to general-knowledge items. For instance, in regard to the item "Which country has the larger population: (a) Finland, (b) Zambia?" a participant may retrieve that Finland lies in Europe, a region with many rich and highly industrialized countries, while Zambia lies in Africa, where most countries are known to be poor and underdeveloped, with poor birth control. In the absence of knowledge of the exact population figures, the participant may believe that a large population is more common among African countries and may therefore decide on Zambia as a best guess. The idea is that answers are selected on the base of probabilistic cues that reflect *knowledge of objects in the world*.

The critical claim by the ecological models is that confidence is based on assessments of the *ecological cue validity* of the cue used in the choice. In PMM theory, as well as in other Brunswik-inspired research on calibration, the ecological cue validity is defined by the relative frequency of cases in the environment where the cue indicates the correct answer. The ecological cue validities are thus determined by the relative frequencies that hold within a reference class of objects in the environment. For example, the choice of an African over a European country in a pair comparison that concerns population will lead to one specific proportion of correct answers when applied to the world countries.

The experience with the natural environment leads to internal or cognitive representations of the ecological cue validities, referred to the *internal cue validities*. These internal cues are in turn translated into overt confidence judgments. A cue that always points to the correct answer (high ecological cue validity) elicits high confidence, whereas a cue that is only slightly better than chance (low ecological cue validity) leads to less confidence. If the participant has reasonably accurate beliefs about the ecological cue validities, the confidence assessments will be appropriate to a distribution of items that is representative of the natural environment (see Figure 36.1A). Realism of confidence can be investigated, however, only for specific item samples generated by the experimenter and presented to the participants in the laboratory. The validity of the cues with these item samples are the *sample cue validities*. In short, ecological cue validity is a property of the environment, internal cue validity is a property of the organism, and the sample cue validities concern the specific laboratory task.

If people are adapted to a natural environment, and this is to be observable in the laboratory, the sample cue validities need to be representative of the ecological cue validities. The controversial argument was that in studies with general knowledge items, the overconfidence phenomenon may to a large extent have been mediated by a violation of representative design; the items have been selected in a manner that overrepresents those situations where the cue-based inferences fail. As a result, the sample cue validities fall below the corresponding ecological cue validities, and — because confidence reflects the ecological cue validities — people appear overconfident.

In Juslin (1994), two samples of general knowledge items were compared: a *representative item sample*, where the objects of judgment (world countries) were sampled randomly from a natural environment (the countries of the world), and a *selected item sample*, intended to be good knowledge-discriminating items. Twelve item-selectors naive to the experimental hypothesis generated the selected sample. The calibration curves from twenty participants who responded to both item samples are presented in Figure 36.1B. For the representative item sample, there was good calibration, but for the selected item set, the proportions correct were too low, thus producing the overconfidence phenomenon (For replications of this experiment, see Winman, 1997; Kleitman & Stankov, 1997).

The initial studies with representative item samples reported proportions correct in the interval .7 to .8 and close to zero over/underconfidence bias (Gigerenzer et al., 1991; Juslin, 1994). Following the lead of Griffin and Tversky (1992), these results were soon dismissed on the grounds

A

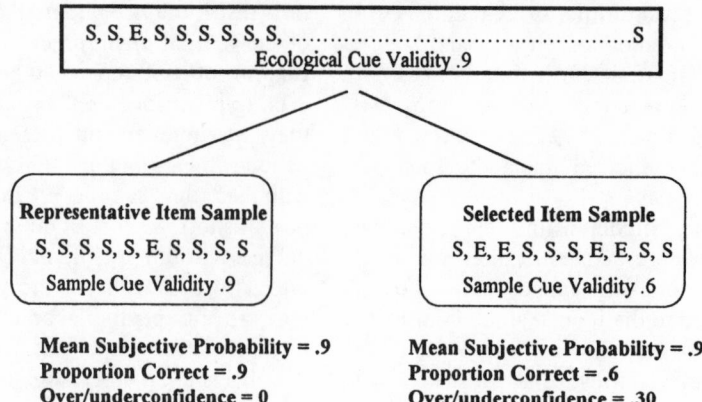

Reference Class of Cue Applications in the Environment

| S, S, E, S, S, S, S, S, S, ...S |
| Ecological Cue Validity .9 |

Representative Item Sample
S, S, S, S, S, E, S, S, S, S
Sample Cue Validity .9

Selected Item Sample
S, E, E, S, S, S, E, E, S, S
Sample Cue Validity .6

Mean Subjective Probability = .9
Proportion Correct = .9
Over/underconfidence = 0

Mean Subjective Probability = .9
Proportion Correct = .6
Over/underconfidence = .30

B

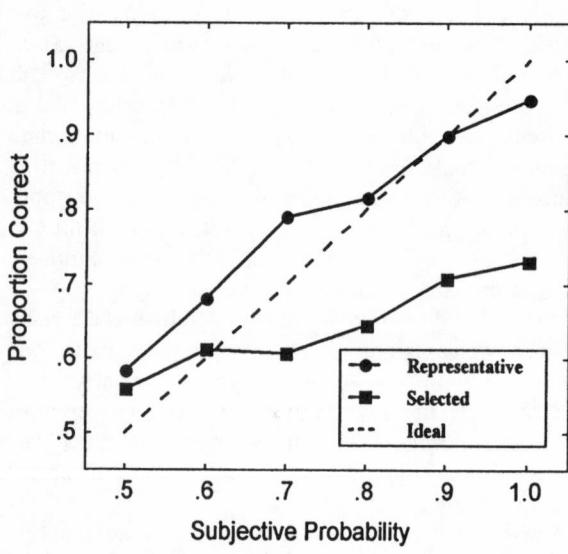

FIGURE 36.1 Panel A illustrates the argument presented by the ecological models, where S denotes applications (items) of the cue that are successful and pick the correct answer, and E denotes cue applications (items) that pick the erroneous answer. Panel B provides one empirical example of the calibration for a representative and a selected sample of general-knowledge items. Panel B is adapted from "The Overconfidence Phenomenon as a Consequence of Informal Experimenter-Guided Selection of Almanac Items" by P. Juslin, 1994, *Organizational Behavior and Human Decision Processes*, **57**, 226–246. Copyright by Academic Press. Adapted with permission.

of a confounding with a well-known empirical regularity, the *hard-easy effect*. According to the hard-easy effect, we should expect more overconfidence for a sample with a lower proportion correct (Lichtenstein & Fischhoff, 1977; but see Juslin, Winman & Olsson, 2000, for a critical discussion of the hard-easy effect). It is obvious from Figure 36.1A that the selected item sample will have a lower proportion correct than the representative item sample. This result, however, is actually a *prediction* by the ecological models.

To evaluate the predictions by the ecological models, we performed a meta-analysis of the data available to us in June 1998 (Juslin et al., 2000). The analysis comprised ninety-five studies with selected item samples (e.g., Lichtenstein & Fischhoff, 1977; Ronis & Yates, 1987) and thirty-five studies with representative item samples (e.g., Brake, Doherty & Kleiter, 1998; Gigerenzer et al., 1991; Griffin & Tversky, 1992), and it included all of the published data on the topic.

In Table 36.1 we see that — as predicted by the ecological models — the mean confidence for selected and representative item samples coincide, indeed with high precision (.73; 95 percent confidence intervals, or CIs, of .01 and .02, respectively). The proportion correct for representative item samples, .72, further agrees with the mean confidence, thus resulting in a close-to-zero over/underconfidence score (.01; 95 percent CI, ± .02). In contrast, there is substantial overconfidence for the selected item samples, (.09; 95 percent CI, ± .02). The last row of Table 36.1 shows that the close-to-zero over/underconfi-

dence score for representative item samples is not a mere consequence of averaging. For the *selected* item samples, the mean absolute bias is .10 (95 percent CI, ± .01); for the *representative* samples, the mean absolute bias is .03 (95 percent CI, ± .01).

A problem with evaluating the argument that the predictions by the ecological models coincide with the hard-easy effect is that, with representative item samples, we seldom expect low proportions correct, while a low proportion correct is a characteristic attribute of selected samples. However, we controlled for difficulty by means of a simple matching procedure for item samples with proportion correct below .7 (hard samples). For each representative item sample with a proportion correct below .7, we entered all selected item samples with the same proportion correct (i.e., as judged by two decimals). The mean over/underconfidence score with *selected hard items* was .10 (95 percent CI, ± .02; proportion correct .65; $N = 29$), and the mean over/underconfidence for *representative hard items* was .05 (95 percent CI, ± .02; proportion correct .65; $N = 12$). There is a difference between selected and representative samples, even if we control for proportion correct (as detailed in Juslin et al., 2000, the "hard-easy effect" that remains with representative samples is mainly explained by statistical artifacts).

Thus, we see that results that originally seemed to demand an explanation in terms of cognitive structure — the confirmatory search of memory, or some unspecified motivational bias — proved to be largely accountable in terms of a more

TABLE 36.1 Means with 95 Percent Confidence Intervals and Standard Deviations for Selected and Representative Item Samples Collected in the Meta-Analysis

	Method for Item Selection	
Dependent Measure	*Selected Item Samples*	*Representative Item Samples*
N (Independent)	95	35
Mean confidence	.73 ± .01 (*sd* = .04)	.73 ± .02 (*sd* = .04)
Proportion correct	.64 ± .02 (*sd* = .08)	.72 ± .02 (*sd* = .07)
Over/underconfidence[a]	.09 ± .02 (*sd* = .08)	.01 ± .02 (*sd* = .05)
Absolute bias[b]	.10 ± .01 (*sd* = .05)	.03 ± .01 (*sd* = .03)

Source: Adapted from P. Juslin, A. Winman, & H. Olsson (2000), 107, 384–396.
[a]The over/underconfidence score is defined as mean confidence minus proportion correct.
[b]Absolute bias is the over/underconfidence score with sign ignored.

careful understanding of the organism-environment relations. The data summarized in Table 36.1 suggest little need to postulate the existence of a processing bias. Moreover, we have experimental control over the "over- or underconfidence" observed for an item sample by item selection procedures that systematically violate representative design (Juslin, 1993).

AUTHOR NOTE

The author is indebted to Patrik N. Juslin, Henrik Olsson, and Anders Winman for discussions of a previous draft of this comment. The research by the author, reviewed in this chapter, was supported by the Swedish Council for Research in the Humanities and Social Sciences.

C.

Examples of Current Brunswikian
Research and Application

37

Assessing the Reliability of Judgments

James H. Hogge and Stephen G. Schilling

Although the technology of judgment analysis within the social judgment theory (SJT) framework (Hammond, Stewart, Brehmer, & Steinmann, 1975) provides a set of statistical parameters corresponding to the elements of Brunswik's lens model (see, for example, Cooksey, 1996b, pp. 205–206), the reliability of judgments, if considered at all, is typically defined as the consistency of repeated ratings of the same cases by the same judges (e.g., Hammond et al., 1975; Stewart, 1988). This approach yields a separate test-retest correlation for each judge and is mainly sensitive to temporal variation.

Reliability could also be assessed in terms of agreement among the judges (interrater reliability), but the decomposition of interjudge agreement by means of the lens model equation (see Cooksey, 1996b, p. 216) is often the focus of such a study. If correlations among judges were treated as reliability estimates, there would be as many sets of interrater reliabilities as occasions. Averaging across occasions is possible, but the resulting judges-by-judges matrix of reliabilities would ignore variance due to occasions.

These alternate and unlinked reliability estimates point to the need for an analytic framework that can simultaneously deal with multiple sources of potential unreliability so that the relative impact of these sources can be assessed and future studies can be designed to minimize error and maximize reliability. Generalizability theory (Cronbach, Gleser, Nanda, & Rajaratnam, 1972; Shavelson & Webb, 1991) offers such a model, which can, for example, help the investigator understand the trade-off between multiple judgment occasions and multiple judges. This chapter contains an example of data from a study conducted within the SJT paradigm, a brief overview of generalizability theory with particular reference to the example data, a demonstration of the application of generalizability theory to the example data, consideration of generalizability theory and representative design, and a discussion of how such an assessment of reliability relates to nomothetic and ideographic levels of analysis.

Example Data: Hail Forecasting

Stewart, Moninger, Grassia, Brady, and Merrem (1989) studied the performance of meteorologists in a limited-information hail-forecasting experiment. Six cues (reflectivity of the storm's core at low level, reflectivity of the storm's core at middle level, presence or absence of a strong echo gradient, presence or absence of tilt, magnitude of rotation, and presence or absence of a favorable differential reflectivity signature), derived from Doppler radar volume scans of 75 storms, were presented to seven meteorologists, who were asked to estimate, for each storm, the probability of any hail and of severe hail. The storms were presented in random order. The meteorologists judged the first 50 storms, took a brief break, and then judged the remaining 25 storms plus an additional 25 storms, consisting of the even-numbered storms from the first 50. Each of the seven meteorologists thus made hail probability estimates for each of the same 25 storms on two occasions.

Generalizability Theory

In contrast to classical test theory, which is based on the notion that each observation (X) is a fallible estimate of a true score (T), generalizability theory is based on the assumption that the investigator wishes to generalize from a single observation to some class of observations. For example, an investigator's interest in test-retest reliabilities (termed *consistency* by SJT researchers, as noted above) may reflect a desire to generalize from a single judgment occasion to all occasions. From a nomothetic perspective, an interest in interjudge agreement may stem from concern about how well one can generalize from an individual judge or a small number of judges to the corresponding population of judges. Because generalization from a particular observation to many different *universes* is possible, an investigator must specify the universe to which generalization is desired before reliability can be studied.

Persons, Conditions, and Facets

Cronbach et al. (1972) used the term *persons* to refer to the entities on which observations are based. In SJT studies, persons correspond to the objects (cases) rated by the judges; in the Stewart et al. hail-forecasting study, the storms correspond to persons. Persons (cases) are assumed to have been randomly sampled from a population to which the investigator wishes to generalize.

As used in generalizability theory, *conditions* is a very general term that can refer to judges, occasions, or situations of observations. Observations (e.g., judgments) are obtained for a particular set of conditions. In the hail-forecasting example, the conditions consist of forecasters (judges) and occasions.

In the terminology of generalizability theory, the persons and conditions are referred to as *facets*; thus, each observation is considered to have been sampled from a multifacet universe. Each probability estimate in the hail-forecasting study was sampled from a three-facet universe: storms (25) by meteorologists (7) by occasions (2).

The Universe Score

If X_{pi} denotes an observation for Person p (in our example, storms correspond to persons) in Condition i, then a *universe score*, M_p, can be defined as the mean of X_{pi} over all the conditions to which the investigator wishes to generalize. For example, from a single meteorologist's estimate of the probability of severe hail in a particular storm observed one time, one might wish to generalize to the probability estimates of all meteorologists observing the storm data an unlimited number of times. The definition of a universe score in generalizability theory is based on the assumptions that (1) the description of the universe makes clear what conditions are included within it, (2) the conditions are experimentally indepen-

dent, (3) the observations (in an SJT study, judgments) are numbers on an interval scale, and (4) both the cases and the conditions are randomly sampled (if one or more facets are fixed, then only the conditions in the other facets are assumed to be randomly sampled).

Generalizability and Decision Studies

An application of generalizability theory begins with a generalizability study (G study), which provides information about the sources of variation in each observation. Ideally, the G study should incorporate as many sources of variation (i.e., conditions) as possible so that the relationship between observed scores and potential universe scores can be explored. In accordance with Stewart's (1988) recommendations, a G study within the SJT framework should thus include, at a minimum, multiple judges and at least two occasions.

Using information from the G study, the investigator plans a decision study (D study) that will apply the measurement procedure (in the SJT case, judgments) to a particular situation. The investigator planning the D study (1) defines the universe of generalization (i.e., all conditions that the investigator would be equally willing to accept), (2) specifies whether the interpretation of the observations is to be relative (based on relative standings or rankings of cases, e.g., identification of the top 10 percent of the cases) or absolute (based on absolute levels of scores, e.g., a pass-fail decision), and (3) uses G study information about the relative magnitudes of various sources of measurement error to assess how well alternative designs would minimize error and thus maximize reliability. The next section illustrates a G study and the planning of a D study for the hail-forecasting data.

Application of Generalizability Theory to Hail Forecasting

Although, as explained above, Stewart et al. (1989) asked the meteorologists in their study to estimate, for each storm, both the probability of any hail and the probability of severe hail, only the latter estimates are considered in this illustration.

The G Study: Interpretation of Estimated Variance Components

The fruit of a G study is a set of estimated variance components corresponding to the facets in the design and the interactions among those facets (see Table 37.1). Because variance components are not measured on a universal metric like correlations, their interpretation is based primarily on their relative sizes. Expression of the variance components as percentages of the total variance facilitates comparisons among them. Also, although not shown here, tests of the statistical significance of individual variance components are possible. Any standard statistics text that deals with random-factor ANOVA (e.g., Neter, Wasserman, & Kutner, 1990) can provide the details.

The largest variance component (368.64; 76.29 percent of the total) in Table 37.1 is associated with storms and indicates that the 25 storms systematically differed with respect to the estimated likelihood of severe hail. The variance component for forecasters (25.76; 5.33 percent) shows the extent to which some forecasters tended to assign higher probabilities than other forecasters. Using the square root of 25.76 (5.08, the standard deviation) as a yardstick, ±3 standard deviations would yield a range of about 30.5 on a 0–100 scale. It would be very unlikely that the probability estimates of any two meteorologists would differ by more than this amount.

The variance component for occasions (0.03; 0.01 percent) was essentially zero. This means that the average estimated likelihood of severe hail was very nearly the same on both occasions. The variance component for the interaction be-tween storms and occasions was also very close to zero and indicates that the relative standings (with respect to the estimated likelihood of severe hail) of the storms were essentially the same on both occasions. The third very small variance component was for the meteorologist-by-occasions interaction (0.79; 0.17 percent). The meteorologists tended to use the same portion of the 0–100 likelihood scale and did so consistently on each occasion.

The variance component for the interaction between storms and meteorologists was comparatively large (53.10; 10.99 percent). Even though the meteorologists used the same standards overall, they disagreed somewhat in regard to the relative standing of the storms with respect to the likelihood of severe hail. The variance component for the residual (34.91; 7.22 percent) is the portion of the variance that is due to the three-way interaction among storms, meteorologists, and occasions and/or unsystematic or unmeasured systematic sources of variation.

The D Study: Estimating the Reliabilities of Alternative Designs

Generalizability theory's distinction between relative and absolute decisions is paralleled by two corresponding reliability-like coefficients that may be computed for a particular number of meteorologists and number of occasions. For relative decisions (e.g., using the forecasts of the likelihood of severe hail to rank-order the storms), the coefficient is referred to as a *generalizability coefficient* (Cronbach et al., 1972); for absolute

TABLE 37.1 Variance Components for Storms × Meteorologists × Occasions G Study

Source of Variation	df	Mean Square	Estimated Variance Component	% of Total
Storms (s)	24	5302.07	368.64	76.29
Meteorologists (m)	6	1449.19	25.76	5.33
Occasions (o)	1	60.07	0.03	0.01
s × m	144	141.10	53.10	10.99
s × o	24	29.77	0.00	0.00
m × o	6	54.87	0.79	0.17
Residual	144	34.91	34.91	7.22
Total variance			483.23	

TABLE 37.2 Generalizability Coefficients for Relative Decisions

Number of Meteorologists	Number of Occasions				
	1	2	3	4	5
1	0.8074	0.8395	0.8508	0.8565	0.8600
2	0.8935	0.9127	0.9194	0.9227	0.9247
3	0.9264	0.9401	0.9448	0.9471	0.9485
4	0.9437	0.9544	0.9580	0.9598	0.9609
5	0.9545	0.9632	0.9661	0.9676	0.9685
6	0.9618	0.9691	0.9716	0.9728	0.9736
7	0.9671	0.9734	0.9756	0.9766	0.9773
8	0.9711	0.9767	0.9785	0.9795	0.9801
9	0.9742	0.9792	0.9809	0.9817	0.9822
10	0.9767	0.9812	0.9828	0.9835	0.9840
20	0.9882	0.9905	0.9913	0.9917	0.9919

decisions (e.g., using the forecasts to characterize a particular storm without regard to the likelihood of severe hail in other storms), as an *index of dependability* (Brennan & Kane, 1977). In each case, however, the coefficient may be interpreted as the universe score variance divided by the sum of universe score variance and error variance and as an approximation of the expected value of the squared correlation between the observed score and the universe score (Cronbach et al., 1972).

Tables 37.2 and 37.3 contain—for relative and absolute decisions, respectively—values of these coefficients for varying numbers of meteorologists combined with varying numbers of occasions. For both tables, a storm's universe score would be based on an unlimited number of meteorolo-gists and an unlimited number of occasions; only the type of decision (relative or absolute) differs. A general comparison of the two tables reveals that, for a given number of meteorologists and number of occasions, forecasts of severe hail are more dependable for relative decisions than for absolute decisions. Also, as would be expected from inspection of the variance components, increasing the number of meteorologists improves dependability more than increasing the number of occasions.

Information from the G study can be used to assess the effectiveness of particular designs. For example, if estimates of the likelihood of severe hail in individual storms without reference to other storms (absolute decisions) are desired, a

TABLE 37.3 Indexes of Dependability for Absolute Decisions

Number of Meteorologists	Number of Occasions				
	1	2	3	4	5
1	0.7630	0.7923	0.8026	0.8078	0.8110
2	0.8655	0.8841	0.8904	0.8937	0.8956
3	0.9061	0.9196	0.9242	0.9265	0.9279
4	0.9278	0.9384	0.9420	0.9438	0.9449
5	0.9414	0.9501	0.9531	0.9545	0.9554
6	0.9507	0.9581	0.9606	0.9618	0.9626
7	0.9574	0.9638	0.9660	0.9671	0.9677
8	0.9625	0.9682	0.9701	0.9711	0.9717
9	0.9665	0.9716	0.9733	0.9742	0.9747
10	0.9697	0.9744	0.9759	0.9767	0.9772
20	0.9846	0.9870	0.9878	0.9882	0.9885

single meteorologist examining the data once would be expected to produce probability estimates that would correlate 0.87 (the square root of 0.7630, from Table 37.3) with the probability estimates of an unlimited number of forecasters examining the data an unlimited number of times. Averaging the probability estimates of two meteorologists on a single occasion would increase the expected correlation to 0.93. Of course, the generalizability coefficients (Table 37.2) and estimated correlations for relative decisions are still higher, but such decisions are not the primary purpose of weather forecasting.

The estimated correlations between observed scores and universe scores reported in the previous paragraph are relatively high. For example, comparable values for nurses' ratings of the professional competence of hypothetical nursing students (Hogge & Schilling, 1995) were 0.71 for a single nurse-rater on a single occasion and 0.77 for two nurse-raters on a single occasion.

Generalizability Theory and Representative Design

Brunswik (1943) was concerned about "the limitation of stimulus-response psychology to narrow-spanning problems of artificially isolated proximal or peripheral technicalities of mediation which are not representative of the larger patterns of life" (p. 262). This approach was operationalized in the fixed-effects factorial designs popularized by Fisher (1925). Instead of relying on such systematic designs, Brunswik argued that it is essential "to insist on representative sampling of situations or tests, just as in the field of individual differences one has to insist on the representative sampling of individuals from a population to ascertain at least some kind of generality for the result"(p. 263).

Generalizability theory's emphasis on random sampling of both cases and conditions yields random-effects designs that, while still factorial designs, address Brunswik's fundamental objection to fixed-effects factorial designs. Because they are factorial designs, however, Brunswik (1955c, p. 203) might have included them among "systematic experiments with representative features" that he suggested "may be considered transitory between systematic and representative design."

Idiographic and Nomothetic Levels of Analysis within Generalizability Theory

Because the application of generalizability theory described in this chapter addresses the question of how well probability estimates obtained from a limited number of meteorologists (e.g., one or two) would approximate the average of the probability estimates of an unlimited number of meteorologists, the level of analysis is nomothetic. As emphasized by numerous Brunswikians (e.g., Brunswik, 1955c; Cooksey, 1996b; Hammond, 1980; Stewart, 1988), such an analysis should be preceded by analyses of data for individual judges (in the example, meteorologists), including significance tests.

Although not originally designed for within-judges analyses, generalizability theory could also be applied in an idiographic fashion. The corresponding G studies would involve separate analyses of each level of the meteorologist facet (i.e., a separate analysis for each judge) and would, of course, require a greater number of levels in the other facets of the design. In fact, it should be noted that although the example in this chapter involves a relatively simple G study with crossed facets, G studies may include nested facets (e.g., a different set of judges making ratings on each of several occasions) and fixed facets (e.g., judges representing several professional specialties). For a detailed discussion of these types of designs, see Cronbach et al. (1972) or Shavelson and Webb (1991).

Conclusion

In this chapter we have demonstrated how generalizability theory provides a comprehensive analytic framework that can be used to estimate the magnitude of multiple sources of error to permit the design of a subsequent study that will yield the required reliability of judgments. The structure of the analytic framework of generalizability is consistent with representative design, and the method can be used at both the idiographic and nomothetic levels.

AUTHOR NOTE

The authors wish to thank Thomas R. Stewart for permission to use his data as the example in this chapter.

38

Vicarious Functioning in Teams

Leonard Adelman, DeVere Henderson, and Sheryl Miller

A number of recent studies (e.g., Hollenbeck et al., 1997; Volpe et al., 1996) have found that, although time pressure has significantly affected team processes, it has had no effect on team performance. Such findings have been surprising, for we are all familiar with cases where time pressure has significantly affected both team processes and team performance. Maule (1997) tried to explain these findings by citing the apparent arbitrariness of the time pressure (or workload) manipulations, for these studies have failed to provide an empirical rationale for why one manipulation is deemed normal and another stressful. More generally, Maule argued that these studies provide no theoretical insights into how teams adapt their processes to increased time pressure, or how process is related to performance. In this brief chapter, we will try to show (1) how Brunswikian theory and methods can be used to understand better how teams adapt their processes to increasing time pressure and (2) why one should not necessarily expect to find a direct relationship between team processes and performance under increasing levels of time pressure.

Relevant Concepts

Three Brunswikian concepts are relevant to our research studying how teams adapt to increasing team pressure: vicarious mediation, vicarious functioning, and constancy. We first describe our task and then show how we incorporated each concept into our research.

Task

Our task was a dynamic aircraft-identification task. A team leader and two subordinate staff members had to track multiple aircraft on their radar screens, pass information about the aircraft to each other, and make recommendations about each aircraft's level of hostility. All three team members initially received five cues about the aircraft when they selected it for examination. Four cues were common to all team members. The three team members had to send the other cues to each other to ensure that (1) both subordinates had all seven cues prior to sending their recommendations to the leader, and (2) the leader had all seven cues and the subordinates' recommendations prior to making a judgment about the aircraft's hostility.[1]

Because aircraft were moving on the participants' radar screens, it became increasingly difficult for the team to make judgments for all aircraft in the allotted time, with increasing time pressure. Consequently, a team's overall performance was a function of both the accuracy of the leader's judgments (called *team accuracy* and defined operationally as r_a), and the percentage of possible identifications made by the leader (called *proportion of judgments made*), that is, both the quality and quantity of its judgments. Performance for a trial was calculated as follows:

Performance $= (7 - |\ \text{Truth} - \text{Judgment}\ |)/7$, averaged over all judgment opportunities for the trial. The number 7 was used because we used a 7-point judgment scale. Higher performance scores represent cases where the judgments were closer to the true outcome for a higher proportion of the aircraft. The team received a 0 score for each case in which they failed to make a judgment in time.

Vicarious Mediation

Brunswik (1952) pointed out that our knowledge of a distal "initial focal variable" (e.g., the cause of an illness) is mediated by the more proximal "cues" (or information) that we have about it (e.g., the patient's symptoms). These cues are often related, having significant correlations among themselves (called *intraecological correlations*) as well as significant correlations with the initial focal (or distal) variable (called *ecological validities*). To take an extreme case, if two cues are perfectly correlated, then they will have the same ecological validity and will therefore be totally redundant in predicting the initial focal variable. Consequently, a person need use only one of these two perfectly substitutable cues.

Brunswik coined the term "vicarious mediation" to reflect the intersubstitutability of cues in the environment. The higher the intraecological correlation between two cues, the more redundant and intersubstitutable the cues. Cue intersubstitutability is critically important because all the cues mediating our knowledge of the distal variable may not be present at the same time. Moreover, individual cues are seldom perfect predictors of the distal variable. Consequently, one's knowledge of the distal, focal variable depends on utilizing multiple, intersubstitutable cues.

We constructed our task to ensure vicarious mediation. Knowledge of the true hostility of each aircraft (i.e., the distal focal variable) was mediated by seven cues: the aircraft's Identification Friend or Foe (IFF) response, speed, course, bearing, range, altitude, and radar type. For consistency with previous team research, we used the following organizing principle, used by Hollenbeck et al. (1997), to relate cue information to the true outcome:

$$\text{Hostility} = 2 \text{ (IFF)} + \text{(Speed} \times \text{Course)} + \text{(Bearing} \times \text{Range)} + \text{(Altitude} \times \text{Radar Type)}$$

Although IFF had the highest validity in predicting the distal variable (i.e., the actual hostility of the aircraft), the other six cues also had significant ecological validities. Task predictability, in terms of R_e in the lens model equation, ranged from 0.95 to 0.98 depending on the trial.

There also were significant intraecological correlations between some of the cues, representative of an actual aircraft identification task outside the laboratory. The size of the intraecological correlations varied somewhat between test trials depending on the set of aircraft comprising a trial, again representing actual identification environments. For example, the intraecological correlations between bearing and course were 0.78 and

0.97 for tempo levels 0.50 and 2.4, which represented the lowest and highest time pressure conditions, respectively. In general, bearing was highly correlated with course and, to a lesser extent, radar and altitude. Since course was very highly correlated with bearing, it was also correlated with radar and altitude. Lastly, IFF was correlated highly with radar and, to a lesser extent, with bearing, course, and altitude. In short, we constructed our task to ensure vicarious mediation, the intersubstitutability of multiple cues.

Vicarious mediation operated in many other ways in our task, one of which is considered here. Specifically, vicarious mediation also operated through the relationship between the outcome and the subordinates' recommendations. Since all three team members were trained to use all seven cues, the task was structured in a way that permitted the leader to make judgments simply by using the subordinates' recommendations (i.e., their judgments of aircraft hostility), not the cues. Said differently, the subordinates' recommendations and the cue values were highly intersubstitutable or redundant. For if the subordinates made accurate recommendations on most aircraft, then knowledge of the true outcome could be mediated by the subordinates' recommendations. Leaders would not have to examine the cues because the subordinates' recommendations would be substitutable for them. It is important to note that the level of intersubstitutability between the subordinates' recommendations and an aircraft's cue values was higher in our study than in others (e.g., Hollenbeck et al., 1997) because all team members in our study knew how to use all the cues and had access to them. Consequently, our task had a higher level of vicarious mediation than many others and, as a result, permitted us to examine a wide range of vicarious functioning in our teams.

Vicarious Functioning

As Brunswik (1952, 1955c) pointed out, the use of multiple intersubstitutable cues when making a judgment or the use of multiple intersubstitutable means (i.e., actions) to accomplish some goal represents vicarious functioning. This does not mean that certain cues are not better predictors than others, or that certain actions are not more appropriate to take in certain situations, for there may be a hierarchy of cues and actions that results in the best possible performance overall. It simply means that the organism can use (or must use) multiple cues and actions to maintain high levels of performance, and that these cues and actions are to some extent redundant or inter-substitutable. To quote Hammond (1966a), "the organism meets the vicarious mediation of the environment with vicarious functioning on its own part" (p. 41).

Vicarious functioning operated in our study in numerous ways. The first two ways parallel those discussed above for vicarious mediation, that is, through the use of intersubstitutable cues and subordinates. In addition, the mediational nature of our task gave team members a range of cognitive and organizational processes that they could adopt to maintain stable performance levels (or "constancy") in the face of increasing time pressure. Consistent with the categorizations found in Payne, Bettman, and Johnson (1993) and in Edland and Svenson (1993), team members could, for example, accelerate their process-ing, that is, try to gather and pass information faster and/or make judgments faster. Alterna-tively, they could decide to omit certain pro-cesses. For example, they might choose to stop sending and/or using certain types of cue informa-tion or stop trying to make judgments for all the aircraft. Third, team members could shift their judgment-processing strategies. For example, team members could make trade-offs between judgment accuracy and the number of judgments they made under increasing levels of time pres-sure. And fourth, from an organizational perspec-tive, teams could modify the way that they did the task. For example, they could divide up the task so that each of the two subordinates made recommendations for only half the aircraft. Or they could redefine the task so that the subordi-nates sent only the cues for the aircraft, but not the recommendations. In short, numerous substi-tutable options were available for adapting to in-creasing levels of time pressure.

Vicarious functioning was possible because the task had a high level of vicarious mediation. The task allowed performance to be mediated (or brought about) by different cognitive and organi-zational approaches (or "means"). Many of the approaches were mutually intersubstitutable and redundant, as in the case where the task permitted the leaders to make their judgments by relying on their subordinates' recommendations, examining the cues themselves, or trying to do both. More-over, these approaches could be more or less successful, depending on the context in which they were used. To quote Brunswik (1952), "They form 'hierarchies' either in the sense that some of the alternatives may be more useful than others (e.g., possessing a greater probability of resulting in the characteristic end state) and/or in the sense that some alternatives are better established in the organism than others (e.g., by more effective learning)" (p. 18). Since many of the approaches were, potentially, equally useful in our task, we focus on "means utilization" in an effort to under-stand how vicarious functioning helps explain the constancy in the time pressure and performance relationship.

Constancy

For Brunswik (e.g., 1952, 1955c), studying how people maintain constancy (i.e., "stabilization" of achievement or performance) in various envi-ronmental contexts was one of the principal goals of a functional psychology. Recently, Hammond (2000) predicted that teams attempt to maintain "correspondence constancy" (i.e., empirical per-formance stabilization) in the face of increasing time pressure by changing their cognitive ap-proach to the task. Moreover, he predicted that different teams adapt in different ways, consistent with Brunswik's concepts of vicarious mediation and functioning. If these different and intersubsti-tutable adaptations were successful—that is, if they maintained correspondence constancy—then one would find significant process differ-ences, but no performance differences, under in-creasing time pressure. Thus, the Brunswikian concepts of vicarious mediation, vicarious func-tioning, and constancy would help explain the findings cited in the introduction to this chapter and, more generally, why one should not neces-sarily expect to find a direct relationship between team processes and team performance under in-creasing time pressure. Processes may change, consistent with the concepts of vicarious media-tion and functioning, but performance stays con-stant.

There is, of course, some point at which the time pressure is so extreme that correspondence constancy can no longer be maintained regardless of teams' process adaptations, and consequently, mean performance deteriorates significantly. Although we had predicted that this mean deterioration would occur at a particular level of time pressure, we realized that this prediction was purely judgmental (or arbitrary, according to Maule, 1997), for we had never run this task and had no empirical data on which to base our prediction. Consequently, we adopted an exploratory design to examine when this point was reached with our task and teams. We had our teams participate over seven consecutive weeks; we consistently increased the time pressure on the teams during that period, so that we could determine the level of time pressure that resulted in a significant decrement in mean performance. We predicted that a second constancy level would be reached, that is, that performance would stabilize again instead of continue to deteriorate.

Method

There were seven three-person teams in the study. Each team was composed of ROTC cadets, who participated for two hours per week for seven weeks. Each team was trained to perform the task in the same way and then required to perform it under increasing levels of time pressure. Time pressure was defined by the number of targets that appeared on the participants' radar scopes per minute for a fifteen-minute time period. Teams trained for the first two weeks of the study at the 0.40 tempo level (six targets for the fifteen-minute scenario). On average, participants had to make two judgments per target, depending on where the targets first appeared on the scopes. Twelve judgments were required for the 0.40 tempo. Teams were considered "trained" when they reached a minimum performance score of 80 percent on scenarios at the 0.40 tempo level.

We began the time pressure manipulation with a 0.50 tempo (i.e., eight targets and fifteen judgments over fifteen minutes) and a performance criterion of 80 percent. Teams failing to obtain a score of 80 percent did the task a second time at the 0.50 tempo level using a second scenario to ensure that they could perform the task before increasing the tempo. Then, we increased the amount of time pressure by increasing the tempo level to 0.60, 0.80, 1.0, 1.2, 1.4, 1.6, 2.0, and, finally, 2.4, over the course of the remaining five weeks. At the highest level of time pressure

(i.e., the 2.4 tempo level), thirty-six targets appeared on the radar scope during the fifteen-minute time period. Although teams had had considerable practice over the five-week period, as they would outside the laboratory, the highest time pressure level was still 4.5 times the initial (low) time pressure level. Although we let team members discuss issues with each other, we set up a competition between the teams to limit the amount of communication between the teams. We thought such an arrangement would foster different team adaptation strategies, if they were going to occur, since the mediational nature of the task permitted substantial vicarious functioning, as we discussed previously.

We lowered the performance criterion to 70 percent at the 0.80 tempo level to ensure that all teams would have enough time to perform all tempos given scheduling problems. In addition, we wanted the teams to have two opportunities to perform the task at higher tempo levels to understand better how they were adapting to increasing levels of time pressure. Before we started the experiment, we thought that all teams would be unable to recover at the 1.0 or 1.2 tempo level. We stopped after one session at the 2.4 tempo level because one of the teams was beginning to exhibit severe interpersonal problems.

Results

A repeated-measures analysis of variance (ANOVA) using the teams' performance score for the first try at each tempo level found that the time pressure manipulation did significantly affect the mean performance of the seven teams. The teams, as a group, could not maintain a constant level of performance over the entire range of the time pressure manipulation. Although important, this finding was not particularly surprising, since we consistently increased the time pressure to see at what tempo level(s) mean performance deteriorated statistically.

Post hoc analyses using the Tukey HSD test found that tempos of 1.6 and higher had statistically lower mean performance scores than tempos of 0.80 and lower. However, the performance differences between tempo levels of 1.6 and higher were not different statistically. The first finding indicates that, on average, the teams were able to maintain constancy beyond the 1.0 or 1.2

tempo levels, which was where we expected mean performance to deteriorate statistically. The second finding indicates that, on average, teams were able to achieve a second constancy level at very high time pressure levels (i.e., between tempo levels of 1.6 and 2.4), as predicted. The observed time pressure effect was mitigated further by practice at a tempo level. Mean performance levels were significantly higher on the second try at tempos 1.6 and 2.0, and over all tempo levels. Conducting the ANOVA again, but this time using a team's best performance at each tempo level, we found that one had to reach a tempo level of 2.0 before one could discriminate between low and high tempo levels statistically. This level was approximately twice as high as we thought would be required for mean performance to deteriorate significantly before the experiment. This finding demonstrates, as Hammond (2000) predicted, that teams could maintain a surprisingly high level of correspondence constancy under increasing levels of time pressure.

We found no difference in the seven teams' mean performance levels over all tempos. However, there were significant team differences on the two subgoals: team accuracy and "proportion of judgments made." In an effort to maintain correspondence constancy, some teams emphasized judgment accuracy (r_a) at the expense of making fewer judgments. In contrast, other teams sacrificed accuracy so that they could make more judgments, and yet other teams tried to balance both under increased time pressure.[2] These process differences illustrate one aspect of vicarious functioning in our task and support Hammond's prediction that teams would adapt in different ways in an effort to maintain correspondence constancy as time pressure increased. The trade-off between "judgment accuracy" and the "proportion of judgments made" is illustrated in Figure 38.1. This figure presents the performance scores, judgment accuracy (r_a), and the proportion of judgments made for all tempo levels run by Teams #3 and #6. These two teams had comparable performance for a number of tempo levels, including the same performance level at tempo 2.0b, that is, the second trial at level 2.0. Yet, the team leaders used very different strategies to accomplish this. Team #3's leader had the highest mean "proportion of judgments made" (0.96) for all seven teams; Team #6's mean was 0.83. In contrast, Team #6's leader had the highest mean judgment accuracy $(r_a = 0.94;\ r_{az} = 1.79)$ for all seven teams; Team #3's mean accuracy (r_a) was 0.66 $(r_{az} = 0.79)$. These mean values were significantly different for both subgoals.

Further examination of Figure 38.1 shows that Team #3's performance was at an almost constant level until the highest time pressure level (i.e., tempo level 2.4). This was a function of the leader's almost constant level of "proportion of judgments made" over increasing levels of time pressure. For example, Team #3's leader made judgments for 95 percent of the cases for tempos 0.6a and 2.0b, which were the second lowest and second highest levels of time pressure, respectively. Team #3's corresponding performance scores were 0.83 and 0.79, respectively.

In contrast, Team #6's performance was constant only until tempo 1.6a, where its performance deteriorated significantly, just as many other teams' performance did according to the post hoc test mentioned earlier. Team #6's performance, however, actually improved under increasingly higher levels of time pressure up to tempo 2.4, where its performance again deteriorated. The increase in performance between tempo 1.6a and 2.0b was caused by an increase in the "proportion of judgments made." For throughout increasing levels of time pressure, Team #6's leader maintained a remarkably high and constant level of judgment accuracy (r_a). For example, his accuracy at the lowest time pressure level (tempo 0.5a) was 0.95; his accuracy at the highest time pressure level (tempo 2.4) was 0.91.

As the above discussion suggests, performance was more dependent on maintaining the "proportion of judgments made" than judgment accuracy. A multiple regression analysis regressing performance on the "proportion of judgments made" and the z transformation of the accuracy scores for all the teams for all the tempos found that the "proportion of judgments made" was three times more important than judgment accuracy in predicting performance. This situation is consistent with Brunswik's position, reflected in our earlier quote, that certain "alternatives" (in our case, subgoals) are more useful than others. Since Team #3's leader maintained constancy in the "proportion of judgments made" instead of judgmental accuracy, he was able to maintain a more constant level of performance than Team #6's

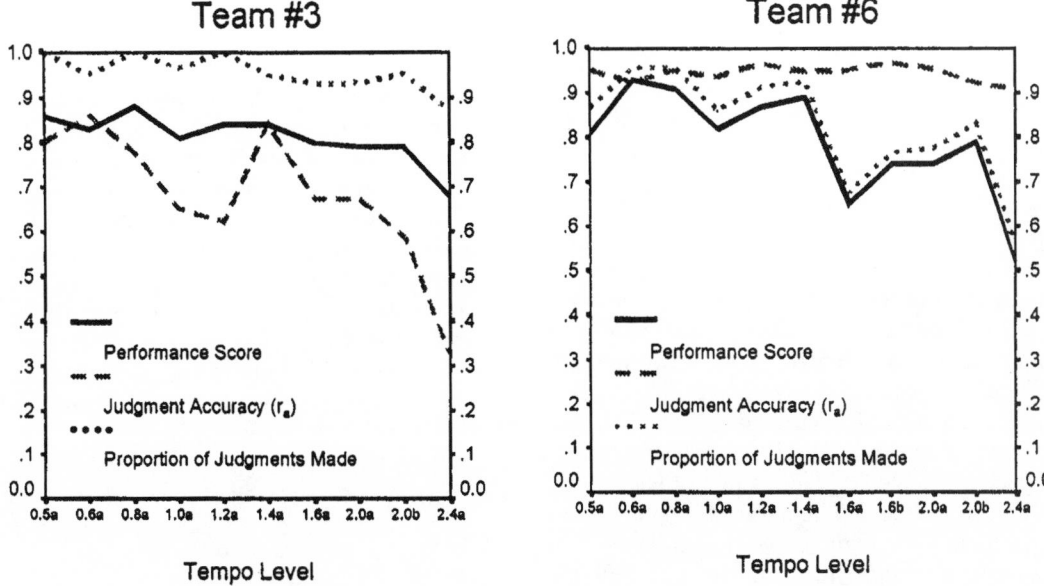

FIGURE 38.1 Team performance, accuracy, and proportion of judgments made for Teams #3 and #6.

leader throughout the range of the time pressure manipulation. However, both teams had the same performance score at tempo 2.0b. At that tempo level, the teams used different, intersubstitutable means (i.e., subgoal trade-offs) to achieve the same end, consistent with Brunswik's concept of vicarious functioning.

Teams #3 and #6 also used different decision-making processes. Team #3's leader relied on the recommendations of his subordinates, as well as his own judgment, just as he had been trained. However, he kept a watchful eye on the radar scope and routinely gave a value of 4, which was the midpoint of the judgment scale, to any aircraft approaching a judgment point for which he did not yet have cue values or recommendations. Thus, his "proportion of judgments made" was always high, but his accuracy (r_a) was some times low. In contrast, Team #6's leader completely dominated his team's process. Because of the poor judgmental accuracy of his subordinates for the first few scenarios, Team #6's leader emphasized having his subordinates send him cue values, not recommendations. Once he had all the cues for an aircraft, he would make his judgment in a relatively slow and deliberate manner; conse-

quently, his accuracy (r_a) was always high, but his "proportion of judgments made" was some times low. Indeed, with this process, one might argue that his team's performance was bound to collapse at some point, as it did at tempo level 2.4.

Three of the other seven teams operated as Team #3 did and tried to perform the task as trained. Two of the teams adapted to the increasing time pressure, however, by having each subordinate make judgments for only half the aircraft. We were particularly interested to see if this strategy would appear because it reduced the workload on the subordinates by half; consequently, we thought it had the potential to maintain the highest levels of performance at the highest levels of time pressure. This did not occur, however, because the subordinates still could not maintain high levels of both judgment accuracy and the proportion of judgments (i.e., recommendations) made. Nevertheless, both teams were able to achieve correspondence constancy at high tempo levels using this strategy. And although lower than expected before the study, these performance levels were comparable to those achieved by other teams using other strategies.

Conclusion

We make seven points in concluding this chapter. First, on average, teams were able to maintain constant levels of performance until high levels of time pressure were reached and then were able to restabilize their performance to achieve correspondence constancy again. Second, although there were no differences in the mean performance of the seven teams, there were significant differences in the teams' mean levels of judgment accuracy, proportion of judgments made, and trade-offs between these two subgoals. Third, there were also significant differences in how the teams decided to do the task as time pressure increased. Fourth, these results support Hammond's (2000) predictions that teams adapt their processes in different ways through vicarious functioning to maintain correspondence constancy (i.e., performance stabilization). Fifth, the mediational characteristics of our task, like many others outside the laboratory, were vicarious and robust enough to permit such vicarious functioning to operate. Sixth, these Brunswikian concepts, when taken together, explain why one should not necessarily expect to find a direct relationship between team processes and performance under increasing time pressure. Teams adapt their processes in different ways to maintain correspondence constancy; consequently, increasing time pressure can significantly affect team processes without necessarily affecting team performance.

Our seventh point is that Brunswik's concepts of vicarious mediation, vicarious functioning, and correspondence constancy naturally lead to future research hypotheses demonstrating the importance of task characteristics to successful functioning. For example, vicarious mediation was high in our current task. There were many intersubstitutable and hence redundant ways to do the task successfully and thereby adjust to increasing levels of time pressure. This permitted vicarious functioning without serious consequences until very high levels of time pressure were reached. However, if the level of vicarious mediation was lowered so that there were only a few ways to perform the task successfully, then vicarious functioning would be constrained, in turn. Consequently, we would hypothesize that the lower the level of vicarious mediation (i.e., intersubstitutability), the tighter the relationship between time pressure, team processes, and team performance.

Moreover, we would hypothesize that tasks with low levels of vicarious mediation would require more training and cognitive support in order to maintain constancy under increasing time pressure. Such hypotheses can be tested in different tasks within and outside the laboratory, for vicarious mediation and vicarious functioning are formal concepts focusing on the importance of task characteristics to successful functioning. They are independent of specific substantive domains or experimental manipulations. Therefore, they and the many other concepts proposed by Brunswik and covered in this volume provide a means of theoretically unifying many disparate studies and thereby developing a cumulative body of scientific research.

NOTES

The authors would like to thank Michael Schoelles, who developed the computer system for conducting this research. They also would like to thank Kenneth R. Hammond for his many helpful comments on earlier drafts of this manuscript. This research was supported under Grant Number F49620-97-1-0353 from the Air Force Office of Scientific Research to George Mason University. The views, opinions, and findings herein are those of the authors and should not be construed as an official Department of the Air Force position.

1. This task can be represented conceptually by the multilevel lens model developed by Brehmer and Hagafors (1986) to represent staff functioning. A static version of the aircraft identification task has been used extensively by Hollenbeck and his associates, for example, Hollenbeck et al. (1995, 1997).

2. The r_a correlations were converted to z scores before we ran the ANOVA. We also ran the ANOVA using the mean square error term (MSE) instead of r_a, consistent with Gigon and Hastie's (1997) argument that MSE is preferred to r_a because the former also accounts for the absolute differences between the judgments and outcomes. We also obtained significant team differences with MSE.

3. Although Teams #3 and #6 showed performance decrements between tempo levels 2.0s and 2.4, mean performance was 0.71 and 0.65, respectively, at these tempos and not different statistically according to the Tukey HSD test. We relied on statistical tests because we were trying to find the level(s) of time pressure where mean performance deteriorated significantly, for at that point, we could argue statistically

that the teams, on average, could no longer maintain correspondence constancy. This maintained the comparability of our research with the studies reported in

the introduction to this chapter. Individual teams could, of course, lose constancy at different levels of time pressure.

39

Probabilistic Functioning and Cognitive Aging

Gérard Chasseigne and Etienne Mullet

Because of its focus on the processing of uncertain information, the Brunswikian probabilistic view of cognition can make a positive and unique contribution to the study of cognitive functioning in the elderly. It is the purpose of this article to demonstrate that contribution.

This is an area heretofore unexplored and apparently unappreciated, despite the obvious relevance of this topic to the performance and well-being of the elderly. Although numerous studies have investigated the ability of the elderly to learn lists of words, prose passages, paired associations of words, paired associations, and symbols, there has been no published work on the learning in the elderly of probability relationships between variables (with the exception of Chasseigne, Mullet & Stewart, 1997; Chasseigne, Grau, Mullet & Cama, 1999). The lens model, however, is superbly qualified to serve as a theoretical point of departure for such studies. Not only does it address the issue directly, but also numerous studies of multiple cue probability learning in normal adults have been carried out for over thirty years and thus provide comparative data (see Cooksey, 1996b, for summaries).

Rather than study the use of differentially weighted cues or the effect of variations in task uncertainty, we centered our investigation on the question of whether the elderly can cope as well as younger people with the problem of making use of cues that have an *inverse* rather than direct positive relation between cue and criterion. On the assumption that inverse relationships demand

greater cognitive control (Hammond & Summers, 1972) and possibly place greater demands on working memory, it seemed reasonable to suppose that such task characteristics would decrease the ability of the elderly to learn them at the same rate as younger adults. In addition, and for much the same reasons, we also investigated the ability of elderly adults to ignore irrelevant cues, a constant problem in everyday life. In this way, we would gain some insight into the question of whether physical aging negatively affects the sort of judgments that require more cognitive effort and control than simple judgments. Finally, we investigated the ability of older people to cope with uncertainty in a learning task. In short, we would gain some insight into the question of cognitive aging.

Detection and Use of Inverse Relations between Cue and Criterion.

The first experiment examined the performance of young people (twenty to thirty years old) and one group of elderly people (sixty-five to seventy-five years old) and a second group (sixty-five to ninety years old), in their ability to detect and use inverse relationships. Participants were presented with three cue values and received outcome feedback (OFB) beginning with the second block of trials. The R^2 value of .93 was maintained in the task throughout blocks of trials. In one condition, the cue-criterion relationships were positive linear for all cues. But in subsequent conditions, the properties of one cue (Cue B) were changed; therefore, we show only the results for performance with regard to Cue B in Figure 39.1.

As shown in the left-hand panel, when Cue B was related to the criterion in a positive linear manner, there was little difference in the utilization of Cue B among the three groups. In a second condition (shown in the center panel), when cue B was related to the criterion in a negative linear manner, the twenty- to thirty-year-old group gradually increased their dependence on Cue B in the appropriate fashion. The sixty-five- to seventy-five-year-old group moved in the correct direction, indicating that they were gaining some information from the OFB, but the seventy-five- to ninety-five-year-old participants failed to do so.

The next step was taken to determine whether the failure of the elderly to use the negative function form of Cue B was due to a failure to *discover* the proper relation of the cue to the criterion as a result of OFB, or whether it was simply due to an inability to *use* the cue in a negative linear manner. This question was investigated by introducing a condition in which the participants were explicitly told—given cognitive feedback—that Cue B was related to the criterion in a negative linear (inverse) manner. As shown in the right-hand panel, as a result of this instruction twenty- to thirty-year-old participants learned to use Cue B appropriately almost immediately, but the elderly participants (sixty-five to seventy-five) were slower to do so, and the very elderly (seventy-five to ninety) never did use it appropriately. Consequently, the difficulties encountered by the elderly in using an inverse relationship—a negative linear function form—can be attributed to their inability to *use* information of this kind, and not merely to their inability to *discover* such information as a result of OFB.

Detection and Nonuse of Inverse Relationships Between Cue and Criterion.

In this study, two cues were valid and two were irrelevant (had zero validity). Participants were given OFB from the second block. As shown in the central part of Figure 39.1, the twenty- to thirty-year-old participants made slightly more use of the irrelevant information in Block 3 than in Block 2 but thereafter learned to progressively

ignore the irrelevant cues. By Block 6, the utilization coefficient was not significantly different from zero. But the elderly participants in both groups were never able to ignore this information.

As in the previous experiment, we then pursued the question of whether the elderly would ignore useless information when directly informed that it was useless. The participants were trained with OFB to use two cues during Blocks 1 and 2. At the beginning of Block 3, half the participants were told that one of the cues had lost its usefulness, but the other half were not so informed. When warned about the loss of the usefulness of the information from one of the cues, all of the older participants immediately ignored the presence of this cue, and their performance did not differ from that of the young adults. Without the warning, however, older adults failed to detect the loss of validity of the irrelevant cue.

Coping with Uncertainty

In this study, participants were presented with three cues and received OFB beginning with block two. Five levels of task predictability were used (0.96, 0.80, 0.64, 0.48, and 0.32). Cues were equally weighted and related to criterion in a positive linear manner. A strong effect of uncertainty on cognitive control was found. Cognitive control decreased at approximately the same rate as did task predictability. This relationship held for all participants, regardless of age.

Summary

The results of these experiments clearly indicate that the elderly have major difficulties in detecting negative linear relationships between cue and criterion from outcome feedback, although young adults do not. In addition, elderly adults have difficulties in applying the knowledge that a negative relationship exists between cue and criterion, even when given the information that such a relationship exists.

Elderly adults were also found to have difficulty in ignoring irrelevant information in an outcome feedback task unless explicitly warned that specific information was indeed irrelevant. Young adults did not have this difficulty. When cue-criterion

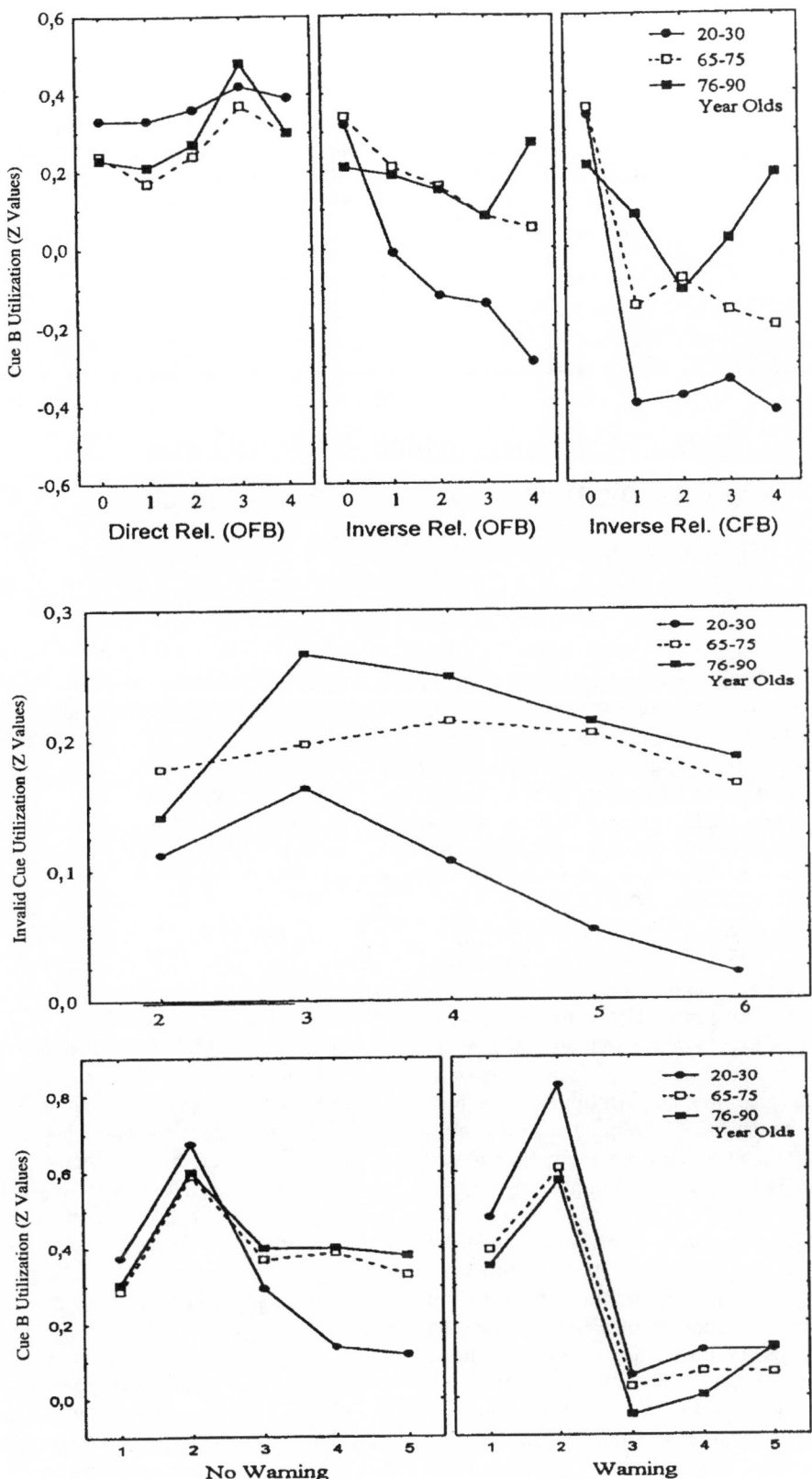

FIGURE 39.1 Summary of results for inverse relation and irrelevant cue.

relations were positive linear, the effect of uncertainty on judgment did not differ across age groups.

These studies illustrate the potential of the Brunswikian approach for increasing our knowledge of cognitive aging, which no other approach ever has. In addition, if confirmed by future studies, the results offer substantive information on the ability of the elderly to cope with properties of probabilistic tasks likely to be encountered in everyday life.

40

A Brunswikian Approach to Emotional Communication in Music Performance

Patrik N. Juslin

Music is probably the most widely practiced and appreciated of all art forms. One possible explanation may be that music offers a powerful means of emotional communication. Yet this is one of the least understood aspects of music, at least as far as scientific explanation goes (Juslin, in press b). As a result, emotional aspects of performance have been sadly neglected in music education (Persson, Pratt, & Robson, 1992; Tait, 1992).

It may be argued that this problem partly stems from the lack of relevant theories about music and emotion. I have recently proposed a theoretical framework—*the functionalist perspective*—that integrates concepts from psychological research on emotions and nonverbal communication with Brunswik's (1956b) theory (Juslin, 1997a, in press a). This framework has generated useful questions, hypotheses, and ways of interpreting results. It represents a Brunswikian point of departure in at least two respects:

First, it focuses on the *functional* relationship between the organism and its environment. It is argued that to understand the nature of emotional communication in music performance, we should consider the functions that emotional communication has served—and continues to serve—in social interaction. The usefulness of such communication is twofold: (1) Emotional expression allows individuals to communicate in-

formation to others, thereby influencing their behaviors, and (2) emotion recognition allows individuals to make inferences about the probable behaviors of others.

Second, the framework aims at decomposing the communicative process in terms of the *probabilistic* relationships among (1) performers, (2) cues in performances, and (3) listeners. It is suggested that we should try to describe and improve the communication in terms of these relationships, and that the relationships should be conceptualized in terms of a Brunswikian *lens model* (Brunswik, 1952; Cooksey, 1996b).

In this chapter, I intend to illustrate how Brunswik's ideas have proved useful in the study of emotional communication in music performance. First, I briefly recapitulate Brunswik's ideas on social perception. Then, I show how these ideas have been applied in studies of music performance. Finally, I consider the implications of this approach for future research.

Brunswik on Social Perception and Communication

Brunswik (1952) clearly recognized the importance of social perception in biological adaptation: "Forced to react quickly or within reasonable limits of time, [the organism] must respond before direct contact with the relevant remote conditions in the environment, such as foodstuffs or traps, friends or enemies, can be established" (p. 22). To come to terms with this social environment, the organism must rely on its ability to make unconscious inferences about the emotional states and personality traits of other individuals.

In a number of experiments initiated in Vienna, Brunswik (1956b) tried to relate physical characteristics of schematized faces to impressions of mood, intelligence, age, and beauty. Interestingly, Brunswik observed that the perception of emotional states seemed to have a higher validity than the perception of personality traits (p. 49). This observation has stood the test of time (e.g., Frick, 1985). Although Brunswik's studies sometimes fell short of his own ideals concerning the "ecological representativeness" of the stimulus (the schematized faces lacked the rich information provided by human faces, e.g., their movements), they at least served to introduce his ideas into the realm of social perception and communication.

Brunswik (1956b) was no stranger to communication theory. As a matter of fact, some authors (e.g., Hake, Rodwan, & Weintraub, 1966) have argued that Shannon and Weaver's (1949) communication theory influenced Brunswik's theoretical views in profound ways. In one sense, his lens model describes a communication system that includes a sender (the distal stimulus), a noisy channel (the proximal cues), and a receiver (the perceiver). Accordingly, veridical perception requires the perceiver to separate the relevant aspects of the input from the irrelevant aspects. Thus, Brunswik (1956b) noted that "the vicariousness of psychological cues . . . may be viewed as a special case of receiving or sending messages through redundant, even though not literally repetitive channels"(p. 142).

Brunswik's ideas may appear genuinely suited to the study of emotional communication. Nevertheless, few researchers in the field seem to know about his work (however; see Scherer, 1986). In the following, I intend to show how Brunswik's ideas have been used in my studies of emotional communication in music performance. The functionalist perspective (e.g., Juslin, 1997a, in press a) is concerned with three aspects of the code used by music performers, namely, its (1) origin, (2) description, and (3) improvement.

What Is the Origin of the Code?

This chapter concerns emotional communication in music performance. How would Brunswik have approached this subject? A Brunswikian approach implies a focus on the *accuracy* of the communication process, as well as on the *strategy* used to attain this accuracy (Brehmer, 1984).

Given the emphasis on communication accuracy, the primary question is whether music performers are able to communicate emotions to listeners at all. The answer to this question, as shown by a number of studies, is a resounding yes (e.g., Gabrielsson & Juslin, 1996; Juslin, 1997a, in press a). In fact, two studies suggest that decoding accuracy for emotional expression in musical performance may be as high as for facial or vocal expression of emotion. The overall accuracy lies at about 75 percent correct, or almost five times the accuracy that would be expected by chance (Juslin, 1997b, 1997c). This actually requires an explanation: What is it that makes this possible? Or more specifically, what is the origin of this communicative code?

It may be hypothesized that music performers communicate emotions to listeners by using the same acoustical code as is used in vocal expression of emotion. This view is supported by similarities in code usage between musical performance and vocal expression, as reported by Juslin (1999). This may, of course, appear to just move the burden of explanation from one modality to another. Luckily, when it comes to vocal expression, the underlying mechanisms are well established: The code is implemented by innate brain programs that function to initiate and organize emotional expressions (e.g., Buck, 1984). The code partly reflects physiological changes in the body associated with specific emotional reactions (Scherer, 1986).

I have recently argued that both expression and recognition of emotions proceed in terms of a limited number of "basic" emotion categories (e.g., Ekman, 1992; Johnson-Laird & Oatley, 1992), which provide the decoder with maximum information and discriminability. To be useful as guides to action, emotional expressions are interpreted in terms of only a few emotion categories related to such fundamental life problems as danger, loss, mating, foraging, and competition (Darwin, 1872; Oatley, 1992; Panksepp, 1989).

The implication is that basic emotions (e.g., fear, sadness, anger, happiness) should be easier to communicate than other emotions—a notion that has received some empirical support (Juslin, 1999).

How May the Code Be Described?

Patrik N. Juslin (1995) has suggested that we should use Brunswik's lens model to illustrate how a music performer *encodes* a certain emotion by means of a number of *probabilistic* but partly *redundant* cues in the performance (e.g., tempo, loudness, timbre, articulation, timing). The emotional expression is *decoded* by the listener, who uses these same cues in order to judge the intended expression. Intercorrelations among the cues reflect both how sounds are produced on musical instruments (e.g., a harder string attack may produce a tone that is both louder and sharper in timbre) and how performers use cues to achieve different emotional expressions.

The redundancy of the cues reduces the uncertainty of the communication process. On the other hand, it also limits the information capacity of the channel. In Brunswik's (1956b) words, the system aims at "smallness of error at the expense of the highest frequency of precision" (p. 146). This leads to "compromise and falling short of precision, but also the relative infrequency of drastic error" (p. 145). It is easy to see how a communication system with this characteristic could have a survival value. It is ultimately more important to avoid making serious mistakes, such as mistaking anger for joy, than to have the ability to make more subtle discriminations among emotional expressions (e.g., detecting many different kinds of anger).

The same characteristic may also explain an apparent paradox found in studies. Performers are rather successful in communicating emotions to listeners despite much inconsistency in cue utilization across performers, musical instruments, pieces of music, and listeners (Juslin, 1997a, 1997c). This (seemingly) contradictory state of affairs is actually predicted by the functionalist perspective: High accuracy in spite of large inconsistency in cue utilization may be explained by reference to the Brunswikian (1957) concept of *vicarious functioning*, that is, the fact that the communication involves many probabi-

listic but partly interchangeable cues that listeners combine in flexible ways to arrive at reliable judgments of the emotional expression.

The beauty of vicarious functioning is that it allows music performers a large amount of artistic freedom, within certain limits. Since there is no pressure toward uniformity in cue utilization (Brehmer, 1989; Dawes & Corrigan, 1974), the performers may communicate successfully without compromising their unique playing styles (Juslin in press a).

Brunswik's lens model provides a new way of seeing an old problem. It has thus been used for descriptive purposes in a series of recent studies. Professional performers have been asked to play short pieces of music so as to communicate specific emotions (e.g., happiness, sadness, anger, fear) to listeners. The resulting performances have been analyzed with regard to acoustical cues. The performances have also been used in experiments in which listeners have judged the expression of each performance. The cue utilization of both performers and listeners has been captured by means of multiple regression analysis. The two systems have then been related to each other by means of the lens model equation (e.g., Stewart, 1988).

These analyses have generated a number of findings: First, linear models provide a good fit to cue utilization, explaining 70–80 percent of the variance in expressions and judgments. Second, the nonlinear component of cue utilization is small, particularly on the listener side. Third, the communication accuracy seems to depend primarily on the extent to which the cue weights of the performer are matched to the cue weights of the listener. Fourth, the cue utilization is more consistent across different pieces of music than across different performers. That is, performers use pretty much the same code regardless of the melody, but there are large inter-individual differences among performers (Gabrielsson & Juslin, in press; Juslin, in press a).

The actual code used by performers and listeners is presented in Table 40.1. To evaluate this code description, I have used *performance synthesis*. The rationale was this: If the performance analysis is an adequate one, it should be possible to recombine the acoustical cues in suitable combinations, and thereby to reconstruct the expressions, as evidenced by listeners' judgments. In a recent study, I showed that synthesized perfor-

TABLE 40.1 A Summary of Cue Utilization for Different Emotional Expressions

Emotion	Cue Utilization
Happiness	Fast tempo, high sound level, bright spectrum, staccato articulation, fast tone onsets, moderate variations in timing, sharp durational contrasts (i.e., between "long" and "short" notes)
Sadness	Legato articulation, low sound level, slow tempo, soft spectrum, slow tone onsets, slow and deep vibrato, soft durational contrasts, relatively large deviations in timing, final ritardando
Anger	High sound level, sharp spectrum, fast tempo, staccato articulation, abrupt tone onsets, mostly sharp durational contrasts, heavy vibrato, spectral noise, no final ritardando
Tenderness	Legato articulation, medium sound level, slow onsets, fairly slow tempo, intense vibrato, fairly large deviations in timing, soft spectrum, mostly soft durational contrasts
Fear	Extremely staccato articulation, very low sound level, low (average) tempo, soft spectrum, large tempo variation, pauses between phrases, much dynamic variation, intense and irregular vibrato.

Note: This is a simplified description of cue utilization. For information about the definition and measurement of each cue, see Juslin (in press a).

mances based on the results from previous investigations yielded predicted judgments of emotional expression from listeners. These performances provide the preliminaries for a computational model of the communication process (Juslin, 1997b).

An interesting combination of analysis and synthesis is afforded by the possibility of resynthesizing human performances by means of computer technology. This method was recently used in a study aimed at exploring the relative importance of timing patterns in communication of emotion through musical performance (Juslin & Madison, 1999). We gradually removed various cues from piano performances with different intended emotional expressions to see how these changes would affect a listener's judgment of the emotional expression. The results indicated that listeners used timing patterns to decode emotional expressions, but that timing patterns were much less effective in communicating emotions to listeners than were tempo and dynamics. Furthermore, a removal of the timing patterns did not necessarily reduce a listener's decoding accuracy due to redundant information provided by other cues.

How Can the Code Be Improved?

Emotional communication—almost by definition—assumes a low level of uncertainty. How-

ever, given that uncertainty is an unavoidable aspect of emotional communication in most real-life situations, one important task could be to minimize this uncertainty as far as possible.

In discussions of the relationship between music psychology and music education, one of the main concerns has been the practical usefulness of research for music teachers. A number of studies (e.g., Persson, Pratt, & Robson, 1992) have suggested that music teachers often fail to consider expressive aspects of performance, instead concentrating their time and effort on technical aspects. One possible explanation is that teachers have difficulties verbalizing their expressive skills. This view is supported by recent research (Tait, 1992). It has been found that, although teachers talk a lot during sessions, the amount of talking is not directly related to the degree of student learning. The problem seems to be that the feedback is not *specific* enough. This problem may be particularly difficult when it comes to the expressive aspects of music performance, because emotions are largely encoded and decoded implicitly.

From a Brunswikian point of view, this problem is best solved by means of *cognitive feedback* (cf. Todd & Hammond, 1965; Balzer, Doherty, & O'Connor, 1989). In other words, we should improve performers' communication by giving them a chance to compare their own cue utilization to an *optimal* model based on listeners' cue utilization. We recently conducted a study to determine whether cognitive feedback could improve the skills of novice performers (Juslin P. N. & Laukka, in press). The feedback was based on the cue weights of the performer and listener models, and we used both behavioral criteria and reaction criteria to measure the efficacy of the feedback (cf. Balzer, Doherty, & O'Connor, 1989).

The main findings were as follows: First, the feedback yielded at least a 50 percent improvement in accuracy after only one feedback session (effect size $d = 1.0$ SD). Second, all of the performers reacted positively to the feedback, believing that it had indeed improved their accuracy. A common "pathology" of the novices was that they concentrated too much on one cue at the expense of all the other cues. We tried to explain to them that the strength of the communication lies in using all cues in combination. Each cue is neither necessary nor sufficient, but the larger the number of cues used, the more reliable the communication (see Doherty, Brake, & Kleiter, this volume).

Implications for Future Research

Viewing emotional communication in music through a Brunswikian lens has a number of important implications. First, previous studies have tended to focus on either performance or perception. However, the Brunswikian paradigm provides the tool for an ultimately more interesting enterprise: how to *relate* performance to perception. Each of these two aspects can be fully understood only in relation to the other. Second, future studies should consider a whole range of cues in order to deal with the complete code used, and thereby to permit performers and listeners to demonstrate their capacity for vicarious functioning. Third, future studies should analyze sufficiently large samples of performers, listeners, and pieces of music to allow for generalizations and the use of such multivariate methods as multiple regression. This recommendation parallels Brunswik's (1952) insistence that we deal with the phenomenon under investigation "on an adequate level of complexity" (p. 1).

Skillful use of lens modeling may provide us with the kind of descriptive high-complexity knowledge that is necessary for more precise models of "micromediation" (Brunswik, 1955c, p. 208). In performance studies, at least, the Brunswikian paradigm has provided us with a far deeper understanding of the process than would have been possible with any other paradigm currently available. Thus, it has provided a fertile ground for more precisely formulated computational models of music performance (e.g., Juslin, Friberg, & Bresin, 2000).

ACKNOWLEDGMENT

Thanks to Pia Wennerholm for useful comments on a previous version of this paper. This research was supported by the Bank of Sweden Tercentenary Foundation through a grant to Alf Gabrielsson.

41

An Application of the Lens Model to Guidance and Counseling of Adolescents

María Teresa Muñoz Sastre and Ludovic Duponchelle

The application of Brunswikian theory is aimed at helping teenagers become aware of (1) the relationships between their job aspirations and expectations, and certain classic determinants of job aspirations and expectations such as prestige, income, and job opportunities; (2) the internal structure of their system of occupational representations; (3) the strong and weak points in their system of information about jobs; and (4) possible conflicts in values or discordance between aspirations and expectations. It can also be used to foster dialogue and greater understanding between parents and students (or classmates) with respect to career guidance.

Theoretical and Methodological Framework

The procedure (known as M-92) draws directly on the lens model (Brunswik, 1952, 1955c). It is an extension of social judgment theory (Brehmer & Joyce, 1988; Hammond Stewart, Brehmer, & Steinmann, 1975; Hammond, 1996c) to the case of paired comparisons.

The principles of the self-knowledge technique depend on Brunswikian methodology in two principal ways: First, they rely on the Brunswikian idiographic-statistical method, and second, they rely on the associated principle of vicarious functioning. A detailed explanation of the idiographic-statistical method and its contrast with the nomothetic method can be found in Hammond, McClelland, and Mumpower (1980). These authors pointed out that "in contrast to the nomothetic assumption that individual judges are replicates of one another . . . the key presumption of the idiographic method is that there exist important and reliable individual differences between judges" (p. 117). And "because of the need

to make separate inferences or model fits for each judge, it is generally advantageous to observe many responses from the same judge" (p. 118). The need for "separate inferences" follows from the principle of vicarious functioning as well because different individuals make use of different items to express their aspirations and expectations. Each individual may express his or her aspirations and expectations over a different set of items, yet the ultimate vocational preferences may be found to be the same. Thus, the procedure draws directly on the lens model (Brunswik 1952, 1955c) and social judgment theory (Cooksey, 1996b; Hammond, 1996c)

More specifically, it also draws on Gottfredson (1981). The Gottfredson framework suggests that determinants of vocational preferences can be grouped under four headings: gender, social status, personal values, and accessibility. Gottfredson also argued that decision making implies a necessary compromise between a person's aspirations and job or training accessibility. This compromise yields more-or-less realistic expectations. Finally, the expert data bank is an application of Batchelder and Romney (1990).

Materials

The material is composed of a general-purpose response sheet—a list of forty-two pairs of occupations, instruction and interpretation sheets for aspirations and expectations (see Figure 41.1, upper part) and for each determinant, and response grids showing expert responses. (A program called PLATON has also been developed.)

The determinants that are ordinarily used are (1) femininity, masculinity (gender determinants in Gottfredson's classification); (2) prestige, in-

---

ASPIRATIONS

Follow all the instructions below as they applied to an ideal situation unaffected by academic standing, age, cost of studies, etc.

A) *Instruction for student on his/her own aspirations*
Look at each pair of occupations. Put an X next to the one in each pair you would least like to hold in the future.

D) *Instruction for mother or father on job aspirations they have for their child*
Look at each pair of occupations. Put an X next to the one in each pair you would least like your son or daughter to hold in the future.

MEETING PEOPLE-BEING ALONE SCALES

I think that I .... rejected the job with the most opportunity for meeting people

Never
X X X X X X X X X X X X X X X X X X X X X X X X
                                                                        Always

In fact You .... rejected the job which appeared to you to provide the most opportunity
for meeting people

Never
0 2 4 6 8 10 12 14 16 18 20 22 24 26 28 30 32 34 36 38 40 42
                                                                        Always

Your information is

of very poor quality
0 2 4 6 8 10 12 14 16 18 20 22 24 26 28 30 32 34 36 38 39
                                                            of very good quality

---

FIGURE 41.1 Part of the Aspirations Instructions Sheet (upper part). Part of the Meeting People Interpretation Sheet (lower part).

---

come, promotion, responsibilities (social status determinants according to Gottfredson); (3) manual/concrete, intellectual/research, artistic, social/altruist, entrepreneurial, clerical (interests determinants); (4) free time, fatigue, meeting-people–being-alone, inside-outside, usefulness to society, altruism (value determinants); and (5) access with respect to current academic status, access with respect to cost and length of studies, job opportunities, possibilities of working abroad (access determinants).

As a result of our Brunswikian orientation, the comparison frame for each result is not a set of results obtained from different subjects for a given dimension but a set of results obtained from a single individual on different dimensions and/or in different situations and/or in response to different instructions (Brunswik, 1940b). The major feature is the fact that the importance a teenager ascribes to a given dimension (such as prestige) is compared to the importance she or he ascribes to other determinants (such as income and free time) in what determines his or her job aspirations or expectations. An individual is not compared with others but is "compared" strictly with himself or herself.

Acknowledging Individual Differences

The technique is not based on the assumption that there is an identity of perception of occupations in all students. In no case does it operate on the principle that "embassy attaché" will be seen by all adolescents as more prestigious than "agronomist" (or the reverse) or that all adolescents will see teachers as more feminine than laboratory assistants. The technique is based on the hypothesis that there is an interdimensional structure shared by all. It is assumed that perceived relationships between dimensions can vary from one student to another. It is of prime importance to discover that prestige is almost entirely linked to income in one adolescent but has practically no link to prestige in another adolescent.

Flexibility

Because of its idiographic character, the technique has variable geometry. The teenager, either alone or together with a teacher or counselor, selects those dimensions that interest him or her and how many. Likewise, any number of dimensions can be examined. The determinants cited above are simply the most common ones. An individual or educator interested in other determinants can simply write the appropriate instructions and develop the expert data bank if needed. It is also entirely open-ended as regards the occupations used for comparison. If certain occupations seem meaningless in a specific context, they can be replaced by more significant ones. The only constraint is to select a representative set of occupations (Brunswik, 1955c). Moreover, the technique is user-friendly. A teenager can ask his or her parents to compare their system of determination of job aspirations to the one he or she has. Brothers and sisters can also take part. Nothing prevents an individual from using the procedure again, using either the same determinants or others. The person can thus measure his or her own evolution (changes in importance, quality of information, disparity between aspirations and expectations). In contrast to most tests, where readministration is not advisable, readministration is both natural and desirable in this case.

Transparency

It is generally considered inadvisable for a subject to know how a test has been constructed. In contrast, grasp of the principles of this technique is the necessary precondition for it to be efficient, for it is nothing more than an empty frame, a field of action. People who take it need to understand that the findings result from the comparison of two sets of their own responses. The pairwise comparison system was specifically chosen for this purpose because it is much easier to interpret a degree of agreement than a correlation coefficient.

Summary

In summary, the self-knowledge technique was built upon Brunswikian principles involving the idiographic-statistical method and vicarious functioning. Application of these principles enabled us to develop a highly useful technique that is specific to an individual and thus allows counseling as well as identification of individual differences, flexibile in its administration and thus permits adaptation to those differences, and transparent in the test construction principles and scoring for the individual who is being counseled. These advantages are not trivial ones.

42

How Probabilistic Functionalism Advances Evolutionary Psychology

Kenneth R. Hammond

Had the term *evolutionary psychology* been invented in Brunswik's time, he would have endorsed it—as he endorsed (or perhaps invented) the concept of *ecological psychology*—as a useful innovation within which his work could be embedded. His evolutionary views are most apparent in his 1957 article in which he took pains to argue for the equal treatment of the environment, theoretically and empirically, with the organism. Brunswik's choice of the term "probabilistic functionalism" as the name for his conceptual framework gives further evidence of placing his own stamp (probabilism) on evolutionary psychology within the Darwinian tradition.

Three issues distinguish a Brunswikian evolutionary psychology from current approaches: first, its domain-independent rather than domain-specific theory of inference; second, its emphasis on the linear model as the organizing cognitive principle that makes domain independence possible; and third, its use of the correspondence and coherence metatheories to distinguish between environmental tasks.

Domain-Independent versus Domain-Specific Approaches in Evolutionary Psychology

The competition between these points of view seems to have been recently settled in favor of domain specificity (see, e.g., Cosmides & Tooby, 1996), despite this settlement's having been reached without any consideration of Brunswikian theory and research. Yet the domain-independent theory goes back as far as Tolman and Brunswik's (1935) landmark paper that expanded psychological theory to include specific characteristics of the environment. Regrettably, the significance of their expanded theoretical framework went completely unrecognized by their contemporaries and remains so by most experimental psychologists today; indeed, it has gone unrecognized even by the prominent evolutionary psychologists of today, almost none of whom ever seem to have heard of Brunswik's work, or the work of his followers.

Tolman and Brunswik began their work by first describing the properties of the environmental circumstances with which the organism must cope, and they then deduced the properties of the "psychological mechanisms" that must necessarily be possessed by surviving organisms. They first postulated a "textured" environment that mediates information in uncertain, interdependent terms and then formulated a theory of cognitive processes that could cope with probabilistic, interdependent information. Brunswik's probabilistic functionalism, as it appears today in the work of the many authors in this volume and others, clearly entails a domain-independent approach to cognition, specifically to judgment under uncertainty. By including the term *probabilistic*, he became the first psychologist to acknowledge the role of uncertainty in the environment (see especially Brunswik, 1952, 1955a, 1956b, 1957), as well as the first to describe in detail—and carry out an experiment (Brunswik, 1938a; see Doherty, this volume) to show—the consequences of that idea for a theory of learning. Brunswik's view of a probabilistic environment is implicitly accepted in much of today's research in judgment and decision making, and in much of cognitive psychology, largely without attribution.

Nevertheless, domain independence of cognitive function flies in the face of much current thinking about evolutionary psychology. For example, in his review of Steven Pinker's (1997) book *How the Mind Works*, Konner (1998) praised Pinker because "he correctly concludes that—contrary to most current cognitive models—the brain cannot be any sort of general information processor, symmetrically repetitive iterator, or global learning machine" (p. 653). Konner added that Pinker should be praised for claiming that "any reasonable expectation informed by evolutionary biology requires domain-specific, functionally restrictive, neural organs and circuits" (p. 653). Such statements (see also Cosmides & Tooby, 1994) by opponents of "general information processors" make it appear as if the proponents of domain-independent models are hopelessly out of touch with, and uninformed by, evolutionary biology and thus entrapped in an outdated psychology. Konner was probably right, however, in pointing out that cognitive psychologists in general accept the domain-independence view, whereas evolutionary psychologists accept the domain-dependence view, a difference that should provoke some thought and perhaps result in productive research. See, for example, the exchange between Gould and Pinker (1997).

But it isn't so much ignorance about evolutionary biology that will divide psychologists as it is ignorance about Brunswikian psychology. For no refutation of, or even acknowledgment of, the theory and empirical data of Brunswikian psychology will be found in any of the attacks on domain-independent models. Indeed, one might say that, because proponents of the domain-specific argument appear to be completely uninformed by that theory and research, they have nothing—in terms of theory or data—to offer to refute it and, indeed, nothing to indicate that they understand it. Yet there have been hundreds of experiments undertaken over the past fifty years that support the concept of a domain-independent cognitive model in *both* in-laboratory and outside-the-laboratory conditions. (See, for example, Holzworth, this volume; see also Cooksey, 1996b; Hammond, 1996c, 1999.)

Fortunately, Cosmides and Tooby (1996, p. 1, 9, 58) seem to take it for granted that conclusions should be based on findings that are general over conditions. They charged, for example, that the results of the "'heuristics and biases' literature" regarding the ineptitude of humans in the use of probabilistic information are to be ignored because they do not appear in the "most ecologically valid condition." Their misuse of the Brunswikian term "ecological validity" supports the suppo-

sition that they are unaware of Brunswikian theory and research. (See the comments on Brunswik's 1949 paper, this volume, for a criticism of the misuse of the term "ecological validity" by Tooby and Cosmides and others.)

Why the Linear Model Was Selected as a Domain-Independent Cognitive Process

Since neither hominids nor Pleistocene *Homo sapiens* have been observed in their natural habitats, we are restricted to observations of monkeys or apes, or to plausibility arguments about "what must have been." Cosmides (1989), for example, made the entirely plausible argument that, for *Homo sapiens*, "the more important the adaptive problem, the more intensely selection should have specialized and improved the performance of the mechanism for solving it" and cited Darwin (1859/1966) and Williams (1966) to support that argument (among others) for domain-specific cognition. Evolutionary biologists on the lookout for "adaptationism" will quarrel with this statement, however; they will argue that selection alone doesn't "specialize and improve" a trait; rather, it is selection plus heritable genetic change that accounts for evolutionary adaptation. But Cosmides's adaptationism shows here, for her statement assumes that there is unlimited genetic variation for the trait to evolve in exactly the direction favored by selection, and that there are no countervailing selective/genetic pressures, a point always emphasized by evolutionary biologists such as Stephen Jay Gould.

But what basis did Tolman and Brunswik have for *their* plausibility argument about "what must have been" that led them to a domain-independent "psychological mechanism"? Where did Brunswik's conception of the nature of the selective environment come from? Did he simply make a guess? The answer is no: His postulation of a probabilistic, multiple cue environment came from his painstaking studies of visual perception, in particular the phenomenon of size constancy carried out in Karl Bühler's laboratory in Vienna as far back as the early 1930s (see Brunswik, 1952, 1956b). It was this work that turned up the various probabilistic, interdependent cues to size and other distal variables in the natural environment and led Brunswik and

Tolman to title their 1935 *Psychological Review* article "The Organism and the Causal Texture of the Environment." The term "causal texture" was intended to indicate the entangled — that is, intercorrelated — relations among perceptual cues such as perspective, interception, and vertical position and their less-than-perfect relation to distance or size. Given the achievement of size constancy as critical to survival, they hypothesized that *Homo sapiens* would be able to make use of such imperfect data (would have a "psychological mechanism" that would enable them to do so). This hypothesis led Brunswik to carry out the first rat experiment on probabilistic learning at Berkeley in 1939 (see Doherty's comments, this volume) and others subsequently, to illustrate the point (see also Brunswik and Herma, 1951, and Bjorkman's comments, this volume). By 1956, Brunswik had decided that the multiple regression model was a reasonable "psychological mechanism" for coping with such tasks (see Brunswik, 1956b, p. 110). Why? Because it is based on (1) data from several variables, (2) all of which have imperfect relations with the criterion in question, (3) all of which may have imperfect redundant relations with one another, and (4) all of which have a functional relationship with the criterion, which may take on various nonlinear (as well as linear) forms, and (5) the equation provides an overall measure of predictability (the multiple R value). All of these statistical parameters thus provide quantitative measures of just the concepts Brunswik was talking about. Within ten years, the lens model equation — an algorithm that makes data from *both* the environment and the organism subject simultaneously to statistical analysis — had been developed and tested and was to be employed on numerous occasions by a wide variety of researchers (see Stewart, this volume, for a description of the lens model equation; see Cooksey, 1996b, for examples). The fit between theory and quantitative expression was a natural one, and it is worth noting that Brunswik first developed the theory and *then* noted the parallel with the multiple regression equation, not the reverse. (See Gigerenzer, 1991, for many examples of the reverse procedure.)

Brunswik's evolutionary psychology thus begins with an empirically based theory of the general characteristics of environmental tasks that challenge organismic perception in general and human judgment in particular. It argues that the natural environment offers a wide variety of interdependent, fallible (or probabilistic) indicators of events or environmental states not directly observable, an argument that has been supported by substantial empirical research over several perceptual domains by many investigators. It is these ubiquitous fallible indicators — not limited to those involved in the visual perception of size, color, and shape that intrigued Brunswik — that must be organized to form the inductive inferences, the judgments that an organism must make about distal variables in order to survive in a probabilistic environment. There is an abundance of empirical laboratory research that illustrates the *capacity* of *Homo sapiens* (and numerous other species) to make use of multiple fallible indicators widely varying in content for such inferences (see Holzworth, this volume). In addition, there is abundant historical evidence of *Homo sapiens*'s ability to — and urge to — *create* multiple fallible indicators in almost every area of endeavor in contemporary society in order to make successful inferences, judgments, or predictions. (For examples, see any textbook in economics, business administration, medicine, or meteorology; indeed, there are so many uses of probabilistic indicators that there is a journal — the *Social Indicators Journal* — for their compilation and use; see Hammond, 1996c, for a discussion and examples.)

Albright and Malloy, Funder, Gillis and Bernieri, and Mumpower (this volume) make the case for the pervasive use of multiple fallible indicators and the linear model in social perception (an area Brunswik opened up in the 1940s). Buss (1989) illustrated this mechanism in mate selection. Moreover, there is abundant evidence of the use of multiple fallible indicators (e.g., wave direction) by migrating species that range from pigeons to turtles. Byrne (1995) described the use of multiple fallible indicators by apes as a means of group communication about the location of food. Torbjorn von Schantz and his colleagues (1989) conducted painstaking field studies of the female pheasants' use of multiple fallible indicators in their choice of mates and found that the linear model successfully accounted for the female pheasant's accurate choices about which male mating would result in the production of the largest number of *viable* eggs. This discovery provides extraordinary support for the linear model as a heritable genetic trait. There is obviously no means by which the pheasant could *learn* to accomplish this feat, and the increased number of viable eggs provides the heritable mechanism. And although no direct studies have been done on the inheritance of the linear model *within* a species, its widespread occurrence *across* species offers plausibility for its inheritance.

The important point here is that the linear model has been found to be general over the wide variety of content of the fallible indicators, from those used in studies carried out in the psychological laboratory to those found by behavioral ecologists. There is a good functionalist reason why the linear model has so often been found to account for the organization of indicators, and that is its *robustness*, a feature of the linear model made apparent to judgment and decision researchers by Dawes and Corrigan (1974). The ability of this form of aggregation to *produce an approximately correct judgment even when it includes incorrect cue weights or function forms, or even the incorrect aggregation rule*, is a truly startling result. Such robustness was well known to statisticians, but the implications of the robustness of the linear model as a *cognitive* model for a wide variety of species — pheasants, turtles, and even mosquitoes (see Wilton, 1968) — have never been brought to the attention of evolutionary psychologists or biologists. The main implications are two: (1) As yet we know of no better data-organizing principle for the *Homo sapiens* who lived in the Pleistocene and earlier to have been endowed with; it would have provided robust inferences that no other procedure known to us even now can match; and (2) if indeed *Homo sapiens* somehow acquired this robust organizing principle, *Homo sapiens would not have to learn* to assign correct weights or function forms between proximal and distal variables; approximately correct judgments would ensue in any event. Indeed, it would have been very difficult for any organism to learn in an environment of this kind were the organism to be equipped with such a robust cognitive principle, because the uncertain environment would not send back reliable information precise enough to disconfirm it. That conclusion is consistent with the well-established finding that our social perception is no more than mediocre in its accuracy and perhaps is why fifty years of research on clinical judgment shows that it is no more accurate than a linear model (Paul Meehl, 1954; Hammond,

1955; Dawes, Faust, & Meehl, 1989; Gardner, Lidz, Mulvey, & Shaw, 1996). It also explains the ineptitude of social policy formation over the centuries; it is very difficult to learn when one possesses a robust organizing principle that is applied to an uncertain environment; clear disconfirmation of plausible alternative hypotheses is infrequent and often impossible.

In short, *any organism endowed with a robust domain-independent linear model as a cognitive system to be used for the purpose of inductive inference would be at a distinct advantage relative to any organism that relied on domain-specific processes. Moreover, any organism so endowed would not have to learn to improve its judgments, nor is it likely, given the uncertainty in the environment, that it could markedly improve them in any event. Cognitive robustness* thus defines what is critically functional and is directly related to the ability to survive and reproduce in a probabilistic environment. And it does so in a manner unanticipated by evolutionary psychologists or biologists.

To say that an organism is "endowed" with a "robust, domain-independent cognitive system," of course, begs the question of how that endowment came about. That endowment is as mysterious as *Homo sapiens*'s endowment of a language ability. The difference is that, so far as we know, *all* warm-blooded creatures are endowed with the linear model as a cognitive system, whereas the language ability is unique to *Homo sapiens*.

What Is Domain-Independent and What Is Domain-Dependent?

It should be clear from the above discussion of robustness that within the Brunswikian framework, domain independence refers to the *organizing principle* (the linear model) used for organizing the data acquired from various multiple fallible indicators. The *content* of the indicators is left unspecified because the process is largely, but not completely, general over the content of indicators. Therefore, it is this principle — the linear model — that is largely domain-independent, for it is highly general over indicator content. And it is the linear model (of which the multiple regression equation is but one example) that is an integral part of the Brunswikian theory that is put forward within the framework of social judgment theory and cognitive continuum theory (see Cooksey, 1996b; Hammond, 1996c, 1999).

The indicators themselves are, of course, *not* domain-independent, a circumstance recognized in the Brunswikian research of the 1960s and made evident by the wide variety of indicators employed in numerous studies of multiple cue probability learning and "policy capturing," in which a linear model is found to be an organizing principle. (For an early study, see Adelman, 1981; for summaries, see Brehmer & Joyce, 1988, and Cooksey 1996b; for examples, see also Holzworth, this volume). Obviously, what is an important indicator in one context often is irrelevant in another.

It has also long been established (see the numerous studies of the application of the lens model to clinical judgment) that accurate inferences require knowledge of which indicators deserve attention and inclusion in the organizing process. Indeed, so obvious has the robustness of the linear model become, and so obvious has the natural use of it become, that Dawes and other students of clinical judgment have long advocated that clinical instructors limit themselves to merely pointing out to students *which* indicators should be noticed and then urging that they should simply *add* them; weighting and organizing should be ignored.

A critical question remains, however. Although wide ranges of differences in the content of indicators have been shown to have little effect on the *form of the process* (the linear model does show great generality), other forms of organization have also been shown to occur; most obvious is the "noncompensatory" organizing principle in which one indicator must be satisfied before others will be taken into account. (See also Anderson, 1981.)

The situation seems to be quite the reverse for those who insist that cognitive processes are domain-dependent. Although Cosmides and others (see Barkow, Cosmides, & Tooby, 1992; Hirschfeld & Gelman, 1994; Cummins & Allen, 1998) acknowledge the use of perceptual "cues" as indicators, they apparently place far less emphasis on their fallible character and redundant (intercorrelated) character than does Brunswikian theory. They base their conclusion on the finding that the form of the process of organizing the information *shifts* according to the content of the indicators (or "cues," or "stimuli"). The results of a wide variety of studies carried out by numerous authors, although no more impervious to criticism than any others, deserve our credence at this point, and I do not wish to quarrel with them. It is my belief that the linear model does possess great generality, but that it does not exhaust all the possibilities of organization, and that the content of indicators *can* affect the form of the organizing process.

Does this mean that I believe that both the domain-independent and the domain-specific theories are correct? The answer is yes; that is because the proponents of each point of view have chosen a different type of task to which they have applied their theory, and each has made significant progress in understanding cognitive activity of relevance to evolutionary psychology. But in order to substantiate that argument, a distinction must be made between two types of environmental tasks: those encompassed by the correspondence and coherence metatheories of truth.

The Importance of Using the Correspondence and Coherence Metatheories to Distinguish between Environmental Tasks

Brunswikian theory is directed toward the psychology of inference, of judgment under environmental uncertainty; it contains a domain-independent organizing principle limited to the *correspondence metatheory* of truth. The correspondence metatheory refers to a class of theories that are focused on the relation between judgment and fact. That means that persons making judgments within the correspondence metatheory are concerned only with the empirical *accuracy* of their judgments, and the researchers who study them focus only on that aspect of their judgments. For example, untutored persons (early *Homo sapiens*, for example) making weather predictions based on multiple fallible indicators (clouds, wind) are concerned only with the accuracy of their judgments, not their justification or the rationality of such predictions. Indeed, persons making such judgments often are unaware of the indicators on which their judgments are made. The lens model is used by researchers in the attempt to understand how that process works.

It is easy to see the applicability of the correspondence metatheory to the cognitive activity of hominids and early *Homo sapiens*. There would be numerous challenges to the empirical accuracy of their judgments, both in physical/biological and social terms. In what must have a been a persistent search for food, and for the avoidance of predators, skill in the use of multiple fallible indicators would have been demanded. Brunswik made this point in his book (1934b), and in his 1952 monograph thus; "any organism has to cope with an environment full of uncertainties. Forced to react quickly or within reasonable limits of time, it must respond before direct contact with the relevant remote conditions in the environment, such as foodstuffs or traps, friends or enemies, can be established The probability character of intra-environmental relationships, their limited "ecological validity," becomes of concern in two regional contexts; on the reception or stimulus side . . . and on the effection or reaction side" (p. 22). (See Adelman, this volume, for a modern example of applying Brunswikian theory to the problem of identifying "friend or foe," still an important cognitive activity relevant to survival.)

Accurate social judgments would also be important in mate selection, as well as in the accurate judgment of friend and foe (see Buss, 1989). But in an environment that made no demands for *coherent* cognitive activity, there would be none, until language, tool use, and social organization became sophisticated enough to demand it (or vice versa). Once the demand for coherence began, however, a new form of cognition would begin, one that would mark *Homo sapiens* off from all the other species. At that point, domain-dependent cognition began, and at that point, a different sort of competence was demanded, a phenomenon that would grow until today, when the coherence metatheory is probably employed by laypersons as frequently as the correspondence metatheory (see Hammond, 1996c, for examples). (Domain-dependent cognition and coherent cognition are, of course, the mainstay of scientific cognition.)

The advocates of domain dependence have emphasized their interest in rationality and reason and thus the coherence metatheory, as they should. For example, after making clear how to make use of the hypotheticodeductive approach to search for psychological mechanisms relevant to evolutionary psychology, Cosmides (1989) stated, "*Evidence for the existence of such mechanisms is: (1) reasoning performance is altered depending on what* content *the subject is asked to reason about; and (2) such* reasoning performance *is altered by specific* content *in the predicted adaptive direction*" (pp. 190–191; italics in original, emphasis mine). I have emphasized the words *reasoning performance* and *content* in each sentence because I believe it was her focus on both terms that inevitably led Cosmides to the restricted research that found that cognition is domain-specific. For her research and that of her colleagues is restricted to tasks requiring coherence competence, that is, to tasks requiring reasoning (such as the Wason card-sorting task), rather than correspondence competence. The study of empirical accuracy was thus set aside in favor of studying rational processes, particularly in what is called the *social contract*. It is my view that when Cosmides asserted that "reasoning performance is altered depending on what content the subject is asked to reason about," she made a critically important statement that is wrongly framed. I believe that the focus on "content" was a mistake; the focus should have been on the *formal properties* of the tasks of interest. That should not have been difficult, for the formal properties of the tasks of interest to Cosmides and her colleagues are those of deductive tasks, namely, the familiar rules of *modus ponens* (if *p* then *q*) and *modus tollens* (if not *p* then not *q*) and therefore straightforward and well-known. Cosmides gave many examples of social behavior in just these terms. The properties of these tasks make them susceptible to solution by well-known rules; the researchers' purpose is to discover the rules (known as descriptive rules) that are actually employed by their subjects in specific social contexts, exactly the same method as used by the coherence theorists in judgment and decision research, whom she severely attacked. (For examples from Cosmides, 1989, see pp. 208–209; cf. numerous examples in Kahneman, Slovic, & Tversky, 1982.)

Precisely the opposite approach was taken by Tolman and Brunswik, and was pursued systematically by Brunswik thereafter. That is, Brunswik focused on the *inductive* leg of the cognitive process (and eschewed his study of rationality or reasoning until much later in his life; see Brunswik, 1956b, pp. 89–99, for his turn near the end of his life to the study of rational, analytical cognition). Furthermore, Brunswik's work centered on the *formal* nature of the cognitive process rather than the *content* of the cues or target object(s).

As a result of these two restrictions of interest (obviously quite different from the restrictions applied by, for example, the authors in Barkow, Cosmides, & Tooby, 1992), Brunswik and later researchers (see Part III of this volume) were led to a belief in a *domain-independent* theory that is focused on cognitive process, in flat opposition to the cue-content-oriented approach advocated by Cosmides and other followers of the *domain-specific* theory. (For further essays by those who support the domain-specific approach, see Cosmides and her collaborator Tooby in Barkow, Cosmides, & Tooby, 1992; see also Hirschfeld & Gelman, 1994, who stated on p. i, "A growing number of researchers now claim that many cognitive abilities are specialized to handle specific types of information," and Cummins & Allen,

1998.) This distinction is well known to philosophers; Isaiah Berlin (1956/1984) made good use of it in his introduction to *The Age of Enlightenment.*

In short, any thorough treatment of the evolution of cognition must take account of the formal properties of tasks, must be prepared to acknowledge their classification into those within the correspondence methatheory and those within the coherence metatheory, and must distinguish the different cognitive demands made by each in different environmental contexts. Fortunately, both the domain-independent approach and the domain-dependent approach already taken, albeit by separate groups of researchers, can accommodate this requirement, as the extensive research carried out by both groups amply demonstrates.

43

Brunswik and Quality of Life: A Brief Note

C. R. B. Joyce

Quality of life (QoL) has been defined in many different ways. One simple and useful definition is this: "The way a person feels and how he or she functions in daily activities" (Kirshner & Guyatt, 1985). Everybody has a QoL, good, average, or poor. Most people would presumably like it to be as good as possible. It varies from one person to another, and from time to time, as do the individual factors in the subject's physical and mental makeup and life history that enter into it. It is also affected by the many factors in the environment.

The scientific study of QoL began, slowly, about thirty years ago, and has accelerated, to the current indexing in MEDLINE of more than 1,000 publications a year with some relevance to the topic. It is now a major, sometimes a unique, outcome measure of the effect on disease of medi-

cal or other interventions, as estimated by controlled clinical trials, and plays an increasingly important part in forming health and other social policies. These applications are demographic or epidemiological in nature, or, in Brunswikian terms, nomothetic.

This approach has led to the following definition: "Individual QoL is what the patient says it is" (Joyce, 1994).

The specific study of individual QoL (IQoL), on the other hand, is much more recent. Its components must attempt a full description of the individual as a physical, thinking, feeling and reacting social being and are often summarized under four headings about which there is general agreement: physical, cognitive, affective, and social. Behavioral, environmental, economic, and spiritual classes of cue are also often used. Each covers specific aspects of behavior (for example, feelings of anxiety or ability to carry out daily tasks) and represents the extent to which these are experienced by the subject. Several instruments have been developed for this kind of idiographic study, of which an early example, the Schedule for the Evaluation of Individual Quality of Life (SEIQoL; Joyce, O'Boyle, & McGee, 1999), makes use of the method of judgment analysis (JA; Cooksey, 1996b).

In a first lightly structured interview, some three to seven cues are identified by the subject as playing a meaningful role in his or her quality of life. The current satisfactoriness of each is evaluated on a scale from 0 to ten, and their current importance may be determined in a variety of ways. The most informative relies on the standard JA procedure, in which the (IQoL) of thirty to fifty hypothetical cases with the individual's selected cues is evaluated by the subject to determine the beta weight of each cue. A set of replicates is included to estimated internal reliability, and validity is assessed, as usual, by R^2. Subsequent examinations usually make use of the same cues, or if it appears that one or more cues have dramatically lost or gained in importance, new cues are incorporated as appropriate. These are given zero weight in the analysis of the initial test, and those dropped are treated in the same way in subsequent tests. The IQoL itself is scored by multiplying the current rate by the appropriate weight and summing the products. In 1997, Browne et al. wrote, "Simpler methods of determining weights (unwillingly satisfying typical demands from medical investigators for speed of administration) entail pie diagrams, such as the use of a flexible model, the divisions of which can be manipulated by the subject until he or she is content with the divisions achieved" (p. 301).

This, of course, gives no information about reliability or validity but may be adequate for monitoring the progress of individual patients in clinical practice. There is also some suggestion that, not surprisingly, it may estimate QoL at what may be called the current, or "state," level rather than the more stable, or "trait," level reached by the full method.

The SEIQoL is intelligible and well accepted. Internal reliability is generally good, r ranging from 0.7 to 0.95. R^2 is of a similarly satisfactory order, from 0.7 to 0.9 in a study of healthy subjects (McGee et al., 1991), with only occasional variances lying outside this range. As expected with a set of vicariously functioning cues, the observations are reasonably well fitted by a linear model. The SEIQoL is being used, or has been used, in more than 200 studies worldwide and is one of ten methods (the only one for IQoL) listed for the purpose by World Health Organization.

This points to one obvious advantage. The cues are personal and are identified by each subject. Apart from the user's manual (the English of which is usually adequate for most investigators; it is, in fact, already available in German and Dutch), there is nothing to translate, and subjects from different ethnic and/or language groups can be combined in the same study.

Disadvantages of the method consist mainly in the time (typically thirty to sixty minutes) required for the first interview; the fact that though the method is direct, it does require an interviewer with some skill and training; and the difficulty of using it with the very young (under eight years old), the demented or others whose cognitive efficiency is questionable. Other methods share these disadvantages, but not the advantage of independence of cultural constraint.

It is considered that the scores derived from individual subjects can be summed and submitted to the same kinds of statistical analysis as those derived from other examinations of mental function (such as the Present State Examination and the Hamilton Depression Rating Scale) with as much (or little) justification.

PART IV

BRUNSWIK THE MAN
AND HIS IDEAS

44

Ideas in Exile: The Struggles of an Upright Man

Gerd Gigerenzer

The sparkling intellectual atmosphere of early-twentieth-century Vienna produced Ludwig Wittgenstein, Karl Popper, Otto Neurath, and Kurt Gödel—in addition to a string of other great thinkers. Among them was Karl Bühler, who, when he founded the Vienna Psychological Institute in 1922, was one of the foremost psychologists in the world. Egon Brunswik began to study psychology in Vienna in 1923 and soon became an active participant in Bühler's famous Wednesday-evening discussion group; Thursdays he went to Moritz Schlick's Thursday-evening discussion group (Leary, 1987). Schlick was the founder and leading member of the European school of positivist philosophers known as the Vienna Circle. In 1927, Brunswik submitted his doctoral thesis to Bühler and Schlick, the same two advisers to whom Karl Popper submitted his thesis a year later.

The intellectual tension between Wednesday and Thursday evenings was vibrant. The logical positivist doctrine of the Vienna Circle posited that the relationship between scientific language and its sense-data referents should and could be unambiguous. Bühler, in contrast, had shown that the relationship between perceptual cues and their objects, as well as between words and their objects, was irreducibly ambiguous. Brunswik sided with Bühler. He did try, though, to resolve the tension by adopting the position of Hans Reichenbach, the leader of the Berlin school of logical positivism, who argued that all knowledge is probabilistic.

Influenced by Bühler's biologically motivated concern with the success of organisms in their world, Brunswik's research in the 1920s and 1930s aimed at studying "perceptual achievement" in the presence of ambiguous cues. The three traditional perceptual constancies—size, shape, and color—were the prototype for achievement, that is, how accurate perception is when

aspects of the environment change. Brunswik extended the question of how well an organism infers size, shape, and color under varying context variables (such as illumination) to the more general problem of studying the invariance of the perception of one characteristic of an object when the others vary. For instance, he studied how the perceived size of coins changed when their value and the number of coins were varied—coins higher in value appeared to be larger in size and greater in number than those of lesser value (Brunswik, 1934b, p. 147). In Brunswik's terms, what we see are *perceptual compromises* that he attributed to the learning of cues from experience (e.g., coins of higher value actually do tend to be larger in size). He manipulated up to four variables simultaneously in factorial designs (he had not yet developed the idea of representative design) and measured how the perception of each variable depended on the values of the others. This Vienna program of "multidimensional psychophysics" measured the context-dependency of judgment (for an introduction, see Gigerenzer & Murray, 1987, pp. 61–81). In contrast, its independence from context was assumed in the one-dimensional psychophysics associated with G. T. Fechner and S. S. Stevens, in which one studied a variable in isolation (such as perceived size), held everything else constant, and then compared the perceived size to the actual size to obtain the psychophysical function.

In the early 1930s, Brunswik was far ahead of mainstream psychophysics in the study of context dependency. This is not to say that there was no room for theoretical development in his multidimensional psychophysics; for instance, Brunswik treated his two explanatory concepts, perceptual compromises and cue learning, as equivalent whereas these actually are different and can lead to contradictory predictions about the effect of context (Gigerenzer & Murray, 1987, pp. 70–74).

However, his Vienna program had virtually no impact on the future of psychophysics, except for a few scattered studies.

One reason for this lack of influence was that the Vienna Psychological Institute's program was destroyed soon after Brunswik had accepted a position at Berkeley in 1937. In early 1938, the Nazis entered Vienna and arrested and dismissed Bühler because of his political views, which were considered dangerous to the "peace and public order of the (Philosophical) Faculty" (Ash, 1987, p. 157). Eventually, he fled to the United States, but no one offered the once-celebrated Karl Bühler an adequate position; his brilliant career crumbled in exile. Schlick had died a few years earlier from gunshot wounds inflicted by a deranged student, and the political pressure of fascism caused the Vienna Circle to disband, with many of its members fleeing to the United States. Brunswik had to start practically from scratch at Berkeley.

Brunswik in the Plural

Unlike the Vienna program, Brunswik's Berkeley program—probabilistic functionalism—is well known. It is so well known, in fact, that there is not just one Brunswik, but several. One is the Brunswik absorbed by contemporary psychology: he-was-one-of-us. These good-natured colleagues spell his name *Brunswick*, confuse his term *ecological validity* with generalizability from the laboratory to the environment, and his term *representative design* with the representativeness heuristic. In their friendly embrace, Brunswik comes out a forerunner and guardian of today's status quo. No conflict surfaces; all is quiet; nothing must be questioned.

There is a more sophisticated image, in which Brunswik's ideas basically boil down to three correlations and one unorthodoxy. The correlations are functional validities, ecological validities, and cue utilization coefficients, and the heresy is representative design—the frightening idea of sacrificing experimental control and, possibly even worse, of leaving one's laboratory to study people in their real-world environments. Correlations are fine; the unorthodoxy is repugnant. This view gets some work done, but it cuts right through the middle of Brunswik's intellectual heart.

There is a third view of Brunswik: opposition by neglect. This is not an active opposition against an intellectual enemy; Brunswik does not seem to have notable intellectual enemies, unlike many other scholars. The opposition takes the form of silence and a lack of understanding of what the fuss is all about. For instance, in his *Sensation and Perception in the History of Experimental Psychology* (1942), Edwin G. Boring, the dean of the history of psychology and an arch-determinist, covered Brunswik's work in Vienna, which had encompassed experimental control in multidimensional designs. But after Brunswik had fleshed out his probabilistic functionalism and representative design, he was not even mentioned in Boring's A *History of Experimental Psychology* (1957) and *History, Psychology, and Science* (1963). As Ken Hammond (1980, p. 9) reported, Boring's verdict was "Brunswik was a brilliant man who wasted his life." Informed neglect can be as toxic to new ideas as an uninformed embrace.

In the following, I describe what I think of when I think of Brunswik. I do not think of correlations; I think of the struggles of an upright man.

Intellectual Integrity

What impresses me deeply is Brunswik's uncompromising intellectual sincerity: the courage to think through the consequences of one's ideas carefully, and to speak out in public even when the scientific community does not want to listen and makes one pay a price for maintaining these standards. And Brunswik did pay dearly. Brunswik's personal struggle was, in my view, about maintaining his *intellectual integrity* in a scientific community in which his ideas fell on hostile ground held by ignorant troops. Great thinkers often learn, to their surprise, that new ideas are less than welcome.

What were these new ideas that inspired so much hostility? Brunswik's probabilistic functionalism can be summarized in the following concepts: achievement, ambiguity of cues, vicarious functioning, and representative design. That is, an organism needs to make inferences about its environment to adjust, survive, and reproduce (achievement); the proximal cues available to it to make these inferences about its environment are uncertain (ambiguity); the organism processes ambiguous cues by substituting or combining them (vicarious functioning); in order to study achievement and vicarious functioning, researchers need to use representative designs. This is Brunswik's linking of biological purpose, environment, cognitive process, and research methodology.

The hostile ground itself was a minefield of dogmas: determinism, the Columbia Bible, and Fisher's experimental design. Determinism was a fading, but still strong, dogma, and the other two were newly emerging dogmas.

Refinancing Determinism

In their struggle to get psychology recognized as a science, many of Brunswik's fellow psychologists in America maintained an old-fashioned ideal no longer characteristic of modern science, from evolutionary biology to quantum physics. This ideal demanded *certain* knowledge and *universal* laws, as Newtonian mechanics had purported to deliver. As an example of this longing for certainty, Edwin Boring declared as late as 1963 that "determinism reigns" (p. 14).

The two debates of Brunswik's program, which were published in the *Psychological Review* in 1943 and 1955, illustrated the way Brunswik's probabilism collided with the leading experimental psychologists' belief in determinism (see Gigerenzer, 1987). Probabilism was interpreted as a confession of failure. For instance, Clark Hull (1943b) declared, in the first debate in Chicago, that he and Kurt Lewin believed in uniform laws of behavior that correspond to correlations of 1.00. Because the effort to isolate deterministic laws is laborious and time-consuming, "All of us may as well give it up, as Brunswik seems already to have done" (p. 204).

Twelve years later, in the second debate in Berkeley, David Krech (1955) confronted Brunswik with his personal confession of faith: "I have always made it a cardinal principle to live beyond my income. And although I have yet to find a one-to-one correlation in psychology . . . I am always ready to make another promissory note and promise that if you bear with us we *will* find uniform laws. . . . And if I can't pay off on my first promissory note I will come seeking refinancing. . . . I have faith that despite our repeated and inglorious failures we will someday come to a theory which is able to give a consistent and complete descrip-

tion of reality. But in the meantime, I repeat, you must bear with us" (p. 230).

Refinancing went on for some time. The fixation on uniform laws of behavior was one of the reasons why many of the commentators did not understand the nature of Brunswik's probabilism—which was located neither in the environment, as Krech (1955) and Hilgard (1955) interpreted Brunswik, nor in the organism, as Hull seemed to do, but rather in the relationship *between* the organism and the environment.

The dogma of determinism did not survive Brunswik very long, but the next two methodological faiths did. They are still entrenched in the minds of most experimental psychologists—and in their hearts, because these methodologies have been taught as if they were moral principles.

The Columbia Bible

The Henry Holt publishing company advertised in 1938, "THE BIBLE IS OUT." Robert S. Woodworth had finally published his long-awaited *Experimental Psychology*. This textbook, which was popularly known as the "Columbia Bible," narrowed the many existing practices of experimentation (see Danziger, 1990) to one and only one legitimate form: Vary an independent variable (or a few), hold all the conditions constant, and observe the effect on the dependent variable. In Brunswik's copy of the Columbia Bible (which Ken Hammond so kindly lent me), on page 2, the passage "all the conditions constant, except for one" is underlined twice, and Brunswik's pencil notation "imposs[ible]!" is in the margin. It is not without irony that Brunswik taught courses for years using Woodworth's textbook, as the notes in his copy indicate. An estimated 100,000 North American psychology majors and graduate students learned what experimental research is from the Woodworth bible and its revised edition (Woodworth & Schlosberg, 1954). The book was translated into many languages and widely used around the world (Evans, 1990). It was enormously successful; many psychologists can no longer envision more than one experimental method in science.

In this book, Woodworth excluded correlation methods and individual differences from the domain of experimental psychology. The bible separated the murky waters of correlation, which obscure the causes of behavior, from the bright sun of experimentation, where cause and effect can be distinguished clearly. The result was a strange institutional partition into "two disciplines of scientific psychology" (Cronbach, 1957), the "Tiny Little Island" of experimental psychology and the "Holy Roman Empire" of correlational psychology.

Brunswik's probabilistic functionalism fitted into neither of these disciplines. His intellectual vision was one of coherence between theory and methodology: to start with the purpose or function (achievement in natural environments) and a subject matter (vicarious functioning of perception and judgment), and to choose a matching methodology (representative design).

There is no such intellectual vision behind the creation of the two "scientific disciplines." Each was, and still is, a historically arbitrary collection of purpose, subject matter, and method that have no necessary logical or psychological affinity with each other (Gigerenzer, 1987). For instance, there is no psychological reason why the study of intelligence is linked with individual differences and correlations, while the study of thinking is linked to general laws and experiments. Nor is there a reason why one group should rarely read or cite the other group's work. Like most ordinary humans who bond with their peers, psychologists in one camp looked down on their colleagues in the other camp, declaring their adversaries' methods inferior and their purpose of little scientific interest and public value. The correlation between psychologists' esteem for their colleagues in one camp and their colleagues in the other camp was −.80 (Thorndike, 1954)—alas, a substantial, but not perfect, correlation.

Brunswik found himself and his ideas exiled from his discipline. Ernest Hilgard (1955), an eminent experimental psychologist, put his lack of regard for Brunswik's methods in no uncertain terms: "Correlation is an instrument of the devil" (p. 228). But methods per se are neither good nor bad; the question is whether they match a theory or not. Brunswik's intellectual integrity demanded that he think for himself, deciding what the proper method was, rather than just climbing on the bandwagon. The tragedy is that he found himself in a no-man's land between the two newly established disciplines.

Fisher's Straightjacket

B. F. Skinner once told me that he had thought of dedicating one of his books to "the statisticians and scientific methodologists with whose help this book would have never been completed." He had second thoughts and, in fact, dedicated the book to those who actually were helpful, "to the pigeon staff." Skinner had had those statisticians in mind who imposed Sir Ronald Fisher's doctrine that the design of an experiment must match the statistical method, such as analysis of variance.

Fisher's randomized control group experiments were tailor-made to Woodworth's ideal of experimentation, and analysis of variance allowed one to study more than one independent variable. Skinner's resistance arose when researchers started to use Fisher's method compulsively rather than in a thoughtful way, that is, as a tool, which is—like all tools—useful only in specific situations. Editors began to make what they believed was good scientific method a sine qua non for publication: factorial designs, large numbers of subjects, and small p values.

Statistical thinking was replaced with a mindless ritual performed in the presence of any set of data (Gigerenzer, 1993). Skinner confessed to me that he once tried a factorial design with some two dozen animals. But only once. He lost experimental control because he could not keep so many animals at the same level of deprivation, and the magnitude of error in his data increased. Why increase error just to have a method that measures error?

The Skinnerians escaped the emerging pressure of editors to publish studies with large numbers of animals by founding a new journal in 1958, the *Journal of the Experimental Analysis of Behavior*. This was not an isolated case. One of the reasons for launching the *Journal of Mathematical Psychology* in 1964 was also to escape the editors' pressure to perform institutionalized null hypothesis testing (Luce, 1989). Somewhat perversely, the best mathematical psychologists were told by their statistically less sophisticated colleagues that they should carry out (as Duncan Luce, 1988, put it) "mindless hypothesis testing in lieu of doing good research: measuring effects, constructing substantive theories of some depth, and developing probability models and statistical procedures suited to these theories" (p. 582).

Brunswik, however, had no following with which he could found his own journal. Like Skinner, he remarked drolly that "our ignorance of Fisher's work on factorial design and its mathematical evaluation . . . paid off" (1956b, p. 102). As almost all great psychologists did, he analyzed individuals rather than comparing group means, and he continued to employ his own nonfactorial representative designs. But he also sometimes felt that he should make concessions, for instance, when he performed "a routine analysis of variance for the factorially orthodox part of our experiment" (1956b, p. 106).

In Brunswik's struggle with Fisher's ideas, unlike Skinner's and Luce's, a classic controversy repeated itself. Karl Pearson, who, with Francis Galton, had founded correlation methods, was involved in a terrible intellectual and personal feud with Fisher. This fight between these towering statisticians repeated itself in psychology between the proponents of their respective tools. Just at the time when Brunswik adopted Pearson's correlation methods around 1940, Fisherian methods began to spread. By 1955, when Brunswik died, Fisherian methods had overrun, conquered, and redefined every branch of experimental psychology (Gigerenzer, 1993).

Then the newly institutionalized tools evolved into new theories of mind. When Brunswik's vision of the mind as an intuitive statistician finally became a great success in experimental psychology, the mind's intuitive statistician was not of the Karl Pearson school, as Brunswik had imagined. Rather, the homunculus statistician used the new laboratory tools, such as analysis of variance. For instance, according to Harold Kelley's (1967) causal attribution theory, the mind attributes a cause to an effect in the same way as researchers have come to do—by calculating an intuitive version of analysis of variance (Gigerenzer, 1991). Brunswik had never been able to persuade his colleagues from experimental psychology that the mind would use the techniques of the competing discipline of correlational psychology.

The Price of Intellectual Integrity

Woodworth's bible had excommunicated Brunswik from experimental psychology, and the institutionalization of Fisher's methods as the sine qua non of scientific method set Brunswik's ideas

outside the realm of what was considered proper scientific method. Brunswik must have soon realized that the edifice he had erected had become, as Ken Hammond (1966b) expressed it succinctly, a significant landmark that "was virtually empty; there were visitors, it is true, but no one stayed" (p. v). Although Brunswik had chosen freely to leave Vienna for the United States, unlike the exiled Bühler, he found his ideas in exile. Unlike in Vienna, at Berkeley he seems not to have had a group of students who worked on his ideas, nor did his working atmosphere support the philosophical and interdisciplinary spirit that continued to enhance his writings. But there was no way back; the Vienna program and the Vienna Circle had been destroyed, and Brunswik himself had moved beyond multidimensional psychophysics. What is one to do if one has lost the old companions and failed to enlist new ones? The obvious easy choice would have been to conform to the new Zeitgeist, but the option of surrendering his ideas seems never to have occurred to Brunswik. It is easy to be true to one's ideas if everyone applauds—I admire Brunswik's intellectual integrity because, in his case, only very, very few applauded. Standing upright must have been difficult, lonely, and depressing.

Do the Ideas Matter?

American psychology would hardly remember Brunswik's ideas had not one of his students, Ken Hammond, kept his memory alive for over half a century. But is the memory of Egon Brunswik of more than historical interest? Are his ideas still exiled, and if so, does it matter?

Representative Sampling

Brunswik (1956b) sadly reported that his success in persuading fellow researchers to shift to representative sampling of stimuli was "very slow going and hard to maintain" (p. 39). He complained that his colleagues practiced "double standards" by being concerned with the sampling of subjects but not of stimulus objects. Representative sampling of stimuli is one aspect of the more general notion of representative design.

It would be an error to introduce representative sampling as a new dogma to replace current methodological dogmas. The point is to choose the appropriate sampling method for the problem under discussion. For instance, representative sampling of objects from a class is indispensable if one wants to make general statements about the degree of "achievement," or its flip side, the fallacies of perception and judgment concerning this class of objects. But if the purpose is testing competing models of cognitive strategies and flat maxima obscure the discriminability of strategies, then using selected stimuli that discriminate between the strategies may be the only choice (see Rieskamp & Hoffrage, 1999).

Is the idea of representative sampling of any relevance to present-day research? Imagine Brunswik browsing through recent textbooks on cognitive psychology and looking for what we have discovered about achievement in judgment—now more fashionably labeled *fallacies* and *cognitive illusions*. It would catch his eye that the stimuli used in the demonstrations of fallacies were typically selected rather than representative, among them, the five letters in Tversky and Kahneman's (1973) study from which the availability heuristic was concluded; the personality sketches in Kahneman and Tversky's (1973) engineer-lawyer study from which base-rate neglect was concluded; and the general-knowledge questions from which the overconfidence bias was concluded (Lichtenstein, Fischhoff, & Phillips, 1982). Brunswik would have objected that if one wants to measure achievement or demonstrate fallacies in a reference class of objects, one needs to take a representative (or random) sample of these objects. If not, one can "demonstrate" almost any level of performance by selecting those objects where performance is at its worst (or at its best). In fact, when one uses representative (rather than selected) samples in these three studies, performance greatly improves: The errors in estimating the frequency of letters largely disappear (Sedlmeier, Hertwig, & Gigerenzer, 1998); the estimated probabilities that a person is an engineer approach Bayes's rule (Gigerenzer, Hell, & Blank, 1988); and the overconfidence bias completely disappears (Gigerenzer, Hoffrage, & Kleinbölting, 1991; Juslin, Winman & Olsson, 2000). These celebrated cognitive illusions, attributed to the subjects, are in part due to the selected sampling done by the experimenters.

These examples illustrate that representative sampling of stimuli is still a blind spot in some areas of research. In survey research, it would be a mistake to present the odd views of a few selected citizens as public opinion; that the same applies to stimulus objects is still not commonly acknowledged. Unreflectively selected samples can produce apparently general phenomena that occupy us for years and then finally dissolve into an issue of mere sampling.

Natural Sampling

Imagine Brunswik looking at the studies on Bayesian reasoning, which emerged about ten years after his death. When he learned that people neglect base rates, he might have been surprised because his rats did not (Brunswik,1939c). His rats were not perfect, but they were sensitive to the difference of the base rates of reinforcement in the two sides of a T-maze, and to the ratio as well. Sensitized by the frequentist Reichenbach, Brunswik's eye would have caught an essential difference between his study and the base rate studies of the 1970s and 1980s: His rats learned the base rates from actual experienced frequencies, whereas the humans in almost all studies that reported base rate neglect could not; they were presented summary information in terms of probabilities or percentages. Rats would not understand probabilities, and humans have only recently in their evolution begun to struggle with this representation of uncertainty. Does representation matter? Christensen-Szalanski and Beach (1982) presented base rates in terms of actual frequencies, sequentially encountered, and reported that base rate neglect largely disappeared. This process of sampling instances from a population sequentially is known as *natural sampling*. Natural sampling is the everyday equivalent—for rats and humans alike—of the representative sampling done by scientific experimenters. When observed frequencies are based on natural sampling—that is, on raw (rather than normalized) counts of events made in an ecological (rather than experimental) setting—then one can show that Bayesian computations become simpler than with probabilities, and that people have more insight into Bayesian problems (Gigerenzer & Hoffrage, 1995).

Structure of Environments

A most important insight I gained from Brunswik's writings is the relevance of the structure of information in environments to the study of judgment. Brunswik tentatively proposed measuring environmental structure by ecological validities, and measuring these in turn by correlation coefficients. Brunswik, though, almost as much as Skinner, hesitated to look into the black box, and so he failed to see the important connection between the structure of environments and that of mediation. Adaptive mental strategies can exploit certain structures. For instance, if there is a match between the structure of the environment and that of a strategy, a simple heuristic that processes much less information than multiple regression can nevertheless make as many (or more) accurate inferences about its environment (Martignon & Hoffrage, 1999). Herbert Simon had emphasized the link between cognitive processes and environmental structure in his famous 1956 *Psychological Review* article on bounded rationality. However, in recent years, bounded rationality has been reduced to cognitive limitations, and the structure of environments has been largely forgotten as an indispensable part of understanding bounded rationality, sometimes even by Simon himself (e.g., 1987). The study of the structure of environments is still in its infancy.

Much of psychology after the cognitive revolution is about what is in our heads: Which logic does human reasoning embody? How many primary emotions should we distinguish? It is little concerned with what cognition, emotion, and behavior are for, and with how they relate to the structure of environments, both physical and social. Brunswik's focus on achievement, in contrast, is functional, focusing on the accuracy of perception and judgment. Accuracy is not the only goal; to be able to act quickly, to come in first, or to establish social relations of trust and cooperation also exemplifies achievement in a broader sense.

The structure of environments is essential for understanding cognition and behavior in terms of adaptation, because adaptations are relative to (past) environments. To flesh out the Darwinian aspect of Brunswikian psychology, one needs to distinguish between past and present environments, between ecological validities in past and in present environments, and between social environments composed of conspecifics (where cues are actually signals) and other environments (e.g., physical environments in which humans do not cooperate or bargain with their inhabitants). For instance, smooth skin in female humans may

have been a highly valid cue for reproductive capability during most of human evolution, signaling good health (Buss, 1987). In current environments with abundant medical technology, the ecological validity of smooth skin may have decreased to almost nil, but men's proximal mechanisms, cognitive and emotional, may still rely on such cues. A Darwinian psychology is a historical psychology, one that looks into the past to learn about the present (e.g., Cosmides & Tooby, 1992).

Brunswik repeatedly alluded to Darwin, and the notions of function, achievement, and environmental structure all relate to evolution by natural selection. Brunswik, however, never developed or carried these ideas any further. Neo-Brunswikians have done little to develop the Darwinian fragment, consistent with the prevailing anxiety about evolution in the American psychology establishment. Given that even Pope John Paul II finally announced in the *Quarterly Review of Biology* (1997) that evolution (of the body, not of the spirit) is a plausible hypothesis, more psychologists might find the courage to think about what we can learn from modern evolutionary theory—even if some of them still consider such thoughts politically incorrect.

Models of Vicarious Functioning

Schlick's Thursday-evening discussion groups seem to have had a lasting effect on Brunswik. The methodological objectivity of the Vienna Circle helped Brunswik to focus his work on the measurement of objective achievement rather than on cognitive processes ("mediation"). He hesitated to speak about the unobservable process of mediation and, even still in 1937, declared that psychology is a science of "what" rather than of "how." The question of how mediation works should be studied only insofar as it throws light upon the question of what an organism achieves. Only later did Brunswik (e.g., 1957) grant a place, though only a second place, to the study of cognitive processes.

Given his reluctance to open the black box, I am not sure how Brunswik would look at the process models of vicarious functions that were inspired by his ideas: multiple regression models, on the one hand (e.g., Hammond, Hursch, & Todd, 1964), and the theory of probabilistic mental models (PMM theory) and the fast and frugal lens model, on the other (Gigerenzer et al., 1991). When Brunswik coined the metaphor of the "intuitive statistician," he tentatively suggested that the process of vicarious functioning might be like multiple regression (Doherty & Kurz, 1996). Brunswik's measurement tool turned into a theory of cognitive processes. In the neo-Brunswikian revival, multiple regression became *the* model of vicarious functioning, and, unfortunately, it remains so. Ken Hammond, like Brunswik, has had second thoughts, but by and large, the tool has become part of the message. It structures our thinking about Brunswik.

Brunswik's reluctance to think about processes may explain why his examples for vicarious functioning vacillated back and forth between two different processes, substitution and combination. Some of his examples (e.g., Hull's habit family hierarchy and the psychoanalytic substitution mechanism in which one cause can manifest itself as various symptoms) referred to substitution without combination, others to the combination of cues. The fast and frugal lens model, based on PMM theory, assumes substitution without combination, emphasizing that judgments need to be made quickly and on the basis of limited knowledge (see Gigerenzer & Kurz, this volume). Here, Egon Brunswik meets Herbert Simon, creating models of bounded rationality in which simple cognitive heuristics exploit environmental structures.

A Love of History, Philosophy, and Methodology

Just as the human species has a history, so do our theories and methods. Not knowing where they come from can blind one to understanding why one propounds a particular theory or uses a specific method. Nevertheless, looking down at history is symptomatic of much of current psychology. Brunswik had written about the history of his field and had published in philosophical journals; possibly, it is just that background that helped him to see that there are differences between methodologies, and that one actually needs to make informed choices. Many psychologists do

not seem to make these choices; rather, they take on the methodological practice of their field and then defend it as if it were religious dogma. If one reads Brunswik, one finds a constant stream of thought about methodology, from preferring matching tasks over numerical response tasks in order to minimize the confounding of perception with judgment, to the larger program of representative design. In contrast, the enthusiasm with which some methods have been mechanically applied as general-purpose tools—factor analysis, multidimensional scaling, and analysis of variance, among others—springs from ignorance of history, philosophy, and the methodologies of other scientific disciplines. Methodology is an art, not the science of compulsive hand washing.

This is not to say that every psychologist must be a master of history, but history can protect one against confusing present-day methodological conventions with the sine qua non of scientific research.

The Search for Objectivity in the Twilight of Uncertainty

John Locke (1690/1959) remarked that "God . . . has afforded us only with the twilight of probability; suitable, I presume, to that state of mediocrity and probationership he has been pleased to place us in here" (vol. 2, p. 360). Bühler's psychology opened the door for Brunswik to the twilight of uncertainty, and the Vienna Circle inspired him to search for objective knowledge behind that door. What Brunswik found there: that we know. What he was looking for is more: not answers, but the right questions. From him, one can learn to rethink that which is taken for granted. I have.

Yet there is another, deeper message in the work of Egon Brunswik: the value of the struggle for intellectual integrity—daring to think ideas through, with all the consequences, and remaining true to them even if they are condemned to exile. Kant's final two words in his lovely essay on the Enlightenment capture the essence of this struggle: *sapere aude*, that is, have the courage to know.

45

Egon Brunswik before and after Emigration: A Study in the History of Science

Mitchell G. Ash

Introduction

In recent years, a wide-ranging body of literature has examined the career trajectories and intellectual development of the scientists who emigrated from Germany and Austria after 1933. The fascination with the impressive accomplishments and contributions of the most prominent of these emigrants endures for good reason. Recent research, however, has shown that various emigrants were able to carry on their work almost without interruption. Consequently, doubts have been raised about whether a causal relation exists between coerced emigration and scientific innovations after 1933 and 1938, respectively.[1] At first glance, Egon Brunswik's intellectual development appears to show uninterrupted continuity. This paper considers the extent to which this was actually the case, and the extent to which Brunswik's emigration was even coerced. To set the scene, I will begin by discussing certain aspects of Brunswik's work before his emigration from Austria.

Toward a Contextualization of Brunswik's Early Works

The situation in which Brunswik found himself as a young scientist at the Vienna Psychological Institute in the 1920s was defined first of all by the relationship between philosophy and psychology in contemporary German-speaking Europe. The establishment of experimental psychology as a viable natural science toward the end of the nineteenth century led to a far-reaching transformation of that relationship. Institutionally, the so-called new psychology remained a specialized subdomain of philosophy. Corresponding with the epistemological disposition of philosophy at that time, and encouraged by the appropriation of certain research techniques from sensory psychology, the initial research projects in this subdomain concentrated predominantly on psychophysical and sensory-psychological questions that were considered relevant to the problem of knowing. It was the philosopher Franz Brentano (1973) who presented a central concept that shaped Brunswik's work. This was the concept of intentionality, (that is, the perpetual "directedness" of consciousness toward a particular object). Brentano and his students construed consciousness generally as the product of the object-directed activity of a subject; this conception would later become known as *act psychology*. The classification and functional analysis of these directed activities, and of the objects correlated with or created by them, were the aims that Brentano articulated in *Psychology from an Empirical Standpoint* (1874).

In the first decade of the twentieth century, Karl Bühler, Egon Brunswik's teacher, extended this research program, in collaboration with the Würzburg School around Oswald Külpe, to the psychology of thought processes. Thus, Bühler construed thought just as Brentano's students construed what they called judgments of perception—as a directed process, which could itself be made the object of intentional scrutiny and analysis through systematic self-observation. In doing so, he drew upon the work of Brentano's student Edmund Husserl (1970), particularly the analysis of "meaning-giving acts" of consciousness in his *Logical Investigations* (Bühler, 1907). A few years later, in 1913, Bühler returned, albeit with different methods, to the original problematic of the Brentano school and became one of the first to determine measurable parameters for the perception of form and proportion. He traced this perception to an act of judgment, which he located between sensations and actual thought processes (Bühler, 1913). To this extent he remained true to Brentano's original project of classifying intentional acts.

Karl Bühler's turn toward developmental psychology, which followed shortly thereafter, made him a leading figure in the second stage of the history of psychology. The establishment of the Vienna Psychological Institute in 1922 was decisively supported by the school reform movement: Psychology, it was maintained, should be made an independent, biological science with its own practical applications.[2] Nonetheless, as will be shown, basic psychological research devoted to epistemological problems continued to play an important role in the work of the Vienna Institute, thanks to the work of Egon Brunswik and others.

Egon Brunswik—Early Life and Works

Egon Brunswik was born in Budapest in 1903, the son of Julius Brunswik von Korompa, a ministry official, and his wife Helene, née Wiser.[3] Brunswik abandoned the noble "von Korompa" in the First Republic, although in the 1930s he occasionally used it in visa applications. Official documents state that he came from an "Austrian civil servant and officer's family" of Roman Catholic confession. For secondary education, he was sent to the exclusive Theresianum in Vienna, so that he, like many children of the contemporary haute bourgeoisie, was on his own at a relatively early age. There, he is said to have learned the history of the Austrian-Hungarian Empire in both of its languages and to have identified discrepancies between the two versions. After 1918, he was sent to Sweden to recuperate following the food shortage in Vienna during World War I. After he received his secondary degree in 1921, he began postsecondary study at Vienna's technical college, where he passed the first state exam in 1923. He then transferred into the philosophy department at the university, where he studied philosophy, psychology, mathematics, and physics; in 1926, he passed the qualifying exam for teachers in the latter two subjects. Subsequently, he worked as a teaching assistant at the elite high school of Vienna's twenty-first district, and by 1927, he had already completed his doctorate. The motivation behind the change in his course of study is unfortunately not revealed in any of the available historical sources. But this turn from

the natural sciences toward philosophy indicates a certain affinity in Brunswik's trajectory with that of Bühler, who was initially a medical student, as well as with the careers of many of the founders of logical empiricism, such as Hans Reichenbach.

In April 1927, Brunswik declared his ambition to become a scientist by applying for a part-time assistant's position at the Vienna Psychological Institute. In 1929, he was named a full-time assistant. From February 1931 until August 1932, he served as visiting docent at the university in Ankara, Turkey, helping to establish the psychology department and organize the curriculum for prospective teachers. In 1933 his application for habilitation was unanimously accepted by the philosophy faculty of the University of Vienna. The faculty explicitly emphasized the relevance of his research on the effects of age on the so-called perceptual constancies to developmental and school psychology. Thus, in the tradition of the Vienna Psychological Institute, Brunswik was manifestly successful at combining basic research in general psychology with pedagogically relevant basic research in developmental psychology. In the following discussion, however, the central focus will be on the former aspect of his work, since this provides a foundation for the analysis of continuity and change after his emigration.[4]

Brunswik's early work at the Vienna Psychological Institute was characterized by the attempt to combine philosophy of science and epistemology with empirical psychological research. On the theoretical level, Brunswik realized this program first by criticizing the primary rival of the Bühler school at the time, the so-called Berlin School of Gestalt psychology. In his empirical research, he developed implications of his critique of Gestalt psychology while simultaneously pursuing the project associated with his teacher and Franz Brentano, the functional analysis of the object-directedness of perception.

In one of his first publications, Brunswik presented a careful historical exposition of the Gestalt concept, from the Greeks and Kant up to the present. As might be expected, he underscored the position of his teacher as "the actual founder of the psychophysics of gestalt" (Brunswik, 1929, p. 92f). Beyond advocating his teacher's priority, Brunswik also offered conceptual analysis. He differentiated Gestalten from forms, concepts, and schemata and argued that this made it possible to elucidate the "logical singularity" of structural laws, as opposed to normative or causal laws (Brunswik, 1929 pp. 95–96, 106). More important than these philosophical issues, however, were the following studies, in which Brunswik elaborated the theoretical and empirical dimensions of the theory of perception sketched by Karl Bühler.

Bühler's positive response to the challenge of Gestalt theory was a biologically oriented version of Brentano's intentional model of consciousness, which already harbored the kernel of his theory of language. Bühler defined sensations as signs or cues of perceptual objects and thus gave them a function analogous to that of the signal concept in biology. In Bühler's conception, words function in the same manner in language. Consequently, there is no one-to-one relation between things and their representations or signs. Both in perception and in language, the goal-directed activity of an organism must be taken into account before meanings can be construed. According to Bühler, a doctrine of signification such as this is better suited to anchor the general category of meaning (Sinn) in psychological research and theory than the contention perpetually repeated by the Berlin school that meaning is simply given in (i.e., intrinsic in) experience. (Bühler, 1927/1978, pp. 119, 124ff.)

In 1933, Brunswik presented a series of studies from the Vienna Psychological Institute intended to provide support for his own version of this conception of perceptual processes. Besides Bühler's doctrine of signification mentioned above, this new approach also built on the thesis, advanced by Fritz Heider in 1926 and 1930, that organisms and objects are separated by a medium by means of which perception is, so to speak, accomplished. According to Heider, this medium has both subjective and objective sides. The signals transmitted to the organism from the thing or object belong to the objective environment, whereas their reception and processing by the sensory and cognitive apparatus belong to the subjective environment (Heider, 1926, 1930). Understood in this manner, sense data become cues by means of which organisms decode the qualities of distal objects, such as color, brightness, and size. Brunswik would later name his own reworking of this idea the "lens model" because, among other things, it describes how peripheral sensors collect such cues and direct them

toward a central point, where the organism mobilizes them so as to effect a "central reaction" (Brunswik, 1933, p. 382; 1934b).

Brunswik formulated the epistemological foundation for all this in his differentiation between "intentional" and "intended" objects. This applied not only to the world of things but also to sensory properties such as color, size, and remoteness. In this view, perceiving subjects are perpetually trying to bring "intentional" and "intended" objects into accord with one another but are rarely entirely successful in doing so. On a general level, this point is exemplified by the long-familiar perceptual constancies. Expressed positively, within certain limits we can discern the size of what Ewald Hering (1964) called the "things of sight" (Sehdinge) independently of their distance from us, their true form despite changes of perspective, and their actual brightness despite changes in illumination. However, the subjectively perceived size, color, illumination, and form of an object correspond with objectively measured properties only within certain parameters. Since the discovery of this set of facts before the turn of the century, the research problem had been to quantify the discrepancy between perceived and "objectively" measurable properties under various conditions.

Brunswik claimed that the problem could be solved by constructing hypothetical "intermediate objects" (Zwischengegenstände) by means of a variation on already-standardized psychophysical scales. Thus, the perception that corresponded with "objective values" was placed at one pole or end point of the scale; in the case of form constancy, this would be the frontal, parallel plane. The experimental task became the measurement of the amount of variation from this end point in subjects' recorded perceptions or perceptual judgments. The respective degrees of precision of these reactions became the yardstick for the achievement of the organism, or, as Brunswik later put it, for the "functional validity" of an act. The core idea that subjects achieve only a relative approximation of the objects they intend would eventually lead to a probabilistic theory of perception, which today is recognized as an important precursor to contemporary, computationally oriented models.[5]

Building on this conception of perception, students at the Vienna Institute produced research concerning the influence of attitude and age on the recognition of perceptual objects. In these, as in the earlier works of other researchers on this subject, individuals' judgments about seen objects under varied conditions constituted the primary set of data. The American Beverly Holaday (1933), for example, used cubes viewed at an angle to test the effects of psychical, somatic, and external conditions on size constancy. Kurt Eissler (1933) did the same with respect to form constancy. Sylvia Klimpfinger's (1933) claim to have determined age-graded developmental curves for both size and form constancy also drew particular attention.

Brunswik, however, emphasized the importance of these results as corroboration of his theoretical project. The subjects in all these experiments, for example, tended, without being instructed to do so, to focus on the intentional, "objective" object. But even when they were explicitly instructed to do so, their assessment of the object's properties did not match but only approached the "objective" values. On the other hand, when subjects were instructed to focus on the "proximal" or "intermediate" object, they felt "pulled" in the opposite direction, that is, toward the "objective" object (Brunswik, 1933 pp. 409–410.) Thus, perception appeared to proceed as a compromise between the two poles of intentionality.

Brunswik had transformed the role of the concept of intentionality. While Bühler had claimed in his earlier works on the psychology of thought processes that the directedness of acts of consciousness was empirically verifiable on the basis of controlled self-observation, for Brunswik, this directedness served simply as one component of a model capable of explaining deviations between two series of measurements. This is the empirical content of his later statement that psychology constitutes a "science of objective relations." Brunswik, however, described this new conception of intentionality in terms of Bühler's theory as a purposive relation (Zweckrelation). Thus, by means of the intended, proximal object the organism searches out, so to speak, the distal, intentional, objective object, albeit rarely entirely successfully. At the end of the programmatic essay with which he introduced these contributions, Brunswik expressed the hope that the results might lead from individual perception and developmental psychology to a general typology of personality, even to a general theory of the state

(Brunswik, 1933, p. 418). But he did not say how such an ambitious agenda might be achieved.

Preliminary Remarks on the Question of Continuity

In order to assess the continuity of Brunswik's thought and research after his emigration, four factors should be kept in mind:

1. The first factor is theoretical and methodological in nature and also touches upon the question of Brunswik's relation to the Vienna Circle. In 1929, the journal *Erkenntnis* published Rudolf Carnap's famous article, "Psychology in Physical Language" (Carnap, 1929/1959, p. 181).[6] The work unleashed a discussion that occupied the Vienna Circle for years concerning the possibilities and limits of a "unified science" *(Einheitswissenschaft)* based on physical language. Carnap argued that a rational theory of science must aim to articulate all experience—including the psychical experiences of people other than ourselves—in physical sentences (i.e., in intersubjectively verifiable protocol-sentences, the objects of which are physical states of affairs). He pointed up the radical difference between his position and that of current European psychological thought by writing that from the epistemological standpoint, his views most closely corresponded with the approach of the American behaviorists (Carnap, 1929/1959, p. 181).

An affinity between Brunswik's precepts and Carnap's "physicalism" seems indisputable and is frequently pointed out. To examine this assumption, it is important to consider what Brunswik meant by calling his own approach "behavioristic." He emphasized in the introduction quoted above that in the empirical investigations of his students, measurements were compared with measurements, while subjects' introspective accounts of their own judgments were disregarded. Since only a "minimum of self-observation" was allowed, such methods satisfied "behavioristic" criteria of precision in psychology (Brunswik, 1933, pp. 409–410, 418). Thus, Brunswik let it be known, at least implicitly, that he was informed about the physicalism discussion in the Vienna Circle. At the time, however, such considerations had not yet moved to the forefront of his work.

2. More important was the rivalry with Gestalt theory—and in particular, the Gestalt theorist

Kurt Koffka, who in his response to Brunswik articulated a challenge to him that would become important for his work after his emigration. Certain similarities between Brunswik's views and those of Gestalt theory are unmistakable. Both approaches present perception as an achievement of the organism. They also agree that the objects of perception are not equivalent to the objects and relations of the external world. Although Brunswik's commitment to methodological "behaviorism" is clearly different from the phenomenological standpoint of Gestalt theory, his actual research methods in the works just discussed differed little from those of his rivals. Thus, it is not surprising that Kurt Koffka's reply in his *Principles of Gestalt Psychology* (1935) was limited in the main to empirical and methodological objections and addressed questions of principle only indirectly (pp. 238–240; Frank, 1928, pp. 102–106).

One of Koffka's criticisms was more fundamental, however; he argued that Brunswik's subjects had been asked to assess only one dimension—size, form, brightness, or distance—at a time and thus paid no heed to possible correlations among them, although it is very well known that size and distance constancy, for example, are highly correlated. Koffka argued that such results were best explained by the hypothesis that the perception of objects located otherwise than in a frontal, parallel position required "special forces," which for their part stood in perpetual rivalry with opposed "forces." Accordingly, the configuration ultimately perceived would result from a balancing of this constellation of forces within the perceptual field (Koffka, 1935, p. 231). Brunswik's later attempt to account for such dimensions of complexity in the process of perception led to the genesis of his concept of "representative design."

3. David Leary (1987) saw in Brunswik's early works the seeds of his later "probabilistic functionalism." Above all, the assertion that objects of perception are only approximately achieved was for Leary a reference to the debate over probability in the philosophical interpretation of theoretical physics. (Leary, 1987, p. 120) However, though Brunswik spoke as early as 1934 of cues being received by the organism as the most probable representations of the properties of the objective world, he did not consistently use probabilistic vocabulary. This he would do for the first time in the United States, after employing measurements of correlation in place of the algebraic

comparisons he had used in Vienna (see below). In any case, these early studies by Brunswik used no probabilistic methods of measurement but an improved version of the long-standing, standard methodology of psychophysics.

4. Finally, in order to assess the status of this phase of Brunswik's trajectory within the history of science, it is appropriate to examine the relation of his "psychology of the object" to the Brentano school in general, and to Alexius Meinong's doctrine of the object in particular. The latter was concerned with what Barry Smith called "formal ontology," that is, logical-ontological analysis of actual and potential objects (Smith, 1982, 1994). Analyses of this kind are essentially unconstrained by empirical-psychological questions of whether and how we might actually perceive such objects. In his early works, Brunswik addressed himself to these questions of principle only very tentatively. In the introduction to the empirical work of his students quoted above, for example, he remained on the level of functional psychological analysis, although he also claimed that the results of this empirical research had significance for epistemology. He grasped the relation between "intentional" and "intended" objects not under the rubric "truth" or "illusion," but purely functionally in a biological sense. By *functional*, he meant, on the one hand, the orientation of the organism in its environment, but he also meant the mode of operation of an organic apparatus— here, the perceptual apparatus—over time, independent of its relation to the external world.

Nevertheless, Brunswik, like Brentano's students and the "Berliner" Gestalt theorists, but in his own particular manner, attempted to maintain the conceptual integration of empirical psychology and epistemologically oriented philosophy. He did this also after his emigration to California, but in a rather different way. First, however, we must consider how and why Brunswik came to the United States.

From Vienna to Berkeley

Although Brunswik is perennially and justifiably counted among the scientists who emigrated from Germany and Austria in 1933 and 1938, his biography does not fit, without some qualification, the picture of the émigré scientist as the victim of political and racial persecution. He was not a

Jew, nor was he compelled by Hitler's invasion to leave Austria. Although he had been engaged to a Jew, Else Frenkel, since the early 1930s, in Austria this was not a sufficiently compelling reason to emigrate before 1938. The mix of push-and-pull factors in Brunswik's story places it somewhere between a "normal" move for the sake of enhanced career opportunities and a forced migration.

First, let us consider the push factors. It is not an exaggeration to say that even for peripheral members of the Vienna Circle, the general political atmosphere had become less accommodating after an authoritarian regime took power in Austria in 1934. Even for those among them who, like Brunswik, had not expressed themselves politically in public and were therefore in no immediate jeopardy, the potential risks of association with Otto Neurath, a reputed Marxist, or with Marie Jahoda and Paul Lazarsfeld, who were openly connected with the Social Democrats, could not be ignored. Even in the absence of other compelling reasons, such risks were sufficient motivation for many Viennese academics to search out better work opportunities elsewhere. Adding to this was the economic crisis, which brought with it increased uncertainty for many people, but especially for younger scientists. Nevertheless—or perhaps precisely because economic uncertainty prevailed everywhere—most scholars and scientists stayed as long as possible in Vienna, the comforting familiarity of which certainly played a role as well. Thus, to explain Brunswik's decision to emigrate even before the Nazi invasion in 1938 requires considering what was pulling at him to go.

The pull factor was named Edward Chace Tolman. During the academic year 1933–1934, the American neobehaviorist from Berkeley spent a few months in Vienna, where he met Brunswik and began an intensive collaboration with him. Tolman was just as well suited to such a collaboration as Brunswik. Many years before, he had begun to develop a variant of behaviorism that not only admitted a cognitive dimension but also incorporated it as an irreducible, independent value. In his main work, *Purposive Behavior in Animals and Men* (1932), he attempted to explain how animals and humans are able to maintain a flexible harmony between their perceptions and their actions without reducing behavior generally to a simple stimulus-response schema or to a chain of conditioned reflexes. Thus, he drew attention to the biological fact that organisms cannot react to all of the stimuli they are able to distinguish, and he attempted to solve the problem of which stimuli actually induce behavior by postulating "intervening variables" in the organism. In this, he transcended the level of perception altogether and even went so far as to speak of rats positing "hypotheses" about the direction to be taken in a maze in order to procure a piece of food. Even before his arrival in Vienna he had made clear that he saw the behavior of white rats and their orientation in laboratory environments as a complex, goal-oriented process, just as Brunswik understood human perception to be.

The collaboration that developed during Tolman's visit resulted in a jointly published essay, "The Organism and the Causal Texture of the Environment" (Tolman & Brunswik, 1935, pp. 43–47). The language of this work demonstrates how both researchers attempted to integrate their respective theoretical vocabularies. They fundamentally agreed that the stimuli with which organisms are confronted are "local representatives" of the objective environment. Therefore, both scientists understood stimuli as "cues" or "signs" (in Tolman's words, "sign-gestalten") that are used by the organism to develop "hypotheses" concerning the contents of its environment that it needs to grasp at a given time. Behavior is thus conceived of entirely in Karl Bühler's sense, as a cognitively mediated, purposive relation. The objects of any given surrounding are, so to speak, "behaved to" and become in turn means to procure other objects. As a particularly suggestive example of what they meant, Tolman and Brunswik evoked the behavior of a child who attempts to "read" from its mother's face what needs to be done and how in order to get a piece of chocolate from her (Tolman & Brunswik, 1935, pp. 50ff). They thus implied a feedback model of behavior, which presupposed the modifiability of cues. This was something entirely distinct from a trial-and-error theory of learning.

Tolman and Brunswik solved the problem of the theoretical integration of behavior and perception by means of a distinction, introduced by Tolman, between two kinds of cues: discriminanda (sensory cues) and manipulanda (i.e., manipulable, serviceable cues). They conceived of both kinds of cues functionally as means to the achievement of a goal. Tolman therefore named them "utilitanda." With an implicit nod to the "unity of science," they concluded their piece with an expression of hope for the formation of an integrated theory applicable to "all of the problems of psychology—not just those of visual perception and learning" (Tolman & Brunswik, 1935, pp. 52, 53, 73).

Tolman articulated the dream that he had evidently conceived during his collaboration with Brunswik in Vienna much later, in a letter to the vice president of the University of California, Monroe Deutsch, on December 2, 1937: "Brunswik sees psychology in general as I do (though with complete originality and independence) and I had looked upon this as the chance of a lifetime (waning, no doubt, in my case—but I hope not too far gone yet!) to build up an experimental and theoretical movement of great importance and of some renown."[7]

This dream could hardly be realized without the mobilization of institutional recourses. A first step in this direction was clearly meant to be accomplished by the Rockefeller stipend that Tolman obtained for Brunswik for the academic year 1935–1936. In principle, such stipends were intended for visits of limited duration, after which the recipient was to return home. But a prospect for Brunswik's longer term appointment already existed when he arrived, because the chair of George Stratton, the most senior psychologist at Berkeley, had just been vacated by his retirement. Stratton was a specialist in the experimental psychology of perception. His work on human visual capacities, including the observation of objects with one or two eyes under otherwise identical conditions, had brought him worldwide acclaim. Thus, as a potential successor in precisely the same field of research, Brunswik had arrived at the right place at the right time; the Rockefeller stipend financed a trial year from the beginning. To be sure, Brunswik was not the only candidate. On June 14, 1935, Kurt Koffka, who had taught at Smith College in Massachusetts since 1927, was recommended as Stratton's successor.[8]

During this time the Rockefeller Foundation gave many stipends to aid emigrants from Nazi Germany. One could classify Brunswik's stipend among them, but Brunswik himself clearly did not. When, at the end of his visit, an assistant professorship was offered to him on a trial basis, Brunswik chose to teach at Berkeley only during the second semester of academic year 1936–1937, in order to avoid jeopardizing his position in Vienna. In November 1936, he postponed his departure yet again because he had not obtained permission to leave Vienna.[9] To Robert Sproul, the president of the University of California, he wrote with remarkable openness: "I would not have hesitated to accept the position immediately in case it would have been a permanent one."[10] In his personal file in Vienna it is stated that he refused "because he was not attracted at this time by the limited duration of the position or the concentration of his teaching duties on the history of psychology."[11]

Shortly afterward, on February 20, 1937, the philosophy faculty of the University of Vienna formally applied, by a vote of fifty-two in favor with one abstention (probably Bühler's), to name Brunswik an associate professor. This promotion came uncommonly early; Brunswik had taught in Vienna only two of the six years normally expected after habilitation. The actual motivation behind this application, which Karl Bühler clearly initiated, shines through at the end of the text: "Brunswik is already a highly esteemed psychologist for whom his circle of colleagues has high hopes. . . . Should he receive our recognition, the prospect exists of keeping him in Europe and indeed within the German-speaking domain."[12]

The same document reports that as early as December 1933—one year before the Austrian fascists' assumption of power—Brunswik had belonged to their leading political formation, the Fatherland Front. This speaks against Brunswik's classification as a politically motivated emigrant. One might interpret this as a precautionary measure and see his political stance as essentially liberal; as far as I know, however, no evidence has appeared to corroborate this assessment.

Already during his first visit to Berkeley, Brunswik had generated controversy. Warner Brown, the chair of the psychology department at the time, said in a meeting with Deutsch in January 1936 that he saw a chance here to acquire a highly talented young representative of a "European perspective" with which American psychology students should be made more familiar.[13] The physicist Victor Lenzen and the legal scholar Max Radin corroborated this assessment in April, 1936.[14] Each writer praised that aspect of Brunswik that lent itself most readily to his own disciplinary standpoint. While the natural scientist Lenzen emphasized that Brunswik had founded a new point of view in psychology that applied the concepts of physics with more legitimacy than all previous approaches, Brown spoke of Brunswik's ability to present a perspective proper to the humanistic disciplines.

One reason for this debate was the economic crisis, which had effectively ended new appointments in Berkeley except in extraordinarily well justified cases. A further complicating factor was skepticism about the actual significance and potential of Brunswik as a scientist. This skepticism was reinforced by a statistical review of Brunswik's teaching in November 1937, which maintained that little need existed for what Brunswik could offer as a teacher, since his two courses had enrolled only twenty-one students: "One might easily conclude that Doctor Brunswik is not contributing a great deal toward meeting the demands for instruction in psychology and that his absence would hardly be felt."[15] Academic politics may also have contributed to this severe assessment. In March 1936, an interdisciplinary committee assembled to appoint Stratton's successor had questioned the necessity of replacing him with a representative of general psychology and instead favored hiring a developmental psychologist. Also, Warner Brown had to admit later that Brunswik's proficiency in English was less than perfect.[16]

Tolman had to intervene personally in order to make things come out as he wanted. In the letter of December 2, 1937, quoted above, he articulated his reasons for his support of Brunswik and went so far as to claim that it would be "not far short of a crime" to let him go. Responding to the criticisms of Brunswik's teaching and English proficiency, he wrote that students had told him that Brunswik's courses were the best they had ever had. What Brunswik had already achieved in rendering his work accessible to an American audience was, Tolman argued, astounding: "He had never seen a rat before he came here on his previous visit, and he has already gone ahead and done outstanding new experiments. And, in general, the ability with which he has caught on to the American scene is extraordinary. In every sense of the word he is a gentleman. This paragraph sounds too strong to be true, but just the same it is my honest and considered judgment. He is truly a top-notcher."[17]

At the conclusion of this exceptional intervention, Tolman emphasized once again his personal interest in Brunswik and stated that he would have to take a decision against Brunswik as a criticism of his own work. Shortly thereafter, Brunswik was named assistant professor with a salary of $2,700. He was also given the prospect, albeit nonbinding, of a quick promotion to associate professor and the transformation of his one-year appointment to one of lifetime tenure.

This story had a sequel that was characteristic not only of the problems emigration imposed on women but also of the status of women in science in the United States at the time. As stated above, Brunswik had already been engaged for years to Else Frenkel. In an interview with Monroe Deutsch and also later in a letter, he called her his wife so that a position might be sought for her without visa problems.[18] Although there was initially no prospect of any such position, she persisted, and as a result the university administration lobbied the American consulate in Vienna and others to secure a quota visa for her and her parents. The couple were married shortly after her arrival in New York.[19] In Berkeley, Else Frenkel-Brunswik, as she would call herself from then on, found employment in 1939 as a research associate at the Institute for Child Welfare at the university. Initially, the position was supported from private funds, while she was listed as an unsalaried assistant at the university; later she was granted a two-thirds salary.[20] Due to the very strict rules against nepotism in American universities at the time, she could not teach at all in the psychology department at first, and she did so later only in an unpaid capacity.[21]

Continuity and Transformation in the United States

Thanks to his favorable institutional situation, Brunswik's subsequent scientific development in the United States progressed with greater continuity than that of many other emigrant scientists. He continued his theoretical and empirical work on perception in accordance with his Viennese research program and progressed with Tolman according to plan on the new projects they had developed in Vienna. However, certain changes occurred that reveal the influence of the American environment in which he found himself. Five of these changes are briefly considered here: an avenue of research that Brunswik discontinued; his brief entrance into animal psychology; his continuation of research on the psychology of perception; the continuation of his empirical critique of Gestalt psychology; and finally, his work on the theoretical foundations of psychology.

1. The most striking of the discontinuities in Brunswik's work after his emigration is the complete disappearance of developmental topics from his research on perception, coupled with his turn toward general psychology. This is probably explained most readily by the change in his institutional situation. Whereas at the Vienna Psychological Institute no fundamental separation between developmental and general psychology had existed, in Berkeley the general psychologists stuck to themselves. Developmental psychology was practiced at the Institute for Child Welfare, while issues of educational psychology were studied at the department of education.

2. The most obvious, but perhaps least considered, transformation in Brunswik's research was his turn toward animal psychology. In studies undertaken immediately on his arrival, which Tolman himself praised in the above-quoted letter as "outstanding new experiments," the influence of the collaboration that Brunswik and the neobehaviorist began in Vienna becomes clear (Brunswik, 1939c). The predominant procedure of the animal laboratory at the time was the maze experiment, in which only affirmative or negative responses were elicited from the animal. In conscious opposition to this, Brunswik attempted to account for the fact that in real life even the so-called lower animals, like the white rats used in Berkeley as elsewhere, tended only to approximate their objectives. Thus, he varied the structure of the common T-maze experiment so as to distribute the probability of reward for a certain behavior (i.e., the choice of one or the other of the directions of the T) from 100/0 to 75/25, 67/33, 50/50, and 0/100. The rats chose correctly most often when the probability was 67/33, or 2 to 1. This was the first step toward the thesis that Brunswik only later would call "probabilistic functionalism." Here, to be sure, he still sought "nomological" rather than probabilistic laws.

3. Brunswik's empirical work in the area of perceptual psychology progressed largely along the lines laid out in *Wahrnehmung und Gegenstandswelt*, although it exhibited early a tendency to move away from the laboratory and toward "representative design." An initial demonstration of this tendency, which reads like a trial run, is a monograph published in 1944 on "distal focusing" in perception (Brunswik, 1944). It drew largely on observations and data collected from two subjects. A doctoral candidate, Johanna Goldsmith, was asked during the course of her daily activities to stop and sketch the linear dimensions of the surfaces that were presented most readily to her field of vision, first "normally" and then "from perspective." Another doctoral candidate, Herbert Bauer, served as both control observer and the experimenter; he made the actual measurements. It turned out that the first series of sketches more closely approximated the "objective" values than the second. With respect to the Vienna experiments discussed above, what was new about this method of measurement was the use of correlation coefficients in place of the subtractive difference or a quotient as the expression of comparison. This demonstrates Brunswik's adaptation to the style of verification then gaining currency in the United States.

4. Brunswik carried forward the empirical critique of Gestalt theory that he began in Vienna in a work published in 1953 with Joe Kamiya, examining the Gestalt law of proximity (Brunswik and Kamiya, 1953). The law, postulated in 1923 by Max Wertheimer, stated in brief that similarly shaped figures or other objects that stand in proximity to one another will be spontaneously perceived as belonging together as a single entity. True to the criterion of "ecological validity" that Brunswik had in the meantime posited, the authors examined the question of the extent to which the proximity of two parallel lines depicted in magazine photos could be taken as a cue that they represented the borders of a single object. Their finding was unequivocal: The closer the lines were to one another, the greater the probability of the above assessment. They took this as an indication of the value of their methodology as well as the verisimilitude of the chosen stimulus object, and also as evidence that organisms do not simply immediately perceive such properties but can also learn them.

5. In Brunswik's work on the theoretical foundations of psychology, the influence of the new environment is noticeable in a different way. Ironically, he expanded and deepened his connection to the Vienna Circle only after his emigration.

This is not the place for a detailed account of the formation of this network. Its result for Brunswik, however, is impressively evident to the reader of *The Conceptual Framework of Psychology* (Brunswik, 1952). In this work, Brunswik tried to resolve a question that is still of the utmost significance: How can psychology's status as a science be explained without doing injustice to the heterogeneity of its subject matter or sacrificing its independence as a discipline? Brunswik (1952) construed the issue as a "problem of objectivity" (p. 1). He saw its solution in a fundamental turn away from the emphasis on intuitive clarity proper to rationalism, or on the supposed self-evidence of immediate perception assumed in Brentano's doctrine of intentionality, as guarantors of scientific rigor, and from the corresponding methodological privileging of self-observation, "to rigor in the sense of inter- and intrasubjective consistency, univocality and coherence as stressed by the empirical sciences" (Brunswik, 1952, p. 12). These are all normative criteria for the "unity of science" proposed by the Vienna Circle.

In this manner, Brunswik also hoped to advance the effort to overcome epistemological and metaphysical dualism. Along with other schools of thought, Gestalt psychology had already made an essential contribution to this process by giving the daily "language of things" a central role in the inventory of immediate experience. The parallel development of positivism from the sensationism of Ernst Mach through the logical atomism of Bertrand Russell to the physicalism of Carnap and Otto Neurath had also led to the reintroduction of a "language of things," this time in the analysis of statements about experience. In both cases, however, the risk of monistic reductionism loomed. According to Brunswik (1952), this could be avoided only by replacing metaphysical dualism with "a simple duality or distinction, within one and the same physicalistically conceived universe of discourse, between organism and environment, or between stimulus and response" (p. 7). Thus, methodological behaviorism, which Brunswik had already professed in Vienna, but which had played only a subsidiary role there, now became the foundation of his theory of science.

In this manner, Brunswik made operationism, which had already been introduced as the symbolic underpinning of all kinds of quantitative methods in psychology and the social sciences at the time, into the connecting link not only for his own discipline but also for the unity of science generally. In accordance with this approach, he established a bridge from experimental cognitive psychology to the test methodology current at the time in personality diagnostics by construing the test as one mode of observation among many and advocating that it be applied to a representative selection of situations. Accordingly, the number of subjects tested would be less important than the number of situations (or experiences), as well as the "maximum reliability coefficients within or between individuals facing a common geographic situation or situational element" (Brunswik, 1952, p. 11).

Thus, Brunswik supported American logical empiricists in their conviction that the dream of a unity of science was realizable, while criticizing Carnap's physicalism. Likewise, although he implicitly criticized the prevailing American style of quantification, which focused on individual differences among subjects rather than on differences among experiences in a single subject, psychologists could cite him as emblematic of the alliance of psychology and logical empiricism and thus as a sign of scientific respectability (Smith, 1986). It was hardly a long stretch, however, from this method-centered grounding of psychology as a science to a model of man as a "calculating-cognizer," that is, as an organism whose strategies of environmental orientation bear an amazing resemblance to precisely those methods of calculating statistical significance by which psychologists certified, and continue to certify, the reliability of their observations (Gigerenzer, 1992).

Brunswik's Legacy

Among the diverse trajectories of Karl Bühler's younger students in the United States, those of Egon Brunswik and Paul Lazarsfeld mark polar extremes. Lazarsfeld's change of discipline from social psychology to sociology became the springboard to a successful career; yet, in many respects, he retained the research inclinations and style of thought of his time in Vienna, purged, to be sure, of their original political motivations (Lazarsfeld, 1969; Neurath, 1988). In comparison, Brunswik's scientific work in America exhibits remarkable continuity. Despite the different disciplinary orientation of psychology in the United States, Brunswik remained true to the project he had set himself in Vienna—to integrate empirical psychology and epistemologically oriented philosophy. However, as we have seen, this does not mean that he stubbornly or rigidly continued his early work; rather, in important ways, he reoriented toward, and responded to feedback from, his new environment.

It has been pointed out many times that Brunswik had only four doctoral students at Berkeley. It is questionable, however, whether this should serve as the sole measure of his influence. As David Leary (1987) contended: "During this time Brunswik was widely acknowledged to be, in essence, the department's intellectual conscience. His deep scholarship and meticulous research provided an exacting model of intellectual and methodological integrity for several generations of students and faculty" (p. 117). Evidence of an indirect impact of this kind on students who did not actually complete their doctoral research under Brunswik's direction has been pointed out in the case of Donald Campbell. Nevertheless, or perhaps for precisely this reason, it must be kept in mind that Brunswik remained marginalized in his own department, for he could not provide easily completed research topics to doctoral candidates, nor did he develop workable models of practical applications of his approach outside the academic setting.

It is here that a tension between the claims articulated in the concept of "representative design" and the realities of university teaching finally makes itself felt. As Roger Barker (1968) and others after him have shown, an ecologically oriented concept of experimental design is altogether practicable, but only on the condition that one pursues field rather than laboratory research. Measured against the dissertation factories of the neobehaviorists at Yale and Iowa at the time, Brunswik's influence must seem inconsequential, but in comparison with the Gestalt psychologists, who had few if any doctoral students, he appears more significant.

Edward Tolman's wish that he and Brunswik might bring to life a new movement in general psychology went unfulfilled. But during the reinvigoration of research into cognition in the 1950s, Brunswik was present at many important symposia as a speaker and participant in panel discussions (see, for example, Brunswik, 1957). One

might even argue that through his theoretical and methodological work, he showed the advocates of this new cognitive approach that it was possible to advocate the methodological operationism that had made behaviorism respectable and also retain cognition as an object of research. In the work of Norbert Bischof and Klaus Holzkamp, there was even a certain reimportation of Brunswik's ideas to Europe (see, for example, Holzkamp, 1981).

Egon Brunswik's persistent commitment to the theoretical and research programs he had already initiated in Vienna was and remains admirable. Judged against the criteria proposed in his own approach, however, this behavior, ironically, does not appear to be entirely functional. While he stayed true to himself, the whole environment around him changed. Thus, Brunswik's intellectual development, like that of so many other émigré scientists of that time, conveys a mixed portrait of tragedy and genius.

NOTES

A longer version of this chapter was originally published as "Egon Brunswik vor und nach der Emigration— wissenschaftshistorische Aspekte." In: Kurt R. Fischer & Friedrich Stadler (Eds.), "Wahrnehmung und Gegenstandswelt": Zum Lebenswerk von Egon Brunswik. Vienna, New York: Springer, 1997. pp. 49–78. Thanks to Springer Verlag for permission to reprint. Translated from the German by Bo Earle and revised by the author.

1. On this point see, for example, Deichmann (1996) and Fischer (1991).

2. Concerning the founding and history of the Vienna Psychological Institute, see Ash (1987) and Benetka (1990).

3. Unless otherwise stated, the following information comes from Egon Brunswik's personal file in the Universitätsarchiv of the University of Vienna [UAUW], 1 Phil PA-249; as well as Tolman (1956; reprinted in Hammond, 1996b).

4. On the significance of topics in developmental psychology for Brunswik's work at the Vienna Institute, see Benetka (1997).

5. On this point, see Leary (1987, especially pp. 119, 121).

6. For a thorough analysis of the transition to physicalism, see Heidelberger (1985).

7. Edward Tolman to Monroe Deutsch, December 2, 1937. Archive of the University of California, Berke-

ley, President's Files. Where not otherwise cited, quotes in the following come from letters in this archive.

8. Warner Brown to Monroe Deutsch, June 14, 1935.

9. Monroe Deutsch, Memorandum to the president re: interview with Egon Brunswik, April 27, 1936.

10. Brunswik to Robert G. Sproul, July 16, 1936.

11. Commission report (of the philosophy faculty) concerning the recommendation to confer the title of associate professor on private docent Dr. Egon Brunswik, 2/20/37: Brunswik's personal file (cited in note 3).

12. Ibid., p. 4. Bühler's leading role in this process is also revealed by the fact that he did not hesitate to sign the names of all but one of the committee members himself.

13. Monroe Deutsch, Memorandum to the president re: Interview with Warner Brown, January 5, 1936.

14. Victor Lenzen to Deutsch, April 18, 1936; Max Radin to Deutsch, April 11, 1936.

15. W. C. Pomeroy to Deutsch, November 27, 1937.

16. Charles B. Lipman to Robert G. Sproul, March 17, 1936; Warner Brown to Deutsch, November 3, 1937.

17. Edward Tolman to Monroe Deutsch, December, 2, 1937.

18. Monroe Deutsch's memorandum of April 27, 1936, to the president cited above reads as follows: "He informed me that his wife was an expert psychologist with a Ph.D. from the University of Vienna and he asked whether she might be employed in the University." In a letter of June 1, 1937, Brunswik wrote to Deutsch, "Though I probably would come alone for the beginning, the remark about an extension of the visa to my wife could remain unchanged."

19. Deutsch to Consul General of the United States, Vienna, Austria, December 17, 1937; Deutsch to Miller Holland, United Press International, November 1, 1938.

20. Harold E. Jones to the president's office, June 29, 1940; Robert M. Underhill to Jones, August 14, 1940, with the budget of the Institute for Child Welfare for 1940–1941.

21. Deutsch to Brown, June 16, 1944; Brown to Deutsch, June 30, 1944. The difficulties that Else Frenkel-Brunswik confronted in the United States warrant an account of their own. For more details, see Heimann and Grant, (1974) and Paier (1993). Concerning the experience of émigré women psychologists generally, see Ash (1995).

46

Expansion of Egon Brunswik's Psychology, 1955–1995

Kenneth R. Hammond

In the eulogy for his colleague Egon Brunswik, Edward Tolman, the famous psychologist at the University of California (Berkeley), noted that Brunswik had studied with Karl Bühler and "came under the influence of Moritz Schlick and the Vienna Circle of logical positivists." (See Hammond, 1966b, pp. 1–12). It was during his 1933–1934 sabbatical in Vienna that Tolman met Brunswik, found that they had much in common, and arranged for Brunswik to visit Berkeley and eventually to become a member of the Berkeley

faculty in 1937. There, Brunswik developed and deepened his interests in Darwinism and functionalist psychology; that led to a Brunswikian psychology that was centered on uncertainty, fallibilism, and vicarious functioning.

Although Brunswik certainly was thoroughly familiar with European psychology, it may well be that he was uncertain about his grasp of American psychology. At least, I have been led to that supposition because I now have in my possession Brunswik's personal copy of the 1938 edition of

Woodworth's *Experimental Psychology*, at that time considered to contain virtually everything of value in academic psychology. Brunswik's notations on the pages of this book are fascinating; one can see that not a line escaped his attention (see Figure 46.1, for an example); he must have been intent on absorbing every idea, every conclusion, every claim. These notations reflect Brunswik's thorough, painstaking approach to his discipline.

As can be seen from his annotations, he did not merely absorb; he commented on, criticized, and challenged every bit of information Woodworth presented in the entire 860 pages of this compendium (which, as an undergraduate in 1938, I found stupifyingly dull—and still do). This textbook, of which American experimental psychology was so proud, was in fact Brunswik's target; he took careful aim at its methods and conclusions and decided both were not only wrong but fundamentally so, and detrimental to the future of psychology. He set out to change matters by introducing two ideas that are still considered radical, the idiographical-statistical analysis of behavior and the representative design of experiments. These ideas shook up, but did not derail (as he had hoped), academic psychology. But his ideas have not been forgotten—far from it. A search of the Social Sciences Citation Index shows that during 1991–1993, Brunswik's work was cited in 79 different journals (see Table 46.1).

In short, although Brunswik may not have succeeded entirely in his efforts during his brief academic life, it may be that patient pursuit and empirical demonstration of the vitality and scope of his ideas will succeed in making significant changes in the future course of psychological theory and research. Brunswik was certainly a revolutionary, but academic revolutions take time.

In this chapter, I want to show how my colleagues and I developed and elaborated on his general theoretical and methodological framework.

I took Brunswik's class in the history of psychology in 1939 and his graduate seminars in 1946 and 1947. I was exposed to Edward Tolman and other luminaries at Berkeley in the late 1930s and again in the 1940s, but for me, Brunswik stood out; he seemed to epitomize the grand, fearless iconoclast; immediately, I wanted to carry on his work, although I wanted to put my own stamp on it—and I like to think that perhaps I have. In an article published while I was a graduate student, without prior consultation with Brunswik, I showed the practical significance of Brunswik's methodological precept of "representative design" by demonstrating the undesirable consequences of ignoring this precept (Hammond, 1948). (Because my brief article expressed Brunswik's ideas—invariably buried in complex, often incomprehensible, language—in simple terms, I was quickly dubbed by my fellow graduate students as "the poor man's Brunswik.")

Much as I admired Brunswik, I dared not carry out my dissertation under his direction; he had a convincing record as a perfectionist, a trait to be admired at a distance, but assuredly not one to be sought in a professor who would control your destiny. Nevertheless, I wanted to apply his ideas, and I saw an opportunity when I saw that the clinical judgments of psychiatrists and psychologists could be decomposed, and thus understood, in terms of the lens model that he had developed for perception. This insight, which appeared in the appendix to my dissertation, would determine the course of my professional life.

The Lens Model and Clinical Judgment

I first presented the application of the lens model to clinical judgment in a paper read at the 1953

Figure is on the following facing pages

FIGURE 46.1 Brunswik's annotations of his copy of Woodworth's *Experimental Psychology*. Note the detailed markings; note especially the double underlining of the words "all the conditions constant, except for one" and the notation "imposs[ible]" in the margin. If these markings were made in 1938, which is highly probable, they suggest that Brunswik's opposition to conventional research design had already begun.

Two important fields offering serious difficulty to the experimenter are those of child development and the genesis of maladjustments. Workers in both these fields employ tests and other laboratory techniques to good advantage in their efforts to trace the course of normal and abnormal development. But a truly incisive experiment in development would be like those in experimental embryology, where the experimenter takes a hand in the process of development by controlling essential conditions and introducing factors which modify the process. In so doing he is able to discover the factors in development. It is true that every educational procedure is experimental—for it may not work in a given case—and the same is true of every mode of treatment applied to a juvenile delinquent, a neurotic or a psychotic patient. The teacher and the psychotherapist would be psychological experimenters if it were feasible for them to know exactly where they started in handling an individual, exactly what they did and exactly where they came out. Their experiments almost necessarily lack precision and do not yield definite data which can be built into a science. "Almost necessarily," we say; hopeful beginnings in the study of the young child presage a day when there will be true experimentation in this field.

An experimenter is said to *control the conditions* in which an event occurs. He has several advantages over an observer who simply follows the course of events without exercising any control.

1. The experimenter makes the event happen at a certain time and place and so is fully *prepared* to make an accurate observation.

2. Controlled conditions being *known* conditions, the experimenter can set up his experiment a second time and *repeat* the observation; and, what is very important in view of the social nature of scientific investigation, he can report his conditions so that another experimenter can duplicate them and check the data.

3. The experimenter can systematically *vary* the conditions and note the concomitant variation in the results. If he follows the old standard "rule of one variable" he holds all the conditions constant except for one factor which is his "experimental factor" or his "independent variable." The observed effect is the "dependent variable" which in a psychological experiment is some characteristic of behavior or reported experience. In an experiment on the effect of noise on mental work, noise is the independent variable controlled by the experimenter, and the dependent variable may be speed or accuracy of work or the subject's report of his feelings.

As regards the rule of one variable, it applies only to the independent variable, for there is no objection to observing a variety of effects of the one experimental factor. With careful planning two or three independent variables can sometimes be handled in a single experiment with economy of effort and with some chance of discovering the interaction of the two or more factors (Fisher, 1936).

Whether one or more independent variables are used, it remains essential that all other conditions be constant. Otherwise you cannot connect the effect observed with any definite cause. The psychologist must expect to encounter difficulties in meeting this requirement of scientific work. He has to contend with differences between individuals, inequalities in the materials used (problems to be solved, for example), and changes due to motivation, practice and fatigue. He can often overcome these difficulties by some system of compensating factors. Suppose the efficiency of work under two conditions, noise and quiet, or, in general, A and B, is to be compared. If the subjects work first under condition A and then under condition B, B will probably show better performance because of the practice effect. We may meet this difficulty in several ways: (1) give the subjects abundant preliminary practice; (2) use the double order of conditions, ABBA; (3) use two groups of subjects, one in the order AB and one in the order BA, and combine the results from the two groups. The experiment must be carefully planned in advance, always with an eye to some defensible way of handling the data.

To be distinguished from the experimental method, and standing on a par with it in value, rather than above or below, is the comparative and correlational method. It takes its start from individual differences. By use of suitable tests it measures the individuals in a sample of some population, distributes these measures and finds their average, scatter, etc. Measuring two or more characteristics of the same individuals it computes the correlation of these characteristics and goes on to factor analysis. This method does not introduce an "experimental factor"; it has no "independent variable" but treats all the measured variables alike. It does not directly study cause and effect. The experimentalist's independent variable is antecedent to his dependent variable; one is cause (or part of the cause) and the other effect. The correlationist studies the interrelation of different effects.

The same psychologists, from the early days, have contributed to the two lines of study, and the contact between the two should remain close. The experimentalist needs to use the statistical techniques devised by the correlationist, or some of them, and the correlationist often bases his tests on laboratory experiments. Some psychological problems can be attacked by both methods, but on the whole the immediate problems are somewhat different. Excellent books are available on the methods and results of the comparative method—on tests, individual differences, correlations and factor analysis. There is good reason for not attempting to cover both lines of study in the same book, and good reason for attempting to bring together the methods and results from a variety of fields which have been cultivated by the experimentalist. Controversies between the schools can be (happily) left aside; experiments contributed by all the schools, as well as by the large number of experimental psy-

TABLE 46.1 Journals Containing Citations of Egon Brunswik: 1991–1993

Academy of Management Review	*Journal of Business Research*
Accident Analysis and Prevention	*Journal of Consumer Research*
Accounting Organizations and Society	*Journal of Environmental Management*
Accounting Review	*Journal of Environmental Psychology*
Advances in Consumer Research	*Journal of Memory and Language*
American Behavioral Scientist	*Journal of Nonverbal Behavior*
American Journal of Psychology	*Journal of Personality*
Annual Review of Psychology	*Journal of Personality and Social Psychology*
Applied Cognitive Psychology	*Journal of Risk and Uncertainty*
Applied Ergonomics	*Journal of Social Behavior and Personality*
Australian Journal of Psychology	*Journal of Social Issues*
Australian Psychologist	*Management Science*
Behavior Research Methods, Instruments, Computers	*Marketing Science*
Behavioral and Brain Sciences	*Medical Care*
Brain and Language	*Medical Decision Making*
British Journal of Social Psychology	*Memory and Cognition*
Canadian Journal of Psychology	*Motivation and Emotion*
Canadian Psychology	*Multivariate Behavioral Research*
Cognitive Development	*Organ Behavior and Human Decision Processes*
Cognitive Psychology	*Perception*
Decision Sciences	*Perception and Psychophysics*
Educational Administration Quarterly	*Perceptual and Motor Skills*
European Journal of Cognitive Psychology	*Personality and Social Psychology Bulletin*
Experimental Aging Research	*Psychological Bulletin*
Human Relations	*Psychological Reports*
IEEE Transactions on Systems, Man, Cybernetics	*Psychological Review*
Infant Behavior and Development	*Psychological Science*
International Journal of Intercultural Relations	*Quarterly Journal of Experimental Psychology:*
International Journal of the Addictions	*Comparative and Physiological Psychology*
Irish Journal of Psychology	*Quality and Quantity*
Journal for the Theory of Social Behavior	*Revista Latinoamericano de Psicologia*
Journal of Consulting and Clinical Psychology	*Scandinavian Journal of Psychology*
Journal of Experimental Psychology: Animal and	*Theory and Psychology*
Behavior Processes	*Transactions of the Institute of British Geographers*
Journal of Experimental Psychology: Human	*Zeitschrift für Hirnforschung*
Perception and Performance	*Zeitschrift für Psychoanalyse*
Journal of Experimental Psychology: General	*Zeitschrift für Psychologie*
Journal of Applied Social Psychology	

meeting of the Symposium on the Probability Approach in Psychology held at the University of California (Berkeley) Conference for the Unity of Science—a descendant of the Vienna Circle. My paper was later published in the *Psychological Review* (Hammond, 1955). Had it not been for Brunswik, I would not, of course, have been invited to present a paper to this August body of scholars (I was by far the youngest at this meeting to read a paper, completely unknown, and baffled by the [to me] incomprehensibly abstract papers given by them). But he was in charge of the program, knew about my research, wanted it to become visible, and took a chance on my being

able to write a presentable paper. Remembering his perfectionism, I sent it to him just before the meeting—too late for him to change anything. With great relief, I found that he had high praise for it.

It was this paper that moved the lens model from the domain of visual perception to the larger topic of human judgment and decision making. Brunswik was impressed with the extrapolation and cited it in his posthumously published 1956 book, *Perception and the Representative Design of Experiments*. I did not know at the time that fourteen years earlier, in 1942, his wife, Else Frenkel-Brunswik, had—most improbably—employed multiple regression statistics (as did I) to decompose clinical judgments. Brunswik never mentioned this to me; I stumbled on the article later. It was certainly improbable for a psychoanalyst, as Frenkel-Brunswik was, to do such research. But she completely buried this idea in her monograph of 145 pages on "Motivation and Behavior," and as a result, her husband may well have been the only one to notice it. He cited it in 1956 as an example of the use of multiple regression statistics: "Further mathematical steps . . . may perhaps be patterned after a model first introduced into the study of functional problems in perception by Else Frenkel-Brunswik in her analysis of clinical intuition" (p. 110). Strangely enough, however, she did not mention her husband's lens model; perhaps the connection was not apparent in 1942. In contrast, my efforts in 1955 became widely known because of my direct application—in plain language—of the lens model to clinical judgment. And it was the use of the lens model that made the difference in the response.

Questions about the competence of clinical judgment had been brought into prominence by another Berkeley professor, Theodore Sarbin (1944). But it was Paul Meehl (1954) who wrote a slender volume that contrasted clinical and actuarial prediction, to the detriment of the former, from which there has been no turning back. (See Dawes, Faust, & Meehl, 1989.) As a result of these publications, numerous studies sharply critical of clinical judgment appeared during the 1950s and 1960s. A great many cited Brunswik and the lens model because of my 1955 article, and many followed, with or without acknowledgment, the general paradigm of the lens model. The lens model was attractive because it offered an organizing principle and a recognizable methodological approach, multiple regression statistics. It became apparent that not only clinical judgment but any set of judgments based on multiple fallible cues, or indicators could be brought under scrutiny.

Learning under Uncertainty

At almost the same time as the lens model was being applied to clinical judgment, several researchers began to see its applicability in the domain of learning under uncertainty. After all,

Brunswik had shown the importance of probability learning in his theorizing (Brunswik, 1943) and had published two articles involving learning (Brunswik 1939c, 1951). Apparently there were three independent efforts undertaken roughly at the same time: Jan Smedslund in Oslo (his dissertation), Björkman in Stockholm, and myself in Boulder, Colorado. Smedslund's dissertation (Smedslund, 1955) was known to Brunswik, and he cited it in 1956. He did not know that Mats Björkman was creating a Brunswikian research group in Stockholm, and that in this group was a student, Berndt Brehmer, who would eventually publish over 100 articles based on Brunswik's theory and method.

Research on learning within the Brunswikian framework became known as multiple cue probability learning (MCPL) and is now an established domain of research in psychology that can be traced directly to Brunswik through the above sources as well as others (see, for example, Brehmer & Joyce, 1988). I will return to the topics of judgment and learning, but we need first to consider a most important development in early 1960s, the mathematical exposition of Brunswik's lens model.

Mathematical Development

In the early 1960s some of my colleagues and I turned our attention to the possibility of providing a mathematical description of the lens model. Brunswik (and Else Frenkel-Brunswik) had already shown that multiple regression statistics might be applied to the circumstances depicted by the lens model (see Brunswik, 1956b; see also Hammond, Hursch, & Todd, 1964). The multiple regression model is easily seen to be applicable to the lens model; it is intended to represent stochastically the relative contribution of several independent variables (cues, in the lens model) to a dependent variable, the subject's judgment on one side of the lens model, and a distal variable on the environmental or ecological side of the lens model. It is the only model of human judgment that incorporates both the model of the subject and the ecology. The equation readily applies to the subject's side of the lens model because it (1) is statistical (thus incorporating probabilism); (2) quantifies the relation of each independent variable to a dependent variable (thus quantifying the relative effects of each cue on the subject's judgments); and (3) specifies a principle by which the cue data are organized (thus providing a model for the cognitive activity of the subject). The equation also readily applies to the ecological side of the lens model because it uses the same concepts to quantify that side of the lens model. That is, the equation specifies the relative contribution of each (palpable) independent variable—each cue—to the distal (impalpable) variable to be inferred by the subject and also specifies an organizing principle for the relationships, namely, a linear, additive one.

The partial lens model equation (LME) states:

$$r_a = G \ R_e R_s,$$

where:

$r_a =$ achievement, the correlation between Y_e, the distal variable, and Y_s, the judge's estimate of the distal variable,

$R_e =$ environmental (linear) predictability, the multiple correlation between the cue variables and the distal variable,

$R_s =$ judgmental (linear) predictability, the multiple correlation between the cue variables and the judge's estimate of the distal variable (sometimes termed *cognitive control*), and

$G =$ (linear) knowledge.

The LME thus provides a descriptive quantitative model for both the organismic and the ecological side of the lens model and therefore makes researchable many questions that were previously beyond our reach. In particular, it informs us about the upper level of achievement we can expect from a person in a task environment of a specified degree of uncertainty. For example, if the R_e in a task is .70, then the upper limit of achievement is .70: Since $r_a = G \ R_e R_s$, achievement (r_a) cannot exceed the highest value of any term on the right side of the equation. But without the knowledge afforded by the LME, one would assume a performance level of .70 to be rather poor and wonder why. The LME, however, shows that such a performance level would be excellent in view of the limit of achievement imposed by the measured uncertainty in the task (R_s).

This conclusion is, however, limited to circumstances in which only a linear model (of both task and subject) is applicable. If nonlinear models

are required, the full lens model equation is appropriate:

$$r_a = G \ R_e R_s + C \ \sqrt{1 - R_e^2} \ \sqrt{1 - R_s^2},$$

where:

$C =$ the correlation between residuals.

Thus, in situations where nonlinear relations exist between cue and distal variable and the subject uses the information for the cue in the same way, C will assume a positive value and achievement (r_a) will be larger than otherwise would be the case. For example, Stewart and his colleagues (1989) found that weather forecasters do make use of nonlinear relations between distal events (e.g., hail) and their cues, a circumstance in which C takes on high positive values. In short, the lens model equation is not limited to the analysis of linear relations. And more recently, in a striking example of the practical use of the lens model and the LME, Donald Burnside (1994), an agricultural scientist, studied the judgments of Australian sheep ranchers (pastoralists) regarding the use of their rangeland. Burnside used both pictorial and verbal descriptions of the land. Both linear and nonlinear phenomena were found.

All of the research within the framework of the lens model, including the lens model equation, has been carried out under the rubric of social judgment theory. It can be described in terms of three varieties of the lens model.

1. The single-system case represents only the subject side of Brunswik's lens model (see Figure 46.2), and it is for this reason it is so labeled. Curiously it is the most frequently employed version of the lens model, and its employment has become know as *policy capturing* (see Brehmer & Brehmer, 1988). Burnside's study, for example, "captured" the judgment policies of pastoralists regarding land use in a hierarchical form of the single-system case. Burnside also "captured" the judgment policies of the pastoralists' professional advisers and found important differences between pastoralists and advisers (see Figure 46.3).

2. The double-system case (Figure 46.4) represents a situation in which the values of the parameters for the ecological side of the lens model are known. It is now frequently used in laboratory studies, for in these circumstances, the researcher can create whatever type (many or few cues, high-

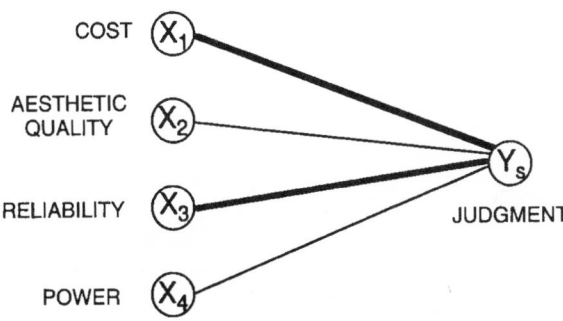

FIGURE 46.2 The single-system case. Example illustrates "capturing" the judgment policy of a person who is purchasing an automobile. Width of the line indicates weight placed on the "cue."

or low-validity cues, linear or nonlinear cues, see Figure 46.5) of judgment task she or he wishes to study. There are numerous examples of this type of research (see Cooksey, 1996b). Cooksey, Freebody, and Davidson's (1986) study of teachers' judgments of students' reading achievement offers an example of research outside the laboratory. Because these authors had data regarding the students' performance, the left-hand side of the lens as well as the right could be quantified, and thus, a double-system case was employed. As a result, they could show that teachers did not make appropriate use of information in such judgments.

Research within the double-system case also produced a new idea about feedback and learning, namely, that probability learning that de-

pended on outcome feedback alone was slow and inefficient. But if subjects were provided with information about task properties (labeled *cognitive feedback*), learning was rapid and intelligent (see Balzer, Doherty, & O'Connor, 1989).

3. The triple-system case. The diagrams for this case represent perhaps the most important expansion of Brunswik's lens model. It is possibly one that Brunswik did not anticipate. A mere glance at the diagram makes it appear to be a natural, perhaps mindless, linear extension of the original model. But it did not come about that way. Rather, this expansion of the lens model resulted from a pursuit of the problem of interpersonal conflict during a problem-solving session. Leon Rappoport, then a graduate student at the University of Colorado, asked, "Can we apply the

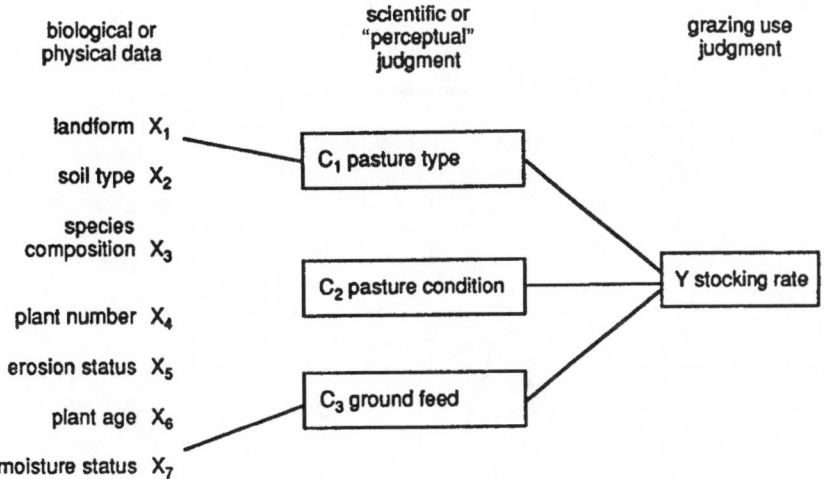

FIGURE 46.3 Burnside's use of the single-system case in a hierarchical form to study range judgments of pastoralists.

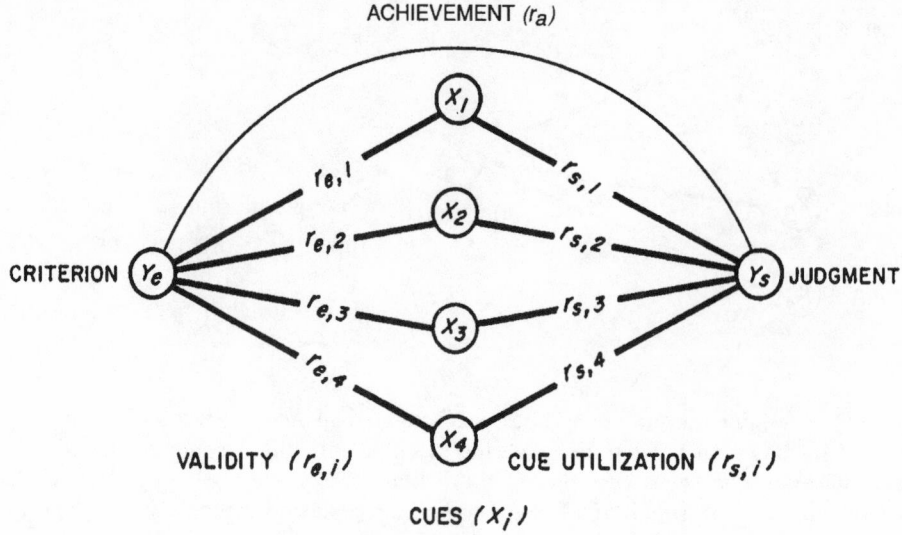

ACHIEVEMENT (r_a)

CRITERION Y_e

VALIDITY $(r_{e,i})$ CUE UTILIZATION $(r_{s,i})$

CUES (X_i)

Y_s JUDGMENT

FIGURE 46.4 The double-system case. Lowercase (r) indicates correlations; uppercase (Y_e, Y_s) indicates task criterion and judgment.

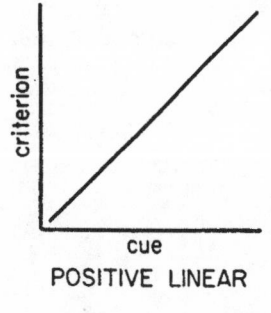

POSITIVE LINEAR

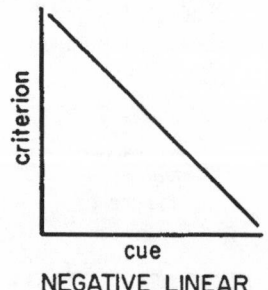

NEGATIVE LINEAR

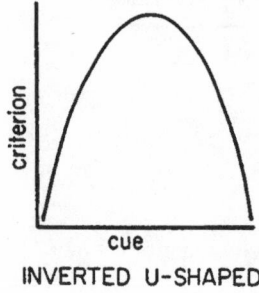

INVERTED U-SHAPED

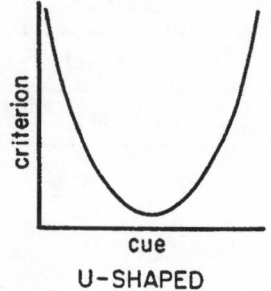

U-SHAPED

FIGURE 46.5 Function forms typically used and examined in lens model studies.

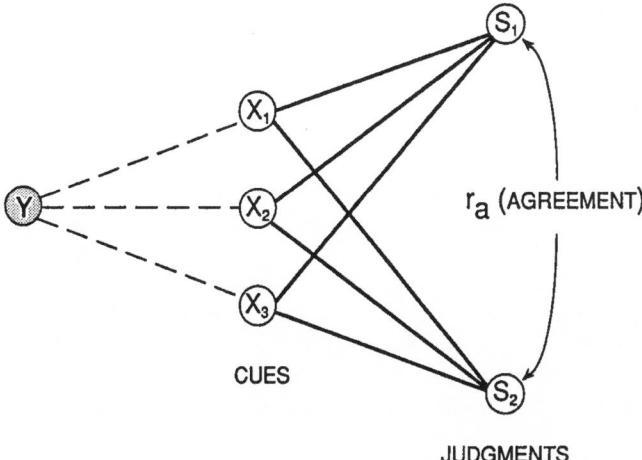

r_a (AGREEMENT)

CUES

JUDGMENTS

FIGURE 46.6 Triple-system case.

lens model to this problem?" The answer to that question led to the construction of the model shown in Figures 46.6 and 46.7. And that in turn led to conceiving of interpersonal conflict at the cognitive, rather than the motivational, level. Might not interpersonal conflict arise out of the differential use of information? The diagram of the "triple-system case"—a task situation and two persons making different use of the same information—established a paradigm for research on interpersonal conflict. Many laboratory studies based on this paradigm were carried out during the 1970s and established the validity of the theory that conflict could arise out of the differential

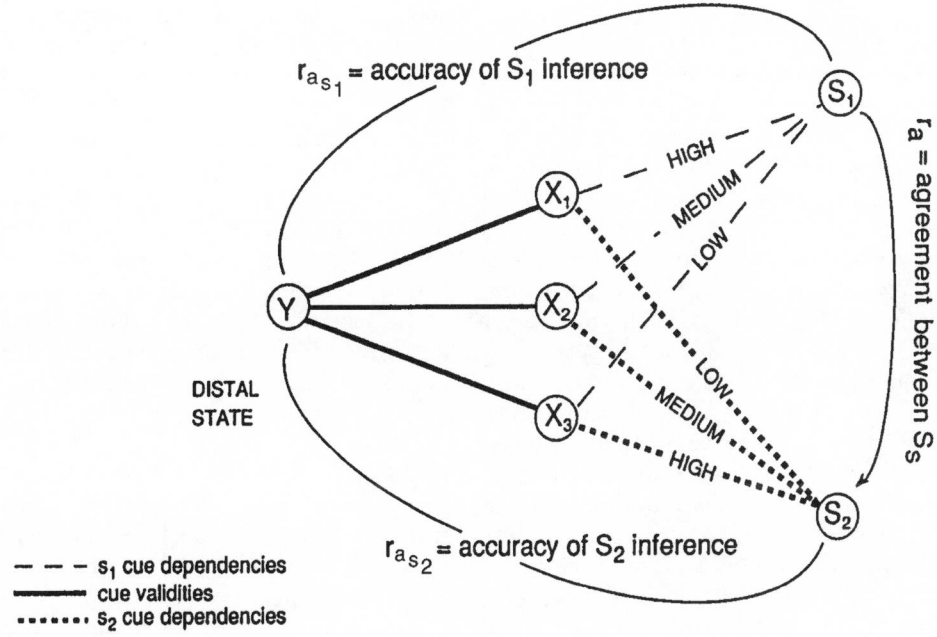

r_{as_1} = accuracy of S_1 inference

r_a = agreement between Ss

DISTAL STATE

r_{as_2} = accuracy of S_2 inference

– – – s_1 cue dependencies
——— cue validities
· · · · · · · s_2 cue dependencies

FIGURE 46.7 Triple-system case used in studying interpersonal conflict due to differential weighting of cues.

use of information. Many practical applications have been made, the most visible one being the study (with Leonard Adelman) of the conflict in a large city over the choice of handgun ammunition by police (Hammond & Adelman, 1976). Jeryl Mumpower has continued to use the triple-system case to study interpersonal learning, that is, how one person learns from and about another person who uses information differently. Perhaps the most interesting and important application of the triple-system case was made by John Gillis (this volume), who successfully used the triple-system case to study the effects of psychotropic drugs on the behavior of adolescent and adult schizophrenics.

Of course, once one sees the expansion of the lens model to include several persons, it becomes possible to study the judgments of individuals in groups, particularly those groups in which individuals find themselves in dispute over policy. Rohrbaugh (Harmon & Rohrbaugh, 1990) has done this. A large number of examples of research that involves the various extensions of the lens model can be found in the book by Brehmer and Joyce (1988).

Cognitive Continuum Theory

Toward the end of the 1970s it had become apparent to me that those of us who had tried to exploit Brunswik's ideas had hardly touched the rich and complex body of ideas put forward by Brunswik. I decided that one important point of entry aside from the lens model would be Brunswik's development of the distinction between perception and thinking, that is, between intuitive and analytical cognition. There were three reasons: First, this distinction has an old and honorable history that reaches back to the Greeks, had been maintained throughout the Middle Ages to the present, and had yet to be dealt with by modern science (psychology) in a productive, scientific manner. Second, Brunswik had made a start on theoretical and empirical analysis of this topic in his address at the 1954 International Congress of Psychology in Montreal and in his 1956 book. And it is clear that at the time of his death in 1955, this was to have been the future center of his attention; had he lived longer, we surely would have seen an elaboration of theory and research on perception versus thinking, as he put it. Third, it seemed to

me that this distinction is central to research on judgment and decision making, particularly in view of psychologists' frequent analysis of judgment and decision making during the 1970s and 1980s.

I made a start in the late 1970s by writing a monograph (as yet unpublished), which was made available as a technical report from the Center for Research on Judgment and Policy at the University of Colorado in 1980. Because of the imposing philosophical work on this topic, and some hard criticism, I was faint-hearted about publishing this monograph. I was encouraged, however, to continue by discovering that the monograph was often requested and cited. The essential ideas in the monograph eventually formed the basis of a large research project and a few discursive articles (e.g., Hammond, 1990b). Because the principal premise of the theory is that there is a continuum—rather than a dichotomy—between intuition and analysis, I named the general theory *cognitive continuum theory* (see Hammond 1996c). So far as I can determine, this is the first time that the traditional dichotomy between intuition and analysis has been challenged. The reason for arguing for a shift from a dichotomy to a continuum lies in Brunswik's early emphasis on "compromise" in perception, and in his later emphasis on compromise in cognition generally. He applied the general term "quasi rationality" to this phenomenon (Brunswik, 1952).

The germ of the idea of cognitive continuum theory can be found on pages 89–96 of Brunswik's 1956 book. In these pages, Brunswik focused on the conceptual differences between perception and thinking, also described as the differences between intuition and analysis. Most important, he demonstrated empirically the differences in the distribution of errors produced by these two modes of cognition (see Figure 46.8).

Five Premises

In my book on "Human Judgment and Social Policy" (Hammond, 1996b) I put forward the following five premises:

First, various modes, or forms, of cognition can be ordered in relation to one another on a continuum that is marked by intuitive cognition at one pole and analytical cognition at the other,

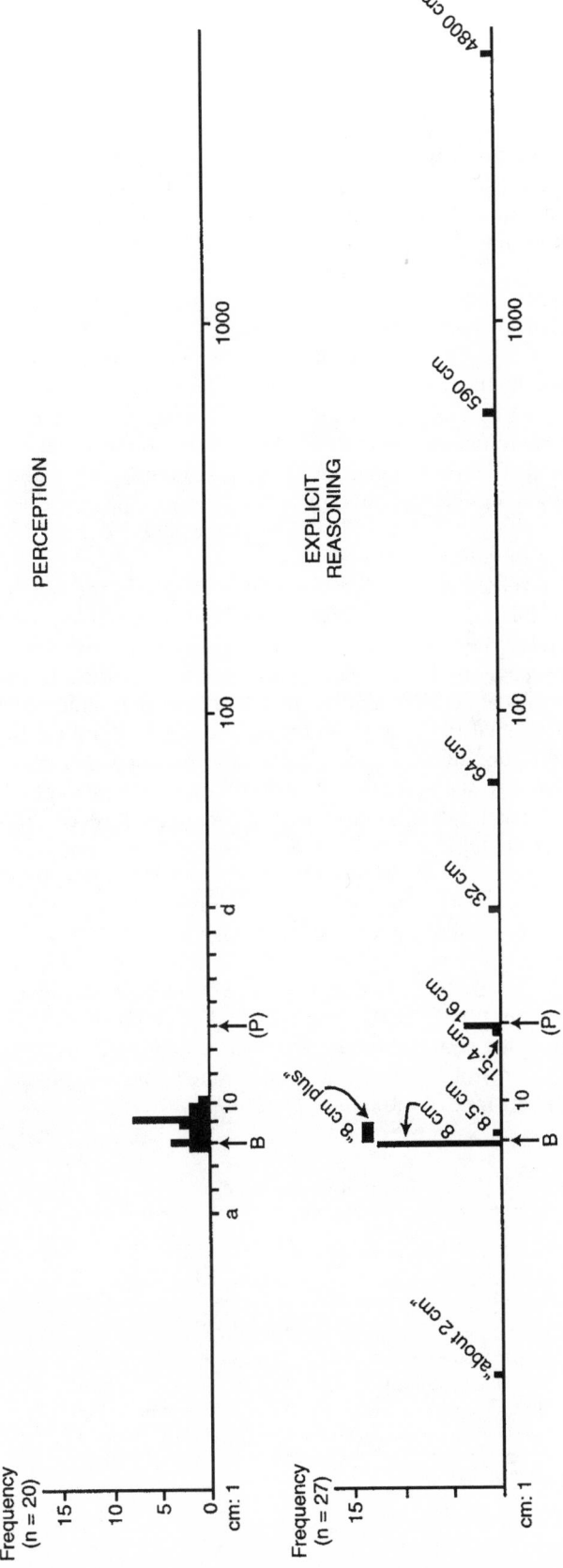

FIGURE 46.8 Distributions of accuracy and error in perception versus thinking. Reproduced from Egon Brunswik, *Perception and the Representative Design of Experiments*. Berkeley, CA: University of California Press 1956. Copyright © 1956 by the Regents of the University of California. Reprinted by permission.

in contrast to the traditional dichotomy, and antinomy, that has existed between these modes of cognition.

Second, the forms of cognition that lie on the continuum between intuition and analysis include elements of both intuition and analysis and are included under the term *quasi rationality*. This is the most common form of cognition: It is known to the layperson as common sense.

Third, cognitive tasks can be ordered on a continuum with regard to their capacity to induce intuition, quasi rationality, and analytical cognition.

Fourth, cognitive activities move along the intuitive-analytical continuum over time; as they do so, the relative contributions to cognition of intuitive and analytic components of quasirationality will change. Successful cognition inhibits movement; failure stimulates it.

Fifth, human cognition is capable of pattern recognition and the use of functional relations.

Premise 1 makes explicit the postulate of a continuum. Once this step is taken it remains to define the properties of intuition and analysis at the poles of the continuum. Tables 46.2 and 46.3 provide these definitions. It also means that the region intermediate to the poles of the cognitive continuum must be defined, a step that was taken in the study of highway engineers. This step was shown to be operationally practical, researchable, and productive.

Premise 2 makes explicit the concept of *compromise*, or *quasi rationality*, that is, cognition that lies on the continuum between the poles of intuition and analysis: It is roughly equivalent to the layperson's notion of common sense. Once it becomes possible to define a point on the continuum, the proportional contribution of intuition and analysis becomes apparent. An index,

the cognitive continuum index (CCI), was developed for this purpose. (Hammond, Hamm, Grassia, & Pearson, 1997)

Premise 3 indicates that judgment tasks as well as cognitive activity can be located on the analytical-intuitive continuum in terms of the ability to induce either. And just as a number can be assigned to the location of cognitive activity (CCI), a number can be assigned to tasks according to their location on the task continuum index (TCI). And once this is done, we can test the hypothesis that task properties induce cognitive properties, specifically, that hypothesis states that a positive correlation will be found between task characteristics and cognitive behavior. We should not expect the correlation to hold over all conditions, however. Stress, for example, may induce cognition to move away from its predicted location in one direction or the other, depending on specifics.

Premise 4 takes account of the fact that cognition is not static, although psychologists have studied cognition almost exclusively under static conditions. Thus, Premise 4 predicts the nature of cognitive activity as task conditions change. Indeed, shifts from analysis to intuition may be found in the most surprising places. For example, on May 1, 1989, at a special session of the annual meeting of the American Physical Society devoted to the "miracle" of "cold fusion," a physicist named Steven Koonin stood up before 2,000 physicists and declared, "Based on my experience, my knowledge of nuclear physics, and my intuition . . . the experiments are just wrong" (Kevles, 1993, p. 82). Thus, contemporary physicists apparently find intuition to be acceptable in the context of verification. Reichenbach surely would have shuddered. But the physicists gave Koonin an ovation.

TABLE 46.2 Properties of Intuition and Analysis

	Intuition	Analysis
Cognitive control	Low	High
Rate of data processing	Rapid	Slow
Conscious awareness	Low	High
Organizing principle	Weighted average	Task-specific
Errors	Normally distributed	Few, but large
Confidence	High confidence in answer	Low confidence in answer
	Low confidence in method	High confidence in method

Source: Hammond, Hamm, Grassia, and Pearson (1987).

TABLE 46.3 Elaboration of Task-Cognition Relation

Task Characteristic	Intuition-Inducing State of Task Characteristic	Analysis-Inducing State of Task Characteristic
1. Number of cues	Large (>5)	Small
2. Measurement of cues	Perceptual measurement	Objective, reliable measurement
3. Distribution of cue values	Continuous, highly variable distribution	Unknown distribution; dichotomous cues; discrete values
4. Redundancy among cues	High redundancy	Low redundancy
5. Decomposition of task	Low	High
6. Degree of certainty in task	Low certainty	High certainty
7. Relation between cues and criterion	Linear	Nonlinear
8. Weighting of cues in environmental model	Equal	Unequal
9. Availability of organizing principle	Unavailable	Available
10. Display of cues	Simultaneous display	Sequential display
11. Time period	Brief	Long

Source: Hammond, Hamm, Grassia, and Pearson (1987).

Premise 5 acknowledges that cognition is capable of pattern recognition as well as the use of multiple probabilistic cues. Bringing concepts invoking coherence or pattern recognition into a Brunswikian theory may well have been resisted by Brunswik. For during most of his academic life, he took pains to deny the validity of Gestalt psychology, the psychology whose basic metaphor was that of patterns, of "good figures." The goal of Gestalt psychology, of course, was to deny the validity of the elementalists. Although that goal was achieved only in part, the empirical research results generated by the Gestaltists were sufficient to shake the foundations of elementalistic psychology.

But Gestalt psychology never was able to produce a sufficiently vigorous research program to recruit new researchers, nor did it ever present a convincing formalization of its theory,[1] and by the 1960s, it seemed to have run its course. Brunswik's own efforts directly challenged even the most vigorous descendent of the Gestaltists, Kurt Lewin, as well as the most vigorous stimulus-response psychologist, Clark Hull. This challenge can be seen in its pure form in the publication of a symposium that included all three of these great psychologists (Brunswik, 1943). In his 1956 book, Brunswik was specific; he reported the results of empirical research in perception that indicated that perceptual judgments that apparently reflected a response to a pattern or organization of visual material could be easily interpreted as reflecting a response to probabilistic cues (e.g., "nearness"). His major point was that he had found evidence for the ecological validity of various Gestalt factors ("symmetry and closedness"). If this were to be generally true—that such "factors" did indeed possess ecological validity—then, from the point of view of probabilistic functionalism, the organism would learn to use them. If so, Gestalt explanations would then become superfluous.

Brunswik wanted his explanation of behavior to begin with a consideration of environmental circumstances, rather than with organismic circumstances. And in this approach, he was, of course, following Darwin. His strong Darwinian point of view can be seen in these sentences:

Furthermore, the successful demonstration of the ecological validity of a Gestalt factor does not automatically imply the legitimacy of its interpretation as a learned cue. It merely shows that an objective basis for probability learning is offered the individual within his surroundings. Since, however, all ecological validities represent a challenge to the organism for utilization, and since it appears that certain cues are on the average being utilized roughly in proportion to the degree of their validity . . . , our findings lend plausibility-support to a viewing of the Gestalt factors as cases of successful cue-utilization subsumable under the principles of [probability] learning theory (Brunswik 1956b, pp. 122–123).

Thus, Brunswik left no doubt that he thought that the question of Gestalt processes, or pattern recognition, would be, or could be, explained in terms of multiple cue probability learning, and that an appeal to pattern recognition was unnecessary.

Although agreeing with Brunswik's conclusions about Gestalt psychology, I find myself in disagreement with Brunswik's dismissal of the concept of pattern recognition. For when the differences between these approaches are put in the context of the differences between the correspondence theory of truth and the coherence theory of truth, I am prepared to find room for both. I do agree with Brunswik's Darwinian framing of the question, however. I do agree that we should investigate the matter by first examining the organism's natural habitat, the task environment in which that organism must function. And I anticipate that we shall find task environments that demand, or at least induce, judgments based on coherence, and that we shall find task environments that induce correspondence judgments.

To summarize: Brunswik's principal ideas persist—they directly guide theory and research—a half century after his death; they are not given mere lip service. And there is a Brunswik Society that has for 16 years held annual meetings. That is a remarkable achievement in a field—psychology—that is well known for the short life of its theoretical systems. What the future holds is uncertain, of course. There is some danger that some of the concepts Brunswik introduced will be silently incorporated into mainstream psychology. One already has been. The concept of ecological validity is now in common use, albeit in a distorted form.[2] Probabilism has been taken for granted by a large section of psychologists—especially those studying judgment and decision making. And within that field, Brunswik's emphasis on the study of a single person over a range of conditions (rather than the reverse, as has been customary for about a century) is now being accepted by psychologists, who are beginning to insist on the use of within-subject experimental designs rather than between-subject designs. As

psychologists pursue the logical implications of these arguments, they will eventually see the deeper significance of Brunswik's claim for the value of the representative design of experiments (Hammond, Hamm, & Grassia, 1986).

I have only touched on the rich resource of ideas—fresh ideas—introduced by Egon Brunswik. Most of these ideas, regrettably, lie untouched in the literature he produced, and I am, at least in part, to blame for this. I made a conscious decision early in my professional life—indeed, while Brunswik was still alive—that it was hopeless to try to persuade psychologists of the value of Brunswik's approach simply by argumentation. His ideas were too complex, too strange, too much opposed to mainstream psychology that at that time (the 1950s) was enjoying a vigorous growth in prestige and productivity; psychology in the 1950s (and 1960s) was in no mood to listen to someone suggesting—as Brunswik was—that it was following a path to nowhere. So I decided that the best hope was to proceed step-by-step; to do the small experiments that the journals would publish, write a few theoretical articles that would not greatly offend the conventional wisdom, and thus eventually gain respectability.

Was that the correct approach? Many colleagues, only a few of whom have been mentioned here, thought so; they joined the endeavor. And the current citations of Brunswik indicated in Table 46.1 offer support for the wisdom of that decision.

It may well be reasonable, then, to conclude that all these against-the-mainstream efforts have been modestly successful in establishing the legitimacy of Brunswikian psychology. If so, it is now time to pursue the wealth of untouched ideas contained in Brunswik's work. I wish success to the brave souls who try.

NOTES

1. For a demonstration of the difficulty of formalizing a coherence theory of truth, see, for example, Rescher (1982).

2. For an attempt to correct the abuse of this concept, see Hammond (1978a). The manuscript was rejected for publication.

47

Notes from Berkeley, 1938, 1945–1948

Kenneth R. Hammond

"You ought to hear this professor from Vienna" was the unlikely suggestion given to me one day in 1938 in the halls of the Life Sciences Building at the University of California at Berkeley. So one day I went to hear him. My best recollection of Egon Brunswik is of a tall, broad-shouldered man addressing a large class of psychology students in hesitating and heavily accented English, accompanied by a rather large woman sitting nearby to whom he turned every so often for the word he needed. I remember nothing of the content of the lecture, of course, but I do remember that it was delivered with great seriousness and dignity. The woman sitting nearby and coaching this professor's English was his wife, Else Frenkel-Brunswik, who would later become very well known in relation to her co-authorship of the exciting book *The Authoritarian Personality* (Adorno, Frenkel-Brunswik, Levinson, and Sanford, 1950). The standard joke among graduate students was that although Egon gradually lost his accent, the coach never lost hers.

I did not see Brunswik again until 1945, the year I returned to Berkeley as a graduate student and began attending his lectures. He was more than impressive; here one saw unmistakably genuine scholarship at work. One had no doubt that this was an opportunity to sit at the feet of a true scholar. I was most impressed with the breadth of his knowledge; it seemed to me that he knew everything about psychology and philosophy. Moreover, he did not simply throw all his knowledge at you (as so many professors did); he tied everything together. Instead of scattered bits of information, he offered coherence (for which all students yearn), a historical description of a pattern of psychological theories, research strategies, tactics, results, disappointments, what led to what, and even personal interactions that had occurred over the years. And then he could walk up to the blackboard and draw a diagram of the whole business that made it all obvious.

Brunswik was both difficult and easy to approach in his office. Difficult, because it was easy to see that he would spot your ignorance immediately (and what graduate student does not secretly fear his or her ignorance), and he had a very serious demeanor; time was not to be squandered. Yet easy, because he was unfailingly polite, dignified, even courteous, and did give every indication of taking you seriously; he seemed to invite and treat your contribution with respect. But you had better be prepared for hard (but not harsh) treatment; he pulled no punches. If your contribution was not a good one, he would tell you, gently but firmly. That was because he was a perfectionist. I mentioned in Chapter 1 that on one occasion, he pointed out a minor error in a diagram I submitted and somewhat apologetically said, "to me, diagrams are sacred." I repeat that remark because it is an understatement: in fact, everything about psychology was sacred and therefore needed to be understood correctly.

His perfectionism was a warning signal to me; I could see that if I undertook a dissertation with this man it would never be completed (and I needed to finish as rapidly as possible). There were precedents that allowed this inference. And there were only a few who did undertake a dissertation with him, and then only in the later years, when apparently he had mellowed somewhat.

Brunswik did offer a seminar (then a rarity for Berkeley professors), in which I participated, but only minimally. The main participant was always Brunswik. I offer one example: James Sakoda and I were friends and admirers of Brunswik, and he seemed to take us seriously. He brought the proofs of his 1947 monograph (Part I of his 1956 book) to us and asked us to read them and indicated that we should comment on them. Sakoda and I were thrilled at this recognition of our wisdom by the wisest man of all, and we dug into this material — hard — indeed as hard as we could. We needed to find a flaw somewhere, somehow —

and we did, or we thought we did. We were elated and could hardly wait for the seminar at which we would demonstrate our critical talents, which had—at last(!)—become so apparent even to those in the highest regions. The day came; Brunswik sat at one end of the table, surrounded by about six or eight graduate students (the cream of the crop), and Sakoda and I sat at the other. Brunswik nodded to indicate that we should begin. Sakoda read his first sentence, carefully crafted and endlessly revised. Brunswik interrupted, with an enthusiastic burst of sentences—and Sakoda never got to say another word during the entire two hours. Nor did I. Nor did anyone else. No one thought there was anything strange about this. Indeed, everyone was grateful—to us for having stimulated this flow of erudition, to Brunswik for providing it.

Brunswik was surprisingly generous with his friendship. I once visited him in Berkeley, and as it became time for me to leave his office, I mentioned that I had an appointment to meet my wife. Brunswik insisted on walking across the campus with me because he wanted to meet her.

And so he did. It was a remarkable demonstration of friendship.

For me, a student struggling to make sense of the perplexing field of psychology, Brunswik saved the day. Without him, I would have given up. His impressive scholarship established his authenticity; his extraordinary ability to provide coherence in an otherwise chaotic endeavor endeared him to me. He did for me what no one else could: he made sense of an endless and disconnected series of books, monographs, articles, theories, quarrels, meaningless dates, and events. Thanks to him, I now could become a scholar and a psychologist.

In his eulogy for his colleague Brunswik, Edward Tolman wrote, "In the coming years, Egon Brunswik will hold an ever increasingly significant and important position in the history of psychology. Those of us who know him and loved him can but be glad that such ever-greater recognition lies ahead, though we grieve that he did not live to see it happen" (see Hammond, 1966b). And I must add, those of us who contributed to this volume also grieve that he did not see it happen.

48

Notes from a Student in Vienna

Ruth Bussey

In the spring of 1936, Egon Brunswik, *Privatdozent* at the University of Vienna, wrote the welcoming letter in answer to that of Leonard Carmichael, professor of psychology at Brown University, in which Dr. Carmichael had said that I, his doctoral candidate and recipient of a traveling fellowship for 1936–1937, wished to study at the University of Vienna. Dr. Carmichael had stated in his original letter to Professors Karl and Charlotte Büehler that it was my intention to study some aspect of the development of perception in infants.

Dr. Brunswik's letter contained information about matriculating at the university as well as the address of the Psychological Institute at I. Liebiggasse 5, where I should come when I first arrived. The letter gave much practical information about living conditions, pensions near the university, and costs of food and housing. Although I did not copy the whole letter, I made note of these suggestions and the list he included of universities and psychologists whom I might want to visit on my way to Vienna. That list had the names of Michotte (Louvain); Piaget (Geneva); Gemelli (Milan); Jaensch (Marburg); and Metzger (Frankfurt).

Before I left for Europe in August, I had heard directly from Professor Bühler and made arrangements to meet her at her new clinic in London, but it was the end of September when we finally met in Vienna. At that time, she informed me that I would be working with Dr. Brunswik in my research on perception, and that Dr. Liselotte Frankl would help us in our work with the infants at the Kinderübernahmestelle.

Soon afterward I had my first conference with Dr. Brunswik, a young man then in his thirties, formally courteous, yet very cordial. We spoke in English. Dr. Brunswik immediately invited me to audit his course in experimental psychology and his seminar on American psychology as often as I could. We did not discuss an area of research for me. I knew that I needed time to familiarize myself with the research publications and resources at the institute.

During that first conference with Dr. Brunswik, he took time to point out to me some of the ways life would be different in Vienna from that in the States. Undoubtedly, he had realized from his stay at the University of California that it would be best to mention these differences immediately. The first item of public etiquette would be that he would always be walking at my left, and that was just what he did at the end of our conference as we walked over to one of his favorite coffee houses.

On the way, Dr. Brunswik stopped in the Rathauspark just south of the main university building to show me the marble bust of the physicist Ernst Mach. My own knowledge of European Geisteswissenschaft was too limited at the time for me to know that Mach was the author of a treatise on the analysis of sensations, one of the almost 200 references in Brunswik's 1929 publication "Prinzipienfragen der Gestalttheorie." I remember, though, that I realized at the time that Dr. Brunswik was not only well versed in areas of knowledge outside modern psychology but also appeared to be a dedicated scholar.

Dr. Brunswik's course in experimental psychology was without doubt the best course I attended during my year in Vienna. Using both demonstrations and lectures, he followed his own textbook, *Experimentelle Psychologie in Demonstrationen*, which had been published the year before. This was the only textbook I knew of in the classes I attended. Students were expected to take their own notes. But illegal though it was, lectures for large classes were transcribed, mimeographed, and sold. The students in Dr. Brunswik's class had in their hands the substance of the course to study as they wished, and they also knew ahead of time the subject of the lecture and the demonstrations they would be able to see in class.

Egon Brunswik was a teacher as well as a lecturer. I remember that in one demonstration in the experimental psychology course, a young woman member of the class proved to be a sensitive *Eidetiker*. Brunswik carefully pointed out her specific ability by questioning her as to what she had seen. This was the only large class that I attended where there was regular student-teacher interaction.

Dr. Brunswik invited me to participate in the course on American psychology by giving a lecture on the topic of maturation and learning as undertaken by American researchers and, specifically, the work of Leonard Carmichael. After I had read my speech, there was considerable discussion. I was asked to continue for a second talk. The next week, I summarized the work of other psychologists, especially those working in the areas of comparative and physiological psychology. I also discussed recent work in electroencephalography and my own work studying the relationship of brain waves and the afterimage and the intensity and duration of a light stimulus. It had been over fifty years since the Austrian scientist Fleischl von Marxow had reported on the electrical variations obtained from outside the skull, but only one year since Rohracher, *Privatdozent* at the University of Innsbruck, had published his study of brain wave variations during mental activity.

For both of these talks, Dr. Brunswik arranged for students to help me. I learned much from them, and they did an excellent job of translating. The young man who did most of the translating for the second talk was amazed at the amount of material I was including in fields in which he had an interest but knew of no course directly associated with the institute where he could pursue. I wonder whether Dr. Karl Bühler, who had a medical degree and took time to attend Rohracher's talk at the university a few months later, might have taken steps toward developing further interaction with other departments in this area had the course of history been different for Austria. Both Dr. Brunswik and Dr. Charlotte

Büehler advised me to attend the public lecture and course Dr. Konrad Lorenz was giving in the department of biology.

Ernest Ligon, professor of psychology at Union College in Schenectady, New York, was also visiting at the institute the fall of 1936 and was a member of many of the courses and seminars I took that fall. Dr. Brunswik, Dr. Ligon, and I frequently stopped after class at a nearby coffee house and talked shop. We discussed in English the question of stimulation and response, the physics of the stimulus, proximal and distal stimuli, the transmission of stimulation, the perception and the assignment of perception to the physical object. This amazing reality of our perception of a "world of things," in Dr. Brunswik's phraseology, is indeed a perplexity. I undoubtedly brought up the question of the underlying physiological and neurological processes occurring in the organism. It was a question that I have never stopped asking. Reality for me was not subdivided into compartments such as divisions in a university, nor was the learning process to be relegated only to those years until one received a doctorate in a specific field.

In one way, I am sure my contacts with Dr. Brunswik were of considerable value to him. That, of course, had to do with our many hours of conversation in English about the problem I eventually selected—the development of size constancy perception in infants. Dr. Brunswik corrected me when he thought my word usage was not precise enough, and I corrected his diction. Conversing with me at my rapid rate of speech, in which I gave no particular thought to whether he was following me, was valuable practice for him. (I had realized that I was learning to listen to and comprehend German in Herr Professor Büehler's lecture in general psychology that fall.) On several occasions, I helped Dr. Brunswik with English composition. I remember editing his communications with Dr. Tolman about his coming appointment at the University of California. The appointment was postponed, I believe, from January of 1937 until the fall of 1937, a change that, as it came about, ensured Brunswik's being in the United States at the time of the Austrian Anschluss.

It took some time for me to choose an area in the study of the development of perception in infants that I could carry out with Dr. Brunswik. Until I had a satisfactory German *Aussprache*, I was not allowed to work with older children. And until I found a way to observe some type of response in infants, any attempt to study perception at a very young age was impossible. The babies I wanted to study were not to be removed from their cribs. I finally worked out behavior repertories to protocol. Dr. Brunswik provided the objects: a small rattle such as used in the Vienna Baby Tests and another rattle similar in form but three times as large which he had the institute technician make. Together, we worked out a simple series of presentation of the two objects at a near and far distance. We had to accept the reality that we could never know how long a given baby would be kept at the Kinderübernahmestelle, since the infants could be returned to their families or placed in other care facilities.

The problem was far more difficult than a presentation of objects in a specified order, to which the child would react by grasping the object (or attempting to grasp), pulling a string attached to the object, or indicating the size verbally. I, of course, was basically interested in the development of size constancy and not just in the degree of size constancy at a given age. I do not believe Brunswik had ever worked with such young infants. He always referred to the babies as Miss Cruikshank's (my maiden name) babies. Just once, he came to the Kinderübernahmestelle to observe the situation and the infants' reactions.

When I analyzed my observations, I remember listing a number of variations that we would check later. At the time, I was planning to return to Vienna in future summer vacations from my teaching in college. Dr. Brunswik deleted this sentence. This was the only overt action on Dr. Brunswik's part that indicated that he realized that serious political changes could be in store for the institute as it was then organized.

The institute met frequently for a late-afternoon colloquium. After a presentation by a staff member, advanced student, or visitor, everybody entered into a lively discussion. Dr. Brunswik could be depended on to add support or criticism by citing references, frequently British or American publications. After our meetings, most of the staff gathered for the evening meal at the restaurant at the Rathaus. If the meal lasted too long, the younger assistants knew that Herr Professor Büehler would soon suggest leaving if they started to talk about the opera.

I don't remember Dr. Brunswik using this ploy

to end the evening, although the opera was one of Egon Brunswik's favorite topics. At one of our coffee house sessions, he had torn a sheet from his pocket notebook and written a list of operas that I should hear during my year in Vienna. In the spring of 1937, he took me to hear *Tristan and Isolde*. It was, he told me, the forty-second time he had heard this opera.

Over the years, I have often wondered what the subsequent careers of all of us there at the University of Vienna in 1936–1937 would have been had World War II not occurred. Karl Büehler, Egon Brunswik, and Jean Piaget were undoubtedly the leading psychologists in Europe in 1937. (I had written to my fellow colleagues at Brown University to this effect in a letter in February 1937.) I have never had any doubt that Egon Brunswik would have become the leading psychologist in Europe. He had such a broad interest in the whole field of psychology and was so able to evaluate and appreciate the research of others that he would have made outstanding contributions from his position there in Vienna. It might have been best had he always been able to list his name as Egon Brunswik, Vienna and Berkeley, as it was on the report of our work, which was presented that summer of 1937 (Brunswik & Cruikshank, 1937). I published a paper on this work in 1941 (Cruikshank, 1941).

EPILOGUE

Kenneth R. Hammond
Thomas R. Stewart

By 2000 the Brunswik Society had conducted its sixteenth annual meeting, an event that must certainly have provided a large measure of satisfaction to those psychologists who placed their confidence in Egon Brunswik's view of psychology. That date signifies a psychological theory with a long life of roughly seventy-five years, if the originating ideas of Brunswik's teacher, Karl Bühler, are included. That is extraordinary, and possibly unique, for a psychology based on empirical research.

In order to understand the course of that long life, it will be helpful to place the past and future of Brunswikian psychology in the context of the distinction between two forms of science characterized in terms of "normal science" and the "scientific paradigm" — concepts introduced by Thomas Kuhn (1962). Kuhn explained that "'normal science' means research firmly based upon one or more past scientific achievements, achievements that some particular scientific community acknowledges as supplying the foundation for its further practice" (p.10). He distinguished such normal science from those efforts that were directed toward the establishment of a new paradigm. And by that he meant those efforts that "were sufficiently unprecedented to attract an enduring group of adherents away from competing modes of scientific activity" (p. 10) and "were sufficiently open-ended to leave all sorts of problems for the redefined group of practitioners to resolve" (p. 10). He further explained the term *paradigm* by suggesting that paradigms " provide models from which spring particular coherent traditions of scientific research" (p. 10).

Kuhn's distinction provides an apt description for the development of the Brunswik Society, for it has been based on a "model from which [a] coherent tradition of scientific research" has sprung. For the fifteen-year existence of the society offers evidence that Brunswik's ideas had indeed been found to be "sufficiently unprecedented to attract an enduring group of adherents away from competing modes of scientific activity" (p. 10). Moreover, the empirical research that resulted from these ideas clearly showed that the paradigm was "sufficiently open-ended to leave all sorts of problems for the redefined group of practitioners to resolve." Thus, the Brunswikian paradigm was striking in that it not only offered a new theoretical and methodological framework for psychologists dissatisfied with conventional psychology but also offered the opportunity for the practice of normal science within its framework. That normal science had provided the "achievements that some particular scientific community [the Brunswik Society] acknowledges as supplying the foundation for its further practice." (p. 10) And as the examples of application in this volume indicate, the Brunswikian paradigm has been offering an opportunity for the practice of normal science within the broad field of judgment and decision making ever since 1955. That date marks the publication of an article (Hammond, 1955) that demonstrated the utility of the application of Brunswik's lens model to clinical judgment.

The productivity of (Brunswikian) normal science was carried out under the rubric of social judgment theory during the period 1960–1990 and is impressive by any standard.

Over 250 studies of multiple cue probability learning were carried out, as well as over 1,000 studies of "judgment analysis" (or "policy capturing"). In addition, studies of conflict resolution and interpersonal learning, as well as studies of the effects of psychoactive drugs (see Albright and Malloy, Funder, Gillis, and Mumpower, this volume, and Hammond and Joyce references), have been carried out in applied as well as academic settings. As might be expected, much of this research remains to be discovered by those still attached to the conventional paradigm, who have not yet read it or can't understand it because of devotion to the conventional paradigm.

Kuhn pointed out that 'twas ever thus; he noted that the change from one paradigm to another is like a "Gestalt switch," and "like the gestalt switch, it must occur all at once (though not necessarily in an instant) or not at all." (p. 10) (Brunswik himself experienced the "Gestalt switch" to which Kuhn referred. In a conversation with Hammond, then a graduate student, he recounted how, when he went to Chicago to explain his point of view to L. L. Thurstone, it all left him: As Hammond recalled Brunswik's remarks: "As I put my hand on the door knob of Thurstone's office, everything turned around, and I could not recall the logic of my position; in fact the opposite seemed correct. I was shaken by this, and turned and walked down the hall in terrible confusion. But after a short distance, everything reversed and it all came back to me, and I went to Thurstone's office in calmness.")

Kuhn further noted that conscious, deliberate changes from one paradigm to another seldom occur in a scientist's lifetime: "Copernicanism made few converts for almost a century after Copernicus' death. Newton's work was not generally accepted . . . for more than half a century after the Principia appeared. Priestly never accepted the oxygen theory, nor Lord Kelvin the electromagnetic theory, and so on. . . . And Darwin . . . wrote: 'Although I am fully convinced of the truth of the views given in this volume . . . , I by no means expect to convince experienced naturalists whose minds are stocked with a multitude of facts all viewed, during a long course of years, from a point of view directly opposite to mine.'" Kuhn further quoted Max Planck, who "sadly remarked that 'a new scientific truth does not triumph by convincing its opponents and making them see the light, but rather because its opponents eventually die, and a new generation grows up that is familiar with it'" (Kuhn, 1962, pp. 150–151).

A shift to the Brunswikian paradigm from that of conventional psychology is apt to be more difficult than shifts in the paradigms of physical science, for two reasons. First, the field of psychology, although strongly orthodox with respect to methodology, is disorganized if not downright chaotic with respect to theory. Brunswik could suffer a Gestalt switch outside Thurstone's office with respect to methodology because a clear, conventional methodology was there to be shifted to. But theoretical psychology, having softened to the point of becoming a morass since the demise of American learning theory and European psychoanalysis, could not offer Brunswik a clear, highly visible Gestalt to which he could switch from his own clear view of probabilistic functionalism. Nor could he make this switch today; Brunswikian theory is firmly organized, but there is no firmly organized theoretical context to which one can switch, at least in the field of cognitive psychology.

Second, Brunswikian concepts such as "ecological validity" and "quasi rationality" have been hijacked—taken over and distorted by careless researchers and textbook writers over the past twenty years; as a result, the acceptance of Brunswikian theory may be further delayed simply because of the confusion engendered (see the commentary on Brunswik, 1949, for further detail). But new events in the 1990s provided a new phase in the history of the Brunswikian paradigm. And those events occurred just prior to the beginning of the decade of the 1990s.

The Decade of the 1990s Brings Change

The decade of the 1990s marked a significant change in the pursuit of Brunswikian ideas. The beginning of the decade saw the culmination of the normal science carried out within the framework of social judgment theory. By 1988, Brehmer and Joyce were sufficiently confident of the visibility of that work they titled their anthology *Human Judgment: The SJT view* (Brehmer & Joyce, 1988), thus presuming that by the beginning of the decade, social judgment theory was sufficiently well known that it would be enough to indicate the content of their anthology merely by use of the initials *SJT*. The contents were inclusive and of high quality, but the book was rarely seen because the publishers priced the book out of the market. But in 1996 an entire issue of the journal *Thinking and Reasoning* appeared that was devoted to social judgment theory. Edited by Michael Doherty, it contained seven contributions that elucidated various aspects of the normal science of the period 1960–1990.

And at the beginning of the decade, Gigerenzer and his colleagues used Brunswikian theory as a point of departure to sharply attack the "heuristics and biases" work by Amos Tversky and Daniel Kaheman, then the dominant approach in the field of judgment and decision making. Throughout the period the vigorous and prolific efforts of Gigerenzer and his colleagues not only provided considerable visibility for the Brunswikian point of view but hammered the then dominant approach of Amos Tversky and Daniel Kahneman. For example, Gigerenzer 1991 article with U. Hoffrage and H. Kleinbolting, titled "Probabilistic Mental Models: A Brunswikian Theory of Confidence," contradicted the Tversky and Kahneman view that people are generally overconfident in their judgments. And Gigerenzer and Hoffrage's (1995) argument that people's judgments under uncertainty generally failed to be "Bayesian" because they were required to cope with probabilities instead of "natural frequencies" (a Brunswikian argument) stood up to criticism. Gigerenzer (1998) continued the ecological tradition apparent in Brunswik's work at the end of the decade by applying it to evolutionary psychology. The range and variety of Gigerenzer's work enriched considerably the vision of what Brunswikian psychology could do. Thus, the decade would provide a form of Brunswikian normal science parallel to, if different from, that provided by social judgment theory.

By any standard, 1996 (twelfth year of the society) was a banner year for the Brunswikian paradigm. By the middle of the decade two "social judgment theory" books appeared, one by R. Cooksey (1996b) and one by K. Hammond (1996c). The appearance of Cooksey's book meant that for the first time researchers could find the basic ideas and technology that are the foundation of social judgment theory between the covers of a book. And for the first time researchers could find the fundamentals of social judgment theory applied to a broad set of social topics in Hammond's book. Moreover, 1999 brought a third social judgment theory book, *Judgments under Stress* (Hammond, 1999) to publication. This book is more firmly and explicitly based on Brunswikian theory inasmuch the concept of stress is defined in terms of the Brunswikian emphasis on "constancy." Thus, at the beginning of the next decade, researchers are able to read the present volume and, perhaps for the first time, read original articles by Brunswik and comments on them, as well as see examples of normal science that have developed from those articles.

In short, the 1990s saw the establishment of two forms of a normal science carried out within the Brunswikian framework. That body of work as well as the appearance and growth of a Brunswik Society was proof that "an enduring [and productive] group of adherents" existed a half century after Brunswik's death, and would continue to exist.

The Future

As Brunswik noted in the first sentence of his 1956 book, "Science has a way of growing in spearheads" (1956b, p. 3). His candidate for a spearhead at the end of the nineteenth century was differential psychology, derived from Galton and Spearman, for it had "supplied the content in terms of which psychologists could develop, or absorb, a general methodology of statistical evaluation" (1956b, p. 3).

Our candidate for the spearhead that appears at the end of the twentieth century is the narrower field of judgment and decision making. It is necessary to use the modifier *narrower* because judgment and decision making appear to be a subfield of cognitive psychology, but reflection will tell us that, although still unformed in many ways, it is the more general aspect of cognitive psychology. And the one paradigm in this subfield that is all-encompassing — for it brings theory, methodology and history together — is the Brunswikian paradigm.

In short, the future will bring the high visibility of the Brunswikian paradigm that forms the foundation of the normal science it fostered in the latter half of the twentieth century. That visibility will be produced in the twenty-first century because the collation of the papers in this volume identify a corpus of a coherent ideas that have proven to be productive at a sufficient level of complexity to gain adherents.

Visibility will bring change, of course. Normal science will continue in its various and complex ways, but the paradigm itself will attract increasing critical analysis, and that, together with the empirical results of normal science, will bring about change in the paradigm itself. If Kuhn was right, the growth of science brought about by the Brunswikian paradigm will result in crisis and a new paradigm. All that remains to be seen, of course. But those who participate should find it to be an exciting time in the history of psychology.

COMPLETE ANNOTATED LIST OF
BRUNSWIK'S PUBLISHED PAPERS

The editors wish to express their appreciation to Bernhard Wolf for contributing references and notes to this list.

Brunswik, E. (1927). Strukturmonismus und Physik. Unpublished dissertation, Philosophische Fakultät der Universität Wien.
   Structure-monism and physics. Faculty of Philosophy. University of Vienna. His doctoral "fathers" (*Doktorvater* is a typical German expression) were the famous Vienna professors Karl Bühler and Moritz Schlick.
Brunswik, E. (1928). Zur Entwicklung der Albedowahrnehmung. *Zeitschrift für Psychologie, 109*, 40–115.
   The development of albedo-perception.
Brunswik, E., & Kardos, L. (1929). Das Duplizitätsprinzip in der Theorie der Farbenwahrnehmung. *Zeitschrift für Psychologie, 111*, 307–320.
   The duplicity principle in the theory of color perception
Brunswik, E., & Kindermann, H. (1929). Eidetik bei taubstummen Jugendlichen. *Zeitschrift für angewandte Psychologie, 34*, 244–274.
   Eidetics in deaf-mute juveniles.
Brunswik, E. (1929). Prinzipienfragen der Gestalttheorie. In E. Brunswik, C. Bühler, H. Hetzer, L. Kardos, E. Köhler, J. Krug, & A. Willwoll (Eds.), *Beiträge zur Problemgeschichte der Psychologie: Festschrift zu Karl Bühlers 50. Geburtstag* (pp. 78–149). Jena: G. Fischer.
   Questions of principle in Gestalt theory. Contributions to the problem history of psychology. Festschrift for Karl Bühler's fiftieth birthday.
Brunswik, E. (1930). Über Farben-, Größen- und Gestaltkonstanz in der Jugend. In H. Volkelt (Ed.), *Bericht über den 11. Kongreß für experimentelle Psychologie in Wien 1929* (pp. 52–56). Jena: G. Fisher.
   On the constancy of color, size, and Gestalt in youth. Proceedings of the eleventh Congress for Experimental Psychology in Vienna, 1929.
Brunswik, E. (1932). Experimente über Kritik: Ein Beitrag zur Entwicklungspsychologie des Denkens. In G. Kafka (Ed.), *Bericht über den 12. Kongreß der Deutschen Gesellschaft für Psychologie in Hamburg 1931* (pp. 300–305). Jena: G. Fischer.
   Experiments on criticism: A contribution to the developmental psychology of thinking. Proceedings of the twelfth Congress of the German Society for Psychology in Hamburg, 1931.
Brunswik, E., Goldscheider, L., & Pilek, E. (1932). Untersuchungen zur Entwicklung des Gedächtnisses bei Knaben und Madchen vom 6–18 Jahren. *Zeitschrift für angewandte Psychologie, Beiheft 64*, VIII+158.
   Studies in the development of memory with boys and girls aged six to eighteen years.
Brunswik, E. (1933). Die Zugänglichkeit von Gegenständen für die Wahrnehmung und deren quantitative Bestimmung. *Archiv für die gesamte Psychologie, 88*, 377–418.
   The accessibility of objects for perception and their quantitative determination.
Brunswik, E. (1934a). Flächeninhalt und Volumen als Gegenstände der Wahrnehmung. In O. Klemm (Ed.), *Bericht über den 13. Kongreß der Deutschen Gesellschaft für Psychologie in Leipzig* (pp. 120–123). Jena: G. Fischer.

Area and volume as objects of perception. Proceedings of the thirteenth Congress of the German Society for Psychology in Leipzig, 1933.

Brunswik, E. (1934b). *Wahrnehmung und Gegenstandswelt: Grundlegung einer Psychologie vom Gegenstand her*. Leipzig and Vienna: F. Deuticke (Habilitationsschrift).
Perception and the world of objects: The foundations of a psychology in terms of objects. The *Habilitation* is a postdoctoral examination, typical at German-speaking universities. A successful candidate becomes *Privatdozent*. The *Habilitationsschrift* is the postdoctoral thesis connected with *Habilitation*. Brunswik's *Habilitations*-father was again Karl Bühler.

Brunswik, E. (1935a). *Experimentelle Psychologie in Demonstrationen*. Vienna: J. Springer.
Experimental psychology in demonstrations

Brunswik, E. (1935b). Prüfung und Übung höherer Wahrnehmungsleistungen (Dingkonstanz). *Bericht über den 8. Internationalen Kongreß für Psychotechnik in Prag 1934* (pp. 684–689). Prague
The verification and use of higher achievements of perception (thing constancy). Proceedings of the eighth International Congress for Psychotechnics in Prague, 1934.

Brunswik, E. (1935c). Psychologie als objektive Beziehungswissenschaft. *Actualitiés Scientifiques et Industrielles*, 389, 7.
Psychology as a science of objective relations.

Tolman, E. C., & Brunswik, E. (1935). The organism and the causal texture of the environment. *Psychological Review*, 42, 43–77.

Brunswik, E. (1936a). Psychologie als objektive Beziehungswissenschaft. *Actes du Congres International de Philosophie Scientifique à Paris 1935. Vol. 2: Unite de la Science* (pp. 15–21). Paris: Hermann.
Psychology as a science of objective relations. Proceedings of the International Congress for Scientific Philosophy in Paris, 1935. Vol. 2: Unity of science.

Brunswik, E. (1936b). Psychologie vom Gegenstand her. *Actes du Huitième Congres International de Philosophie à Prague 1934* (pp. 840–845). Prague: Orbis.
Psychology in terms of objects. Proceedings of the eighth International Congress for Philosophy in Prague, 1934.

Brunswik, E. (1936c). Psychology in terms of objects. In H. W. Hill (Ed.), *Proceedings of the 25th Anniversary Celebration of the Inauguration of Graduate Studies* (pp. 122–126). University of Southern California.

Brunswik, E. (1937). Psychology as a science of objective relations. *Philosophy of Science*, 4, 227–260.
Errata: *Philosophy of Science* (1938), 5, 110.

Brunswik, E., & Cruikshank, R. M. (1937). Perceptual size-constancy in early infancy. *Psychological Bulletin*, 34, 713–714.

Brunswik, E., & Reiter, L. (1937). Eindruckscharaktere schematisierter Gesichter. *Zeitschrift für Psychologie*, 142, 67–134.
Impression characteristics of schematized faces.

Brunswik, E. (1938a). Das Induktionsprinzip in der Wahrnehmung. In H. Pieron & J. Meyerson (Eds.), *11ième Congres International de Psychologie à Paris 1937. Rapports et Comptes Rendus* (pp. 346–347). Paris: Alcan.
The principle of induction in perception. Proceedings of the eleventh International Congress for Psychology in Paris, 1937.

Brunswik, E. (1938b). Die Eingliederung der Psychologie in die exakten Wissenschaften. *Einheitswissenschaft*, 6, 17–34.
The position of psychology within the exact sciences.

Brunswik, E. (1939a). The conceptual focus of some psychological systems. *Journal of Unified Science (Erkenntnis)*, 8, 36–49.
Also in M. H. Marx, (Ed.) (1936). *Theories in Contemporary Psychology*. New York: Macmillan, pp. 226–237. (Paper sent in for the fourth International Congress for the Unity of Science, Cambridge, England, 1938.)

Brunswik, E. (1939b). Perceptual characteristics of schematized human figures. *Psychological Bulletin*, 36, 553.

Abstract: Twelve variations of a graphic, crudely schematized human figure, about half of them involving changes of facial appearance besides those of stature were presented to 58 students using the method of paired comparison. Among the six apparent characteristics tested, greatest agreement among the subjects was found for "good-lookingness," followed in declining order by "age," "energy", "likeability", "happiness", "intelligence." In approximately the same order there is an increase in the relative influence of the face, although even for the last two of these qualities, apparent happiness and apparent intelligence, significant differences can be found for pairs differing only in stature and not in facial proportion. Besides the general tendency to perceive as more intelligent the standard medium figure, men seem to rate athletic more intelligent than leptosomatic figures with little emphasis on height, women are more intelligent than short figures with little emphasis on breadth. For such qualities as happy, good-looking, and energetic, however, women seem to be favorably impressed also by breadth. An example of the tendency toward ambivalent effects is shown by the addition of spectacles to the standard face which increases apparent intelligence and decreases good-lookingness of the figure. (15 min. slides).

Brunswik, E. (1939c). Probability as a determiner of rat behavior. *Journal of Experimental Psychology*, 25, 175–197.

Brunswik, E. (1940a). A random sample of estimated sizes and their relation to corresponding size measurements. *Psychological Bulletin*, 37, 585–586.

Abstract: A subject was asked to give intuitive as well as critical estimates — each in different attitudes — of the extension of an object most conspicuous to him at the moment. The conditions included indoor and outdoor situations representative of the activities pursued during a normal day. The material comprises a total of 180 of such situations. Objective measurements of the objects as well as of their distances from the eye were also obtained, showing approximately normal distributions. Almost perfect correlations between measured and estimated sizes were found, indicating the presence of perceptual size-constancy in an unbiased sample of "natural" test situations.

Brunswik, E. (1940b). Thing constancy as measured by correlation coefficients. *Psychological Review*, 47, 69–78.

Brunswik, E. (1941). Perceptual size-constancy in life situations. *Psychological Bulletin*, 38, 611–612.

Abstract: A sample of 93 frontal objects of various sizes and distances representative of perceptial situations in everday life was secured by obtaining from a subject, at irregular intervals during normal activities, reports of the incidental perceptual contents. Immediate perceptual estimates (as well as critical ones) of object-size (distal stimulus), visual angle (proximal, "retinals," stimulus), and of distance were given by both subject and experimenter. The latter also secured the corresponding objective measures. The sizes range from a few mm. to more that 100 m. and show a normal distribution when plotted logarithmically, and the distances range from 25 cm to about 1500 m.

Perceptual estimates show, on the whole, much better agreement with the corresponding stimulus variable when this variable is distant object-size (indicating good perceptual size-constancy), or when it is distance, than when it is proximal size (supporting evidence against the "constancy-hypothesis"). Various correlations computed between the estimates and the environmental variables after elimination of the environmental correlation between object-size and retinal size are between .95 and 1.00 in the case of object-size and of distance, and between 0 and .7 when retinal size is involved, with good agreement between the coefficients representing the perceptual achievements of the two observers. Averages of errors follow a similar pattern.

The generality of further findings of laboratory experimentation, such as the comparative overestimation of near objects (perceptual compromise between distal and proximal size), and the improvement of estimates by shifting from the purely perceptual to the critically controlled attitudes was also demonstrated by our random sample of size estimates. There also is some indication of the relative independence of the distance functionally "taken into consideration" in the establishment of size-constancy, and the explicat ("conscious") estimates of distance.

Overestimation of vertical as contrasted to horizontal extensions was not borne out by our data. (15 min., slides.)

Brunswik, E. (1943). Organismic achievement and environmental probability. *Psychological Review, 50,* 255–272.

Part of "Symposium on Psychology and Scientific Method," held in 1941. Other speakers were C. Hull and K. Lewin. Reported as "The Probability Point of View" in M. H. Marx, (Ed.) (1951). *Psychological Theory.* New York: Macmillan, pp. 188–202.

Brunswik, E. (1944). Distal focussing of perception: Size constancy in a representative sample of situations. *Psychological Monographs, 56*(254), 1–49.

Brunswik, E. (1945). Social perception of traits from photographs. *Psychological Bulletin, 42,* 535–536.

Abstract: Psychology classes totalling 95 subjects judged standardized photographs of 46 Army STP students (IQ approximately 90 to 140) unknown to them. Correlating "real" traits (mutual ASTP ratings, for intelligence also tests) with corresponding average intuitive estimates shows social perceptual validity ("achievement") to be negligible for intelligence (under .10), statistically significant for personality traits such as energy and likeability (about 35). Goodlookingness yields .65. Halos among judgments are strong, and unrealistic considering low corresponding real-trait relationships (added in parenthesis): intelligence with energy, 84 (.28) with likeability, .62 (.01); with goodlookingness, .59 (.05) Among possible cues, height (stature) correlates .25 with intuited intelligence; if confirmed, this possibly indicates utilization of low but established height IQ relationship of about .15 also found here. Among facial features, forehead-height shows only .18 (compare with popular prejudice!) versus .22, nose-height .20 versus .13.

Brunswik, E. (1946a). Four types of experiment. *American Psychologist, 1,* 457.

Brunswik, E. (1946b). Points of view: Components of psychological theorizing. In P. L. Harriman (Ed.), *Encyclopedia of Psychology* (pp. 523–537). New York Philosophical Library.

Brunswik, E. (1947). *Systematic and Representative Design of Psychological Experiments: With Results in Physical and Social Perception.* Berkeley: University of California Press.

Also published in J. Neyman, (Ed.) (1949). *Proceedings of the Berkeley Symposium on Mathematical Statistics and Probability* (pp. 143–202). Berkeley: University of California Press.

The symposium was held at the Statistical Laboratory, Department of Mathematics, University of California, August 13–18, 1945, and January 27–29, 1946.

Brunswik, E. (1948). Statistical separation of perception, thinking, and attitudes. *American Psychologist, 3,* 342.

Brunswik, E. (1949). Discussion: Remarks on functionalism in perception. *Journal of Personality, 18,* 56–65.

A contribution to a Symposium on Personal and Social Factors in Perception held during the 1949 meetings of the American Psychological Association in Denver. Also appears in J. S. Bruner, & D. Krech, (Eds.) (1950). *Perception and Personality: A Symposium.* Durham, NC: Duke University Press (pp. 56–65).

Brunswik, E. (1950). Discussion: Remarks on functionalism in perception. In J. S. Bruner & D. Krech (Eds.), *Perception and Personality: A Symposium* (pp. 56–65). Durham, NC: Duke University Press.

Same as: Brunswik, E. (1949). Discussion: Remarks on functionalism in perception. *Journal of Personality, 18,* 56–65.

Brunswik, E. (1951). Note on Hammond's analogy between "relativity and representativeness." *Philosophy of Science, 18,* 212–217.

Brunswik, E., & Herma, H. (1951). Probability learning of perceptual cues in the establishment of a weight illusion. *Journal of Experimental Psychology, 41,* 281–290.

Brunswik, E. (1952). The conceptual framework of psychology. *International Encyclopedia of Unified Science*. Chicago: University of Chicago Press.
Prepublication announced as *Methodological Foundations of Psychology* and earlier as E. Brunswik and A. Ness, *Theory of Behavior*.

Brunswik, E., & Kamiya, J. (1953). Ecological cue-validity of "proximity" and of other Gestalt factors. *American Journal of Psychology, 66*, 20–32.

Brunswik, E. (1955a). In defense of probabilistic functionalism: A reply. *Psychological Review, 62*, 236–242.

Brunswik, E. (1955b). "Ratiomorphic" models of perception and thinking. *Acta Psychologica, 11*, 108–109.
Also published in N. Maillouw (Ed.) (1955). *Proceedings of the 14th International Congress on Psychology, Montreal, 1954*. Amsterdam: North-Holland.

Brunswik, E. (1955c). Representative design and probabilistic theory in a functional psychology. *Psychological Review, 62*(3), 193–217.

Brunswik, E. (1956a). Historical and thematic relations of psychology to other sciences. *Scientific Monthly, 83*, 151–161.
Also Chapter 17 in Hammond (1966b).

Brunswik, E. (1956b). *Perception and the Representative Design of Psychological Experiments*. Berkeley: University of California Press.
Part I is a reprint of Brunswik (1947). Part II is entitled "Perception: The Ecological Generality of Its Distal Aim."

Brunswik, E. (1957). Scope and aspects of the cognitive problem. In H. Gruber, K. R. Hammond, & R. Jessor (Eds.), *Contemporary Approaches to Cognition* (pp. 5–31). Cambridge: Harvard University Press.
Contributors to this volume were J. S. Bruner, E. Brunswik, L. Festinger, F. Heider, K. F. Muenzinger, C. E. Osgood, and D. Rapaport.

Brunswik, E. (1959). Ontogenetic and other developmental parallels to the history of science. In H. M. Evans (Ed.), *Men and Moments in the History of Science* (pp. 3–21). Seattle: University of Washington Press.

Brunswik, E. (1963). The conceptual focus of psychological systems (Reprint of Brunswik, 1939a). In M. Marx (Ed.), *Contemporary Theories in Psychology* (pp. 226–239). New York: Macmillan.
Reprint of E. Brunswik (1939a). The conceptual focus of some psychological systems. *Journal of Unified Science (Erkenntnis), 8*, 36–49.

Brunswik, E. (1966). Reasoning as a universal behavior model and a functional differentiation between "perception" and "thinking." In K. R. Hammond (Ed.), *The Psychology of Egon Brunswik* (pp. 487–494). New York: Holt, Rinehart, & Winston.
Read at the International Congress of Psychology in Montreal, 1954.

REFERENCES

Abernathy, C. M., & Hamm, R. M. (1995). *Surgical intuition: What it is and how to get it*. Philadelphia: Hanley & Belfus.

Adelman, L., Stewart, T. R., & Hammond, K. R. (1975). A case history of the application of social judgment theory to policy formation. *Policy Sciences, 6,* 137–159.

Adelman, L. (1977). *Information about task properties: A necessary, but not a sufficient condition for high levels of achievement in multiple-cue probability learning tasks* (Center for Research on Judgment and Policy Report No. 199). Boulder: Institute of Behavioral Science, University of Colorado.

Adelman, L. (1981). The influence of formal, substantive, and contextual task properties on the relative effectiveness of different forms of feedback in multiple-cue probability learning tasks. *Organizational Behavior and Human Performance, 27,* 423–442.

Adelman, L. (1988). Separation of facts and values. In B. Brehmer & C. R. B. Joyce (Eds.), *Human judgment: The SJT view* (pp. 443–464). New York: North-Holland.

Adorno, T. W., Frenkel-Brunswik, E., Levinson, D. J., & Sanford, R. N. (1950). *The authoritarian personality*. New York: Harper.

Ahl, V. A., Moore, C. F., & Dixon, J. A. (1992). Development of intuitive and numerical proportional reasoning. *Cognitive Development, 7,* 81–108.

Aitken, M. (1980). A note on the selection of log-linear models. *Biometrics, 36,* 173–178.

Allport, F. H. (1955). *Theories of perception and the concept of structure*. New York: Wiley.

Allport, G. W. (1937). *Personality: A psychological interpretation*. New York: Holt.

Allport, G. W. (1958). What units shall we employ? In G. Lindzey (Ed.), *Assessment of human motives* (pp. 239–260). New York: Rinehart.

Allport, G. W. (1962). The general and the unique in psychological science. *Journal of Personality, 30,* 405–422.

Allport, G. W. (1966). Traits revisited. *American Psychologist, 21,* 1–10.

Ambady, N., & Rosenthal, R. (1992). Thin slices of expressive behavior as predictors of interpersonal consequences: A meta-analysis. *Psychological Bulletin, 111,* 256–274.

Ambady, N., & Rosenthal, R. (1993). Half a minute: Predicting teacher evaluations from thin slices of nonverbal behavior and physical attractiveness. *Journal of Personality and Social Psychology, 64,* 431–441.

Andersen, S. M. (1984). Self-knowledge and social inference: II. The diagnosticity of cognitive/affective and behavioral data. *Journal of Personality and Social Psychology, 46,* 294–307.

Anderson, N. H. (1981). *Foundations of information integration theory*. New York: Academic Press.

Asch, S. E. (1946). Forming impressions of personality. *Journal of Abnormal and Social Psychology, 9,* 258–290.

Ash, M. G. (1987). Psychology and politics in interwar Vienna: The Vienna Psychological Institute, 1922–1942. In M. G. Ash & W. R. Woodward (Eds.), *Psychology in twentieth-century thought and society*. Cambridge: Cambridge University Press.

Ash, M. G. (1995). Emigré women psychologists and psychoanalysts in the United States. In S. Quack (Ed.), *Between sorrow and strength: Women refugees of the Nazi period* (pp. 239–264). Cambridge: Cambridge University Press.

Ashby, F. G., Alfonso-Reese, L. A., Turken, A. U., & Waldron, E. M. (1998). A neuropsychological theory of multiple systems in category learning. *Psychological Review, 105,* 442–481.

Ashton, R. H. (1992). Effects of justification and a mechanical aid on judgment performance. *Organizational Behavior and Human Decision Processes, 52,* 292–306.

Baldessarini, R. J. (1978). Chemotherapy. In A. M. Nicholi (Ed.), *The Harvard guide to modern psychiatry* . Cambridge: Harvard University Press.

Balke, W. M., Hammond, K. R., & Meyer, G. D. (1973). An alternate approach to labor-management relations. *Administrative Science Quarterly, 18,* 311–327.

Ball, G. H., & Hall, D. J. (1967). A clustering technique for summarizing multivariate data. *Behavioral Science, 12,* 153–155.

Balzer, W. K., Doherty, M. E., & O'Connor, R. O. (1989). The effects of cognitive feedback on performance. *Psychological Bulletin, 106,* 410–433.

Balzer, W. K., Sulsky, L. M., Hammer, S., & Sumner, K. (1992). Task information, cognitive information, or functional validity information: Which components of cognitive feedback affect performance? *Organizational Behavior and Human Decision Processes, 53,* 35–54.

Balzer, W. K., Hammer, L. B., Sumner, K. E., Birchenough, T. R., Martens, S. P., & Raymark, P. H. (1994). Effects of cognitive feedback components, display format, and elaboration on performance. *Organizational Behavior and Human Decision Processes, 58,* 369–385.

Banaji, M. R., & Crowder, R. G. (1989). The bankruptcy of everyday memory. *American Psychologist, 44,* 1185–1193.

Barker, R. (1968). *Ecological psychology: Concepts and methods for studying the environment of human behavior.* Stanford, CA: Stanford University Press.

Barkow, J., Cosmides, L., & Tooby, J. (1992). *The adapted mind: Evolutionary psychology and the generation of culture.* New York: Oxford University Press.

Bartlett, M. S., Hager, J. C., Ekman, P., & Sejnowski, T. J. (1999). Measuring facial expressions by computer image analysis. *Psychophysiology, 36,* 253–263.

Batchelder, W. H., & Romney, A. K. (1990). New results in test theory without an answer key. In E. E. E. Roskam (Ed.), *Mathematical psychology in progress.* New York: Springer-Verlag.

Beal, D., Gillis, J. S., & Stewart, T. (1978). The lens model: Computational procedures and applications. *Perceptual and Motor Skills, 46,* 3–28.

Bean, W. B. (1961). *Sir William Osler, aphorisms.* Springfield, IL: Charles C Thomas.

Beck, S. J. (1953). The science of personality: Nomothetic or idiographic? *Psychological Review, 60,* 353–359.

Benetka, G. (1990). *Zur Geschichte der Institutionalisierung der Psychologie in Österreich.* Vienna-Salzburg: Geyer-Edition.

Benetka, G. (1995). *Psychologie in Wien: Sozial- und Theoriegeschichte des Wiener Psychologischen Instituts 1922–1938.* Vienna: Wiener Universitätsverlag.

Benetka, G. (1997). Vor der Emigration: Zum wissenschaftlichen Werdegang Egon Brunswiks. In K. R. Fischer & F. Stadler (Eds.), *Wahrnehmung und Gegenstandswelt: Zum Lebenswerk von Egon Brunswik.* Vienna: Springer.

Bergmann, G. (1952). Review of Egon Brunswik's "The conceptual framework of psychology." *Psychological Bulletin, 49,* 654–656.

Berlin, I. (1956/1984). *The Age of Enlightenment.* Meridian, NY: New American Library.

Berlin, I. (1969). *Four essays on liberty.* New York: Oxford University Press.

Bernieri, F. J., Zuckerman, M., Koestner, R., & Rosenthal, R. (1994). Measuring person perception accuracy: Another look at self-other agreement. *Personality and Social Psychology Bulletin, 20,* 367–378.

Bernieri, F. J., & Gillis, J. S. (1995a). The judgment of rapport: A cross-cultural comparison between Americans and Greeks. *Journal of Nonverbal Behavior, 19,* 115–130.

Bernieri, F. J., & Gillis, J. S. (1995b). Personality correlates of accuracy in a social perception task. *Perceptual and Motor Skills, 81,* 168–170.

Bernieri, F. J., Gillis, J. S., Davis, J. M., & Grahe, J. E. (1996). Dyad rapport and the accuracy of its judgment across situations: A lens model analysis. *Journal of Personality and Social Psychology, 70,* 110–129.

Bernieri, F. J., Gillis, J., & Curtis, M. (1998). *Issues in assessing rapport judgments: Construct definition, target focus, and gender.* (Manuscript submitted for publication.)

Berretty, P. M., Todd, P. M., & Martignon, L. (1999). Categorization by elimination: Using few cues to choose. In G. Gigerenzer, P. M. Todd, & the ABC Research Group, *Simple heuristics that make us smart*. New York: Oxford University Press.

Björkman, M. (1965). Studies in predictive behavior: Explorations into predictive judgments based on functional learning and defined by estimation, categorization, and choice. *Scandinavian Journal of Psychology, 6,* 129–156.

Björkman, M. (1967). Stimulus-event learning and event learning as concurrent processes. *Organizational Behavior and Human Performance, 2,* 219–236.

Björkman, M. (1969). Individual performances in a single-cue probability learning task. *Scandinavian Journal of Psychology, 10,* 113–123.

Björkman, M. (1987). A note on cue probability learning: What conditioning data reveal about cue contrast. *Scandinavian Journal of Psychology, 28,* 226–232.

Björkman, M. (1994). Internal cue theory: Calibration and resolution of confidence in general knowledge. *Organizational Behavior and Human Decision Processes, 58,* 386–405.

Blackman, M. C., & Funder, D. C. (1998). The effect of information on consensus and accuracy in personality judgment. *Journal of Experimental Social Psychology, 34,* 164–181.

Blattberg, R. C., & Hoch, S. J. (1990). Database models and managerial intuition: 50% model + 50% manager. *Management Science, 36,* 887–899.

Boring, E. G. (1942). *Sensation and perception in the history of experimental psychology.* New York: Appleton-Century-Crofts.

Boring, E. G. (1957). *A history of experimental psychology.* New York: Appleton-Century-Crofts.

Boring, E. G. (1963). *History, psychology, and science: Selected papers.* New York: Wiley.

Bossomaier, T., & Green, D. (1998). *Patterns in the sand: Computers, complexity and life.* St. Leonards, NSW, Australia: Allen & Unwin.

Brake, G. L., Doherty, M. E., & Kleiter, G. (1997). *A Brunswikian approach to the calibration of subjective probabilities.* Unpublished manuscript.

Brake, G. L. (1998). *Calibration of probability judgments: Effects of number of focal hypotheses and predictability of the environment.* Unpublished doctoral dissertation, Bowling Green State University.

Brake, G. L., Doherty, M. E., & Kleiter, G. D. (1998). Overconfidence: Rethinking a fundamental bias in judgment yet again. (Unpublished manuscript.)

Brehmer, A., & Brehmer, B. (1988). What have we learned about human judgment from thirty years of policy capturing? In B. Brehmer & C. R. B. Joyce (Eds.), *Human Judgment: The SJT View* (pp. 75–114). New York: North-Holland.

Brehmer, B. (1972a). Cue utilization and cue consistency in multiple-cue probability learning. *Organizational Behavior and Human Performance, 8,* 286–296.

Brehmer, B. (1972b). Policy conflict as a function of policy similarity and policy complexity. *Scandinavian Journal of Psychology, 13,* 208–221.

Brehmer, B. (1974). Hypotheses about relations between scaled variables in the learning of probabilistic inference tasks. *Organizational Behavior and Human Performance, 11,* 1–27.

Brehmer, B. (1976). Social judgment theory and the analysis of interpersonal conflict. *Psychological Bulletin, 83,* 985–1003.

Brehmer, B. (1980a). In one word: Not from experience. *Acta Psychologica, 45,* 223–241.

Brehmer, B. (1980b). Probabilistic functionalism in the laboratory: Learning and interpersonal (cognitive) conflict. In K. R. Hammond & N. E. Wascoe (Eds.), *Realizations of Brunswik's representative design.* San Francisco: Jossey-Bass.

Brehmer, B. (1984). Brunswikian psychology for the 1990's. In K. M. J. Lagerspetz & P. Niemi (Eds.), *Psychology in the 1990's* (pp. 383–398). Amsterdam: North-Holland Elsevier.

Brehmer, B., & Hagafors, R. (1986). Use of experts in complex decision making: A paradigm for the study of staff work. *Organizational Behavior and Human Decision Processes, 38,* 181–195.

Brehmer, B. (1987). Note on subjects' hypotheses in multiple-cue probability learning. *Organizational Behavior and Human Decision Processes, 40,* 323–329.

Brehmer, B. (1988). The development of social judgment theory. In B. Brehmer & C. R. B. Joyce (Eds.), *Human judgment: The social judgment theory view* (pp. 13–40). Amsterdam: North-Holland.

Brehmer, B., & Joyce, C. R. B. (Eds.). (1988). *Human judgment: The social judgment theory view*. Amsterdam: North-Holland.

Brehmer, B. (1989). The psychology of linear judgment models. *Acta Psychologica, 87,* 137–154.

Brehmer, B. (1992). Dynamic decision making: Human control of complex systems. *Acta Psychologica, 81,* 211–241.

Brehmer, B. (1996). Man as a stabiliser of systems: From static snapshots of judgment processes to dynamic decision making. *Thinking and Reasoning, 2,* 225–238.

Brennan, R. L., & Kane, M. T. (1977). An index of dependability for mastery tests. *Journal of Educational Measurement, 14,* 277–289.

Brennan, J. F. (1986). *History and systems of psychology*. London: Prentice-Hall.

Brentano, F. (1973). *Psychology from an Empirical Standpoint*. Trans. L. McAlister. London: Routledge and Kegan Paul. First published 1874.

Brookhouse, K. J., Guion, R. G., & Doherty, M. E. (1986). Social desirability response bias as one source of the discrepancy between subjective and regression weights. *Organizational Behavior and Human Decision Processes, 37,* 297–315.

Browne, B. A., & Gillis, J. S. (1982). Evaluating the quality of instruction in art: A social judgment analysis. *Psychological Reports, 50,* 955–962.

Browne, J. P., O'Boyle, C. A., McGee, H. M., McDonald, N. J., & Joyce, C. R. B. (1997). Development of a direct weighting procedure for quality of life domains. *Quality Life Research, 6,* 301–309.

Bruner, J., & Krech, D. (1949/1950). *Perception and personality*. Durham: Duke University Press.

Bryk, A. S., & Raudenbush, S. W. (1992). *Hierarchical linear models: Application and data analysis methods*. Newbury Park, CA: Sage.

Buck, R. (1984). *The communication of emotion*. New York: Guilford Press.

Bühler, K. (1907). Tatsachen und Probleme zu einer Psychologie der Denkvorgänge. I. Über Gedanken. *Archiv für die gesamte Psychologie, 9,* 297–365.

Bühler, K. (1913). *Die Gestaltwahrnehmungen*. Stuttgart: Spemann.

Bühler, K. (1927/1978). *Die Krise der Psychologie*. Berlin: Ullstein.

Burnside, D. (1994). *A study of land management judgments in the rangelands of Western Australia and South Australia*. Doctoral dissertation, University of Queensland, Brisbane.

Bush, R. R., & Estes, W. K. (1959). *Studies in mathematical learning theory*. Stanford: Stanford University Press.

Buss, A. H. (1961). *The psychology of aggression*. New York: Wiley.

Buss, D. M. (1987). Sex differences in human mate selection criteria: An evolutionary perspective. In C. Crawford, M. Smith, & D. Krebs (Eds.), *Sociobiology and psychology: Ideas, issues and applications* (pp. 335–351). Hillsdale, NJ: Erlbaum.

Buss, D. M. (1989). Sex differences in human mate preferences: Evolutionary hypotheses tested in 37 cultures. *Behavioral and Brain Sciences, 12,* 1–49.

Byrne, R. (1995). *The thinking ape: Evolutionary origins of intelligence*. New York: Oxford University Press.

Campbell, D. T., & Fiske, D. W. (1959). Convergent and discriminant validity by the multitrait-multimethod matrix. *Psychological Bulletin, 56,* 81–105.

Campbell, D. T. (1966). Pattern matching as an essential in distal knowing. In K. R. Hammond (Ed.), *The psychology of Egon Brunswik* (pp. 81–106). New York: Holt, Rinehart, & Winston.

Carnap, R. (1929/1959). Psychology in Physical Language. In A. J. Ayer (Ed.), *Logical Positivism*. New York: Free Press.

Carroll, J. S., & Johnson, E. J. (1990). *Decision research: A field guide*. Newbury Park, CA: Sage.

Carroll, J. (1991). Introduction: The Kittle House manifesto. In J. Carroll (Ed.), *Designing interaction* (pp. 1–16). Cambridge: Cambridge University Press.

Castellan, N. J., Jr. (1972). The analysis of multiple criteria in multiple-cue judgment tasks. *Organizational Behavior and Human Performance, 8,* 242–261.

Castellan, N. J., Jr. (1973). Comments on the "lens model" equation and the analysis of multiple-cue judgment tasks. *Psychometrika, 38,* 87–100.

Castellan, N. J., Jr. (1992). Relations between linear models: Implications for the lens model. *Organizational Behavior and Human Decision Processes, 51,* 364–381.

Chasseigne, G., Grau, S., Mullet, E., & Cama, V. (1999). How do elderly people cope with uncertainty in a learning task? *Acta Psychologica, 103,* 229–238.

Chasseigne, G., Mullet, E., & Stewart, T. R. (1997). Aging and multiple cue probability learning: The case of inverse relationships. *Acta psychologica, 97,* 235–252.

Checkland, P. (1981). *Systems thinking, systems practice.* Chichester, UK: Wiley.

Christal, R. E., & Bottenberg, R. A. (1968). Grouping criteria: A method which retains maximum predictive efficiency. *Journal of Experimental Education, 36,* 28–34.

Christensen-Szalanski, J. J. J., & Beach, L. R. (1982). Experience and the base-rate fallacy. *Organizational Behavior and Human Performance, 29,* 270–278.

Churchman, C. W. (1971). *The design of inquiring systems: Basic concepts of systems and organizations.* New York: Basic Books.

Clover, W. (1979). *Cognitive feedback and the selection interview: Applying social judgment theory in the field.* Unpublished doctoral dissertation, Bowling Green State University.

Cohen, G. (1996). *Memory in the real world* (2nd ed.). East Sussex, UK: Psychology Press.

Colvin, C. R. (1993a). Childhood antecedents of young-adult judgability. *Journal of Personality, 61,* 611–635.

Colvin, C. R. (1993b). Judgable people: Personality, behavior, and competing explanations. *Journal of Personality and Social Psychology, 64,* 861–873.

Cook, R., & Stewart, T. R. (1975). A comparison of seven methods for obtaining subjective descriptions of judgment policy. *Organizational Behavior and Human Performance, 13,* 31–45.

Cooksey, R. W. (1982). *A modified version of the ISODATA program* (Unpublished manuscript). Armidale, NSW, Australia: University of New England.

Cooksey, R. W., & Freebody, P. (1985). Generalized multivariate lens model analysis for complex human inference tasks. *Organizational Behavior and Human Performance, 35,* 46–72.

Cooksey, R., Freebody, P., & Davidson, G. (1986). Social judgment theory: Teacher expectations concerning children's early reading potential. *American Educational Research Journal, 23,* 41–64.

Cooksey, R. W., Freebody, P., & Bennett, A. J. (1990). The ecology of spelling: A lens model analysis of spelling errors and student judgments of spelling difficulty. *Reading Psychology: An International Quarterly, 11,* 293–322.

Cooksey, R. W., & Gates, G. R. (1995). HRM: A management science in need of discipline. *Asia Pacific Journal of Human Resources, 33,* 15–38.

Cooksey, R. W. (1996a, November). *Beyond judgment analysis: Brunswik, complex systems, and the human dimension.* Paper presented at the 12th Annual International Invitational Meeting of the Brunswik Society, Chicago.

Cooksey, R. W. (1996b). *Judgment analysis: Theory, methods, and applications.* New York: Academic Press.

Cooksey, R. W. (1996c). The methodology of social judgement theory. *Thinking and Reasoning, 2,* 141–173.

Cooksey, R. W. (2000). The complex texture of managerial decision making: A complex dynamic decision perspective. *Emergence, 2,* 102–122.

Coombs, C. H. (1958). On the use of inconsistency of preferences in psychological measurement. *Journal of Experimental Psychology, 55,* 1–7.

Cooper, R. P., & Werner, P. D. (1990). Predicting violence in newly admitted inmates: A lens model analysis of staff decision making. *Criminal Justice and Behavior, 17,* 431–447.

Cosmides, L. (1989). The logic of social exchange: Has natural selection shaped how humans reason: Studies with the Wason selection task. *Cognition, 31,* 187–276.

Cosmides, L., & Tooby, J. (1992). Cognitive adaptations for social exchange. In J. Barkow, L. Cosmides, & J. Tooby (Ed.), *The adapted mind: Evolutionary psychology and the generation of culture* (pp. 163–228). New York: Oxford University Press.

Cosmides, L., & Tooby, J. (1994). Beyond intuition and instinct blindness: Towards an evolutionary rigorous cognitive science. *Cognition, 50,* 41–77.

Cosmides, L., & Tooby, J. (1996). Are humans good intuitive statisticians after all? Rethinking some conclusions from the literature on judgment under uncertainty. *Cognition, 58,* 1–73.

Cronbach, L. J. (1955). Processes affecting scores of "understanding of others" and "assumed similarity." *Psychological Bulletin, 52,* 177–193.

Cronbach, L. J. (1957). The two disciplines of scientific psychology. *American Psychologist, 12,* 671–684.

Cronbach, L. J., Gleser, G. C., Nanda, H., & Rajaratnam, N. (1972). *The dependability of behavioral measurements: Theory of generalizability for scores and profiles.* New York: Wiley.

Cronbach, L. J. (1975). Beyond the two disciplines of scientific psychology. *American Psychologist, 30,* 116–127.

Cruikshank, R. M. (1941). The development of visual size constancy in early infancy. *Journal of Genetic Psychology, 58,* 327–351.

Cummins, D., & Allen, C. (1998). *The evolving mind.* New York: Oxford University Press.

Cutting, J. E. (1986). *Perception with an eye for motion.* Cambridge: MIT Press.

Czerlinski, J., Gigerenzer, G., & Goldstein, D. G. (1999). How good are simple heuristics? In G. Gigerenzer, P. M. Todd, & ABC Research Group, *Simple heuristics that make us smart* (pp. 97–118). New York: Oxford University Press.

Danziger, K. (1990). *Constructing the subject: Historical origins of psychological research.* New York: Cambridge University Press.

Darling, T. A., Mumpower, J. L., Rohrbaugh, J., & Vari, A. (1999). Negotiation support for multi-party resource allocation: Developing recommendations for decreasing transportation-related air pollution in Budapest. *Group Decision and Negotiation, 8,* 51–75.

Darlington, R. B. (1968). Multiple regression in psychological research and practice. *Psychological Bulletin, 69,* 161–182.

Darwin, C. (1859/1966). *On the origin of species.* Cambridge: Harvard University Press.

Darwin, C. (1872). *The expression of the emotions in man and animals.* London: John Murray.

Dawes, R. M., & Corrigan, B. (1974). Linear models in decision making. *Psychological Bulletin, 81,* 95–106.

Dawes, R. M. (1979). The robust beauty of improper linear models in decision making. *American Psychologist, 34,* 571–582.

Dawes, R., Faust, D., & Meehl, P. (1989). Clinical versus actuarial judgment. *Science, 243,* 1668–1673.

Dawes, R. (1996). The purpose of experiments: Ecological validity versus competing hypotheses. *Brain and Behavioral Sciences, 19,* 20.

Dawes, R. (1998). Behavioral decision making and judgment. In D. Gilbert, S. Fiske, & G. Lindzey (Eds.), *Handbook of social psychology* (4th ed., Vol. 1, pp. 497–548). New York: McGraw-Hill.

Dean, D. H., Hammond, K. R., & Summers, D. A. (1972). Acquisition and application of knowledge in complex inference tasks. *Journal of Experimental Psychology, 92,* 20–26.

Deichmann, U. (1992). *Biologen unter Hitler: Vertreibung, Karrieren, Forschung.* Frankfurt: Campus.

DeShon, R. P., & Alexander, R. A. (1996). Goal setting effects on implicit and explicit learning of complex tasks. *Organizational Behavior and Human Decision Processes, 65,* 18–36.

Dhir, K. S., & Markman, H. J. (1984). Application of social judgment theory to understanding and treating marital conflict. *Journal of Marriage and the Family, 46,* 597–610.

Doherty, M. E. (2001). Self Insight. In K. R. Hammond, & T. R. Stewart (Ed.), *The esssential Brunswik: Beginnings, explications, applications.* New York: Oxford University Press.

Doherty, M. E., & Balzer, W. K. (1988). Cognitive feedback. In B. Brehmer & C. R. B. Joyce (Eds.), *Human judgment: The SJT view* (pp. 163–197). Amsterdam: North-Holland Elsevier.

Doherty, M. E. (Ed.). (1996). *Social Judgement Theory (Special Issue of Thinking and Reasoning)* (Vol. 2, Issues 2/3). East Sussex, UK: Psychology Press.

Doherty, M. E., Chadwick, R., Garavan, H., Barr, D., & Mynatt, C. R. (1996). On people's understanding of the diagnostic implications of probabilistic data. *Memory and Cognition, 24,* 644–654.

Doherty, M. E., & Kurz, E. (1996). Social judgment theory. *Thinking and Reasoning, 2,* 109–140.

Doherty, M. E., & Brehmer, B. (1997). The Paramorphic representation of human judgment: A 30 year retrospective. In W. M. Goldstein & R. M. Hogarth (Eds.), *Research on judgment and decision making: Currents, contents, and controversies* (pp. 537–551). Cambridge: Cambridge University Press.

Dowell, J., & Long, J. (1998). Conception of the cognitive engineering design problem. *Ergonomics, 41,* 126–139.

Dudycha, A. L., & Naylor, J. C. (1966). Characteristics of the human inference process in complex choice behavior. *Organizational Behavior and Human Performance, 1,* 110–128.

Earle, T. C. (1973). Interpersonal learning. In L. Rappoport & D. Summers (Eds.), *Human judgment and social interaction* (pp. 240–266). New York: Holt, Rinehart, & Winston.

Edgell, S. E. (1993). Using configural and dimensional information. In N. J. Castellan, Jr. (Ed.), *Individual and group decision making* (pp. 43–64). Hillsdale, NJ: Erlbaum.

Edland, A., & Svenson, O. (1993). Judgment and judgment making under time pressure: Studies and findings. In O. Svenson & A. J. Maule (Eds.), *Time pressure and stress in human judgment and judgment making.* Mahwah, NJ: Erlbaum.

Edwards, W. (1983). Human cognitive capabilities, representative design, and ground rules for research. In P. Humphreys, O. Svenson, & A. Vari (Eds.), *Analysing and aiding decision processes* (pp. 507–513). Amsterdam: North-Holland Elsevier.

Edwards, R. H. (1992). Model building. In R. Colwell (Ed.), *Handbook of research on music teaching and learning* (pp. 38–47). New York: Schirmer Books.

Einhorn, H. J., & Hogarth, R. M. (1981). Behavioral decision theory: Processes of judgment and choice. *Annual Review of Psychology, 32,* 53–88.

Eissler, K. (1933). Die Gestaltkonstanz der Sehdinge bei Variation der Objekte und ihrer Einwirkungsweise auf den Wahrnehmenden. *Archiv für die gesamte Psychologie, 88,* 487–550.

Ekman, P. (1992). An argument for basic emotions. *Cognition and Emotion, 6,* 169–200.

Endsley, M. R. (1995). Towards a theory of situation awareness in dynamic systems. *Human Factors, 37,* 32–64.

Epstein, S. (1994). Integration of the cognitive and the psychodynamic unconscious. *American Psychologist, 49,* 709–724.

Ericsson, K. A., & Simon, H. A. (1993). *Protocol analysis: Verbal reports as data* (2nd ed.). Cambridge: MIT Press.

Estes, W. K. (1950). Toward a statistical theory of learning. *Psychological Review, 57,* 94–117.

Estes, W. K. (1959). The statistical approach to learning theory. In S. Koch (Ed.), *Psychology: A study of science* (Vol. 2). New York: McGraw-Hill.

Estes, W. K. (1964). Probability learning. In A. W. Melton (Ed.), *Categories of human learning.* New York: Academic Press.

Estes, W. K. (Ed.). (1975). *Handbook of learning and cognitive processes* (Vol. 2). Hillsdale, NJ: Erlbaum.

Estes, W. K. (1976). The cognitive side of probability learning. *Psychological Review, 83,* 37–64.

Evans, R. B. (1990). Robert Sessions Woodworth and the "Columbia Bible": How the psychological experiment was redefined. *American Journal of Psychology, 103,* 391–401.

Eysenck, H. J. (1954). The science of personality: Nomothetic! *Psychological Review, 61,* 339–342.

Falk, J. (1956). Issues distinguishing idiographic from nomothetic approaches to personality. *Psychological Review, 63,* 53–62.

Feinstein, A. R. (1967). *Clinical judgment.* Baltimore, MD: Williams and Wilkins.

Fero, D. (1975). *A lens model analysis of the effects of the amount of information and mechanical decision making aid on clinical judgment and confidence.* Unpublished doctoral dissertation, Bowling Green State University.

Fiedler, K., & Walka, I. (1993). Training lie detectors to use nonverbal cues instead of global heuristics. *Human Communication Research, 20,* 199–223.

Fischer, K. (1991). Die Emigration von Wissenschaftlern nach 1933: Möglichkeiten und Grenzen einer Bilanzierung. *Vierteljahresschrift für Zeitgeschichte, 39,* 535–549.

Fischhoff, B., Slovic, P., & Lichtenstein, S. (1980). Knowing what you want: Measuring labile values. In T. S. Wallston (Ed.), *Cognitive processes in choice and decision behavior* (pp. 117–141). New York: Erlbaum.

Fischhoff, B. (1991). Value elicitation: Is there anything in there? *American Psychologist, 46,* 835–847.

Fisher, R. A. (1921). On the probable error of a coefficient of correlation deduced from a small sample. *Metron, 1,* 3–32.

Fisher, R. A. (1925). *Statistical methods for research workers.* London: Oliver & Boyd.

Flach, J., & Dominguez, C. (1995). Use-centered design: Integrating the user, instrument, and goal. *Ergonomics and Design,* 19–24.

Fodor, J. A. (1983). *The modularity of mind: An essay on faculty psychology.* Cambridge: MIT Press.

Frank, H. (1928). Die Sehgrößenkonstanz bei Kindern. *Psychologische Forschung, 10,* 102–106.

Frenkel-Brunswik, E. (1942). Motivation and behavior. *Genetic Psychology Monographs, 26,* 121–265.

Frenkel-Brunswik, E. (1951). Personality theory and perception. In R. R. Blake & G. V. Ramsey (Eds.), *Perception: An Approach to Personality.* New York: Ronald Press.

Frick, R. W. (1985). Communicating emotion: The role of prosodic features. *Psychological Bulletin, 97,* 412–429.

Funder, D. C. (1980). On seeing ourselves as others see us: Self-other agreement and discrepancy in personality ratings. *Journal of Personality, 48,* 473–493.

Funder, D. C. (1987). Errors and mistakes: Evaluating the accuracy of social judgment. *Psychological Bulletin, 101,* 75–90.

Funder, D. C., & Dobroth, K. M. (1987). Differences between traits: Properties associated with interjudge agreement. *Journal of Personality and Social Psychology, 52,* 409–418.

Funder, D. C., & Colvin, C. R. (1988). Friends and strangers: Acquaintanceship, agreement, and the accuracy of personality judgment. *Journal of Personality and Social Psychology, 55,* 149–158.

Funder, D. C., & Colvin, C. R. (1991). Explorations in behavioral consistency: Properties of persons, situations, and behaviors. *Journal of Personality and Social Psychology, 60,* 773–794.

Funder, D. C. (1993). Judgments as data for personality and developmental psychology: Error versus accuracy. In D. C. Funder, R. D. Parke, C. Tomlison-Keasey, & K. Widaman (Eds.), *Studying lives through time: Personality and development* (pp. 121–146). Washington, DC: American Psychological Association.

Funder, D. C., & Sneed, C. D. (1993). Behavioral manifestations of personality: An ecological approach to judgmental accuracy. *Journal of Personality and Social Psychology, 64,* 479–490.

Funder, D. C., & West, S. G. (1993). Consensus, self-other agreement, and accuracy in personality judgment: An introduction. *Journal of Personality, 64,* 457–476.

Funder, D. C. (1995). On the accuracy of personality judgment: A realistic approach. *Psychological Review,* 652–670.

Funder, D. C. (1996). *The personality puzzle.* New York: Norton.

Funder, D. C., Furr, R. M., & Colvin, C. R. (1998). *The behavioral Q-sort: A tool for the description of social behavior.* (Unpublished manuscript.) Riverside: University of California.

Funder, D. C. (1999). *Personality judgment: A realistic approach to social perception.* San Diego, CA: Academic Press.

Gabrielsson, A., & Juslin, P. N. (1996). Emotional expression in music performance: Between the performer's intention and the listener's experience. *Psychology of Music, 24,* 68–91.

Gabrielsson, A., & Juslin, P. N. (in press). Emotional expression in music. In R. J. Davidson, H. H. Goldsmith, & K. R. Scherer (Eds.), *Handbook of the affective sciences.* Oxford: Oxford University Press.

Gangestad, S. W., Simpson, J. A., DiGeronimo, K., & Biek, M. (1992). Differential accuracy in person perception across traits: Examination of a functional hypothesis. *Journal of Personality and Social Psychology, 62,* 688–698.

Garcia, J. (1990). Learning without memory. *Journal of Cognitive Neuroscience, 2,* 287–305.

Gardner, W., Lidz, C., Mulvey, E., & Shaw, E. (1996). Clinical versus actuarial predictions of violence in patients with mental illnesses. *Journal of Consulting and Clinical Psychology, 64,* 1–8.

Gibson, J. J. (1957). Survival in a world of probable objects. *Contemporary Psychology, 2,* 33–35.

Gibson, J. J. (1966). *The senses considered as perceptual systems.* Boston: Houghton Mifflin.

Gibson, J. J. (1979). *The ecological approach to visual perception.* New York: Harper & Row.

Gifford, R., Ng, C. F., & Wilkinson, M. (1985). Nonverbal cues in the employment interview: Links between applicant qualities and interviewer judgments. *Journal of Applied Psychology, 70,* 729–736.

Gifford, R. (1991). Mapping nonverbal behavior on the interpersonal circle. *Journal of Personality and Social Psychology, 61,* 279–288.

Gifford, R. (1994). A lens mapping framework for understanding the encoding and decoding of interpersonal dispositions in nonverbal behavior. *Journal of Personality and Social Psychology, 66,* 398–412.

Gigerenzer, G. (1987). Survival of fittest probabilist: Brunswik, Thurstone, and the two disciplines of psychology. In L. Krüger, G. Gigerenzer, & M. S. Morgan (Eds.), *The probabilistic revolution: Vol. 2: Ideas in the sciences* (pp. 49–72). Cambridge: MIT Press.

Gigerenzer, G., & Murray, D. J. (1987). *Cognition as intuitive statistics.* Hillsdale, NJ: Erlbaum.

Gigerenzer, G., Hell, W., & Blank, H. (1988). Presentation and content: The use of base rates as a continuous variable. *Journal of Experimental Psychology: Human Perception and Performance, 14,* 513–525.

Gigerenzer, G. (1991). From tools to theories: A heuristic of discovery in cognitive psychology. *Psychological Review, 98,* 254–267.

Gigerenzer, G., Hoffrage, U., & Kleinbölting, H. (1991). Probabilistic mental models: A Brunswikian theory of confidence. *Psychological Review, 98,* 506–528.

Gigerenzer, G. (1992). Discovery in cognitive psychology: New tools inspire new theories. *Science in Context, 5,* 329–350.

Gigerenzer, G. (1993). The superego, the ego, and the id in statistical reasoning. In G. Keren & C. Lewis (Eds.), *A handbook for data analysis in the behavioral sciences: Methodological issues* (pp. 311–339). Hillsdale, NJ: Erlbaum.

Gigerenzer, G. (1994). Where do new ideas come from? In M. A. Boden (Ed.), *Dimensions of creativity* (pp. 53–74). Cambridge: MIT Press.

Gigerenzer, G., & Hoffrage, U. (1995). How to improve Bayesian reasoning without instruction: Frequency formats. *Psychological Review, 102,* 684–704.

Gigerenzer, G. (1996). From tools to theories: Discovery in cognitive psychology. In C. F. Graumann & K. J. Gergen (Eds.), *Historical dimensions of psychological discourse.* Cambridge: Cambridge University Press.

Gigerenzer, G., & Goldstein, D. (1996). Reasoning the fast and frugal way: Models of bounded rationality. *Psychological Review, 103,* 650–669.

Gigerenzer, G. (1998). Ecological intelligence: An adaptation for frequencies. In D. Cummings & C. Allen (Eds.), *The evolution of mind* (pp. 9–29). New York: Oxford University Press.

Gigerenzer, G., & Hoffrage, U. (1999). Overcoming difficulties in Bayesian reasoning. *Psychological Review, 106,* 425–430.

Gigerenzer, G., Czerlinski, J., & Martignon, L. (1999). How good are fast and frugal heuristics? In J. Shanteau, B. Mellers, & D. Schum (Eds.), *Decision research from Bayesian approaches to normative systems: Reflections on the contributions of Ward Edwards* (pp. 81–103). Norwell, MA: Kluwer.

Gigerenzer, G., Todd, P. M., & ABC Research Group. (1999). *Simple heuristics that make us smart.* New York: Oxford University Press.

Gigone, D., & Hastie, R. (1993). The common knowledge effect: Information sharing and group judgment. *Journal of Personality and Social Psychology, 65,* 959–974.

Gigone, D., & Hastie, R. (1996). The impact of information on group judgment: A model and computer simulation. In E. Witte, J. H. Davis (Ed.), *Understanding group behavior: Vol. 1: Consensual action by small groups.* Hillsdale, NJ: Erlbaum.

Gigone, D., & Hastie, R. (1997). Proper analysis of the accuracy of group judgments. *Psychological Bulletin, 121,* 149–176.

Gillis, J. S. (1969). Schizophrenic thinking in a probabilistic situation. *Psychological Record, 19,* 211–224.

Gillis, J. S. (1975). Effects of chlorpromazine and thiothixene on acute schizophrenic patients. In K. R. Hammond & C. R. B. Joyce (Eds.), *Psychoactive drugs and social judgment: Theory and research.* New York: Wiley.

Gillis, J. S., & Moss, C. D. (1975). Effects of therapeutic dose levels of psychoactive drugs on chronic schizophrenic patients. In K. R. Hammond, & C. R. B. Joyce (Eds.), *Psychoactive drugs and social judgment: Theory and research.* New York: Wiley.

Gillis, J. S. (1977). The effects of selected antipsychotic drugs on human judgment. *Current Therapeutic Research, 21,* 224–232.

Gillis, J. S., & Davis, H. G. (1977). The effects of thioridazine and mesoridazine on the interpersonal learning of acute schizophrenics. *Current Therapeutic Research, 21,* 507–517.

Gillis, J. S., & Parkison, S. C. (1977). The effects of phenothiazines on complex learning. *Current Therapeutic Research, 22,* 348–355.

Gillis, J. S. (1978). Selected combinations of amitriptyline and antipsychotic drugs and complex learning. *Current Therapeutic Research, 23,* 407–416.

Gillis, J. S., & Moss, C. D. (1978). An experimental study of the effects of amitriptyline-perphenazine and amitriptyline-haloperidol combinations in interpersonal learning. *Current Therapeutic Research, 23,* 261–270.

Gillis, J. S., & Parkison, S. C. (1979, April 7). *The effects of fluphenazine injection and chlorpromazine on symptom severity and interpersonal learning in outpatient schizophrenics.* Paper presented at the Western Psychological Association, San Diego.

Gillis, J. S. (1979a). Antipsychotic drugs and conflict resolution: A study of the comparative effects of trifluoperazine, haloperidol and thioridazine. *Research Communications in Psychology, Psychiatry and Behavior, 4,* 3–20.

Gillis, J. S. (1979b). Antipsychotic drugs and interpersonal learning: A five-year progress report. In R. Shulman (Ed.), *Sociopharmacology.* Dordrecht, Holland: Reidel Press.

Gillis, J. S. (1980). Understanding the effects of psychiatric drugs on social judgment. In K. R. Hammond & N. E. Wascoe (Eds.), *Realizations of Brunswik's representative design.* San Francisco: Jossey-Bass.

Gillis, J., & Parkison, S. (1981). The effects of fluphenazine injection and chlorpromazine on symptom severity and learning in outpatient schizophrenics. *Current Therapeutic Research, 29,* 1–16.

Gillis, J. S., Bernieri, F. J., & Wooten, E. (1995). The effects of stimulus medium and feedback on the judgment of rapport. *Organizational Behavior and Human Decision Processes, 63,* 33–45.

Goldman, L., Cook, E. F., Brand, D. A., Lee, T. H., Rouan, G. W., Weisberg, M. C., et al. (1988). A computer protocol to predict myocardial infaction in emergency department patients with chest pain. *New England Journal of Medicine, 318,* 797–803.

Goldstein, W. M., & Hogarth, R. M. (Eds.). (1997). *Research on judgment and decision making.* New York: Cambridge University Press.

Goodale, M. A., & Milner, D. A. (1992). Separate visual pathways for perception and action. *Trends in Neurosciences, 15*, 20–25.

Goodale, M. A. (1993). Visual pathways supporting perception and action in the primate cerebral cortex. *Current Opinion in Neurobiology, 3*, 578–585.

Gottfredson, L. S. (1981). Circumscription and compromise: A developmental theory of occupational aspiration (monograph). *Journal of Counseling Psychology, 28*, 545–579.

Gould, S. J., & Pinker, S. (1997). Evolutionary psychology: An exchange. *New York Review of Books, 44*, 55–58.

Grahe, J. E., Bernieri, F. J., Gillis, J. S., Gada-Jain, N., Ahadi, S. A., El Hajje, R., Vance, M., Williams, K. D., & Yuliandari, E. (1999). *Varying cultures, similar judgment policies: A cross-cultural study of rapport perception.* (Unpublished manuscript.)

Graves, L. M., & Karren, R. J. (1992). Interviewer decision processes and effectiveness: An experimental policy capturing investigation. *Personnel Psychology, 45*, 313–340.

Green, D. M., & Swets, J. (1966). *Signal detection theory and psychophysics.* New York: Wiley.

Griffin, D., & Tversky, A. (1992). The weighting of evidence and the determinants of confidence. *Cognitive Psychology, 24*, 411–435.

Hake, H. W., Rodwan, A., & Weintraub, D. (1966). Noise reduction in perception. In K. R. Hammond (Ed.), *The psychology of Egon Brunswik* (pp. 277–316). New York: Holt, Rinehart, & Winston.

Hall, G. S. (1923). *Life and confessions of a psychologist.* New York: Appleton.

Hamm, R. M. (1983). *Task conditions versus stable individual differences as determinants of experts' judgment policies* (Report No. 249). Boulder: Center for Research on Judgment and Policy, University of Colorado.

Hamm, R. M. (1988). Clinical intuition and clinical analysis: Expertise and the cognitive continuum. In J. Dowie & A. Elstein (Eds.), *Professional judgment: A reader in clinical decision making* (pp. 78–105). Cambridge: Cambridge University Press.

Hammer, L. B. (1991). *The effects of task complexity and the components of cognitive feedback on judgment performance.* Unpublished doctoral dissertation, Bowling Green State University.

Hammond, K. (1948). Subject and object sampling: A note. *Psychological Bulletin, 45*, 530–533.

Hammond, K. R. (1954). Representative design vs. systematic design in clinical psychology. *Psychological Bulletin, 51*, 150–159.

Hammond, K. R. (1955). Probabilistic functionalism and the clinical method. *Psychological Review, 62*, 255–262.

Hammond, K. R., Hursch, C. J., & Todd, F. J. (1964). Analyzing the components of clinical inference. *Psychological Review, 71*, 438–456.

Hammond, K. R. (1965). New directions in research on conflict resolution. *Journal of Social Issues, 21*, 44–66.

Hammond, K. R. (1966a). Probabilistic functionalism: Egon Brunswik's integration of history, theory, and method of psychology. In K. R. Hammond (Ed.), *The psychology of Egon Brunswik* (pp. 15–80). New York: Holt, Rinehart, & Winston.

Hammond, K. R. (Ed.). (1966b). *The psychology of Egon Brunswik.* New York: Holt, Rinehart, & Winston.

Hammond, K. R., Wilkins, M. M., & Todd, F. J. (1966). A research paradigm for the study of interpersonal learning. *Psychological Bulletin, 65*, 221–232.

Hammond, K. R. (1971). Computer graphics as an aid to learning. *Science, 172*, 903–908.

Hammond, K. R., & Summers, D. A. (1972). Cognitive control. *Psychological Review, 79*, 58–67.

Hammond, K. R. (1973). The cognitive conflict paradigm. In L. Rappoport & D. Summers (Eds.), *Human judgment and social interaction* (pp. 188–205). New York: Holt, Rinehart, & Winston.

Hammond, K. R. (1975). Social judgment theory: Its use in the study of psychoactive drugs. In K. R. Hammond & C. R. B. Joyce (Eds.), *Psychoactive drugs and social judgment: Theory and research.* New York: Wiley.

Hammond, K. R., & Joyce, C. R. B. (Eds.). (1975). *Psychoactive drugs and social judgment: Theory and research*. New York: Wiley.

Hammond, K. R., Stewart, T. R., Brehmer, B., & Steinmann, D. O. (1975). Social judgment theory. In M. Kaplan & S. Schwartz (Eds.), *Human judgment and decision processes* (pp. 271–312). San Diego: Academic Press.

Hammond, K. R., & Adelman, L. (1976). Science, values, and human judgment. *Science, 194,* 389–396.

Hammond, K. R., Rohrbaugh, J., Mumpower, J., & Adelman, L. (1977). Social judgment theory: Applications in policy formation. In M. Kaplan & S. Schwartz (Eds.), *Human judgment and decision processes in applied settings* (pp. 1–29). New York: Academic Press.

Hammond, K. R. (1978a). *Psychology's scientific revolution: Is it in danger?* (Tech. Rep. No. 211). Boulder: University of Colorado, Center for Research on Judgment and Policy.

Hammond, K. R. (1978b). Toward increasing competence of thought in public policy formation. In K. Hammond (Ed.), *Judgment and decision making in public policy formation*. Boulder, CO: Westview, 11–32.

Hammond, K. R. (1980). Introduction to Brunswikian theory and methods. In K. R. Hammond & N. E. Wascoe (Eds.), *Realizations of Brunswik's representative design* (pp. 1–11). San Francisco: Jossey-Bass.

Hammond, K. R., McClelland, G. H., & Mumpower, J. (1980). *Human judgment and decision making: Theories, methods, and procedures*. New York: Praeger.

Hammond, K. R., & Grassia, J. (1985). The cognitive side of conflict: From theory to resolution of policy disputes. In S. Oskamp (Ed.), *Applied social psychology annual: Vol. 6: International conflict and national public policy issues* (pp. 233–254). Beverly Hills, CA: Sage.

Hammond, K. R. (1986). Generalization in operational contexts: What does it mean? Can it be done? *IEEE Transactions on Systems, Man, and Cybernetics, SMC-16,* 428–433.

Hammond, K. R., Hamm, R. M., & Grassia, J. (1986). Generalizing over conditions by combining the multitrait-multimethod matrix and representative design of experiments. *Psychological Bulletin, 100,* 257–269.

Hammond, K. R., Hamm, R. M., Grassia, J., & Pearson, T. (1987). Direct comparison of the efficacy of intuitive and analytical cognition in expert judgment. *IEEE Transactions on Systems, Man, and Cybernetics, SMC-17,* 753–770.

Hammond, K. R. (1988). Judgment and decision making in dynamic tasks. *Information and Decision Technologies, 14,* 3–14.

Hammond, K. R., Frederick, E., Robillard, N., & Victor, D. (1989). Application of cognitive theory to the student-teacher dialogue. In D. A. V. L. P. Evans (Ed.), *Cognitive science in medicine: Biomedical modeling* (pp. 173–210). Cambridge: MIT Press.

Hammond, K. R. (1990a). Functionalism and illusionism: Can integration be usefully achieved? In R. Hogarth (Ed.), *Insights in decision making: A tribute to Hillel J. Einhorn* (pp. 227–261). Chicago: University of Chicago Press.

Hammond, K. R. (1990b). Intuitive and analytical cognition: Information models. In A. P. Sage (Ed.), *Concise encyclopedia of information processing in systems and organizations*. Oxford: Pergamon Press.

Hammond, K. R., Harvey, L. O., & Hastie, R. (1992). Making better use of scientific knowledge: Separating truth from justice. *Psychological Science, 3,* 80–87.

Hammond, K. R. (1996a). Expansion of Egon Brunswik's psychology (1955–1996). In K. Fischer & F. Stadler (Eds.), *Wahrnehmung und gegenstandswelt: Zum Lebenswerk von Egon Brunswik (1903–1955)* (pp. 79–105). Vienna: Springer-Verlag.

Hammond, K. R. (1996b). How convergence of research paradigms can improve research on diagnostic judgment. *Medical Decision Making, 16,* 281–287.

Hammond, K. R. (1996c). *Human judgment and social policy: Irreducible uncertainty, inevitable error, unavoidable injustice*. New York: Oxford University Press.

Hammond, K. R. (1996d). Upon reflection. *Thinking and Reasoning, 2,* 239–248.

Hammond, K. R. (1997). Expansion of Egon Brunswik's psychology. In K. F. F. Stadler (Ed.), *Wahrnemung und Gegenstandswelt: Zum Lebenswerk von Egon Brunswik (1903–1955)* (pp. 79–105). Vienna: Springer-Verlag.

Hammond, K. R., Hamm, R., Grassia, J., & Pearson, T. (1997). Direct comparison of the efficacy of intuitive and analytical cognition in expert judgment. In W. Goldstein & R. Hogarth (Eds.), *Research in judgment and decision making* (pp. 144–180). New York: Cambridge University Press.

Hammond, K. R., & Schneider, V. (1997, November). *One J/DM society or two: Drift, or judgment and decision?* Paper presented at the J/DM Symposium presented at the Annual Conference of Society for Judgment and Decision Making, Philadelphia.

Hammond, K. R. (1998, September). Ecological validity: Then and now (http://www.albany.edu/cpr/brunswik/essay2.html).

Hammond, K. R. (2000). *Judgments under stress.* New York: Oxford University Press.

Harlow, H. (1959). Learning set and error factor theory. In S. Koch (Ed.), *Psychology: A study of a science* (Vol. 2, pp. 492–537). New York: McGraw-Hill.

Harmon, J., & Rohrbaugh, J. (1990). Social judgment analysis and small group decision making: Cognitive feedback effects on individual and collective performance. *Organizational Behavior and Human Decision Processes, 46,* 34–54.

Harries, C., Evans, J., & Dennis, I. (1997, November). *On self-insight in multi-cue judgement making.* Paper presented at the 13th Annual International Invitational Meeting of the Brunswik Society, Philadelphia.

Harries, C., & Dhami, M. K. (1998, November). *Models of human judgment: Why "take the best"? Or the fast and frugal fetish: Fructiferous freethinking or futile fracas?* Paper presented at the 14th Annual International Invitational Meeting of the Brunswik Society, Dallas.

Harries, C., Evans, J. S. B. T., & Dennis, I. (in press). Measuring doctors' self-insight into their treatment decisions. *Applied Cognitive Psychology.*

Hart, P. M., & Wearing, A. J. (1995). Occupational stress and well-being: A systematic approach to research, policy, and practice. In P. Cotton (Ed.), *Psychological health in the workplace* (pp. 185–216). Melbourne: APS.

Hart, P. M., & Wearing, A. J. (in press). Using employee opinion surveys to identify control mechanisms in organisations. In W. J. Perrig & A. Grob (Eds.), *Control of human behavior, mental processes and consciousness.* Mahwah, NJ: Erlbaum.

Hartlage, L. C. (1965). Effects of chlorpromazine on learning. *Psychological Bulletin, 64,* 235–245.

Hastie, R., Ostrom, T. M., Ebbesen, E. B., Wyer, R. S., Hamilton, D. L., & Carlston, D. E. (1980). *Person memory: The cognitive basis of social perception.* Hillsdale, NJ: Erlbaum.

Hebb, D. O. (1949). *The organization of behavior.* New York: Wiley.

Hedlund, J., Ilgen, D. R., & Hollenbeck, J. R. (1998). Decision accuracy in computer-mediated versus face-to-face decision-making teams. *Organizational Behavior and Human Decision Processes, 76,* 30–47.

Heidbreder, E. (1993). *Seven psychologies.* New York: Appleton-Century.

Heidelberger, M. (1985). Zerspaltung und Einheit: Vom logischen Aufbau der Welt zum Physikalismus. In H.-J. Dahms (Ed.), *Philosophie, Wissenschaft, Aufklärung. Beiträge zur Geschichte und Wirkung des Wiener Kreises* (pp. 144–189). Berlin: de Gruyter.

Heider, F. (1926). *Ding und Medium. Symposion, 1,* 109–157. English translation in Heider (1959), 1–34.

Heider, F. (1930). Die Leistung des Wahrnehmungssystems. *Zeitschrift für Psychologie, 114,* 371–394. English translation in Heider (1959), 35–52.

Heider, F. (1958). *The psychology of interpersonal relations.* Hillsdale, NJ: Erlbaum.

Heider, F. (1959). On Perception, Event-Structure and Psychological Environment. *Selected Papers. Psychological Issues, 1,* No. 3.

Heimann, N., & Grant, J. (1974). Introduction (Else Frenkel-Brunswik, selected papers). *Psychological Issues, 8,* Monograph 31.

Henry, R. A. (1995). Improving group judgment accuracy: Information sharing and determining the best member. *Organizational Behavior and Human Decision Processes, 62,* 190–197.

Hepworth, S. (1991). The assessment of student nurses. *Nurse Education Today, 11,* 46–52.

Hergenhahn, B. R. (1992). *An introduction to the history of psychology.* Belmont, CA: Wadsworth.

Hering, E. (1964). *Outlines of a Theory of the Light-Sense.* Trans. L. M. Hurvich & D. Jameson. Cambridge, Mass.: Harvard University Press. First published 1905.

Herrnstein, R. J. (1979). Derivatives of matching. *Psychological Review, 86,* 486–495.

Herrnstein, R. J. (1990). Behavior, reinforcement and utility. *Psychological Science, 1,* 217–224.

Hertwig, R., Hoffrage, U., & Martignon, L. (1999). Quick estimation: Letting the environment do the work. In G. Gigerenzer, P. M. Todd, & the ABC Research Group, *Simple heuristics that make us smart* (pp. 209–239). New York: Oxford University Press.

Hilgard, E. R. (1955). Discussion of probabilistic functionalism. *Psychological Review, 62,* 226–228.

Hillner, K. P. (1984). *History and systems of modern psychology.* New York: Gardner.

Hinze, V. B., Tindale, R. S., & Vollrath, D. A. (1997). The emerging conceptualization of groups as information processors. *Psychological Bulletin, 121,* 43–64.

Hirschfeld, L. A., & Gelman, S. A. (1994). *Mapping the mind: Domain specificity in cognition and culture.* New York: Cambridge University Press.

Hoch, S. J., & Schkade, D. A. (1996). A psychological approach to decision support systems. *Management Science, 42,* 51–64.

Hochberg, J. (1954). Review of "The conceptual framework of psychology" by Egon Brunswik. *American Journal of Psychology, 67,* 386–388.

Hochberg, J. (1966). Representative sampling and the purposes of perceptual research: Pictures of the world and the world of pictures. In K. R. Hammond (Ed.), *The psychology of Egon Brunswik* (pp. 361–381). New York: Holt, Rinehart, & Winston.

Hoffman, P. J. (1960). The paramorphic representation of clinical judgment. *Psychological Bulletin, 57,* 116–131.

Hoffrage, U., & Martignon, L. (1999). *Fast, frugal and fit: Simple heuristics for paired comparison.* Manuscript submitted for publication.

Hogge, J. H., & Murrell, J. (1991, November). *Exploring values underlying the assessment of teaching competence: An application of social judgment theory.* Paper presented at the poster presentation at Annual Meeting of Mid-South Educational Research Association, Lexington, KY.

Hogge, J. H., & Murrell, J. (1994, November). *A look at nursing competence through Brunswik's lens.* Paper presented at the Poster presentation at Annual Meeting of Society for Judgment and Decision Making, St. Louis, MO.

Hogge, J. H., & Schilling, S. G. (1995, November). *The application of generalizability theory to judgment analysis.* Paper presented at the Poster presentation at Annual Meeting of Society for Judgment and Decision Making, Los Angeles.

Hogge, J. H., & Schilling, S. G. (1998). Multilevel judgment and reliability analysis: Hierarchical linear models as a bridge between generalizability theory and the lens model. (Unpublished manuscript).

Holaday, B. E. (1933). Die Größenkonstanz der Sehdinge bei Variation der inneren und äußeren Wahrnehmungsbedingungen. *Archiv für die gesamte Psychologie, 88,* 419–486.

Hollenbeck, J. R., Ilgen, D. R., et al. (1995). Multilevel theory of team judgment making: Judgment performance in teams incorporating distributed expertise. *Journal of Applied Psychology, 80,* 292–316.

Hollenbeck, J. R., Sego, D. J., Ilgen, D. R., Major, D. A., Hedlund, J., & Phillips, J. (1997). Team judgment-making accuracy under difficult conditions: Construct validation of potential manipulations using the TIDE2 simulation. In T. Brannick, E. Salas, & C. Prince (Eds.), *Team performance assessment and measurement: Theory, methods, and applications.* Mahwah, NJ: Erlbaum.

Hollenbeck, J. R., Ilgen, D. R., LePine, J. A., Colquitt, J. A., & Hedlund, J. (1998). Extending the multilevel theory of team decision making: Effects of feedback and experience in hierarchical teams. *Academy of Management Journal, 41,* 269–282.

Holt, R. (1962). Individuality and generalization in the psychology of personality. *Journal of Personality, 30*, 377–404.

Holzkamp, K. (1981). *Theorie und Experiment in der Psychologie. Eine grundlagenkritische Untersuchung* (2nd ed.). Berlin and New York: de Gruyter.

Holzworth, R. J., & Doherty, M. E. (1976). Feedback effects in a metric multiple cue probability learning task. *Bulletin of the Psychonomic Society, 8*, 557–559.

Holzworth, R. J. (1980). Reversal of order of information in a multiple-cue probability learning task. *Journal of General Psychology, 102*, 211–223.

Holzworth, R. J. (1996). Policy capturing with ridge regression. *Organizational Behavior and Human Decision Processes, 68*, 171–179.

Hull, C. L. (1943a). The problem of intervening variables in molar behavior theory. *Psychological Review, 50*, 273–291.

Hull, C. L. (1943b). The uniformity point of view. *Psychological Review, 50*, 203–216.

Hunt, M. (1993). *The story of psychology.* New York: Doubleday.

Hunter, W. S. (1928). *Human behavior.* Chicago: University of Chicago Press.

Hunter, W. S. (1932). The psychological study of behavior. *Psychological Review, 39*, 1–24.

Hursch, C. J., Hammond, K. R., & Hursch, J. L. (1964). Some methodological considerations in multiple-cue probability learning studies. *Psychological Review, 71*, 42–60.

Husserl, E. (1970). *Logical Investigations.* Trans. J. N. Findlay. London: Routledge and Kegan Paul. First published 1900.

Ignatieff, M. (1997). *The warrior's honor.* New York: Henry Holt.

Ittelson, W. H. (1951). The constancies in perceptual theory. *Psychological Review, 58*, 285–294.

Jenkins, J. (1974). Remember that old theory of memory? *American Psychologist, 29*, 785–795.

Jick, T. J. (1979). Mixing qualitative and quantitative methods: Triangulation in action. *Administrative Science Quarterly, 24*, 602–611.

John, O. P., & Robins, R. W. (1993). Determinants of interjudge agreement on personality traits: The Big Five domains, observability, evaluativeness, and the unique perspective of the self. *Journal of Personality, 61*, 521–551.

John Paul II. (1997). The pope's message on evolution and four commentaries. *Quarterly Review of Biology, 72*, 381–406.

Johnson-Laird, P. N. (1983). *Mental models: Towards a cognitive science of language, inference, and consciousness* (Vol. 6). Cambridge: Harvard University Press.

Johnson-Laird, P. N., & Oatley, K. (1992). Basic emotions, rationality, and folk theory. *Cognition and Emotion, 6*, 201–223.

Jones, E. E. (1985). Major developments in social psychology during the past five decades. In G. Lindzey & E. Aronson (Eds.), *The handbook of social psychology* (3rd ed., pp. 47–107). New York: Random House.

Jones, E. E. (1990). *Interpersonal perception.* New York: Freeman.

Joyce, C. R. B. (1994). Health status or quality of life: Which matters to the patient? *Journal of Cardiovascular Pharmacology, 23*, S26–S33.

Joyce, C. R. B., O'Boyle, C. A., & McGee, H. M. (1999). *Individual quality of life.* London: Harwood.

Juslin, P. (1993). An explanation of the easy-hard effect in studies of realism of confidence in one's general knowledge. *European Journal of Cognitive Psychology, 5*, 55–71.

Juslin, P. (1994). The overconfidence phenomenon as a consequence of informal experimenter-guided selection of almanac items. *Organizational Behavior and Human Decision Processes, 57*, 226–246.

Juslin, P., Olsson, H., & Björkman, M. (1997). Brunswikian and Thurstonian origins of bias in probability assessment: On the interpretation of stochastic components of judgment. *Journal of Behavioral Decision Making, 10*, 189–209.

Juslin, P., Olsson, H., & Winman, A. (1998). The calibration issue: Theoretical comments on Suantak, Bolger, and Ferrell (1996). *Organizational Behavior and Human Decision Processes, 73*, 3–26.

Juslin, P., Winman, A., & Olsson, H. (2000). Naive empiricism and a priori dogmatism in confidence research: A critical examination of the hard-easy effect. *Psychological Review, 107,* 384–396.

Juslin, P. N. (1995). Emotional communication in music viewed through a Brunswikian lens. In G. Kleinen (Ed.), *Musical expression. Proceedings of the Conference of ESCOM and DGM* (pp. 21–25). University of Bremen, Bremen, Germany.

Juslin, P. N. (1997a). Emotional communication in music performance: A functionalist perspective and some data. *Music Perception, 14,* 383–418.

Juslin, P. N. (1997b). Perceived emotional expression in synthesized performances of a short melody: Capturing the listener's judgment policy. *Musicae Scientiae, 1,* 225–256.

Juslin, P. N. (1997c). Can results from studies of perceived expression in musical performances be generalized across response formats? *Psychomusicology, 16,* 77–101.

Juslin, P. N. (1997d). Perceived emotional expression in synthesized performances of a short melody: Capturing the listener's judgment policy. *Musicae Scientiae, 1,* 225–256.

Juslin, P. N. (1999). *Communication of emotion in vocal expression and music performance: Different channels, same code?* (Manuscript submitted for publication.)

Juslin, P. N., & Madison, G. (1999). The role of timing patterns in recognition of emotional expression from musical performance. *Music Perception, 17,* 197–221.

Juslin, P. N., Friberg, A., & Bresin, R. (2000). *Towards a computational model of music performance: The GERM model.* (Manuscript submitted for publication.)

Juslin, P. N. (in press). Can results from studies of perceived expression in musical performances be generalized across response formats? *Psychomusicology.*

Juslin, P. N. (in press a). Cue utilization in communication of emotion in music performance: Relating performance to perception. *Journal of Experimental Psychology: Human Perception and Performance.*

Juslin, P. N. (in press b). Communicating emotions in music performance: Research findings and a theoretical framework. In P. N. Juslin & J. A. Sloboda (Eds.), *Music and emotion: Theory and research.* New York: Oxford University Press.

Juslin, P. N., & Laukka, P. (in press). Improving emotional communication in music performance through cognitive feedback. *Musicae Scientiae.*

Kahneman, D., & Tversky, A. (1973). On the psychology of prediction. *Psychological Review, 80,* 237–251.

Kahneman, D., & Tversky, A. (1979). Prospect theory: An analysis of decision under risk. *Econometrica, 47,* 263–291.

Kahneman, D., Slovic, P., & Tversky, A. (1982). *Judgments under uncertainty: Heuristics and biases.* New York: Cambridge University Press.

Kamouri, J. (1986). *Passive versus active information retrieval: The effects on multiple cue probability learning in the presence of irrelevant cues.* Unpublished doctoral dissertation, Bowling Green State University.

Kantowitz, B., & Sorkin, R. (1983). *Human factors: Understanding people-system relationships.* New York: Wiley.

Kelley, H. H. (1967). Attribution theory in social psychology. In D. Levine (Ed.), *Nebraska Symposium on Motivation* (Vol. 15). Lincoln: University of Nebraska Press.

Kenny, D. A., & Albright, L. (1987). Accuracy in interpersonal perception: A social relations analysis. *Psychological Bulletin, 102,* 390–402.

Kenny, D. A. (1994). *Interpersonal perception: A social relations analysis.* New York: Guilford Press.

Kevles, D. (1993, August 2). Cold Facts Review of "Bad Science: The Short Life and Weird Times of Cold Fusion." *New Yorker,* 82.

Kirlik, A. (1995). Requirements of psychological models to support design: Toward ecological task analysis. In J. Flach, P. Hancock, J. Caird, & K. Vicente (Eds.), *Global perspectives on the ecology of human-machine systems* (pp. 68–120). Hillsdale, NJ: Erlbaum.

Kirlik, A., & Bisantz, A. (1999). Cognition in human-machine systems: Experiential and environmental aspects of adaptation. In P. A. Hancock (Ed.), *Handbook of perception and cognition: Human performance and ergonomics* (Vol. 17, pp. 47–68). New York: Academic Press.

Kirlik, A., Fisk, A. D., Walker, N., & Rothrock, L. (1999). Feedback augmentation and part-task practice in training dynamic decision making skills. In J. Cannon-Bowers & E. Salas (Eds.), *Decision making in complex environments* (pp. 91–114). Washington, DC: APA Press.

Kirlik, A. (in press). The design of everyday life environments. In W. Bechtel & G. Graham (Eds.), *A companion to cognitive science*. Cambridge, UK: Blackwell.

Kirshner, B., & Guyatt, G. (1985). A methodological framework for assessing health indices. *Journal of Chronic Disease, 38*, 27–36.

Klayman, J. (1988). Learning from experience. In B. Brehmer & C. R. B. Joyce (Eds.), *Human judgment: The SJT view* (pp. 115–162). Amsterdam, North-Holland: Elsevier.

Klein, G., Orasanu, J., Calderwood, R., & Zsambok, C. (Eds.). (1993). *Decision making in action: Models and methods*. Norwood, NJ: Ablex.

Kleitman, S., & Stankov, L. (1997). *Ecological and person-oriented aspects of metacognitive processes in test-taking.* (Unpublished manuscript.) Sydney: University of Sydney, Department of Psychology.

Klimpfinger, S. (1933). Über den Einfluß von intentionaler Einstellung und Übung auf die Gestaltkonstanz. *Archiv für die gesamte Psychologie, 88*, 551–598.

Kling, J. W., & Riggs, L. A. (1971). *Woodworth and Schlossberg's experimental psychology* (3rd ed.). New York: Holt, Rinehart, & Winston.

Knapp, M. L., & Hall, J. A. (1997). *Nonverbal communication in human interaction* (4th ed.). Fort Worth: Harcourt Brace College.

Knaus, W. A., Harrell, F. E., Lynn, J., Goldman, L., Phillips, R. S., Connors, A. F., Dawson, N. V., et al. (1995). SUPPORT prognostic model. Objective estimates of survival for seriously ill hospitalized adults. *Annals of Internal Medicine, 122*, 191–203.

Knez, I. (1992). Subjects' inferential performance and the interaction of data and hypotheses in probabilistic inference tasks. *Scandinavian Journal of Psychology, 33*, 56–67.

Knight, H. C. (1921). *A comparison of reliability of group and individual judgments.* Unpublished M.A. thesis, Columbia University.

Koehler, J. J. (1996). The base rate fallacy reconsidered: Descriptive, normative, and methodological challenges. *Behavioral and Brain Sciences, 19*, 1–53.

Koffka, K. (1935). *Principles of Gestalt psychology.* New York: Harcourt Brace.

Kohler, W. (1929). *Gestalt psychology.* New York: Liveright.

Konner, M. (1998). A piece of your mind. *Science, 281*, 653–654.

Krech, D. (1955). Discussion: Theory and reductionism. *Psychological Review, 62*, 229–231.

Kuhn, T. S. (1962). *The structure of scientific revolutions.* Chicago: University of Chicago Press.

Kuhn, T. S. (1970). *The structure of scientific revolutions* (2nd ed.). Chicago: University of Chicago Press.

Kurz, E. M., & Tweney, R. D. (1997). The heretical psychology of Egon Brunswik. In W. G. Bringmann, H. E. Lueck, R. Miller, & C. E. Early (Ed.), *A pictorial history of psychology* (pp. 221–232). Carol Stream, IL: Quintessence.

Kurz, E. M., & Martignon, L. (1998). Weighing, then summing: The triumph and trumbling of a modeling practice in psychology. Paper presented at Model-based Reasoning in Scientific Discovery (MBR '98), Pavia, Italy.

Lakoff, G. (1987). *Women, fire, and dangerous things: What categories reveal about the mind.* Chicago: University of Chicago Press.

Lamiell, J. T. (1997). Individuals and the differences between them. In R. Hogan, J. Johnson, & S. Briggs (Eds.), *Handbook of personality psychology* (pp. 117–141). New York: Academic Press.

Lamiell, J. T. (1998). "Nomothetic" and "idiographic": Contrasting Windelband's understanding with contemporary usage. *Theory and Psychology, 23–38.*

Langer, E. J. (1989). *Mindfulness.* Reading, MA: Addison-Wesley.

Lazarsfeld, P. F. (1969). An episode in the history of empirical social research: A memoir. In D. Fleming & B. Baily (Eds.), *The intellectual migration: Europe and America* (pp. 270–337). Cambridge: Harvard University Press.

Leahey, T. H. (1987). *A history of psychology.* Englewood Cliffs, NJ: Prentice Hall.

Leary, D. E. (1987). From act psychology to probabilistic functionalism: The place of Egon Brunswik in the history of psychology. In M. G. Ash & W. R. Woodward (Eds.), *Psychology in twentieth-century thought and society* (pp. 115–142). Cambridge: Cambridge University Press.

Ledley, R. S., & Lusted, L. B. (1959). Reasoning foundations of medical diagnosis. *Science, 130,* 9–21.

Lee, D. (1976). A theory of visual control of braking based on information about time to collision. *Perception, 5,* 437–459.

Lee, J. W., & Yates, J. F. (1992). How quantity judgment changes as the number of cues increases: An analytical framework and review. *Psychological Bulletin, 112,* 363–377.

Leeper, R. W. (1955). Complex intermediate processes between situation and response: Their methodological implications. *Acta Psychologica, 11,* 110–111.

Leeper, R. W. (1966). A critical consideration of Egon Brunswik's probabilistic functionalism. In K. R. Hammond (Ed.), *The psychology of Egon Brunswik* (pp. 405–454). New York: Holt, Rinehart, & Winston.

Lewin, K. (1943). Defining the "field at a given time." *Psychological Review, 50,* 292–310.

Lichtenstein, S., & Fischhoff, B. (1977). Do those who know more also know more about how much they know? *Organizational Behavior and Human Performance, 20,* 159–183.

Lichtenstein, S., Fischhoff, B., & Phillips, L. D. (1982). Calibration of probabilities: The state of the art to 1980. In D. Kahneman, P. Slovic, & A. Tversky (Eds.), *Judgment under uncertainty: Heuristics and biases* (pp. 306–334). Cambridge: Cambridge University Press.

Locke, J. (1690/1959). *An essay concerning human understanding (Edited by Alexander Campbell Fraser).* New York: Dover.

Luce, R. D. (1988). The tools-to-theory hypothesis. Review of G. Gigerenzer and D. J. Murray, "Cognition as intuitive statistics." *Contemporary Psychology, 33,* 582–583.

Luce, R. D. (1989). Autobiography. In G. Lindzey (Ed.), *Psychology in autobiography* (Vol. 8, pp. 245–289). Stanford: Stanford University Press.

Lusk, C. M., & Hammond, K. R. (1991). Judgment in a dynamic task: Microburst forecasting. *Journal of Behavioral Decision Making, 4,* 55–73.

Machiavelli, N. (1513/1950). *The prince.* New York: Random House.

MacIntyre, A. (1981). *After virtue* (2nd ed.). Notre Dame: University of Notre Dame Press.

Malloy, T. E., & Albright, L. (1990). Interpersonal perception in a social context. *Journal of Personality and Social Psychology, 58,* 419–428.

Marr, D. (1982). *Vision: A computational investigation into the human representation and processing of visual information.* San Francisco: Freeman.

Martignon, L., & Hoffrage, U. (1998). *Lexicographic comparison: A satisficing cognitive strategy* (Manuscript).

Martignon, L., & Hoffrage, U. (2000). Why does one-reason decision making work? A case study in ecological rationality. In G. Gigerenzer, P. M. Todd, & ABC Research Group, *Simple heuristics that make us smart* (p. 119–140). New York: Oxford University Press.

MathSoft Inc. (1998). *S-Plus 4.5 Professional Release 1.* Cambridge, MA: Mathsoft.

Matlin, M. W. (1989). *Cognition* (2nd ed.). New York: Harcourt Brace.

Matlin, M. W. (1997). *Cognition* (4th ed.). New York: Harcourt Brace.

Maule, A. J. (1997). Strategies for adapting to time pressure. In R. Flin, E. Salas, M. Strub, & L. Martin (Eds.), *Judgment making under stress: Emerging themes and applications* (pp. 271–279). Aldershot, Hampshire, England: Ashgate.

McCartt, A. T., & Rohrbaugh, J. (1995). Managerial openness to change and the introduction of GDSS: Explaining initial success and failure in decision conferencing. *Organization Science, 6,* 569–584.

McClelland, A. G. R., & Bolger, F. (1994). The calibration of subjective probabilities: Theories and models 1980–1993. In G. Wright & P. Ayton (Eds.), *Subjective probability* (pp. 453–482). Chichester, England: Wiley.

McGee, H. M., O'Boyle, C. A., Hickey, A., Joyce, C. R. B., & O'Malley, K. (1991). Assessing the quality of life of the individual: The SEIQol with a healthy and a gastroenterology unit population. *Psychological Medicine, 21,* 749–759.

McGeoch, J. A. (1942). *The psychology of human learning.* New York: Longmans, Green.

McGeoch, J. A., & Irion, A. L. (1952). *The psychology of human learning* (2nd ed.). New York: David McKay.

McGrath, J. E. (1984). *Groups: Interaction and performance.* Englewood Cliffs, NJ: Prentice-Hall.

McNamara, R. (1995). *In retrospect: The tragedy and lessons of Viet Nam.* New York: Times Books.

Meehl, P. (1954). *Clinical vs. statistical prediction: A theoretical analysis and a review of the evidence.* Minneapolis: University of Minnesota Press.

Miller, G. A. (1956). The magical number seven, plus or minus two: Some limits of our capacity for processing information. *Psychological Review, 63,* 81–97.

Miller, M. (1973). Interpersonal learning: Laboratory and field investigations. In L. Rappoport & D. Summers (Eds.), *Human judgment and social interaction* (pp. 267–294). New York: Holt, Rinehart, & Winston.

Milter, R. G., Darling, T. A., & Mumpower, J. L. (1966). The effects of substantive task characteristics on negotiators' ability to reach efficient agreements. *Acta Psychologica, 93,* 207–228.

Milter, R. G., & Rohrbaugh, J. (1988). Judgment analysis and decision conferencing for administrative review: A case study of innovative policy making in government. In R. L. Cardy, S. M. Puffer, & J. M. Newman (Eds.), *Advances in information processing in organizations.* Greenwich, CT: JAI Press.

Mische, A., & Pattison, P. E. (in press). The plurality of civic relations: Publics, projects and social settings. *Poetics.*

Müller-Merbach, H. (1994). A system of systems approaches. *Interfaces, 24,* 16–25.

Mulligan, K. (1997). Konstanz und Kriterien: Brunswiks Beitrag. In K. R. Fischer & F. Stadler (Eds.), *Wahrnehmung und Gegenstandswelt: Zum Lebenswerk von Egon Brunswik.* Vienna: Springer.

Mumpower, J. L., & Rohrbaugh, J. (1996). Negotiation and design: Supporting resource allocation decisions through analytical mediation. *Group Decision and Negotiation, 5,* 385–410.

Mumpower, J. L. (1988). An analysis of the judgmental components of negotiation and a proposed judgmentally oriented approach to mediation. In B. Brehmer & C. R. B. Joyce (Eds.), *Human judgment: The SJT view* (pp. 465–502). Amsterdam: North-Holland.

Mumpower, J. L., Schuman, S. P., & Zumbolo, A. (1988). Analytical mediation: An application in collective bargaining. In R. M. Lee, A. M. McCosh, & P. Migliarese (Ed.), *Organisational decision support systems* (pp. 61–73). Amsterdam: North-Holland.

Mumpower, J. L. (1991). The judgment policies of negotiators and the structure of negotiations. *Management Science, 37,* 1304–1324.

Mumpower, J. L., & Stewart, T. R. (1996). Expert judgment and expert disagreement. *Thinking and Reasoning, 2,* 191–212.

Munsterberg, H. (1914). *Psychology and social sanity.* Garden City, NY: Doubleday.

Murphy, G. (1955). The boundaries between the individual and his world. *Acta Psychologica, 11,* 111–113.

Murphy, G. (1956). The boundaries between the person and the world. *British Journal of Psychology, 47,* 88–94.

Neisser, U. (1976). *Cognition and reality: Principles and implications of cognitive psychology.* San Francisco: Freeman.

Neter, J., Wasserman, W., & Kutner, M. H. (1990). *Applied linear statistical models: Regression, analysis of variance, and experimental designs.* Boston: Irwin.

Neurath, P. (1988). Paul Lazarsfeld in emigration and (teilweiser) remigration. In F. Stadler (Ed.), *Vertriebene Vernunft II. Emigration und Exil österreichischer Wissenschaft* (pp. 360–372). Vienna: Verlag Jugend & Volk.

Nisbett, R. E., & Wilson, T. D. (1977). Telling more than we can know: Verbal reports on mental processes. *Psychological Review, 84,* 234–259.

Nunnally, J. C. (1978). *Psychometric theory* (2nd ed.). New York: McGraw-Hill.

Oatley, K. (1992). *Best laid schemes: The psychology of emotions.* Cambridge: Cambridge University Press.

O'Boyle, C. A., McGee, H., Hickey, A., O'Malley, K., & Joyce, C. R. B. (1992). Individual quality of life in patients undergoing hip replacement. *Lancet, 339,* 1088–1091.

O'Connor, R., Doherty, M. E., & Tweney, R. D. (1989). The effects of system failure error on predictions. *Organizational Behavior and Human Decision Processes, 44,* 1–11.

O'Connor, R. (1990). *The effects of task complexity on feedforward and cognitive feedback.* Unpublished doctoral dissertation, Bowling Green State University.

Paier, D. (1993, November). "Else Frenkel-Brunswik." *Archiv für die Geschichte der Soziologie in Österreich, Newsletter 9,* pp. 12–18.

Panksepp, J. (1989). The neurobiology of emotions: Of animal brains and human feelings. In H. Wagner & A. Manstead (Eds.), *Handbook of social psychophysiology* (pp. 5–26). New York: Wiley.

Parkin, J. V. (1993). *Judging plans and projects.* Aldershot, UK: Avebury.

Pattison, P. E. (in preparation). *Algebraic decompositions of binary arrays.*

Payne, J. W., Bettman, J. R., & Johnson, E. J. (1993). *The adaptive decision maker.* New York: Cambridge University Press.

Persson, R. S., Pratt, G., & Robson, C. (1992). Motivational and influential components of musical performance: A qualitative analysis. *European Journal for High Ability, 3,* 206–217.

Petrinovich, L. (1979). Probabilistic functionalism: A concept of research method. *American Psychologist, 34,* 373–390.

Pinker, S. (1997). *How the mind works.* New York: Norton.

Poses, R. M., Cebul, R. D., & Wigton, R. S. (1995). You can lead a horse to water—Improving physicians' knowledge of probabilities may not affect their decisions. *Medical Decision Making, 15,* 65–75.

Postman, L., & Tolman, E. C. (1959). Brunswik's probabilistic functionalism. In S. Koch (Ed.), *Psychology: A study of science: Sensory, perceptual, and physiological formulations* (Vol. 1). New York: McGraw-Hill.

Preston, R. A., Materson, B. J., Reda, D. J., Williams, D. W., et al. (1998). Age-race subgroup compared with renin profile as predictors of blood pressure response to antihypertensive therapy. *Journal of the American Medical Association, 280,* 1168–1172.

Raiffa, H. (1982). *The art and science of negotiation.* Cambridge, MA: Belknap/Harvard.

Rasmussen, J. (1990). Cognitive engineering, a new profession? In L. P. Goodstein, S. E. Olsen, & H. B. Anderson (Eds.), *Tasks, errors, and mental models* (pp. 325–334). New York: Taylor & Francis.

Reagan, P., & Rohrbaugh, J. (1990). Group decision process effectiveness: A competing values approach. *Group and Organization Studies, 15,* 20–43.

Reagan-Cirincione, P., & Rohrbaugh, J. (1992a). Decision conferencing: A unique approach to the behavioral aggregation of expert judgment. In G. Wright & F. Bolger (Eds.), *Expertise and decision support.* New York: Plenum.

Reagan-Cirincione, P., & Rohrbaugh, J. (1992b). Task bias and the accuracy of judgment: Setting a baseline for expected group performance. *Journal of Behavioral Decision Making, 5,* 233–252.

Reagan-Cirincione, P. (1994). Improving the accuracy of group judgment: A process intervention combining group facilitation, social judgment analysis, and information technology. *Organizational Behavior and Human Decision Processes, 58,* 246–270.

Reilly, B. A., & Doherty, M. E. (1989). A note on the assessment of self-insight in judgment research. *Organizational Behavior and Human Decision Processes, 44,* 123–131.

Reilly, B. A., & Doherty, M. E. (1992). The assessment of self-insight in judgment policies. *Organizational Behavior and Human Decision Processes, 53,* 285–309.

Reilly, B. A. (1996). Self-insight, other-insight, and their relation to interpersonal conflict. *Thinking and Reasoning, 2,* 213–223.

Rescher, N. (1982). *The coherence theory of truth.* Washington, DC: University Press of America.

Reyna, V. F., & Brainerd, C. J. (1995). Fuzzy-trace theory: An interim synthesis. *Learning and Individual Differences, 7,* 1–75.

Riesen, A. H. (1954). Vision. In C. P. Stone & Q. McNemar (Eds.), *Annual review of psychology* (Vol. 5). Palo Alto, CA: Annual Reviews.

Rieskamp, J., & Hoffrage, U. (1999). When do people use simple heuristics and how can we tell? In G. Gigerenzer, P. M. Todd, & ABC Research Group, *Simple heuristics that make us smart* (pp. 141–167). New York: Oxford University Press.

Rohrbaugh, J. (1977). Cognitive maps: Describing the policy ecology of a community. *Great Plains-Rocky Mountain Geographical Journal, 6,* 64–73.

Rohrbaugh, J. (1979). Improving the quality of group judgment: Social judgment analysis and the Delphi technique. *Organizational Behavior and Human Performance, 24,* 73–92.

Rohrbaugh, J. (1981). Improving the quality of group judgment: Social judgment analysis and the nominal group technique. *Organizational Behavior and Human Performanc, 28,* 272–288.

Rohrbaugh, J. (1984). Making decisions about staffing standards: An analytical approach to human resource planning in health administration. In L. G. Nigro (Ed.), *Decision making in the public sector.* New York: Marcel Dekker.

Rohrbaugh, J. (1988). Cognitive conflict tasks and small group processes. In B. Brehmer & C. R. B. Joyce (Eds.), *Human judgment: The SJT view* (pp. 199–226). Amsterdam: North-Holland.

Rohrbaugh, J. (1992). Cognitive challenges and collective accomplishments. In R. P. Bostrom, R. Watson, & S. T. Kinney (Eds.), *Computer augmented teamwork: A guided tour.* New York: Van Nostrand Reinhold.

Rohrbaugh, J. (1997). Beyond the triple system case: Cognitive conflict tasks and small group processes. In K. R. Fischer & F. Stadler (Eds.), *Perception and universal themes: The life work of Egon Brunswik.* Vienna: Springer.

Ronis, D. L., & Yates, J. F. (1987). Components of probability judgment accuracy: Individual consistency and effects of subject matter and assessment method. *Organizational Behavior and Human Decision Processes, 40,* 193–218.

Rousseau, J. J. (1755/1964). Discourse on the origin and foundations of inequality among men. In R. D. Masters (Ed.), *Jean-Jacques Rousseau: The first and second discourses* (pp. 76–248). New York: St. Martin's Press.

Ruble, T. L., & Crosier, R. A. (1990). Effects of cognitive styles and decision setting on performance. *Organizational Behavior and Human Decision Processes, 46,* 283–295.

Sandel, M. (1996). *Democracy's discontent.* Cambridge: Harvard University Press.

Sarbin, T. (1941). Clinical Psychology. Art or Science? *Psychometrik, 6,* 391–401.

Sarbin, T. (1942). A contribution to the study of actuarial and individual methods of prediction. *American Journal of Sociology, 48,* 593–602.

Sarbin, T. (1944). The logic of prediction in psychology. *Psychological Review, 51,* 210–228.

SAS Institute Inc. (1990). SAS *language reference, version 6, first edition.* Cary, NC: SAS Institute.

Scherer, K. R. (1977). Methods of research on vocal communication: Paradigms and parameters. In K. R. Scherer & P. Ekman (Eds.), *Handbook of methods in nonverbal behavior research* (pp. 136–198). Cambridge: Cambridge University Press.

Scherer, K. R. (1986). Vocal affect expression: A review and a model for future research. *Psychological Bulletin, 99,* 143–165.

Schumacker, T. E., & Lomax, R. G. (1996). *A beginner's guide to structural equation modeling.* Mahwah, NJ: Erlbaum.

Sedlmeier, P., Hertwig, R., & Gigerenzer, G. (1998). Are judgments of the positional frequencies of letters systematically biased due to availability? *Journal of Experimental Psychology: Learning, Memory, and Cognition, 24,* 754–770.

Selker, H. P., Beshansky, J. R., Griffith, J. L., Aufderheide, T. P., et al. (1998). Use of the acute cardiac ischemia time-insensitive predictive instrument (ACI-TIPI) to assist with triage of patients with chest pain or other symptoms suggestive of acute cardia ischemia. *Annals of Internal Medicine, 129,* 845–855.

Senge, P. M. (1990). *The fifth discipline:The art and practice of the learning organization.* New York: Doubleday/Currency.

Sengupta, K., & Te'eni, D. (1993). Cognitive feedback in GDSS: Improving control and convergence. *MIS Quarterly, 17,* 87–109.

Shannon, C. E., & Weaver, W. (1949). *The mathematical theory of communication.* Urbana: University of Illinois Press.

Shavelson, R. J., & Webb, N. M. (1991). *Generalizability theory: A primer.* Newbury Park, CA: Sage.

Shepard, R. N. (1984). Ecological constraints on internal representation: Resonant kinematics of perceiving, imagining, thinking, and dreaming. *Psychological Review, 91,* 417–447.

Shepard, R. N. (1994). Perceptual-cognitive universals as reflections of the world. *Psychonomic Bulletin and Review, 1,* 2–28.

Simon, H. A. (1955). A behavioral model of rational choice. *Quarterly Journal of Economics, 69,* 99–118.

Simon, H. A. (1956). Rational choice and the structure of environments. *Psychological Review, 63,* 129–138.

Simon, H. A. (1969). *The sciences of the artificial.* Cambridge: MIT Press.

Simon, H. A. (1987). Bounded rationality. In J. Eatwell, M. Milgate, P. K. Newman, & R. H. I. Palgrave (Eds.), *The New Palgrave. A dictionary of economics* (pp. 266–268). London: Macmillan.

Skinner, B. F. (1938). *The behavior of organisms.* New York: Appleton.

Skinner, B. F. (1938/1966). *The behavior of organisms: An experimental analysis.* New York: Appleton-Century-Crofts.

Slegers, D. W., Brake, G. L., & Doherty, M. E. (2000). Probabilistic mental models with continuous predictors. *Organizational Behavior and Human Decision Processes, 81,* 98–114.

Sloman, S. A. (1996). The empirical case for two systems of reasoning. *Psychological Bulletin, 119,* 3–22.

Slovic, P., & Lichtenstein, S. (1971). Comparison of bayesian and regression approaches to the study of information processing in judgment. *Organizational Behavior and Human Performance, 6,* 649–744.

Smedslund, J. (1955). *Multiple probability learning.* Oslo, Norway: Oslo University Press.

Smith, B. (1994). *Austrian philosophy: The legacy of Franz Brentano.* Chicago: La Salle, Open Court.

Smith, L. D. (1986). *Behaviorism and logical positivism: A reassessment of the alliance.* Stanford: Stanford University Press.

Smith, B. (1988). Gestalt Theory: An Essay in Philosophy. In B. Smith (ed.), Foundations of Gestalt Theory (pp. 11–18). Munich: Philosophia Verlag.

Sniezek, J. A. (1986). The role of variable labels in cue probability learning tasks. *Organizational Behavior and Human Performance, 38,* 141–161.

Snow, R. E. (1968). Brunswikian approaches to research on teaching. *American Educational Research Journal, 5,* 475–489.

Snow, R. E. (1974). Representative and quasi-representative designs for research on teaching. *Review of Educational Research, 44,* 265–291.

Soll, J. B. (1996). Determinants of overconfidence and miscalibration: The roles of random error and ecological structure. *Organizational Behavior and Human Decision Processes, 65,* 117–137.

Steiner, I. D. (1972). *Group process and productivity.* New York: Academic Press.

Steinmann, D. O. (1974). Transfer of lens model training. *Organizational Behavior and Human Peerformance, 12,* 1–16.

Stenson, H. H. (1974). The lens model with unknown cue structure. *Psychological Review, 81,* 257–264.

Stewart, T. R. (1976). Components of correlations and extensions of the lens model equation. *Psychometrika, 41*, 101–120.

Stewart, T. R. (1988). Judgment analysis: Procedures. In B. Brehmer & C. R. B. Joyce (Eds.), *Human judgment: The SJT view* (pp. 41–74). Amsterdam: North-Holland Elsevier.

Stewart, T. R., Moninger, W. R., Grassia, J., Brady, R. H., & Merrem, F. H. (1989). Analysis of expert judgment and skill in a hail forecasting experiment. *Weather and Forecasting, 4*, 24–34.

Stewart, T. R. (1990). A decomposition of the correlation coefficient and its use in analyzing forecasting skill. *Weather and Forecasting, 5*, 661–666.

Stewart, T. R., Moninger, W. R., Heideman, K. F., & Reagan-Cirincione, P. (1992). Effects of improved information on the components of skill in weather forecasting. *Organizational Behavior and Human Decision Processes, 53*, 107–134.

Stewart, T. R., & Lusk, C. M. (1994). Seven components of judgmental forecasting skill: Implications for research and the improvement of forecasts. *Journal of Forecasting, 13*, 575–599.

Stewart, T. R., Roebber, P. J., & Bosart, L. F. (1997). The importance of the task in analyzing expert judgment. *Organizational Behavior and Human Decision Process, 69*, 205–219.

Stiell, I. G., McKnight, R. D., Greenberg, G. H., & McDowell, I. (1994). Implementation of the Ottawa ankle rules. *Journal of the American Medical Association, 271*, 827–832.

Stigler, S. M. (1986). *The history of statistics: The measurement of uncertainty before 1900*. Cambridge: Harvard University Press.

Suantak, L., Bolger, F., & Ferrell, W. R. (1996). The hard-easy effect in subjective probability calibration. *Organizational Behavior and Human Decision Processes, 67*, 201–221.

Sunstein, C. (1997). Behavioral Analysis of Law. *University of Chicago Law Review, 64*, 1175–1195.

Swets, J. A., Tanner, W. P., & Birdsall, T. G. (1961). Decision processes in perception. *Psychological Review, 68*, 301–340.

Tagiuri, R., & Petrullo, L. (Eds.). (1958). *Person perception and interpersonal behavior*. Palo Alto, CA: Stanford University Press.

Tait, M. (1992). Teaching strategies and styles. In R. Colwell (Ed.), *Handbook of research on music teaching and learning* (pp. 525–534). New York: Schirmer Books.

Tape, T. G., Heckerling, P. S., Ornato, J. P., & Wigton, R. S. (1991). Use of clinical judgment analysis to explain regional variations in physicians' accuracies in diagnosing pneumonia. *Medical Decision Making, 11*, 189–197.

Tape, T. G., Kripal, J., & Wigton, R. S. (1992). Comparing methods of learning clinical prediction from case simulations. *Medical Decision Making, 12*, 213–221.

Taylor, C. (1985). *How is mechanism conceivable? Human agency and language*. Cambridge: Cambridge University Press.

Taylor, F. (1957). Psychology and the design of machines. *American Psychologist, 12*, 249–258.

Thaler, R. H. (1991). *Quasi rational economics*. New York: Russell Sage Foundation.

The Concise Oxford Dictionary of Current English (9th ed.). (1995). Oxford: Clarendon Press; New York: Oxford University Press.

Thompson, D. (Ed.). (1995). *The concise Oxford dictionary of current English* (9th ed.). New York: Oxford University Press.

Thorndike, R. L. (1954). The psychological value system of psychologists. *American Psychologist, 9*, 787–790.

Tickle-Degnen, L., & Rosenthal, R. (1990). The nature of rapport and its nonverbal correlates. *Psychological Inquiry, 1*, 285–293.

Todd, F. J. (1954). *A methodological analysis of clinical judgment*. Doctoral dissertation, University of Colorado, Boulder.

Todd, F. J., & Hammond, K. R. (1965). Differential effects in two multiple-cue probability learning tasks. *Behavioral Science, 10*, 429–435.

Tolman, E. C. (1932). *Purposive behavior in animals and men*. New York: Appleton-Century-Crofts.

Tolman, E., & Brunswik, E. (1935). The organism and the causal texture of the environment. *Psychological Review, 42,* 43–77.

Tolman, E. C. (1956). Egon Brunswik: 1903–1955. *American Journal of Psychology, 69,* 315–342.

Tucker, L. R. (1964). A suggested alternative formulation in the developments by Hursch, Hammond, & Hursch and by Hammond, Hursch, & Todd. *Psychological Review, 71,* 528–530.

Tversky, A. (1969). Intransitivity of preferences. *Psychological Review, 76,* 31–48.

Tversky, A., & Kahneman, D. (1973). Availability: A heuristic for judging frequency and probability. *Cognitive Psychology, 5,* 207–232.

Ungerleider, L. G., & Mishkin, M. (1982). Two cortical visual systems. In D. G. Ingle, M. A. Goodale, & R. J. W. Mansfield (Eds.), *Analysis of visual behavior.* Cambridge: MIT Press.

Urban, J. M., Weaver, J. L., Bowers, C. A., & Rhodenizer, L. (1996). Effects of workload and structure on team processes and performance: Implications for complex team judgment making. *Human Factors, 38,* 300–310.

Vicente, K. J., Christoffersen, K., & Pereklita, A. (1995). Supporting operator problem solving through ecological interface design. *IEEE Transactions on Systems, Man, and Cybernetics, 25,* 529–545.

Vicente, K. J. (1997). Heeding the legacy of Meister, Brunswik & Gibson: Toward a broader view of human factors research. *Human Factors, 39,* 323–328.

Volpe, C. E., Cannon-Bowers, J. A., Salas, E., & Spector, P. E. (1996). The impact of cross-training on team functioning: An empirical investigation. *Human Factors, 38,* 87–100.

Von Schantz, T., Goransson, G., Anderson, G., Froberg, I., Grahn, M., Helgee, A., & Witzell, H. (1989). Female choice selects for a viability male trait in pheasants. *Nature, 337,* 166–169.

Waldrop, M. M. (1992). *Complexity: The emerging science at the edge of order and chaos.* London: Viking.

Wallsten, T. S. (1996). An analysis of judgment research analyses. *Organizational Behavior and Human Decision Processes, 65,* 220–226.

Wertheimer, M. (1998). Opus magnificentissimum. *Contemporary Psychology, 43,* 7–10.

Whitecotton, S. M., Sanders, D. E., & Norris, K. B. (1998). Improving predictive accuracy with a combination of human intuition and mechanical decision aids. *Organizational Behavior and Human Decision Processes, 76,* 325–348.

Whitehead, A. N. (1932). *Adventures of ideas.* Cambridge: Cambridge University Press.

Wickens, C. (1992). *Engineering psychology and human performance* (2nd ed.). New York: HarperCollins.

Wigton, R. S., Connor, J. L., & Centor, R. M. (1986). Transportability of a decision rule for the diagnosis of streptococcal pharyngitis. *Archives of Internal Medicine, 146,* 81–83.

Wigton, R. S. (1988). Use of linear models to analyze physicians' decisions. *Journal of Medical Decision Making, 8,* 241–252.

Wigton, R. S., Poses, R. M., Collins, M., & Cebul, R. D. (1990). Teaching old dogs new tricks: Using cognitive feedback to improve physicians' diagnostic judgments on simulated cases. *Academic Medicine, 65,* S5–S6.

Wigton, R. S. (1996). Social judgement theory and medical judgement. *Thinking and Reasoning, 2,* 175–190.

Williams, G. C. (1966). *Adaptation and natural selection: A critique of some current evolutionary thought.* Princeton: Princeton University Press.

Wilson, E. O., & Kellert, S. R. (1993). *The biophilia hypothesis.* Washington, DC: Island Press.

Wilton, D. (1968). Oviposition site selection by the tree-hole mosquito, Aedes triseriatus. *Journal of Medical Entomology, 5,* 189–194.

Windelband, W. (1894/1904). *Geschichte und Naturwissenschaft* (3rd unaltered ed.). Strassburg: Heitz.

Windelband, W. (1998). History and natural science. *Theory and Psychology, 8,* 5–22.

Winman, A. (1997). The importance of item selection in "knew-it-all-along" studies of general knowledge. *Scandinavian Journal of Psychology, 38,* 63–72.

Winston, A. S. (1990). Robert Session Woodworth and the "Columbia Bible": How the psychological experiment was redefined. *American Journal of Psychology, 103,* 391–401.

Woods, D. (1995). Toward a theoretical base for representation design in the computer medium: Ecological perception and aiding human cognition. In J. Flach, Hancock, P., Caird, J., & Vicente, K. (Ed.), *Global perspectives on the ecology of human-machine systems* (pp. 157–188). Hillsdale, NJ: Erlbaum.

Woodworth, R. S. (1938). *Experimental psychology.* New York: Holt.

Woodworth, R. S., & Schlosberg, H. (1954). *Experimental psychology* (Rev. ed.). New York: Holt, Rinehart, & Winston.

York, K. M., Doherty, M. E., & Kamouri, J. (1987). The influence of cue unreliability on judgment in a multiple cue probability learning task. *Organizational Behavior and Human Decision Processes, 39,* 303–317.

Young, M. F. (1982). *Faculty evaluation: An assessment of departmental values.* Unpublished master's equivalency paper, Peabody College of Vanderbilt University, Nashville.

Zebrowitz, L. A., & Collins, M. A. (1997). Accurate social perception at zero acquaintance: The affordances of a Gibsonian approach. *Personality and Social Psychology Review, 1,* 204–233.

Zsambok, C. E., & Klein, G. (Eds.). (1997). *Naturalistic decision making.* Mahwah, NJ: Erlbaum.

INDEX

References to figures are printed in italic type; tables are indicated by the letter t.

abilities, 102, 251
abortion, 354, 356
absolutism, 303–304
abstractions, 277–279, 353, 373
  level of, 110–111, 267, 268
abstractive relevance, 32n3
academic psychology, 113–114, 121–122
accuracy
  of communication, 427
  measurement of, 330, 331
  vs. proportion of judgments, 420–421, *421*, 422
  of social perception, 388
achievement, 57–66, 94, 227, 349. *See also* attainment
  attainment and, 65–66n7, 251
  cognitive, 301–302, 351–356
  constancy mechanism and, 185
  correlation coefficients for, 184–185, 189–190
  distal, 135–143, 268
  ecological, 302–303
  in groups, 385–388
  in judgment, 450
  organism-environment relations and, 53–56, 65n7, 300–301, 302–303
  perceptual, 94–99, 141–142, *142*
  probability and, 57–66
  ratiomorphic model and, 146–147, 356–357
  thing constancy and, 41, 129
  veridical perception and, 239
  vicarious functioning and, 327
actions, 102, 241
act-psychology, 109, 129, 250, 453
actualgenesis, 273, 275, 279
adaptation
  domain-dependent cognition and, 435
  of hypotheses, 28–30, 31–32
  information structure and, 451
  organisms and environment in, 37, 239
  social perception and, 426–427
adaptive toolbox, 347
Adelman, Leonard, 326, 374–375, 474
  on vicarious functioning in teams, 416–423
Adler, Alfred, 111
adolescent counseling, occupational, 431–433, *432*
aging, 423–427, 455–456

Ahl, V. A., 254
aircraft identification studies, 416, 417, 418–422
Akaike information criterion, 335, 341
Albright, Linda, on interpersonal perception, 328–332
Allport, Floyd, *Theories of Perception and the Concept of Structure*, 212–213
Allport, Gordon, 281, 332–333, 366
Ambady, N., 381
ambiguity, zone of, 299
ambiguous cues, 23, *23*, 26–27, 54n30
  learning and, 196, 209n2
American functionalism, 250, 251
American psychology, 464–465, 481
Ames, Adelbert, 144
analysis of variance. *See* ANOVA
analysis, vs. intuition, 37
Anatomy of Melancholy (Burton), 290
animal magnetism, 275
animation intensity cues, 383
ANOVA, 145–146, 295, 376, 413, 420, 422n2
Ansbacher, Heinz, 144
Anschauung, 352, 353, 356
antidepressant drugs, 399
antiperistasis, 276
Anzeichen. See cues
appearance, modes of, 47, 48–49
Aristotelian thought, 64, 118, 279, 284, 290
Aristotle, 118, 276, 302, 303, 305
Ash, Mitchell G., on Brunswik's career, 453–464
Ashby, F., *Design for a Brain*, 294
Ashton, R. H., 359
association theory, 116
atomic theory, 290
attainment. *See also* achievement
  achievement and, 65–66n7, 251
  of distal variables, 129
  functionalism and, 250–251
  intentional, 19, 44–45, 46–47, 52n10, 129
  mediation and, 54n27
attitudes
  analytical perceptual, 71
  betting, 71, 74t, 88–89
  biological, 102